MIND AND BEHAVIOR

Readings from
**SCIENTIFIC
AMERICAN**

MIND AND BEHAVIOR

With *Introductions* by
Rita L. Atkinson
Richard C. Atkinson
University of California, San Diego

W. H. Freeman and Company
San Francisco

All of the SCIENTIFIC AMERICAN articles in *Mind and Behavior* are available as separate Offprints. For a complete list of articles now available as Offprints, write to W. H. Freeman and Company, 660 Market Street, San Francisco, California 94104.

Library of Congress Cataloging in Publication Data

Main entry under title:

Mind and behavior.

  Bibliography: p.
  Includes index.
  1. Psychology—Addresses, essays, lectures.
2. Mind and body—Addresses, essays, lectures.
3. Brain—Psychological aspects—Addresses, essays, lectures. I. Atkinson, Rita L.   II. Atkinson, Richard C.   III. Scientific American.   [DNLM: 1. Mental processes—Collected works.   2. Psychology—Collected works.   3. Behavior—Collected works.   BF121 M663]
BF149.M49   150   80–15307
ISBN 0–7167–1215–6
ISBN 0–7167–1216–4 (pbk.)

PREFACE

Each article in this book presents intriguing new discoveries in the search for an understanding of the processes that govern human thought and behavior. Although most of the articles are written by psychologists, research by other specialists—neurobiologists, psychiatrists, and anthropologists—is also included. The very diversity of topics covered in this volume points up the scope of psychology as both a scientific and an applied discipline. For the layman this book will serve as an introduction to the rapidly expanding field of psychology. For the psychology student it will present a variety of possibilities for future study and research. For either it should provide fascinating reading.

The 28 articles in this volume have been selected from more than 350 articles on psychology and related topics published in *Scientific American* during the past two decades. *Scientific American* has gained wide recognition for its excellence in scientific reporting; significant discoveries are presented clearly and accurately, but with a minimum of technical detail. The articles are organized into four sections. Section I, "Biological and Developmental Determiners of Behavior," deals with how the brain and nervous system are related to psychological processes and how these processes change as the organism matures. Section II, "Perception and Awareness," discusses the sensory mechanisms that make it possible for us to be aware of events around us and how sensory inputs are organized into perceptions. Because vision is our predominant sense, most of the articles are concerned with visual perception. Section III, "Memory, Learning, and Thinking," deals with the cognitive processes specified in its title as well as the use of language. Section IV, "Personality, Abnormality, and Social Behavior," covers a wide range of topics concerned with personality (both normal and abnormal), methods for modifying abnormal behavior, and the ways in which people interact with and influence each other.

The organization of the articles into sections was necessarily somewhat arbitrary. For example, "Brain Mechanisms of Vision" would have been as appropriate in Section II as Section I. Similarly, "Specializations of the Human Brain" could have been placed in Section I rather than in Section III. The order of the sections need not be followed, since in most cases the later articles do not depend on earlier ones.

Rita L. Atkinson
Richard C. Atkinson

February 1980

CONTENTS

IV   PERSONALITY, ABNORMALITY, AND SOCIAL BEHAVIOR

Note on cross-references to SCIENTIFIC AMERICAN *articles:* Articles included in this book are referred to by title and page number; articles not included in this book but available as Offprints are referred to by title and offprint number; articles not included in this book and not available as Offprints are referred to by title and date of publication.

MIND AND BEHAVIOR

BIOLOGICAL AND DEVELOPMENTAL DETERMINERS OF BEHAVIOR

I

I   BIOLOGICAL AND DEVELOPMENTAL DETERMINERS OF BEHAVIOR

INTRODUCTION

To understand human behavior and mental functioning, we need to know something about the underlying biological processes and how these processes develop as the individual matures from infancy to adulthood. The human brain with its billions of nerve cells and virtually infinite number of interconnections and pathways may well be the most complex structure in the universe. In principle, all psychological events are related to activities of the brain and nervous system in conjunction with the other body systems. We know, for example, that emotions, such as fear and rage, can be produced in animals and humans by mild electrical stimulation of specific areas of the brain. Stimulation of different brain regions will produce sensations of pleasure and pain and even vivid memories of past experience. But only in recent years have techniques been developed that allow us to explore, as never before, the activities of individual nerve cells and of microscopic neural pathways. Thus, an understanding of current developments in psychology requires a familiarity with neurobiology. Some understanding of developmental processes is also required. The saying "The child is father of the man" points up the importance of early experiences in determining adult behavior. Since the time of Sigmund Freud, psychologists have been aware that the events of infancy are of great significance for personality development. Recent research indicates that early experience may be crucial for many areas of human functioning. The articles in this section present some of the research relating psychological phenomena to neurobiological and developmental processes.

Ultimately, our ability to feel, think, learn, and remember may be shown to reside in the precise patterns of connections between nerve cells, or neurons, in the brain. Because the human brain is so incredibly complex, researchers have resorted to studying neural connections in lower organisms, which have far fewer brain cells. In "Small Systems of Neurons" Eric Kandel describes some learning experiments with the sea snail *Aplysia*. By identifying individual neurons and their connections, it was possible to study the neural circuits controlling specific behaviors and to determine what happens to these circuits as the result of experience. An important discovery is that even very simple forms of learning appear to involve changes in the strength of the connections between neurons—more specifically, changes in the amount of certain chemicals, called neurotransmitters, released by the nerve cell at its synapse (the slight space between adjacent neurons). These chemicals determine whether or not the neural impulse will be transmitted across the synapse to the neighboring neurons.

If learning involves changes in neural connections, then we might expect an organism's experiences to produce observable changes in the brain. Mark

Rosenzweig, Edward Bennett, and Marian Diamond ("Brain Changes in Response to Experience") exposed two groups of young rats to quite different early experiences. Rats in the "enriched" environment lived together in a large cage furnished with a variety of objects that they could play with; a new set of playthings was placed in the cage each day. Rats in the "impoverished" environment lived alone in bare cages. When the rats' brains were examined after several months of such experience, the two groups were found to differ significantly in a number of ways; for example, the rats with the enriched experience had a thicker cerebral cortex.

The next two articles describe research on specific areas of the brain. In "The Reward System of the Brain" Aryeh Routtenberg discusses the brain's "pleasure centers"—and their role in learning and memory. The highly organized structure of the brain's visual system is discussed by David Hubel and Torsten Wiesel in "Brain Mechanisms of Vision." These authors recorded the responses of individual nerve cells as an animal viewed various visual patterns; recordings were taken at progressive levels of the visual system, starting with cells in the retina of the eye and proceeding up the optic nerve to cells of the visual cortex (the area where vision is represented in the brain). They found that the nerve cells at each successive level in the system respond to increasingly complex stimuli. Thus, whereas neurons in the retina respond to almost any pattern of light, cells of the visual cortex are more discriminating, responding only to very specific patterns of stimulation. For example, some cortical cells fire only when stimulated by a narrow slit of light oriented in a horizontal direction; others are activated by a vertical slit; and yet others respond to stimuli moving only in one direction or forming a certain angle.

Many of the behavior patterns displayed by animals—mating rituals, nest building, feeding and caring for the young—seem to be "instinctive," that is, to occur with little opportunity for learning. In the past the word *instinct* was used to refer to any unlearned, patterned, goal-directed behavior characteristic of a species. And the word was often used to describe human behavior as well—a mother's love for a child illustrating a "parental instinct," warfare an "aggressive instinct," social behavior a "herd instinct," and so on. The question of whether or not there were human instincts was a topic of intense controversy during the 1920s. The argument became part of a larger controversy over the relative contributions of heredity and environment to development. Those who believed in instincts considered heredity the most important developmental influence. Those who did not believe in them prevailed, because the instinct theorists failed to agree with one another on either the number or the kinds of instincts human beings possessed.

Because human beings have a much longer infancy than other species, during which all kinds of learning can take place, the concept of instinct has not proved very useful in studying or understanding human behavior. The study of instincts in animals, however, has taken on renewed interest as the result of a group of psychologists and zoologists who call themselves *ethologists*. These scientists study animals in their native environments rather than in the laboratory where the artificiality of the situation often prevents behavior patterns from appearing in their natural form. Ethologists prefer the term *species-specific behavior* to the more controversial term *instinct*; they study behavior that is specific to a certain species and that appears in the same form in all members of the species. One of the concepts ethologists have introduced is *imprinting*, which refers to a type of early learning that forms the basis for the young animal's attachment to its parents. The clearest example is the tendency of a young duckling to follow its "mother" shortly after it is hatched and thereafter to follow only this particular female duck. A newly hatched duckling that has been artificially incubated without the presence of a mother duck will follow a human being, a wooden decoy, or almost any other moving object that it first sees after birth. Following a wooden decoy for as little as ten minutes is enough to "imprint" the duckling on the decoy so that it will remain attached to this object, following it even under adverse circumstances and preferring it to a live duck. Eckhard Hess in his article "Imprinting in a Natural Laboratory" reviews recent research on imprinting and examines the implications for psychological theory.

The last two articles in this section are concerned with developmental processes. In "The Object in the World of the Infant" T. G. R. Bower examines how infants come to know something about the solidity and permanence of objects. As adults we know that the vase we see on the table is a solid object even before we reach out to grasp it. If someone hides the vase from view by placing a screen in front of it, we are fairly certain that the object is still there, even though we can't see it. And if the vase is moved from the table to the floor, we still recognize it as the same object despite the change in location. But for infants, this knowledge is a matter of learning. Bower has devised some ingenious procedures to investigate how the concept of an object's permanence develops and changes at different ages.

In "Repetitive Processes in Child Development" Bower looks at some abilities that appear at an early age, are lost, and then reappear later. For example, if a six-day-old infant is supported above a flat surface, he or she will make walking movements. This response disappears at about eight weeks and does not reappear until the end of the child's first year. To take another example, during the first few weeks of life infants can reach out to touch visible objects and will occasionally even grasp them. This type of eye-hand coordination disappears at about four weeks and does not reappear until the age of twenty weeks. These disappearances are puzzling, because we think of development as a continuous growth process. Although the author's explanations vary, depending on the nature of the particular ability, he concludes that, despite apparent reversals and repetitions, psychological growth is a continuous, additive process.

Small Systems of Neurons

by Eric R. Kandel
September 1979

Such systems are the elementary units of mental function. Studies of simple animals such as the large snail Aplysia show that small systems of neurons are capable of forms of learning and memory

Many neurobiologists believe that the unique character of individual human beings, their disposition to feel, think, learn and remember, will ultimately be shown to reside in the precise patterns of synaptic interconnections between the neurons of the brain. Since it is difficult to examine patterns of interconnections in the human brain, a major concern of neurobiology has been to develop animal models that are useful for studying how interacting systems of neurons give rise to behavior. Networks of neurons that mediate complete behavioral acts allow one to explore a hierarchy of interrelated questions: To what degree do the properties of different neurons vary? What determines the patterns of interconnections between neurons? How do different patterns of interconnections generate different forms of behavior? Can the interconnected neurons that control a certain kind of behavior be modified by learning? If they can, what are the mechanisms whereby memory is stored?

Among the many functions that emerge from the interactions of neurons, the most interesting are the functions concerned with learning (the ability to modify behavior in response to experience) and with memory (the ability to store that modification over a period of time). Learning and memory are perhaps the most distinctive features of the mental processes of advanced animals, and these features reach their highest form in man. In fact, human beings are what they are in good measure because of what they have learned. It is therefore of theoretical importance, for the understanding of learning and for the study of behavioral evolution, to determine at what phylogenetic level of neuronal and behavioral organization one can begin to recognize aspects of the learning and memory processes that characterize human behavior. This determination is also of practical importance. The difficulty in studying the cellular mechanisms of memory in the brain of man or other mammals arises because such brains are immensely complex. For the

human brain ethical issues also preclude this kind of study. It would therefore be congenial scientifically to be able to examine these processes effectively in simple systems.

It could be argued that the study of memory and learning as it relates to man cannot be pursued effectively in simple neuronal systems. The organization of the human brain seems so complex that trying to study human learning in a reduced form in simple neuronal systems is bound to fail. Man has intellectual abilities, a highly developed language and an ability for abstract thinking, which are not found in simpler animals and may require qualitatively different types of neuronal organization. Although such arguments have value, the critical question is not whether there is something special about the human brain. There clearly is. The question is rather what the human brain and human behavior have in common with the brain and the behavior of simpler animals. Where there are points of similarity they may involve common principles of brain organization that could profitably be studied in simple neural systems.

The answer to the question of similarity is clear. Ethologists such as Konrad Lorenz, Nikolaas Tinbergen and Karl von Frisch have shown that human beings share many common behavioral patterns with simpler animals, including elementary perception and motor coordination. The capacity to learn, in particular, is widespread; it has evolved in many invertebrate animals and in all vertebrates. The similarity of some of the learning processes suggests that the neuronal mechanisms for a given learning process may have features in common across phylogeny. For example, there appear to be no fundamental differences in structure, chemistry or func-

tion between the neurons and synapses in man and those of a squid, a snail or a leech. Consequently a complete and rigorous analysis of learning in such an invertebrate is likely to reveal mechanisms of general significance.

Simple invertebrates are attractive for such investigation because their nervous systems consist of between 10,000 and 100,000 cells, compared with the many billions in more complex animals. The cells are collected into the discrete groups called ganglia, and each ganglion usually consists of between 500 and 1,500 neurons. This numerical simplification has made it possible to relate the function of individual cells directly to behavior. The result is a number of important findings that lead to a new way of looking at the relation between the brain and behavior.

The first major question that students of simple systems of neurons might examine is whether the various neurons of a region of the nervous system differ from one another. This question, which is central to an understanding of how behavior is mediated by the nervous system, was in dispute until recently. Some neurobiologists argued that the neurons of a brain are sufficiently similar in their properties to be regarded as identical units having interconnections of roughly equal value.

These arguments have now been strongly challenged, particularly by studies of invertebrates showing that many neurons can be individually identified and are invariant in every member of the species. The concept that neurons are unique was proposed as early as 1912 by the German biologist Richard Goldschmidt on the basis of his study of the nervous system of a primitive worm, the intestinal parasite *Ascaris*. The brain

GROUP OF NEURONS appears in the photomicrograph on the following page, which shows the dorsal surface of the abdominal ganglion of the snail *Aplysia*. The magnification is 100 diameters. A particularly large, dark brown neuron can be seen at the right side of the micrograph. It is the cell identified as R2 in the map of the abdominal ganglion of *Aplysia* on page 8.

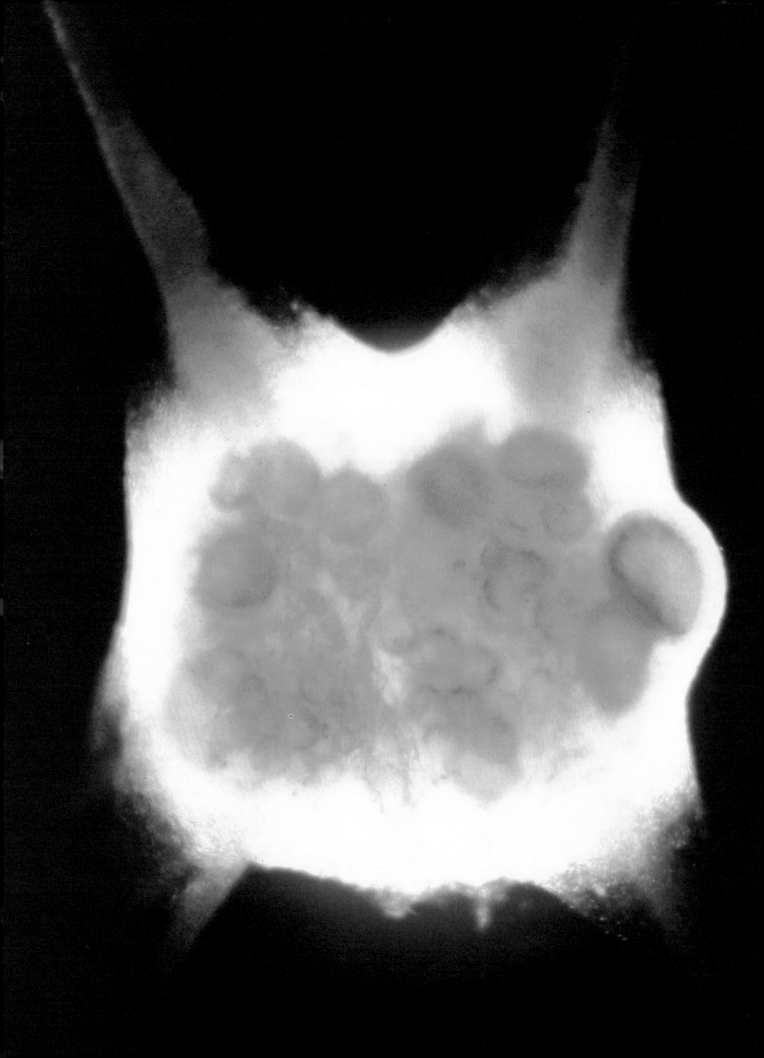

of this worm consists of several ganglia. When Goldschmidt examined the ganglia, he found they contained exactly 162 cells. The number never varied from animal to animal, and each cell always occupied a characteristic position. In spite of this clear-cut result Goldschmidt's work went largely unheeded.

More than 50 years later two groups at the Harvard Medical School returned to the problem independently. Masanori Otsuka, Edward A. Kravitz and David D. Potter, working with the lobster, and Wesley T. Frazier, Irving Kupfermann, Rafiq M. Waziri, Richard E. Coggeshall and I, working with the large marine snail *Aplysia,* found a similar but less complete invariance in the more complex nervous systems of these higher invertebrates. A comparable invariance was soon found in a variety of invertebrates, including the leech, the crayfish, the locust, the cricket and a number of snails. Here I shall limit myself to considering studies of *Aplysia,* particularly studies of a single ganglion: the abdominal ganglion. Similar findings have also emerged from the studies of other invertebrates.

In the abdominal ganglion of *Aplysia* neurons vary in size, position, shape, pigmentation, firing patterns and the chemical substances by which they transmit information to other cells. On the basis of such differences it is possible to recognize and name specific cells (R1, L1, R15 and so on). The firing patterns illustrate some of the differences. Certain cells are normally "silent" and others are spontaneously active. Among the active ones some fire regular action potentials, or nerve impulses, and others fire in recurrent brief bursts or trains. The different firing patterns have now

been shown to result from differences in the types of ionic currents generated by the membrane of the cell body of the neurons. The cell-body membrane is quite different from the membrane of the axon, the long fiber of the neuron. When the membrane of the axon is active, it typically produces only an inflow of sodium ions and a delayed outflow of potassium ions, whereas the membrane of the cell body can produce six or seven distinct ionic currents that can flow in various combinations.

Whether or not most cells in the mammalian nervous system are also unique individuals is not yet known. The studies in the sensory systems of mammals reviewed by David Hubel and Torsten Wiesel in this book, however, have revealed fascinating and important differences between neighboring neurons [see "Brain Mechanisms of Vision," by David H. Hubel and Torsten N. Wiesel, page 32]. Studies of the development of the vertebrate brain reviewed by Maxwell Cowan lead to a similar conclusion [see "The Development of the Brain," by W. Maxwell Cowan; SCIENTIFIC AMERICAN Offprint 1440].

The finding that neurons are invariant leads to further questions. Are the synaptic connections between cells also invariant? Does a given identified cell always connect to exactly the same follower cell and not to others? A number of investigators have examined these questions in invertebrate animals and have found that cells indeed always make the same kinds of connections to other cells. The invariance applies not only to the connections but also to the "sign," or functional expression, of the connections, that is, whether they are excitatory or inhibitory.

Therefore Frazier, James E. Blan-

kenship, Howard Wachtel and I next worked with identified cells to examine the rules that determine the functional expression of connections between cells. A single neuron has many branches and makes many connections. We asked: Are all the connections of a neuron specialized for inhibition or excitation, or can the firing of a neuron produce different actions at different branches? What determines whether a connection is excitatory or inhibitory? Is the sign of the synaptic action determined by the chemical structure of the transmitter substance released by the presynaptic neuron, or is the nature of the postsynaptic receptor the determining factor? Does the neuron release the same transmitter from all its terminals?

One way to explore these questions is to look at the different connections made by a cell. The first cell we examined gave a clear answer: it mediated different actions through its various connections. The cell excited some follower cells, inhibited others and (perhaps most unexpectedly) made a dual connection, which was both excitatory and inhibitory, to a third kind of cell. Moreover, it always excited precisely the same cells, always inhibited another specific group of cells and always made a dual connection with a third group. Its synaptic action could be accounted for by one transmitter substance: acetylcholine. The reaction of this substance with different types of receptors on the various follower cells determined whether the synaptic action would be excitatory or inhibitory.

The receptors determined the sign of the synaptic action by controlling different ionic channels in the membrane: primarily sodium for excitation and chloride for inhibition. The cells that received the dual connection had two types of receptor for the same transmitter, one receptor that controlled a sodium channel and another that controlled a chloride channel. The functional expression of chemical synaptic transmission is therefore determined by the types of receptor the follower cell has at a given postsynaptic site. (Similar results have been obtained by JacSue Kehoe of the École Normale in Paris, who has gone on to analyze in detail the properties of the various species of receptors to acetylcholine.) Thus, as was first suggested by Ladislav Tauc and Hersch Gerschenfeld of the Institute Marey in Paris, the chemical transmitter is only permissive; the instructive component of synaptic transmission is the nature of the receptor and the ionic channels it interacts with. This principle has proved to be fairly general. It applies to the neurons of vertebrates and invertebrates and to neurons utilizing various transmitters: acetylcholine, gamma-aminobutyric acid (GABA), serotonin, dopamine and histamine. (The principle

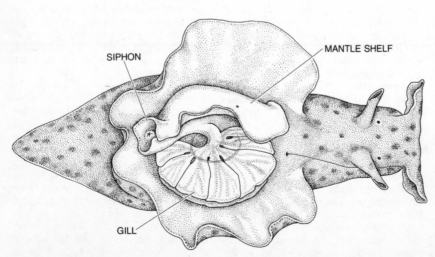

SIPHON

MANTLE SHELF

GILL

GILL-WITHDRAWAL REFLEX of *Aplysia* results when the siphon or the mantle shelf is somehow stimulated. The animal then retracts the gill to the position that is indicated in color.

also applies to the actions of certain peptide hormones on neurons, a subject to which I shall return.)

The discovery in invertebrate ganglia of identifiable cells that make precise connections with one another has led to the working out of the "wiring diagram" of various behavioral circuits and has therefore made possible an exact study of the causal relation of specific neurons to behavior. The term behavior refers to the observable actions of an organism. These range from complex acts such as talking or walking to simple acts such as the movement of a body part or a change in heart rate. Types of behavior that have been at least partly worked out in leeches, crayfishes and snails include feeding, various locomotor patterns and a variety of escape and defensive reactions.

The first finding to emerge from these studies is that individual cells exert a control over behavior that is specific and sometimes surprisingly powerful. The point can be illustrated by comparing the neural control of the heart in *Aplysia* with that in human beings.

The human heart beats spontaneously. Its intrinsic rhythm is neuronally modulated by the inhibitory action of cholinergic neurons (acetylcholine is the transmitter substance) with their axons in the vagus nerve and the excitatory action of noradrenergic neurons with their axons in the accelerator nerve. The modulation involves several thousand neurons. In *Aplysia* the heart also beats spontaneously; it is neuronally modulated by the inhibitory action of cholinergic neurons and the excitatory action of serotonergic neurons, but the modulation is accomplished by only four cells! Two cells excite the heart (only the "major excitor" cell is really important) and two inhibit it. Three other cells give rise to a constriction of the blood vessels and thereby control the animal's blood pressure.

Since individual cells connect invariably to the same follower cells and can mediate actions that have a different sign, certain cells at a critical point in the nervous system are in a position to control an entire behavioral sequence. As early as 1938 C. A. G. Wiersma, working with the crayfish at the California Institute of Technology, had appreciated the importance of single cells in behavior and had called them "command cells." Such cells have now been found in a variety of animals. A few of them have proved to be dual-action neurons. Hence John Koester, Earl M. Mayeri and I, working with *Aplysia* at the New York University School of Medicine, found that the dual-action neuron described above is a command cell for the neural circuit controlling the circulation. This one cell increases the rate and output of the heart by exciting the

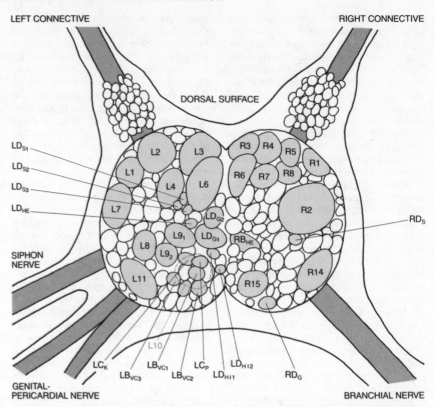

MAP OF ABDOMINAL GANGLION in *Aplysia californica* shows the location of the identified neurons, which have been labeled L or R (for left or right hemiganglion) and assigned a number. Neurons that are members of a cluster, consisting of cells with similar properties, are further identified by a cluster letter (LD) and a subscript representing the behavioral function of the neuron, such as HE for heart excitor and G1 and G2 for two gill motor neurons.

major cell that excites the heart while inhibiting the cells that inhibit the heart and the cells that constrict the major blood vessels. As a result of the increased activity of this one cell the heart beats faster and pumps more blood.

This is only a simple example of the behavioral functions of a command cell. In the crayfish and even in a more complex animal, the goldfish, a single impulse in a single command neuron causes the animal to flee from threatened danger. Recently Vernon Mountcastle of the Johns Hopkins University School of Medicine has suggested in this context that small groups of cells may serve similar command functions in the primate brain to control purposeful voluntary movements.

Hence a functional purpose of dual-action cells is to bring about a constellation of different physiological effects. A similar constellation can be achieved by the action of neuroendocrine cells, neurons that release hormones (the chemical substances that are usually carried in the bloodstream to act at distant sites). The abdominal ganglion of *Aplysia* contains two clusters of neuroendocrine cells, which are called bag cells because each cluster is bag-shaped. Kupfermann, working in our division at the Columbia University College of Physicians and Surgeons, has shown, as have

Stephen Arch of Reed College and Felix Strumwasser and his colleagues at Cal Tech, that the bag cells release a polypeptide hormone that controls egg laying. Mayeri has found that this hormone has long-lasting actions on various cells in the abdominal ganglion, exciting some and inhibiting others.

One of the cells excited by this hormone is the dual-action command cell that controls the heart rate. As a result the heart speeds up to provide the extra flow of blood to the tissues that the animal requires during egg laying. Thus superimposed on a precise pattern of connections that provide short-range interaction of neurons is an equally precise pattern of long-range interactions achieved by the hormones released by neuroendocrine cells. The precise effect of each hormone seems to be determined, as synaptic effects are, by the nature of the receptors on the target cells.

The finding that behavior is mediated by invariant cells interconnecting in precise and invariant ways might suggest that simple animals differ from more complex ones in having stereotyped and fixed repertories of activity. It is not so. Studies in different invertebrates have shown that behavior in simple animals is quite capable of being modified by learning.

We have explored this subject most

fully in one of *Aplysia*'s simplest kinds of behavior: a defensive reflex action in which the gill is withdrawn after a stimulus. The gill is in a respiratory chamber called the mantle cavity. The chamber is covered by a protective sheet, the mantle shelf, that terminates in a fleshy spout, the siphon. When a weak or a moderately intense stimulus is applied to the siphon, the gill contracts and withdraws into the mantle cavity. This reflex is analogous to the withdrawal responses found in almost all higher animals, such as the one in which a human being jerks a hand away from a hot object. *Aplysia* and the other animals exhibit two forms of learning with such reflexes: habituation and sensitization.

Habituation is a decrease in the strength of a behavioral response that occurs when an initially novel stimulus is presented repeatedly. When an animal is presented with a novel stimulus, it at first responds with a combination of orienting and defensive reflexes. With repeated stimulation the animal readily learns to recognize the stimulus. If the stimulus proves to be unrewarding or innocuous, the animal will reduce and ultimately suppress its responses to it. Although habituation is remarkably simple, it is probably the most widespread of all forms of learning. Through

habituation animals, including human beings, learn to ignore stimuli that have lost novelty or meaning; habituation frees them to attend to stimuli that are rewarding or significant for survival. Habituation is thought to be the first learning process to emerge in human infants and is commonly utilized to study the development of intellectual processes such as attention, perception and memory.

An interesting aspect of habituation in vertebrates is that it gives rise to both short- and long-term memory and has therefore been employed to explore the relation between the two. Thomas J. Carew, Harold M. Pinsker and I found that a similar relation holds for *Aplysia*. After a single training session of from 10 to 15 tactile stimuli to the siphon the withdrawal reflex habituates. The memory for the stimulus is short-lived; partial recovery can be detected within an hour and almost complete recovery generally occurs within a day. Recovery in this type of learning is equivalent to forgetting. As with the repetition of more complex learning tasks, however, four repeated training sessions of only 10 stimuli each produce profound habituation and a memory for the stimulus that lasts for weeks.

The first question that Vincent Castellucci, Kupfermann, Pinsker and I asked

was: What are the loci and mechanisms of short-term habituation? The neural circuit controlling gill withdrawal is quite simple. A stimulus to the skin of the siphon activates the 24 sensory neurons there; they make direct connections to six motor cells in the gill, and the motor cells connect directly to the muscle. The sensory neurons also excite several interneurons, which are interposed neurons.

By examining these cells during habituation we found that short-term habituation involved a change in the strength of the connection made by the sensory neurons on their central target cells: the interneurons and the motor neurons. This localization was most fortunate, because now we could examine what happened during habituation simply by analyzing the changes in two cells, the presynaptic sensory neuron and the postsynaptic motor neuron, and in the single set of connections between them.

The strength of a connection can be studied by recording the synaptic action produced in the motor cells by an individual sensory neuron. It is possible to simulate the habituation training session of from 10 to 15 stimuli by stimulating a sensory neuron following the exact time sequence used for the intact animal. The stimulus can be adjusted so that it generates a single action potential. The first time the neuron is caused to fire an action potential it produces a highly effective synaptic action, which is manifested as a large excitatory postsynaptic potential in the motor cell. The subsequent action potentials initiated in the sensory neuron during a training session give rise to progressively smaller excitatory postsynaptic potentials. This depression in the effectiveness of the connection parallels and accounts for the behavioral habituation. As with the behavior, the synaptic depression resulting from a single training session persists for more than an hour. Following a second training session there is a more pronounced depression of the synaptic potential, and further training sessions can depress the synaptic potential completely.

What causes the changes in the strength of the synaptic connection? Do they involve a change in the presynaptic sensory neuron, reflecting a decrease in the release of the transmitter substance, or a change in the postsynaptic cell, reflecting a decrease in the sensitivity of the receptors to the chemical transmitter? The questions can be answered by analyzing changes in the amplitude of the synaptic potential in terms of its quantal components.

As was first shown by José del Castillo and Bernhard Katz at University College London, transmitter is released not as single molecules but as "quanta," or multimolecular packets. Each packet contains roughly the same amount

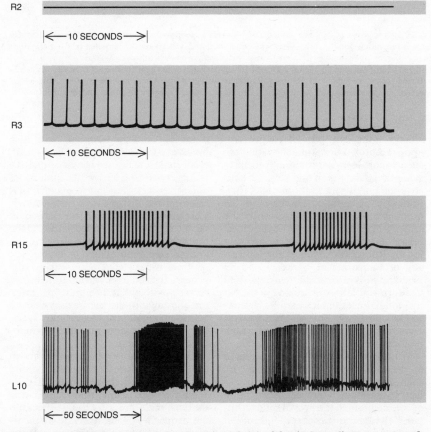

R2

|← 10 SECONDS →|

R3

|← 10 SECONDS →|

R15

|← 10 SECONDS →|

L10

|← 50 SECONDS →|

FIRING PATTERNS of identified neurons in *Aplysia*'s abdominal ganglion are portrayed. R2 is normally silent, R3 has a regular beating rhythm, R15 a regular bursting rhythm and L10 an irregular bursting rhythm. L10 is a command cell that controls other cells in the system.

a

b

RB_{HE}
LD_{HI}
L10

← FIVE SECONDS →

L7

L10

← FIVE SECONDS →

c

RB_{HE}
LD_{HI}
L10

← 50 MILLISECONDS →

L7

L10

← 50 MILLISECONDS →

INVARIANCE OF CONNECTIONS between cell L10 and some of its follower cells was ascertained (*a*) by an arrangement in which double-barrel microelectrodes for recording and passing current were inserted in L10, which is a presynaptic neuron, and three of its follower cells. L10 produces excitation (*white*) in RB, inhibition (*black*) in LD and both excitation and inhibition in L7. The respective firing patterns are shown at *b*. Several superposed sweeps (*at the left in* c) illustrate the brief but constant latency between an impulse in the presynaptic neuron and the response of two follower cells. Superposed traces from L10 and L7 (*at the right in* c) show that effect is excitatory when L10 fires initially, as indicated by tall and narrow impulses, and inhibitory when it fires repeatedly, as shown by short and broad impulses.

of transmitter (several thousand molecules). The quanta are thought to be stored in subcellular organelles called synaptic vesicles that are seen in abundance at synaptic endings examined with the electron microscope. Since the number of transmitter molecules in each quantum does not ordinarily change, the number of quanta released by each action potential is a fairly reliable index of the total amount of transmitter released. Each quantum in turn produces a miniature excitatory postsynaptic potential of characteristic size in the postsynaptic cell. The size is an indication of how sensitive the postsynaptic receptors are to the several thousand molecules of transmitter released by each packet.

Castellucci and I, working with *Aplysia,* found that the decrease in the amplitude of the synaptic action potential with habituation was paralleled by a decrease in the number of chemical quanta released. In contrast, the size of the miniature postsynaptic potential did not change, indicating that there was no change in the sensitivity of the postsynaptic receptor. The results show that the site of short-term habituation is the presynaptic terminals of the sensory neurons and that the mechanism of habituation is a progressive decrease in the amount of transmitter released by the sensory-neuron terminals onto their central target cells. Studies in the crayfish by Robert S. Zucker of the University of California at Berkeley and by Franklin B. Krasne of the University of California at Los Angeles and in the cat by Paul B. Farel and Richard F. Thompson of the University of California at Irvine indicate that this mechanism may be quite general.

What is responsible for the decrease in the number of quanta released by each action potential? The number is largely determined by the concentration of free calcium in the presynaptic terminal. Calcium is one of three kinds of ion involved in the generation of each action potential in the terminal. The depolarizing upstroke of the action potential is produced mainly by the inflow of sodium ions into the terminal, but it also involves a lesser and delayed flow of calcium ions. The repolarizing downstroke is largely produced by the outflow of potassium ions. The inflow of calcium is essential for the release of transmitter. Calcium is thought to enable the synaptic vesicles to bind to release sites in the presynaptic terminals. This binding is a critical step preliminary to the release of transmitter from the vesicles (the process termed exocytosis). It therefore seems possible that the amount of calcium coming into the terminals with each action potential is not fixed but is variable and that the amount might be modulated by habituation.

The best way to examine changes in the flow of calcium into terminals would be to record from the terminals directly. We have been unable to do so because the terminals are very small. Because the properties of the calcium channels of the cell body resemble those of the terminals, however, one of our graduate students, Marc Klein, set about examining the change in the calcium current of the cell body that accompanies the synaptic depression.

The calcium current turns on slowly during the action potential and so is normally overlapped by the potassium current. To unmask the calcium current we exposed the ganglion to tetraethylammonium (TEA), an agent that selectively blocks some of the delayed potassium current. By blocking the repolarizing action of the potassium current the agent produces a significant increase in the duration of the action potential. Much of this prolongation is due to the unopposed action of the calcium current. The duration of the action potential prolonged by TEA is a good assay for changes in calcium current.

We next examined the release of transmitter by the terminals of the sensory neurons, as measured by the size of the synaptic potential in the motor cell, and the changes recorded simultaneously in the calcium current, as measured by the duration of the action potential. We found that repeated stimulation of the sensory neuron at rates that produce habituation led to a progressive decrease in the duration of the calcium component of the action potential that paralleled the decrease in the release of transmitter. Spontaneous recovery of the synaptic potential and of the behavior were accompanied by an increase in the calcium current.

What we have learned so far about the mechanisms of short-term habituation indicates that this type of learning involves a modulation in the strength of a previously existing synaptic connection. The strength of the connection is determined by the amount of transmitter released, which is in turn controlled by the degree to which an action potential in the presynaptic terminal can activate the calcium current. The storage of the memory for short-term habituation therefore resides in the persistence, over minutes and hours, of the depression in the calcium current in the presynaptic terminal.

What are the limits of this change? How much can the effectiveness of a given synapse change as a result of learning, and how long can such changes endure? I have mentioned that repeated training sessions can completely depress the synaptic connections between the sensory and the motor cells. Can this condition be maintained? Can long-term habituation give rise to a complete and prolonged inactivation of a previously functioning synapse?

These questions bear on the long-standing debate among students of learning about the relation of short- and long-term memory. The commonly accepted idea is that the two kinds of memory involve different memory processes. This idea is based, however, on rather indirect evidence.

Castellucci, Carew and I set out to

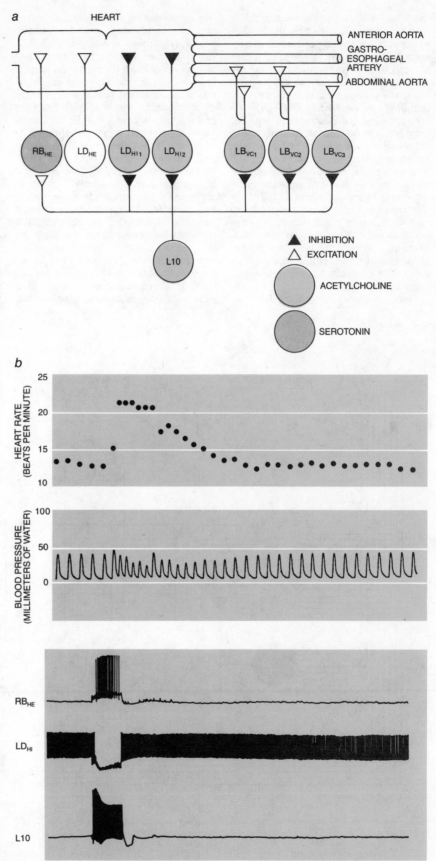

BEHAVIORAL CONTROL exerted by the single neuron L10 is shown by its effect on cardiovascular motor neurons of *Aplysia*. L10 is known to make synaptic connections (*a*) with six of the cells (LD$_{HE}$ has not yet been examined for this synaptic connection); the color of each cell indicates what chemical transmitter it utilizes. It can be seen (*b*) that activity in L10 increases the animal's heart rate and blood pressure by exciting RB$_{HE}$ and inhibiting LD$_{HI}$.

examine the hypothesis more directly by comparing the effectiveness of the connections made by the population of sensory neurons on an identified gill motor cell, L7, in four groups of *Aplysia*: untrained animals that served as controls, and groups examined respectively one day, one week and three weeks after long-term habituation training. We found that in the control animals about 90 percent of the sensory neurons made extremely effective connections to L7, whereas in the animals examined one day and one week after long-term habituation the figure was 30 percent. Even in the three-week group only about 60 percent of the cells made detectable connections to L7. Here, then, are previously effective synaptic connections that become inactive and remain that way for more than a week as a result of a simple learning experience.

Hence whereas short-term habitua-

tion involves a transient decrease in synaptic efficacy, long-term habituation produces a more prolonged and profound change, leading to a functional disruption of most of the previously effective connections. The data are interesting for three reasons: (1) they provide direct evidence that a specific instance of long-term memory can be explained by a long-term change in synaptic effectiveness; (2) they show that surprisingly little training is needed to produce a profound change in synaptic transmission at synapses critically involved in learning, and (3) they make clear that short- and long-term habituation can share a common neuronal locus, namely the synapses the sensory neurons make on the motor neurons. Short- and long-term habituation also involve aspects of the same cellular mechanism: a depression of excitatory transmission. One now needs to determine whether the

long-term synaptic depression is presynaptic and whether it involves an inactivation of the calcium current. If it does, it would support on a more fundamental level the notion that short- and long-term memory can involve a single memory trace.

Sensitization is a slightly more complex form of learning that can be seen in the gill-withdrawal reflex. It is the prolonged enhancement of an animal's preexisting response to a stimulus as a result of the presentation of a second stimulus that is noxious. Whereas habituation requires an animal to learn to ignore a particular stimulus because its consequences are trivial, sensitization requires the animal to learn to attend to a stimulus because it is accompanied by potentially painful or dangerous consequences. Therefore when an *Aplysia* is presented with a noxious stimulus

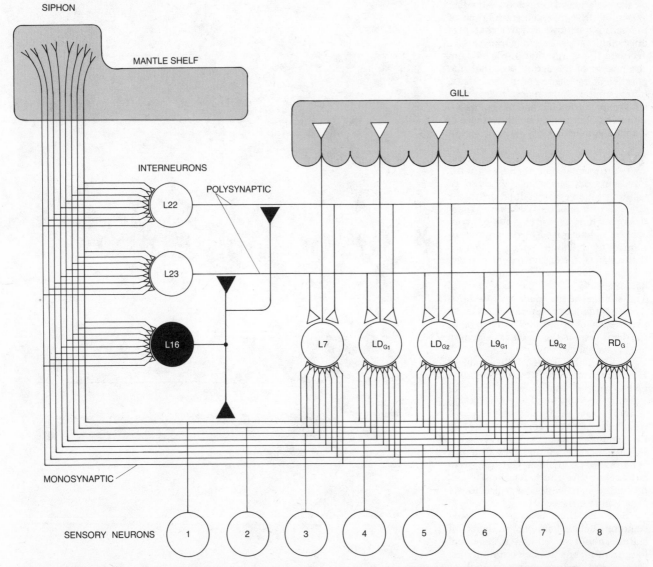

NEURAL CIRCUITRY of a behavioral reflex of *Aplysia*, the gill-withdrawal reflex, is depicted schematically. In the reflex action the animal withdraws its gill when a fleshy spout (the siphon) on a protective sheet (the mantle shelf) is stimulated in some way. The skin of the siphon is innervated by about 24 sensory neurons; the diagram has been simplified to focus on only eight of them. The sensory neurons make monosynaptic, or direct, connections to six identified gill motor neurons, which are shown in the row beginning with L7, and to at least one inhibitory cell (L16) and two interposed excitatory interneurons (L22 and L23), which make synapses with motor neurons.

to the head, the gill-withdrawal reflex response to a repeated stimulus to the siphon is greatly enhanced. As with habituation, sensitization can last from minutes to days and weeks, depending on the amount of training. Here I shall focus only on the short-term form.

Castellucci and I found that sensitization entails an alteration of synaptic transmission at the same locus that is involved in habituation: the synapses made by the sensory neurons on their central target cells. Our physiological studies and subsequent morphological studies by Craig Bailey, Mary C. Chen and Robert Hawkins indicate that the neurons mediating sensitization end near the synaptic terminals of the sensory neurons and enhance the release of transmitter by increasing the number of quanta turned loose by each action potential in the sensory neuron. The process is therefore called presynaptic facilitation. It is interesting because it illustrates (as does the earlier finding of presynaptic inhibition in another system by Joseph Dudel and Stephen Kuffler of the Harvard Medical School) that neurons have receptors to transmitters at two quite different sites. Receptors on the cell body and on the dendrites determine whether a cell should fire an action potential, and receptors on the synaptic terminals determine how much transmitter each action potential will release.

The same locus—the presynaptic terminals of the sensory neurons—can therefore be regulated in opposite ways by opposing forms of learning. It can be depressed as a result of the intrinsic activity within the neuron that occurs with habituation, and it can be facilitated by sensitization as a result of the activity of other neurons that synapse on the terminals. These findings at the level of the single cell support the observation at the behavioral level that habituation and sensitization are independent and opposing forms of learning.

This finding raises an interesting question. Sensitization can enhance a normal reflex response, but can it counteract the profound depression in the reflex produced by long-term habituation? If it can, does it restore the completely inactivated synaptic connections produced by long-term habituation? Carew, Castellucci and I examined this question and found that sensitization reversed the depressed behavior. Moreover, the synapses that were functionally inactivated (and would have remained so for weeks) were restored within an hour by a sensitizing stimulus to the head.

Hence there are synaptic pathways in the brain that are determined by devel-opmental processes but that, being predisposed to learning, can be functionally inactivated and reactivated by experience! In fact, at these modifiable synapses a rather modest amount of training or experience is necessary to produce profound changes. If the finding were applicable to the human brain, it would imply that even during simple social experiences, as when two people speak with each other, the action of the neuronal machinery in one person's brain is capable of having a direct and perhaps long-lasting effect on the modifiable synaptic connections in the brain of the other.

Short-term sensitization is particularly attractive from an experimental point of view because it promises to be amenable to biochemical analysis. As a first step Hawkins, Castellucci and I have identified specific cells in the abdominal ganglion of *Aplysia* that produce presynaptic facilitation. By injecting an electron-dense marker substance to fill the cell and label its synaptic endings we found that the endings contain vesicles resembling those found in *Aplysia* by Ludmiela Shkolnik and James H. Schwartz in a neuron whose transmitter had previously been established to be serotonin. Consistent with the possible serotonergic nature of this cell, Marcel-

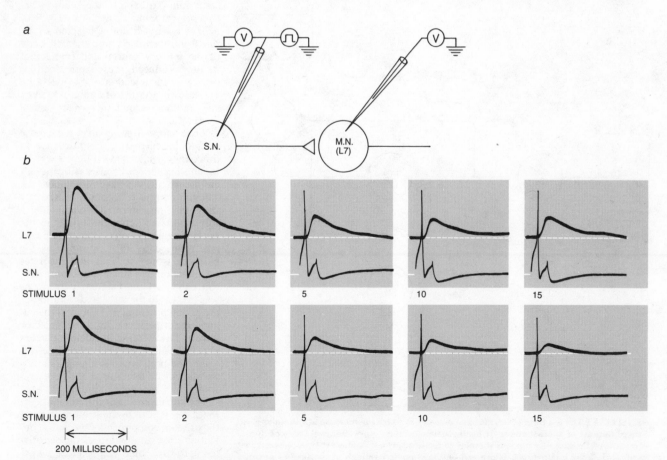

HABITUATION PROCESS, in which an animal's response to a stimulus gradually declines if the stimulus proves to be unimportant, is an elementary form of learning and memory that can be seen at the level of the single motor neuron. Here a sensory neuron (*S.N.*) from *Aplysia* that synapses on motor neuron L7 has been set up (*a*) so that the sensory neuron can be stimulated every 10 seconds. Selected records from two consecutive training sessions of 15 stimuli, separated by 15 minutes, show that the response of L7 declines and vanishes.

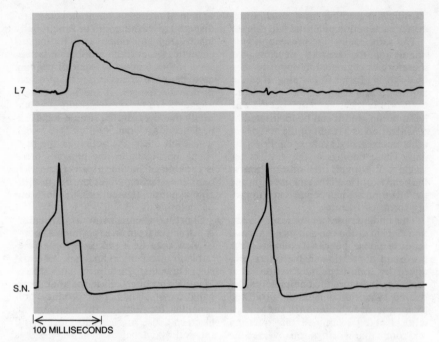

L7

S.N.

|←——→| 100 MILLISECONDS

LONG-TERM HABITUATION is revealed in a comparison of synaptic connections between a sensory neuron (*S.N.*) and the motor neuron L7 in untrained *Aplysia* (*left*), which served as controls, and in *Aplysia* that had received long-term habituation training (*right*). In the control animals an impulse in the sensory neuron is followed by a large excitatory synaptic response from the motor neuron. In the trained animals the synaptic connection is almost undetectable.

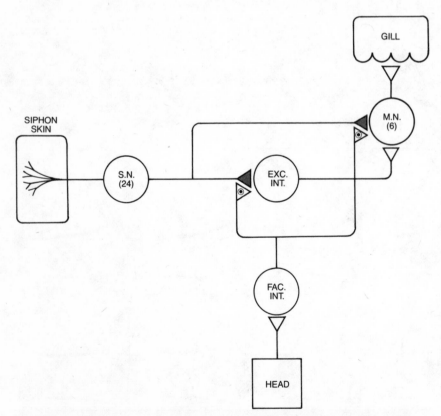

SENSITIZATION is a form of learning and memory in which the response to a stimulus is enhanced because of another and more noxious stimulus. Here gill-withdrawal reflex of *Aplysia* is intensified because of a noxious stimulus to the head. This stimulus activates neurons that excite facilitating interneurons, which end on the synaptic terminals of the sensory neurons. Those neurons are plastic, that is, capable of changing the effectiveness of their synapse. The transmitter of the facilitating interneurons, thought to be serotonin (*circled dots*), modulates the release of sensory-neuron transmitter to the excitatory interneurons and motor neurons.

lo Brunelli, Castellucci, Tom Tomosky-Sykes and I found that serotonin enhanced the monosynaptic connection between the sensory neuron and the motor cell L7, whereas other likely transmitters did not.

We next uncovered an interesting link between serotonin and the intracellular messenger cyclic adenosine monophosphate (cyclic AMP). It has been known since the classic work of Earl W. Sutherland, Jr., and his colleagues at Vanderbilt University that most peptide hormones do not enter the target cell but instead act on a receptor on the cell surface to stimulate an enzyme called adenylate cyclase that catalyzes the conversion in the cell of adenosine triphosphate (ATP) into cyclic AMP, which then acts as a "second messenger" (the hormone is the first messenger) at several points inside the cell to initiate a set of appropriate changes in function.

Howard Cedar, Schwartz and I found that strong and prolonged stimulation of the pathway from the head that mediates sensitization in *Aplysia* gave rise to a synaptically mediated increase in cyclic AMP in the entire ganglion. Cedar and Schwartz and Irwin Levitan and Samuel Barondes also found that they could generate a prolonged increase in cyclic AMP by incubating the ganglion with serotonin. To explore the relation between serotonin and cyclic AMP, Brunelli, Castellucci and I injected cyclic AMP intracellularly into the cell body of the sensory neuron and found that it also produced presynaptic facilitation, whereas injection of 5'-AMP (the breakdown product of cyclic AMP) or still another second messenger, cyclic GMP, did not.

Since habituation involves a decrease in calcium current, it was attractive to think that cyclic AMP might exert its facilitating actions by increasing the calcium current. As I have mentioned, the calcium current is normally masked by the potassium current. Klein and I therefore examined action potentials in the sensory neurons with the potassium current reduced by TEA. Stimulating the pathway from the head that mediates sensitization or a single facilitating neuron enhanced the calcium current, as was evident in the increased duration of the action potential in TEA, and the enhancement persisted for 15 minutes or longer. The increase in calcium current paralleled the enhanced transmitter release, and both synaptic changes in turn paralleled the increase in the reflex response to a sensitizing stimulus.

The enhancement of the calcium current, as it is seen in the prolongation of the calcium component of the action potential after stimulation of the sensitizing pathway, could be produced by extracellular application of either serotonin or two substances that increase the intracellular level of cyclic AMP by inhibiting phosphodiesterase, the enzyme that breaks down cyclic AMP. Similar effects were observed after direct intracellular injection of cyclic AMP, but not of 5'-AMP.

On the basis of these results Klein and I have proposed that stimulation of the facilitating neurons of the sensitizing pathway leads to the release of serotonin, which activates a serotonin-sensitive enzyme (adenylate cyclase) in the membrane of the sensory-neuron terminal. The resulting increase in cyclic AMP in the terminal leads to a greater activation of the calcium current either directly by activation of the calcium channel or indirectly by a decrease in an opposing potassium current. With each action potential the influx of calcium rises and more transmitter is released.

The availability of large cells whose electrical properties and interconnections can be thoroughly studied was the major initial attraction for using *Aplysia* to study behavior. The size of these cells might now prove to be an even greater advantage for exploring the subcellular and biochemical mechanisms of learning on the one hand and possible changes in membrane structure on the other. For example, it will be interesting to see more precisely how the increase in the level of cyclic AMP during sensitization is linked to the activation of a calcium current, because the linkage could provide the first step toward a molecular understanding of this simple form of short-term learning.

A number of mechanisms come to mind. The channels through which ions traverse the neuronal membranes are thought to consist of protein molecules. An obvious possibility is therefore that

cyclic AMP activates one or more protein kinases, enzymes that Paul Greengard of the Yale University School of Medicine has suggested may provide a common molecular mechanism for mediating the various actions of cyclic AMP within the cell. Protein kinases are enzymes that phosphorylate proteins, that is, they link a phosphoryl group to a side chain of the amino acids serine or threonine in the protein molecule, thereby changing the charge and configuration of proteins and altering their function, activating some and inactivating others. Phosphorylation could serve as an effective mechanism for the regulation of memory. One way sensitization might work is that the calcium-channel protein becomes activated (or the opposing potassium-channel protein becomes inactivated) when it is phosphorylated by a protein kinase that is dependent on cyclic AMP.

Sensitization holds an interesting position in the hierarchy of learning. It is frequently considered to be a precursor form of classical conditioning. In both sensitization and classical conditioning a reflex response to a stimulus is enhanced as a result of the activation of another pathway. Sensitization differs from conditioning in being nonassociative; the sensitizing stimulus is effective in enhancing reflex responsiveness whether or not it is paired in time with the reflex stimulus. Several types of associative learning have now been demonstrated in mollusks by Alan Gelperin of Princeton University, by George Mpitsos and Stephen Collins of Case Western Reserve University and by Terry Crow and Daniel L. Alkon of the National Institutes of Health. Recently Terry Walters, Carew and I have

obtained evidence for associative conditioning in *Aplysia*. We may therefore soon be in a position to analyze precisely how the mechanisms of sensitization relate to those of associative learning.

Another direction that research can now take is to examine the relation between the initial development of the neural circuit in the embryo and its later modification by learning. Both development and learning involve functional changes in the nervous system: changes in the effectiveness of synapses and in other properties of neurons. How are such changes related? Are the mechanisms of learning based on those of developmental plasticity, or do completely new processes specialized for learning emerge later?

Whatever the answers to these intriguing questions may be, the surprising and heartening thing that has emerged from the study of invertebrate animals is that one can now pinpoint and observe at the cellular level, and perhaps ultimately at the molecular level, simple aspects of memory and learning. Although certain higher mental activities are characteristic of the complex brains of higher animals, it is now clear that elementary aspects of what are regarded as mental processes can be found in the activity of just a very few neurons. It will therefore be interesting both philosophically and technically to see to what degree complex forms of mentation can be explained in terms of simpler components and mechanisms. To the extent that such reductionist explanations are possible it will also be important to determine how the units of this elementary alphabet of mentation are combined to yield the language of much more complex mental processes.

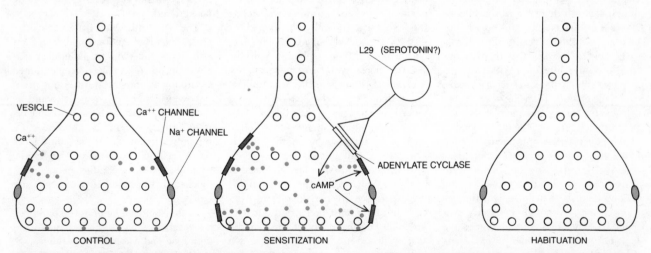

SHORT-TERM SENSITIZATION AND HABITUATION at the level of the single sensory neuron are modeled, beginning with what happens in a control situation (*left*) in which a cell fires before either sensitization or habituation has set in. A nerve impulse in the terminal membrane of the neuron opens up a number of channels for calcium ions (*Ca⁺⁺*) in parallel with the sodium channels (*Na⁺*). Sensitization is produced by cell group L29 (perhaps more) that are believed to release the transmitter serotonin. It acts on an adenylate cyclase, an enzyme that catalyzes the synthesis of cyclic adenosine monophosphate (cyclic AMP) in the neuron terminals. The cyclic AMP increases the influx of calcium ions, perhaps by making more calcium channels available. The calcium causes a greater binding of transmitter-bearing vesicles to release sites, increasing the probability that the neuron will release transmitter. In habituation repeated impulses in the terminals could decrease the number of open calcium channels, depressing the calcium influx and inactivating the synapse.

2

Brain Changes in Response to Experience

by Mark R. Rosenzweig, Edward L. Bennett
and Marian Cleeves Diamond
February 1972

*Rats kept in a lively environment for 30 days show
distinct changes in brain anatomy and chemistry
compared with animals kept in a dull environment.
The implications of these effects for man are assessed*

Does experience produce any observable change in the brain? The hypothesis that changes occur in brain anatomy as a result of experience is an old one, but convincing evidence of such changes has been found only in the past decade. It has now been shown that placing an experimental animal in enriched or impoverished environments causes measurable changes in brain anatomy and chemistry. How these changes are related to learning and memory mechanisms is currently being studied by an interdisciplinary approach that involves neurochemical, neuroanatomical and behavioral techniques.

The earliest scientific account of brain changes as a result of experience that we have been able to find was written in the 1780's by an Italian anatomist, Michele Gaetano Malacarne. His experimental design is worth describing briefly, since it resembles the one we are using in our laboratory at the University of California at Berkeley. He worked with two dogs from the same litter and with two parrots, two goldfinches and two blackbirds, each pair of birds from the same clutch of eggs. He trained one member of each pair for a long period; the other member of the pair was left untrained. He then killed the animals and examined their brains. He reported that there were more folds in the cerebellum of the trained animals than in that of the untrained ones. Although his study was noted by some of his contemporaries, we have not found any evidence that others attempted to carry out similar experiments. Knowledge of Malacarne's experiment quickly faded away.

During the 19th century there was considerable interest in the relation between the size of the human head and intellectual ability and training. In the 1870's Paul Broca, a famous French physician and anthropologist, compared the head circumference of medical students and male nurses and found that the students had larger heads. Since he believed the two sets of young men were equal in ability, he concluded that the differences in head size must have been due to the differences in training. Clearly Broca's logic was not impeccable, and there are other possible explanations for the differences he found. His critics pointed to the lack of correspondence between skull size and brain volume, the important roles of age and body size in determining brain size and the relative stability of the size of the brain in comparison with the size of most other organs. By the beginning of the 20th century not only had experimenters failed to prove that training resulted in changes in the gross anatomy of the brain but also a consensus had developed that such changes could not be detected, and so the search was generally abandoned.

With the development of new biochemical tools and techniques in the 1950's, some investigators began to ask if chemical changes in the brain following training could be detected. They looked for changes at the synapses that transmit impulses from one nerve cell to another or for changes in the nucleic acids (RNA and DNA) of nerve cells. The techniques used to find chemical or anatomical changes in the brain following experience are not difficult in principle but they must be carried out with precision because many of the changes that occur are not large. Here is how a basic experiment is conducted with laboratory rats of a given strain. (In our experiments we have worked with several strains of rats and with laboratory mice and gerbils; we have observed similar effects in all these animals.) At a given age, often at weaning, sets of three males are taken from each litter. Usually a dozen sets of three males are used in an experiment. This yields stabler and more reliable results than working with a single set, as Malacarne did.

The use of rodents for these studies is convenient for several reasons. Brain dissection is simpler in rodents than it is in carnivores or primates because the cerebral cortex of rodents is smooth and not convoluted like the cortex of higher mammals. The gray cortex can be stripped away from the underlying white matter more readily in rodents than it can in higher mammals. Rodents are small, inexpensive and bear large litters, so that littermates with the same genetic background can be assigned to different conditions. In addition, geneticists have developed inbred lines of rats and mice, and working with these inbred lines gives us further control over the genetic background.

The three male rats from each litter are assigned at random so that one rat remains in the standard laboratory colony cage, one rat is placed in an enriched environment and the third is put in an impoverished environment. It should be noted that "enriched" and "impoverished" are not used in an absolute sense but only in relation to the standard laboratory colony environment that is the usual baseline for studies in anatomy, biochemistry, physiology, nutrition and behavior.

In the standard laboratory conditions a few rats live in a cage of adequate size with food and water always present [*see illustration on following page*]. In the enriched environment several rats live in a large cage furnished with a variety of objects they can play with. A new set of playthings, drawn out of a pool of 25 objects, is placed in the cage every day. In the impoverished environment each rat lives alone in a cage. Originally the isolated rats were kept in a separate quiet room, but this turned out to be unnecessary.

At the end of a predetermined experimental period, which can be from a few days to several months, the rats are sacrificed and their brains are removed. The brain dissection and analysis of each set of three littermates are done in immediate succession but in a random order and identified only by code number so that the person doing the dissection does not know which cage the rat comes from. With practice a skillful worker can do dissections with considerable precision and reliability. To delineate the various cortical regions a small plastic calibrated T square is used [*see illustration on page 19*]. Samples removed from a cortical region are weighed to the nearest tenth of a milligram and then placed on dry ice. The samples are kept frozen until chemical analysis is performed to determine the activity of the neurotransmitter enzymes in them.

If the rat brains are to be used for anatomical studies, the animal is anesthetized and perfused with a fixative solution. Later sections of the brain are prepared for microscopy.

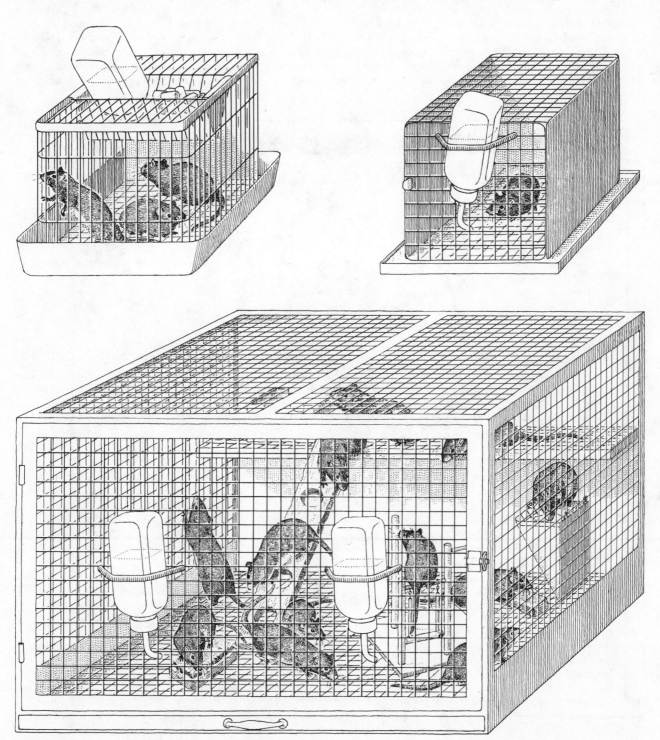

THREE LABORATORY ENVIRONMENTS that produce differences in brain anatomy of littermate rats are depicted. In the standard laboratory colony there are usually three rats in a cage (*upper left*). In the impoverished environment (*upper right*) a rat is kept alone in a cage. In the enriched environment 12 rats live together in a large cage furnished with playthings that are changed daily. Food and water are freely available in all three environments. The rats typically remain in the same environment for 30 days or more.

In the 1950's we had been attempting to relate individual differences in the problem-solving behavior of rats to individual differences in the amount of the enzyme acetylcholinesterase in the brain. (At the time and until 1966 the psychologist David Krech was a member of the research group.) The enzyme rapidly breaks down acetylcholine, a substance that acts as a transmitter between nerve cells. The excess transmitter must be neutralized quickly because nerve impulses can follow each other at a rate of hundreds per second. This enzymatic activity is often measured in terms of tissue weight, and so in our early experiments we recorded the weight of each sample of brain tissue we took for chemical analysis. We found indications that the level of brain acetylcholinesterase was altered by problem-solving tests, and this led us to look for effects of more extensive experience. To our surprise we found that different experiences not only affected the enzymatic activity but also altered the weight of the brain samples.

By 1964 we had found that rats that had spent from four to 10 weeks in the enriched or the impoverished environments differed in the following ways: rats with enriched experience had a greater weight of cerebral cortex, a greater thickness of cortex and a greater total activity of acetylcholinesterase but less activity of the enzyme per unit of tissue weight. Moreover, rats with enriched experience had considerably greater activity of another enzyme: cholinesterase, which is found in the glial cells and blood capillaries that surround the nerve cells. Glial cells (named from the Greek word for "glue") perform a variety of functions, including transportation of materials between capillaries and nerve cells, formation of the fatty insulating sheath around the neural axons and removal of dead neural tissue.

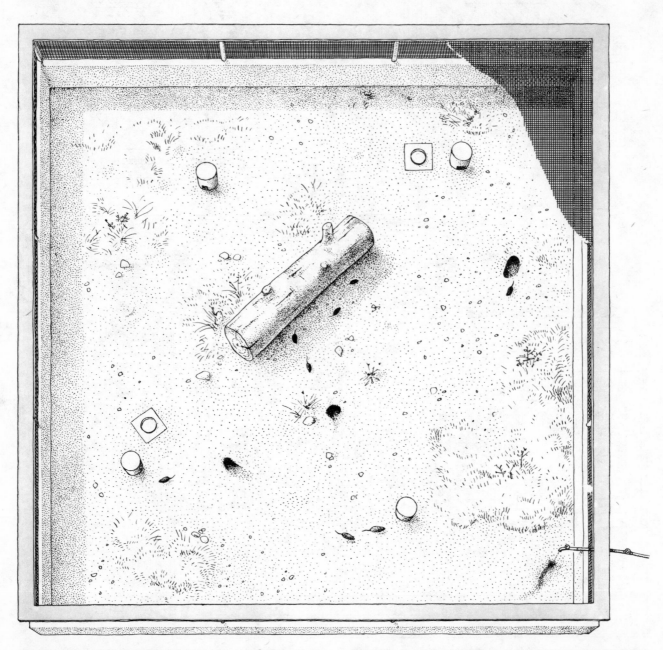

SEMINATURAL ENVIRONMENT for studying the effects of experience on the brain is provided by outdoor enclosures at the Field Station for Research in Animal Behavior at the University of California at Berkeley. The enclosures have a concrete base 30 feet by 30 feet with a screen over the top. Inbred laboratory rats thrive in the outdoor setting when food and water are provided. The rats revert to burrowing, something that their ancestors, which had lived in laboratory cages, had not done for more than 100 generations.

We later found that there were more glial cells in rats from the enriched environment than there were in rats from the impoverished one, and this may account for the increased activity of cholinesterase. Although differences in experience did not change the number of nerve cells per unit of tissue, the enriched environment produced larger cell bodies and nuclei. These larger cell bodies indicate higher metabolic activity. Further chemical measures involving RNA and DNA pointed in the same direction. The amount of DNA per milligram of tissue decreased, presumably because the bulk of the cortex increased as the number of neurons, whose nuclei contain a fixed amount of DNA, remained relatively constant. The amount of RNA per milligram remained virtually unchanged, yielding a significant increase in the ratio of RNA to DNA, and this suggests a higher metabolic activity. In most of the experiments the greatest differences between enriched and impoverished experience were found in the occipital cortex, which is roughly the rear third of the cortical surface.

We do not know why the occipital region of the cortex is affected by enriched experience more than other regions. At first we thought that differences in visual stimulation might be responsible, but when we used blinded rats, the occipital cortex still showed significant differences between littermates from the enriched and the impoverished environments. We found the same effects when normal rats were placed in the different environments and kept in darkness for the entire period. This is not to say that deprivation of vision did not have an effect on the anatomy and chemistry of the brain. The occipital cortex of rats that were blinded or kept totally in the dark gained less weight than the occipital cortex of littermates that were raised in standard colony conditions with a normal light-dark cycle, but this did not prevent the occurrence of the enrichment-impoverishment effect.

Although the brain differences induced by environment are not large, we are confident that they are genuine. When the experiments are replicated, the same pattern of differences is found repeatedly. For example, in 16 replications between 1960 and 1969 of the basic enriched-environment-v.-impoverished-environment experiment, using the same strain of rat exposed to the experimental conditions from the age of 25 to 105 days, each experiment resulted in a greater occipital-cortex weight for the rats in the enriched environment. Twelve

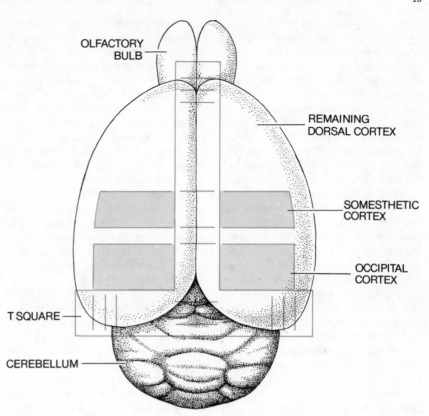

OLFACTORY BULB

REMAINING DORSAL CORTEX

SOMESTHETIC CORTEX

OCCIPITAL CORTEX

T SQUARE

CEREBELLUM

CORTICAL AREAS of a rat brain are located for dissection with the aid of a calibrated plastic T square to ensure uniform samples. The desired sections are removed, weighed and stored on dry ice. The remaining cortex and the subcortex also are weighed and frozen.

of the 16 replications were significantly at better than the .05 level, that is, for each of the 12 experiments there was less than one chance in 20 that the difference was due simply to chance or biological variability. For weight of the total cortex, 13 of the 16 experiments showed significant differences [*see top illustration on page 22*].

The most consistent effect of experience on the brain that we found was the ratio of the weight of the cortex to the weight of the rest of the brain: the subcortex. It appears that the cortex increases in weight quite readily in response to an enriched environment, whereas the weight of the rest of the brain changes little. Moreover, since rats with larger bodies tend to have both a heavier cortex and a heavier subcortex than smaller rats, the ratio of the cortex to the rest of the brain tends to cancel the influence of body weight. For animals of a given strain, sex, age and environment the cortex/subcortex ratio tends to be the same even if the animals differ in body weight. When the environment is such that the cortex grows, the cortex/subcortex ratio shows the change very clearly and reliably. On this measure 14 of the 16 experiments were significant at the .01 level.

One of the major problems for mea-

suring the effects of experience on the brain is finding an appropriate baseline. Initially we took the standard laboratory colony condition as the baseline, as most other investigators have. The cortex/subcortex-weight ratio in rats from the enriched environment is greater than the ratio in rats from the standard colony environment, and this ratio in turn is greater than the ratio in rats from the impoverished environment. Where thickness of cortex is concerned, both environmental enrichment and impoverishment are effective but on different regions of the cortex.

Suppose that the natural environment in which the animals evolved were taken as the baseline. Compared with the laboratory environments, even the enriched one, a natural environment may be much richer in learning experiences. For inbred laboratory animals, however, it is no longer clear what the natural environment is. Laboratory rats and mice have been kept for more than 100 generations in protected environments, and inbreeding has made their gene pool different from the natural one. For this reason we have begun to study wild deer mice (*Peromyscus*). The mice are trapped in the San Francisco area and brought to our laboratory; some are kept in almost natural conditions at an outdoor station and others are put into laboratory cages. The work with deer mice is still in progress, but we have also placed laboratory rats in the outdoor setting. We found that when food is provided, laboratory rats can thrive in an outdoor enclosure even in a wet winter when the temperature drops to the freezing point. When the ground was not too wet, the rats dug burrows, something their ancestors had not done for more than 100 generations. In each of eight experiments the rats kept for one month in the outdoor setting showed a greater brain development than their littermates that had been kept in enriched laboratory cages. This indicates that even the enriched laboratory environment is indeed impoverished in comparison with a natural environment.

It is possible that the brain changes we found are not the result of learning and memory but are due to other aspects of the experimental situation, such as the amount of handling and stress, or perhaps an altered rate of maturation. For example, simply handling rats, particularly young ones, is known to increase the weight of their adrenal glands. Rats in the enriched environment are handled each day when they are removed from their cage while their playthings are being changed, whereas rats in the impoverished environment are handled only once a week for weighing. We tested the effects of handling on brain changes some years ago. Some rats were handled for several minutes a day for either 30 or 60 days; their littermates were never handled. There were no differences between the handled rats and the nonhandled ones in brain weight or brain-enzyme activity. More recently rats from both the enriched and the impoverished environments were handled once a day and the usual brain differences developed.

Stress was another possible cause of the cerebral effects. Rats from the impoverished environment might have suffered from "isolation stress" and rats from the enriched environment may have been stressed by "information overload." To test this notion Walter H. Riege subjected rats to a daily routine of stress. The rats were briefly tumbled in a revolving drum or given a mild electric shock. The stress produced a significant increase in the weight of the adrenal glands but did not give rise to changes in the brain measures that we use. It seems clear that stress is not responsible for the cerebral changes we have found.

It was also possible, since some of the brain changes we have found go in the same direction as changes that occur in normal maturation, that enriched experience simply accelerates maturation or that isolation retards it. Changes in the depth of the cerebral cortex and certain other changes resulting from an enriched environment go in the opposite direction to what is found in normal growth. The cortical thickness of standard colony rats reaches a maximum at 25 days after birth and then decreases slightly with age, whereas enriched experience causes cortical thickness to increase even in year-old rats. In fact, Riege has found that an enriched environment will produce as great an increase in brain weight in fully mature rats as it does in young rats, although the adult rats require a longer period of environmental stimulation to show the maximum effect.

The effect of enriched environment on very young rats has been tested by Dennis Malkasian. He puts sets of three litters of six-day-old rat pups and their mother either into an unfurnished cage or into a cage containing play objects. Brains were taken for anatomical analysis at 14, 19 and 28 days of age. At each age pups from the enriched environment showed a greater thickness of cerebral cortex, and in some parts of the cortex the differences were larger than those found in experiments with rats examined after weaning.

When we first reported our results other investigators were understandably skeptical, since the effect of experience on the brain had not been previously demonstrated. After our findings had been replicated, some investigators began to think that the brain may be so plastic that almost any treatment can modify it, for example merely placing a rat for 15 minutes a day in any apparatus other than its home cage. This does not happen; although cerebral changes are easier to induce than we had supposed at first, a moderate amount of experience is still necessary. We recently demonstrated that two hours of daily enriched experience over a 30-day period is sufficient to produce the typical changes in brain weight. On the other hand, placing a group of 12 rats in a large unfurnished cage for two hours a day for 30 days did not bring about significant changes in our usual brain measures. Moreover, putting rats alone in large cages with play objects for two hours a day is not very effective, probably because a single rat does not play with the objects much and tends to rest or to groom itself. The enriched environment will produce cerebral changes in a single rat if the rat is stimulated to interact with the objects. This can be done by giving the rat a moderate dose of an excitant drug or by putting it into the enriched environment during the dark part of its daily cycle (rats are nocturnal animals). A recent experiment indicates that cerebral changes can also be achieved by putting the rat into the enriched environment after several hours of food deprivation and placing tiny pellets of food on and in the play objects.

There can now be no doubt that many aspects of brain anatomy and brain chemistry are changed by experience. Some of our most recent efforts have been directed toward determining the changes that occur at the synaptic level in the occipital cortex, a region of the brain that shows relatively large changes with experience in enriched environments. Over the past few years Albert Globus of the University of California at Irvine has been counting the number of dendritic spines in brain sections from rats that have been exposed to an enriched environment or an impoverished one in our laboratory. Most of the synaptic contacts between nerve cells in the cortex are made on the branchlike dendrites of the receiving cell or on the dendritic spines, which are small projections from the dendrites. Globus made his counts on the cortical neuron called a pyramidal cell [see top illustration on opposite page]. He found more spines, particularly on the basal dendrites, in rats exposed to an enriched environment than in littermates from the impoverished environment.

An even more detailed view of changes in the synaptic junctions has come out of a study we have done in collaboration with Kjeld Møllgaard of the University of Copenhagen, who spent a year in our laboratory. He prepared electron micrographs of brain sections from the third layer of the occipital cortex of rats. Measurement of the synaptic junctions revealed that rats from enriched environments had junctions that averaged approximately 50 percent larger in cross section than similar junctions in littermates from impoverished environments. The latter, however, had more synapses per unit area [see illustration on page 23].

William T. Greenough, Roger West and T. Blaise Fleischmann of the University of Illinois have also found that there is increased synaptic contact in enriched-experience rats. Some other workers have reported that increased size of synapse is associated with a decreased number of synapses, whereas decreased size of synapse is associated with an increased number. It seems that memory

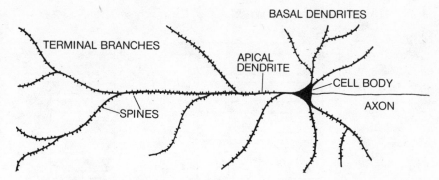

DENDRITIC SPINES, tiny "thorns," or projections, from the dendrites of a nerve cell, serve as receivers in many of the synaptic contacts between neurons. The drawing is of a type of cortical neuron known as the pyramidal cell. Rats from an enriched environment have more spines on these cells than their littermates from an impoverished environment.

or learning may be encoded in the brain either by the selective addition of contacts between nerve cells or by the selective removal of contacts, and that both processes may go on at the same time.

Does an enriched environment or an impoverished environment alter learning ability? Although some studies suggest that experience in an enriched environment usually improves subsequent learning, the effects are often short-lived. The result depends on many factors, for example the measure of learning that is used, the age at which the enriched experience is provided and the type of task that is learned. Early enrichment may improve subsequent learning of one task, have no effect on another task and actually impair learning in a third. Perhaps we should not expect much transfer of capacity among entirely different kinds of behavior. Nor should we expect experience in an enriched environment to lead to an increase in "general ability"; every environment is specific and so are abilities. Harry F. Harlow of the University of Wisconsin has shown that early problem-solving in monkeys may have the deleterious effect of fixating infantile behavior patterns; such monkeys may never reach the efficient adult performance that they would have attained without the early training. Again, this result is specific and should be generalized only with caution.

Formal training of rats, such as teaching them to press a lever in response to a signal or to run a maze, produces changes in brain anatomy and chemistry, but the type of training seems to determine the kind of changes. Victor Fedorov and his associates at the Pavlov Institute of Physiology near Leningrad found changes in brain weight and in the activity of acetylcholinesterase and cholinesterase after prolonged training of rats, but the pattern of changes is different from what we found with enriched and impoverished environments. In our laboratory we have given rats daily formal training in either operant-conditioning devices or in a series of mazes for a month or more and have found changes in brain weight and brain enzymes. These changes, however, were rather small and also had a pattern different from the changes induced by environmental experience. This is clearly a problem that requires more research.

The effect of experimental environments on the brains of animals has sometimes been cited as bearing on problems of human education. We should like to sound a cautionary note in this regard. It is difficult to extrapolate from an experiment with rats under one set of conditions to the behavior of rats under another set of conditions, and it is much riskier to extrapolate from a rat to a mouse to a monkey to a human. We have found generally similar brain changes as a result of experience in several species of rodents, and this appears to have fostered the assumption that similar results may be found with carnivores and with primates, including man. Only further research will show whether or not this is so. Animal research raises questions and allows us to test concepts and techniques, some of which may later prove useful in research with human subjects.

If this research leads to knowledge of how memories are stored in the brain, it will have obvious implications for the study of conditions that favor learning and memory and also of conditions that impair learning and the laying down of memories. Among the unfavorable conditions that are of great social concern are mental retardation and senile decline in ability to form new memories. Clues to the prevention or amelioration of these conditions could be of great social value. Let us also consider two other areas into which such research on brain plasticity may extend.

One of these areas concerns the effects of malnutrition on the development of the brain and of intelligence. Some investigators, such as R. H. Barnes and David A. Levitsky of the Cornell University Graduate School of Nutrition, have proposed that certain effects of malnutrition may actually be secondary effects of environmental impoverishment. That is,

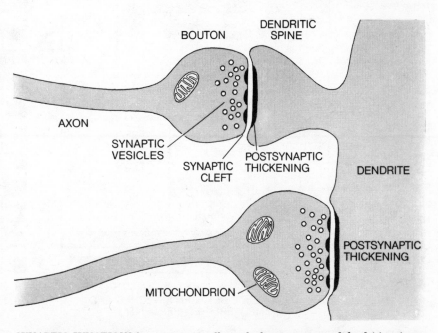

SYNAPTIC JUNCTIONS between nerve cells can be between axon and dendritic spine or between axon and the dendrite itself. The vesicles contain a chemical transmitter that is released when an electrical signal from the axon reaches the end bouton. The transmitter moves across the synaptic cleft and stimulates the postsynaptic receptor sites in the dendrite. The size of the postsynaptic membrane is thought to be an indicator of synaptic activity.

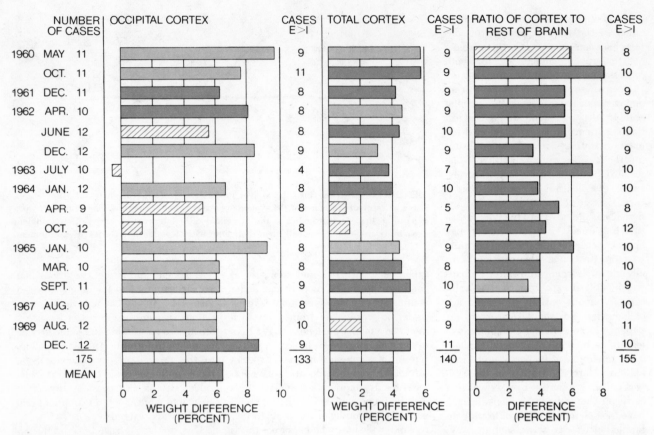

	NUMBER OF CASES	OCCIPITAL CORTEX	CASES E>I	TOTAL CORTEX	CASES E>I	RATIO OF CORTEX TO REST OF BRAIN	CASES E>I
1960 MAY	11		9		9		8
OCT.	11		11		9		10
1961 DEC.	11		8		9		9
1962 APR.	10		8		9		9
JUNE	12		8		10		10
DEC.	12		9		9		9
1963 JULY	10		4		7		10
1964 JAN.	12		8		10		10
APR.	9		8		5		8
OCT.	12		8		7		12
1965 JAN.	10		8		9		10
MAR.	10		8		8		10
SEPT.	11		9		10		9
1967 AUG.	10		8		9		10
1969 AUG.	12		10		9		11
DEC.	12		9		11		10
	175		133		140		155
MEAN							

BRAIN-WEIGHT DIFFERENCES between rats from enriched environments and their littermates from impoverished environments were replicated in 16 successive experiments between 1960 and 1969 involving an 80-day period and the same strain of rat. For the occipital cortex, weight differences in three of the replications were significant at the probability level of .01 or better (*dark colored bars*), nine were significant at the .05 level (*light colored bars*) and four were not significant (*hatched bars*). The ratio of the weight of the cortex to the rest of the brain proved to be the most reliable measure, with 14 of the 16 replications significant at the .01 level.

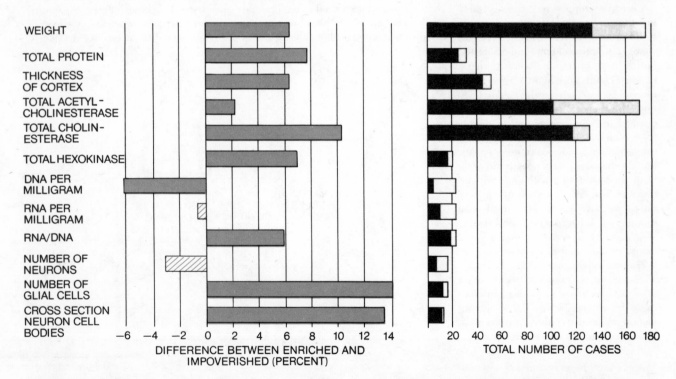

OCCIPITAL CORTEX of rats kept in enriched or impoverished environments from 25 to 105 days showed the effects of the different experiences. The occipital cortex of rats from the enriched environment, compared with that of rats from the impoverished one, was 6.4 percent heavier. This was significant at the .01 level or better, as were most other measures (*dark colored bars*). Only two measures were not significant (*hatched bars*). The dark gray bars on the right show the number of cases in which the rat from the enriched environment exceeded its littermate from the impoverished environment in each of the measures that are listed.

since a prominent effect of malnutrition is to make the person or animal apathetic and unresponsive to the environment, the individual then suffers from lack of stimulation, and this may be the direct cause of some of the symptoms usually associated with malnutrition. Current research suggests that some of the effects of malnutrition may be offset by programs of environmental stimulation or increased by environmental impoverishment.

Another possibly beneficial result of our research findings would be to stimulate a resurgence of attempts to determine relations between experience and brain anatomy in man. This was a topic of some interest late in the 19th century, and a number of reports were published. For example, in 1892 there was a publication on the postmortem examination of the brain of a blind deaf-mute, Laura Bridgman. It was found that the parts of her cortex that were involved in vision and hearing were thin and lacked the pattern of folding found in the normal human brain. In contrast, the region of her cortex devoted to touch had a normal appearance. It would be of interest to see if such results could be generalized by a large-scale modern postmortem study of brains of people who had been deprived of one or more senses. It would be even more interesting to find out if heightened employment of a sense leads to supranormal development of the associated brain region. Would musicians as a group, for example, show an enhanced development of the auditory cortex?

The human brain, because of the specialization of the two cerebral hemispheres, is more likely to provide answers to such questions than animal brains. Spoken words are analyzed in the auditory region of the left cerebral hemisphere, whereas music is analyzed in the auditory region of the right hemisphere. (These hemispheric functions are reversed in a few people.) The relative development of different regions in the same brain could be measured, so that the subjects would be their own control. In recent investigations Norman Geschwind and Walter Levitsky of the Harvard Medical School have found that 65 percent of the human brains they examined showed a greater anatomical development of the auditory area in the left hemisphere, 11 percent showed a greater auditory development in the right hemisphere and 24 percent showed equal development on the two sides. On the other hand, behavioral and physiological tests indicate that 96 percent of the people tested have left-hemisphere speech dom-

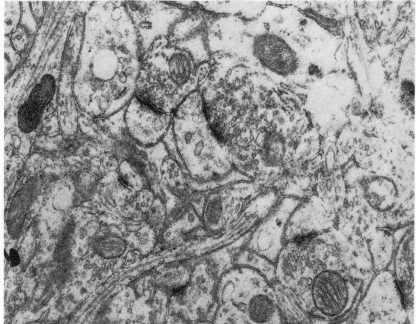

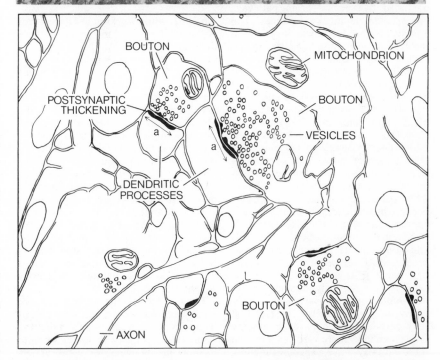

BRAIN SECTION from the occipital cortex of a rat is enlarged 37,000 times in this electron micrograph by Kjeld Møllgaard. The map identifies some of the components. Measurement of the postsynaptic thickening is shown in the map of the section by the arrow (a). The number of synaptic junctions was also counted. It was found that rats reared in an enriched environment had junctions approximately 50 percent larger than littermates from an impoverished environment, and the latter had more junctions, although smaller ones, per unit area.

inance and presumably have a greater development of the auditory area on that side. Is it possible that people with musical training account for most of the cases in which size of the right auditory area equals or exceeds the size of the left? In order to find out investigators will have to measure sufficient numbers of brains of individuals whose major abilities and disabilities are known. In

fact, such a program was proposed 100 years ago by Broca, but the techniques available then were not adequate to carrying out the project. Today the results of our animal studies can serve as a guide, and investigators can look more penetratingly for the anatomical and chemical changes in the human brain that are correlated with experience and learning.

3

The Reward System of the Brain

by Aryeh Routtenberg
November 1978

*Two decades ago it was discovered that the brain has
"pleasure centers." These centers are now seen as
belonging to a system of pathways that appear to play
a role in learning and memory*

Neuroscientists have learned much about the anatomy, physiology and chemistry of the brain. Does this knowledge relate to human learning, pleasure and mood? Is it possible that these complex processes are mediated by specific brain pathways and specific chemical substances? The answer appears to be yes, largely as a result of an intriguing but puzzling discovery made some 20 years ago at McGill University by James Olds and Peter Milner. They demonstrated that a rat with an electrode inserted into a certain area of its brain would press a treadle to stimulate itself [see "Pleasure Centers in the Brain," by James Olds; SCIENTIFIC AMERICAN Offprint 30]. Olds, a pioneer in the study of the relation between brain function and behavior, died in a swimming accident in 1976; his death was particularly tragic because he was engaged in exciting new explorations of brain physiology.

The phenomenon discovered by Olds and Milner, which is now referred to as brain reward, can be localized in particular nerve cells and their fibers. The brain-reward system is affected by drugs that interact with the substances secreted by these nerve cells. The fact that only certain nerve-fiber pathways are implicated in brain reward suggests that these pathways have a specific function. This parallels what is known of the visual system and the movement system, each of which has a specified set of component pathways.

Olds, first at the University of California at Los Angeles and then at the University of Michigan, took the initial steps toward identifying the pathways that support brain reward. He confirmed that self-stimulating behavior in laboratory animals is prompted only by the stimulation of particular brain areas and is not a general effect due simply to the electrical stimulation of brain tissue. For example, stimulation of the medial forebrain bundle, a group of nerve fibers that pass through the hypothalamus, gave rise to the highest rates of treadle-pressing in response to the lowest electric currents: shocks from electrodes in

this area could produce response rates of more than 100 presses a minute. There were also areas characterized by milder effects; for example, stimulation of the septal area caused the animals to respond only about 10 times a minute.

In 1962, while working in Olds's laboratory, I became interested in these different response rates for stimulation of different brain regions and set about studying them. A rat was given a choice between two treadles, one delivering rewarding brain stimulation and the other delivering the only food available to the animal during the experiment. I found that the animals would forgo food essential to their survival in order to obtain brain stimulation. This behavior was observed, however, only if the electrode was within the medial forebrain bundle. If the electrode was as little as half a millimeter away from this area, or in other areas whose stimulation yielded a reward, such as the septal area, the animals pressed both the food-delivering and the brain-stimulation treadles and were able to maintain their body weight and survive.

I wondered whether an animal more intelligent than the rat, if it were placed in the same situation, would show the same maladaptive behavior or whether its more highly developed cerebral cortex would enable it to achieve a balance between self-stimulation and feeding. Eliot Gardner and I were able to demon-

strate self-starvation in the rhesus monkey, an animal with a cortex far more advanced than that of the rat. This powerful effect implies that higher primates, perhaps even human beings, will stop eating in order to obtain rewarding brain stimulation. Such results suggest that the neural mechanisms subserving self-stimulation exert a powerful and perhaps dominant influence on behavior, particularly activities of the moment. Since the behavior is so compulsive, one wonders whether the reward system may play a role in drug addiction. For example, there is some evidence that certain regions of the brain that are sensitive to morphine and contain the morphinelike substance enkephalin are in the same location as the regions supporting brain reward.

The brain's functioning is obscured by its enormously complex array of nerve cells and their fibers, and so in order to identify the cells involved in self-stimulation it is necessary to combine the study of brain reward with the study of brain anatomy. In my laboratory at Northwestern University we have been pursuing this approach by making lesions with the stimulating electrode under light anesthesia at brain sites in rats where self-stimulation has been demonstrated. Within a few days the neural elements near the tip of the stimulating electrode begin to degenerate. We then perfuse the animals with formaldehyde, use a special stain for degenerating tis-

TWO TYPES OF NERVE FIBERS in the frontal cortex of the human brain are revealed in the fluorescent micrographs on the opposite page. The images were obtained by chemically treating thin sections of brain tissue so that the neurotransmitter substances in the nerve fibers fluoresced when they were illuminated with ultraviolet radiation. This technique has been an essential tool in mapping the neural pathways that mediate brain reward. The micrograph at the top shows a nerve fiber containing the neurotransmitter dopamine. The green-fluorescent dopamine fiber is typically thin and sinuous, with irregularly spaced spindle-shaped swellings. (The bright yellow blobs in the background represent not neurotransmitter but granules of the fatty pigment lipofuscin, which are present in many cell types and fluoresce in the absence of chemical treatment.) The micrograph at the bottom shows a nerve fiber containing the neurotransmitter norepinephrine. This fiber too has a green glow, but it can be distinguished from the dopamine fiber by the closely spaced swellings, which are intensely fluorescent. Both the dopamine and the norepinephrine pathways in the frontal cortex have been implicated in the reward system of the brain. These micrographs, magnified approximately 1,000 diameters, were made by Brigitte Berger of Neuropathology Laboratory at Pitié-Salpêtrière Hospital in Paris.

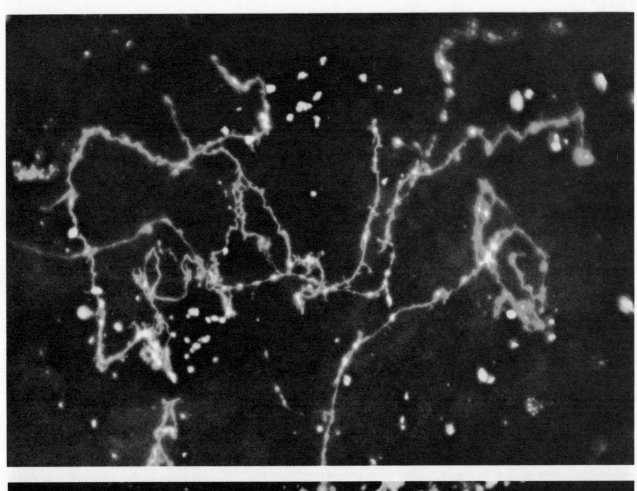

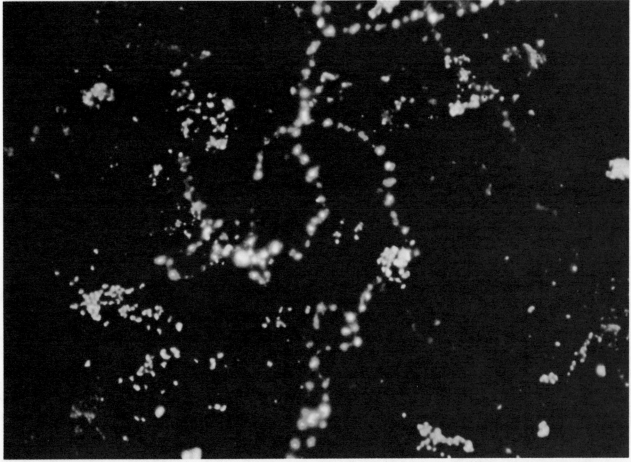

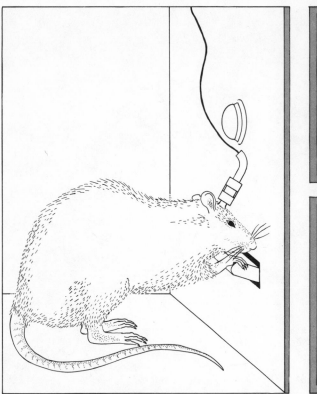
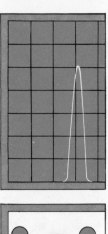
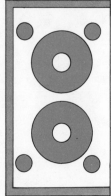

SKINNER-BOX APPARATUS is utilized to study the behavioral effects of brain reward. A metal electrode is implanted in the reward system of the rat, and the animal is allowed to trigger an electric stimulus to its brain by pressing the treadle. The curve on the oscilloscope screen indicates the delivery of the stimulus. If the stimulating electrode is implanted in the medial forebrain bundle of the hypothalamus, the rat will stimulate itself nearly continuously for days, neglecting food, water and sleep. Other parts of reward system give rise to less dramatic effects.

sue and see which neural elements are associated with the reward effects.

An example of this approach linking self-stimulation to specific pathways is provided by our study of the cerebral cortex in the frontal lobe of the brain. Although it had been doubted that the frontal cortex was important to brain reward, there are two regions of it in the rat that we have found to support self-stimulation. We made lesions at frontal-cortex self-stimulation sites and traced a pathway through the caudate nucleus and the internal capsule on its medial side. At the level of the hypothalamus this pathway is intermingled with the medial forebrain bundle. This work offers evidence that brain reward in the medial forebrain bundle results from stimulation of these frontal-cortex fibers. There is reason to believe from other work that this system may be only one of several brain-reward systems passing through the medial forebrain bundle.

The involvement of the frontal cortex in brain reward has been demonstrated in monkeys as well as in rats. Edmund Rolls of the University of Oxford has discovered self-stimulation points in the frontal cortex of the squirrel monkey similar to the regions that have been mapped in the rat. Even

though the brain locations where self-stimulation has been observed are similar in a rodent (the rat) and a primate (the squirrel monkey), the great difference among species in the size of the frontal cortex creates the potential for great variation in the significance to a given species of brain-reward stimulation.

Brain reward can be found not only in the frontal cortex and the hypothalamus but also deep within the brain stem: in the pons and the medulla. Such findings indicate that although brain reward is present only at specific locations, it extends from the forebrain to the midbrain and into the hindbrain. In 1969 Charles Malsbury and I showed that self-stimulation could be obtained with electrodes positioned in the output pathway of the cerebellum and at sites in the dorsal pontine tegmentum of the brain stem. Some of these regions were also close to newly discovered pathways that were associated with catecholamine neurotransmitters: substances that transmit the nerve impulse from one nerve cell to another. We therefore began to suspect that neurotransmitters of this type were involved in self-stimulation.

In 1971 Urban Ungerstedt of the Karolinska Institute in Stockholm described new catecholamine pathways in the forebrain, the midbrain and the

hindbrain. He worked with the technique known as histofluorescence, in which the location of specific substances in a tissue is revealed by inducing them to emit light of a characteristic color. The technique was developed in 1962 by B. Falck of the University of Lund and N.-Å. Hillarp of the Karolinska Institute, who built on earlier work by O. Eränkö of the University of Helsinki and Arvid Carlsson of the University of Göteborg. In 1974 Olle Lindvall and Anders Björklund of the University of Lund applied more sensitive techniques to establish the existence in the central nervous system of mammals of several pathways associated with the catecholamine norepinephrine and several pathways associated with another catecholamine, dopamine.

To obtain histofluorescent micrographs of brain tissue the tissue is first treated with aldehyde or glyoxylic acid, which react with catecholamines to form fluorophores, substances that fluoresce when they are excited by ultraviolet radiation. When a thin section of the tissue is exposed to ultraviolet in the fluorescence microscope, the fluorophore is excited and emits light. With the aid of a special wavelength detector norepinephrine can be seen to emit in the green-yellow region of the spectrum and dopamine in the green region. Although the color difference is difficult to determine without a special detector, the shape of the nerve fiber containing one substance or the other is different. Thus when the fluorescent fibers are observed in a histofluorescent micrograph, they reveal the anatomical location of the chemical substance. The histofluorescence technique is therefore based on histochemical principles: it is chemical in that it reveals brain pathways through a chemical reaction with neurotransmitters and histological in that the reaction takes place in a thin section of brain tissue on a microscope slide.

The existence of catecholamine pathways has been confirmed by the application of histofluorescence to the human brain. Working with tissue from an unviable fetus, Lars Olson, L. O. Boréus and Ake Seiger of the Karolinska Institute and Hospital have found the analogous catecholamine brain pathways in humans that have been observed in the brain of rats and monkeys.

The evidence for the similar location of catecholamine pathways and areas of self-stimulation is not the sole reason for supposing there is a connection between catecholamines and the brain-reward system. The rate at which rats with an electrode implanted in their brain will press a treadle to stimulate themselves is affected by certain drugs that are known to interfere with the function of catecholamines. The same drugs are also known to affect mood in human beings; indeed, they are sometimes administered to control anxiety and psychotic behavior. Since there is a connection between these mood-altering drugs and the catecholamines and also between the catecholamines and the brain-reward system, there would seem to be one between the brain-reward system and mood and personality.

Norepinephrine and dopamine are two major catecholamines that have been identified as neurotransmitters in the brain. When a nerve cell in a catecholamine system is activated, it releases one of these substances. The neurotransmitter crosses the synapse, the gap between the axon terminal of one nerve cell and the cell body of the next nerve cell. In so doing it changes the permeability of the membrane of the second nerve cell to ions in the extracellular fluid and so changes its excitability. The catecholamine is then either destroyed by an enzyme or is taken back into the axon terminal of the first cell.

Drugs that manipulate the catecholamine system have a powerful effect on mood. It is generally believed such drugs act to modify catecholamine transmission at the synapse, thereby altering the neurotransmitter's ability to influence other nerve cells. Studies involving a variety of drugs that modify catecholamine synaptic transmission have revealed a straightforward relation: agents that elevate catecholamine levels or mimic the action of catecholamines facilitate self-stimulation; agents that lower these levels depress self-stimulation. For example, the drug *d*-amphetamine potentiates both the action of catecholamines and self-stimulation. The drug chlorpromazine blocks the action of catecholamines and also blocks self-stimulation.

Chlorpromazine has been effective as an antipsychotic agent, and so a link has been suggested between psychoses and the catecholamine-connected self-stimulation pathways. It seems possible that because of either genetic or environmental factors abnormalities in the brain-reward pathways could lead to permanent changes in mental state. Larry Stein and C. David Wise of the Wyeth Laboratories have suggested that the cause of schizophrenia is an enzymatic deficiency that allows the production of a toxic substance, 6-hydroxydopamine, which destroys norepinephrine pathways thought to be associated with brain reward. They argue that these pathways, which can be seen in histofluorescent micrographs, are essential for adaptive behavioral responses. In support of their hypothesis they have demonstrated that synthetic 6-hydroxydopamine injected directly into the brain of a rat reduces the rate at which the rat presses a treadle to get a brain reward. This hypothesis is of special value because it explicitly relates schizophrenia to abnormalities in particular brain-reward pathways that

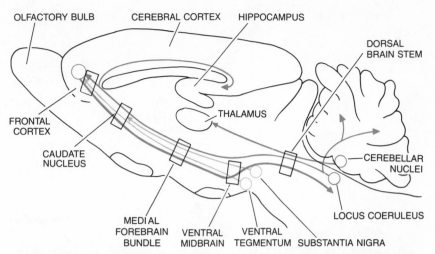

PATHWAYS OF REWARD in the rat brain are outlined schematically in this longitudinal section. The pathways extend in both directions from nerve-cell bodies in the hindbrain, the midbrain and the frontal cortex, passing through the medial forebrain bundle in the hypothalamus. The circles indicate the locations of the cell bodies; the rectangles indicate regions where reliable self-stimulation behavior has been obtained in studies with the Skinner-box apparatus.

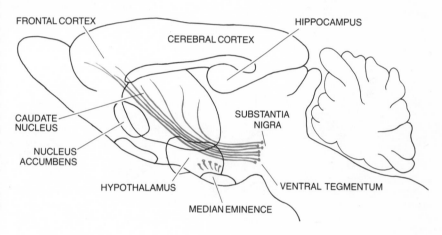

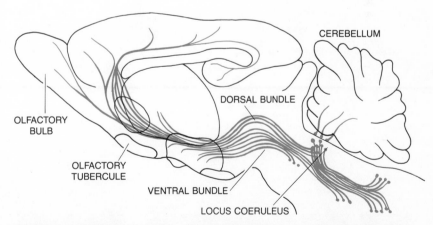

NEUROTRANSMITTER PATHWAYS implicated in the reward system of the rat brain were mapped by fluorescence microscopy. The nerve cells that secrete dopamine (*top*) have their cell bodies concentrated in the substantia nigra and the ventral tegmentum of the midbrain; their axons project primarily to the caudate nucleus, the frontal cortex and the entorhinal cortex. The nerve cells that secrete norepinephrine (*bottom*) have their cell bodies localized primarily in the locus coeruleus of the brain stem; they project to the cerebellum, the cerebral cortex and the hypothalamus. Both the norepinephrine and the dopamine systems overlap much of the area that gives rise to self-stimulation behavior in rats. The dopamine fibers are found only in areas that mediate brain reward, whereas the norepinephrine fibers extend into other regions. This and other evidence points to a more critical role for dopamine in brain reward.

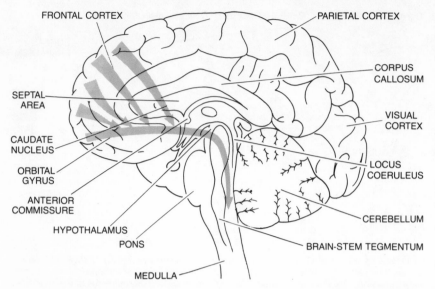

REWARD SYSTEM OF THE HUMAN BRAIN has been roughly localized in the regions shown in color. These areas correspond to the parts of the rat brain that support self-stimulation behavior. As in rodent brain, the pathways extend between hindbrain and frontal cortex.

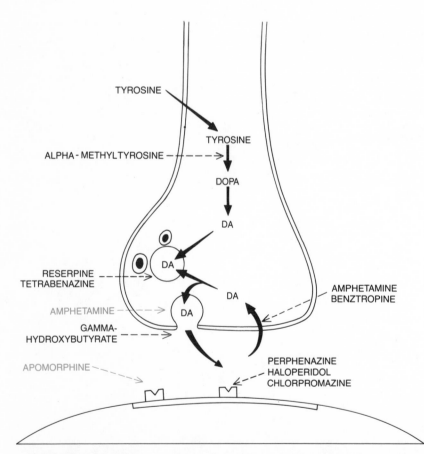

DOPAMINE TRANSMISSION across the synapse, the tiny gap between the terminal of one cell and the receptive surface of another, can be enhanced or inhibited by psychoactive drugs. Thus the effects of these drugs on self-stimulation behavior shed some light on the neurochemical mechanisms underlying brain reward. Inhibitory drugs are shown in black, enhancers in color. Dopamine transmission can be inhibited by agents that block its synthesis (alpha-methyltyrosine), prevent its storage in vesicles (reserpine, tetrabenazine), prevent its release (gamma-hydroxybutyrate) or block its attachment to receptor sites on the postsynaptic membrane (perphenazine, haloperidol, chlorpromazine). Dopamine transmission is enhanced by drugs that increase its release (amphetamine, cocaine), facilitate receptor activation (apomorphine) or inhibit reuptake of dopamine into the terminal from the synapse (amphetamine, benztropine).

contain a particular transmitter substance.

A question that has generated much interest among investigators of brain reward has to do with possible differences among the roles played by different catecholamines. Various hypotheses have been put forward: that self-stimulation is mediated solely by either norepinephrine or dopamine, that they are both involved but independently, or that they act in concert. Ronald M. Clavier and I have approached the problem anatomically. We examined the contribution made to self-stimulation by two major norepinephrine systems known as the dorsal and ventral bundles. First we demonstrated that self-stimulation in the brain stem is associated with the dorsal norepinephrine bundle. We made lesions at sites that supported self-stimulation and found they gave rise to a change in the histochemical fluorescence of the dorsal bundle, indicating that this region is associated with pathways that mediate brain reward. Similar changes in the histochemical fluorescence of the ventral bundle resulted only from lesions in brain areas that were not involved in self-stimulation. Therefore whereas the ventral bundle is not associated with brain reward, the dorsal norepinephrine bundle does appear to be associated with it.

Even though the dorsal bundle is associated with self-stimulation, is it an essential component of the brain-reward system? If brain reward results from an activation of the axons in the dorsal bundle, one would expect that the destruction of the nerve-cell bodies of these axons, which are found in an area called the locus coeruleus, would reduce self-stimulation. Clavier and I found this did not happen: the almost total destruction of the locus coeruleus had little effect on the rate of self-stimulation in rats. Interestingly enough, however, a lesion limited to the medial forebrain bundle drastically reduced self-stimulation. This effect may be related to the medial forebrain bundle's acting as a "pleasure relay station" for other brain pathways that do not contain norepinephrine.

These results indicate the norepinephrine pathways may not be critical to self-stimulation. That a dopamine system plays a more crucial role is suggested by the fact that the lesion in the medial forebrain bundle reducing self-stimulation also damaged two components of the dopamine system in the midbrain: the ventral tegmentum and the substantia nigra, pars compacta. Olds and Ephraim Peretz had shown in 1960 that the ventral tegmentum could support self-stimulation, and Malsbury and I, surveying the midbrain, the pons and the anterior medulla, had demonstrated in 1969 that the highest rates of self-stimulation were obtained from electrodes placed in the ventral tegmentum.

We also discovered brain reward in the other component of the dopamine system, the substantia nigra, pars compacta. Yung H. Huang, who was then a graduate student in my laboratory, demonstrated the involvement of the substantia nigra by means of low currents delivered through electrode wires that were considerably smaller than those implanted in earlier experiments. C. L. E. Broekkamp of the University of Nijmegen has shown that self-stimulation in the substantia nigra is blocked by the injection into the caudate nucleus of the drug haloperidol, which selectively blocks dopamine transmission. Self-stimulation is increased by the injection of amphetamine, which enhances dopamine transmission. These results indicate that the drugs influence brain reward by acting on nerve cells in the caudate nucleus. They also indicate an important role for dopamine systems in self-stimulation mechanisms.

It has been learned only recently that both norepinephrine and dopamine systems send their axons into the cerebral cortex. This finding is a critically important one because it relates the cerebral cortex to primitive structures deep within the midbrain and hindbrain that arose much earlier in the evolution of the brain. It raises the possibility that the highly complex and intricate patterns of intellectual activity in the cortex are influenced by evolutionarily primitive catecholamine systems.

By exploiting recent improvements in the sensitivity of the fluorescence technique it is now possible to distinguish between norepinephrine axons and dopamine axons in the cerebral cortex of both experimental animals and man. There are differences in the visual appearance of the two networks: the norepinephrine fibers are thicker and have more swellings than the dopamine fibers, which are thin and sinuous.

Although both catecholamine systems are found at self-stimulation sites, the norepinephrine system is distributed evenly throughout the layers of the frontal cortex and is found in areas where self-stimulation cannot be demonstrated. The dopamine system, on the other hand, has been shown by Brigitte Berger, Ann-Marie Thierry and Jacques Glowinski of the Collège de France to be unevenly distributed, with its highest concentration of axons and axon terminals located in the medial and sulcal cortex: precisely those areas in the frontal cortex where brain reward was observed. Recently Timothy Collier and I have studied islands of dopamine fluorescence in the entorhinal cortex, a region of the temporal lobe where we have demonstrated brain-reward effects.

The involvement of certain regions of the cerebral cortex in self-stimulation may therefore be related, at least in part, to their input from dopamine systems. It is tempting to think that dopamine-affecting drugs that manipulate mood and alleviate psychotic behavior may

achieve part of their effect through those catecholamine systems of the cortex that support brain reward.

The fact that our recent brain-reward studies have implicated the entorhinal cortex as an area supporting self-stimulation is one of considerable interest. Fibers in this region project to the hippocampus, a brain structure thought to be involved in the formation of memory and recently shown to be connected with memory of spatial relations. A connection between brain reward and learning has been recognized since 1961, when Olds and his wife Marianne E. Olds showed that the stimulation of reward sites disrupted learning in experimental animals. Since then neuroscientists have gained in their understanding not only of the link between reward and learning but also of the role played by the self-stimulation pathways in memory formation.

I have speculated that the pathways of brain reward may function as the pathways of memory consolidation. By this I mean that when something is learned, activity in the brain-reward pathways facilitates the formation of memory. If these pathways are electrically stimulated in the course of the learning process, in effect jamming the circuits and altering the normal physiological activity associated with the process, one would expect memory of what is being learned to be impaired. This expectation has been confirmed

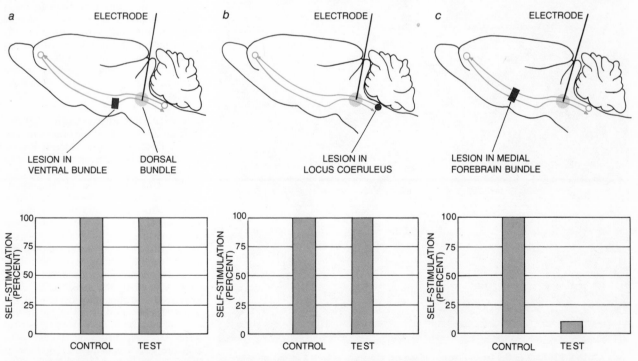

EFFECTS OF BRAIN LESIONS on self-stimulation behavior in the rat were determined in experiments performed by the author and Ronald M. Clavier in the author's laboratory at Northwestern University. An electrode was implanted in the dorsal brain stem of the rat, and the animal was allowed to stimulate itself by pressing a treadle in a Skinner box. Lesions in the ventral bundle of the norepineph-rine system (*a*) had no effect on self-stimulation behavior 10 days after surgery, nor did removal of the locus coeruleus (*b*), where the norepinephrine cell bodies giving rise to the dorsal bundle are concentrated. On the other hand, destruction of the medial forebrain bundle (*c*) resulted in a dramatic decline in self-stimulation, suggesting that the dopamine fibers in this region are essential for brain reward.

DOPAMINE FIBERS in the frontal cortex of the rat brain are revealed in this montage of fluorescent micrographs. The surface of the brain is at the top of the montage, with the deep layers at the bottom. Only dopamine fibers appear, because several weeks before the micrographs were taken a lesion was made in the locus coeruleus of the animal that destroyed all the norepinephrine fibers in the frontal cortex. Note that density of dopamine fibers is greatest in deep layers of the cortex. Micrographs were made by Olle Lindvall of the University of Lund.

to a remarkable degree by work I have done with Elaine Bresnahan, Nancy Holzman and Rebecca Santos-Anderson. We found that continuous stimulation of brain-reward regions in the medial forebrain bundle, the substantia nigra or the frontal cortex applied in the course of learning a simple task disrupts the ability of an experimental animal to remember the task 24 hours later. On the other hand, stimulation of the locus coeruleus, which apparently is not involved in brain reward, had no effect on the retention of the task.

The involvement of the substantia nigra in memory processes is surprising because it is usually associated with the control of movement. (A malfunction of the substantia nigra has been specifically related to Parkinson's disease.) Haing-Ja Kim has shown in my laboratory, however, that injections of substances specifically overactivating the substantia nigra cause the release of dopamine and lead to the disruption of memory. It seems likely that the substantia nigra system plays a role in behavioral processes beyond the control of movement and that the system is also important in the formation of memory.

Collier and I found that the entorhinal cortex plays an interesting part in the relation between self-stimulation and memory formation. Artificial stimulation applied to this area during learning has no effect on memory, but when it is applied after learning, it impairs memory. The finding is remarkable because it means brain stimulation does not have the same effect on memory in all brain areas and at all times. The evidence from our research on the entorhinal cortex suggests that stimulation must be applied both in the appropriate brain region and at the right moment in the learning process in order to hinder memory.

One puzzling question raised by this research is that if the brain stimulation is rewarding, why does it impair learning rather than enhance it? The problem is currently being investigated, and it seems the effect is related, at least in part, to how the stimulation is administered. Norman White of McGill has shown that if animals are given the opportunity after learning to press a treadle to get rewarding brain stimulation, rather than receiving it continuously as in our memory-reward experiments, they remember the task better. The improved learning may be due to the fact that the animals self-regulate the amount of stimulation, thereby self-reinforcing their behavior. Other work also supports a view held in my laboratory, namely that this enhancement of memory is to a large extent mediated by the dopamine system of the substantia nigra.

The role of self-stimulation pathways

DRUG	TRADE NAME	NEUROTRANSMITTERS AFFECTED	MODE OF ACTION	EFFECT ON SELF-STIMULATION	EFFECT ON LEARNING AND MEMORY
ALPHA-METHYL-TYROSINE	—	DOPAMINE NOREPINEPHRINE	INHIBITS SYNTHESIS OF CATECHOLAMINES	DECREASES RATE	IMPAIRMENT
RESERPINE	SERPASIL	DOPAMINE NOREPINEPHRINE	PREVENTS STORAGE OF CATECHOLAMINES	DECREASES RATE	IMPAIRMENT
6-HYDROXYDOPAMINE	—	DOPAMINE NOREPINEPHRINE	KILLS NERVE CELLS CONTAINING CATECHOLAMINES	DECREASES RATE	IMPAIRMENT
CHLORPROMAZINE	THORAZINE	DOPAMINE NOREPINEPHRINE	BLOCKS CATECHOLAMINE RECEPTORS	DECREASES RATE	IMPAIRMENT
AMPHETAMINE	DEXEDRINE	DOPAMINE NOREPINEPHRINE	ENHANCES RELEASE OF CATECHOLAMINES INTO SYNAPSE	INCREASES RATE	FACILITATION (AT LOW DOSES)
IMIPRAMINE	TOFRANIL	DOPAMINE NOREPINEPHRINE	PREVENTS REUPTAKE OF CATECHOLAMINES FROM SYNAPSE	INCREASES RATE	UNCERTAIN (INSUFFICIENT INFORMATION)
PHENOXYBENZAMINE	DIBENZYLINE	NOREPINEPHRINE	BLOCKS ALPHA-NOREPINEPHRINE RECEPTORS	DECREASES RATE	UNCERTAIN
PROPRANOLOL	INDERAL	NOREPINEPHRINE	BLOCKS BETA NOREPINEPHRINE RECEPTORS	DECREASES RATE	UNCERTAIN
CLONIDINE	CATAPRES	NOREPINEPHRINE	DECREASES NOREPINEPHRINE RELEASE	DECREASES RATE	UNCERTAIN
HALOPERIDOL	HALDOL	DOPAMINE	BLOCKS DOPAMINE RECEPTORS	DECREASES RATE	IMPAIRMENT
APOMORPHINE	—	DOPAMINE	STIMULATES DOPAMINE RECEPTORS	INCREASES RATE	FACILITATION (AT LOW DOSES)

EFFECTS OF PSYCHOACTIVE DRUGS on self-stimulation behavior and on learning and memory in the rat are summarized in this table. Drugs that enhance transmission at dopamine and norepineph-rine synapses tend to potentiate self-stimulation behavior; blocking drugs tend to inhibit it. The drugs seem to have parallel effects on learning and memory, although in some cases data are inconclusive.

in learning and memory remains a strong interest of several investigators of brain reward. Before his death Olds had been recording the activity of single nerve cells throughout the brain during learning in freely moving rats, and this research is being continued by Marianne Olds. James Olds had discovered certain nerve cells that "fire" 20 milliseconds or less after the presentation of a cue the animal has learned earlier is a signal for food. A number of these cells were in the substantia nigra, the region my research had connected with brain-reward pathways.

The evidence clearly shows that the brain-reward pathways play an important role in learning and memory. Much of the research strategy in the study of brain reward itself can be applied in this area, including the anatomical analysis of brain pathways and the use of drugs that affect the function of specific neurotransmitters. In this connection it is of considerable interest that certain amphetaminelike compounds potentiating the self-stimulation system are the principal therapeutic drugs prescribed for children with neurological disorders of attention and learning. These considera-tions suggest that as more is learned about self-stimulation pathways and their relation to learning new therapeutic tools for assisting people with learning and memory disabilities may be discovered.

To sum up, new information about the catecholamine-fiber system has made it possible to chart the brain pathways of self-stimulation as explicitly as the pathways of well-known sensory and motor systems. Evidence for the reward effects of localized electrical stimulation, for the control of brain reward by psychoactive drugs and for the association of reward pathways with memory formation indicates that the neural substrates of self-stimulation play a vital role in the guidance of behavior. And it has been shown that reward systems are present at all levels of the brain, from the medulla oblongata to the cerebral cortex.

Since the time when the medial forebrain bundle alone was designated as the pleasure center, the boundaries of the brain-reward system have been extended deep into the brain stem and far forward into the cortex of the frontal lobe of the cerebrum. All the reward systems do, however, have pathways through the medial forebrain bundle, suggesting that this region of the hypothalamus may be described as the relay station through which the brain-reward pathways course.

It would obviously be highly desirable if brain-stimulation technology and the information derived from the study of the anatomy of the reward system could be applied to the alleviation of neurological diseases caused by disorders of the reward system. Such applications, however, have been misused in the past. All neuroscientists share the responsibility for limiting the use of brain-stimulation techniques in human beings to therapeutic purposes, and for guarding against the unwarranted or unethical applications of those techniques. Yet neuroscientists must also be prepared to communicate the positive character of their work in a society suspicious of "mind control." The potential value to society of applying such knowledge to physiological disorders of personality and mental function calls both for continued basic research and for efforts to build bridges to the clinic.

4

Brain Mechanisms of Vision

by David H. Hubel and Torsten N. Wiesel
September 1979

*A functional architecture that may underlie processing
of sensory information in the cortex is revealed by
studies of the activity and the organization in
space of neurons in the primary visual cortex*

Viewed as a kind of invention by evolution, the cerebral cortex must be one of the great success stories in the history of living things. In vertebrates lower than mammals the cerebral cortex is minuscule, if it can be said to exist at all. Suddenly impressive in the lowest mammals, it begins to dominate the brain in carnivores, and it increases explosively in primates; in man it almost completely envelops the rest of the brain, tending to obscure the other parts. The degree to which an animal depends on an organ is an index of the organ's importance that is even more convincing than size, and dependence on the cortex has increased rapidly as mammals have evolved. A mouse without a cortex appears fairly normal, at least to casual inspection; a man without a cortex is almost a vegetable, speechless, sightless, senseless.

Understanding of this large and indispensable organ is still woefully deficient. This is partly because it is very complex, not only structurally but also in its functions, and partly because neurobiologists' intuitions about the functions have so often been wrong. The outlook is changing, however, as techniques improve and as investigators learn how to deal with the huge numbers of intricately connected neurons that are the basic elements of the cortex, with the impulses they carry and with the synapses that connect them. In this article we hope to sketch the present state of knowledge of one subdivision of the cortex: the primary visual cortex (also known as the striate cortex or area 17), the most elementary of the cortical regions concerned with vision. That will necessarily lead us into the related subject of visual perception, since the workings of an organ cannot easily be separated from its biological purpose.

The cerebral cortex, a highly folded plate of neural tissue about two millimeters thick, is an outermost crust wrapped over the top of, and to some extent tucked under, the cerebral hemispheres. In man its total area, if it were spread out, would be about 1.5 square feet. (In a 1963 article in *Scientific American* one of us gave the area as 20 square feet and was quickly corrected by a neuroanatomist friend in Toronto, who said he thought it was 1.5 square feet—"at least that is what Canadians have.") The folding is presumably mainly the result of such an unlikely structure's having to be packed into a box the size of the skull.

A casual glance at cortical tissue under a microscope shows vast numbers of neurons: about 10^5 (100,000) for each square millimeter of surface, suggesting that the cortex as a whole has some 10^{10} (10 billion) neurons. The cell bodies are arranged in half a dozen layers that are alternately cell-sparse and cell-rich. In contrast to these marked changes in cell density in successive layers at different depths in the cortex there is marked uniformity from place to place in the plane of any given layer and in any direction within that plane. The cortex is morphologically rather uniform in two of its dimensions.

One of the first great insights about cortical organization came late in the 19th century, when it was gradually realized that this rather uniform plate of tissue is subdivided into a number of different regions that have very different functions. The evidence came from clinical, physiological and anatomical sources. It was noted that a brain injury, depending on its location, could cause paralysis or blindness or numbness or speech loss; the blindness could be total or limited to half or less of the visual world, and the numbness could involve one limb or a few fingers. The consistency of the relation between a given defect and the location of the lesion gradually led to a charting of the most obvious of these specialized regions, the visual, auditory, somatic sensory (body sensation), speech and motor regions.

In many cases a close look with a microscope at cortex stained for cell bodies showed that in spite of the relative uniformity there were structural variations, particularly in the layering pattern, that correlated well with the clinically defined subdivisions. Additional confirmation came from observations of the location (at the surface of the brain) of the electrical brain waves produced when an animal was stimulated by touching the body, sounding clicks or tones in the ear or flashing light in the eye. Similarly, motor areas could be mapped by stimulating the cortex electrically and noting what part of the animal's body moved.

This systematic mapping of the cortex soon led to a fundamental realization: most of the sensory and motor areas contained systematic two-dimensional maps of the world they represented. Destroying a particular small region of cortex could lead to paralysis of one arm; a similar lesion in another small region led to numbness of one hand or of the upper lip, or blindness in one small part of the visual world; if electrodes were placed on an animal's cortex, touching one limb produced a correspondingly localized series of electric potentials. Clearly the body was systematically mapped onto the somatic sensory and motor areas; the visual world was mapped onto the primary visual cortex, an area on the occipital lobe that in man and in the macaque monkey (the animal in which our investigations have mainly been conducted) covers about 15 square centimeters.

In the primary visual cortex the map is uncomplicated by breaks and discontinuities except for the remarkable split of the visual world down the exact middle, with the left half projected to the right cerebral cortex and the right half projected to the left cortex. The map of the body is more complicated and is still perhaps not completely understood. It is nonetheless systematic, and it is similarly crossed, with the right side of the body projecting to the left hemisphere and the left side projecting to the right hemisphere. (It is worth remarking that no one has the remotest idea why there should be this amazing tendency for nervous-system pathways to cross.)

An important feature of cortical maps is their distortion. The scale of the maps varies as it does in a Mercator projection, the rule for the cortex being that

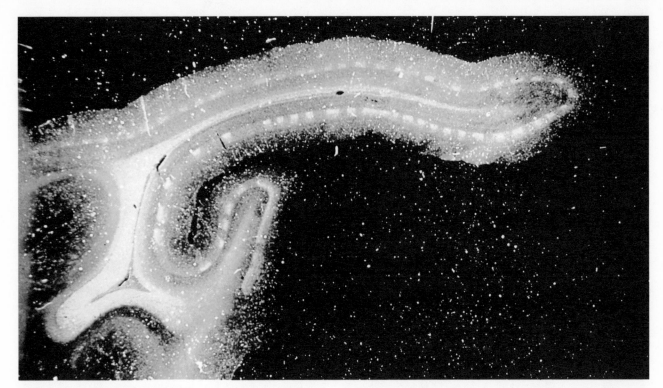

OCULAR-DOMINANCE COLUMNS, one of the two major systems that characterize the functional architecture of the primary visual cortex, are revealed as periodic bright patches in this dark-field autoradiograph of a section of macaque monkey cortex. The columns (actually curving slabs of cortex, seen here in cross section in a brain slice cut perpendicularly to the surface) are regions in which all neurons respond more actively to the right eye than to the left one; dark regions separating the bright patches are columns of left-eye prefer-

ence. The autoradiograph was made by injecting a radioactively labeled amino acid into the right eye of an anesthetized animal. The amino acid was taken up by cell bodies in the retina and transported via the lateral geniculate nucleus, a way station in the brain, to cells in the cortex. A brain slice was coated with a photographic emulsion, which was exposed for several months and then developed. Exposed silver grains overlying the regions of radioactivity form the light-scattering patches that represent ocular-dominance columns.

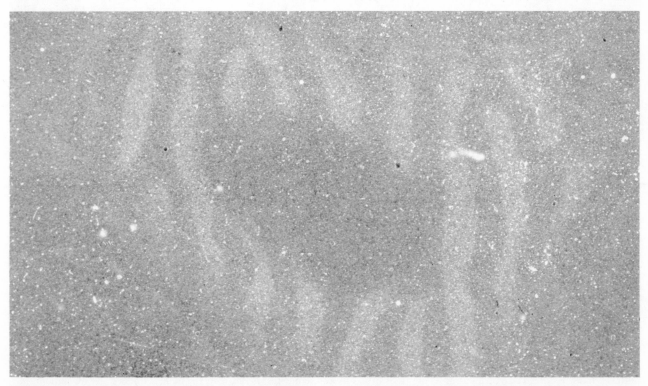

DOMINANCE PATTERN is seen face on in an axonal-transport autoradiograph of a brain section parallel, rather than perpendicular, to the surface of the primary visual cortex. As can be seen in the autoradiograph at the top of the page, the label is brightest in one layer of the folded cortex, layer IV. This is the level at which the axons bringing visual information to the cortex terminate and where

the label therefore accumulates. This section was cut in a plane tangential to the dome-shaped surface of the cortex and just below layer IV, which therefore appears as a ring of roughly parallel bright bands. These are the radioactively labeled ocular-dominance regions, which are now seen from above instead of edge on. The actual width of the ocular-dominance regions is typically about .4 millimeter.

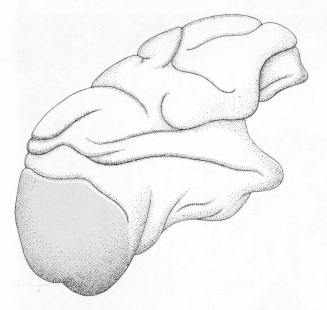

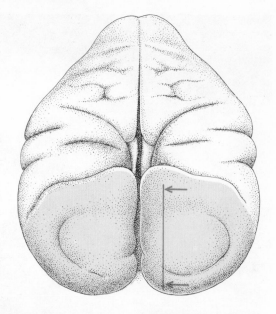

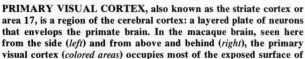

PRIMARY VISUAL CORTEX, also known as the striate cortex or area 17, is a region of the cerebral cortex: a layered plate of neurons that envelops the primate brain. In the macaque brain, seen here from the side (*left*) and from above and behind (*right*), the primary visual cortex (*colored areas*) occupies most of the exposed surface of the two occipital lobes. It also curves around the medial surface between the two cerebral hemispheres. It continues in a complex fold underneath the convex outer surface, as is shown in a parasagittal section (*see top illustration on opposite page*) that was cut along the colored line and is viewed in the direction indicated by the arrows.

the regions of highest discrimination or delicacy of function occupy relatively more cortical area. For the body surface, a millimeter of surface on the fingers, the lips or the tongue projects to more cortex than a millimeter of trunk, buttocks or back; in vision the central part of the retina has a representation some 35 times more detailed than the far peripheral part.

Important as the advances in mapping cortical projections were, they tended for some time to divert thought from the real problem of just how the brain analyzes information. It was as though the representation could be an end in itself instead of serving a more subtle purpose—as though what the cortex did was to cater to some little green man who sat inside the head and surveyed images playing across the cortex. In the course of this article we shall show that, for vision at least, the world is represented in a far more distorted way; any little green man trying to glean information from the cortical projection would be puzzled indeed.

The first major insight into cortical organization was nonetheless the recognition of this subdivision into areas having widely different functions, with a tendency to ordered mapping. Just how many such areas there are has been a subject of wide speculation. Anatomists' estimates have on the whole been rather high—up to several hundred areas, depending on the individual worker's sensitivity to fine differences in microscopic patterns and sometimes also on his ability to fool himself. Physiologists began with lower estimates, but lately, with more powerful mapping methods, they

have been revising their estimates upward. The important basic notion is that information on any given modality such as sight or sound is transmitted first to a primary cortical area and from there, either directly or via the thalamus, to successions of higher areas. A modern guess as to the number of cortical areas might be between 50 and 100.

The second major insight into cortical organization came from the work of the anatomist Santiago Ramón y Cajal and his pupil Rafael Lorente de Nó. This was the realization that the operations the cortex performs on the information it receives are local. What that means can best be understood by considering the wiring diagram that emerged from the Golgi method used by Cajal and Lorente de Nó. In essence the wiring is simple. Sets of fibers bring information to the cortex; by the time several synapses have been traversed the influence of the input has spread vertically to all cell layers; finally several other sets of fibers carry modified messages out of the area. The detailed connections between inputs and outputs differ from one area to the next, but within a given area they seem to be rather stereotyped. What is common to all regions is the local nature of the wiring. The information carried into the cortex by a single fiber can in principle make itself felt through the entire thickness in about three or four synapses, whereas the lateral spread, produced by branching trees of axons and dendrites, is limited for all practical purposes to a few millimeters, a small proportion of the vast extent of the cortex.

The implications of this are far-reaching. Whatever any given region of the cortex does, it does locally. At stages where there is any kind of detailed, systematic topographical mapping the analysis must be piecemeal. For example, in the somatic sensory cortex the messages concerning one finger can be combined and compared with an input from elsewhere on that same finger or with input from a neighboring finger, but they can hardly be combined with the influence from the trunk or from a foot. The same applies to the visual world. Given the detailed order of the input to the primary visual cortex, there is no likelihood that the region will do anything to correlate information coming in from both far above and far below the horizon, or from both the left and the right part of the visual scene. It follows that this cannot by any stretch of the imagination be the place where actual perception is enshrined. Whatever these cortical areas are doing, it must be some kind of local analysis of the sensory world. One can only assume that as the information on vision or touch or sound is relayed from one cortical area to the next the map becomes progressively more blurred and the information carried more abstract.

Even though the Golgi-method studies of the early 1900's made it clear that the cortex must perform local analyses, it was half a century before physiologists had the least inkling of just what the analysis was in any area of the cortex. The first understanding came in the primary visual area, which is now the best-understood of any cortical region and is still the only one where the analysis and consequent transformations of information are known in any detail. After describing the main transformations that take place in the primary visual cortex we shall go on to show how increasing understanding of these cortical functions has revealed an entire world of architectural order that is otherwise inaccessible to observation.

We can best begin by tracing the visual path in a primate from the retina to the cortex. The output from each eye is conveyed to the brain by about a million nerve fibers bundled together in the optic nerve. These fibers are the axons of the ganglion cells of the retina. The messages from the light-sensitive elements, the rods and cones, have already traversed from two to four synapses and have involved four other types of retinal cells before they arrive at the ganglion cells, and a certain amount of sophisticated analysis of the information has already taken place.

A large fraction of the optic-nerve fibers pass uninterrupted to two nests of cells deep in the brain called the lateral geniculate nuclei, where they make synapses. The lateral geniculate cells in turn send their axons directly to the primary visual cortex. From there, after several synapses, the messages are sent to a number of further destinations: neighboring cortical areas and also several targets deep in the brain. One contingent even projects back to the lateral geniculate bodies; the function of this feedback path is not known. The main point for the moment is that the primary visual cortex is in no sense the end of the visual path. It is just one stage, probably an early one in terms of the degree of abstraction of the information it handles.

As a result of the partial crossing of the optic nerves in the optic chiasm, the geniculate and the cortex on the left side are connected to the two left half retinas and are therefore concerned with the right half of the visual scene, and the converse is the case for the right geniculate and the right cortex. Each geniculate and each cortex receives input from both eyes, and each is concerned with the opposite half of the visual world.

To examine the workings of this visual pathway our strategy since the late 1950's has been (in principle) simple. Beginning, say, with the fibers of the optic nerve, we record with microelectrodes from a single nerve fiber and try to find out how we can most effectively influence the firing by stimulating the retina with light. For this one can use patterns of light of every conceivable size, shape and color, bright on a dark background or the reverse, and stationary or moving. It may take a long time, but sooner or later we satisfy ourselves that we have found the best stimulus for the cell being tested, in this case a ganglion cell of the retina. (Sometimes we are

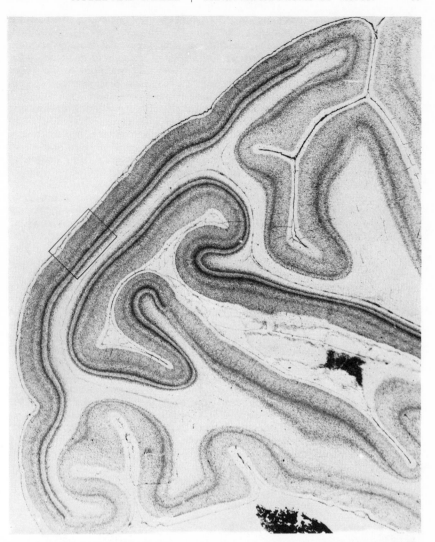

SECTION OF VISUAL CORTEX along the colored line in the illustration on the opposite page was stained by the Nissl method, which makes cell bodies but not fibers visible. The visual cortex is seen to be a continuous layered sheet of neurons about two millimeters thick. The black rectangle outlines a section like the one that is further enlarged in the illustration below.

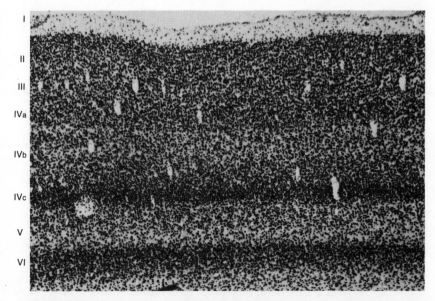

CROSS SECTION OF PRIMARY VISUAL CORTEX in the macaque, stained here by the Nissl method and enlarged about 35 diameters, shows the layered structure and gives the conventional designations of the six layers (left). The white gaps are sectioned blood vessels.

wrong!) We note the results and then go on to another fiber. After studying a few hundred cells we may find that new types become rare. Satisfied that we know roughly how the neurons at this stage work, we proceed to the next stage (in this case the geniculate) and repeat the process. Comparison of the two sets of results can tell us something about what the geniculate does. We then go on to the next stage, the primary cortex, and repeat the procedure.

Working in this way, one finds that both a retinal ganglion cell and a geniculate cell respond best to a roughly circular spot of light of a particular size in a particular part of the visual field. The size is critical because each cell's receptive field (the patch of retinal receptor cells supplying the cell) is divided, with an excitatory center and an inhibitory surround (an "on center" cell) or exactly the reverse configuration (an "off center" cell). This is the center-surround configuration first described by Stephen W. Kuffler at the Johns Hopkins University School of Medicine in 1953. A spot exactly filling the center of an on-center cell is therefore a more effective stimulus than a larger spot that invades the inhibitory area, or than diffuse light. A line stimulus (a bar of light) is effective if it covers a large part of the center region and only a small part of the surround. Because these cells have circular symmetry they respond well to such a line stimulus whatever its orientation. To sum up, the retinal ganglion cells and the cells of the lateral geniculate—the cells supplying the input to the visual cortex—are cells with concentric, center-surround receptive fields. They are primarily concerned not with assessing levels of illumination but rather with making a comparison between the light level in one small area of the visual scene and the average illumination of the immediate surround.

The first of the two major transformations accomplished by the visual cortex is the rearrangement of incoming information so that most of its cells respond not to spots of light but to specifically oriented line segments. There is a wide variety of cell types in the cortex, some simpler and some more complex in their response properties, and one soon gains an impression of a kind of hierarchy, with simpler cells feeding more complex ones. In the monkey there is first of all a large group of cells that behave (as far as is known) just like geniculate cells: they have circularly symmetrical fields. These cells are all in the lower part of one layer, called layer IV, which is precisely the layer that receives the lion's share of the geniculate input. It makes sense that these least sophisticated cortical cells should be the ones most immediately connected to the input.

Cells outside layer IV all respond best to specifically oriented line segments. A typical cell responds only when light falls in a particular part of the visual world, but illuminating that area diffusely has little effect or none, and small spots of light are not much better. The best response is obtained when a line that has just the right tilt is flashed in the region or, in some cells, is swept across the region. The most effective orientation varies from cell to cell and is usually defined sharply enough so that a change of 10 or 20 degrees clockwise or counterclockwise reduces the response markedly or abolishes it. (It is hard to convey the precision of this discrimination. If 10 to 20 degrees sounds like a wide range, one should remember that the angle between 12 o'clock and one o'clock is 30 degrees.) A line at 90 degrees to the best orientation almost never evokes any response.

Depending on the particular cell, the stimulus may be a bright line on a dark background or the reverse, or it may be a boundary between light and dark regions. If it is a line, the thickness is likely to be important; increasing it beyond some optimal width reduces the response, just as increasing the diameter of a spot does in the case of ganglion and geniculate cells. Indeed, for a particular part of the visual field the geniculate receptive-field centers and the optimal cortical line widths are comparable.

Neurons with orientation specificity vary in their complexity. The simplest, which we call "simple" cells, behave as though they received their input directly from several cells with center-surround, circularly symmetrical fields—the type of cells found in layer IV. The response properties of these simple cells, which respond to an optimally oriented line in a narrowly defined location, can most easily be accounted for by requiring that the centers of the incoming center-surround fields all be excitatory or all be inhibitory, and that they lie along a straight line. At present we have no direct evidence for this scheme, but it is attractive because of its simplicity and because certain kinds of indirect evidence support it. According to the work of Jennifer S. Lund of the University of Washington School of Medicine, who in the past few years has done more than anyone else to advance the Golgi-stain anatomy of this cortical area, the cells in layer IV project to the layers just above, which is roughly where the simple cells are found.

The second major group of orientation-specific neurons are the far more numerous "complex" cells. They come in a number of subcategories, but their main feature is that they are less particular about the exact position of a line.

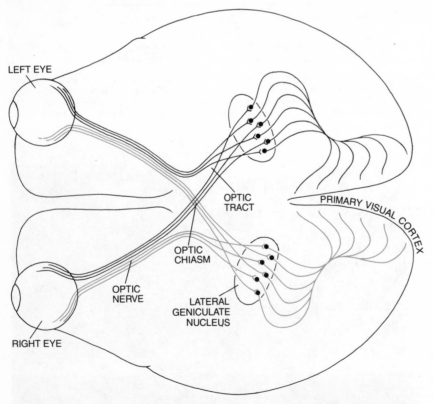

VISUAL PATHWAY is traced schematically in the human brain, seen here from below. The output from the retina is conveyed, by ganglion-cell axons bundled in the optic nerves, to the lateral geniculate nuclei; about half of the axons cross over to the opposite side of the brain, so that a representation of each half of the visual scene is projected on the geniculate of the opposite hemisphere. Neurons in the geniculates send their axons to the primary visual cortex.

LEFT EYE

OPTIC TRACT

PRIMARY VISUAL CORTEX

OPTIC CHIASM

OPTIC NERVE

LATERAL GENICULATE NUCLEUS

RIGHT EYE

RIGHT EYE LEFT EYE RIGHT EYE

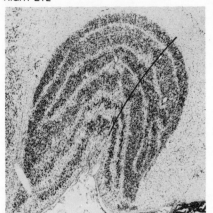 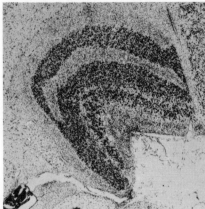 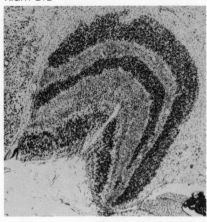

LATERAL GENICULATE NUCLEUS of a normal monkey (*left*) is a layered structure in which cells in layers 1, 4 and 6 (numbered from bottom to top) receive their input from the eye on the opposite side and those in layers 2, 3 and 5 receive information from the eye on the same side. The maps are in register, so that the neurons along any radius (*black line*) receive signals from the same part of the visual scene. The layered nature of the input is demonstrated in the two geniculates of an animal that had vision in the left eye only (*two micrographs at right*): in each geniculate cells in the three layers with input from right eye have atrophied. Geniculates are enlarged 10 diameters.

Complex cells behave as though they received their input from a number of simple cells, all with the same receptive-field orientation but differing slightly in the exact location of their fields. This scheme readily explains the strong steady firing evoked in a complex cell as a line is kept in the optimal orientation and is swept across the receptive field. With the line optimally oriented many cells prefer one direction of movement to the opposite direction. Several possible circuits have been proposed to explain this behavior, but the exact mechanism is still not known.

Although there is no direct evidence that orientation-sensitive cells have anything to do with visual perception, it is certainly tempting to think they represent some early stage in the brain's analysis of visual forms. It is worth asking which cells at this early stage would be expected to be turned on by some very simple visual form, say a dark blob on a light background. Any cell whose receptive field is entirely inside or outside the boundaries of such an image will be completely unaffected by the figure's presence because cortical cells effectively ignore diffuse changes in the illumination of their entire receptive fields.

The only cells to be affected will be those whose field is cut by the borders. For the circularly symmetrical cells the ones most strongly influenced will be those whose center is grazed by a boundary (because for them the excitatory and inhibitory subdivisions are most unequally illuminated). For the orientation-specific cells the only ones to be activated will be those whose optimal orientation happens to coincide with the prevailing direction of the border. And among these the simple cells will be much more exacting than the complex ones, responding optimally only when the border falls along a line separating an excitatory and an inhibitory region. It is important to realize that this part of the cortex is operating only locally, on bits of the form; how the entire form is analyzed or handled by the brain—how this information is worked on and synthesized at later stages, if indeed it is—is still not known.

The second major function of the monkey visual cortex is to combine the inputs from the two eyes. In the lateral geniculate nuclei a neuron may re-

a 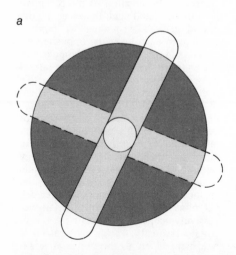 *b* 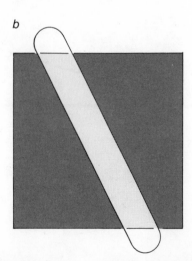 *c*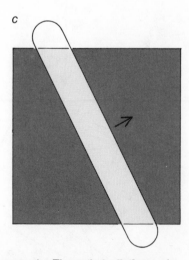

RECEPTIVE FIELDS of various cells in the visual pathway are compared. Retinal ganglion cells and neurons in the lateral geniculate nucleus have circular fields with either an excitatory center and an inhibitory surround (*a*) or the opposite arrangement. A spot of light falling on the center stimulates a response from such a cell; so does a bar of light falling on the field in any orientation, provided it falls on the center. In the visual cortex there is a hierarchy of neurons with increasingly complex response properties. The cortical cells that receive signals directly from the geniculate have circularly symmetrical fields. Cortical cells farther along the pathway, however, respond only to a line stimulus in a particular orientation. A "simple" cell (*b*) responds to such a line stimulus only in a particular part of its field. A "complex" cell (*c*) responds to a precisely oriented line regardless of where it is in its field and also to one moving in a particular direction (*arrow*).

spond to stimulation of the left eye or of the right one, but no cell responds to stimulation of both eyes. This may seem surprising, since each geniculate receives inputs from both eyes, but the fact is that the geniculates are constructed in a way that keeps inputs from the two eyes segregated. Each geniculate body is divided into six layers, three left-eye layers interdigitated with three right-eye ones. The opposite-side half of the visual world is mapped onto each layer (with the six maps in precise register, so that in a radial pathway traversing the six layers the receptive fields of all the cells encountered have virtually identical positions in the visual field). Since any one layer has input from only one eye, the individual cells of that layer must be monocular.

Even in the visual cortex the neurons to which the geniculate cells project directly, the circularly symmetrical cells in layer IV, are all (as far as we can tell) strictly monocular; so are all the simple cells. Only at the level of the complex cells do the paths from the two eyes converge, and even there the blending of information is incomplete and takes a special form. About half of the complex cells are monocular, in the sense that any one cell can be activated only by stimulating one eye. The rest of the cells can be influenced independently by both eyes.

If one maps the right-eye and left-eye receptive fields of a binocular cell (by stimulating first through one eye and then through the other) and compares the two fields, the fields turn out to have identical positions, levels of complexity, orientation and directional preference; everything one learns about the cell by stimulating one eye is confirmed through the other eye. There is only one exception: if first one eye and then the other are tested with identical stimuli, the two responses are usually not quantitatively identical; in many cases one eye is dominant, consistently producing a higher frequency of firing than the other eye.

From cell to cell all degrees of ocular dominance can be found, from complete monopoly by one eye through equality to exclusive control by the other eye. In the monkey the cells with a marked eye preference are somewhat commoner than the cells in which the two eyes make about equal contributions. Apparently a binocular cell in the primary visual cortex has connections to the two eyes that are qualitatively virtually identical, but the density of the two sets of connections is not necessarily the same.

It is remarkable enough that the elaborate sets of wiring that produce specificity of orientation and of direction of movement and other special properties

should be present in two duplicate copies. It is perhaps even more surprising that all of this can be observed in a newborn animal. The wiring is mostly innate, and it presumably is genetically determined. (In one particular respect, however, some maturation of binocular wiring does take place mostly after birth.)

We now turn to a consideration of the way these cells are grouped in the cortex. Are cells with similar characteristics—complexity, receptive-field position, orientation and ocular dominance—grouped together or scattered at random? From the description so far it will be obvious that cells of like complexity tend to be grouped in layers, with the circularly symmetrical cells low in layer IV, the simple cells just above them and the complex cells in layers II, III, V and VI. Complex cells can be further subcategorized, and the ones found in each layer are in a number of ways very different.

These differences from layer to layer take on added interest in view of the important discovery, confirmed by several physiologists and anatomists during the past few decades, that fibers projecting from particular layers of the cortex have particular destinations. For example, in the visual cortex the deepest layer, layer VI, projects mainly (perhaps only) back to the lateral geniculate body; layer V projects to the superior colliculus, a visual station in the midbrain; layers II and III send their projections to other parts of the cortex. This relation between layer and projection site probably deserves to be ranked as a third major insight into cortical organization.

The next stimulus variable to be considered is the position of the receptive field in the visual field. In describing the lateral geniculate nucleus we pointed out that in each layer the opposite-half visual field forms an ordered topographical map. In the projection from lateral geniculate to primary visual cortex this order is preserved, producing a cortical map of the visual field. Given this ordered map it is no surprise that neighboring cells in this part of the cortex always have receptive fields that are close together; usually, in fact, they overlap. If one plunges a microelectrode into the cortex at a right angle to the surface and records from cell after cell (as many as 100 or 200 of them) in successively deeper layers, again the receptive fields mostly overlap, with each new field heaped on all the others. The extent of the entire pile of fields is usually several times the size of any one typical field.

There is some variation in the size of these receptive fields. Some of the variation is tied to the layering: the largest fields in any penetration tend to be in

POSITIONS OF RECEPTIVE FIELDS (*numbered from 1 to 9*) of cortical neurons mapped by an electrode penetrating at roughly a right angle to the surface are essentially the same (*left*), although the fields are different sizes and there is some scatter. In an oblique penetration (*right*) from two to four cells were recorded, at .1-millimeter intervals, at each of four sites (*numbered from 1 to 4*) one millimeter apart. Each group includes various sizes and some scatter, but now there is also a systematic drift: fields of each successive group of cells are somewhat displaced.

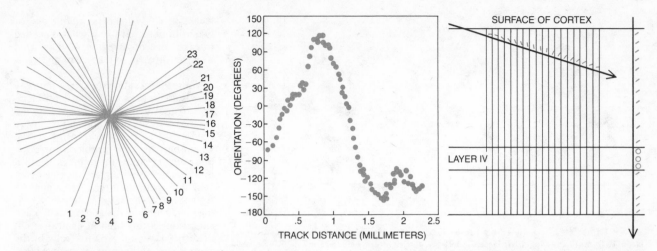

ORIENTATION PREFERENCES of 23 neurons encountered as a microelectrode penetrated the cortex obliquely are charted (*left*); the most effective tilt of the stimulus changed steadily in a counterclockwise direction. The results of a similar experiment are plotted (*center*); in this case, however, there were several reversals in direction of rotation. The results of a large number of such experiments, together with the observation that a microelectrode penetrating the cortex perpendicularly encounters only cells that prefer the same orientation (apart from the circularly symmetrical cells in layer IV, which have no preferred orientation), suggested that the cortex is subdivided into roughly parallel slabs of tissue, with each slab, called an orientation column, containing neurons with like orientation specificity (*right*).

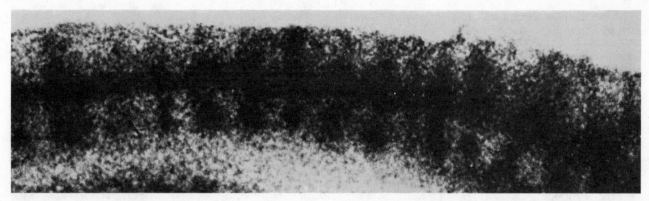

ORIENTATION COLUMNS are visualized as anatomical structures in a deoxyglucose autoradiograph made by the authors and Michael P. Stryker. Radioactively labeled deoxyglucose was injected into a monkey; it was taken up primarily by active neurons, and an early metabolite accumulated in the cells. Immediately after the injection the animal was stimulated with a pattern of vertical stripes, so that cells responding to vertical lines were most active and became most radioactive. In this section perpendicular to surface active-cell regions are narrow bands about .5 millimeter apart. Layer IV (with no orientation preference) is, as expected, uniformly radioactive.

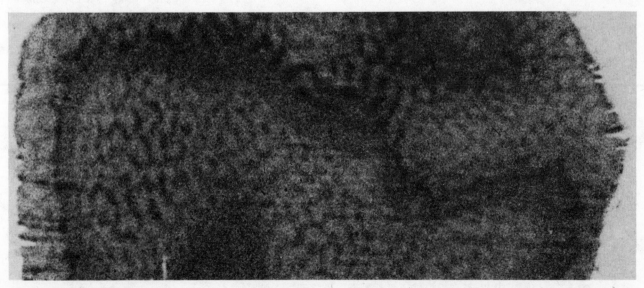

ORIENTATION PATTERN, seen face on, is unexpectedly complex. This deoxyglucose autoradiograph is of a section tangential to the somewhat curved layers of the cortex. The darker regions represent continuously labeled layer IV. In the other layers the orientation regions are intricately curved bands, something like the walls of a maze seen from above, but distance from one band to next is uniform.

40

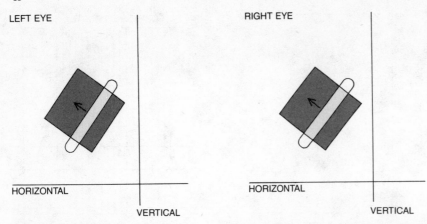

LEFT EYE   RIGHT EYE

HORIZONTAL   HORIZONTAL

VERTICAL   VERTICAL

BINOCULAR CELL in the cortex can be influenced independently by both eyes or more strongly by both eyes together. Here the left-eye and right-eye fields are mapped for a complex cell whose receptive field is in the upper left quadrant of the visual field. (The lines represent the horizontal and vertical meridians of the field, intersecting at the point of fixation.) The two receptive fields are identical, but the amount of response may differ depending on whether the left eye or the right eye is stimulated. Preference for one eye is called ocular dominance.

layers III, V and VI. The most important variation, however, is linked to eccentricity, or the distance of a cell's receptive field from the center of gaze. The size of the fields and the extent of the associated scatter in the part of the cortex that maps the center of gaze are tiny compared to the size and amount of scatter in the part that maps the far periphery. We call the pile of superimposed fields that are mapped in a penetration beginning at any point on the cortex the "aggregate field" of that point. The size of the aggregate field is obviously a function of eccentricity.

If the electrode penetrates in an oblique direction, almost parallel to the surface, the scatter in field position from cell to cell is again evident, but now there is superimposed on the scatter

a consistent drift in field position, its direction dictated by the topographical map of the visual fields. And an interesting regularity is revealed: it turns out that moving the electrode about one or two millimeters always produces a displacement in visual field that is roughly enough to take one into an entirely new region. The movement in the visual field, in short, is about the same as the size of the aggregate receptive field. For the primary visual cortex this holds wherever the recording is made. At the center of gaze the fields and their associated scatter are tiny, but so is the displacement corresponding to a one-millimeter movement along the cortex. With increasing eccentricity (farther out in the visual field) both the field and scatter and the displacement become larger, in parallel fashion. It seems that every-

where a block of cortex about one or two millimeters in size is what is needed to take care of a region of the visual world equivalent to the size of an aggregate field.

These observations suggest the way the visual cortex solves a basic problem: how to analyze the visual scene in detail in the central part and much more crudely in the periphery. In the retina, which has the same problem, for obvious optical reasons the number of millimeters corresponding to a degree of visual field is constant. The retina handles the central areas in great detail by having huge numbers of ganglion cells, each subserving a tiny area of central visual field; the layer of ganglion cells in the central part of the retina is thick, whereas in the outlying parts of the retina it is very thin. The cortex, in contrast, seems to want to be uniform in thickness everywhere. Here there are none of the optical constraints imposed on the retina, and so area is simply allotted in amounts corresponding to the problem at hand.

The machinery in any square millimeter of cortex is presumably about the same as in any other. A few thousand geniculate fibers enter such a region, the cortex does its thing and perhaps 50,000 fibers leave—whether a small part of the visual world is represented in great detail or a larger part in correspondingly less detail. The uniformity of the cortex is suggested, as we indicated at the outset, by the appearance of stained sections. It is compellingly confirmed when we examine the architecture further, looking specifically at orientation and at ocular dominance.

For orientation we inquire about groupings of cells just as we did with field position, looking first at two cells sitting side by side. Two such cells almost invariably have the same optimal stimulus orientation. If the electrode is inserted in a direction perpendicular to the surface, all the cells along the path of penetration have identical or almost identical orientations (except for the cells deep in layer IV, which have no optimal orientation at all). In two perpendicular penetrations a millimeter or so apart, however, the two orientations observed are usually different. The cortex must therefore be subdivided by some kind of vertical partitioning into regions of constant receptive-field orientation. When we came on this system almost 20 years ago, it intrigued us because it fitted so well with the hierarchical schemes we had proposed to explain how complex cells are supplied by inputs from simple cells: the circuit diagrams involve connections between cells whose fields cover the same part of the visual world and that respond to the same line orientation. It seemed eminently reasonable that strongly inter-

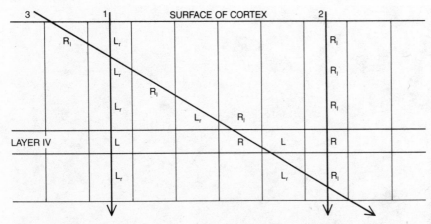

SURFACE OF CORTEX

LAYER IV

GROUPING OF CELLS according to ocular dominance was revealed by physiological studies. In one typical vertical penetration of the cortex (1) a microelectrode encounters only cells that respond preferentially to the left eye (L_r) and, in layer IV, cells that respond only to the left eye (L); in another vertical penetration (2) the cells all have right-eye dominance (R_l) or, in layer IV, are driven exclusively by the right eye (R). In an oblique penetration (3) there is a regular alternation of dominance by one eye or the other eye. Repeated penetrations suggest that the cortex is subdivided into regions with a cross-sectional width of about .4 millimeter and with walls perpendicular to the cortical surface and layers: the ocular-dominance columns.

connected cells should be grouped together.

If the cortex is diced up into small regions of constant receptive-field orientation, can one say anything more about the three-dimensional shape of the regions than that their walls are perpendicular to the surface? Are neighboring regions related in any systematic way or are regions subserving all the possible orientations scattered over the cortex at random? We began to study these questions simply by penetrating the cortex obliquely or parallel to the surface. When we first did this experiment in about 1961, the result was so surprising that we could hardly believe it. Instead of a random assortment of successive orientations there was an amazing orderliness. Each time the electrode moved forward as little as 25 or 50 micrometers (thousandths of a millimeter) the optimal orientation changed by a small step, about 10 degrees on the average; the steps continued in the same direction, clockwise or counterclockwise, through a total angle of anywhere from 90 to 270 degrees. Occasionally such a sequence would reverse direction suddenly, from a clockwise progression to a counterclockwise one or vice versa. These reversals were unpredictable, usually coming after steady progressions of from 90 to 270 degrees.

Since making this first observation we have seen similar order in almost every monkey. Either there is a steady progression in orientation or, less frequently, there are stretches in which orientation stays constant. The successive changes in orientation are small enough so that it is hard to be sure that the regions of constant orientation are finite in size; it could be that the optimal orientation changes in some sense continuously as the electrode moves along the cortex.

We became increasingly interested in the three-dimensional shape of these regional subdivisions. From considerations of geometry alone the existence of small or zero changes in every direction during a horizontal or tangential penetration points to parallel slabs of tissue containing cells with like orientation specificity, with each slab perpendicular to the surface. The slabs would not necessarily be planar, like slices of bread; seen from above they might well have the form of swirls, which could easily explain the reversals in the direction of orientation changes. Recording large numbers of cells in several parallel electrode penetrations seemed to confirm this prediction, but it was hard to examine more than a tiny region of brain with the microelectrode.

Fortunately an ideal anatomical method was invented at just the right time for us. This was the 2-deoxyglucose technique for assessing brain activity, devised by Louis Sokoloff and his group

at the National Institute of Mental Health [see "The Chemistry of the Brain," by Leslie L. Iversen; SCIENTIFIC AMERICAN Offprint 1440]. The method capitalizes on the fact that brain cells depend mainly on glucose as a source of metabolic energy and that the closely similar compound 2-deoxyglucose can to some extent masquerade as glucose. If deoxyglucose is injected into an animal, it is taken up actively by neurons as though it were glucose; the more

active the neuron, the greater the uptake. The compound begins to be metabolized, but for reasons best known to biochemists the sequence stops with a metabolite that cannot cross the cell wall and therefore accumulates within the cell.

The Sokoloff procedure is to inject an animal with deoxyglucose that has been labeled with the radioactive isotope carbon 14, stimulate the animal in a way calculated to activate certain neurons

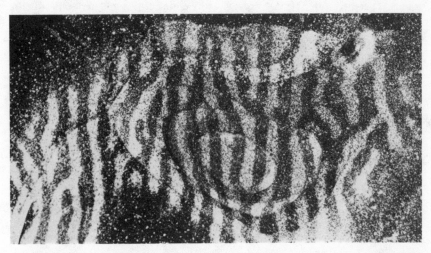

ANATOMICAL CONFIRMATION of ocular-dominance columns came from various staining methods and from axonal-transport autoradiographs such as those shown in color on page 33. This composite autoradiograph visualizing the pattern over an area some 10 millimeters wide was made by cutting out and pasting together the regions representing layer IV in a number of parallel sections; the one in bottom illustration on page 33 and others at different depths.

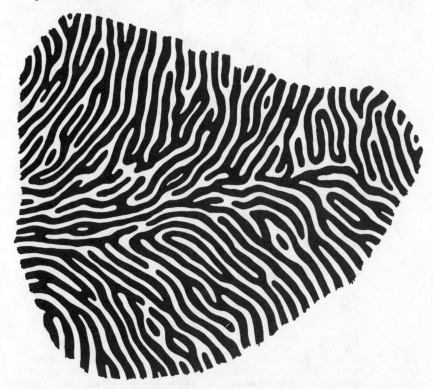

RECONSTRUCTION of the ocular-dominance pattern over the entire exposed part of the right primary visual cortex was made by the authors and Simon LeVay from a series of sections stained by a reduced-silver method he developed. The left-hand margin is at the medial edge of occipital lobe, where cortex folds downward; pattern is enlarged about six diameters.

and then immediately examine the brain for radioactivity, which reveals active areas where cells will have taken up more deoxyglucose than those in quiescent areas. The usual way of examining the brain for this purpose is to cut very thin slices of it (as one would for microscopic examination) and press them against a photographic plate sensitive to the radioactive particles. When the film is developed, any areas that were in contact with radioactive material are seen as dark masses of developed silver grains. Together with Michael P. Stryker we adapted the Sokoloff method to our problem, injecting an anesthetized animal with deoxyglucose and then moving a pattern of black and white vertical stripes back and forth 1.5 meters in front of the animal for 45 minutes. We then cut the brain into slices, either perpendicular to the surface of the cortex or parallel to it.

The autoradiographs quickly confirmed the physiological results. Sections cut perpendicular to the surface showed narrow bands of radioactivity about every 570 micrometers (roughly half a millimeter), extending through the full thickness of the cortex. Evidently these were the regions containing cells responsive to vertical lines. The deep part of layer IV was uniformly radioactive, as was expected from the fact that the cells in the layer have circularly symmetrical receptive fields and show no orientation selectivity.

Sections cut parallel to the surface showed an unexpectedly complex set of periodically spaced bands, often swirling, frequently branching and rejoining, only here and there forming regular parallel slabs. What was particularly striking was the uniformity of the distance from one band to the next over the entire cortex. This fitted perfectly with the idea of a uniform cortex. Moreover, the distance between stripes fitted well with the idea that the cortical machinery must repeat itself at least every millimeter. If the distance were, for example, 10 millimeters from vertical through 180 degrees and back to vertical, sizable parts of the visual field would lack cells sensitive to any given orientation, making for a sketchy and extremely bizarre representation of the visual scene.

The final variable whose associated architecture needs to be considered is eye preference. In microelectrode studies neighboring cells proved almost invariably to prefer the same eye. If in vertical penetrations the first cell we encountered preferred the right eye, then so did all the cells, right down to the bottom of layer VI; if the first cell preferred the left eye, so did all the rest. Any penetration favored one eye or the other with equal probability. (Since the cells of layer IV are monocular, there it was a matter not of eye preference but of eye monopoly.) If the penetration was oblique or horizontal, there was an alternation of left and right preferences, with a rather abrupt switchover about every half millimeter. The cortex thus proved to be diced up into a second set of regions separated by vertical walls that extend through the full cortical thickness. The ocular-dominance system was apparently quite independent of the orientation system, because in oblique or tangential penetrations the two sequences had no apparent relation to each other.

The basis of these ocular-dominance columns, as they have come to be called, seems to be quite simple. The terminals of geniculate fibers, some subserving the left eye and others the right, group themselves as they enter the cortex so that in layer IV there is no mixing. This produces left-eye and right-eye patches at roughly half-millimeter intervals. A neuron above or below layer IV receives connections from that layer from up to about a millimeter away in every direction. Probably the strongest connections are from the region of layer IV closest to the neuron, so that it is presumably dominated by whichever eye feeds that region.

Again we were most curious to learn what these left-eye and right-eye regions might look like in three dimensions; any of several geometries could lead to the cross-sectional appearance the physiology had suggested. The answer first came from studies with the silver-degeneration method for mapping connections, devised by Walle J. H. Nauta of the Massachusetts Institute of Technology. Since then we have found three other independent anatomical methods for demonstrating these columns.

A particularly effective method (because it enables one to observe in a single animal the arrangement of columns over the entire primary visual cortex) is based on the phenomenon of axonal transport. The procedure is to inject a radioactively labeled amino acid into an area of nervous tissue. A cell body takes up the amino acid, presumably incorporates it into a protein and then transports it along the axon to its terminals. When we injected the material into one eye of a monkey, the retinal ganglion cells took it up and transported it along their axons, the optic-nerve fibers. We could then examine the destinations of these fibers in the lateral geniculate nuclei by coating tissue slices with a silver emulsion and developing the emulsion; the radioactive label showed up clearly in

BLOCK OF CORTEX about a millimeter square and two millimeters deep (*light color*) can be considered an elementary unit of the primary visual cortex. It contains one set of orientation slabs subserving all orientations and one set of ocular-dominance slabs subserving both eyes. The pattern is reiterated throughout the primary visual area. The placing of the boundaries (at the right or the left eye, at a vertical, horizontal or oblique orientation) is arbitrary; representation of the slabs as flat planes intersecting at right angles is an oversimplification.

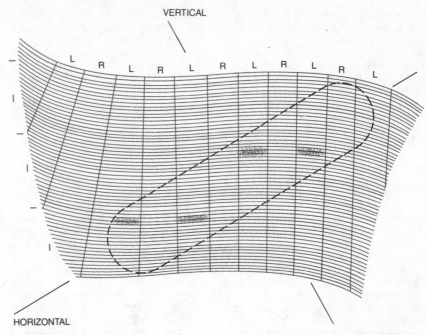

VERTICAL

HORIZONTAL

HYPOTHETICAL PATTERN OF CORTICAL ACTIVITY that might result from stimulation of the left eye with a single short horizontal line, placed in the upper left quadrant of the visual field, is shown by the colored patches on a diagram of an area of the right cortex, seen face on. The area receiving input from the object in the visual field is indicated by the broken black line. If ocular-dominance and orientation columns are arrayed as shown, activated cells will be those that respond optimally to approximately horizontal stimuli from the left eye.

the three complementary layers of the geniculate on each side.

This method does not ordinarily trace a path from one axon terminal across a synapse to the next neuron and its terminals, however, and we wanted to follow the path all the way to the cortex. In 1971 Bernice Grafstein of the Cornell University Medical College discovered that after a large enough injection in the eye of a mouse some of the radioactive material escaped from the optic-nerve terminals and was taken up by the cells in the geniculate and transported along their axons to the cortex. We had the thought that a similarly large injection in a monkey, combined with autoradiography, might demonstrate the geniculate terminals from one eye in layer IV of the visual cortex.

Our first attempt yielded dismayingly negative results, with only faint hints of a few silver grains visible in layer IV. It was only after several weeks that we realized that by resorting to dark-field microscopy we could take advantage of the light-scattering properties of silver grains and so increase the sensitivity of the method. We borrowed a dark-field condenser, and when we looked at our first slide under the microscope, there shining in all their glory were the periodic patches of label in layer IV [see top illustration on page 33].

The next step was to try to see the pattern face on by sectioning the cortex parallel to its surface. The monkey cortex is dome-shaped, and so a section parallel to the surface and tangent to layer IV shows that layer as a circle or an oval, while a section below layer IV shows it as a ring. By assembling a series of such ovals and rings from a set of sections one can reconstruct the pattern over a wide expanse of cortex.

From the reconstructions it was immediately obvious that the main overall pattern is one of parallel stripes representing terminals belonging to the injected eye, separated by gaps representing the other eye. The striping pattern is not regular like wallpaper. (We remind ourselves occasionally that this is, after all, biology!) Here and there a stripe representing one eye branches into two stripes, or else it ends blindly at a point where a stripe from the other eye branches. The irregularities are commonest near the center of gaze and along the line that maps the horizon. The stripes always seem to be perpendicular to the border between the primary visual cortex and its neighbor, area 18, and here the regularity is greatest. Such general rules seem to apply to all macaque brains, although the details of the pattern vary from one individual to the next and even from one hemisphere to the other in the same monkey.

The width of a set of two stripes is constant, about .8 millimeter, over the entire primary visual cortex, once more emphasizing the uniformity of the cortex. Again the widths fit perfectly with the idea that all of the apparatus needed to look after an area the size of an aggregate field must be contained within any square millimeter of cortex. The two techniques, deoxyglucose labeling and amino acid transport, have the great advantage of being mutually compatible, so that we have been able to apply both together, one to mark orientation lines and the other to see the ocular-dominance columns. The number of brains examined so far is too small to justify any final conclusions, but the two systems appear to be quite independent, neither parallel nor at right angles but intersecting at random.

The function served by ocular-dominance columns is still a mystery. We know there are neurons with all grades of eye preference throughout the entire binocular part of the visual fields, and it may be that a regular, patterned system of converging inputs guarantees that the distribution will be uniform, with neither eye favored by accident in any one place. Why there should be all these grades of eye preference everywhere is itself not clear, but our guess is that it has something to do with stereoscopic depth perception.

Given what has been learned about the primary visual cortex, it is clear that one can consider an elementary piece of cortex to be a block about a millimeter square and two millimeters deep. To know the organization of this chunk of tissue is to know the organization for all of area 17; the whole must be mainly an iterated version of this elementary unit. Of course the elementary unit should not be thought of as a discrete, separable block. Whether the set of orientation slabs begins with a slab representing a vertical orientation, an oblique one or a horizontal one is completely arbitrary; so too is whether an ocular-dominance sequence begins with a left-plus-right pair of dominance slabs or a right-plus-left pair. The same thing is true for a unit crystal of sodium chloride or for any complex repetitive pattern such as is found in wallpaper.

What, then, does the visual scene really look like as it is projected onto the visual cortex? Suppose an animal fixes its gaze on some point and the only object in the visual field is a straight line above and a bit to the left of the point where the gaze is riveted. If each active cell were to light up, and if one could stand above the cortex and look down at it, what would the pattern be? To make the problem more interesting, suppose the pattern is seen by one eye only. In view of the architecture just described the pattern turns out to be not a line but merely a set of regularly spaced patches [see illustration above]. The reasoning can be checked directly by exposing a monkey with one eye closed to a set of vertical stripes and making a deoxyglucose autoradiograph. The resulting pattern should not be a great surprise: it is a set of regularly spaced patches, which simply represents the intersection of the two sets of column systems. Imagine the surprise and bewilderment of a little green man looking at such a version of the outside world!

Why evolution has gone to the trouble of designing such an elaborate architecture is a question that continues to fascinate us. Perhaps the most plausible notion is that the column systems are a solution to the problem of portraying more than two dimensions on a two-dimensional surface. The cortex is dealing with at least four sets of values: two for the x and y position variables in the visual field, one for orientation and one for the different degrees of eye preference. The two surface coordinates are used up in designating field position; the other two variables are accommodated by dicing up the cortex with subdivisions so fine that one can run through a complete set of orientations or eye preferences and meanwhile have a shift in visual-field position that is small with respect to the resolution in that part of the visual world.

The strategy of subdividing the cortex with small vertical partitions is certainly not limited to the primary visual area. Such subdivisions were first seen in the somatic sensory area by Vernon B. Mountcastle of the Johns Hopkins University School of Medicine about 10 years before our work in the visual area. In the somatic sensory area, as we pointed out above, the basic topography is a map of the opposite half of the body, but superimposed on that there is a twofold system of subdivisions, with some areas where neurons respond to the movement of the joints or pressure on the skin and other areas where they respond to touch or the bending of hairs. As in the case of the visual columns, a complete set here (one area for each kind of neuron) occupies a distance of about a millimeter. These subdivisions are analogous to ocular-dominance columns in that they are determined in the first instance by inputs to the cortex (from either the left or the right eye and from either deep receptors or receptors in the upper skin layers) rather than by connections within the cortex, such as those that determine orientation selectivity and the associated system of orientation regions.

The columnar subdivisions associated with the visual and somatic sensory systems are the best-understood ones, but there are indications of similar vertical subdivisions in some other areas: several higher visual areas, sensory parietal regions recently studied by Mountcastle and the auditory region, where Thomas J. Imig, H. O. Adrián and John F. Brugge of the University of Wisconsin Medical School and their colleagues have found subdivisions in which the two ears seem alternately to add their information or to compete.

For most of these physiologically defined systems (except the visual ones) there are so far no anatomical correlates. On the other hand, in the past few years several anatomists, notably Edward G. Jones of the Washington University School of Medicine and Nauta and Patricia Goldman at M.I.T., have shown that connections from one region of the cortex to another (for example from the somatic sensory area on one side to the corresponding area on the other side) terminate in patches that have a regular periodicity of about a millimeter. Here the columns are evident morphologically, but one has no idea of the physiological interpretation. It is clear, however, that fine periodic subdivisions are a very general feature of the cerebral cortex. Indeed, Mountcastle's original observation of that feature may be said to supply a fourth profound insight into cortical organization.

It would surely be wrong to assume that this account of the visual cortex in any way exhausts the subject. Color, movement and stereoscopic depth are probably all dealt with in the cortex, but to what extent or how is still not clear. There are indications from work we and others have done on depth and from work on color by Semir Zeki of University College London that higher cortical visual areas to which the primary area projects directly or indirectly may be specialized to handle these variables, but we are a long way from knowing what the handling involves.

What happens beyond the primary visual area, and how is the information on orientation exploited at later stages? Is one to imagine ultimately finding a cell that responds specifically to some very particular item? (Usually one's grandmother is selected as the particular item, for reasons that escape us.) Our answer is that we doubt there is such a cell, but we have no good alternative to offer. To speculate broadly on how the brain may work is fortunately not the only course open to investigators. To explore the brain is more fun and seems to be more profitable.

There was a time, not so long ago, when one looked at the millions of neurons in the various layers of the cortex and wondered if anyone would ever have any idea of their function. Did they all work in parallel, like the cells of the liver or the kidney, achieving their objectives by pure bulk, or were they each doing something special? For the visual cortex the answer seems now to be known in broad outline: Particular stimuli turn neurons on or off; groups of neurons do indeed perform particular transformations. It seems reasonable to think that if the secrets of a few regions such as this one can be unlocked, other regions will also in time give up their secrets.

ACTUAL PATTERN of cortical activity was elicited by exposing only the left eye to a set of vertical stripes. The deoxyglucose autoradiograph is of a tangential section in the outer layers of the cortex. The pattern of regularly spaced dark patches of radioactivity represents intersection of ocular-dominance and orientation systems. Magnification is about eight diameters.

5

"Imprinting" in a Natural Laboratory

by Eckhard H. Hess
August 1972

A synthesis of laboratory and field techniques has led to some interesting discoveries about imprinting, the process by which newly hatched birds rapidly form a permanent bond to the parent

In a marsh on the Eastern Shore of Maryland, a few hundred feet from my laboratory building, a female wild mallard sits on a dozen infertile eggs. She has been incubating the eggs for almost four weeks. Periodically she hears the faint peeping sounds that are emitted by hatching mallard eggs, and she clucks softly in response. Since these eggs are infertile, however, they are not about to hatch and they do not emit peeping sounds. The sounds come from a small loudspeaker hidden in the nest under the eggs. The loudspeaker is connected to a microphone next to some hatching mallard eggs inside an incubator in my laboratory. The female mallard can hear any sounds coming from the laboratory eggs, and a microphone beside her relays the sounds she makes to a loudspeaker next to those eggs.

The reason for complicating the life of an expectant duck in such a way is to further our understanding of the phenomenon known as imprinting. It was through the work of the Austrian zoologist Konrad Z. Lorenz that imprinting became widely known. In the 1930's Lorenz observed that newly hatched goslings would follow him rather than their mother if the goslings saw him before they saw her. Since naturally reared geese show a strong attachment for their parent, Lorenz concluded that some animals have the capacity to learn rapidly and permanently at a very early age, and in particular to learn the characteristics of the parent. He called this process of acquiring an attachment to the parent *Prägung*, which in German means "stamping" or "coinage" but in English has been rendered as "imprinting." Lorenz regarded the phenomenon as being different from the usual kind of learning because of its rapidity and apparent permanence. In fact, he was hesitant at first to regard imprinting as a form of learn-

ing at all. Some child psychologists and some psychiatrists nevertheless perceived a similarity between the evidence of imprinting in animals and the early behavior of the human infant, and it is not surprising that interest in imprinting spread quickly.

From about the beginning of the 1950's many investigators have intensively studied imprinting in the laboratory. Unlike Lorenz, the majority of them have regarded imprinting as a form

of learning and have used methods much the same as those followed in the study of associative learning processes. In every case efforts were made to manipulate or stringently control the imprinting process. Usually the subjects are incubator-hatched birds that are reared in the laboratory. The birds are typically kept isolated until the time of the laboratory imprinting experience to prevent interaction of early social experience and the imprinting experience. Various objects

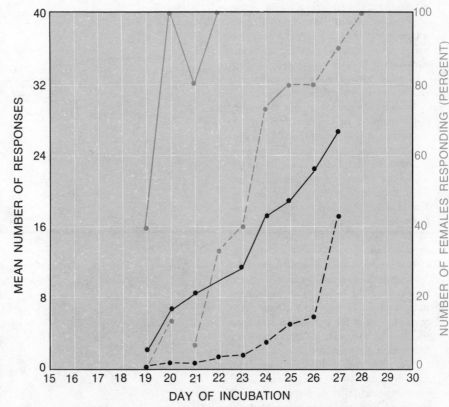

VOCAL RESPONSES to hatching-duckling sounds of 15 female wild mallards (*broken curves*) and five human-imprinted mallards (*solid curves*), which were later released to the wild, followed the same pattern, although the human-imprinted mallards began responding sooner and more frequently. A tape recording of the sounds of a hatching duckling was played daily throughout the incubation period to each female mallard while she was on her nest. Responses began on the 19th day of incubation and rose steadily until hatching.

have been used as artificial parents: duck decoys, stuffed hens, dolls, milk bottles, toilet floats, boxes, balls, flashing lights and rotating disks. Several investigators have constructed an automatic imprinting apparatus into which the newly hatched bird can be put. In this kind of work the investigator does not observe the young bird directly; all the bird's movements with respect to the imprinting object are recorded automatically.

Much of my own research during the past two decades has not differed substantially from this approach. The birds I have used for laboratory imprinting studies have all been incubated, hatched and reared without the normal social and environmental conditions and have then been tested in an artificial situation. It is therefore possible that the behavior observed under such conditions is not relevant to what actually happens in nature.

It is perhaps not surprising that studies of "unnatural" imprinting have produced conflicting results. Lorenz' original statements on the permanence of natural imprinting have been disputed. In many instances laboratory imprinting experiences do not produce permanent and exclusive attachment to the object selected as an artificial parent. For example, a duckling can spend a considerable amount of time following the object to which it is to be imprinted, and immediately after the experience it will follow a completely different object.

In one experiment in our laboratory we attempted to imprint ducklings to ourselves, as Lorenz did. For 20 continuous hours newly hatched ducklings were exposed to us. Before long they followed us whenever we moved about. Then they were given to a female mallard that had hatched a clutch of ducklings several hours before. After only an hour and a half of exposure to the female mallard and other ducklings the human-imprinted ducklings followed the female on the first exodus from the nest. Weeks later the behavior of the human-imprinted ducks was no different from the behavior of the ducks that had been hatched in the nest. Clearly laboratory imprinting is reversible.

We also took wild ducklings from their natural mother 16 hours after hatching and tried to imprint them to humans. On the first day we spent many hours with the ducklings, and during the next two months we made lengthy attempts every day to overcome the ducklings' fear of us. We finally gave up. From the beginning to the end the ducks

remained wild and afraid. They were released, and when they had matured, they were observed to be as wary of humans as normal wild ducks are. This result suggests that natural imprinting, unlike artificial laboratory imprinting, is permanent and irreversible. I have had to conclude that the usual laboratory imprinting has only a limited resemblance to natural imprinting.

It seems obvious that if the effects of natural imprinting are to be understood, the phenomenon must be studied as it operates in nature. The value of such studies was stressed as long ago as 1914 by the pioneer American psychologist John B. Watson. He emphasized that field observations must always be made to test whether or not conclusions drawn from laboratory studies conform to what actually happens in nature. The disparity between laboratory results and what happens in nature often arises from the failure of the investigator to really look at the animal's behavior. For years I have cautioned my students against shutting their experimental animals in "black boxes" with automatic recording devices and never directly observing how the animals behave.

This does not mean that objective laboratory methods for studying the behavior of animals must be abandoned. With laboratory investigations large strides have been made in the development of instruments for the recording of behavior. In the study of imprinting it is not necessary to revert to imprecise naturalistic observations in the field. We can now go far beyond the limitations of traditional field studies. It is possible to set up modern laboratory equipment in actual field conditions and in ways that do not disturb or interact with the behavior being studied, in other words, to achieve a synthesis of laboratory and field techniques.

The first step in the field-laboratory method is to observe and record the undisturbed natural behavior of the animal in the situation being studied. In our work on imprinting we photographed the behavior of the female mallard during incubation and hatching. We photographed the behavior of the ducklings during and after hatching. We recorded

CLUCKS emitted by a female wild mallard in the fourth week of incubating eggs are shown in the sound spectrogram (*upper illustration*). Each cluck lasts for about 150 milliseconds

all sounds from the nest before and after hatching. Other factors, such as air temperature and nest temperature, were also recorded.

A detailed inventory of the actual events in natural imprinting is essential for providing a reference point in the assessment of experimental manipulations of the imprinting process. That is, the undisturbed natural imprinting events form the control situation for assessing the effects of the experimental manipulations. This is quite different from the "controlled" laboratory setting, in which the ducklings are reared in isolation and then tested in unnatural conditions. The controlled laboratory study not only introduces new variables (environmental and social deprivation) into the imprinting situation but also it can prevent the investigator from observing factors that are relevant in wild conditions.

My Maryland research station is well suited for the study of natural imprinting in ducks. The station, near a national game refuge, has 250 acres of marsh and forest on a peninsula on which there are many wild and semiwild mallards. Through the sharp eyes of my technical assistant Elihu Abbott, a native of the Eastern Shore, I have learned to see much I might otherwise have missed. Initially we looked at and listened to the undisturbed parent-offspring interaction of female mallards that hatched their own eggs both in nests on the ground and in specially constructed nest boxes. From our records we noticed that the incubation time required for different clutches of eggs decreased progressively between March and June. Both the average air temperature and the number of daylight hours increase during those months; both are correlated with the incubation time of mallard eggs. It is likely, however, that temperature rather than photoperiod directly influences the duration of incubation. In one experiment mallard eggs from an incubator were slowly cooled for two hours a day in a room with a temperature of seven degrees Celsius, and another set of eggs was cooled in a room at 27 degrees C. These temperatures re-spectively correspond to the mean noon temperatures at the research station in March and in June. The eggs that were placed in the cooler room took longer to hatch, indicating that temperature affects the incubation time directly. Factors such as humidity and barometric pressure may also play a role.

We noticed that all the eggs in a wild nest usually hatch between three and eight hours of one another. As a result all the ducklings in the same clutch are approximately the same age in terms of the number of hours since hatching. Yet when mallard eggs are placed in a mechanical incubator, they will hatch over a two- or three-day period even when precautions are taken to ensure that all the eggs begin developing simultaneously. The synchronous hatching observed in nature obviously has some survival value. At the time of the exodus from the nest, which usually takes place between 16 and 32 hours after hatching, all the ducklings would be of a similar age and thus would have equal motor capabilities and similar social experiences.

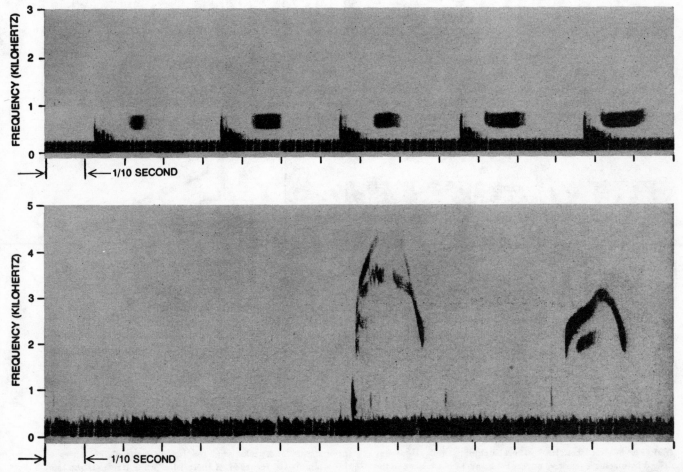

and is low in pitch: about one kilohertz or less. Sounds emitted by ducklings inside the eggs are high-pitched, rising to about four kilohertz (*lower illustration*). Records of natural, undisturbed imprinting events in the nest provide a control for later experiments.

Over the years our laboratory studies and actual observations of how a female mallard interacts with her offspring have pointed to the conclusion that imprinting is related to the age after hatching rather than the age from the beginning of incubation. Many other workers, however, have accepted the claim that age from the beginning of incubation determines the critical period for maximum effectiveness of imprinting. They base their belief on the findings of Gilbert Gottlieb of the Dorothea Dix Hospital in Raleigh, N.C., who in a 1961 paper described experiments that apparently showed that maximum imprinting in ducklings occurs in the period between 27 and 27½ days after the beginning of incubation. To make sure that all the eggs he was working with started incubation at the same time he first chilled the eggs so that any partially developed embryos would be killed. Yet the 27th day after the beginning of incubation can hardly be the period of maximum imprinting for wild ducklings that hatch in March under natural conditions, because such ducklings take on the average 28 days to hatch. Moreover, if the age of a duckling is measured from the beginning of incubation, it is hard to explain why eggs laid at different times in a hot month in the same nest will hatch within six to eight hours of one another under natural conditions.

Periodic cooling of the eggs seems to affect the synchronization of hatching. The mallard eggs from an incubator that were placed in a room at seven degrees C. hatched over a period of a day and a half, whereas eggs placed in the room at 27 degrees hatched over a period of two

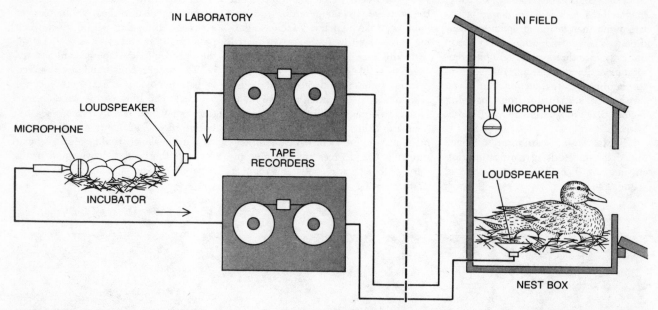

FEMALE MALLARD sitting on infertile eggs hears sounds transmitted from mallard eggs in a laboratory incubator. Any sounds she makes are transmitted to a loudspeaker beside the eggs in the laboratory. Such a combination of field and laboratory techniques permits recording of events without disturbing the nesting mallard and provides the hatching eggs with nearly natural conditions.

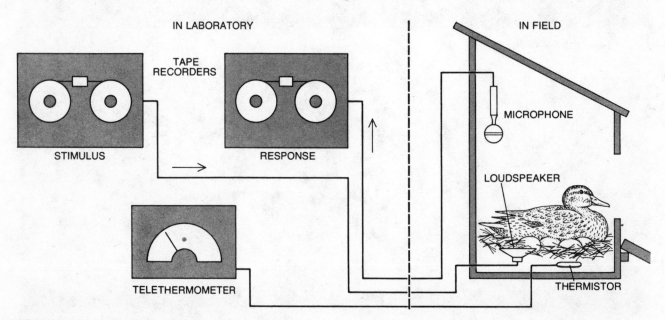

REMOTE MANIPULATION of prehatching sounds is accomplished by placing a sensitive microphone and a loudspeaker in the nest of a female wild mallard who is sitting on her own eggs. Prerecorded hatching-duckling sounds are played at specified times through the loudspeaker and the female mallard's responses to this stimulus are recorded. A thermistor probe transmits the temperature in the nest to a telethermometer and chart recorder. The thermistor records provide data about when females are on nest.

and a half days (which is about normal for artificially incubated eggs). Cooling cannot, however, play a major role. In June the temperature in the outdoor nest boxes averages close to the normal brooding temperature while the female mallard is absent. Therefore an egg laid on June 1 has a head start in incubation over those laid a week later. Yet we have observed that all the eggs in clutches laid in June hatch in a period lasting between six and eight hours.

We found another clue to how the synchronization of hatching may be achieved in the vocalization pattern of the brooding female mallard. As many others have noted, the female mallard vocalizes regularly as she sits on her eggs during the latter part of the incubation period. It seemed possible that she was vocalizing to the eggs, perhaps in response to sounds from the eggs themselves. Other workers had observed that ducklings make sounds before they hatch, and the prehatching behavior of ducklings in response to maternal calls has been extensively reported by Gottlieb.

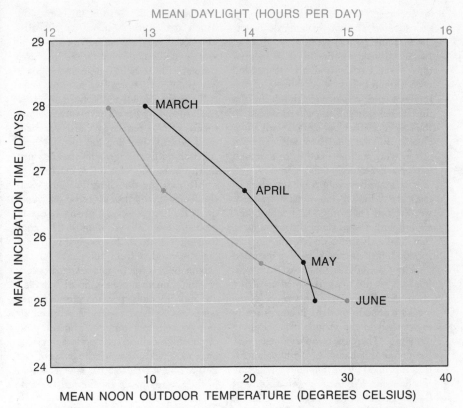

INCUBATION TIME of mallard eggs hatched naturally in a feral setting at Lake Cove, Md., decreased steadily from March to June. The incubation period correlated with both the outdoor temperature (*black curve*) and the daily photoperiod (*colored curve*).

We placed a highly sensitive microphone next to some mallard eggs that were nearly ready to hatch. We found that the ducklings indeed make sounds while they are still inside the egg. We made a one-minute tape recording of the sounds emitted by a duckling that had pipped its shell and was going to hatch within the next few hours. Then we made a seven-minute recording that would enable us to play the duckling sounds three times for one minute interspersed with one-minute silences. We played the recording once each to 37 female mallards at various stages of

NEST EXODUS takes place about 16 to 32 hours after hatching. The female mallard begins to make about 40 to 65 calls per minute and continues while the ducklings leave the nest to follow her. The ducklings are capable of walking and swimming from hatching.

incubation. There were no positive responses from the female mallards during the first and second week of incubation. In fact, during the first days of incubation some female mallards responded with threat behavior: a fluffing of the feathers and a panting sound. In the third week some females responded to the recorded duckling sounds with a few clucks. In the fourth week maternal clucks were frequent and were observed in all ducks tested.

We found the same general pattern of response whether the female mallards were tested once or, as in a subsequent experiment, tested daily during incubation. Mallards sitting on infertile eggs responded just as much to the recorded duckling sounds as mallards sitting on fertile eggs did. Apparently after sitting on a clutch of eggs for two or three weeks a female mallard becomes ready to respond to the sounds of a hatching duckling. There is some evidence that the parental behavior of the female mallard is primed by certain neuroendocrine mechanisms. We have begun a study of the neuroendocrine changes that might accompany imprinting and filial behavior in mallards.

To what extent do unhatched ducklings respond to the vocalization of the female mallard? In order to find out we played a recording of a female mallard's vocalizations to ducklings in eggs that had just been pipped and were scheduled to hatch within the next 24 hours. As before, the sounds were interspersed with periods of silence. We then recorded all the sounds made by the ducklings during the recorded female mallard vocalizations and also during the silent periods on the tape. Twenty-four hours before the scheduled hatching the ducklings emitted 34 percent of their sounds during the silent periods, which suggests that at this stage they initiate most of the auditory interaction. As hatching time approaches the ducklings emit fewer and fewer sounds during the silent periods. The total number of sounds they make, however, increases steadily. At the time of hatching only 9 percent of the sounds they make are emitted during the silent periods. One hour after hatching, in response to the same type of recording, the ducklings gave 37 percent of their vocalizations during the silent periods, a level similar to the level at 24 hours before hatching.

During the hatching period, which lasts about an hour, the female mallard generally vocalizes at the rate of from zero to four calls per one-minute interval. Occasionally there is an interval in which she emits as many as 10 calls. When the duckling actually hatches, the female mallard's vocalization increases dramatically to between 45 and 68 calls per minute for one or two minutes.

Thus the sounds made by the female mallard and by her offspring are complementary. The female mallard vocalizes most when a duckling has just hatched. A hatching duckling emits its cries primarily when the female is vocalizing.

After all the ducklings have hatched the female mallard tends to be relatively quiet for long intervals, giving between zero and four calls per minute. This continues for 16 to 32 hours until it is time for the exodus from the nest. As the exodus begins the female mallard quickly builds up to a crescendo of between 40 and 65 calls per minute; on rare occasions we have observed between 70 and 95 calls per minute. The duration of the high-calling-rate period depends on how quickly the ducklings leave the nest to follow her. There is now a change in the sounds made by the female mallard. Up to this point she has been making clucking sounds. By the time the exodus from the nest takes place some of her sounds are more like quacks.

The auditory interaction of the female mallard and the duckling can begin well before the hatching period. As I have indicated, the female mallard responds to unhatched-duckling sounds during the third and fourth week of incubation. Normally ducklings penetrate a membrane to reach an air space inside the eggshell two days before hatching. We have not found any female mallard that vocalized to her clutch before the duckling in the egg reached the air space. We have found that as soon as the duckling penetrates the air space the female begins to cluck at a rate of between zero and four times per minute. Typically she continues to vocalize at this rate until the ducklings begin to pip their eggs (which is about 24 hours after they have entered the air space). As the eggs are being pipped the female clucks at the rate of between 10 and 15 times per minute. When the pipping is completed, she

SOUND SPECTROGRAM of the calls of newly hatched ducklings in the nest and the mother's responses is shown at right. The high-pitched peeps of the ducklings are in the

DISTRESS CALLS of ducklings in the nest evoke a quacklike response from the female mallard. The cessation of the distress calls and the onset of normal duckling peeping sounds

drops back to between zero and four calls per minute. In the next 24 hours there is a great deal of auditory interaction between the female and her unhatched offspring; this intense interaction may facilitate the rapid formation of the filial bond after hatching, although it is quite possible that synchrony of hatching is the main effect. Already we have found that a combination of cooling the eggs daily, placing them together so that they touch one another and transmitting parent-young vocal responses through the microphone-loudspeaker hookup between the female's nest and the laboratory incubator causes the eggs in the incubator to hatch as synchronously as eggs in nature do. In fact, the two times we did this we found that all the eggs in the clutches hatched within four hours of one another. It has been shown in many studies of imprinting, including laboratory studies, that auditory stimuli have an important effect on the development of filial attachment. Auditory stimulation, before and after hatching, together with tactile

stimulation in the nest after hatching results in ducklings that are thoroughly imprinted to the female mallard that is present.

Furthermore, it appears that auditory interaction before hatching may play an important role in promoting the synchronization of hatching. As our experiments showed, not only does the female mallard respond to sounds from her eggs but also the ducklings respond to her clucks. Perhaps the daily cooling of the eggs when the female mallard leaves the nest to feed serves to broadly synchronize embryonic and behavioral development, whereas the auditory interaction of the mother with the ducklings and of one duckling with another serves to provide finer synchronization. Margaret Vince of the University of Cambridge has shown that the synchronization of hatching in quail is promoted by the mutual auditory interaction of the young birds in the eggs.

Listening to the female mallards vocalize to their eggs or to their newly hatched offspring, we were struck by the

fact that we could tell which mallard was vocalizing, even when we could not see her. Some female mallards regularly emit single clucks at one-second intervals, some cluck in triple or quadruple clusters and others cluck in clusters of different lengths. The individual differences in the vocalization styles of female mallards may enable young ducklings to identify their mother. We can also speculate that the characteristics of a female mallard's voice are learned by her female offspring, which may then adopt a similar style when they are hatching eggs of their own.

The female mallards not only differ from one another in vocalization styles but also emit different calls in different situations. We have recorded variations in pitch and duration from the same mallard in various nesting situations. It seems likely that such variations in the female mallard call are an important factor in the imprinting process.

Studies of imprinting in the laboratory have shown that the more effort a duckling has to expend in following the im-

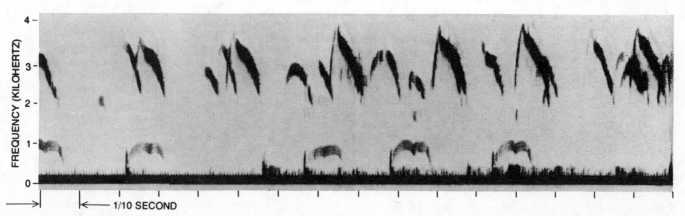

two-to-four-kilohertz range. They normally have the shape of an inverted V. The female mallard's clucks are about one kilohertz

and last about 130 milliseconds. After the eggs hatch the vocalization of the female changes both in quantity and in quality of sound.

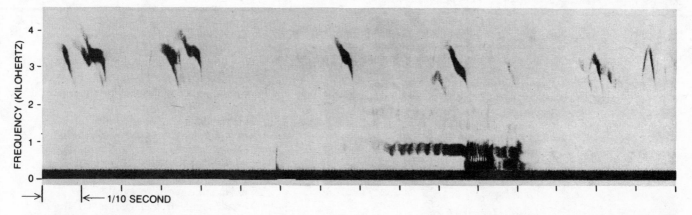

is almost immediate, as can be seen in this sound spectrogram. The female mallard's quacklike call is about one kilohertz in pitch and

has a duration of approximately 450 milliseconds. The call is emitted about once every two seconds in response to distress cries.

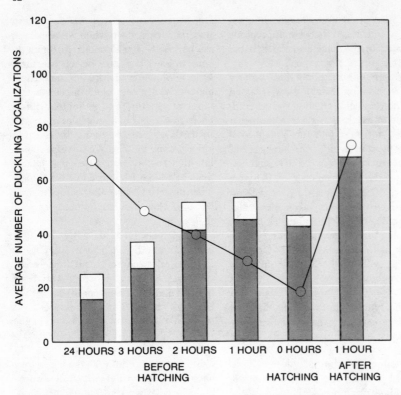

NUMBER OF SOUNDS from ducklings before and after hatching are shown. The ducklings heard a recording consisting of five one-minute segments of a female mallard's clucking sounds interspersed with five one-minute segments of silence. The recording was played to six mallard eggs and the number of vocal responses by the ducklings to the clucking segments (*gray bars*) and to the silent segments (*white bars*) were counted. Twenty-four hours before hatching 34 percent of the duckling sounds were made during the silent interval, indicating the ducklings initiated a substantial portion of the early auditory interaction. As hatching time approached the ducklings initiated fewer and fewer of the sounds and at hatching vocalized most in response to the clucks of the female mallard.

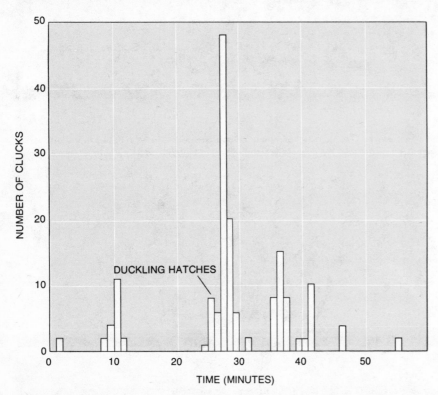

CLUCKING RATE of a wild, ground-nesting female mallard rose dramatically for about two minutes while a duckling hatched and then slowly declined to the prehatching rate. Each bar depicts the number of clucks emitted by the female during a one-minute period.

printing object, the more strongly it prefers that object in later testing. At first it would seem that this is not the case in natural imprinting; young ducklings raised by their mother have little difficulty following her during the exodus from the nest. Closer observation of many nests over several seasons showed, however, that ducklings make a considerable effort to be near their parent. They may suffer for such efforts, since they can be accidentally stepped on, squeezed or scratched by the female adult. The combination of effort and punishment may actually strengthen imprinting. Work in my laboratory showed that chicks given an electric shock while they were following the imprinting object later showed stronger attachment to the object than unshocked chicks did. It is reasonable to expect similar results with ducklings.

Slobodan Petrovich of the University of Maryland (Baltimore County) and I have begun a study to determine the relative contributions of prehatching and posthatching auditory experience on imprinting and filial attachment. The auditory stimuli consist of either natural mallard maternal clucks or a human voice saying "Come, come, come." Our results indicate that prehatching stimulation by natural maternal clucks may to a degree facilitate the later recognition of the characteristic call of the mallard. Ducklings lacking any experience with a maternal call imprint as well to a duck decoy that utters "Come, come, come" as to a decoy that emits normal mallard clucks. Ducklings that had been exposed to a maternal call before hatching imprinted better to decoys that emitted the mallard clucks. We found, however, that the immediate posthatching experiences, in this case with a female mallard on the nest, can highly determine the degree of filial attachment and make imprinting to a human sound virtually impossible.

It is important to recognize that almost all laboratory imprinting experiments, including my own, have been deprivation experiments. The justification for such experiments has been the ostensible need for controlling the variables of the phenomenon, but the deprivation may have interfered with the normal behavioral development of the young ducklings. Whatever imprinting experiences the experimenter allows therefore do not produce the maximum effect.

Although our findings are far from complete, we have already determined enough to demonstrate the great value of studying imprinting under natural conditions. The natural laboratory can be profitably used to study questions about imprinting that have been raised but not answered by traditional laboratory experiments. We must move away from the in vitro, or test-tube, approach to the study of behavior and move toward the in vivo method that allows interaction with normal environmental factors. Some of the questions are: What is the optimal age for imprinting? How long must the imprinting experience last for it to have the maximum effect? Which has the greater effect on behavior: first experience or the most recent experience? Whatever kind of behavior is being studied, the most fruitful approach may well be to study the behavior in its natural context.

6

The Object in the World of the Infant

by T. G. R. Bower
October 1971

*At what stage of development does an infant begin
to associate qualities such as solidity with objects
that he sees? Experiments with infants reveal that
this occurs much earlier than expected*

According to most traditional theories of how we come to perceive the world around us, the quality of solidity belongs to the sense of touch in the same way that the quality of color belongs to the sense of vision or the quality of pitch to the sense of hearing. Only the sense of touch has the intrinsic ability to distinguish solids from nonsolids. The ability to identify solid objects visually is the result of learning to associate visual clues with tactile impressions, or so the traditional arguments have asserted. The classic version of the theory was presented by Bishop Berkeley. It was espoused in the 19th century by Hermann von Helmholtz and more recently by J. McV. Hunt, Burton White and Richard L. Gregory.

If the ability to associate touch and sight is learned, then at what stage of human development does the learning occur? Since young children clearly exhibit a unity of the senses, such learning must take place at some early stage of infancy. The infant who has not yet made the association must therefore live in a world of clouds, smoke puffs and insubstantial images of objects rather than in a world of solid, stable objects.

A similar situation holds when we observe an object move behind another object and disappear from sight. An adult knows that the object is still there, that it has not ceased to exist. This can be verified simply by removing the obstructing object or looking around it. It is hard to understand how an infant could know that the object is still there by using vision alone; how can vision provide information about the location of an invisible object? Touch must play a critical role in the development of the ability to deal with hidden objects. The hand can go around obstacles to reach such objects, and only as a result of such

explorations can an infant come to know that the object is still there. So, again, goes the traditional argument, and very plausible it seems.

These aspects of objects—solidity and permanence—present deep problems to the student of human development. Not the least formidable of the problems is finding ways to measure a naïve infant's response to objects. The infant, with his limited repertory of responses, is a refractory subject for psychological investigation. Recent advances in techniques of studying space perception and pattern recognition in infants are inherently unsuitable. These methods mostly determine whether or not the infant discriminates between two presentations, for example a regular pattern and an irregular one. One could present a solid object and, say, a bounded air space with the same external contour to an infant. Undoubtedly an infant of any age could discriminate between the two objects. The mere fact of discrimination would not tell us that the infant knew the object was solid, tangible and would offer resistance to his touch. There are visual differences between solids and nonsolids, and the infant could pick up these differences without realizing that they signify solidity. Indeed, according to some theories there must be such a stage, where the infant does perceive differences but is not aware of their significance.

The methods I adopted to measure the infant's expectation of solidity involve the element of surprise and the use of an optical illusion. The illusion is produced with a binocular shadow-caster, a device consisting of two light projectors with polarizing filters and a rear-projection screen. The object, made of translucent plastic, is suspended be-

tween the lights and the screen so that it casts a double shadow on the rear of the screen. The small subject sits in front of the screen and views the shadows through polarizing goggles that have the effect of making only one shadow visible to each eye. The two retinal images are combined by the normal processes of binocular vision to yield a stereoscopic percept of the object. This virtual object appears in front of the screen and looks very real and solid. It is nonetheless an illusion and is therefore intangible. When the infant attempts to grasp it, his hand closes on empty air. To reach out for a seemingly solid object and come in contact with nothing is startling for anyone. The surprise clearly is a consequence of the nonfulfillment of the expectation that the seen object will be tangible.

Since even very young infants display the startle response, it can serve as an indicator of surprise. If the infant is startled by the absence of solidity in the virtual object, that can be taken as an index of an expectation that the seen object will be tangible. In contrast, a startle response on contact with the real object could be taken as an indication that the seen object is not expected to be tangible.

In the first experiment the infant sat before a screen and was presented with the virtual object or the real object. The two situations were presented several times, always beginning with the virtual object. We looked for evidence of startle behavior. The startle response can be measured in numerous ways, some of which are sophisticated and expensive, but in this experiment we used very simple indicators: facial expression and crying. These measures, so simple as to seem unscientific, are in fact as reliable as the more complex ones we used later.

Our subjects were infants between 16 and 24 weeks old. The results were quite unambiguous. None of the infants showed any sign of surprise when he touched the real object in front of him. Every infant showed marked surprise when his hand failed to make contact with the perceived virtual object. Whenever the infant's hand reached the place where the virtual object seemed to be, within a fraction of a second he emitted a coo, a whoop or a cry, accompanied by a change in facial expression so marked as to seem a caricature. The older infants reacted even more: they stared at their hand, rubbed their hands together or banged their hand on the chair before reaching again for the virtual object. All of this supports the idea that the infants expected to be able to touch a seen object and were very surprised when their attempts to do so produced no tactile feedback.

Although these results are interesting, they do not resolve the problem under investigation. They merely indicate that learning to coordinate vision and touch must take place, if it takes place at all, before the age of 16 weeks. We therefore attempted to study coordination between vision and touch in even younger infants, hoping to find a period of noncoordination. The communication problem is intensified in very young infants, since their behavioral repertory is even more limited than that of older infants.

Some investigators have reported that an infant less than six weeks old will not show defensive or avoidance behavior when an object approaches him. Other studies, however, have shown that an infant can discriminate changes in the position of objects in space well before the age of six weeks [see "The Visual World of Infants," by T. G. R. Bower; Scientific American Offprint 502]. The lack of defensive behavior may indicate the absence of the expectation that the seen object would produce tactile consequences, and it seemed to us that the infant's response to approaching objects would be a promising area to investigate.

Our preliminary investigations were highly encouraging. We took infants in their second week of life, placed them on their back and moved objects toward their face. We used objects of a wide variety of sizes and a wide variety of speeds. Some objects were moved noisily, some silently. All of this was to no avail. The infants, more than 40 of them, did not even blink. These two-week-old infants certainly did not seem to expect a seen object to have tactile consequences. It appeared that we had indeed found a period when vision and touch were not coordinated.

At this point in the research I became aware of the work of Heinz Prechtl, who

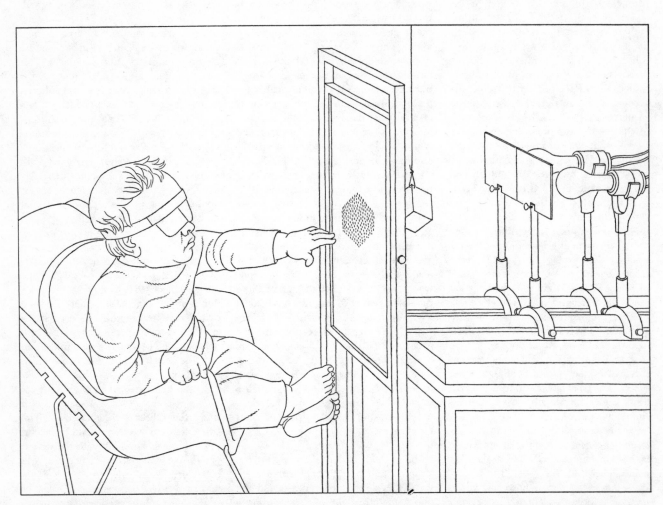

INTANGIBLE OBJECT is produced by a shadow-caster, in which two oppositely polarized beams of light cast a double shadow of an object on a rear-projection screen. An infant views the double shadows through polarizing goggles that make a different shadow visible to each eye. The innate processes of stereopsis fuse the two images to make the infant think he is seeing a solid object in front of the screen. When the infant tries to grasp the virtual image, he is startled when his hand closes on empty air; within a fraction of a second he cries and his face expresses marked surprise. When a real object is placed in front of the screen, none of the infants show any signs of surprise when they touch it. These results indicate that the infants expect a seen object to be solid and tangible.

had gathered evidence that implied infants under two weeks old are never fully awake while they are lying on their back. Since one could not expect defensive behavior from infants who were half-asleep, we repeated the experiment with infants of the same age who were held in an upright or semiupright position. With this modification the results were totally different. The infants clearly showed a defensive response to an approaching object. They pulled their head back and put their hands between their face and the object. These responses were accompanied by distress and crying so intense that the experiment had to be terminated earlier than had been planned. We were nonetheless able to try a few variations. We found that the defensive behavior was specific to an approaching object; if an object moved away, it produced neither defensive behavior nor crying. Moreover, the response was specific to a seen object. A moving solid object displaces air, which presumably causes pressure changes at the surface of the skin. In order to rule out the possibility that such pressure changes were the effective stimulus, we had a group of infants view an approaching virtual object produced by a

shadow-caster. An object behind a translucent screen was moved away from the infant toward a projector. When the infant is placed at the same distance in front of the screen as the projectors are behind it, a shadow on the screen produces an image on the infant's retina that is identical with the image produced by a real object moving toward the baby, without the displacement of air and other nonvisual changes that accompany the movement of a real object.

The results were that seven out of seven infants in their second week of life exhibited defensive behavior when they saw the approaching virtual object. In our study the intensity of the infant's response to the virtual object seems somewhat less than the response to the real object, but a replication of the experiment by E. Tronick and C. Ball of Harvard University showed that the two responses are not that different. As a further check on the role of air movement another group of infants was presented with air displacement alone (produced by an air hose) with no object in the field of vision. None of these infants exhibited any defensive behavior or marked distress.

Taken together, these results suggest

that by the second week of life an infant expects a seen object to have tactile consequences. The precocity of this expectation is quite surprising from the traditional point of view. Indeed, it seems to me that these findings are fatal to traditional theories of human development. In our culture it is unlikely that an infant less than two weeks old has been hit in the face by an approaching object, so that none of the infants in the study could have been exposed to situations where they could have learned to fear an approaching object and expect it to have tactile qualities. We can only conclude that in man there is a primitive unity of the senses, with visual variables specifying tactile consequences, and that this primitive unity is built into the structure of the human nervous system.

In an effort to further test this hypothesis we repeated the original virtual-object experiment with a group of newborn infants. It was not easy to do this, since the infants had to meet the criterion that they would wear the polarizing goggles without fussing. Newborn infants do not reach for objects in the same way that older infants do. They will, however, reach out and grasp ob-

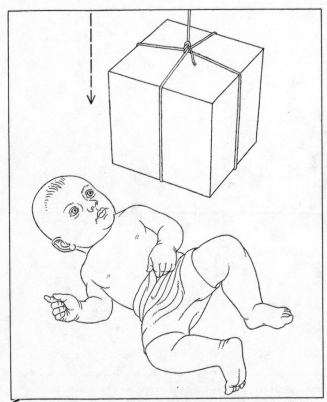

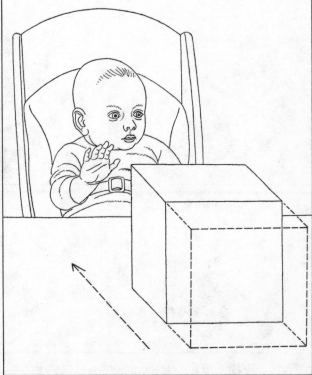

NO RESPONSE was observed when objects were moved toward the face of two-week-old infants who were lying on their back. At first this was taken to mean that infants at this age do not expect seen objects to have tactile qualities, but the author learned later that very young infants are never fully awake when on their back.

DEFENSIVE RESPONSE and marked distress to an approaching object was exhibited by upright two-week-old infants, even when the approaching object was an illusion produced by a shadow-caster. This evidence contradicts the theory that the perception of solidity is learned by associating tactile impressions and vision.

58

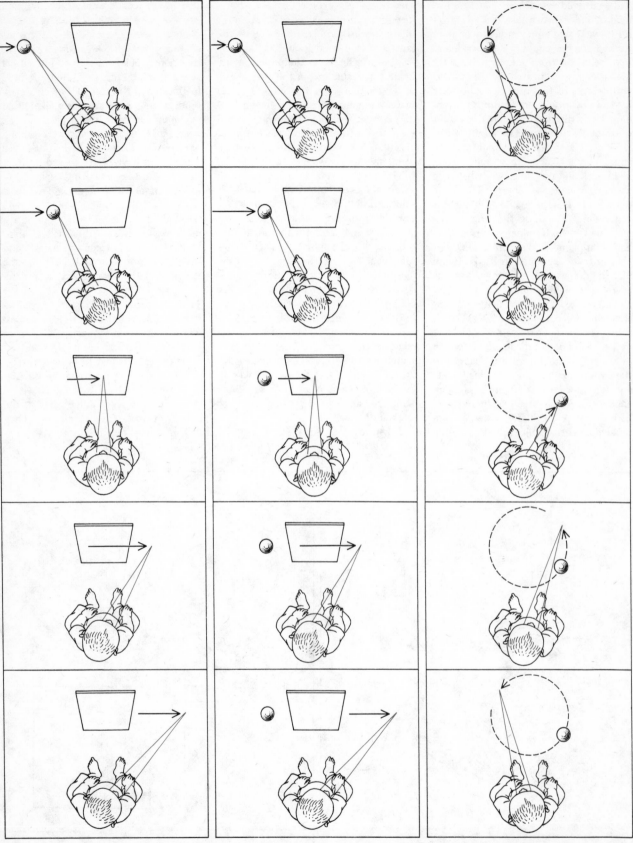

INFANT'S ANTICIPATION of the reappearance of an object that moves behind a screen and stops (*left*) seems to prove that the infant knew the object was still behind the screen. When the object stops before it reaches the screen, however, the infant continues to track the path of motion as if he could not arrest his head movement (*middle*). Next the infant was shown an object moving in a circle. If inability to arrest head movement were responsible for the continuation of tracking, then when the object stops halfway up the arc (*right*), the infant's gaze should continue tangentially to the circular path. Instead the infant's gaze paused on the stopped object for half a second and then continued along the circular path. It seems that the eight- and 16-week-old infants did not identify an object as being the same object when it was moving and when it was stationary and so they continued to look for the moving object.

jects if they are supported so that their hands and arms are free to move to the objects in front of them. (They also reach out and grasp at empty air, but that does not affect the argument.)

We found that all the newborn infants touched and grasped real objects without any sign of being disturbed. The virtual object, however, produced a howl as soon as the infant's hand went to the intangible object's location. Here too, then, in dealing with the absence of tactile input in a situation where it normally would be expected, we have evidence of a primitive unity of the senses. This unity is unlikely to have been learned, given the early age and the history of the infants studied.

These results were surprising and interesting. They showed that at least one aspect of the eye-and-hand interaction is built into the nervous system. If it is built in, might not a more complex aspect of objects, namely permanence, also be built in? Is it possible that inborn structural properties ensure that an infant knows an object moving out of sight behind another object is still there? In order to find out we again used the startle response as an indicator of surprise. We sat an infant in front of an object. A screen moved in from one side and covered the object. After various intervals (1.5, 3, 7.5 or 15 seconds) the screen moved away. In half of the trials the object was still there when the screen moved away. In the other trials the object was no longer there when the screen moved away. If the infant knew that the object was still there behind the screen, its absence when the screen moved should have surprised him. If, on the other hand, the infant thought the object had ceased to exist when it was covered by the screen, its reappearance when the screen moved away should have been surprising.

In this experiment surprise was determined by a more quantitative index: a change in the heart rate. It is well known that the heart rate of an adult changes when he is surprised, and the same is true of infants. We measured the change in the heart rate of an infant by comparing his average heart rate over the 10 seconds after the moment of revelation with the average heart rate over the 10 seconds before the object was covered with the screen. Our subjects were infants who were 20, 40, 80 and 100 days old.

The results revealed an interesting pattern. When the object had been occluded for 1.5 seconds, all the infants manifested greater surprise at its non-reappearance than at its reappearance.

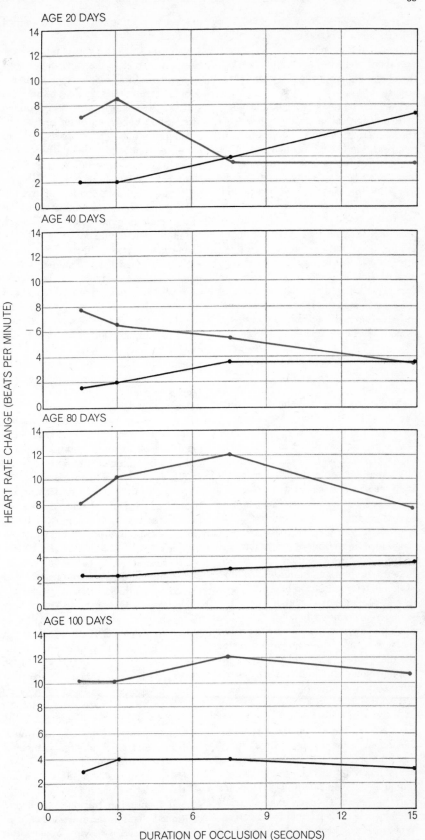

CHANGES IN HEART RATE reveal the degree of surprise in infants at the reappearance or disappearance of an object after it has been covered by a moving screen for various periods of time. Older infants are not surprised at the reappearance (*black curves*) of the object when the screen moves on, regardless of the duration of occlusion, and show little change in their heart rate. They are surprised when the object does not reappear (*colored curves*) from behind the moving screen. The youngest infants also are surprised by the object's failure to reappear when the occluding period is brief; when the time is increased to 15 seconds, they seem to forget about the object and show surprise at its reappearance.

In short, they expected the object to still be there. When the object failed to reappear, the change in the heart rate was about seven beats per minute; when the object did reappear, the change was very slight.

The oldest infants expected the object to reappear even after the longest occlusion period; when the object did not reappear, the change in their heart rate was 11 beats per minute. Curiously, the youngest infants exhibited a reverse effect after the longest occlusion period. They showed more surprise at the object's reappearance than at its nonreappearance. It seems that even very young infants know that an object is still there after it has been hidden, but if the time of occlusion is prolonged, they forget the object altogether. The early age of the infants and the novelty of the testing situation make it unlikely that such a response has been learned.

If object permanence is a built-in property of the nervous system, then it should show up in other situations. If the object was moved behind a stationary screen instead of the screen's moving to cover a stationary object, the same neural process should inform the infant that the object was behind the screen. We tested this assumption by having an eight-week-old infant watch an object that could be moved from side to side in front of him. A screen hid the center segment of the object's path. We reasoned that if the infant knew that the object had gone behind the screen rather than disappearing into some kind of limbo, he should be able to anticipate its reappearance on the other side of the screen. On the other hand, if the infant did not know that the object was behind the screen, he should not look over to the place where it would reappear; his eye movement should be arrested at the point of disappearance.

Two television cameras were lined up with the infant's face in order to record what side of the screen the infant was looking at. In the first part of the experiment the object would begin at one side, move slowly toward the screen, go behind it, emerge and continue to move for some distance. Then on random trials the object stopped behind the screen. Would such eight-week-old infants look over to the side where the object was due to emerge, or would they halt their gaze at the point of disappearance? The answer was quite straightforward: all the infants anticipated the reappearance of the object. Their behavior supported the hypothesis that a built-in neural

process had informed them the object was behind the screen.

Unfortunately this result might have been an artifact of the experiment. Perhaps the infant following the object could not stop the movement of his head and the movement simply continued after it had begun. In order to test this possibility we ran a comparison series of experiments in which the object stopped in full view before it reached the screen. We reasoned that if the infant's apparent anticipation of the object's reappearance had been the result of the continuing movement of his head, the movement should continue after the object had stopped. On the other hand, if the infant had been genuinely anticipating the reappearance of the object, he would not look at the other side of the screen for an object he had just seen stop before reaching the screen. To our great disappointment the infants all looked over to the other side of the screen. This result seemed to rule out the hypothesis that eight-week-old infants seeing an object go behind a screen know that the object is still there and will reappear. Further studies indicated that infants up to 16 weeks old also were likely to look for the object to reappear in both experimental situations.

The inability to arrest head movement is an intrinsically unsatisfying explanation, particularly since it does not explain the results from the experiment with the stationary object and the moving screen. We therefore tried a variety of other experiments. In one test infants were presented with an object that moved in a circular trajectory at right angles to their line of sight. After a time the object stopped in full view at a point halfway up the arc. If the continuation of tracking was the result of an inability to arrest ongoing movement, a pause in the object's movement on a circular path should have produced head movements tangential to the path. Every infant, however, continued to look along the circular trajectory. Furthermore, frame-by-frame analysis of motion pictures of the head movements and eye movements revealed that the infant's fixation on the object was held for about half a second before the tracking movement continued. This bizarre behavior, continuing to track a moving object after seeing it stop, cannot be the result of an inability to arrest head movement. Every infant was able to momentarily hold his gaze on the object when it stopped. Therefore the infants must at least have noticed that the object had stopped. Yet they continued to track the path the ob-

ject would have taken had it continued to move.

The explanation of this behavior was not, and is not, obvious. Superficially the infant's behavior appears to reflect an inability to identify a stationary object with the same object when it is moving. It was as if the infants had been tracking a moving object, had noticed the stationary object that the moving object had become, had looked at it for a while and then had looked farther on to find the moving object again. It seems that they had not been aware that the stationary object was in fact the same as the moving object.

Could the converse be true? Would infants look for an object in the place where it had been stationary after seeing it move off to a new location? In order to find out we seated an infant in front of a toy railroad track that had a train on it. The train carried flashing lights to attract the infant's attention. At the beginning of the experiment the train was stationary in the middle of the track. After 10 seconds the train moved slowly to the left and stopped at a new position, where it remained for 10 seconds, and then returned to its original position. The cycle was repeated 10 times.

How would this simple to-and-fro movement be seen by a three-month-old infant? Our hypothesis was that an infant of this age fails to recognize the identity of a moving object and the same object standing still. Initially the infant should see a stationary object in a particular place. Then the object would disappear and a new moving object would appear. Then the moving object would disappear and a stationary object would appear in a new place. After a time that too would disappear and a new moving object would appear, which in turn would give way to the original object in the original place again. To the infant the cycle would seem to involve perhaps four objects, whereas in reality there is only one. An infant quickly learns to look from one place to another as an object moves between them. If our hypothesis is correct, the infant is not following an object from place to place; rather he is applying a rule in the form, "Object disappears at A, object will reappear at B."

Suppose now that after the 10th cycle the train moves to the right to an entirely new position instead of moving to the left as usual. A subject who was following a single object would have no trouble. If an infant is applying the rule above, he should make an error. Specifically, when the stationary object moves to the right for the first time, thereby disappearing at the middle, the infant should look for the stationary object to the left in the place where it has reappeared before. When we tested three-month-old infants, every infant made the error predicted by our hypothesis. That is, when the train moved to the right, the infant looked to the left and

stared at the empty space where the train had stopped before. Meanwhile the train with its flashing lights was in full view in its new place to the right.

This last result, together with those from our earlier studies, confirms the hypothesis that three-month-old infants do not recognize the identity of an object at a standstill and the same object in motion, and vice versa. Note that I am using "identity" in a rather special

sense, meaning to recognize an object as being the same object rather than another identical object. If an infant does not identify a stationary object with a moving object when they are the same object, how does he identify a stationary object with itself when it is stationary in the same place later? How does he identify a moving object with itself when it is moving along a continuous trajectory? We began a new series of experiments to answer this fundamental question. The most obvious features of an object are its size, shape and color. These seem to serve as identification elements for adults. For an infant their role would seem to be somewhat different.

We presented infants with four situations: (1) An object (a small white mannikin) moved along a track, went behind a screen, emerged on the other side, moved on for a short distance, stopped and then returned to its original position. (2) The object moved along the track, went behind a screen and at the moment when the object should have emerged on the other side of the screen a totally different object (a stylized red lion) emerged, moved on for a short distance before reversing and repeating the entire cycle in the opposite direction. In this sequence there were differences of size, shape and color between the two objects, but there was only one kind of movement in any one direction. (3) The object moved along a track as before, except that at a time when, according to its speed before occlusion, it should still have been behind the screen, an identical object moved out. Here the objects were identical but there were two kinds of movement and evidence that there were two different objects since a single object could not have moved quickly enough to get across the screen in such a short time. (4) The object moved along a track as before, and at a time when it still should have been behind the screen a totally different object moved out. Here there were two kinds of difference in movement and features to indicate that there were two different objects. In all the situations only one object was visible at a time.

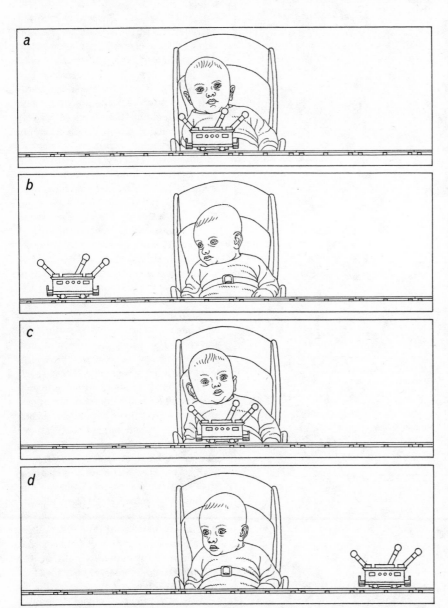

DISAPPEARING TRAIN confirms the hypothesis that infants 12 weeks old do not watch a single object when the object is at first stationary, then moves and stops. They do not follow the moving object from place to place but rather apply a cognitive rule that can be stated: "Object disappears at *A*; object reappears at *B*." In the experimental test the infant sat watching a toy train with flashing lights at rest in the middle of the track (*a*). After 10 seconds the train moved to the left and stopped (*b*) and remained there for 10 seconds before returning to the center again. The cycle was repeated 10 times. On the next cycle (*c, d*) the train moved slowly to the right and stopped. If the infant had been following the moving object, he would have looked to the right, but if he had been following the hypothesized cognitive rule, he would have looked to the left in the place where the train had stopped before. Every 12-week-old infant tested made the error predicted by the hypothesis.

We conducted the experiment with groups of infants between six and 22 weeks old. The older infants tracked the moving object in Situation 1 quite happily; when the object stopped, they stopped tracking it. In Situation 2, where a different object emerged, they also followed the object in motion, although some glancing back and forth between

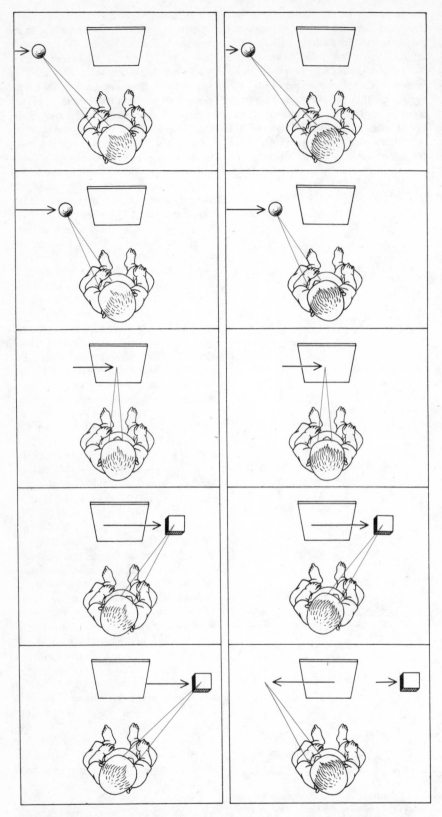

MOVEMENT AND FEATURES mean different things in the perceptual worlds of young and older infants. Infants less than 16 weeks old tracked a moving object (*left*) until it went behind a screen and anticipated its reappearance; when a different object emerged, they continued to track its motion with no sign of surprise. Older infants also tracked the object in motion when a different object emerged from behind the screen (*right*), but when the object stopped, the older infants often glanced to the other side of the screen as if they were looking for the first object. This indicates that the younger infants do not respond to moving objects but to movements, and not to stationary objects but to places. Older infants have learned to recognize an object by its features rather than by its place or movement.

the sides of the screen was noticeable. When the object stopped, at least 25 percent of the time they looked to the other side of the screen as if they were looking for the object that had disappeared. Their responses in Situation 3 and Situation 4 were similar, with the difference that when the object stopped, on every trial the infants looked to the other half of the track in apparent anticipation of the appearance of the other object.

Infants less than 16 weeks old showed a complete contrast in behavior. In Situation 1 they followed the moving object with no sign of being disturbed. When the object stopped, they continued to follow its path of movement. In Situation 2, when a different object emerged, they also continued to track it with no sign of being disturbed. When the object stopped, they continued to track it. In Situation 3, however, where the object came out from behind the screen sooner than it should have, they were upset and refused to look any more. They also refused to look in Situation 4. In both cases when the object stopped, the infants did not continue to follow its path as they had in the first two situations. This was largely due to their refusal to track at all.

These results show that younger infants are not affected by feature differences. For them movement is predominant. They respond to a change in motion but not to a change in size, shape or color. They ignore features to such an extent that I would suggest they respond not to moving objects but to movements. Similarly, I would suggest that they respond not to stationary objects but to places. In contrast, older infants have learned to define an object as something that can go from place to place along pathways of movement. They identify an object by its features rather than by its place or movement. For them different features imply different objects that can move independently, so that the stopping of one does not imply the stopping of the other.

This attainment is obviously one of tremendous significance. It transforms the perceptual world of the infant at one stroke into something very close to the perceptual world of the adult. According to these studies it seems that infants less than 16 weeks old live in a world articulated in terms of solids that are stably arranged in space according to their location, with a constancy of existence when they occlude one another. It is, however, a grossly overpopulated world. An object becomes a different object as soon as it moves to a new location. In this world every object is unique. The infant must cope with a large number of objects when only one is really there.

In the last experiment I shall describe infants sat in front of an arrangement of mirrors that produced two or three images of a person. In some instances the infant was presented with two or three images of his mother; in others he would see his mother and one or two strangers who were seated so that they were in a position identical with the earlier additional images of his mother.

In the multiple-mother presentation infants less than 20 weeks old happily responded with smiles, coos and arm-waving to each mother in turn. In the mother-stranger presentation the infants were also quite happy and interacted with their mother, and they normally ignored the strangers. This demonstrates that young infants can recognize features in recognizing their mother, but they recognize the mother as one of many identical mothers. They do not recognize the identity of the multi-

ple mothers in the special sense in which I have used the word "identity," that is, they do not identify the multiple images of the mother as belonging to one and the same person.

Infants more than 20 weeks old also ignored the strangers and interacted with their mothers. In the multiple-mother situation, however, the older infants became quite upset at the sight of more than one mother. This shows, I would argue, that the younger infants do identify objects with places and hence think they have a multiplicity of mothers. Because the older infants identify objects by features, they know that they have only one mother, and this is why they are upset by the sight of multiple mothers.

The discovery of the object concept must simplify the world of the infant more than almost any subsequent intellectual advance. Two pressing questions arise from this research. We do not know why the object concept must be discovered rather than being built into the neural system (as so many other kinds of perceptual knowledge are), nor

do we know how the discovery is made. There are indications that built-in analyzers are limited to the initial input areas of the brain and their cross-connections. It is known that place and movement are separately coded in the visual system. Moreover, errors of the kind made by young infants persist in adults in some form. The late Baron Albert Michotte of the University of Louvain found that adults who are shown an impossible sequence such as the one described in Situation 3, where an object reappears from behind the screen sooner than it should, will say something like, "It looks as if it is the same object, but I know. . . ." This kind of response indicates that the infant's error persists in the adult's perceptual system and is overcome by a cognitive rule. We do know that particular environments can speed or slow the acquisition of such conceptual behavior. In line with this fact there is evidence that nonhuman primates never overcome perceptual errors and remain much like the young infants we studied. The object concept may thus be outside the limits of intrinsic neural specification.

MULTIPLE MOTHERS were presented to infants by an arrangement of mirrors. In other instances the infant would see his mother and two unfamiliar women seated in the same position as the mirror images of the mother. Infants less than 20 weeks old waved their arms, smiled and called to each of the mother images in turn. Older infants, however, became quite disturbed by the sight of more than one mother. All the infants ignored the strangers and interacted only with the mother. It seems that the younger infants think they have a multiplicity of mothers because they identify objects with places. Older infants identify objects by features and know they have only one mother. Learning to identify objects by features is one of the major intellectual advances made by infants.

7

Repetitive Processes in Child Development

by T. G. R. Bower
November 1976

As an infant grows he acquires certain skills, loses them and then acquires them again. How does this phenomenon fit the concept that behavioral growth is roughly comparable to physical growth?

For many years students of child development have conducted their research and formed their theories on the basis of one major assumption: that as a child gets older and progressively bigger he also gets progressively better at any kind of perceptual, intellectual or motor task set for him. That assumption underlies the entire concept of intelligence tests. Such tests are constructed on the notion that the average nine-year-old can do everything the average eight-year-old can do, plus something more, and that the average eight-year-old can do everything the average seven-year-old can do, plus something more, and so forth.

The assumption of progressive development seems to be quite obvious. After all, if one looks at children at various stages in their development, they always get bigger. Although growth is not a continuous or steady process, it never happens that a child who is four feet tall one year shrinks back to a height of three feet six inches the next year. Since such a regression is never seen in physical growth, we would hardly expect to see an analogous regression in behavioral or intellectual growth. Or would we?

Numerous studies, particularly several undertaken in recent years, appear to indicate that behavioral and intellectual development may not be strictly cumulative and incremental. Such studies seem to imply that the pattern of psychological growth may be quite different from the pattern of physical growth. One familiar example is the development of walking. Newborn infants, if they are properly supported, will march along a flat surface, an ability that demonstrates the remarkable sensory-motor coordination of the newborn infant. Yet the ability normally disappears at the age of about eight weeks. Walking of any kind will not usually be seen again until the end of the child's first year.

On a somewhat more complex level, during the first few weeks of life infants can reach out to touch visible objects and will occasionally even grasp them. That eye-hand coordination also disappears at the age of about four weeks and will not be seen again until the age of some 20 weeks. Similarly, young infants have appreciable ear-hand coordination. They are quite willing and able to reach out and grasp objects they can hear but not see, whether they are blind or have normal vision. That ability, which is of obvious practical use to the blind infant in particular, disappears when the infant reaches five or six months, and for the blind infant it may not return at all.

In the area of sensory-motor coordination but at a still higher level of complexity one must include the fact that newborn infants show an extraordinary capacity for imitating the behavior of an adult. For example, they are quite able to imitate an adult sticking out his tongue, opening his mouth or widening his eyes. Indeed, this ability is the most remarkable example known of the competence of the newborn infant's perceptual system. Consider what is involved in imitating someone's sticking out his tongue. The infant must identify the thing he sees in the adult's mouth as being a tongue. (I shall ask the reader to bear with me in my not saying "he or she sees," which makes this kind of discourse unduly cumbersome.) He must realize that the thing he cannot see but can feel in his own mouth is also a tongue, the homologue of the thing he sees. He must then execute fairly complex muscular movements in order to imitate what he sees. The activity of imitation seems to be basically a social ability. The infant and his mother become raptly involved with each other as they play games of imitation. In spite of the fact that the ability manifests itself so early in life it soon seems to fade away, reappearing only toward the end of the child's first year.

The apparent loss of abilities is not limited to sensory-motor skills. It is also not limited to the period of infancy. The pattern of loss and reacquisition of capacities extends to abstract intellectual abilities and persists all the way through childhood. For example, adults know perfectly well that the weight of a lump of modeling clay does not change with changes in its shape. This is a fact a child must discover not once but three times in the course of his development.

If a one-year-old child is presented with a ball of modeling clay, he will probably misjudge its weight the first time he picks it up. After he has been presented with the ball two or three times, however, his behavior will clearly show that he knows the weight of the object. He can pick it up without his arm wavering and put it unerringly wherever he wants. Suppose that the ball of clay is then rolled into the shape of a sausage with the child watching. What happens when he picks up the sausage? Typically his arm will fly up over his head, indicating that he thinks the object has become much heavier because it has become longer. He makes the opposite kind of mistake if the experimenter begins with a sausage-shaped piece of clay and then molds it into a ball. In short, a one-year-old child has not mastered the concept of the conservation of weight.

If one gives the same child the same task at 18 months, he makes no mistakes at all. If his behavior is taken to be an index of what he knows, one can say that the 18-month-old child knows that the weight of an object does not change when the shape of the object is changed. In short, an 18-month-old child does.apprehend the concept of the conservation of weight.

If the same child is asked two years later what happens to the weight of a ball of clay when it is rolled into the shape of a sausage, he will probably answer that the sausage is heavier than the ball because it is longer. Furthermore, if the child is then presented with the identical behavioral test he was given as an infant, he will once again make the mistakes he made at the age of a year—mistakes he did not make at 18 months. Again if the child's behavior is taken as an index of what he knows, it seems as though he has once more lost the concept of the conservation of weight.

Normally the child reacquires the concept of the conservation of weight, exhibited both behaviorally and verbally, at the age of seven or eight. The acquisition of the concept, however, is not complete at that stage. If the child is given the same test at 11 or 12, he will again give the wrong verbal response, just as he did at the age of four. It is not known whether his performance in the behavioral test will decline as well, because no one has yet tested it. It seems likely, however, that it would decline, because behavior usually follows language. Not until age 13 or 14 does the child arrive at a stable concept of the conservation of weight.

Observations such as those I am de-scribing seem to be at odds with the view that psychological growth is a continuous incremental process like physical growth. Abilities seem to appear and then disappear, leaving the child worse off than he was when he was younger, perhaps even no better off than he was as an infant.

There is evidence, however, that the various phases of development are connected. It has been shown, for example, that if an infant practices walking at the very early phase, the experience will accelerate the appearance of walking later. It has been suggested that the acquisition of certain concepts in infancy is necessary for the permanent emergence of those concepts later in life, and that a child who does not acquire normal concepts during infancy may be permanently unable to acquire them. There are data that appear to support this suggestion. It would therefore seem that the study of repetitive processes in devel-opment has a practical value. The observations, however, complicate the theoretical puzzle. How can something that disappears be critical for subsequent development?

I personally have been fascinated by repetitive processes in development for many years. When I began studying them, I made the naïve assumption that a repetition is a repetition, and that studying any specific type of repetition, either sensory-motor or cognitive, would ultimately yield a general theory of repetition in development. Therefore I concentrated on the simplest and quickest of the repetitive processes: reaching.

There are two obvious questions involved in studying any repetitive process. First, why does the earliest phase of gaining an ability—let us call it Phase 1—come to an end? Second, what is the relation between Phase 1 and Phase 2 or

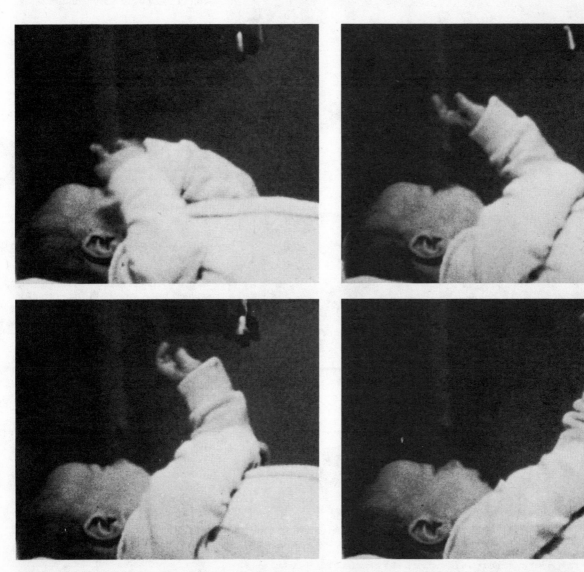

NEWBORN MALE INFANT REACHES out and touches a bell with no hesitation at the age of 10 days, demonstrating the remarkable organization of the newborn perceptual system and a high degree of eye-hand coordination. Yet when the infant attains the age of four weeks, the ability will disappear, and it does not reappear for another four months. These photographs, which read from left to right and top to bottom, are frames from a motion picture of the infant made in the author's laboratory at the University of Edinburgh.

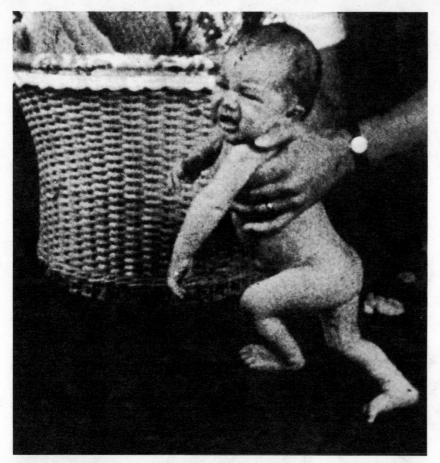

SIX-DAY-OLD FEMALE INFANT WALKS much like an older child if she is properly supported on a flat surface. This remarkable sensory-motor ability disappears at the age of about eight weeks and does not reappear in any form until the end of the child's first year.

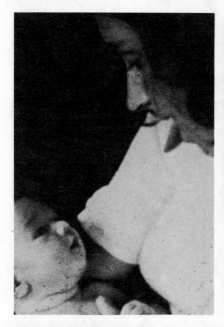 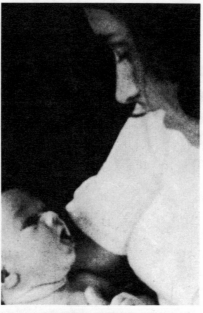

SIX-DAY-OLD FEMALE INFANT IMITATES her mother's protruding her tongue. The ability to imitate is a much more complex achievement than either reaching or walking: it requires the infant to recognize that what she sees in her mother's mouth is a tongue (*left*) and that what she feels in her own mouth but cannot see is also a tongue. Then the infant must execute complex muscular actions required for her to protrude her own tongue (*right*). The ability to imitate also seems to disappear early, reappearing only near the age of one year.

any succeeding phase? On the basis of the methods of study available it is in fact difficult to establish that there is any relation between two phases of behavior that are separated in the full span of development. About the only paradigm that is of any value is the hypothesis of early practice; if one can show that practicing one type of behavior in Phase 1 affects the emergence of Phase 2 of that behavior, then one has made a case in favor of the hypothesis that the two phases are connected. It is not a water-tight case, to be sure, but it is a case.

Accordingly I gave several groups of infants intensive practice in reaching during Phase 1, the first four weeks of life. The results were moderately clear and were in accord with what earlier investigators had concluded from studies of walking: the more the behavior was practiced in Phase 1, the earlier it appeared in Phase 2. In my own studies there were even cases where reaching ability was not lost after Phase 1.

Such results pointed to the possibility that the reason abilities disappear is that they are not exercised. Given practice and reinforcement, I hypothesized, the abilities might not disappear at all. If they did not, that would confirm the traditional theory that psychological development is a continuous and incremental process like physical growth.

To test this hypothesis my colleagues and I at the University of Edinburgh administered a selection of various tasks to a number of infants only days or weeks old and gave them intensive practice in performing the tasks as soon as their abilities appeared. The results were mixed, to say the least. For example, practice of ear-hand coordination in Phase 1 actually accelerated the disappearance of the coordination and retarded its reappearance in Phase 2. This seemed to be true both for normal infants tested in darkness and for one blind infant. On more cognitive tasks the results were inconsistent. Sometimes practice during the early phase of an ability accelerated the reappearance of that ability, but increasing the amount of practice did not increase the rate of acceleration.

As an example, one task we gave the infants was a counting problem that involved a form of conservation. A child was shown candies in pairs of rows in which the length of the rows, the spacing between the candies and the number of candies varied. The child was then allowed to choose the row he wanted. If he always chose the row with more candies, it was concluded that he had a primitive ability to count. A high proportion of children between the ages of two and two and a half can give correct verbal responses to the problem. Thereafter they are unable to respond correctly until they are nearly five. Even before the age of two there is a phase in which children can respond correctly to such tasks (although at that age they cannot respond verbally). It was this initial phase that we investigated. With practice the children's choice responses became quite exact. Yet at the usual age of two or two and a half, when other children can give correct verbal responses, only a small proportion of the children with practice responded correctly. The proportion of the children who finally did acquire the ability to give correct verbal responses by age five, however, did not seem to be affected.

Disappointed that our first explanation of repetitive processes in development had failed, we decided to return to our previous study of reaching and to reexamine the characteristics of reaching in Phase 1 with respect to the characteristics of reaching in Phase 2. We had found that the infants who had practiced reaching in Phase 1 were better at reaching when the ability reappeared in Phase 2 than infants who had not been given any practice in Phase 1. Specifically, they were more skilled than untrained infants at seizing dangling objects presented in a variety of positions. They were particularly good at reaching under conditions of visual distraction.

In one study we fitted the infants with specially constructed glasses consisting of two thin wedge prisms instead of lenses. The prisms displace the apparent location of an object with respect to its real location. Normal infants who had had no practice in reaching would reach toward the apparent location of the object, thereby missing it. Then they would lie still for a time, with both the object and their hand in their visual field, before pulling their hand back, reaching again and missing again. These infants seemed quite incapable of using the sight of their hand to correct their behavior in reaching.

In contrast, older infants who had had no practice in reaching and somewhat younger ones who had been given early practice would first reach toward the incorrect location and then as soon as their hand came into view would correct its motion and home in on the object with perfect accuracy. They were thus able to use the visible position of their hand to correct its motion. Normal infants who have had no practice acquire this ability at an average age of 24 weeks, whereas the infants who had been given early practice succeeded at the task at an average age of 19 weeks.

This accelerated flexibility was acquired at a price, as a second experiment soon showed. For the experiment the infants were put in an illuminated but light-tight room. They were shown a toy but were kept from reaching for it until

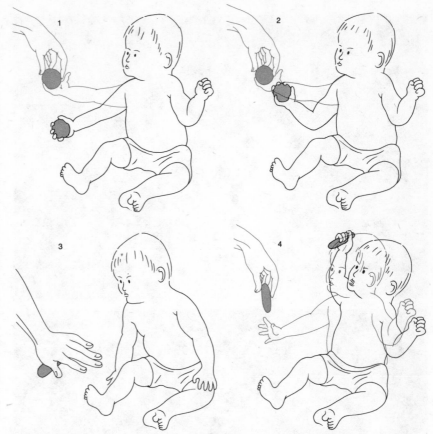

CONCEPT OF THE CONSERVATION OF WEIGHT may be acquired not just once but three times in the course of a child's development. If a one-year-old child is handed a ball of modeling clay, he will typically misjudge its weight the first time it is presented to him (1). Soon, however, his behavior indicates that he has learned to estimate the weight of the object before he holds it (2). The ball of clay is then rolled into the shape of a sausage with the child watching (3). When the child holds the sausage, typically his arm flies up (4), indicating that he thinks the sausage is heavier than the ball because it is longer. This erroneous behavior disappears by the age of about 18 months, only to reappear and disappear twice more much later. A child finally acquires a stable concept of the conservation of weight early in his teens.

after the room lights had been switched off. They therefore had to reach for it in the dark. Their behavior in the dark was monitored with an infrared television camera. The younger infants, as one might expect from our wedge-prism experiment, were not distracted by the darkness: their hands went straight out to grasp the object. The older infants and the accelerated ones were quite un-

certain. Although they too reached out, their reaching was not at all direct; they fumbled for the object instead of grasping it. It seemed that their ability to employ visual guidance had brought them to rely on it, so that without visual guidance they were lost.

If the main change in the development of a child's ability to reach is the acquisition of visual control, how did

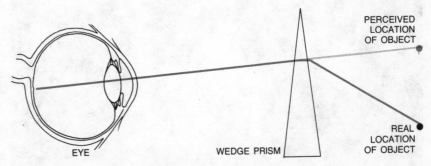

WEDGE PRISM fitted to glasses displaces the apparent location of an object from its actual location. The effect of wedge prisms on infants can be seen in illustrations on next two pages.

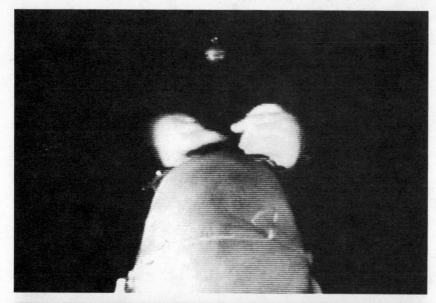

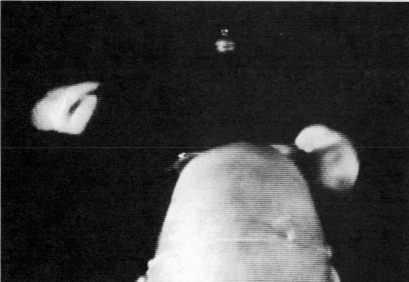

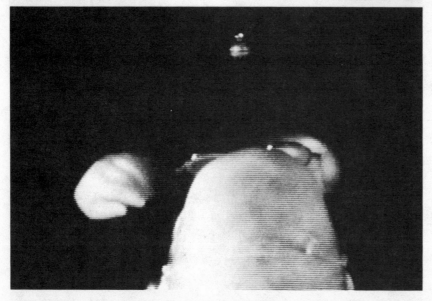

YOUNG INFANT WEARING WEDGE PRISMS reaches toward the place where he perceives an object to be and misses. After resting for a while with both his hand and the object in his field of view, he reaches and misses again. He seems unable to use his vision to correct the position of his hand. Horizontal lines across photograph are scan lines of television camera.

practice during Phase 1 of reaching accelerate the appearance of visual control in Phase 2? It is clear that reaching for an object with visual guidance calls for more attention than reaching without such guidance: for the infant to attend to both his hand and the object will take up more of his attentional space than if he simply attends to the object. It is also clear that infants cannot initially attend to both their hand and an object. At some age the hand and the object actually seem to compete for attention. The early practice would therefore result in the hand's being in the visual field much more often than it was without such practice. For the accelerated infants the hand would thus be a more familiar sight. It is known from many other studies that familiar objects require less attentional space than unfamiliar ones. Hence it is possible that practice during Phase 1 of reaching accelerated the appearance of Phase 2 of reaching by making the infants more familiar with the sight of their own hand.

Even if this explanation for the development of reaching is correct, there is no reason to expect that the same explanation will apply to the repetitive appearance of abilities other than reaching. It seemed necessary to look for additional explanations for the other repetitions, thereby forsaking the hope of constructing a general theory of repetition in development. Indeed, different specific explanations for different specific abilities were readily forthcoming. For example, the remarkable ability of newborn infants to imitate adults disappears at a certain age. Colwyn Trevarthen of Edinburgh has pointed out, however, that infants in the age group that will not imitate adults are nonetheless delighted if they themselves are imitated. If an infant is to recognize that he is being imitated, he must have at his disposal exactly the same perceptual tools he would need in order to be able to imitate someone else. The decline in an infant's imitative behavior hence may not imply any loss of ability but rather may indicate a change in motivation. The infant still has the ability to imitate, but he chooses to employ it to detect others' imitation of him.

Including changes in motivation in the list of possible hypotheses for seeming repetitions in development led us to what I believe is the correct explanation for the sometimes permanent decline in ear-hand coordination. The explanation stems from the difference between the normal conditions of visual stimulation and those of auditory stimulation. The situation of the infant with respect to visual stimulation is normally an active one: he can look at things that interest him and he can look away from things that bore or disturb him. He can close his eyes if he wants to. His situation with respect to auditory stimulation is quite different: it is a passive one. The infant cannot switch on sounds he likes or switch off sounds he dislikes. There is no way for him to shut his ears as he can shut his eyes. In short, he has no control over auditory input.

Passive situations of this type have important effects on development. The classic experiments on the effects of passivity were done with vision, using kittens as the subjects [see "Plasticity in Sensory-Motor Systems," by Richard Held; SCIENTIFIC AMERICAN Offprint 494]. Kittens that were raised for as short a period as 30 hours in conditions where they were not allowed to respond actively to visual stimulation became functionally blind. When they were presented with any type of visual stimulation, they showed no response.

The results of the kitten experiments suggested to us that the reason human infants lose their auditory-manual coordination is that they are passive in the presence of auditory stimulation. How could we present auditory information to the infant in such a way as to give him an active role?

After some trial and error we found that the answer was to fit the infant with an ultrasonic echo-location device. The device sent out pulses of sound waves at ultrasonic frequencies in a cone with a width of 80 degrees. Since the frequency of the sound was so high, the pulses could not be heard. Ultrasonic echoes bounced off any object in the field of the device. The device itself converted the ultrasonic echoes into audible sounds that were channeled directly into the ears of the infant. The closer the object was to him, the lower the pitch of the sound he heard was, and the larger the object was, the louder the sound was. Objects to the right of the infant produced a louder sound in his right ear, and objects to the left produced a louder sound in his left ear. Objects that were straight ahead produced sounds that were equally loud in both ears. Hard

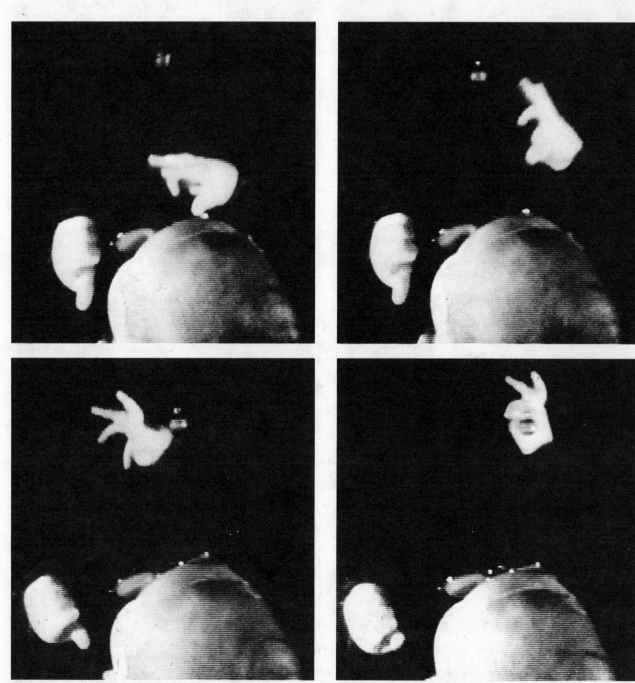

OLDER INFANT WEARING WEDGE PRISMS reaches toward the apparent location of an object and also starts to miss the object.

As soon as his hand enters his field of view, however, he uses his vision to correct its trajectory and to accurately home in on the object.

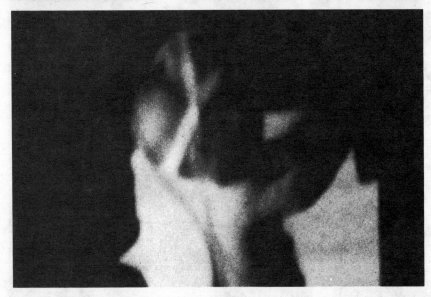

BLIND INFANT WEARING SONAR DEVICE has active control over his auditory inputs, much as a normal infant can control his visual inputs by closing his eyes or looking away. The device sends out ultrasonic waves that are reflected from objects. The echoes are then converted by the device itself into audible tones. The nature of the tones depends on the distance, size and texture of the objects. In this sequence of photographs when the blind infant is moved by an adult toward a metal pole, he puts out his hands as he gets close, as a normal child would.

objects made a clear sound and soft objects made a somewhat fuzzier one.

The most important characteristic of the device, however, is that anyone wearing it has direct control over the sounds it channels to his ears. The wearer can focus on interesting objects; he can turn away from boring objects and thereby silence them; he can inspect objects by moving past them, and so on. In other words, the wearer has active control over at least this type of auditory stimulation. If our hypothesis about the disappearance of normal auditory-manual coordination is correct, behavior guided by the ultrasonic device should not disappear.

The device has been tested only on one infant who is congenitally blind. The results, however, were quite satisfactory. Not only did auditory-manual behavior not decline but also the infant actually developed some skills comparable to those acquired by a normal infant of the same age. Furthermore, the experiment clearly showed the flexibility of the newborn infant's perceptual system. No organism in the history of life had ever received the inputs this infant was given, yet he began making sense of the sounds within seconds after the device had been put on.

Of the major types of repetitive processes I have described, the only type for which I have offered no explanation is the cognitive repetitions. We do, in fact, have an explanation for them, but it is extremely complex. Some of the experiments we have devised to test the explanation, however, have shed a most intriguing light on the nature of intellectual development, particularly that in infancy.

Our explanation for the repetitions in cognitive development is based on data from experiments on short-term perceptual development. Consider a simple experiment on habituation. If one shows an infant a cube in a constant orientation 10 times for a period of 30 seconds each time, he will look at the cube progressively less and less. This decreasing level of attention indicates that the infant has recognized that he is seeing the same object each time. Suppose one now shows the infant a cube 10 times but each time the cube is in a different orientation. The result is that the infant shows exactly the same decline in the amount of time he spends looking at the cube.

This phenomenon yields a great deal of information about how an infant remembers objects. Clearly the infant cannot have in his memory a very specific image of the cube in a specific orientation, because every time the cube is presented the orientation is different. This means that the infant must remember from one presentation to the next what shape a cube is without remembering the orientation of the cube. This kind of

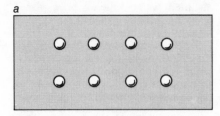 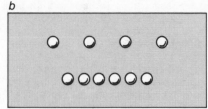 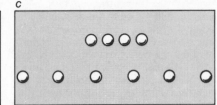

COUNTING TASK, administered to children old enough to talk, involves the concept of number. The experimenter first shows the child two equally long rows of candy (*a*) and makes sure that the child agrees there are the same number of pieces of candy in each row. Then the child is shown a different pair of rows (*b or c*) and is al-lowed to pick whichever row he wants. The object is to see whether or not he will choose the row with more candies in it without regard to how long the row is and how close together the candies are. If child always chooses row with more candies in it regardless of arrange-ment of pieces, one can assume that he has a primitive ability to count.

memory is actually rather abstract; indeed, it must be almost as abstract as a word is. It also lacks the details of the object, even details as important as orientation. Nevertheless, if the infant is given enough time, he can internally work up a quite detailed description of the object, so that even a very slight change in it will arrest the decline in his looking behavior. Thus the infant's internal description of an object can change from being rather abstract to being quite specific.

My colleagues and I propose that there is a similar kind of process underlying cognitive development: as the child grows older he progressively elaborates his internal descriptions of events to make them more specific. Such a change in favor of more specific description acts to decrease the likelihood of a smooth transfer from one skill to another, thereby increasing the likelihood of a seeming repetition. Consider the problem presented to an infant by the sight of an object entering one end of a tunnel and emerging from the other end. Initially the infant may refuse to look at this kind of display. Once he has recognized that the object he sees at either end of the tunnel is the same object, which is no easy feat, he must then figure out what is happening to the object when it is out of his sight [see "The Object in the World of the Infant," by T. G. R. Bower, page 55].

I propose that the infant's first discov-ery is that one object can go inside an-other and still exist. That is a relatively abstract hypothesis about the world; it will not particularly improve the in-fant's skill at tracking the object through the tunnel. What the hypothesis will do is allow the infant to shift his under-standing from the tracking situation to other situations. Suppose an infant who understands this hypothesis now sees a toy placed under one of two cups. He should now know that the toy is under a specific cup and therefore be able to re-trieve it. If the toy is placed under the other cup, he should be able to retrieve it from under that cup. That is exactly what happens if the infant is given this transfer task.

If the infant is then given more prac-

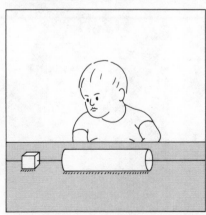  

TRACKING TASK presents an infant with an object going into one end of a tunnel and then after several seconds reappearing at the other end. At first infants may be surprised and disturbed by this kind of display (*three panels at top*). They may even refuse to look at it until they learn that one object can go inside another and still ex-ist. After they acquire the concept they can with practice track the object so accurately that they can move their eyes unerringly to in-tercept the object at any point in space (*three panels at bottom*).

tice with the tunnel-tracking task, however, something quite different happens. After a while he readily works out specific sensory-motor rules enabling him to track the object quite efficiently. He shows by his behavior that he knows that in order to see the object that has vanished at the left end of the tunnel he must look for it at the right end of the tunnel after x seconds. His knowledge of the spatial and temporal nature of the tracking task becomes very detailed indeed. Infants who have had weeks of

experience with tracking tasks do not spend much time looking at the display, but they can move their eyes unerringly to catch the object at any point in space.

If such infants are again given the toy-under-the-cup transfer task, they do better than infants with no experience in the tracking task. They do not do as well, however, as other infants who are given the transfer task after having had some tracking experience but not as much as they had had. In particular, if

the infant watches the toy being placed under the second cup after a few trials of seeing it placed under the first cup, he will still tend to look for it under the first cup. Thus the infant seems to repeat a phase in his development, failing to understand for a second time the relation between two objects when one is inside the other. What causes such a repetition, I suggest, is that with so much practice at tracking an object going through the tunnel the infant has evolved such specific rules in dealing with the tracking

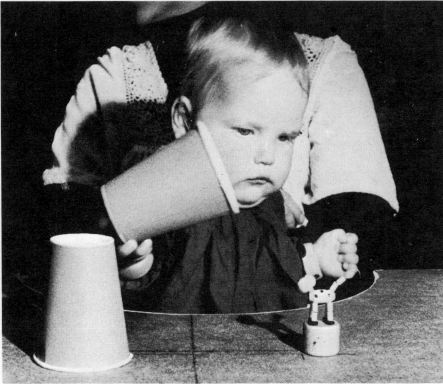

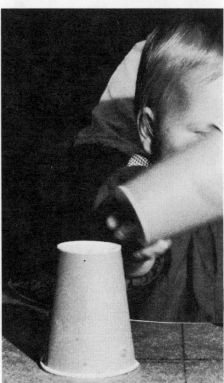

TRANSFER TASK makes use of the concept that one object can go inside another and still exist, acquired in the tracking task. An infant watches an adult place a toy under one of two cups and then is en-couraged to choose the cup concealing the toy. A child with some tracking experience does very well (*three photographs at top*). A child with a great deal of tracking experience, however, does less well, al-

task that he is actually hampered by them when he is faced with a similar but not identical situation. An infant who has had less practice with tracking has the initial conceptual discovery (one object can go inside another and continue to exist) still at the front of his mind to help him perform the transfer task.

This kind of model of cognitive development can explain puzzling instances of repetitive processes in which young children give correct verbal responses to a problem whereas somewhat older children give incorrect responses. Here the underlying concept has been acquired late in infancy. When the verbal tests are first given, there has not been enough time for the initial discovery to have been specified to the extent that the child is incapable of applying the discovery to other situations. With older children, however, the initial discovery has been made highly specific. The relation between the initial problem and the new problem is therefore obscured. They must dredge the initial discovery from their memory, erring until they do, and they will seem to repeat an earlier phase of their cognitive development.

The various explanations of repetitive processes in development thus seem to differ depending on the specific repetition to be explained. What all the explanations have in common, however, is that they preserve the assumption that psychological growth, in spite of its apparent reversals and repetitions, is a continuous and additive process.

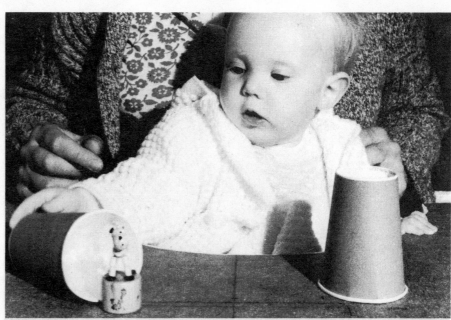

though he performs better than a child without tracking experience. In particular, if the child watches the toy being placed under the second cup after seeing it placed under the first cup a few times, he will still tend to look for it under the first cup (*three photographs at bottom*). Concept acquired in tracking task has become so specified with practice it actually hampers child in performing transfer task.

II

PERCEPTION
AND AWARENESS

PERCEPTION AND AWARENESS   II

INTRODUCTION

Awareness of the environment depends on the ability of our sense organs to change various forms of physical energy into nerve impulses. Complex structures in the ear transduce the mechanical energy of sound waves into the electrical energy of nerve impulses. Certain specialized cells on the skin's surface change the mechanical energy of pressure into nerve impulses that convey the sensation of touch. Receptor cells in the eye transform the electromagnetic energy of light into nerve impulses. But the activation and transmission of nerve impulses by the sensory systems is only the first step in awareness. Our brain integrates these messages with messages from other parts of the body and then interprets the total information in the light of experience. Perception thus requires interaction between sensory mechanisms and those parts of the brain that are concerned with storage and retrieval of past experiences.

The mechanisms by which different perceptual systems receive, transduce, and interpret a stimulus input are complex and varied. We could not possibly survey the variety of research on all the senses in one section on perception. Therefore, this section is concerned primarily with visual perception—the perceptual system that normally dominates our awareness of the world and the one that has been most thoroughly investigated.

As we have said, perception involves more than the transmission of nerve impulses by the sensory systems. The brain must interpret the information it receives. The image projected on the retina is not a faithful representation of all that we perceive. We normally perceive a coin as unvarying in size—whether it is in our hand or lying on a table across the room—even though the retinal image is actually quite different in the two instances. As Ulric Neisser points out in "The Processes of Vision," our visual world is not a photographic copy of the retinal image. What we perceive is somehow constructed by the brain from a composite of information—information that is extracted from rapidly changing retinal patterns as our eyes move about, as well as information from past visual inputs that is retrieved from memory. Neisser discusses the properties of stimuli that determine what we perceive and then considers visual imagery, the memory of visual events not immediately present.

If you stare at a bright light and then look away at a neutral surface, you will see a dark image of the light. This is called a negative afterimage (negative because the object was light and the image is dark). A similar phenomenon occurs if you stare for a few minutes at something moving uniformly in one direction, such as a waterfall. When you shift your gaze, the scene you are observing will appear to move slowly in the opposite direction. This is a negative aftereffect. In "Negative Aftereffects in Visual Perception" Olga Favreau and Michael Corballis describe a number of such phenomena and discuss the clues they provide about how the sense organs and the nervous system process information. For example, there is evidence that some aftereffects may result from fatigue of feature-detecting neurons in the visual cortex. (See the article by Hubel and Wiesel in Section I.)

Sometimes even though our sense receptors are functioning properly, they may deceive us. Our perceptions may not depict reality accurately and we experience an illusion. In "Visual Illusions" Richard Gregory describes some of the most common optical illusions and offers one explanation of why such illusions occur. Perception may be a search for the best interpretation of sensory information, based on our knowledge of object characteristics. In other words, a perceived object may be a *hypothesis* suggested by the sensory data. The notion of hypothesis-testing suggests that the perceptual system is active rather than passive; the system does not merely receive input, but searches for the percept that is most consistent with the sensory data. In most situations there is only one reasonable interpretation, and the search for the correct percept proceeds so quickly and automatically that we are unaware of it. Only under unusual conditions, for instance, when viewing an illusion or ambiguous figure, does the hypothesis-testing nature of perception become apparent.

Employing a similar approach, Fred Attneave in "Multistability in Perception" examines various kinds of pictures and geometric forms that spontaneously shift in their principal aspect when looked at steadily. Some of the most striking of these are pictures that can be seen as either of two familiar objects, for example, a figure that may look like a duck at one moment and a rabbit the next. Attneave's analysis of this phenomenon elaborates on the hypothesis-testing view of perception and suggests that the perceptual system is "motivated" to represent the world as economically as possible, within the constraints of the input received and the limitations of its encoding capabilities.

In "The Perception of Distorted Figures" Irvin Rock provides additional evidence for the active nature of perception. He argues persuasively that perception of form cannot be reduced to the detection of a set of component features. Although the detection of features does play an important role in perception (as noted in the article by Hubel and Wiesel in Section I), features themselves do not constitute form. Rock's findings suggest that the perception of form is based to a much greater extent on cognitive processes than most current theories maintain.

While illusions represent misinterpretations of sensory data, hallucinations are false sensory perceptions in the *absence* of appropriate external stimulation. Seeing animals, people, or strange shapes when nothing of the sort is present or hearing voices when no one is there are examples of hallucinations. Such sensations may be induced by extreme fatigue, stress, illness, or drugs. In his article "Hallucinations" Ronald Siegel examines the kinds of visual imagery people experience under the influence of such hallucinogenic drugs as LSD, mescaline, and THC (the active ingredient in marijuana). He reports some consensus in the kinds of images experienced and reviews several theories about the origin of hallucinations.

The last article in this section, "Sources of Ambiguity in the Prints of Maurits C. Escher," is quite different from the others. It is not concerned with psychological research but rather with the work of the Dutch graphic artist Escher. The author, Marianne Teuber, discusses Escher's use of visual ambiguity in his prints—the ambiguity of figure and ground, of two and three dimensions on a flat surface, and of the reversible cube. Escher's novel use of ambiguity illustrates several aspects of perception. This is not surprising since, as Teuber shows, Escher was greatly influenced by psychological research on perception. There is little doubt that he was familiar with the early experiments of the Gestalt psychologists, in particular with Kurt Koffka's book, *Principles of Gestalt Psychology*.

The significance of stimulus patterns in producing a perceptual experience was recognized by proponents of Gestalt psychology, a school of psychology that arose in Austria and Germany near the end of the nineteenth century. *Gestalt* is a German word that has no exact translation, though "form," "configuration," or "pattern" come close. The word itself helps to emphasize the idea that properties of the whole affect the way in which parts are perceived. Perception "draws together" *(gestalten)* the sensory data into a holistic pattern; for this reason, it is sometimes said that "the whole is different from the sum of its parts"—a favorite phrase of Gestalt psychologists. Escher's work illustrates many of the principles of Gestalt psychology, and his use of psychological research helps us appreciate his unusual contribution to modern art.

8

The Processes of Vision

by Ulric Neisser
September 1968

*Light enables us to see, but optical images on the retina
are only the starting point of the complex activities of
visual perception and visual memory*

It was Johannes Kepler who first compared the eye to a "camera" (a darkened chamber) with an image in focus on its rear surface. "Vision is brought about by pictures of the thing seen being formed on the white concave surface of the retina," he wrote in 1604. A generation later René Descartes tried to clinch this argument by direct observation. In a hole in a window shutter he set the eye of an ox, just in the position it would have had if the ox had been peering out. Looking at the back of the eye (which he had scraped to make it transparent), he could see a small inverted image of the scene outside the window.

Since the 17th century the analogy between eye and camera has been elaborated in numerous textbooks. As an account of functional anatomy the analogy is not bad, but it carries some unfortunate implications for the study of vision. It suggests all too readily that the perceiver is in the position of Descartes and is in effect looking through the back of his own retina at the pictures that appear there. We use the same word—"image"—for both the optical pattern thrown on the retina by an object and the mental experience of seeing the object. It has been all too easy to treat this inner image as a copy of the outer one, to think of perceptual experiences as images formed by the nervous system acting as an optical instrument of extraordinarily ingenious design. Although this theory encounters insurmountable difficulties as soon as it is seriously considered, it has dominated philosophy and psychology for many years.

Not only perception but also memory has often been explained in terms of an image theory. Having looked at the retinal picture, the perceiver supposedly files it away somehow, as one might put a photograph in an album. Later, if he is lucky, he can take it out again in the form of a "memory image" and look at it a second time. The widespread notion that some people have a "photographic memory" reflects this analogy in a particularly literal way, but in a weaker form it is usually applied even to ordinary remembering. The analogy suggests that the mechanism of visual memory is a natural extension of the mechanisms of vision. Although there is some truth to this proposition, as we shall see below, it is not because both perception and memory are copying processes. Rather it is because *neither* perception *nor* memory is a copying process.

The fact is that one does not see the retinal image; one sees with the aid of the retinal image. The incoming pattern of light provides information that the nervous system is well adapted to pick up. This information is used by the perceiver to guide his movements, to anticipate events and to construct the internal representations of objects and of space called "conscious experience." These internal representations are not, however, at all like the corresponding optical images on the back of the eye. The retinal images of specific objects are at the mercy of every irrelevant change of position; their size, shape and location are hardly constant for a moment. Nevertheless, perception is usually accurate: real objects appear rigid and stable and appropriately located in three-dimensional space.

The first problem in the study of visual perception is therefore the discovery of the stimulus. What properties of the incoming optic array are informative for vision? In the entire distribution of light, over the retina and over a period of time, what determines the way things look? (Actually the light is distributed over two retinas, but the binocularity of vision has no relevance to the variables considered here. Although depth perception is more accurate with two eyes than with one, it is not fundamentally different. The world looks much the same with one eye closed as it does with both open; congenitally monocular people have more or less the same visual experiences as the rest of us.)

As a first step we can consider the patterns of reflected light that are formed when real objects and surfaces are illuminated in the ordinary way by

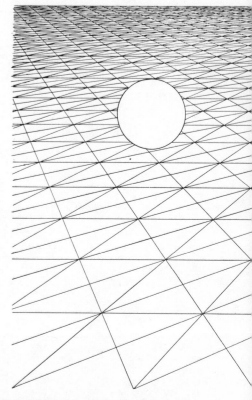

PERCEPTION OF SIZE relies heavily on cues provided by a textured surface. These five disks, if seen alone, would appear to lie

sunshine or lamplight. J. J. Gibson of Cornell University, who has contributed much to our understanding of perception, calls this inquiry "ecological optics." It is an optics in which point sources, homogeneous fields and the other basic elements of classical optics rarely appear. Instead the world we ordinarily look at consists mostly of *surfaces,* at various angles and in various relations to one another. This has significant consequences for the visual input.

One of these consequences (the only one we shall examine here) is to give the visual field a microstructure. Most surfaces have some kind of texture, such as the grain in wood, the individual stalks of grass in a field or the weave in a fabric. These textures structure the light reaching the eye in a way that carries vital information about the layout of environmental objects. In accordance with the principles of perspective the texture elements of more distant surfaces are represented closer to one another on the retina than the elements of surfaces nearby. Thus the microstructure of a surface that slants away from the observer is represented on the retina as a gradient of density—a gradient that carries information about the orientation of the surface.

Consider now an ordinary scene in which discrete figures are superposed on textured surfaces. The gradient of increasing texture density on the retina, corresponding to increasing distance from the observer, gives a kind of "scale" for object sizes. In the ideal case when the texture units are identical, two figures of the same real size will always occlude the same number of texture units, regardless of how far away either one may be. That is, the relation between the retinal texture-size and the dimensions of the object's retinal image is invariant, in spite of changes of distance. This relation is a potentially valuable source of information about the real size of the object—more valuable than the retinal image of the object considered alone. That image, of course, changes in dimension whenever the distance between the object and the observer is altered.

Psychologists have long been interested in what is called "size constancy": the fact that the sizes of real objects are almost always perceived accurately in spite of the linear dependence of retinal-image size on distance. It must not be supposed that this phenomenon is fully explained by the scaling of size with respect to texture elements. There are a great many other sources of relevant information: binocular parallax, shifts of retinal position as the observer moves, relative position in the visual field, linear perspective and so on. It was once traditional to regard these sources of information as "cues" secondary to the size of the object's own retinal image. That is, they were thought to help the observer "correct" the size of the retinal image in the direction of accuracy. Perhaps this is not a bad description of Descartes's situation as he looked at the image on the back of the ox's eye: he may have tried to "correct" his perception of the size of the objects revealed to him on the ox's retina. Since one does not see one's own retina, however, nothing similar need be involved in normal perceiving. Instead the apparent size of an object is determined by information from the entire incoming light pattern, particularly by certain properties of the input that remain invariant with changes of the object's location.

The interrelation of textures, distances and relative retinal sizes is only one example of ecological optics. The example may be a misleadingly simple one, because it assumes a stationary eye, an eye fixed in space and stably oriented in a particular direction. This is by no means a characteristic of human vision. In normal use the eyes are rarely still for long. Apart from small tremors, their

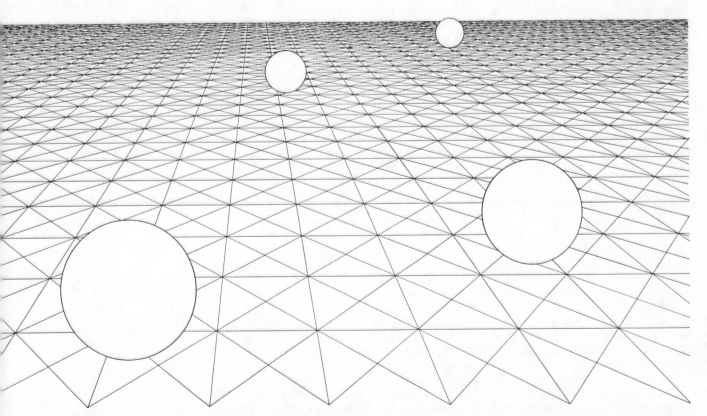

in one plane and be of different sizes. Against this apparently receding surface, however, they seem to lie in five different planes. Since each disk masks the same amount of surface texture, there is a tendency to see them as being equal in size. This illustration, the one at the bottom of the next two pages and the one on page 84 are based on the work of J. J. Gibson of Cornell University.

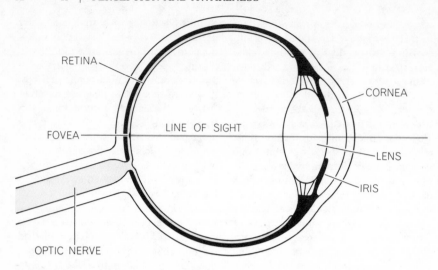

SITE OF OPTICAL IMAGE is the retina, which contains the terminations of the optic nerve. In the tiny retinal depression known as the fovea the cone nerve endings are clustered. Their organization and dense packing make possible a high degree of visual acuity.

most common movement is the flick from one position to another called a "saccade." Saccades usually take less than a twentieth of a second, but they happen several times each second in reading and may be just as frequent when a picture or an actual scene is being inspected. This means that there is a new retinal image every few hundred milliseconds.

Such eye movements are necessary because the area of clear vision available to the stationary eye is severely limited. To see this for oneself it is only necessary to fixate on a point in some unfamiliar picture or on an unread printed page. Only a small region around the fixation point will be clear. Most of the page is seen peripherally, which means that it is hazily visible at best. Only in the fovea, the small central part of the retina, are the receptor cells packed close enough together (and appropriately organized) to make a high degree of visual acuity possible. This is the reason one must turn one's eyes (or head) to look directly at objects in which one is particularly interested. (Animals with non-foveated eyes, such as the horse, do not find this necessary.) It is also the reason why the eye must make several fixations on each line in reading, and why it roves widely over pictures.

Although it is easy to understand the function of saccadic movements, it is difficult or impossible to reconcile them with an image theory of perception. As long as we think of the perceiver as a homunculus looking at his retinal image, we must expect his experience to be one of almost constant interruption and change. Clearly this is not the case; one sees the page or the scene as a whole without any apparent discontinuity in

space or time. Most people are either unaware of their own eye movements or have erroneous notions about them. Far from being a copy of the retinal display, the visual world is somehow *constructed* on the basis of information taken in during many different fixations.

The same conclusion follows, perhaps even more compellingly, if we consider the motions of external objects rather than the motions of the eyes. If the analogy between eye and camera were valid, the thing one looked at would have to hold still like a photographer's model in order to be seen clearly. The opposite is true: far from obscuring the shapes and spatial relations of things, movement generally clarifies them. Consider the visual problem presented by a distant arrow-shaped weather vane. As long as the weather vane and the observer remain motionless, there is no way to tell whether it is a short arrow oriented at right angles to the line of sight or a longer arrow slanting toward (or away from) the observer. Let it begin to turn in the wind, however, and its true shape and orientation will become visible immediately. The reason lies in the systematic distortions of the retinal image produced by the object's rotation. Such distortions provide information that the nervous system can use. On the basis of a fluidly changing retinal pattern the perceiver comes to experience a rigid object. (An interesting aspect of this example is that the input information is ambiguous. The same retinal changes could be produced by either a clockwise or a counterclockwise rotation of the weather vane. As a result the perceiver may alternate between two perceptual experiences, one of which is illusory.)

Some years ago Hans Wallach and D. N. O'Connell of Swarthmore College showed that such motion-produced changes in the input are indeed used as a source of information in perceiving; in fact this kind of information seems to be a more potent determiner of what we see than the traditionally emphasized cues for depth are. In their experiment the subject watched the shadow of a wire form cast on a translucent screen. He could not see the object itself. So long as the object remained stationary the subject saw only a two-dimensional shadow on a two-dimensional screen, as might be expected. The form was mounted in such a way, however, that it could be swiveled back and forth by a small electric motor. When the motor was turned on, the true three-dimensional shape of the form appeared at once, even though the only stimulation reaching the subject's eyes came from a distorting shadow on a flat screen. Here the kinetic depth effect, as it has been called, overrode binocular stereoscopic information that continued to indicate that all the movement was taking place in a flat plane.

In the kinetic depth effect the constructive nature of perception is particularly apparent. What one sees is somehow a composite based on information accumulated over a period of time. The same is true in reading or in any instance where eye movements are involved: information from past fixations is used together with information from the present fixation to determine what is seen. But if perception is a temporally extended act, some storage of information, some kind of memory, must be involved in it. How shall we conceive of this storage? How is it organized? How

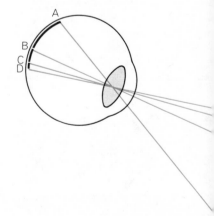

CONTRACTION OF IMAGE takes place as the distance between the viewer and the

long does it last? What other functions might it serve?

With questions like these, we have moved beyond the problem of specifying the visual stimulus. In addition to identifying the sources of information for vision, we want to know how that information is processed. In the long run, perhaps, questions about processes should be answered in neurological terms. However, no such answers can be given at present: The neurophysiology of vision has recently made great strides, but it is still not ready to deal with the constructive processes that are central to perception. We shall have to be content with a relatively abstract account, one that does not specify the neural locus of the implicated mechanisms.

Although seeing requires storage of information, this memory cannot be thought of as a sequence of superposed retinal images. Superposition would give rise only to a sort of smear in which all detail is lost. Nor can we assume that the perceiver keeps careful track of his eye movements and thus is able to set each new retinal image in just the right place in relation to the older stored ones. Such an alignment would require a much finer monitoring of eye motion than is actually available. Moreover, the similar synthesis of information that is involved in the kinetic depth effect could not possibly be explained that way. It seems, therefore, that perceiving involves a memory that is not representational but schematic. During a series of fixations the perceiver synthesizes a model or schema of the scene before him, using information from each successive fixation to add detail or to extend the construction. This constructed whole is what guides his

movements (including further eye movements in many cases) and it is what he describes when he is being introspective. In short, it is what he sees.

Interestingly enough, although the memory involved in visual synthesis cannot consist simply of stored retinal afterimages, recent experiments indicate that storage of this kind does exist under certain circumstances. After a momentary exposure (too short for eye movement) that is followed by a blank field the viewer preserves an iconic image of the input pattern for some fraction of a second. George Sperling of the Bell Telephone Laboratories has shown that a signal given during this postexposure period can serve to direct a viewer's attention to any arbitrary part of the field, just as if it were still present.

The displays used in Sperling's experiments consisted of several rows of letters—too many to be reported from a single glance. Nevertheless, subjects were able to report any *single row*, indicated by the postexposure signal, rather well. Such a signal must come quickly; letters to which the observer does not attend before the brief iconic memory has faded are lost. That is why the observer cannot report the entire display: the icon disappears before he can read it all.

Even under these unusual conditions, then, people display selectivity in their use of the information that reaches the eye. The selection is made from material presented in a single brief exposure, but only because the experimental arrangements precluded a second glance. Normally selection and construction take place over a series of glances; no iconic memory for individual "snapshots" can survive. Indeed, the presentation of a

second stimulus figure shortly after the first in a brief-exposure experiment tends to destroy the iconic replica. The viewer may see a fusion of the two figures, only the second, or an apparent motion of the figures, depending on their temporal and spatial relations. He does not see them separately.

So far we have considered two kinds of short-term memory for visual information: the iconic replica of a brief and isolated stimulus, and the cumulative schema of the visible world that is constructed in the course of ordinary perception. Both of these processes (which may well be different manifestations of a single underlying mechanism) involve the storage of information over a period of time. Neither of them, however, is what the average man has in mind when he speaks of memory. Everyday experience testifies that visual information can be stored over long periods. Things seen yesterday can be recalled today; for that matter they may conceivably be recalled 20 years from now. Such recall may take many forms, but perhaps the most interesting is the phenomenon called visual imagery. In a certain sense one can see again what one has seen before. Are these mental images like optical ones? Are they revived copies of earlier stimulation? Indeed, does it make any sense at all to speak of "seeing" things that are not present? Can there be visual experience when there is no stimulation by light?

To deal with these problems effectively we must distinguish two issues: first, the degree to which the mechanisms involved in visual memory are like those involved in visual perception and, second, the degree to which the perceiver

B   C   D

object in view increases. The texture elements of a distant surface are also projected closer together than similar elements nearby.

Thus a textured surface slanting away from the viewer is represented optically as a density gradient (*see illustration on next page*).

is willing to say his images look real, that is, like external things seen. Although the first issue is perhaps the more fundamental—and the most relevant here—the second has always attracted the most attention.

One reason for the perennial interest in the "realness" of images is the wide range of differences in imaging capacity from person to person and from time to time. When Francis Galton conducted the first empirical study of mental im-agery (published in 1883), he found some of his associates skeptical of the very existence of imagery. They assumed that only poetic fancy allowed one to speak of "seeing" in connection with what one remembered; remembering consisted simply in a knowledge of facts. Other people, however, were quite ready to describe their mental imagery in terms normally applied to perception. Asked in the afternoon about their breakfast table, they said they could see it clearly, with colors bright (although perhaps a little dimmer than in the original experience) and objects suitably arranged.

These differences seem to matter less when one is asleep; many people who report little or no lifelike imagery while awake may have visual dreams and believe in the reality of what they see. On the other hand, some psychopathological states can endow images with such a compelling quality that they dominate the patient's experience. Students of per-

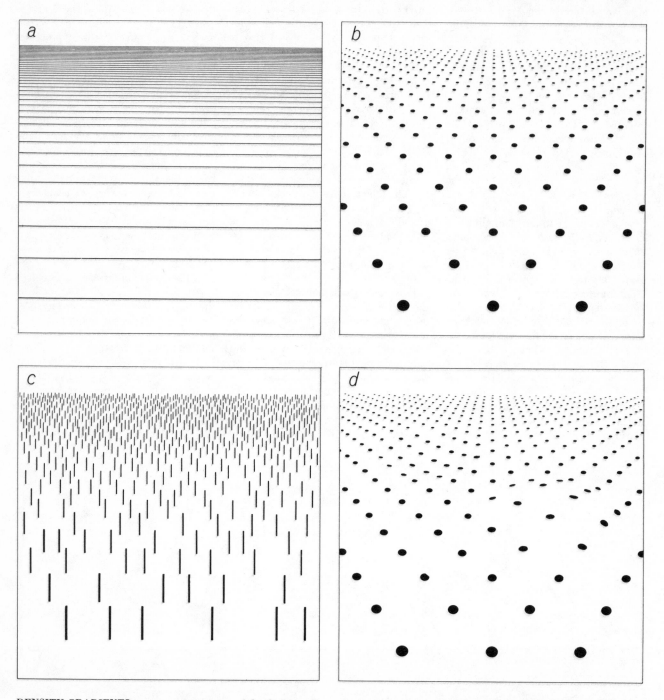

DENSITY GRADIENTS convey an impression of depth. Depending on the size, shape and spacing of its textural elements, the gradient may create the impression of a smooth flat surface (a, b), a rough flat surface (c) or a surface broken by an elevation and a depression (d). Like the gradients depicted, the textured surfaces of the visual world (by structuring the light that falls on the retina) convey information concerning the orientation of the surface. Textured surfaces also provide a scale for gauging the size of objects.

ception have often disregarded dreams and phantasms, considering them "hallucinatory" and thus irrelevant to normal seeing. However, this is a difficult position to defend either logically or empirically. Logically a sharp distinction between perception and hallucination would be easy enough if perceptions were copies of the retinal image; hallucinations would then be experiences that do *not* copy that image. But since perception does more than mirror the stimulus (and since hallucinations often incorporate stimulus information), this distinction is not clear-cut. Moreover, a number of recent findings seem to point up very specific relations between the processes of seeing and of imagining.

Perhaps the most unexpected of these findings has emerged from studies of sleep and dreams. The dreaming phase of sleep, which occurs several times each night, is regularly accompanied by bursts of rapid eye movements. In several studies William C. Dement and his collaborators have awakened experimental subjects immediately after a period of eye motion and asked them to report their just-preceding dream. Later the eye-movement records were compared with a transcript of the dream report to see if any relation between the two could be detected. Of course this was not possible in every case. (Indeed, we can be fairly sure that many of the eye movements of sleep have no visual significance; similar motions occur in the sleep of newborn babies, decorticated cats and congenitally blind adults.) Nevertheless, there was appreciably more correspondence between the two kinds of record than could be attributed to chance. The parallel between the eye movements of the dreamer and the content of the dream was sometimes striking. In one case five distinct upward deflections of the eyes were recorded just before the subject awoke and reported a dream of climbing five steps!

Another recent line of research has also implicated eye movements in the processes of visual memory. Ralph Norman Haber and his co-workers at Yale University reopened the study of eidetic imagery, which for a generation had remained untouched by psychological research. An eidetic image is an imaginative production that seems to be external to the viewer and to have a location in perceived space; it has a clarity comparable to that of genuinely perceived objects; it can be examined by the *"Eidetiker,"* who may report details that he did not notice in the original presentation of the stimulus. Most *Eidetikers*

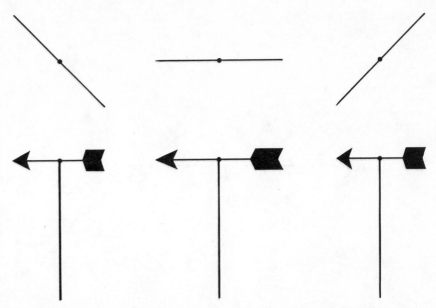

AMBIGUOUS VISUAL INPUT can arise from a stationary weather vane. The weather vane in three different orientations is shown as it would be seen from above (*top*) and in side view (*bottom*). If the vane begins to rotate, its real length will become apparent.

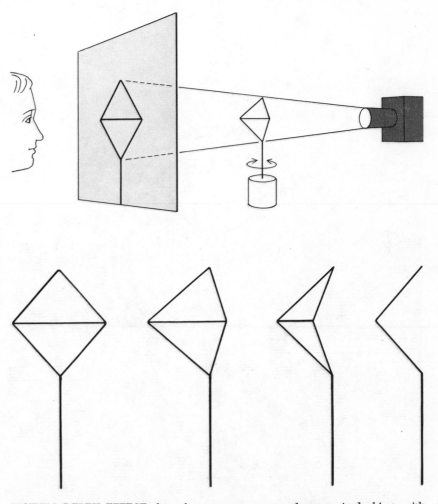

KINETIC DEPTH EFFECT shows how movement can endow perceived objects with three-dimensional shape. The shadow of a bent wire form (*shown at bottom in four different orientations*) looks as flat as the screen on which it is cast so long as the form remains stationary. When it is swiveled back and forth, the changing shadow is seen as a rigid rotating object with the appropriate three-dimensionality. The direction of rotation remains ambiguous, as in the case of the weather vane in the illustration at top of the page.

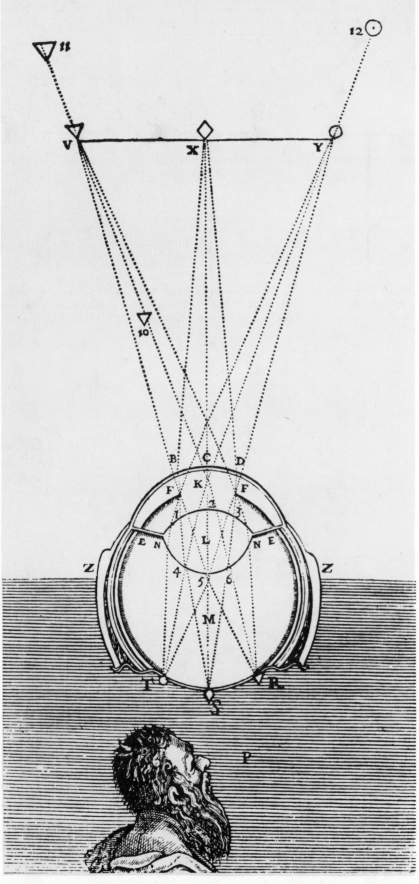

OPTICAL ANALYSIS BY DESCARTES included an experiment in which he removed the eye of an ox, scraped the back of the eye to make it transparent and observed on the retina the inverted image of a scene. The illustration is from Descartes's essay *La Dioptrique*.

are children, but the developmental course of this rather rare ability is not well understood. What is most interesting about these images for the present argument is that the *Eidetiker* scans them with his eyes. Asked about a detail in one or another corner of the image, he moves his eyes to look at the appropriate part of the blank wall on which he has "projected" it. That is, he does just what anyone would do who was really looking at something.

Are these esoteric phenomena really relevant to the study of vision? It might be argued that they do not provide a safe basis for inference; dreaming is a very special physiological state and eidetic imagery is restricted to very special types of people. It is not difficult, however, to show that similar processes occur in persons who do not have vivid visual imagery at all. A simple demonstration suggested by Julian Hochberg of New York University helps to make this point: Try to remember how many windows there are in your own house or apartment.

If you have never considered this question before, it will be hard to find the answer without actively looking and counting. However, you will probably not need to look at the windows themselves. Most people, even those who say they have no visual imagery, can easily form and scan an *internal representation* of the walls, counting off the windows as they appear in them. This process evidently uses stored visual information. It seems to involve mechanisms much like those used for seeing and counting real windows.

We can draw three conclusions from this demonstration. First, seeing and imagining employ similar—perhaps the same—mechanisms. Second, images can be useful, even when they are not vivid or lifelike, even for people who do not have "good imagery." Third, mental images are constructs and not copies. This last point may have been obvious in any case—you might just as well have been asked to imagine a gryphon and to count its claws—but it bears further emphasis. All the windows could not have been optically imaged on the retina simultaneously, and they may not even have appeared there in rapid succession. The image (or series of images) developed in solving this problem is new; it is not a replica of any previous stimulus.

The first two of these points have received additional confirmation in a recent experiment by Lee R. Brooks of McMaster University, whose method puts imagery and visual perception in direct competition. In one of his studies the subjects were shown a large block *F* and told to remember what it looked like. After the *F* was removed from view they were asked to describe the succession of corner points that would be encountered as one moved around it, responding "Yes" for each point that was either on the extreme top or the bottom of the *F*, and "No" for each point in between. This visual-memory task proved to be more difficult when the responses were made by *pointing* to a printed series of yeses and noes than when a spoken "Yes" or "No" was allowed. However, the difficulty was not intrinsic to the act of pointing; it resulted from the conflict between pointing and simultaneously visualizing the *F*. In another of Brooks's tasks the subjects had to respond "Yes" for each noun and "No" for each non-noun in a memorized sentence.

In this case they tended to rely on verbal-auditory memory rather than visual memory. As a result spoken response was the more difficult of the two.

We would not have been surprised to find a conflict between visually guided pointing and corner-counting on an *F* the viewer was *looking at*. After all, he could not be expected to look in two places at once. Even if the *F* had appeared on the same sheet of paper with the yeses and noes, interference would have been easy to understand: the succession of glances required to examine the corners of the *F* would have conflicted with the visual organization needed to point at the right succession of responses. What Brooks has shown, rather surprisingly, is that this conflict exists even when the *F* is merely imagined. Visual images are apparently produced by the same integrative processes that make ordinary perception possible.

In short, the reaction of the nervous system to stimulation by light is far from passive. The eye and brain do not act as a camera or a recording instrument. Neither in perceiving nor in remembering is there any enduring copy of the optical input. In perceiving, complex patterns are extracted from that input and fed into the constructive processes of vision, so that the movements and the inner experience of the perceiver are usually in good correspondence with his environment. Visual memory differs from perception because it is based primarily on stored rather than on current information, but it involves the same kind of synthesis. Although the eyes have been called the windows of the soul, they are not so much peepholes as entry ports, supplying raw material for the constructive activity of the visual system.

9

Negative Aftereffects in Visual Perception

by Olga Eizner Favreau and Michael C. Corballis
December 1976

You will see one if you stare at a waterfall for a short time and then look away; the surrounding scene will seem to move slowly upward. The study of such illusions yields information on perceptual systems

It is a common experience to look at a bright light and to find that a dark image of the object remains in the visual field for some time afterward. The phenomenon is called a negative afterimage (negative because the object was bright and the image is dark). A similar phenomenon can be experienced by staring for several minutes at something that is moving in a uniform direction, as a waterfall does, and then turning the gaze away; the surrounding scene will appear to drift slowly in the opposite direction. This is a negative aftereffect. Afterimages and aftereffects are illusions, reminding one that the senses are sometimes imperfect mediators between the external world and one's perception of it. The study of such illusions is valuable in psychology for the clues they provide to how the sense organs and the nervous system function in processing information.

Afterimages and aftereffects are encountered in a variety of forms. For example, afterimages of colored objects appear in colors that are complementary to the colors of the objects. If you stare at a patch of green for a minute or so and then look at a blank field, you can expect to see a reddish patch of the same shape [*see illustration on opposite page*].

In addition to motion aftereffects of the kind evoked by watching a waterfall one can experience figural aftereffects. For example, if you look at a line that is tilted about 15 degrees from the vertical, a line that is actually vertical may appear to be tilted in the opposite direction [*see bottom illustration on page 93*]. A related aftereffect can be observed if you look at a curved line for a time; a straight line then seems to curve the other way.

Aftereffects are by no means limited to vision. If someone is blindfolded and then runs a finger back and forth along a curved rod, a straight rod will seem to be curved the other way. Similarly, as has been demonstrated by Stuart M. Anstis of York University, if one listens repeatedly to a tone that increases in intensity, a tone of constant intensity is likely to sound as though it is decreasing in intensity. Here we shall focus on visual aftereffects, since they have been the most intensively examined.

A number of investigators in the 19th century thought motion aftereffects might be related to movements of the eyes. Exposure to a moving pattern induces the eyes to follow the motion of the pattern. If the eyes tend to persist in the same pattern of scanning when the movement is no longer there, a stationary pattern might then seem to move in the opposite direction.

In 1850, however, this hypothesis was discredited by the Belgian physicist Joseph Plateau on the basis of work with rotating spirals. Such a spiral appears either to expand or to contract, depending on the direction of rotation. Plateau found that if one watches an expanding spiral for a few minutes, a stationary spiral then seems to contract; conversely, a contracting spiral induces an aftereffect of expansion. The spiral aftereffect cannot be explained simply in terms of eye movements, because both expansion and contraction consist of movement in all directions at once.

Another explanation for aftereffects is the concept of normalization proposed by J. J. Gibson of Cornell University. He argued that a prolonged exposure to a stimulus that deviates in some way from an established norm might serve to redefine the norm. For example, an exposure to a line that is tilted slightly from the vertical might induce the observer to recalibrate his conception of the vertical toward the line. A truly vertical line would then be seen as being tilted in the other direction. This hypothesis may be partly correct, but it cannot easily account for aftereffects that arise when no obvious norm is involved. As Donald E. Mitchell and Darwin W. Muir of Dalhousie University have shown, the tilt aftereffect induced with a stimulus of oblique lines is similar in both magnitude and direction to the aftereffects induced with vertical and horizontal lines.

In recent years attempts to understand visual aftereffects have drawn increasingly on concepts derived from the growing body of knowledge of the neurophysiology of the visual system. Although most of this work is based on recordings made with microelectrodes from individual neurons, or nerve cells, in the visual system of such animals as cats and monkeys, a number of psychologists have been quick to extrapolate the findings to human vision. The exchange has also gone the other way: concepts derived from work on aftereffects in human beings preceded fundamental discoveries in the neurophysiology of vision in other primates. We hope to convey something of the flavor of this exchange between disciplines.

Light reaching the eye is focused by the lens to form a two-dimensional image on the retina. Light-sensitive receptors there convert the image into a spatial pattern of neural impulses. The impulses are transmitted from the receptors to a layer of neurons called bipolar cells and then to another layer called retinal ganglion cells. Fibers from the retinal ganglion cells make up the optic nerve, which carries the neural information from the retina to the brain.

Negative and complementary afterimages probably depend largely on the properties of cells in the retina. It is easy to demonstrate that an afterimage moves about as one moves one's eyes and that its location is perfectly correlated with the position of the eyes; it is as though the afterimage were painted on the retina. In contrast, objects actually present in the visual field appear to remain fixed if one moves one's eyes. These observations hold only for normal, voluntary eye movements. The situation is reversed if one moves an eye passively, as by pressing at the corner of the eye with a finger; then objects in the real world appear to move but an afterimage remains motionless. Both kinds of observation show that afterimages are formed at a level of processing preceding the one where the perceived location of objects in space is "corrected" for voluntary eye movements.

It is also easy to show that afterimages do not transfer from one eye to the other. The reader can verify this finding by looking at the illustration at the right for about 40 seconds with a hand over one eye. The afterimage will then be visible against a plain surface only to the exposed eye.

One can explain these phenomena by supposing cells in the retina, including the receptors, become temporarily fatigued or adapted after a long stimulation. According to this reasoning, if one looks at, say, a white patch, cells responsive to white light become less responsive, leaving an impression of a dark patch if the gaze is shifted to a uniform field. Complementary afterimages (red following green, for example) can be explained in a similar way.

Neurons beyond the receptors may also contribute to afterimages. They include the bipolar and ganglion cells in the retina and possibly cells in the lateral geniculate nucleus, a relay station in the brain that receives its input directly from the retinal ganglion cells. Among the retinal ganglion cells and the lateral geniculate cells are cells that typically exhibit what is termed "opponent process" organization, meaning that a cell increases its normal rate of firing in response to one color but decreases it in response to the complementary color. Opponent-process cells might contribute to afterimages in two ways. Suppose one views a uniform green field for a period of time. The cells that fire at an increased rate for green (they are called green-on, red-off cells) may become fatigued, so that if one subsequently views a uniform white field, the reduced firing of these cells is interpreted as redness. Conversely, red-on, green-off cells would be depressed while one was looking at a green field and might subsequently "rebound" to enhance the impression of redness.

Whereas afterimages depend on the fatigue of cells in the early stages of visual processing, figural and motion aftereffects appear to depend on properties of neurons at a higher level, perhaps in the visual cortex. The study of such aftereffects was greatly stimulated by the pioneering discoveries of David H.

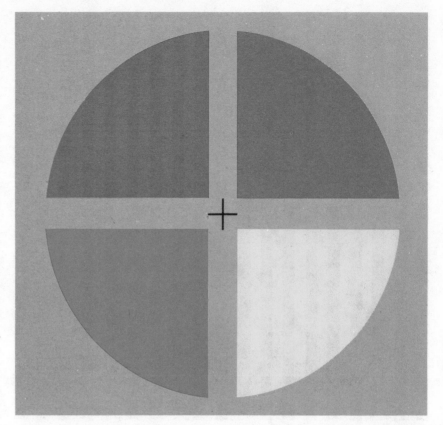

NEGATIVE AFTERIMAGE is the simplest kind of negative aftereffect. Here the afterimage will appear in the color that is complementary to the color you look at. If you fix your gaze on the cross at the center of the colors for about a minute and then look at the gray field at the bottom of the page, you should see patches that are in the complementary colors of the original: the green, yellow, blue and red will be replaced respectively by red, blue, yellow and green.

CONTINGENT AFTEREFFECT is demonstrated by these two grids and the pattern in the illustration on the opposite page. Look alternately at one grid and then the other for about 10 seconds each for 10 minutes. Then look at the pattern on the opposite page. Its horizontal lines should appear reddish and its vertical lines greenish. If the page is turned 90 degrees, the color relations reverse. The phenomenon is termed an orientation-contingent color aftereffect.

Hubel and Torsten N. Wiesel of the Harvard Medical School on the properties of neurons in the visual cortex of the cat brain [see "The Visual Cortex of the Brain," by David H. Hubel; SCIENTIFIC AMERICAN, Offprint 168]. Hubel and Wiesel found cells that they classified hierarchically as simple, complex and hypercomplex. Simple cells respond to edges, slits or lines. The edge, slit or line must be precisely located and oriented in the visual field to cause a given cell to fire at the maximum rate. Although location is not so critical for complex and hypercomplex cells, they have the added characteristic of responding maximally when the preferred stimulus is in motion in a direction perpendicular to its orientation. Many of these cells are also directionally selective in that they respond to motion in one direction but not to motion in the opposite direction.

In 1961, two years after the first report by Hubel and Wiesel, N. Stuart Sutherland, who is now at the University of Sussex, suggested that cortical cells of the kind described by the Harvard workers might underlie aftereffects of motion and orientation. His explanation, like the one we have described for afterimages, invoked the concept of neural fatigue. According to Sutherland, the perception of the orientation of a line would involve a kind of averaging of the activity of all the line detectors that respond to the line. If one looks at, say, a vertical line, the neurons most sensitive to verticalness are the most active and there is no overall bias due to the activity of cells sensitive to other orientations. The decision about the orientation of the line therefore corresponds to reality.

Now suppose the observer looks for some time at a line that is tilted 15 degrees clockwise. Line detectors maximally sensitive to the 15-degree line become fatigued, so that when the observer looks at the vertical line, the balance of activity is shifted counterclockwise away from the vertical. A similar process could underlie motion aftereffects.

The recognition that single cells in the cat's brain are simultaneously sensitive to more than one specific feature of environmental stimuli, such as orientation and brightness, introduced the possibility of discovering aftereffects with multiple components. The possibility was first realized by Celeste McCollough of Oberlin College. She reasoned that human beings probably have line detectors similar to the ones found in cats and that since people, unlike cats, also have color vision it might not be unreasonable to suppose that human line detectors are specialized for color as well as for orientation. If they are, one might be able to demonstrate aftereffects that depend on both the orientation and the color of lines.

McCollough accomplished the demonstration in the following way. Subjects looked at grids of horizontal blue and black lines alternating every few seconds with grids of vertical orange and black lines. After about 10 minutes they were shown grids of horizontal and of vertical white and black lines. The horizontal grids appeared to have a faint orange color and the vertical grids were tinged with blue. This result can be described as an orientation-contingent color aftereffect; it is generally known as the McCollough effect.

It is unlikely that the McCollough effect is retinal in origin. For one thing it is clear that the perceived colors are not simply complementary afterimages, since either color can be seen in the same retinal location, depending only on the orientation of the lines in the grid. Moreover, it is not necessary to gaze fixedly at the figures in order to get the McCollough effect.

Another aspect of the McCollough effect that differentiates it from simple afterimages is its extreme persistence. With an adaptation period of 10 or 15 minutes the effect may still be visible days or even weeks later. Because of these properties it is generally believed that the mechanisms responsible for the McCollough effect are localized in the visual cortex of the cerebrum. Three years after McCollough's discovery Hubel and Wiesel reported that the visual cortex of the monkey does in fact contain neurons sensitive to both the orientation and the color of a stimulus.

Other reports of contingent aftereffects have followed McCollough's work. Norva Hepler of McGill University and Charles F. Stromeyer and R. J. W. Mansfield of Harvard University independently discovered that color aftereffects can be made contingent on the direction of motion of a pattern. For example, if an observer alternately watches a spiral rotating clockwise in green light and counterclockwise in red light, a black-and-white spiral may subsequently appear pinkish if it is rotated clockwise and greenish if it is rotated counterclockwise.

We and Victor F. Emerson, working at McGill, discovered that it is possible to induce the converse of this contingency. (The finding was also reported by Anstis and John E. W. Mayhew.) After watching a green clockwise spiral alternating with a red counterclockwise spiral observers report that a stationary spiral appears to move briefly counterclockwise when it is green and clockwise when it is red. This is a color-contingent motion aftereffect. Like the motion-contingent color aftereffect, it is long-lasting, that is, although it is brief for any one exposure to a colored spiral, it can reappear when the spiral is looked at again. Both the color-contingent motion aftereffect and the motion-contingent color aftereffect can reappear if an ob-

BLACK-AND-WHITE PATTERN, viewed in conjunction with grids on opposite page, produces the orientation-contingent color aftereffect. Such multiple-component aftereffects are called McCollough effects after Celeste McCollough of Oberlin College, who discovered them.

server is shown the test patterns 24 hours after adaptation.

The evidence we have reviewed so far seems to support the view that aftereffects depend on the properties of feature detectors that bear a close functional resemblance to the neurons described by Hubel and Wiesel. Nevertheless, investigators in both neurophysiology and human perception have recently sought to prove the existence of detectors that respond to more integrated properties of the visual display. Indeed, some workers now believe the neurons studied by Hubel and Wiesel do not function simply as edge, slit or line detectors but also contribute to an analysis of the spatial frequencies (the spacing of more or less regularly repeating elements) in the total display. It has been found that individual neurons in the visual cortex of the cat respond selectively to sinusoidal gratings (parallel bars having a brightness that varies in a sinusoidal manner across the grating) only within a narrow range of spatial frequencies [see "Contrast and Spatial Frequency," by Fergus W. Campbell and Lamberto Maffei; SCIENTIFIC AMERICAN Offprint 1308].

A number of aftereffects can be attributed to detectors of spatial frequency. For example, Colin Blakemore and Peter Sutton of the University of Cambridge discovered that if one looks at a

striped pattern for some minutes and then views a grating with the same orientation but slightly narrower bars, the bars seem even narrower and more closely spaced than they really are. Conversely, broader bars seem broader [see *bottom illustration on page 94*].

The explanation proposed by Blakemore and Sutton was similar to the one advanced by Sutherland to explain tilt and motion aftereffects. They suggested that a grating of a particular frequency arouses activity in a subpopulation of frequency-detecting neurons. The distribution of activity is averaged to provide a perceptual impression of what the displayed frequency is. Preadaptation to some other spatial frequency would have depressed the activity of neurons sensitive to that frequency and so would skew the distribution away from the distribution normally evoked by the displayed pattern.

Color aftereffects can also be made contingent on spatial frequency. W. J. Lovegrove and Ray F. Over of the University of Queensland had subjects watch a vertical grating of one spatial frequency in red light alternating with a vertical grating of a different spatial frequency in green light. Afterward a black-and-white test grating of the first frequency appeared greenish and a grating of the second frequency appeared

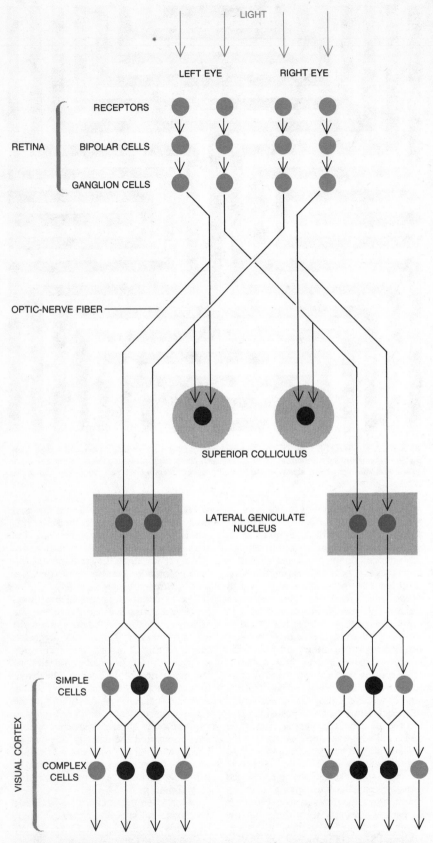

LIGHT

LEFT EYE   RIGHT EYE

RECEPTORS

RETINA   BIPOLAR CELLS

GANGLION CELLS

OPTIC-NERVE FIBER

SUPERIOR COLLICULUS

LATERAL GENICULATE NUCLEUS

SIMPLE CELLS

VISUAL CORTEX

COMPLEX CELLS

VISUAL SYSTEM is depicted schematically to show the flow of information. The neurons, or nerve cells, represented in color are driven by only one eye, whereas the ones shown in black are driven by both eyes. Hence if an aftereffect that has been induced in one eye is observed to transfer to the other eye, one can infer that it is mediated by cells either in the visual cortex of the brain or in the superior colliculus. Afterimages, in contrast to aftereffects, do not transfer from one eye to the other, so that they evidently originate in early stages of visual processing.

pinkish. Color aftereffects occurred, however, only if the frequency of one grating was at least twice that of the other and if the frequency of at least one grating was higher than three cycles per degree of visual angle. Lovegrove and Over suggested that their results could be explained in terms of the adaptation of neural units tuned for both color and spatial frequency.

A useful way to check on the location in the visual system of the neurons responsible for aftereffects is to test for interactions of the eyes. For example, one can induce an aftereffect in one eye and then ask whether the observer sees it when he looks with the other eye. Neurons in the visual pathway from the retina to the visual cortex are driven by one eye up to and including the lateral geniculate nucleus. In the visual cortex some neurons are driven monocularly (by an input to one eye only) and others are driven binocularly (by an input to either eye). Most of the cells in the superior colliculus (another part of the visual-processing system) are driven binocularly. Hence if an aftereffect is observed to transfer from one eye to the other, one can infer that it is mediated by cells in either the visual cortex or the superior colliculus. Since neurons in the superior colliculus appear to be sensitive mainly to motion, however, their role (if they have one) would be confined to motion aftereffects.

It has generally been found that figural and motion aftereffects, unlike afterimages, do transfer from one eye to the other, although their strength is reduced in the process. These aftereffects are therefore probably mediated by both monocularly and binocularly driven neurons. In the eye that was exposed to the adapting pattern both kinds of neurons would mediate the effect. In the other eye, however, only the neurons driven binocularly would be involved, which accounts for the reduction in strength.

Contingent aftereffects where one of the components is color apparently do not transfer from one eye to the other. This finding suggested that they may be mediated by monocularly driven neurons. Some evidence indicates, however, that this hypothesis may not be altogether correct. Experiments conducted by T. R. Vidyasagar of the University of Manchester have indicated that orientation-contingent color aftereffects can involve neurons that require an input to both eyes. Such neurons are binocular, but they could not mediate an interocular transfer. It seems possible that other contingent aftereffects may also involve binocular neurons of this type.

Gerald M. Murch of Portland State University has demonstrated that the color and motion components of an aftereffect can be dissociated. He has also shown that the motion component transfers from one eye to the other and the color component does not. Murch's procedure involved an adaptation phase and a test phase. In the adaptation phase he presented to the right eye a spiral whose motion was alternated between clockwise and counterclockwise, and at the same time he presented to the left eye the contingent color, alternately red and green. In the test phase the observer looked at stationary red or green spirals with first one eye and then the other. The contingent aftereffect (clockwise movement of the green spiral and counterclockwise movement of the red one) was reported only when the observer used his left eye. The adaptation to motion thus transferred from one eye to the other but the information about the contingent colors did not.

Murch's elegant experiment raises a general question about the nature of contingent aftereffects. Until recently it had been widely assumed that they are due solely to the adaptation of "multiple duty" neurons tuned to the different components, such as color and orientation, that underlie the aftereffects. Murch and other workers have questioned this assumption, suggesting instead that the contingency may depend on associative connections between different classes of neurons, each type tuned to a single component of the visual experience. Although Murch's experiment does not rule out the participation of multiple-duty neurons in the mediation of contingent aftereffects, it does introduce the possibility that such aftereffects can also be mediated by associations among previously independent neurons.

The possibility that contingent aftereffects may depend on the formation of associative connections rather than (or perhaps in addition to) fatigue has been suggested for another reason, namely the persistence of many contingent aftereffects. As we have mentioned, they can be detected days or even weeks after the adaptation period. We know of no neurophysiological evidence that fatigue or the adaptation of single neurons ever persists for such a long time.

Indeed, the persistence may not be confined to contingent aftereffects, although the question of whether or not an aftereffect is contingent is sometimes a fine point. Richard F. Masland of McGill showed that features of the spiral aftereffect can persist for as long as 24 hours. One of us (Favreau) has found that it may still be present a week later. The decrease in magnitude of the spiral aftereffect is rapid during the first few minutes, but thereafter the rate of decrease is markedly slower. For this reason Masland suggested that the aftereffect has two components: a rapidly

SPIRAL AFTEREFFECT is caused by putting a spiral on a turntable and rotating it at $33\frac{1}{3}$ revolutions per minute. When the spiral is stopped, it seems to move in the other direction.

decaying component directly due to the adaptation of motion detectors and a more slowly decaying, more persistent component caused by the conditioned adaptation of the detectors. In conditioned adaptation, although the motion detectors would not remain fatigued for the entire period during which the aftereffect persists, the spiral configuration, having become associated with fatigue,

could cause the detectors to return to a state resembling fatigue.

Although the concept of conditioned adaptation or fatigue could be useful in explaining the long-term persistence of negative aftereffects, it presents a stumbling block. If the various attributes of the inducing stimulus, such as spiral configuration and clockwise motion, become associated with one another, one

TILT AFTEREFFECT appears when one has looked steadily for about five minutes at the tilted lines. Thereafter lines that are actually vertical will seem to tilt in the opposite direction.

94

CURVE AFTEREFFECT results from looking at curved lines for 10 minutes, moving the eyes only along the central portion. The straight lines will then appear to curve the opposite way.

would expect to obtain positive aftereffects rather than negative ones. Thus, for example, a stationary spiral would appear to rotate in the direction in which the spiral was previously seen rotating and a colorless vertical grating employed to test for the McCollough effect

would appear green if the vertical orientation had been paired with green. The striking feature of negative aftereffects, however, is that when two attributes are combined in a stimulus, one of them subsequently becomes associated with an opposite quality of the other (move-

SPATIAL VARIATIONS can also cause aftereffects, apparently because certain neurons in the visual system are sensitive to spatial frequencies, that is, the spacing of more or less regular features of something one is looking at. One can obtain the aftereffect by first looking at the two sets of vertical bars at the left to determine whether they are the same. Then move your eyes back and forth along the horizontal bar between the two sets of vertical bars for about five minutes. When you shift your gaze to the horizontal bar between the vertical grids at the right, the spatial frequency of the grid at the top will appear to be higher than that of the grid at the bottom. If the illustration is turned upside down, the spatial relations will then reverse.

ment in the other direction, the complementary color and so on).

It is plausible that fatigue could become associated with aspects of the adapting stimulus, since it is known that the processes of fatigue start operating as soon as one looks at a stimulus. When one views something that is constantly moving, the perceived velocity decreases. When one looks at a colored surface, the color appears to become desaturated. (The reader can verify this relation by looking at one of the colored patches in the illustration on page 89. If half of the patch is obscured by a piece of gray paper that is removed after about 30 seconds, the part of the patch that was covered appears to be brighter than the part that was exposed.)

We have now examined two possible explanations of negative aftereffects: fatigue and conditioned fatigue. Possibly they both play a role. Masland's work on the spiral aftereffect showed that it has two components. One of us (Favreau) has conducted experiments that suggest a further dissociation of the short- and long-term components of this aftereffect. The simple aftereffect is observable immediately after one looks at a spiral, and it also decreases steadily in strength. The color-contingent spiral aftereffect is not seen immediately and does not reach full strength for several minutes. The finding suggests that during an exposure to spirals of alternating motion and colors, visual units sensitive to both directions of motion may become fatigued and hence prevent the rapid appearance of a motion aftereffect. As the fatigue wears off, the effects of mechanisms underlying the color contingency may be revealed.

If contingent aftereffects do depend on the formation of associative connections between visual units, the question arises of how such connections are established. One possibility is that information from different sets of feature-extracting neurons converges in a mutually interactive way at a higher level of visual processing. The interaction (between, say, color and motion) would be recorded by a relative adaptation across a bank of neurons at the higher level. Thereafter the activation of this system by either of the original sets of neurons could re-create the impression of adaptation in the other set, thereby yielding the appropriate negative aftereffect.

This account still relies on the notion of adaptation, or habituation, of neurons. These hypothetical neurons, however, are at least removed from the feature-analyzing neurons that have been studied intensively and have not been observed to exhibit long-term adaptation effects. Neurons of this kind, which store patterns of interaction by means of long-term habituation, may play a rather general role in learning and memory.

10

Visual Illusions

by Richard L. Gregory
November 1968

*Why do simple figures sometimes appear distorted
or ambiguous? Perhaps because the visual system
has to make sense of a world in which everyday
objects are normally distorted by perspective*

A satisfactory theory of visual perception must explain how the fleeting patterns of light reaching the retina of the eye convey knowledge of external objects. The problem of how the brain "reads" reality from the eye's images is an acute one because objects are so very different from images, which directly represent only a few of the important characteristics of objects. At any instant the retinal image represents the color of an object and its shape from a single position, but color and shape are in themselves trivial. Color is dependent on the quality of the illumination, and on the more subtle factors of contrast and retinal fatigue. Shape, as we all know, can be strongly distorted by various illusions. Since it is obviously not in the best interests of the possessor of an eye to be tricked by visual illusions, one would like to know how the illusions occur. Can it be that illusions arise from information-processing mechanisms that under normal circumstances make the visible world easier to comprehend? This is the main proposition I shall examine here.

Illusions of various kinds can occur in any of the senses, and they can cross over between the senses. For example, small objects feel considerably heavier than larger objects of exactly the same weight. This can be easily demonstrated by filling a small can with sand and then putting enough sand in a much larger can until the two cans are in balance. The smaller can will feel up to 50 percent heavier than the larger can of precisely the same weight. Evidently weight is perceived not only according to the pressure and muscle senses but also according to the expected weight of the object, as indicated by its visually judged size. When the density is unexpected, vision produces the illusion of weight. I believe all systematic-distortion illusions are essentially similar to this size-weight illusion.

Although several visual illusions were known to the ancient Greeks, they have been studied experimentally for only a little more than a century. The first scientific description in modern times is in a letter to the Scottish physicist Sir David Brewster from a Swiss naturalist, L. A. Necker, who wrote in 1832 that a drawing of a transparent rhomboid reverses in depth: sometimes one face appears to be in front and sometimes the other. Necker noted that although changes of eye fixation could induce this change in perception, it would also occur quite spontaneously. This celebrated effect is generally illustrated with an isometric cube rather than with Necker's original figure [*see top illustration on page 97*].

Somewhat later W. J. Sinsteden reported an equally striking effect that must have long been familiar to Netherlanders. If the rotating vanes of a windmill are viewed obliquely or directly from the side, they spontaneously reverse direction if there are no strong clues to the direction of rotation. This effect can be well demonstrated by projecting on a screen the shadow, seen in perspective, of a slowly rotating vane. In the absence of all clues to the direction of rotation the vane will seem to reverse direction spontaneously and the shadow will also at times appear to expand and contract on the plane of the screen. It is important to note that these effects are not perceptual distortions of the retinal image; they are alternative interpretations of the image in terms of possible objects. It is as though the brain entertains alternative hypotheses of what object the eye's image may be representing. When sensory data are inadequate, alternative hypotheses are entertained and the brain never "makes up its mind."

The most puzzling visual illusions are systematic distortions of size or shape. These distortions occur in many quite simple figures. The distortion takes the same direction and occurs to much the same extent in virtually all human observers and probably also in many animals. To psychologists such distortions present an important challenge because they must be explained by a satisfactory theory of normal perception and because they could be important clues to basic perceptual processes.

Distortion Illusions

The simplest distortion illusion was also the first to be studied. This is the horizontal-vertical illusion, which was described by Wilhelm Wundt, assistant to Hermann von Helmholtz at Heidelberg and regarded as the father of experimental psychology. The illusion is simply that a vertical line looks longer than a horizontal line of equal length. Wundt attributed the distortion to asymmetry in the system that moves the eye. Although this explanation has been invoked many times since then, it must be ruled out because the distortions occur in afterimages on the retina and also in normal images artificially stabilized so as to remain stationary on the retina. In addition, distortions can occur in several directions at the same time, which could hardly be owing to eye movements. It is also difficult to see how curvature distortions could be related to eye movements. All the evidence suggests that the distortions originate not in the eyes but in the brain.

Interest in the illusions became general on the publication of several figures showing distortions that could produce errors in the use of optical instruments. These errors were an important concern to physicists and astronomers a centu-

ZÖLLNER ILLUSION was published in 1860 by Johann Zöllner; the first of the special distortion illusions.

ry ago, when photographic and other means of avoiding visual errors were still uncommon. The first of the special distortion figures was the illusion published by Johann Zöllner in 1860 [*see illustration above*]. The same year Johann Poggendorff published his line-displacement illusion [*see middle illustration on page 97*]. A year later Ewald Hering presented the now familiar illusion in which parallel lines appear bowed; the converse illusion was conceived in 1896 by Wundt [*see illustrations on page 99*].

Perhaps the most famous of all distortion illusions is the double-headed-arrow figure devised by Franz Müller-Lyer

and presented in 15 variations in 1889 [*see illustration, page 100*]. This figure is so simple and the distortion is so compelling that it was immediately accepted as a primary target for theory and experiment. All kinds of theories were advanced. Wundt again invoked his eye-movement theory. It was also proposed that the "wings" of the arrowheads drew attention away from the ends of the central line, thus making it expand or contract; that the heads induced a state of empathy in the observer, making him feel as if the central line were being either stretched or compressed; that the distortion is a special case of a supposed general principle that acute angles tend

to be overestimated and obtuse angles underestimated, although why this should be so was left unexplained.

All these theories had a common feature: they were attempts to explain the distortions in terms of the stimulus pattern, without reference to its significance in terms of the perception of objects. There was, however, one quite different suggestion. In 1896 A. Thiery proposed that the distortions are related to the way the eye and brain utilize perspective to judge distances or depths. Thiery regarded the Müller-Lyer arrows as drawings of an object such as a saw-horse, seen in three dimensions; the legs would be going away from the observer in the acute-angled figure and toward him in the obtuse-angled figure. Except for a brief discussion of the "perspective theory" by Robert S. Woodworth in 1938, Thiery's suggestion has seldom been considered until recently.

Woodworth wrote: "In the Müller-Lyer figure the obliques readily suggest perspective and if this is followed one of the vertical lines appears farther away and therefore objectively longer than the other." This quotation brings out the immediate difficulties of developing an adequate theory along such lines. The distortion occurs even when the perspective suggestion is not followed up, because the arrows generally appear flat and yet are still distorted. Moreover, no hint is given of a mechanism responsible for the size changes. An adequate theory based on Thiery's suggestion must show how distortion occurs even though the figures appear flat. It should also indicate the kind of brain mechanisms responsible.

The notion that geometric perspective—the apparent convergence of parallel lines with distance—has a bearing on the problem is borne out by the occurrence of these distortions in photographs of actual scenes in which perspective is pronounced. Two rectangles of equal size look markedly unequal if they are superposed on a photograph of converging railroad tracks [see illustration on page 98]. The upper rectangle in the illustration, which would be the more distant if it were a real object lying between the tracks, looks larger than the lower (and apparently nearer) one. This corresponds to the Ponzo illusion [see bottom illustration on this page].

Similarly, the eye tends to expand the inside corner of a room, as it is seen in a photograph, and to shrink the outside corners of structures [see illustration on page 105]. The effect is just the same as the one in the Müller-Lyer figures, which in fact resemble outline drawings of corners seen in perspective. In both cases the regions indicated by perspective as being distant are expanded, whereas those indicated as being closer are shrunk. The distortions are opposite to the normal shrinking of the retinal image when the distance to an object is increased. Is this effect merely fortuitous, or is it a clue to the origin of the illusions?

Paradoxical Pictures

Before we come to grips with the problem of trying to develop an adequate theory of perspective it will be helpful to consider some curious fea-

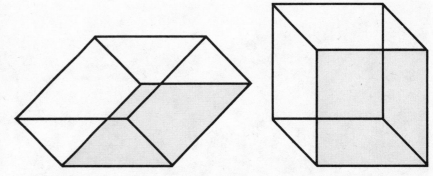

NECKER ILLUSION was devised in 1832 by L. A. Necker, a Swiss naturalist. He noticed that a transparent rhomboid (*left*) spontaneously reverses in depth. The area lightly tinted in color can appear either as an outer surface or as an inner surface of a transparent box. The illusion is now more usually presented as a transparent cube (*right*), known as a Necker cube.

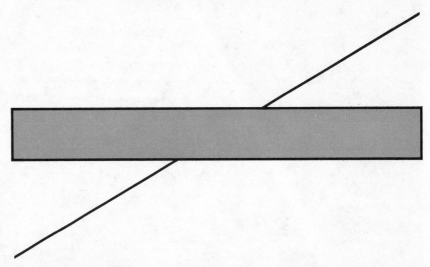

POGGENDORFF ILLUSION was proposed by Johann Poggendorff in 1860, the same year that Johann Zöllner proposed the figure shown on page 96. In Poggendorff's figure the two segments of the diagonal line seem to be offset.

PONZO ILLUSION, also known as the railway lines illusion, was proposed by Mario Ponzo in 1913. It is the prototype of the illusion depicted in the photograph on the following page.

ILLUSION INVOLVING PERSPECTIVE is remarkably constant for all human observers. The two rectangles superposed on this photograph of railroad tracks are precisely the same size, yet the top rectangle looks distinctly larger. The author regards this illusion as the prototype of visual distortions in which the perceptual mechanism, involving the brain, attempts to maintain a rough size constancy for similar objects placed at different distances. Since we know that the distant railroad ties are as large as the nearest ones, any object lying between the rails in the middle distance (the upper rectangle) is unconsciously enlarged. Indeed, if the rectangles were real objects lying between the rails, we would know immediately that the more distant was larger.

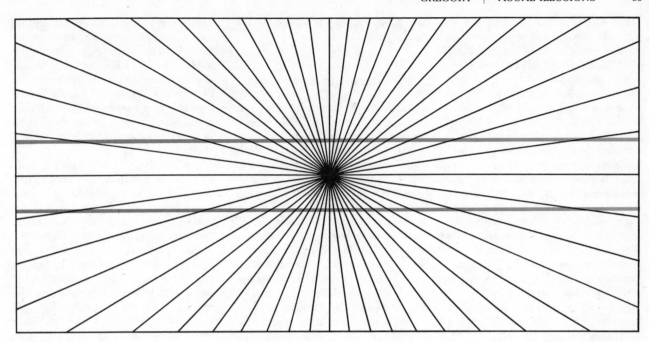

HERING ILLUSION was published in 1861 by Ewald Hering. The horizontal lines are of course straight. Physicists and astronomers of that period took a lively interest in illusions, being concerned that visual observations might sometimes prove unreliable.

tures of ordinary pictures. Pictures are the traditional material of perceptual research, but all pictures are highly artificial and present special problems to the perceiving brain. In a sense all pictures are impossible because they have a dual reality. They are seen both as patterns of lines lying on a flat background and as objects depicted in a quite different three-dimensional space. No actual object can be both two-dimensional and three-dimensional, yet pictures come close to it. Viewed as patterns they are seen as being two-dimensional; viewed as representing other objects they are seen in a quasi-three-dimensional space. Pictures therefore provide a paradoxical visual input. They are also ambiguous, because the third dimension is never precisely defined.

The Necker cube is an example of a picture in which the depth ambiguity is so great that the brain never settles for a single answer. The fact is, however, that any perspective projection could represent an infinity of three-dimensional shapes. One would think that the perceptual system has an impossible task! Fortunately for us the world of objects does not have infinite variety; there is usually a best bet, and we generally interpret our flat images more or less correctly in terms of the world of objects.

The difficulty of the problem of seeing the third dimension from the two dimensions of a picture, or from the

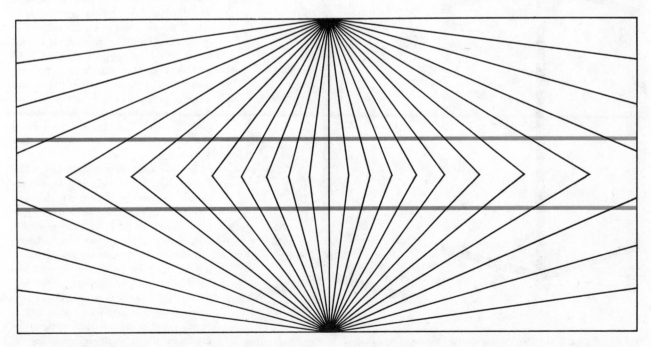

CONVERSE OF HERING ILLUSION was conceived in 1896 by Wilhelm Wundt, who introduced experimentation into psychology. Wundt earlier described the simplest of the visual illusions: that a vertical line looks longer than a horizontal line of equal length.

retinal images of normal objects, is ingeniously brought out by special "impossible pictures" and "impossible objects." They show what happens when clearly incompatible distance information is presented to the eye. The impossible triangle devised by Lionel S. Penrose and R. Penrose cannot be perceptually interpreted as an object in normal three-dimensional space [*see illustration on page 101*]. It is, however, perfectly possible to make actual three-dimensional objects, not mere pictures, that give rise to the same perceptual confusion—provided that they are viewed with only one eye. For example, the Penrose triangle can be built as an open three-dimensional structure [*see top illustration on page 103*] that looks like an impossible closed structure when it is viewed with one eye (or photographed) from exactly the right position [*see bottom illustration on page 103*].

Ordinary pictures are not so very different from obviously impossible pictures. All pictures showing depth are paradoxical: we see them both as being flat (which they really are) and as having a kind of artificial depth that is not quite right. We are not tempted to touch objects shown in a picture through the surface of the picture or in front of it. What happens, however, if we remove the surface? Does the depth paradox of pictures remain?

The Removal of Background

To remove the background for laboratory experiments we make the pictures luminous so that they glow in the dark. In order to deprive the brain of stereoscopic information that would reveal that the pictures are actually flat the pictures are viewed with one eye. They may be wire figures coated with luminous paint or photographic transparencies back-illuminated with an electroluminescent panel. In either case there is no visible background, so that we can discover how much the background is responsible for the depth paradox of pictures, including the illusion figures.

Under these conditions the Müller-Lyer arrows usually look like true corners according to their perspective. They may even be indistinguishable from actual luminous corners. The figures are not entirely stable: they sometimes reverse spontaneously in depth. Nonetheless, they usually appear according to their perspective and without the paradoxical depth of pictures with a background. The distortions are still present. The figure that resembles a dou-

ble-headed arrow looks like an outside corner and seems shrunk, whereas the figure with the arrowheads pointing the wrong way looks like an inside corner and is expanded. Now, however, the paradox has disappeared and the figures look like true corners. With a suitable apparatus one can point out their depth as if they were normal three-dimensional objects.

Having removed the paradox, it is possible to measure, by quite direct means, the apparent distance of any selected part of the figures. This we do by using the two eyes to serve as a range finder for indicating the apparent depth of the figure, which is visible to only one eye. The back-illuminated picture is placed behind a polarizing filter so that one eye is prevented from seeing the picture by a second polarizing filter oriented at right angles to the first. Both eyes, however, are allowed to see one or more small movable reference lights that are optically introduced into the picture by means of a half-silvered mirror set at 45 degrees to the line of sight. The distance of these lights is given by stereoscopic vision, that is, by the convergence angle of the eyes; by moving the lights so that they seem to coincide with the apparent distance of selected parts of the picture we can plot the visual space of the observer in three dimensions [*see top illustration on page 101*].

When this plotting is done for various angles of the "fin," or arrowhead line, in the Müller-Lyer illusion figure, it becomes clear that the figures are perceived as inside and outside corners. The illusion of depth conforms closely to the results obtained when the magnitude of the illusion is independently measured by asking subjects to select comparison lines that match the apparent length of the central line between two kinds of arrowhead [*see bottom illustration on page 101*]. In the latter experiment the figures are drawn on a normally textured background, so that they appear flat.

The two experiments show that when the background is removed, depth very closely follows the illusion for the various fin angles. The similarity of the plotted results provides evidence of a remarkably close connection between the illusion as it occurs when depth is not seen and the depth that is seen when the background is removed. This suggests that Thiery was essentially correct: perspective can somehow create distortions. What is odd is that perspective produces the distortions according to *indicated* perspective depth even when depth is *not* consciously seen.

MÜLLER-LYER ILLUSION was devised by Franz Müller-Lyer in 1889. Many theories were subsequently invoked in an attempt to explain why reversed arrowheads (*right*) seem to lengthen a connecting shaft whereas normal arrowheads seem to shrink the shaft (*left*).

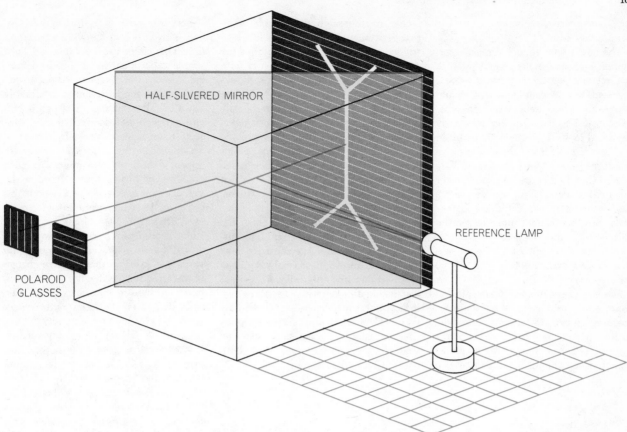

HALF-SILVERED MIRROR

REFERENCE LAMP

POLAROID
GLASSES

APPARATUS FOR STUDYING ILLUSIONS was devised by the author. The objective is to present figures such as the Müller-Lyer arrows with the background removed so that the figures seem suspended in space. Under these conditions the Müller-Lyer arrows generally look like true corners. The subject can adjust a small light so that it appears to lie at the same depth as any part of the figure. The light, which the subject sees in three-dimensional space with both eyes, is superposed on the illuminated figure by means of a half-silvered mirror. A polarizing filter is placed over the figure and the subject wears polarizing glasses that allow him to see the figure with only one eye. Thus he has no way of telling whether the figure is really two-dimensional or three-dimensional.

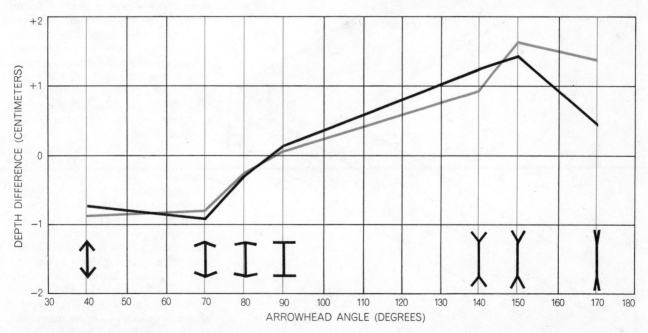

DEPTH DIFFERENCE (CENTIMETERS)

ARROWHEAD ANGLE (DEGREES)

QUANTITATIVE MEASUREMENT OF ILLUSION produced the results plotted here for Müller-Lyer arrows. The black curve shows the average results for 20 subjects who were asked to select a comparison line that matched the length of a central shaft to which were attached arrowheads set at the angles indicated. When arrowheads were set at less than 90 degrees, the comparison lines were as much as one centimeter shorter. When the arrowhead was set at 150 degrees, the comparison line was more than 1.5 centimeters longer. The colored curve shows the maximum depth difference perceived for the same set of arrows when displayed, with the background removed, in the apparatus shown in the illustration at the top of the page. The two curves match quite closely except at the extreme setting of 170 degrees, when the figure no longer resembles a true corner when presented in the light box.

Size Constancy

The next step is to look for some perceptual mechanism that could produce this relation between perspective and apparent size. A candidate that should have been obvious many years ago is size constancy. This phenomenon was clearly described in 1637 by René Descartes in his *Dioptrics*. "It is not the absolute size of images [in the eyes] that counts," he wrote. "Clearly they are 100 times bigger [in area] when objects are very close than when they are 10 times farther away, but they do not make us see the objects 100 times bigger. On the contrary, they seem almost the same size, at any rate as we are not deceived by too great a distance."

We know from many experiments that Descartes is quite right. What happens, however, when distance information, such as perspective, is presented to the eye but two components of the scene, one of which should be shrunk by distance, are the same size? Could it be that perspective presented on a flat plane triggers the brain to compensate for the expected shrinking of the images with distance even though there is no shrinking for which to compensate? If some such thing happens, it is easy to see why figures that suggest perspective can give rise to distortions. This would provide the start of a reasonable theory of illusions. Features indicated as being distant would be expanded, which is just what we find, at least for the Müller-Lyer and the Ponzo figures.

It is likely that this approach to the problem was not developed until recently because, although size constancy was quite well known, it has always been assumed that it simply follows apparent distance in all circumstances. Moreover, it has not been sufficiently realized how very odd pictures are as visual inputs. They are highly atypical and should be studied as a special case, being both paradoxical and ambiguous.

Size constancy is traditionally identified with an effect known as Emmert's law. This effect can be explained by a simple experiment involving the apparent size of afterimages in vision. If one can obtain a good afterimage (preferably by briefly illuminating a test figure with an electronic flash lamp), one can "project" it on screens or walls located at various distances. The afterimage will appear almost twice as large with each doubling of distance, even though the size of the image from the flash remains constant. It is important to note, however, that there *is* a change in retinal stimulation for each screen or wall lying at a different distance; their images *do* vary. It is possible that the size change of the afterimage is due not so much to a brain mechanism that changes its scale as to its size on the retina with respect to the size of the screen on which it appears to lie. Before we go any further, it is essential to discover whether Emmert's law is due merely to the relation between the areas covered by the afterimage and the screen, or whether the visual information of distance changes the size of the afterimage by some kind of internal scaling. This presents us with a tricky experimental problem.

As it turns out, there is a simple solution. We can use the ambiguous depth phenomenon of the Necker cube to establish whether Emmert's law is due to a central scaling by the brain or is merely an effect of relative areas of stimulation of the retina. When we see a Necker cube that is drawn on paper reverse in depth, there is no appreciable size change. When the cube is presented on a textured background, it occupies the paradoxical depth of all pictures with visible backgrounds; it does not change in size when it reverses in pseudo-depth.

What happens, however, if we remove the cube's background? The effect is dramatic and entirely repeatable: with each reversal in depth the cube changes its apparent shape, even though there is no change in the retinal image. Whichever face appears to be more distant always appears to be the larger. The use of depth-ambiguous figures in this way makes it possible to separate what happens when the pattern of stimulation of the retina is changed. The answer is that at least part of size constancy, and of Emmert's law, is due to a central size-scaling mechanism in the brain that responds to changes in apparent distance although the retinal stimulation is unchanged.

Apparent size, then, is evidently established in two ways. It can be estab-

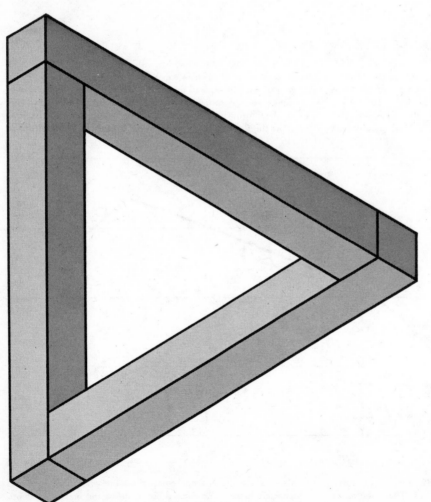

IMPOSSIBLE TRIANGLE was devised by Lionel S. Penrose and R. Penrose of University College London. It is logically consistent over restricted regions but is nonsensical overall. The author sees a certain similarity between such impossible figures and ordinary photographs, which provide the illusion of a third dimension even though they are flat.

lished purely by apparent distance. It can also be established directly by visual depth features, such as perspective in two-dimensional pictures, even though depth is not seen because it is countermanded by competing depth information such as a visible background. When atypical depth features are present, size scaling is established inappropriately and we have a corresponding distortion illusion.

The size scaling established directly by depth features (giving systematic distortions when it is established inappropriately) we may call "depth-cue scaling." It is remarkably consistent and independent of the observer's perceptual "set." The other system is quite different and more subtle, being only indirectly related to the prevailing retinal information. It is evidently linked to the interpretation of the retinal image in terms of what object it represents. When it appears as a different object, the scaling changes at once to suit the alternative object. If we regard the seeing of an object as a hypothesis, suggested (but never strictly proved) by the image, we may call the system "depth-hypothesis scaling," because it changes with each change of the hypothesis of what object is represented by the image. When the hypothesis is wrong, we have an illusion that may be dramatic. Such alternations in hypotheses underlie the changes in direction, and even size, that occur when one watches the shadow of a rotating vane.

Observers in Motion

The traditional distortion illusions can be attributed to errors in the setting of the depth-cue scaling system, which arise when figures or objects have misleading depth cues, particularly perspective on a flat plane. Although these illusions might occasionally bother investigators making visual measurements, they are seldom a serious hazard. The other kind of illusion—incorrect size-scaling due to an error in the prevailing perceptual hypothesis—can be serious in unfamiliar conditions or when there is little visual information available, as in space flight. It can also be important in driving a car at night or in landing an airplane under conditions of poor visibility. Illusions are most hazardous when the observer is in rapid motion, because then even a momentary error may lead to disaster.

So far little work has been done on the measurement of illusions experienced by observers who are in motion with respect to their surroundings. The ex-

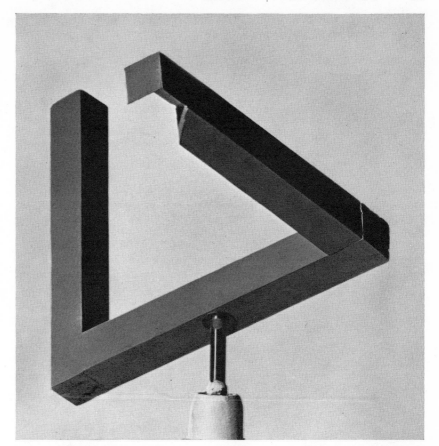

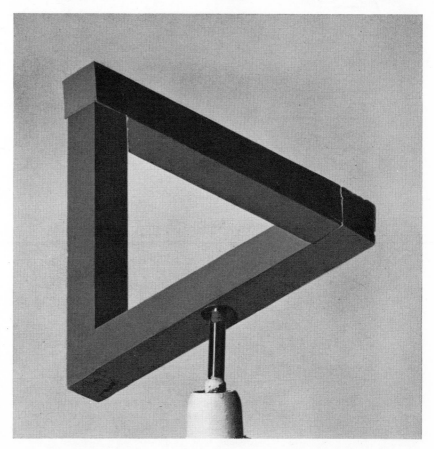

ACTUAL IMPOSSIBLE TRIANGLE was constructed by the author and his colleagues. The only requirement is that it be viewed with one eye (or photographed) from exactly the right position. The top photograph shows that two arms do not actually meet. When viewed in a certain way (*bottom*), they seem to come together and the illusion is complete.

perimental difficulties involved in making such measurements are severe; nevertheless, we have been tackling the problem with support from the U.S. Air Force. The equipment, which is fairly elaborate, can move the observer with controlled velocity and acceleration through various visual environments, including the blackness of space (with or without artificial stars presented optically at infinite distance).

We measure the observer's visual sense of size constancy as he is moving by having him look at a projected display that changes size as he approaches or recedes from it. As he moves away from it, the display is made to expand in size; as he approaches it, the display is made to shrink. The change in size is adjusted until, to the moving observer, the display appears fixed in size. If there were no perceptual mechanism for constancy scaling, the size of the display would have to be adjusted so that its image on the observer's retina would be the same size regardless of his distance from it. If, at the other extreme, the size-

constancy effect were complete, we could leave the display unchanged and it would still appear to be the same size regardless of its actual distance from the observer. In practice some size change between these limits provides the illusion of an unchanging display, and this gives us a measure of the size-constancy effect as the observer is moved about.

We find that when the observer is in complete darkness, watching a display that is projected from the back onto a large screen, there is no measurable size constancy when the observer is moving at a fixed speed. When he is accelerated, size constancy does appear but it may be wildly wrong. In particular, if he interprets his movement incorrectly, either in direction or in amount, size constancy usually fails and can even work in reverse. This is rather similar to the reversal of size constancy with reversal of the depth of the luminous Necker cube. In the conditions of space, perception may be dominated by the prevailing hypothesis of distance and velocity. If either is wrong, as it may well be for

lack of reliable visual information, the astronaut may suffer visual illusions that could be serious.

The Nonvisual in Vision

Visual perception involves "reading" from retinal images a host of characteristics of objects that are not represented directly by the images in the eyes. The image does not convey directly many important characteristics of objects: whether they are hard or soft, heavy or light, hot or cold. Nonvisual characteristics must somehow be associated with the visual image, by individual learning or conceivably through heredity, for objects to be recognized from their images. Psychologists now believe individual perceptual learning is very important for associating the nonoptical properties of objects with their retinal images. Such learning is essential for perception; without it one would have mere stimulus-response behavior.

Perception seems to be a matter of looking up information that has been stored about objects and how they behave in various situations. The retinal image does little more than select the relevant stored data. This selection is rather like looking up entries in an encyclopedia: behavior is determined by the contents of the entry rather than by the stimulus that provoked the search. We can think of perception as being essentially the selection of the most appropriate stored hypothesis according to current sensory data.

Now, a look-up system of this kind has great advantages over a control system that responds simply to current input. If stored information is used, behavior can continue in the temporary absence of relevant information, or when there is inadequate information to provide precise control of behavior directly. This advantage has important implications for any possible perceptual system, including any future "seeing machine": a robot equipped with artificial eyes and a computer and designed to control vehicles or handle objects by means of artificial limbs. Even when enough direct sensory information is available for determining the important characteristics of surrounding objects (which is seldom the case), it would require a rate of data transmission in excess of that provided by the human nervous system (or current computers) to enable a robot to behave appropriately. Hence there are strong general design reasons for supposing that any effective seeing system—whether biological or man-made—should use current sensory

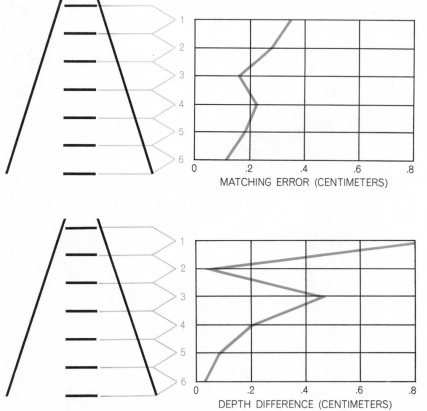

RAILWAY LINES ILLUSION can also be studied quantitatively. The methods are the same as those described in the bottom illustration on page 101. Subjects were presented with a horizontal line at one of the indicated positions and asked to select a second line that seemed to match it in length. The matching error for different pairs is plotted in the top curve. Pairs of lines were then presented in the apparatus shown at the top of page 101 and the subjects adjusted the light to match the apparent depth of each line. Under these conditions (*bottom curve*) the illusion of depth is much more dependent on where a given pair of lines is located with respect to the "rails," but the trend of the top curve is preserved.

THEORY OF MÜLLER-LYER ILLUSION favored by the author suggests that the eye unconsciously interprets the arrow-like figures as three-dimensional skeleton structures, resembling either an outside (*left*) or inside corner (*right*) of a physical structure. A perceptual mechanism evidently shrinks the former and enlarges the latter to compensate for distortion caused by perspective.

information for selecting preformed hypotheses, or models, representing important features of the external world of objects as opposed to controlling behavior directly from sensory inputs.

If we consider the problems of storing information about objects, it soon becomes clear that it would be most uneconomical to store an independent model of each object for every distance and orientation it might occupy in surrounding space. It would be far more economical to store only typical characteristics of objects and to use current sensory information to adjust the selected model to fit the prevailing situation.

The model must be continually scaled for distance and orientation if the owner of the perceptual system is to interact with the object.

We might guess that depth-cue scaling represents this adjustment of the selected model in the light of the available depth information. When the available information is inappropriate (as in the case of perspective features on a flat plane), it will scale the perceptual model wrongly. There will be a systematic error: a distortion illusion due to inappropriate depth-cue scaling. There will also be errors—possibly very large ones—whenever a wrong model is selected. We

see this happening in a repeatable way in the ambiguous figures, such as the luminous Necker cube, that change shape with each depth reversal even though the sensory input is unchanged.

If this general account of perception as essentially a look-up system is correct, we should expect illusions similar to our own to arise in any effective perceptual system, including future robots. Illusions are not caused by any limitation of our brain. They are the result of the imperfect solutions available to any data-handling system faced with the problem of establishing the reality of objects from ambiguous images.

Multistability in Perception

11

by Fred Attneave
December 1971

*Some kinds of pictures and geometric forms
spontaneously shift in their principal aspect
when they are looked at steadily. The reason
probably lies in the physical organization
of the perceptual system*

Pictures and geometric figures that spontaneously change in appearance have a peculiar fascination. A classic example is the line drawing of a transparent cube on this page. When you first look at the cube, one of its faces seems to be at the front and the other at the back. Then if you look steadily at the drawing for a while, it will suddenly reverse in depth and what was the back face now is the front one. The two orientations will alternate spontaneously; sometimes one is seen, sometimes the other, but never both at once.

When we look steadily at a picture or a geometric figure, the information received by the retina of the eye is relatively constant and what the brain perceives usually does not change. If the figure we are viewing happens to be an ambiguous figure, what the brain perceives may change swiftly without any change in the message it is receiving from the eye. The psychologist is interested in these perceptual alternations not as a curiosity but for what they can tell us about the nature of the perceptual system.

It is the business of the brain to represent the outside world. Perceiving is not just sensing but rather an effect of sensory input on the representational system. An ambiguous figure provides the viewer with an input for which there are two or more possible representations that are quite different and about equally good, by whatever criteria the perceptual system employs. When alternative representations or descriptions of the input are equally good, the perceptual system will sometimes adopt one and sometimes another. In other words, the perception is multistable. There are a number of physical systems that have the same kind of multistable characteristics, and a comparison of multistability in physical and perceptual situations

may yield some significant clues to the basic processes of perception. First, however, let us consider several kinds of situations that produce perceptual multistability.

Figure-ground reversal has long been used in puzzle pictures. It is often illustrated by a drawing that can be seen as either a goblet or a pair of faces [*see top illustration on page 109*]. This figure was introduced by the Danish psychologist Edgar Rubin. Many of the drawings and etchings of the Dutch artist Maurits C. Escher are particularly elegant examples of figure-ground reversal [*see bottom illustration on page 109*]. These examples are somewhat misleading because they suggest that the components of a figure-ground reversal must be familiar objects. Actually you can make a perfectly good reversing figure by scribbling a meaningless line down the middle of a circle. The line will be seen as a contour or a boundary, and its appearance is quite different depending on which side of the contour is seen as the inside and which as the outside [*see top illustration on page 111*]. The difference is so fundamental that if a person first sees one side of the contour as the object or figure, the probability of his recognizing the same contour when it is shown as part of the other half of the field is little better than if he had never seen it at all; this was demonstrated by Rubin in a classic study of the figure-ground dichotomy.

Note that it is quite impossible to see both sides of the contour as figures at the same time. Trying to think of the halves as two pieces of a jigsaw puzzle that fit together does not help; the pieces are still seen alternately and not simultaneously. What seems to be involved here is an attribution of surface properties to some parts of a field but not to others. This kind of distinction is of cen-

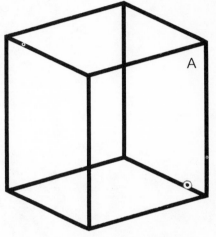

NECKER CUBE, a classic example of perspective reversal, is named after Louis Albert Necker, who in 1832 reported that line drawings of crystals appeared to reverse in depth spontaneously. Corner *A* alternates from front to back when gazed at steadily.

tral importance in the problem of scene analysis that Marvin Lee Minsky of the Massachusetts Institute of Technology and other investigators of computer simulation have been grappling with lately. The figure made by drawing a line through a circle is actually tristable rather than bistable; the third possibility is being able to see the line as a thing in itself, as a twisted wire rather than the boundary of a figure.

PAINTING BY SALVADOR DALI on the following page is an example of the use of ambiguous figures by a serious artist. The illustration is a portion of "Slave Market with Apparition of the Invisible Bust of Voltaire." It is reproduced with the permission of the Dali Museum in Cleveland. When viewed at close range, the figures of people predominate; when viewed at a distance, bust of Voltaire becomes apparent.

The point of basic interest in figure-ground reversal is that one line can have two shapes. Since an artist's line drawing is readily identifiable with the object it is supposed to portray, and since a shape has much the same appearance whether it is white on black, black on white or otherwise colored, many workers have suggested that the visual system represents or encodes objects primarily in terms of their contours. As we have seen, however, a contour can be part of two shapes. The perceptual representation of a contour is specific to which side is regarded as the figure and which as the ground. Shape may be invariant over a black-white reversal, but it is not invariant over an inside-outside reversal.

Under natural conditions many factors cooperate to determine the figure-ground relationship, and ambiguity is rare. For example, if one area encloses another, the enclosed area is likely to be seen as the figure. If a figure is divided into two areas, the smaller of the areas is favored as the figure [*see middle illustration on page 111*].

The visual field usually consists of many objects that overlap and occlude one another. The perceptual system has an impressive ability to segregate and sort such objects from one another. Along with distinguishing figure from ground, the system must group the fragments of visual information it receives into separate sets that correspond to real objects. Elements that are close to one another or alike or homogeneous in certain respects tend to be grouped together. When alternative groupings are about equally good, ambiguity results.

For example, if a set of dots are aligned, the perceptual system tends to group them on the basis of this regularity. When the dots are in regular rows and columns, they will be seen as rows if the vertical distance between the dots is greater than the horizontal distance, and they will seem to be in columns if the horizontal distance is greater than the vertical distance. When the spacing both ways is the same, the two groupings—rows and columns—tend to alternate. What is interesting and rather puzzling about the situation is that vertical and horizontal groupings are competitive at all. Geometrically the dots form both rows and columns; why, then, does seeing them in rows preclude seeing them in columns at the same moment? Whatever the reason is in terms of perceptual mechanisms, the principle involved appears to be a general one: When elements are grouped percep-

REVERSIBLE GOBLET was introduced by Edgar Rubin in 1915 and is still a favorite demonstration of figure-ground reversal. Either a goblet or a pair of silhouetted faces is seen.

WOODCUT by Maurits C. Escher titled "Circle Limit IV (Heaven and Hell)" is a striking example of both figure-ground reversal and competition between rival-object schemata. Devils and angels alternate repeatedly but neither seems to be able to overpower the other.

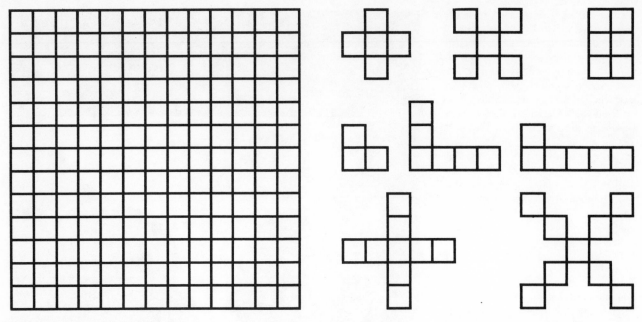

FIGURAL GROUPINGS occur when one stares at a matrix of squares. The simple figures organize themselves spontaneously and with effort more complex figures can be perceived. Some figures, however, are so complex that they are difficult to maintain.

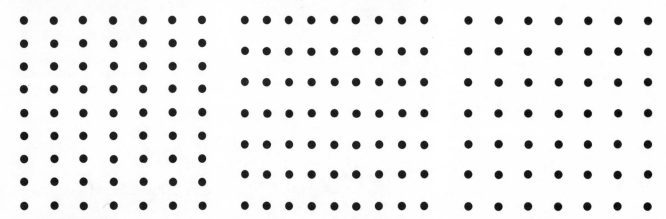

ALIGNED DOTS fall into a regular pattern when viewed. Depending on the spacing, dots can be seen as columns (*left*) or as rows (*middle*). When vertical and horizontal spacing are equal, dots can be seen as rows or columns but not as both at the same time.

EQUILATERAL TRIANGLES appear in one of three orientations depending on the dominant axis of symmetry (*left*). Usually all point in the same direction at one time, although the direction can change spontaneously. The scalene triangles (*middle*) fluctuate in orientation even though they are asymmetrical because they can also appear as isosceles or right triangles that point down or up. The same shape can be seen as either diamonds or tilted squares (*right*) depending on the orientation of the local reference system.

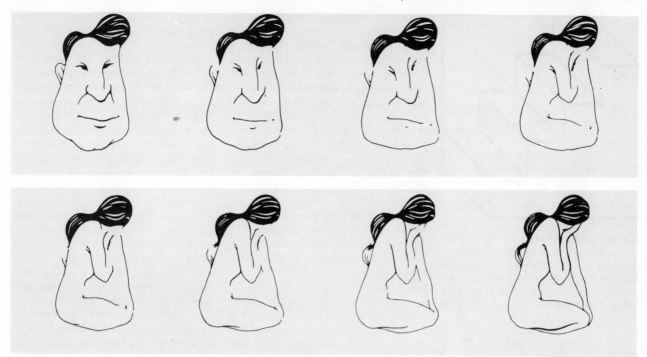

MAN-GIRL FIGURES are part of a series of progressively modified drawings devised by Gerald Fisher in 1967. He found that the last drawing in the top row has equal probability of being seen as a man or as a girl. Perception of middle pictures can be biased toward the man by viewing series in sequence beginning from top left and can be biased toward the girl by starting from bottom right.

fixation, "the point of distinct vision" being perceived as the closer. Although the fixation point is indeed important, it has been shown that depth reversal will readily occur without eye movement.

If we want to understand how depth relationships can be multistable, we must first consider the more general question of how the perceptual system can derive a three-dimensional representation from a two-dimensional drawing. A straight line in the outside world casts a straight line on the retina. A given straight line on the retina, however, could be the image of any one of an infinite number of external lines, and not necessarily straight lines, that lie in a common plane with one another and the eye. The image on a single retina is always two-dimensional, exactly as a photograph is. We should not be surprised, therefore, that depth is sometimes ambiguous; it is far more remarkable that the perceptual system is able to select a particular orientation for a line segment (or at worst to vacillate between two or three orientations) out of the infinite number of legitimate possibilities that exist.

On what basis does the system perform this feat? According to the Gestalt psychologists the answer is to be found in a principle of *Prägnanz:* one perceives the "best" figure that is consistent with a given image. For most practical purposes "best" may be taken to mean "simplest." The advantage of this interpretation is that it is easier to find objective standards for complexity than for such qualities as being "best." One observes a particular configuration of lines on paper, such as the Necker cube, and assigns a three-dimensional orientation to the lines such that the whole becomes a cube (although an infinite number of noncubical forms could project the same form) because a cube is the simplest of the possibilities. In a cube the lines (edges) are all the same length; they take only three directions, and the angles they form are all equal and right

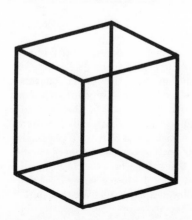
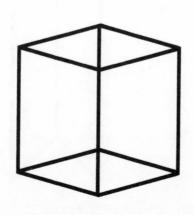
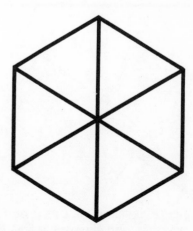

PROJECTIONS OF A CUBE onto a two-dimensional surface are nearly always seen in depth when they resemble the Necker cube (*left*). As the projection becomes simpler and more regular it is more likely to be seen as a flat figure, such as a hexagon (*right*).

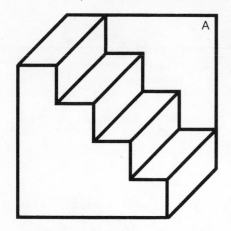

SCHRÖDER STAIRS line drawing is another classic example of perspective reversal. Corner *A* is part of the rear wall when the staircase goes up to the left; when reversal occurs, corner *A* becomes part of the front wall and the bottom of the stairway is seen.

angles. No other interpretation of the figure, including the two-dimensional aspect itself, is as simple and regular. In cases of reversible perspective two maximally simple tridimensional constructions are permissible, each being symmetrical with the other in depth.

If this reasoning is correct, simple projections of a given solid should be perceived as being flat more often than complex projections of the same solid. Julian Hochberg and his colleagues at Cornell University studied various two-dimensional projections of a cube and other regular solids [*see bottom illustra-tion on preceding page*]. Relatively complex projections are nearly always perceived in depth. A figure such as a regular hexagon divided into equilateral triangles, which is simple and regular in two dimensions, stays two-dimensional because seeing it as a cube does not make it any simpler. Intermediate figures become tristable; they are sometimes seen as being flat and sometimes as being one or another aspect of a cube. The measure of complexity devised by Hochberg and Virginia Brooks involved the number of continuous lines in the figure, the number of interior angles and the number of different angles. This measure predicted with considerable accuracy the proportion of the time that a figure was seen in depth rather than as being flat.

I have been emphasizing the importance of simplicity, but it is obvious that familiarity also plays an important role in instances of ambiguous depth. The two factors are hard to disentangle. Simple structures are experienced with great frequency, particularly in man-made environments. As Alvin G. Goldstein of the University of Missouri has shown by experiment, within limits a nonsense shape is judged to be simpler the more often it is experienced. In my view familiarity and simplicity become functionally equivalent in the perceptual system when a given input corresponds closely to a schema that is already well established by experience and can therefore be encoded or described (in the language of the nervous system) most simply in terms of that schema.

Depth reversal does not occur only with two-dimensional pictures. As the Austrian physicist and philosopher Ernst Mach pointed out, the perspective of many real objects will reverse when the object is viewed steadily with one eye. A transparent glass half-filled with water is a particularly dramatic example, but it requires considerable effort to achieve the reversal and the stability of the reversal is precarious. Mach discovered an easier reversal that is actually more instructive. Take a white card or a small piece of stiff paper and fold it once along its longitudinal axis [*see bottom illustration on this page*]. Place the folded card or paper in front of you on a table so that it makes a rooflike structure. Close one eye and view the card steadily for a while from directly above. It will reverse (or you can make it reverse) so that it appears as if the fold is at the bottom instead of the top. Now view the card with one eye from above at about a 45-degree angle so that the front of the folded card can be seen. After a few seconds the card will reverse and stand up on end like an open book with the inside toward you. If the card is asymmetrically illuminated and is seen in correct perspective, it will appear to be more or less white all over, as it is in reality, in spite of the fact that the illuminated plane reflects more light than the shadowed one. When the reversal occurs, the shadowed plane looks gray instead of white and the illuminated plane may appear luminous. In the perspective reversal the perceptual mechanism that preserves the constancy of reflectance is fooled; in order to maintain the relation between light source and the surfaces the perceptual system makes corrections that are erroneous because they are based on incorrect information.

Another remarkable phenomenon involving the folded card seems to have escaped Mach's notice. Recently Murray Eden of the Massachusetts Institute of Technology found that if after you make the folded card reverse you move your head slowly from side to side, the card will appear to rock back and forth quite as convincingly as if it were physically in motion. The explanation, very roughly, is that the mechanism that makes allowance for head movements, so that still objects appear still even though the head moves, is operating properly but on erroneous premises when the perspective is reversed. The perceived rocking of the card is exactly what would

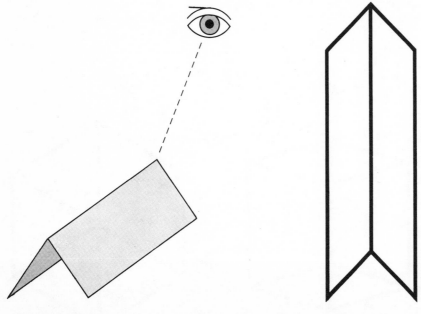

DEPTH REVERSAL OF A REAL OBJECT can occur when it is viewed from above with one eye, an effect discovered by Ernst Mach. When a folded card is viewed from above and the front, it will appear to stand on end like an open book when it reverses. The same kind of depth reversal occurs with a simple line drawing of a folded card (*above right*).

have to happen objectively if the card were really reversed to account for the sequence of retinal images accompanying head movement. What is remarkable about this is not that the mechanism can be wrong but rather that it can function so efficiently as a "lightning calculator" of complex problems in projective geometry and compensate so completely to maintain the perceived orientation. It seems to me that this capacity is a good argument for the existence of some kind of working model of three-dimensional space within the nervous system that solves problems of this type by analogue operations. Indeed, the basic concept of *Prägnanz*, of a system that finds its way to stable states that are simple by tridimensional criteria, is difficult to explain without also postulating a neural analogue model of three-dimensional space. We have no good theory at present of the nature of the neural organization that might subserve such a model.

A few years ago I stumbled on a principle of ambiguity that is different from any we have been considering. While planning an experiment on perceptual grouping I drew a number of equilateral triangles. After looking at them for a time I noticed that they kept changing in their orientation, sometimes pointing one way, sometimes another and sometimes a third way [see bottom illustration on page 110]. The basis for this tristable ambiguity seems to be that the perceptual system can represent symmetry about only one axis at a time, even though an equilateral triangle is objectively symmetrical about three axes. In other words, an equilateral triangle is always perceived as being merely an isosceles triangle in some particular orientation. Compare any two sides or any two angles of an equilateral triangle and you will find that the triangle immediately points in the direction around which the sides and angles are

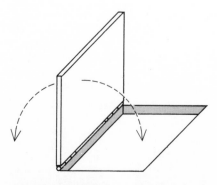

PHYSICAL SYSTEM that exhibits a simple form of multistability is a trapdoor that is stable only when it is either open or shut.

symmetrical. When a group of equilateral triangles points upward, the triangles cease to fluctuate; the perceptual system strongly prefers the vertical axis of symmetry. Indeed, any perceived axis of symmetry seems to have the character of a locally rotated vertical.

When scalene triangles (triangles with three unequal sides) are grouped together with their corresponding sides parallel, they also appear to fluctuate in orientation after a brief inspection [see bottom illustration on page 110]. This is at first puzzling since they have no axes of symmetry at all. The answer to the puzzle involves the third dimension: When the triangles are seen to point in a given direction, they simultaneously go into depth in such a way that they look like isosceles triangles seen at an angle. Perspective reversal doubles the possibilities, so that there are six ways the scalene triangles can be seen as isosceles. The same triangles may also be seen as right triangles in depth, with the obtuse angles most easily becoming the right angles.

These observations begin to make sense if we suppose the perceptual system employs something quite like a Cartesian coordinate system to locate and describe things in space. (To call the system Cartesian is really putting the issue backward, since Descartes clearly took the primary perceptual directions of up-down, left-right and front-back as his reference axes.) The multistable states of triangles thus appear to involve simple relations between the figure and the reference system. The reference system may be tilted or rotated locally by the perceptual system and produce the apparent depth or orientation of the triangles.

In the same way we can explain how the same shape can appear to be so different when it is seen as a square or as a diamond. The square is perceived as having horizontal and vertical axes along its sides; the diamond is perceived as being symmetrical about a vertical axis running through opposite corners. Yet in certain kinds of grouping the perceptual axes can be locally rotated and the diamond can look like a tilted square [see bottom illustration on page 110].

It should be evident by now that some principle of *Prägnanz*, or minimum complexity, runs as a common thread through most of the cases. It seems likely that the perceptual machinery is a teleological system that is "motivated" to represent the outside world as economically as possible, within the constraints of the input received and the

limitations of its encoding capabilities.

A good reason for invoking the concept of multistability to characterize figural ambiguity is that we know a great deal about multistable physical and electronic systems and may hope to apply some of this knowledge to the perceptual processes. The multistable behavior of the perceptual system displays two notable characteristics. The first is that at any one moment only one aspect of the ambiguous figure can be seen; mixtures or intermediate states occur fleetingly if at all. The second is that the different percepts alternate periodically. What accounts for this spontaneous alternation? Once the perceptual system locks into one aspect of the figure, why does it not remain in that state? An analogous physical system is a trapdoor that is stable only when it is either open or closed.

As Necker pointed out, changing the point of visual fixation may cause perspective to reverse. In the instances where the input is being matched against more than one schema visual fixation on a feature that is more critical to one representation than the other may lock perception into only one aspect of the ambiguous figure. Since the percepts can alternate without a change in the point of fixation, however, some additional explanation is needed. The most likely is that the alternative aspects of the figure are represented by activity in different neural structures, and that when one such structure becomes "fatigued," or satiated or adapted, it gives way to another that is fresher and more excitable. Several investigators have noted that a reversing figure alternates more rapidly the longer it is looked at, presumably because both alternative neural structures build up some kind of fatigue. In some respects the neural structures behave like a multistable electronic circuit. A common example of multistability in electronic circuitry is the multivibrator flip-flop circuit, which can incorporate either vacuum tubes or transistors. In the vacuum tube version [see illustration on opposite page] when one tube is conducting a current, the other tube is prevented from conducting by the low voltage on its grid. The plates and the grids of the two tubes are cross-coupled through capacitors, and one tube continues to conduct until the charge leaks from the coupling capacitor sufficiently for the other tube to start conducting. Once this tube begins to conduct, the positive feedback loop quickly makes it fully conducting and the other tube is cut off and becomes nonconducting. The process reverses and the system flip-flops between one state and the other.

What is "fatigued" in the multivibrator is the suppressive linkage. In other words, the inhibition of the nonconducting tube slowly weakens until it is no longer strong enough to prevent conduction. The possibility of an analogous neural process, in which the inhibition of the alternative neural structure progressively weakens, is worth considering.

Brain lesions may affect the perception of ambiguous figures. The finding most generally reported is that in people who have suffered brain damage the rate of alternation is lower, more or less independently of the locus of the lesion. On the other hand, a study of a group of brain-damaged war veterans conducted by Leonard Cohen at New York University indicated that damage to both frontal lobes increases the rate of alternation of a reversible figure, whereas damage to only one frontal lobe decreases the rate. The theoretical implications of these neurological findings are quite obscure and will doubtless remain so until we have some fundamental picture of the way the nervous system represents form and space.

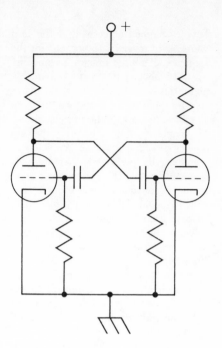

MULTIVIBRATOR CIRCUIT spontaneously alternates between two states. When one vacuum tube is conducting, the other is inhibited. A charge leaking from the coupling capacitor eventually starts the inhibited tube conducting. The positive feedback loop quickly makes it fully conducting and cuts off conduction in the first tube. The entire process is repeated in reverse, and the circuit flops from one state to the other.

The Perception of Disoriented Figures

by Irvin Rock
January 1974

*Many familiar things do not look the same when their
orientation is changed. The reason appears to be that
the perception of form embodies the automatic assignment
of a top, a bottom and sides*

Many common experiences of everyday life that we take for granted present challenging scientific problems. In the field of visual perception one such problem is why things look different when they are upside down or tilted. Consider the inverted photograph on the opposite page. Although the face is familiar to most Americans, it is difficult to recognize when it is inverted. Even when one succeeds in identifying the face, it continues to look strange and the specific facial expression is hard to make out.

Consider also what happens when printed words and words written in longhand are turned upside down. With effort the printed words can be read, but it is all but impossible to read the longhand words [*see top illustration on page 119*]. Try it with a sample of your own handwriting. One obvious explanation of why it is hard to read inverted words is that we have acquired the habit of moving our eyes from left to right, and that when we look at inverted words our eyes tend to move in the wrong direction. This may be one source of the difficulty, but it can hardly be the major one. It is just as hard to read even a single inverted word when we look at it without moving our eyes at all. It is probable that the same factor interfering with the recognition of disoriented faces and other figures is also interfering with word recognition.

The partial rotation of even a simple figure can also prevent its recognition, provided that the observer is unaware of the rotation. A familiar figure viewed in a novel orientation no longer appears to have the same shape [*see bottom illustration on page 119*]. As Ernst Mach pointed out late in the 19th century, the appearance of a square is quite different when it is rotated 45 degrees. In fact, we call it a diamond.

Some may protest that a familiar shape looks different in a novel orientation for the simple reason that we rarely see it that way. But even a figure we have not seen before will look different in different orientations [*see top illustration on page 120*]. The fact is that orientation affects perceived shape, and that the failure to recognize a familiar figure when it is in a novel orientation is based on the change in its perceived shape.

On the other hand, a figure can be changed in various ways without any effect on its perceived shape. For example, a triangle can be altered in size, color and various other ways without any change in its perceived shape [*see middle illustration on page 120*]. Psychologists, drawing an analogy with a similar phenomenon in music, call such changes transpositions. A melody can be transposed to a new key, and although all the notes then are different, there is no change in the melody. In fact, we generally remain unaware of the transposition. Clearly the melody derives from the relation of the notes to one another, which is not altered when the melody is transposed. In much the same way a visual form is based primarily on how parts of a figure are related to one another geometrically. For example, one could describe a square as being a four-sided figure having parallel opposite sides, four right angles and four sides of equal length. These features remain unchanged when a square is transposed in size or position; that is why it continues to look like a square. We owe a debt to the Gestalt psychologists for emphasizing the importance in perception of relations rather than absolute features.

Since a transposition based on rotation also does not alter the internal geometric relations of a figure, then why does it look different in an altered orientation? At this point we should consider the meaning of the term orientation. What changes are introduced by altering orientation? One obvious change is that rotating a figure would result in a change in the orientation of its image on the retina of the eye. Perhaps, therefore, we should ask why different retinal orientations of the same figure should give rise to different perceived shapes. That might lead us into speculations about how the brain processes information about form, and why differently oriented projections of a retinal image should lead to different percepts of form.

Before we go further in this direction we should consider another meaning of the term orientation. The inverted and rotated figures in the illustrations for this article are in different orientations with respect to the vertical and horizontal directions in their environment. That part of the figure which is normally pointed upward in relation to gravity, to the sky or to the ceiling is now pointed downward or sideways on the page. Perhaps it is this kind of orientation that is responsible for altered perception of shape when a figure is disoriented.

It is not difficult to separate the retinal and the environmental factors in an experiment. Cut out a paper square and tape it to the wall so that the bottom of the square is parallel to the floor. Compare the appearance of the square first with your head upright and then with your head tilted 45 degrees. You will see that the square continues to look like a square when your head is tilted. Yet when your head is tilted 45 degrees, the retinal image of the square is the same as the image of a diamond when the diamond is viewed with the head upright. Thus it is not the retinal image that is responsible for the altered appearance of a square when the square is rotated 45 degrees. The converse experiment points to the same conclusion. Rotate the square on the wall so that it becomes a diamond. The diamond viewed with your head tilted 45 degrees produces a retinal image of a square, but the diamond still looks like a diamond. Needless to say, in these simple demonstrations one continues to perceive correctly where the top, bottom and sides of the figures are even when one's posture changes. It is therefore the change of a figure's perceived orientation in the environment that affects its apparent shape and not the change of orientation of its retinal image.

These conclusions have been substantiated in experiments Walter I. Heimer and I and other colleagues have conducted with numerous subjects. In one series of experiments the subjects were shown unfamiliar figures. In the first part of the experiment a subject sat at a table and simply looked at several figures shown briefly in succession. Then some of the subjects were asked to tilt their head 90 degrees by turning it to the side and resting it on the table. In this position the subject viewed a series of figures. Most of the figures were new, but among them were some figures the subject had seen earlier. These figures were shown in either of two orientations: upright with respect to the room (as they had been in the first viewing) or rotated 90 degrees so that the "top" of the figure corresponded to the top of the subject's tilted head. The subject was asked to say whether or not he had seen each figure in the first session. He did not know that the orientation of the figures seen previously might be different. Other subjects viewed the test figures while sitting upright.

When we compared the scores of subjects who tilted their head with subjects who sat upright for the test, the results were clear. Tilted-head subjects recognized the environmentally upright (but retinally tilted) figures about as well as the upright observers did. They also failed to recognize the environmentally tilted (but retinally upright) figures about as often as the upright subjects did. In other words, the experiments confirmed that it is rotation with respect to the up-down and left-right coordinates in the environment that produces the change in the perceived shape of the figure. It is not rotation of the retinal image that produces the change, since altering the image's orientation does not adversely affect recognition and preserving it does not improve recognition.

In another experiment subjects viewed an ambiguous or reversible figure that could be perceived in one of two ways depending on its orientation. For example, when one figure that looked like a map of the U.S. was rotated 90 degrees, it looked like the profile of a bearded man. Subjects were asked to rest their head on the table when viewing the ambiguous figures. The question we asked ourselves was: Which "upright" would dominate, the retinal upright or the environmental upright? The results were decisive. About 80 percent of the subjects reported seeing only the aspect of the ambiguous figure that was environmentally upright, even though the alternative was upright on their retina [see bottom illustration on page 121].

Why does the orientation of a figure with respect to the directional coordinates of the environment have such a profound effect on the perceived shape of the figure? The answer I propose is that perceived shape is based on a cognitive process in which the characteristics of the figure are implicitly described by the perceptual system. For example, the colored figure at the left in the top illustration on page 111 could be described as a closed figure resting on a horizontal base with a protrusion on the figure's left side and an indentation on its right side. The colored figure to the right of it, although it is identical and only rotated 90 degrees, would be described quite differently, as being symmetrical with two bumps on the bottom and with left and right sides more or less straight and identical with each other. I am not suggesting that such a description is conscious or verbal; obviously we would be aware of the descriptive process if it were either. Furthermore, animals and infants who are nonverbal perceive shape much as we do. I am proposing that a process analogous to such a description does take place and that it is not only based on the internal geometry of a figure but also takes into account the location of the figure's top, bottom and sides. In such a description orienta-

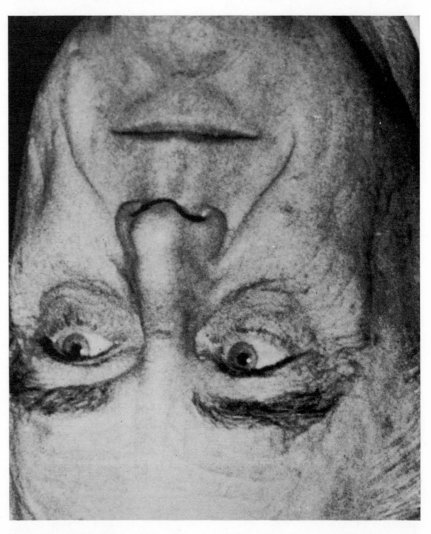

INVERTED PHOTOGRAPH of a famous American demonstrates how difficult it is to recognize a familiar face when it is presented upside down. Even after one succeeds in identifying the inverted face as that of Franklin D. Roosevelt, it continues to look strange.

orientation, say 45 or 90 degrees. Interestingly enough, inversions or rotations of 180 degrees often have only a slight effect on perceived shape, perhaps because such changes will usually not alter perceived symmetry or the perceived orientation of the long axis of the figure.

There is one kind of orientation change that has virtually no effect on perceived shape: a mirror-image reversal. This is particularly true for the novel figures we used in our experiments. How can this be explained? It seems that although the "sides" of visual space are essentially interchangeable, the up-and-down directions in the environment are not. "Up" and "down" are distinctly different directions in the world we live in. Thus a figure can be said to have three main perceptual boundaries: top, bottom and sides. As a result the description of a figure will not be much affected by whether a certain feature is on the left side or the right. Young children and animals have great difficulty learning to discriminate between a figure and its mirror image, but they can easily distinguish between a figure and its inverted counterpart.

Related to this analysis is a fact observed by Mach and tested by Erich Goldmeier: A figure that is symmetrical around one axis will generally appear to be symmetrical only if that axis is vertical. Robin Leaman and I have demonstrated that it is the perceived vertical axis of the figure and not the vertical axis of the figure's retinal image that produces this effect. An observer who tilts his head will continue to perceive a figure as being symmetrical if that figure is symmetrical around an environmental vertical axis. This suggests that perceived symmetry results only when the two equivalent halves of a figure are located on the two equivalent sides of perceptual space.

If, as I have suggested, the description of a figure is based on the location of its top, bottom and sides, the question arises: How are these directions assigned in a figure? One might suppose that the top of a figure is ordinarily the area uppermost in relation to the ceiling, the sky or the top of a page. In a dark room an observer may have to rely on his sense of gravity to inform him which way is up.

Numerous experiments by psychologists have confirmed that there are indeed two major sources of information for perceiving the vertical and the horizontal: gravity (as it is sensed by the vestibular apparatus in the inner ear, by the pressure of the ground on the body and by feedback from the muscles)

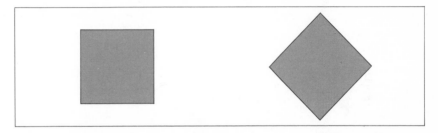

INVERTED WORDS are difficult to read when they are set in type, and words written in longhand are virtually impossible to decipher. The difficulty applies to one's own inverted handwriting in spite of a lifetime of experience reading it in the normal upright orientation.

tion is therefore a major factor in the shape that is finally perceived.

From experiments I have done in collaboration with Phyllis Olshansky it appears that certain shifts in orientation have a marked effect on perceived shape. In particular, creating symmetry around a vertical axis where no symmetry had existed before (or vice versa), shifting the long axis from vertical to horizontal (or vice versa) and changing the bottom of a figure from a broad horizontal base to a pointed angle (or vice versa) seemed to have a strong effect on perceived shape. Such changes of shape can result from only a moderate angular change of

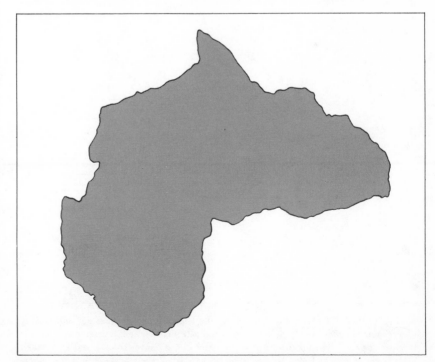

SQUARE AND DIAMOND are two familiar shapes. The two figures shown here are identical; their appearance is so different, however, that we call one a square and the other a diamond. With the diamond the angles do not spontaneously appear as right angles.

"UNFAMILIAR" SHAPE shown here becomes a familiar shape when it is rotated clockwise 90 degrees. In a classroom experiment, when the rotated figure was drawn on the blackboard, it was not recognized as an outline of the continent of Africa until the teacher told the class at the end of the lecture that the figure was rotated out of its customary orientation.

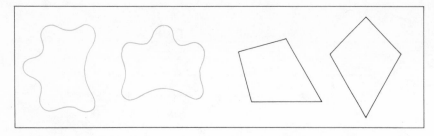

NOVEL OR UNFAMILIAR FIGURES look different in different orientations, provided that we view them naïvely and do not mentally rotate them. The reason may be the way in which a figure is "described" by the perceptual system. The colored figure at left could be described as a closed shape resting on a horizontal base with a protrusion on its left side and an indentation on its right side. The colored figure adjacent to it, although identical, would be described as a symmetrical shape resting on a curved base with a protrusion at the top. The first black figure could be described as a quadrilateral resting on a side. The black figure at right would be described as a diamondlike shape standing on end.

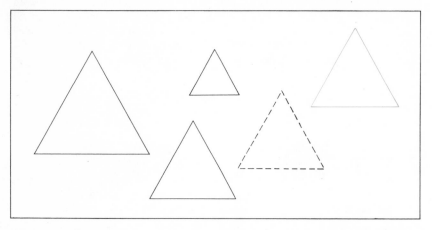

ALTERATION IN SIZE, color or type of contour does not change the perceived shape of a triangle. Even varying the location of the triangle's retinal image (by looking out of the corner of your eyes or fixating on different points) does not change perceived shape.

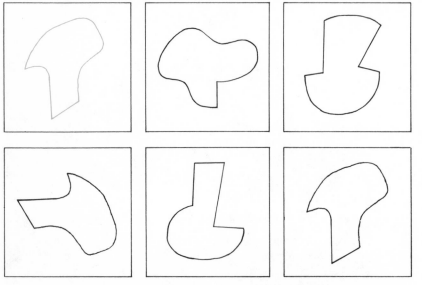

ROTATION OF RETINAL IMAGE by tilting the head 90 degrees does not appreciably affect recognition of a novel figure (color). Subjects first viewed several novel targets while sitting upright. Then they were shown a series of test figures (black) and were asked to identify those they had seen before. Some subjects tilted their head 90 degrees; others viewed the test figures with their head upright. Tilted-head subjects failed to recognize figures that were retinally "upright" (for example figure at bottom left) about as much as upright viewers did (to whom such figures were not retinally upright). Tilted-head subjects recognized environmentally upright figures (bottom right) as often as upright viewers did.

and information from the scene itself. We have been able to demonstrate that either can affect the perceived shape of a figure. A luminous figure in a dark room will not be recognized readily when it is rotated to a new orientation even if the observer is tilted by exactly the same amount. Here the only source of information about directions in space is gravity. In a lighted room an observer will often fail to recognize a figure when he and the figure are upright but the room is tilted. The tilted room creates a strong impression of where the up-down axis should be, and this leads to an incorrect attribution of the top and bottom of the figure [see "The Perception of the Upright," [by Herman A. Witkin; SCIENTIFIC AMERICAN Offprint 410].

Merely informing an observer that a figure is tilted will often enable him to perceive the figure correctly. This may explain why some readers will not perceive certain of the rotated figures shown here as being strange or different. The converse situation, misinforming an observer about the figures, produces impressive results. If a subject is told that the top of a figure he is about to see is somewhere other than in the region uppermost in the environment, he is likely not to recognize the figure when it is presented with the orientation in which he first saw it. The figure is not disoriented and the observer incorrectly assigns the directions top, bottom and sides on the basis of instructions.

Since such knowledge about orientation will enable the observer to shift the directions he assigns to a figure, and since it is this assignment that affects the perception of shape, it is absolutely essential to employ naïve subjects in perception experiments involving orientation. That is, the subject must not realize that the experiment is concerned with figural orientation, so that he does not examine the figures with the intent of finding the regions that had been top, bottom and sides in previous viewings of it. There are, however, some figures that seem to have intrinsic orientation in that regardless of how they are presented a certain region will be perceived as the top [see top illustration on next page]. It is therefore difficult or impossible to adversely affect the recognition of such figures by disorienting them.

In the absence of other clues a subject will assign top-bottom coordinates according to his subjective or egocentric reference system. Consider a figure drawn on a circular sheet of paper that is lying on the ground. Neither gravity nor visual clues indicate where the top and bottom are. Nevertheless, an observer will assign a top to that region of the figure which is uppermost with respect to his egocentric coordinate reference system. The vertical axis of the figure is seen as being aligned with the long axis of the observer's head and body. The upward direction corresponds to the position of his head. We have been able to demonstrate that such assignment of direction has the same effect on the recognition that other bases of assigning direction do. A figure first seen in one orientation on the circular sheet will generally not be recognized if its egocentric orientation is altered.

Now we come to an observation that seems to be at variance with much of what I have described. When a person lies on his side in bed to read, he does not hold the book upright (in the environmental sense) but tilts it. If the book is not tilted, the retinal image is disoriented and reading is quite difficult. Similarly, if a reader views printed matter or photographs of faces that are environmentally upright with his head between his legs, they will be just as difficult to recognize as they are when they are upside down and the viewer's head is upright. The upright pictures, however, are still perceived as being upright even when the viewer's head is inverted. Conversely, if the pictures are upside down in the environment and are viewed with the head inverted between the legs, there is no difficulty in recognizing them. Yet the observer perceives the pictures as being inverted. Therefore in these cases it is the orientation of the retinal image and not the environmental assignment of direction that seems to be responsible for recognition or failure of recognition.

Experiments with ambiguous figures conducted by Robert Thouless, G. Kanizsa and G. Tampieri support the notion that retinal orientation plays a role in recognition of a figure [see illustration on page 124]. Moreover, as George Steinfeld and I have demonstrated, the recognition of upright words and faces falls off in direct proportion to the degree of body tilt [see illustration on opposite page]. With such visual material recognition is an inverse function of the degree of disorientation of the retinal image. As we have seen, the relation between degree of disorientation and recognizability does not hold in cases where the assignment of direction has been altered. In such cases the greatest effect is not with a 180-degree change but with a 45- or 90-degree change.

The results of all these experiments

FIGURES WITH INTRINSIC ORIENTATION appear to have a natural vertical axis regardless of their physical orientation. A region at one end of the axis is perceived as top.

IMPRESSION OF SYMMETRY is spontaneous only when a figure is symmetrical around a vertical axis. Subjects were asked to indicate which of two figures (*middle and right*) was most like the target figure (*left*). The figure at right was selected most frequently, presumably because it is symmetrical around its vertical axis. If the page is tilted 90 degrees, the figure in the middle will now be selected as being more similar to the target figure. Now if the page is held vertically and the figures are viewed with the head tilted 90 degrees, the figure at right is likely to be seen as being the most similar. This suggests that it is not the symmetry around the egocentric vertical axis on the retina but rather the symmetry around the environmental axis of the figure that determines perceived symmetry.

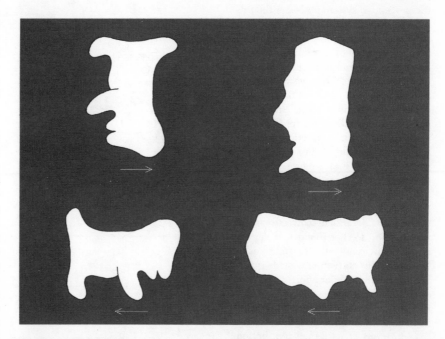

AMBIGUOUS FIGURES can be perceived in different ways depending on the orientation assigned to them. Figure at left can look like the profile of a man's head with a chef's hat (*top left*) or, when rotated 90 degrees, like a dog (*bottom left*). Figure at right can look like the profile of a bearded man's head (*top right*) or like a map of the U.S. (*bottom right*). When subjects with their head tilted 90 degrees to one side viewed these ambiguous figures (*direction of subject's head is shown by arrow*), they preferentially recognized the figure that was upright in the environment instead of the figure that was upright on the retina.

have led me to conclude that there are two distinct factors involved in the perception of disoriented figures: an assignment-of-direction factor and a retinal factor. I believe that when we view a figure with our head tilted, we automatically compensate for the tilt in much the same way that we compensate for the size of distant objects. An object at a moderate distance from us does not appear small in spite of the fact that its retinal image is much smaller than it is when the object is close by. This effect usually is explained by saying that the information supplied by the retinal image is somehow corrected by allowing for the distance of the object from us. Similarly, when a vertical luminous line in a dark room is viewed by a tilted observer, it will still look vertical or almost vertical in spite of the fact that the retinal image in the observer's eye is tilted. Thus the tilt of the body must be taken into account by the perceptual system. The tilted retinal image is then corrected, with the result that the line is perceived as being vertical. Just as the correction for size at a distance is called size constancy, so can correction for the vertical be called orientation constancy.

When we view an upright figure with our head tilted, before we have made any correction, we begin with the information provided by an image of the figure in a particular retinal orientation. The first thing that must happen is that the perceptual system processes the retinal image on the basis of an egocentrically assigned top, bottom and sides, perhaps because of a primitive sense of orientation derived from retinal orientation. For example, when we view an upright square with our head tilted, which yields a diamondlike retinal image, we may perceive a diamond for a fleeting moment before the correction goes into operation. Head orientation is then automatically taken into account to correct the perception. Thus the true top of the figure is seen to be one of the sides of the square rather than a corner. The figure is then "described" correctly as one whose sides are horizontal and vertical in the environment, in short as a "square." This correction is made quickly and usually without effort. In order to describe a figure the viewer probably must visualize or imagine it in terms of its true top, bottom and sides rather than in terms of its retinal top, bottom and sides.

If the figure is relatively simple, the correction is not too difficult to achieve. If we view an upright letter with our head tilted, we recognize it easily; it is of interest, however, that there is still

something strange about it. I believe the dual aspect of the perception of orientation is responsible for this strangeness. There is an uncorrected perception of the letter based on its retinal-egocentric orientation and a corrected perception of it based on its environmental orientation. The first perception produces an unfamiliar shape, which accounts for

the strange appearance of the letter in spite of its subsequent recognition. In our experiments many of the figures we employed were structurally speaking equivalent to letters, and in some cases we actually used letters from unfamiliar alphabets.

With a more complex figure, such as an inverted word or an upright word

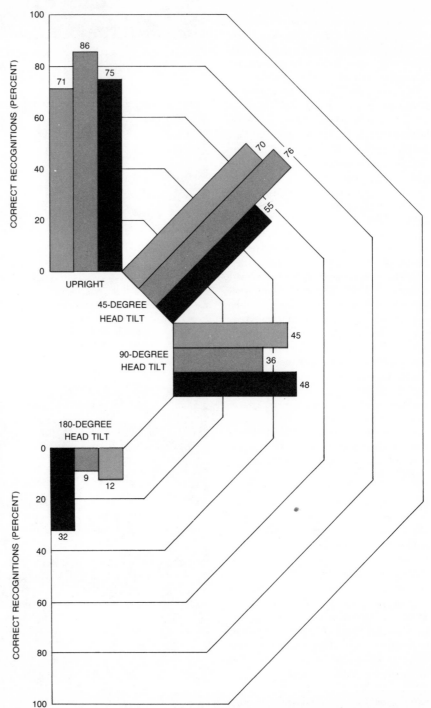

RECOGNITION OF CERTAIN KINDS OF VISUAL MATERIAL decreases almost in direct proportion to the degree of head tilt of the observer. In a series of experiments the number of correct recognitions of faces (*colored bars*), written words (*gray*) and fragmented figures (*black*) were recorded for various degrees of head tilt. Subject saw several examples of each type of test material in each of the head positions. For this visual material recognition is an inverse function of the degree of disorientation of the retinal image.

viewed by an inverted observer, the corrective mechanism may be entirely overtaxed. Each letter of the word must be corrected separately, and the corrective mechanism apparently cannot cope simultaneously with multiple components. It is true that if an observer is given enough time, an inverted word can be deciphered, but it will never look the same as it does when it is upright. While one letter is being corrected the others continue to be perceived in their uncorrected form. There is a further difficulty: letter order is crucial for word recognition, and inverting a word reverses the normal left-to-right order.

The recognition of inverted longhand writing is even more difficult. When such writing is turned upside down, many of the inverted "units" strongly resemble normal upright longhand letters. Moreover, since the letters are connected, it is difficult to tell where one letter ends and another begins. Separating the letters of the inverted word makes recognition easier. Even so, it is all too easy to confuse a *u* and an *n*. This type of confusion is also encountered with certain printed letters, namely, *b* and *q*, *d* and *p* and *n* and *u*, although not as frequently. In other words, if a figure is recognized on the basis of its upright retinal-egocentric orientation, this may tend to stabilize the perception and block the correction process. The dominance of the retinally upright faces in the illustration on the opposite page probably is an effect of just this kind.

There may be a similar overtaxing of the corrective mechanism when we view an inverted face. It may be that the face contains a number of features each of which must be properly perceived if the whole is to be recognized [see "The Recognition of Faces," by Leon D. Harmon; SCIENTIFIC AMERICAN Offprint 555]. While attention is focused on correcting one feature, say the mouth, other features remain uncorrected and continue to be perceived on the basis of the image they form on the retina. Of course, the relation of features is also important in the recognition of a face, but here too there are a great number of such relations and the corrective mechanism may again be overtaxed.

Charles C. Bebber, Douglas Blewett and I conducted an experiment to test the hypothesis that it is the presence of multiple components that creates the difficulty of correcting figures. Subjects were briefly shown a quadrilateral figure and asked to study it. They viewed the target figure with their head upright. Then they were shown a series of test

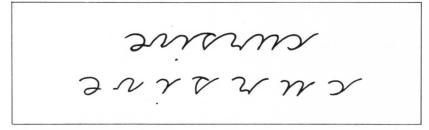

SINGLE LETTER that is tilted can be easily identified once it is realized how it is oriented. A strangeness in its appearance, however, remains because the percept arising from the uncorrected retinal image continues to exist simultaneously with the corrected percept.

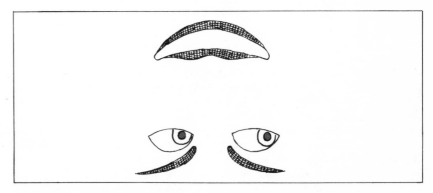

INVERTED LONGHAND WRITING is difficult to decipher because many inverted units resemble written upright letters. For example, an inverted *u* will look like an *n* and an inverted *c* like an *s*. Moreover, the connection between letters leads to uncertainty about where a letter begins and ends. Several inverted units can be grouped together and misperceived as an upright letter. Separating the inverted letters makes them easier to decipher.

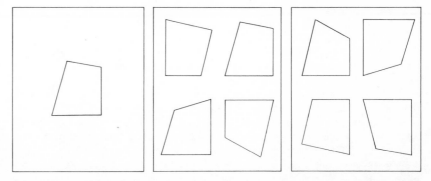

INVERTED FACIAL FEATURES are difficult to interpret because while attention is focused on correcting one feature other features remain uncorrected. For example, one might succeed in correcting the eyes shown here so that they are perceived as gazing downward and leftward, but at that very moment the mouth is uncorrected and expresses sorrow rather than pleasure. Conversely, one might correct the mouth and misperceive the eyes.

MULTIPLE ITEMS were found to have an adverse effect on recognition of even simple figures. Subjects sitting upright viewed the target (*left*). Then they were briefly shown test cards, some of which contained the target figure (*middle*) and some of which did not (*right*). The subjects were to indicate when they saw a figure that was identical with the target figure. Half of the test cards were viewed with the head upright and half with the head inverted. Recognition was poor when inverted subjects viewed the test cards. In other experiments with a single test figure head inversion did not significantly affect recognition.

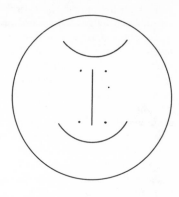

AMBIGUOUS FACES are perceived differently when their images on the retina of the observer are inverted. If you hold the illustration upright and view it from between your legs with your head inverted, the alternative faces will be perceived even though they are upside down in terms of the environment. The same effect occurs when the illustration is inverted and viewed from an upright position. Such tests provide evidence that figures such as faces are recognized on the basis of their upright retinal orientation.

cards each of which had four quadrilateral figures. The test cards were viewed for one second, and the subjects were required to indicate if the target figure was on the card.

The subjects understood that they were to respond affirmatively only when they saw a figure that was identical with the target figure both in shape and in orientation. (Some of the test figures were similar to the target figure but were rotated by 180 degrees.) Half of the test cards were seen with the subject's head upright and half with the subject's head inverted. It was assumed that the subject would not be able to correct all four test figures in the brief time that was allowed him while he was viewing them with his head down. He had to perceive just as many units in the same brief time while he was viewing them with his head upright, but he did not have to correct any of the units. We expected that target figures would often not be recognized and that incorrect figures would be mistakenly identified as the target when the subjects viewed the test cards with their head inverted.

The results bore out our prediction. When multiple components have to be corrected, retinal disorientation has an adverse effect on recognition. The observer responded to twice as many test cards correctly when he was upright than he did when he was inverted.

As I have noted, when we look at figures that are difficult to recognize when they are retinally disoriented, the difficulty increases as the degree of disorientation increases. Why this happens may also be related to the nature of the correction process. I suggested that the observer must suppress the retinally (egocentrically) upright percept and substitute a corrected percept. To do this, however, he must visualize or imagine

how the figure would look if it were rotated until it was upright with respect to himself or, what amounts to the same thing, how it would look if he rotated himself into alignment with the figure. The process of mental rotation requires visualizing the entire sequence of angular change, and therefore the greater the angular change, the greater the difficulty.

As every parent knows, children between the ages of two and five seem to be quite indifferent to how a picture is oriented. They often hold a book upside down and seem not at all disturbed by it. On the basis of such observations and the results of some early experiments, many psychologists concluded that the orientation of a figure did not enter into its recognition by young children. More recent laboratory experiments, however, do not confirm the fact that children recognize figures equally well in any orientation. They have as much difficulty as, or more difficulty than, adults in recognizing previously seen figures when the figure is shown in a new orientation. Why then do young children often spontaneously look at pictures upside down in everyday situations? Perhaps they have not yet learned to pay attention to orientation, and do not realize that their recognition would improve if they did so. When children learn to read after the age of six, they are forced to pay attention to orientation because certain letters differ only in their orientation.

In summary, the central fact we have learned about orientation is that the perceived shape of a figure is not simply a function of its internal geometry. The perceived shape is also very much a function of the up, down and side directions we assign to the figure. If there is a change in the assigned directions, the figure will take on a different per-

ceptual shape. I have speculated that the change in perceived shape is based on a new "description" of the figure by the perceptual system. The directions assigned are based on information of various kinds about where the top, bottom and sides of a figure are and usually do not depend on the retinal orientation of the image of the figure. When the image is not retinally upright, a process of correction is necessary in order to arrive at the correct description, and this correction is difficult or impossible to achieve in the case of visual material that has multiple components.

All of this implies that form perception in general is based to a much greater extent on cognitive processes than any current theory maintains. A prevailing view among psychologists and sensory physiologists is that form perception can be reduced to the perception of contours and that contour perception in turn can be reduced to abrupt differences in light intensity that cause certain neural units in the retina and brain to fire. If this is true, then perceiving form results from the specific concatenation of perceived contours. Although the work I have described does not deny the possible importance of contour detection as a basis of form perception, it does suggest that such an explanation is far from sufficient, and that the perception of form depends on certain mental processes such as description and correction. These processes in turn are necessary to account for the further step of recognition of a figure. A physically unchanged retinal image often will not lead to recognition if there has been a shift in the assigned directions. Conversely, if there has been no shift in the assigned directions, even a very different retinal image will still allow recognition.

Hallucinations

by Ronald K. Siegel
October 1977

These false perceptions, which can occur in any of the senses, turn out to be much alike from one person to another. Apparently they have their roots in excitations of the central nervous system

A motorist who drives alone at night in a state of extreme fatigue may well perceive things that are not there: people, animals, vehicles or strange forms. Such a percept is characterized as a hallucination. Although the definition of the word (which comes from the Latin *hallucinari,* meaning to prate, to dream or to wander in mind) is far from precise, one that is widely accepted in psychiatry is: "A false sensory perception in the absence of an actual external stimulus. May be induced by emotional and other factors such as drugs, alcohol and stress. May occur in any of the senses."

By this definition it is likely that everyone has had a hallucination at one time or another. Lonely explorers, isolated hunters in the Arctic and prisoners in dark cells have reported experiencing them. Some people seek out the experience by taking hallucinogenic drugs. Under the right social circumstances the perceptions may be regarded as valid. Joan of Arc became a saint because of her visions, and the flashes of light perceived by the astronauts were taken quite seriously. (They were actually caused by cosmic rays.) On the other hand, negative evaluations are applied to similar perceptions by inmates of correctional institutions. All such reports, however, are necessarily subjective. When one has a hallucination, one does so alone, in the privacy of one's mind.

Do the hallucinations of one person have anything in common with those of another? My colleagues and I in the Neuropsychiatric Institute of the University of California at Los Angeles have attempted to answer the question by means of experiment. We find that hallucinations do have a great deal in common. Moreover, the experiments point to underlying mechanisms in the central nervous system as the source of a universal phenomenology of hallucinations.

One of the earliest classifications of hallucinations was offered in 1853 by Brierre de Boismont of France. He found that hallucinations occurring in states of insanity, delirium tremens, drug intoxication, nervous disorders, nightmares, dreams, ecstasies and fevers were all characterized by excitation and the production of images from memory and the imagination. His countryman Jacques Moreau described hallucinations as being similar to dreams in which imagined visual, auditory and tactile stimuli seem to be real. Foretelling what future neurophysiological research would reveal, he maintained that hallucinations resulted from excitation of the brain. Moreau's technique, which he described in 1845, was to take hashish, which put him in a hallucinatory state while leaving him able to report his experiences. (Moreau also tried to persuade his medical colleagues and friends to take hashish. His colleagues were hesitant because they did not view the taking of hashish as an acceptable form of objective experimentation. The Bohemian artists and writers of 19th-century Paris were more receptive. One of them, the novelist Théophile Gautier, went on to organize the Club des Haschichins, whose members included Balzac, Baudelaire, the younger Dumas and Victor Hugo. Some of the club members' writings testify to the richness of the imagery induced by hashish.)

In Germany and the U.S. early students of hallucinations followed a similar course of self-experimentation and focused mainly on visual hallucinations. Using mescaline, a hallucinogenic alkaloid derived from the peyote cactus *Lophophora williamsii,* Heinrich Klüver began a series of investigations at the University of Chicago in 1926. He reported that mescaline-induced imagery could be observed with the eyes either closed or open and that with the eyes open it was impossible to look at a blank wall without seeing it as being covered with various forms.

Among these forms Klüver found four constant types. One he described with terms such as grating, lattice, fretwork, filigree, honeycomb and chessboard. A second type resembled cobwebs. A third was described with terms such as tunnel, funnel, alley, cone and vessel. The fourth type consisted of spirals. The form constants were further characterized by varied and saturated colors, intense brightness and symmetrical configurations. The visions seemed to be located at reading distance. They varied greatly in apparent size. In general they could not be consciously controlled.

Klüver made the crucial observation that these form constants appear in a wide variety of hallucinatory conditions. He listed a number of the conditions, and other investigators have added to his list, which now includes falling asleep, waking up, insulin hypoglycemia, the delirium of fever, epilepsy, psychotic episodes, advanced syphilis, sensory deprivation, photostimulation, electrical stimulation, crystal gazing, migraine headaches, dizziness and of course a variety of drug intoxications.

Most of the drugs that give rise to such imagery are classifed as hallucinogens. Other drugs and substances can give rise to similar effects, however, and so most psychoactive compounds (to the extent that they cause the mind or the attention to wander) can be regarded as hallucinogens. In this category are alcohol, carbon dioxide, cocaine, cortisol, digitalis, scopolamine and even tobacco with a high concentration of nicotine.

The form constants appear in the first of two stages of drug-induced imagery. The images of the second stage, which are more complex but can incorporate the simple constants, include landscapes, faces and familiar objects and places. The complex images, which are perhaps the most dramatic aspect of the hallucinatory experience, are usually regarded as an activation of images already recorded in the memory.

One would expect the forms and scenes of complex imagery to be almost infinitely diverse. Actually constants appear even at this stage. Indeed, a review of more than 500 hallucinations induced by lysergic acid diethylamide (LSD) revealed that whereas between 62 and 72 percent of the subjects experienced the simple form constants, more than 79 percent reported quite similar complex images. They included religious symbols and images (72 percent) and images of small animals and human beings (49 percent), most of them friendly and many in the nature of cartoons and caricatures.

Most of the investigators and the subjects did not describe the complex imagery in detail. Moreover, before Klüver's classic work little was said about the geometry of even simple hallucinatory images. Klüver attributed this omission to the novelty of the visions, expressing the view that many hallucinating people are so overwhelmed by the color or brightness of the images that they do not articulate the basic forms. It was this inarticulateness that challenged Klüver to describe the simple first stage of hallucinatory imagery. The apparent complexity of the second-stage images challenged us to do the same for them. We believed the study of such phenomena might point to a common visual imagery underlying hallucinations and so might help us understand the origin of these percepts and related ones.

Our first experiments were designed to see if the hallucinatory phenomena I have described appeared when hallucinations were induced in untrained subjects by drugs. Each subject was given either a standard dose of a hallucinogen (usually marihuana or its active principle, tetrahydrocannabinol) or an inactive placebo. (The subject did not know which substance he was receiving.) He was then asked to lie on a bed in a light-proof and soundproof chamber and to report his experiences. We recorded the reports on tape and analyzed them according to the frequency of different

HALLUCINATORY SHAPES AND COLORS are represented in this yarn painting made by a member of the Huichol Indian group in Mexico. The picture was made to show visions of the kind experienced in hallucination brought on by taking peyote. The Indian at the left is carrying a basket of freshly harvested peyote and viewing a vision that is exploding with color and streaks and flashes of light. The peyote cactus is represented at the right. The picture was made by putting beeswax on wood and then pressing yarn into the beeswax.

forms, colors, movements and complex images.

The results showed that normal imagery (that is, imagery not induced by drugs) is characterized by amorphous black-and-white forms (sometimes including lines and curves) that move about randomly in the visual field. Anyone who closes his eyes or goes into a dark room is likely to experience a baseline imagery of this kind. Indeed, one can induce similar imagery, some of it brightly colored and geometric, by gently rubbing one's closed eyelids.

With hallucinogenic drugs, however, the number of images reported by the subjects rose sharply. The consensus was that the imagery resembled what one would see in a motion picture or a slide show. A number of the subjects had difficulty in describing the imagery, but they agreed that there were many geometric forms in it. The imagery was characterized by a bright light in the center of the field of vision that obscured details but allowed images on the periphery to be observed.

The location of this point of light created a tunnel-like perspective. The subjects reported viewing much of their imagery in relation to a tunnel. According to their reports, the images tended to pulsate, moving toward the center of the tunnel or away from the bright light and sometimes moving in both directions.

When the images appeared in color, all colors were reported, although the incidence of reports that the color was red increased as the dosage of the drug increased. Geometric forms frequently combined, duplicated and superimposed. At times the flow of imagery was so rapid that most subjects found it difficult to maintain a running commentary.

The geometric forms were soon replaced by complex imagery. The complex images reported included recognizable scenes, people and objects, many in cartoon or caricature form, with some degree of depth and symmetry. The images were often projected against a background of geometric forms.

In listening to these reports we encountered certain difficulties. The subjects differed widely in their choice of words. Moreover, the reports were riddled with idiosyncratic experiences. We therefore decided to facilitate the ease and accuracy of reporting by training our subjects to use a standard descriptive code.

Efforts along this line had previously been made at Harvard University by the psychologists Ogden R. Lindsley and Timothy Leary. They employed the

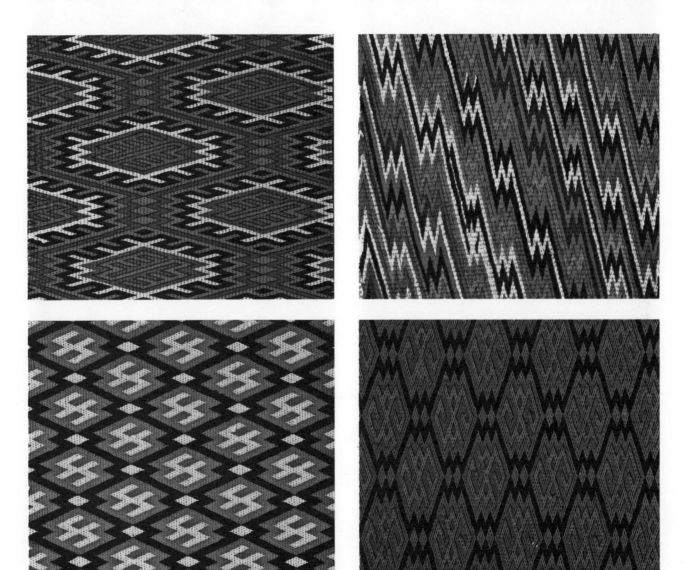

LATTICE FORMS, one of several form constants reported during drug-induced hallucinations, are depicted in four samples of Huichol Indian embroidery. The patterns illustrate designs commonly found in the hallucinatory visions induced by peyote. Some pictures made by schizophrenics exhibit a similar preoccupation with geometric designs, which are often distorted and repeated in symmetrical patterns.

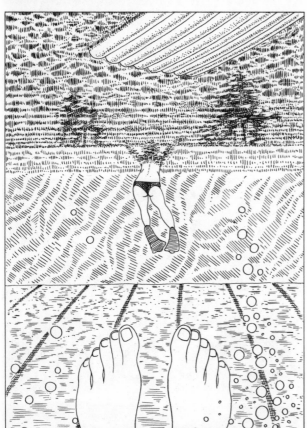

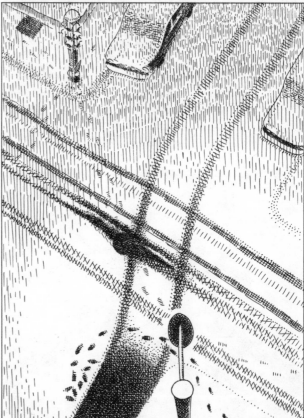

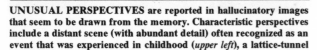

UNUSUAL PERSPECTIVES are reported in hallucinatory images that seem to be drawn from the memory. Characteristic perspectives include a distant scene (with abundant detail) often recognized as an event that was experienced in childhood (*upper left*), a lattice-tunnel pattern with complex memory images at the periphery (*upper right*), a scene viewed as if the subject were under water, looking up toward and through the surface (*lower left*) and an aerial perspective (*lower right*), which may be accompanied by sensations of floating and flying.

operant key press as a reporting device; each key was equated with the occurrence of a subjective state. A hallucinating subject who wanted to report that he "saw" or "heard" something would press a given key for each condition. Lindsley and his colleagues had already demonstrated that the key-pressing technique provided a continuous and objective method for the study of gross behavior in altered states of consciousness.

Nevertheless, a method for obtaining detailed information on subjective phenomena was not developed until Lindsley and Leary devised the "experiential typewriter." This apparatus consisted of a 20-key typewriter connected to a recording instrument. The keys served to code various subjective states, including modes of perception, internal images, external images, images seen with the eyes closed and with the eyes open, hallucinations, colors and so on. Training consisted of having the subjects memorize the categories and the corresponding keys. When a subject felt a bodily sensation such as "pain," he pressed a specific key to signify the event. A hallucination with oscillating colors could be signified by pressing a different key.

In tests with the hallucinogens LSD and dimethyltryptamine Leary found that the muscular discoordination associated with those drugs interfered with pressing the keys. The problem could have been avoided with lower doses, and the key press could have been replaced by a verbal report. (Leary had found that verbal reporting was not disrupted by the drugs.) Therefore we decided to develop a verbal code for reporting drug-induced hallucinations.

On the basis of the previous results we constructed a list of eight forms (random, line, curve, web, lattice, tunnel, spiral and kaleidoscope), eight colors (black, violet, blue, green, yellow, orange, red and white) and eight patterns of movement (aimless, vertical, horizontal, oblique, explosive, concentric, rotational and pulsating) for subjects to employ in describing visual imagery. We then selected a group of subjects and trained them with slides illustrating the different categories. For example, in training related to the tunnel form we showed hundreds of different slides of tunnels so that the subjects would have a broad concept of the tunnel form. In this way new instances of the form, which might not have been perceived before, could be appropriately classified on the basis of common features. The subjects were trained to recognize all three categories (form, color and movement) in displays projected for eight milliseconds, with a one-second pause between displays. Our aim in making the displays brief was to simulate the rapid changes of imagery in hallucinations.

WHITE LIGHT seen during the early stages of intoxication with a hallucinogenic drug is portrayed. The visual imagery is reported to explode from the center to the periphery. Pattern appears initially in black and white, but bright colors may develop as the experience progresses.

SPIRAL TUNNEL is another of the early form constants in drug-induced hallucination. The main patterns of movement accompanying the form are reported as pulsation and rotation.

LATTICE-TUNNEL FORM CONSTANT is depicted in a painting made to show a pattern that is often reported during the early stages of intoxication from marihuana and tetrahydrocannabinol (the active principle of marihuana). It is possible that the blue color is related to the initial lowering of the body temperature and to the absorption of blue light by hemoglobin in "floater" cells in the retina. Colors tend to become red with time and with increasing dosage.

All the subjects, including some who were untrained so that we could see if their reports of visual experiences were comparable to those of the trained subjects, then participated in a series of weekly test sessions in each of which they received either a hallucinogen, a stimulant, a depressant or a placebo. No subject knew what he was receiving. Both high and low doses were tested. The subjects were tested in the light-proof chamber I have mentioned. All the subjects were instructed to report what they "saw" with their eyes open, but the trained subjects were restricted to the descriptive code. In the middle of the session the trained subjects were tested with slides of real images to ensure that the drugs and dosages were not impairing the skills they had acquired in training. (We found no indication of impairment.)

The results were intriguing. We found that the trained subjects could keep abreast of the rapid flow of imagery and could readily classify most of the images into the categories of the reporting code. These subjects averaged 20 reports per minute; the untrained subjects reported only about five times per minute. (The duration of a typical session was six hours.)

The imagery associated with placebos, the stimulant *d*-amphetamine and the depressant phenobarbital was described as black-and-white random forms moving about aimlessly. The hallucinogens tetrahydrocannabinol, psilocybin, LSD and mescaline induced dramatic changes. Here the forms became less random and more organized and geometric as the experience progressed. The black-and-white images began to take on blue hues, and movement became more organized and pulsating. At 30 minutes after the administration of the drug the subjects reported a significant increase in lattice and tunnel forms and a slight increase in kaleidoscopic forms. By 90 and 120 minutes most forms were lattice-tunnels. Concomitantly the colors shifted to red, orange and yellow. Movement continued to be pulsating but became more organized, with explosive and rotational patterns.

Complex imagery usually did not appear until well after the shift to the lat-tice-tunnel forms was reported. Thereafter complex forms constituted from 43 to 75 percent of the forms reported by trained subjects who had received hallucinogens. The complex images first appeared in the reports as overlying the lattice-tunnels and situated on the periphery of those images.

Common complex images included childhood memories and scenes associated with strong emotional experiences that the subjects had undergone. These hallucinatory images were more than pictorial replicas; many of them were elaborated and embellished into fantastic scenes. This constructive aspect of imagery can be illustrated by a simple exercise. Recall the last time you went swimming in the ocean. Now ask yourself if this memory includes a picture of yourself running along the beach or moving about in the water. Such a picture is obviously fictitious, since you could not have been looking at yourself, but images in the memory often include fleeting pictures of this kind. Our subjects often reported equally improbable images, such as aerial perspectives and underwater views.

It has not been established where such constructions arise, but contributions are probably made in the encoding, storage and retrieval stages of the memory process. Much of the content of complex imagery can also be influenced by environmental stimuli. Since our subjects were in an isolated chamber, most of their images came from their memory. Occasionally, however, we escorted the subjects (at the peak of the hallucinatory experience) to a botanical garden. There they wore goggles through which they could not see, lay on the grass and reported what they "saw" with their eyes open. At these times the imagery from memory was reduced significantly, and reports of birds, airplanes, trees and so on increased. In other experiments we have shaped and guided drug-induced imagery by giving the subjects suggestive words or music. Nevertheless, even these primed complex images were usually reported as appearing in lattice-tunnel arrangements and moving in explosive or rotational configurations.

During the peak hallucinatory periods the subjects frequently described themselves as having become part of the imagery. At such times they stopped using similes in their reports and asserted that the images were real. This point marked the transition from pseudohallucination to true hallucination. Highly creative and fantastic combinations of imagery were reported, sometimes with as many as 10 changes of image per second. The subjects frequently reported feeling dissociated from their bodies.

The remarkable constancies of drug-induced hallucinations lead naturally to an inquiry into how universal they may be. Some of them are strikingly similar to the primordial or archetypal forms (such as the mandala, the mystic symbol of the universe employed in Hinduism and Buddhism as an aid to meditation) that the psychoanalyst C. G. Jung described as part of man's collective unconscious. Moreover, as many anthropologists have noted, the hallucinogen-inspired art of many primitive peoples often contains constants of form, color and movement.

We examined this phenomenon by traveling to the Sierra Madre of Mexico to study a group of Huichol Indians who take peyote. They have remained relatively isolated since Aztec times. We interviewed them during their peyote ceremonies, eliciting reports on their visual imagery. The images proved to be virtually identical to the symmetrical, repeat-

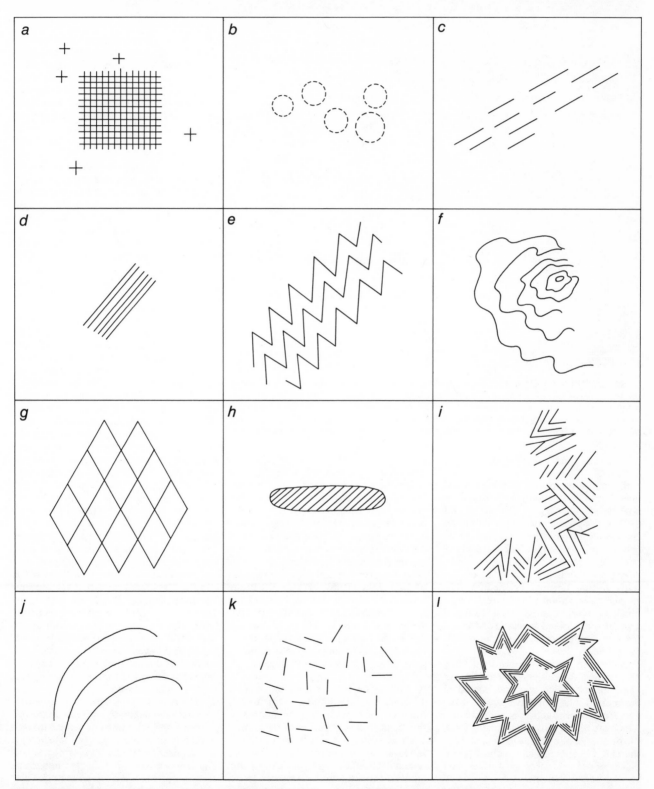

VISUAL HALLUCINATIONS seen during controlled intoxication with cocaine were drawn by people who served as subjects in the author's experiments. The patterns were usually seen with the eyes open in a dark room; they appeared as transitory black-and-white spots in the periphery of the visual field. Patterns *c, e, f, g, i, k* and *l* are virtually identical to the patterns seen in the hallucinations accompanying migraine attacks. Indeed, pattern *l* is the "fortification illusion" that is frequently reported by people who are suffering migraine headaches.

```
        It looks like several different whirlpools, with lots of spirals divided

up into checks.  It's pretty black.  There's purple and green glowing areas in the

middle of the spirals, kind of clouds around.  There are lines going from top to

bottom, kind of a grid, but the lines squiggle around.  There's odd shapes, but still

lots of right angles in them.  Seems really bright....  There's like an explosion,

yellow in the middle, like a volcano gushing out lava, yellow, glowing.  There's a

black square with yellow light coming behind it.  There's a regular pattern

superimposed on everything, lots of curlicues, with dots in the middle.  Lot of

little paisley things that fill up the spaces between the patterns of triangles,

squares, or crown-shaped things.  And there's a little white star that floats around

the picture and sometimes goes behind what's on the screen and illuminates from behind.


        Now there's a kind of landscape.  Very flat, flat country.  The picture is

very narrow.  In the middle part a tree at the left and then flat with green grass

and blue sky above.  There are orange dots, oranges hanging all over, in the sky, on

the tree, on the ground.  A bicycle! Oh, my!  It's headed down, not horizontal, like

someone's holding it up on end....  There's a checkerboard superimposed on everything,

like the flags they wave at the races.


        I can see the street out there....  Well, it's old--golly--interesting!  It's

like in the forties, I guess, or maybe the fifties....  And there are people riding

their bicycles, and there are, like, boys, in plaid vests and those funny kind of

hats....  I was at the side walking on the sidewalk, so it wasn't like I was in the

middle of the street and (laughter) you can't laugh very long in the middle of the

street in the city, so that image kind of went away (laughter).
```

PARTIAL TRANSCRIPT of the remarks made by a subject who had taken 20 milligrams of the hallucinogen psilocybin shows an increasing complexity of imagery. The first paragraph is from an initial segment of the experience, which began about 25 minutes after the subject had taken the drug. The simple geometric forms are supplemented several minutes later (*second paragraph*) by complex images. They are later replaced (*third paragraph*) by dreamlike scenes.

ing patterns found in Huichol weaving and art.

In attempting to explain the origin of the simple hallucinatory constants a number of investigators have described them as the product of events within the eye resulting from the visualization of certain structures when light strikes the eye in a particular way. For example, horizontal bands are said to be due to folds in the corneal epithelium that change with motion of the eyelid, and a black lacework seen against a red background is attributed to shadows cast on the rods and cones by blood vessels of the retina.

Since such causes require light, they cannot have figured prominently in our experiments, which were conducted in darkness. Light is not necessary, however, for the production of phosphenes, which are visual sensations arising from the discharge of neurons in structures of the eye. Phosphenes can include spots, disks, concentric arcs or circles and checkerboard patterns.

The constants are also highly similar to the patterns found in hallucinations accompanying migraine attacks. Migraine patterns include lines, grids, concentric circles and the "fortification illusion," which is a horseshoe-shaped area consisting of bright zigzag lines appearing at an expanding outer edge. Migraine hallucinations can also be brightly colored and explosive and can include complex images of people and objects. The most plausible explanation of migraine phenomena is that they reflect the electrical excitation of organized groups of cells in the visual cortex of the brain. Indeed, the work of Wilder Penfield and his colleagues at McGill University has shown that the direct electrical stimulation of the visual cortex or the temporal lobes gives rise to moving colored lights, geometric forms, stars and lines.

Most of the investigators undertaking to explain complex hallucinatory imagery have described the images as the result of an excitation of the central nervous system. As early as 1845 Moreau was maintaining that hallucinations resulted from cerebral excitation that enabled thoughts and memories to become transformed into sensory impressions. Recent electrophysiological research has confirmed that hallucinations are directly related to states of excita-tion and arousal of the central nervous system, which are coupled with a functional disorganization of the part of the brain that regulates incoming stimuli. Behaviorally the result is an impairment of the discrimination normally based on external stimuli and a preoccupation with internal imagery.

This hallucinatory process has been described by such terms as "memory flashback" and "involuntary reminiscence." Certain psychoanalysts have postulated that it is the result of a general regression to primitive or childlike thinking, coupled with the emergence of repressed information and memories. Students of psychedelic phenomena have postulated that hallucinogens release normally suppressed information and memories.

Perhaps the most integrated explanation has been provided by the perceptual-release theory of hallucinations, which was formulated by the British neurologist Hughlings Jackson in 1931. As recently brought up to date by Louis Jolyon West of UCLA, the hypothesis assumes that normal memories are suppressed by a mechanism that acts as a gate to the flow of information from the outside. An input of new information inhibits the emergence and awareness of previous perceptions and processed information. If the input is decreased or impaired while awareness remains, such perceptions are released and may be dynamically organized and experienced as hallucinations, dreams or fantasies.

West has offered an analogy to illustrate the process. Picture a man in his living room, standing at a closed window opposite his fireplace and looking out at the sunset. He is absorbed by the view of the outside world and does not visualize the interior of the room. As darkness falls outside, however, the images of the objects in the room behind him can be seen reflected dimly in the window. With the deepening of darkness the fire in the fireplace illuminates the room, and the man now sees a vivid reflection of the room, which appears to be outside the window. As the analogy is applied to the perceptual-release hypothesis, the daylight (the sensory input) is reduced while the interior illumination (the general level of arousal of the central nervous system) remains bright, so that images originating within the rooms of the brain may be perceived as though they came from outside the windows of the senses.

Through such research and hypotheses we have begun to understand the nature of hallucinations as stored images in the brain. Like a mirage that shows a magnificent city, the images of hallucinations are actually reflected images of real objects located elsewhere. The city is no less intriguing and no less worthy of study because it is not where we think it is. Further experiments will help localize it.

14

Sources of Ambiguity in the Prints of Maurits C. Escher

by Marianne L. Teuber
July 1974

The fascinating graphic inventions of the late Dutch artist reflect a strong mathematical and crystallographic influence. Their original inspiration, however, came from experiments on visual perception

If ambiguity is a sign of our time, the late Dutch graphic artist Maurits C. Escher managed to represent it in striking visual terms. In Escher's art there is the ambiguity of figure and ground; the ambiguity of two and three dimensions on the flat surface; the ambiguity of the reversible cube; the ambiguous limits of the infinitely small and the infinitely large. In his prints visual ambiguity goes hand in hand with ambiguity of meaning. Good and evil are contemplated in the figure-ground reversal of black devils and white angels. Day changes into night; sky becomes water; fish metamorphose into fowl.

Escher's regular subdivisions of the surface have been compared to the packed periodic structures of crystals and to the mathematical transformations of topology and non-Euclidean geometry [see "Mathematical Games," SCIENTIFIC AMERICAN, April, 1961, and April, 1966]. The original inspiration for his unusual ambiguous patterns, however, can be traced to contemporary sources more familiar to the student of psychology and visual perception. Psychological studies of the relation of figure and ground—in turn encouraged by the positive and negative forms of Art Nouveau—were for Escher the primary stimulus. Only after he had mastered reversible figure-ground constructions of his own invention did he recognize their similarity to certain principles of crystallography, and his interest in mathematics was aroused.

Figure-ground designs appear at an early stage in Escher's work—as early as 1921, when he was only 23 years old. It was not until the late 1930's, however, when Escher "rediscovered" the style that made him famous, that the figure-ground ambiguity clearly became the dominant feature of his art. The well-known woodcuts *Development I, Day and Night* and *Sky and Water I*, among others, date from this period.

From Escher's own commentary on these prints in *The Graphic Work of M. C. Escher* one must conclude that he knew the pertinent psychological literature. In particular he seems to have been familiar with the early experiments on figure and ground by the Danish psychologist Edgar Rubin, with Kurt Koffka's 1935 book *Principles of Gestalt Psychology*, where Rubin's results are summarized, and with the studies of Molly R. Harrower, a student of Koffka's. Patterns related to crystallography and geometry turn out to be a later development.

One of Rubin's best-known patterns, presented in his 1915 monograph dealing with visually perceived form as a function of the relation of figure to ground, can be seen either as a vase in the center or as two profiles facing each other [*see illustration at left*]. When the profiles are seen, the vase becomes ground, and vice versa. It is impossible, as Rubin points out, to see vase and profiles simultaneously as figures.

Rubin's book was published in a German translation in Copenhagen in 1921. The following year, when the young Escher was completing his training at the School of Architecture and Ornamental Design in Haarlem, he carved a

 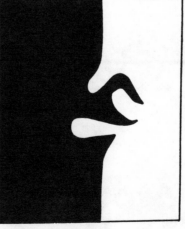

REVERSIBLE PATTERNS published originally in 1915 by the Danish psychologist Edgar Rubin in a study of the role of the figure-ground relation in visual perception were presumably familiar to Escher at an early stage. The pattern at left can be seen either as a vase in the center or as two profiles facing each other. The more abstract pattern at right can be seen either as a black figure against a white background or vice versa. In each case it is impossible, said Rubin, to see both the black and the white areas simultaneously as figures.

134

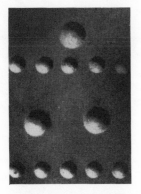 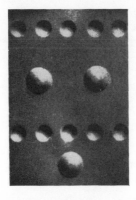 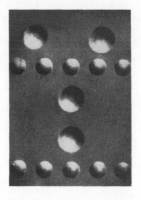 

EXPERIMENTAL PATTERNS designed to study the crater illusion were published by the Finnish psychologist Kai von Fieandt in 1938. The patterns test the changes in depth perception from concave to convex, depending on the direction of the illumination.

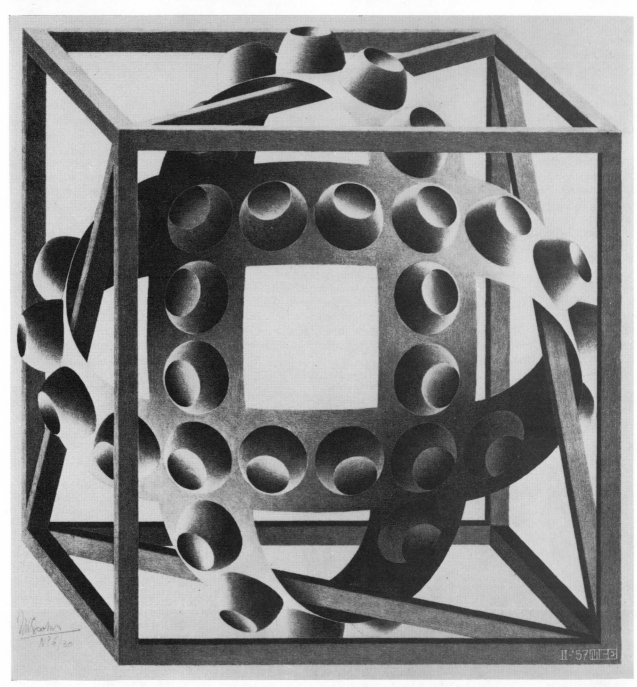

"CUBE WITH MAGIC RIBBONS," a 1957 Escher lithograph in the Roosevelt collection at the National Gallery, uses strips of small "buttonlike protuberances" just like those illustrated in the von Fieandt study to explore "inversions" of concave and convex.

woodcut called *Eight Heads* [*see illustration below*]. Each head fills exactly the space left between neighboring heads and acts alternately as figure and ground, depending on the viewer's attitude. Escher is quite explicit about his purpose. In *The Graphic Work of M. C. Escher* the artist himself provides an introduction and comments on his prints. These explanations reflect the technical language of his scientific sources. The wording here leaves no doubt about the

specific psychological studies that contributed to the formation of his unique style.

One can easily discern the link with Rubin's experiments when Escher classifies *Eight Heads* and his later reversible patterns of fish and bird in *Sky and Water I* or *Day and Night* under the heading "The Function of Figures as a Background." Escher comments: "Our eyes are accustomed to fixing on a specific object. The moment this happens every-

thing round about becomes reduced to background." This description is in keeping with Rubin's analysis of his ambiguous vase-profile pattern.

Whereas Escher insisted on meaningful, if fantastic, creatures for his basic reversible units, Rubin, in his attempt to find general principles of figure formation, actually preferred more abstract designs. In his 1915 book Rubin even cites Wassily Kandinsky's contemporary abstract paintings as good examples of the

"EIGHT HEADS," a woodcut carved by Escher in 1922, the year he finished his training at the School of Architecture and Ornamental Design at Haarlem in the Netherlands, bears a strong resemblance to Rubin's diagrams. Each of the four male and four female heads can act alternately as figure or ground. *Eight Heads* was Escher's first attempt at an infinitely repeating subdivision of a plane surface. This reproduction is from a print in the Escher Foundation collection in the Haags Gemeentemuseum at The Hague.

MAJOLICA TILES at the Alhambra in Spain were sketched by Escher during a trip in 1936. The internal symmetry and the am-biguous contours of the Moorish designs appear to have helped revive Escher's early fascination with the figure-ground problem.

equivalence of color fields. By means of abstract test patterns Rubin hoped to isolate basic characteristics of form perception without the distractions caused by figurative images. As he points out, it is always the form with the greater realistic or emotional appeal that tends to attract our attention; in the vase-profile pattern, for instance, the profiles will win out when the reversals are observed over prolonged periods.

To avoid these pitfalls Rubin derived the main principles of what makes for figure and what for ground from his abstract patterns. According to Rubin, one usually sees the smaller enclosed form as figure by contrast with the larger surrounding expanse of the ground. The figure has "solid-object quality," whereas the ground takes on a "film quality." The figure protrudes; the ground recedes and stretches behind the figure. The contour is seen as belonging to the figure and not to the ground.

In ambiguous patterns, however, the one-sided function of the contour is challenged. Rubin's analysis of contours can be recognized in Escher's description of the difficulties he encountered in drawing his ambiguous creatures. In discussing the borderline between two adjacent shapes having a double function Escher notes that "the act of tracing such a line is a complicated business. On either side of it, simultaneously, a recognizability takes shape. But the human eye and mind cannot be busy with two things at the same moment, and so there must be a quick and continual jumping from one side to the other.... This difficulty is perhaps the very moving-spring of my perseverance."

After his early exposure to Rubin's work in 1921 and 1922, Escher left his native Netherlands to live in Italy until

"METAMORPHOSIS I," a woodcut designed by Escher in 1937, represents an abrupt change in his style from the flat periodic sub-divisions he had invented up to 1936 to the development of forms from flat to plastic on the two-dimensional plane. This new ap-

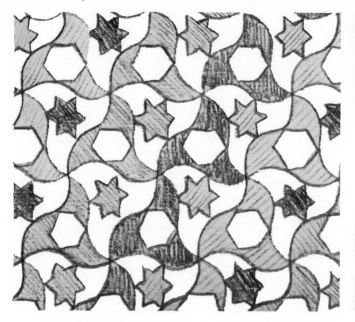

Unlike the Moorish artists, however, Escher continued to design his flat tessellations with contiguous human and animal forms.

Escher's original color drawings of the Alhambra tiles are part of the Escher Foundation collection in the Haags Gemeentemuseum.

1934. An extraordinarily skillful craftsman, he created a large series of woodcuts and lithographs; they represent landscapes, architecture and portraiture in brilliantly realistic style, in which the traditional Renaissance picture space prevails. Only once during his Italian period did the figure-ground problem return: in 1926 he designed some interlocking animal shapes, very similar to his later periodic structures on the picture surface. Escher claims that the departure from Italy in 1934 was responsible for his change in style. He felt that landscape in the North did not attract him as

it had in Italy; instead, he writes, "I concentrated...on personal ideas...and inner visions." He lived for more than a year in Switzerland and for five years in Belgium before settling in 1941 at Baarn in the Netherlands, where he remained until his death in 1972, except for brief visits to Britain, the U.S. and Canada.

As I have noted, the major turning point in Escher's style came in the late 1930's after he left Italy. What caused that change? It is evident that at some time between 1935 and 1938 Escher became acquainted with Koffka's *Princi-*

ples of Gestalt Psychology. That Escher was indebted to Koffka can be documented from his graphic work and written comments. Koffka, one of the three chief proponents of Gestalt psychology (with Max Wertheimer and Wolfgang Köhler), relied heavily on Rubin's work, although Rubin never counted himself among the Gestalt psychologists. In *Principles of Gestalt Psychology* an entire chapter is devoted to the topic of figure and ground. Thus, through Koffka, an old and fascinating preoccupation of Escher's was revived.

Escher's development can be appre-

proach appears to have been influenced by his reading of Kurt Koffka's 1935 book *Principles of Gestalt Psychology*. The design is

reproduced here from an original print in the National Gallery of Art in Washington, D.C. (gift of Cornelius Van Schaak Roosevelt).

ciated by considering drawings the artist made in 1936 on a trip to Spain when he copied majolica tiles at the Alhambra [*see top illustration on preceding two pages*]. These examples of Moorish art with their internal symmetry and obviously ambiguous contours must have attracted him precisely because he had been familiar with the figure-ground problem since 1921. He looked at the Alhambra tiles with eyes trained by Rubin's experiments. As in the case of Rubin's abstract patterns, however, he regretted that the Moorish artists were not allowed to make "graven images" and "always restricted themselves...to designs of an abstract geometrical type. Not one single Moorish artist...ever made so bold...as to use concrete, recognizable, naturalistically conceived figures of fish, birds, reptiles or human beings as elements in their surface coverage."

Instead Escher preferred to design his flat tessellations with contiguous human and animal forms. In the course of the next year or so, however, he abruptly transformed this flat motif into three-dimensional cubes and an entire town in his woodcut *Metamorphosis I* [*see bottom illustration on preceding two pages*]. One of the new aspects noticeable in Escher's post-1937 work, in contrast with the flat periodic subdivisions he had invented up to 1936, is the development

of forms from flat to plastic on the two-dimensional plane. In *Principles of Gestalt Psychology* Koffka demonstrates the compelling three-dimensional organization of two-dimensional lines and planes under certain conditions. He shows, among other examples, how a hexagon, depending on the internal arrangement of its lines, can change from a flat pattern to a cube, just as in Escher's *Metamorphosis I*. In summarizing experiments by Hertha Kopfermann and himself, Koffka points out that it is the intrinsic tendency toward simplicity of organization that makes one see one array of forms as two-dimensional and a slightly altered one as three-dimensional.

Many of Escher's prints of the following years are based on just such a change of forms from flat to plastic. A noteworthy example is the lithograph *Reptiles*, designed in 1943 [*see illustration below*]. Escher describes this series of prints in words that echo Koffka's text: "The chief characteristics of these prints is the transition from flat to spatial and vice versa." Escher goes on to show how in such designs the individual creatures free themselves from the flat ground in which they are rigidly embedded. He writes: "We can think in terms of an interplay between the stiff, crystallized two-dimensional figures of a regular pattern and the individual freedom of three-dimensional creatures capable of mov-

ing about in space without hindrance. On the one hand, the members of the planes of collectivity come to life in space; on the other, the free individuals sink back and lose themselves in the community."

In the same manner Koffka speaks in the last chapter of his book of the embracing ground and the protruding figure as paradigms for the relation between personality and "behavioral social field." The reptiles in Escher's lithograph thus free themselves from the contiguous design on the flat page to venture into three-dimensional space, only to return to the flat surface where their individuality is again submerged. On their way they pass the paraphernalia of smoking and other ephemeral artifacts drawn in hard illusionistic style; they crawl over one of the Platonic solids (a dodecahedron). These forms fascinated Escher because, as he said, geometric shapes were timeless and not man-made.

During the same period (1936–1938) Escher also became aware of an experimental study by Harrower, who in April, 1936, published an article titled "Some Factors Determining Figure-Ground Articulation" in the *British Journal of Psychology*. She varied Rubin's pattern in the following manner. Several test cards emphasized the outline of the vase and let the profiles recede into the background; other cards emphasized the profiles and allowed the vase to become ground; the center card showed the vase and profiles as being equivalent. Two years later, in 1938, Escher created two of his most striking woodcuts, *Sky and Water I* [*see illustration at top right on opposite page*] and *Day and Night* [*see bottom illustration on opposite page*], according to the same principle; in these works the ground slowly becomes figure and the figure becomes ground; the forms in the center, however, remain equivalent. In his interpretation of *Sky and Water I* Escher employs Harrower's terminology when he says: "In the horizontal central strip there are birds and fish equivalent to each other."

This principle of equivalence, first discussed by Rubin and emphasized by Harrower, is an important ingredient of Escher's many inventive preparatory drawings for his woodcuts. When explaining his compositions, Escher would frequently refer to the fact that his forms had to be "equivalent." The crystallographic terms "distinct" and "equivalent" should not, of course, be confused with the simple notion of equivalence Escher (and Harrower) had in mind. The ingenious basic drawing of *Fish and*

"REPTILES," a lithograph designed in 1943, is a notable example of Escher's increasing preoccupation after 1937 with the transformation of forms from flat to plastic. This reproduction is from a print in the Lessing J. Rosenwald collection at the National Gallery.

"FISH AND FOWL," a preliminary drawing for the woodcut *Sky and Water I*, is a good example of Escher's interest in the "equivalence" of visual forms, a notion he adapted from Molly R. Harrower, a student of Koffka's. The original is in the Gemeentemuseum.

"SKY AND WATER I," carved in 1938, is one of Escher's best-known woodcuts. Unlike the preliminary watercolor drawing at left, the forms of the birds and the fish are equivalent only in the center. This reproduction is from a print in the Gemeentemuseum.

Fowl for *Sky and Water I* is a good example of equivalence; the surfaces of the individual birds and fish are approximately equal in extent, internal design, light-dark contrast and simplicity of contour [*see illustration at top left on this page*]. Such equivalence makes the figures ambiguous, and a rapid reversal is the result.

In her 1936 article Harrower tested the relation of figure to ground by introducing a number of variables, among them increasing and decreasing brightness contrast (or graded grays). Escher's

woodcut *Development I*, made in 1937, shows how faint gray squares arranged along the periphery gain in black-and-white contrast as well as distinctness of shape until they become four black and white reptiles in the center [*see top illustration on next page*]. The two "factors"

"DAY AND NIGHT," another 1938 woodcut, represents the same slow transformation of ground into figure and figure into ground, with only the forms in the center remaining equivalent. The prin-

ciple of transformation is the same as that discussed by Harrower in her 1936 article in the *British Journal of Psychology*. The original print is in the Rosenwald collection at the National Gallery.

"DEVELOPMENT I," a 1937 Escher woodcut, incorporates two basic variables from Harrower's experiments: brightness gradient and development from shapeless ground to distinct figure. This print is in the John D. Merriam collection at the Boston Public Library.

from Harrower's experiments, brightness gradient and development from shapeless ground to distinct figure, are the basic compositional principles of this impressive work. Escher's comment on the print is again couched in the technical language of Harrower's study. He writes: "Scarcely visible gray squares at the edges evolve in form and contrast toward the center."

Escher groups several additional prints under the category "Development of Form and Contrast," in keeping with Harrower's analysis. One of these is the lithograph *Liberation,* designed in 1955 [*see illustration on opposite page*]. He describes this print in terms that are reminiscent of Harrower's test cards and Koffka's text: "On the uniformly gray strip of paper that is being unrolled, a simultaneous development in form and contrast is taking place. Triangles—at first scarcely visible—change into more complicated figures, whilst the color contrast between them increases. In the middle they are transformed into white and black birds, and from there fly off into the world as independent creatures, and so the strip of paper on which they are drawn disappears."

In *Liberation* Escher presents us with a surrealist situation; the birds freed from the gray scroll are caught, nevertheless, on the surface on which the lithograph is printed. The artist reflects here on the visual absurdity of his own craft, as he had implicitly in *Reptiles.*

To summarize this important phase in Escher's artistic development, starting in 1937, he transforms his ambiguous figurative patterns in three ways: (1) from flat to plastic, derived from Koffka's *Principles of Gestalt Psychology* of 1935; (2) from shaped form to shapeless ground, derived from Harrower's study of 1936; (3) from strong black-and-white contrast to gray, also derived from Harrower.

Sky and Water I and *Day and Night,* both done in 1938, exhibit these categories of transformation of shape. In *Day and Night* the square gray fields in the foreground gain in articulation of shape and contrast; they become an equivalent pattern of distinct black birds and white birds in the upper center and from there develop into three-dimensional creatures flying off into the "real" world of day or night. In *Sky and Water I* the strongly articulated plastic single bird and single fish, above and below, evolve from the flat equivalent strip in the middle. What was bird becomes watery ground and what was fish becomes sky. Here Escher enhances the individuality, or object quality, of the figure compared with the film quality of the ground, features already emphasized by Rubin in 1915.

It is difficult to reconstruct by what route Escher came in such close contact with the technical aspects of figure-ground experiments. He may have had a mentor. The artist himself belonged to a family where professional and intellectual achievement were the rule, and he may have come across Koffka's and Harrower's experiments because of his own strong interests. The year in the French-speaking part of Switzerland (1936), near the universities of Geneva and Lau-

"SWANS," a 1956 woodcut, is a good example of how, in experimenting with space-filling tessellations on a flat surface, Escher often relied on crystallographic rules of transformation. He himself classified this print under the heading "Glide Reflexion." The print used to make this reproduction is in the Roosevelt collection at the National Gallery.

sanne, and the five years in Ukkel, not far from the University of Brussels (1937–1941), were the period of his "conversion," when he made the figure-ground problem a permanent feature of his style. Whatever his contacts may have been, by the 1930's not only was the impact of Gestalt psychology widespread at European universities but also it had become fashionable among intellectuals.

The figure-ground studies of the Gestalt psychologists were not, however, Escher's only source of inspiration. He varied his fantastic tessellations on the picture plane by following the structural principles of periodic packing in crystals. Caroline H. MacGillavry analyzed Escher's inventions in these terms in her 1965 monograph *Symmetry Aspects of M. C. Escher's Periodic Drawings*. In *Color and Symmetry*, published in 1971, A. L. Loeb selects striking instances of form and color symmetry from Escher's work to accompany his text. Escher himself recognized the similarities of his regular subdivisions on the plane to principles of crystallography. They had been pointed out to him by his brother, B. G. Escher, professor of geology at the University of Leyden. By that time, however, the artist had created his own figure-ground patterns based on Rubin's visual analyses and the Moorish tiles at the Alhambra. As the mathematician H. S. M. Coxeter has remarked, the Moors had already made use of all 17 crystallographic groups of symmetry structures, subsequently established by E. S. Fedorov in 1891.

In experimenting with space-filling creatures on the flat surface, Escher arrived at many intriguing compositions that follow crystallographic rules of transformation; a good example is his woodcut *Swans,* designed in 1956 [*see bottom illustration on opposite page*]. Again Escher writes a commentary, as he had done for his figure-ground inventions. He groups these prints under the heading "Glide Reflexion" and acknowledges the "three fundamental principles of crystallography"; they are, in his words, "repeated shifting (translation), turning about axes (rotation) and glide mirror image (reflexion)." Among

"LIBERATION," a lithograph designed in 1955, was classified by Escher under the heading "Development of Form and Contrast," in keeping with the technical terms of Harrower's analysis. This print is in Merriam collection at Boston Public Library.

scientists this aspect of Escher's graphic work is probably the best known.

Yet the origin of his compositions from playful manipulations of the figure-ground ambiguity has so far been noted only once before—by the art historian E. H. Gombrich in his article "Illusions and Visual Deadlock" (reprinted in his 1963 book *Meditations on a Hobby Horse*). This oversight is understandable, since Escher's later prints suggest mathematical prototypes as a primary source for his work. Such an interpretation is offered, for example, by Coxeter. In his essay "The Mathematical Implications of Escher's Prints" (reprinted in *The World of M. C. Escher*) Coxeter marvels at Escher's ability to extend the theory of crystallographic groups beyond Fedorov's original 17 by anticipating "through artistic intuition" the added principle of color symmetry.

Escher, however, was led to these extensions by his earlier sources from the psychological literature. Thus he knew how to combine both the figurative reversals and the crystallographic rules of regular and semiregular tessellations in one and the same composition on the flat picture surface. In *Reptiles* and in many other drawings he achieved such a feat. The fundamental region of a tessellation is a polygon (triangle, square or hexagon) or a combination of polygons; they must meet corner to corner. In *Reptiles* three heads, three elbows and three toes abut exactly at the corners of a hexagon, which forms the fundamental region of this regular tessellation on the plane. Escher looked at these solutions, some more difficult than others, with a great deal of pride.

A similar close association between crystallographic principles and the design of densely packed surfaces was recognized by Paul Klee and later by Victor Vasarely. Both painters based certain pictures and diagrams on Johannes Kepler's humorous treatise *De Nive Sexangula* (*The Six-cornered Snowflake*), published in 1611. Kepler's neo-Platonic concept of an underlying order or harmony—the belief in a mathematical structure of the universe—was shared by Escher. Occasionally one or another of his graphic works illustrates that idea, for example *Reptiles* or *Stars*, a 1948 wood engraving in the style of the early 17th century, Kepler's period [*see illustration on this page*]. This work depicts a star-studded sky in which the stellar bodies are composed of the Platonic solids cherished by Kepler. In such prints Escher intends to draw a contrast between the permanent laws of mathematics and the incidentals of debris or the changing colors of chameleons. "There is something in such laws that takes the breath away," Escher wrote in his essay "Approaches to Infinity." He continued: "They are not discoveries or inventions of the human mind but exist independently of us." Thus had Socrates explained the intrinsic beauty of geometric forms in Plato's *Philebus*. The abstract laws or principles of simplicity of form that attracted Escher to the perceptual analyses of the Gestalt psychologists were also essentially Platonic in concept.

Through his new interest in mathematics and contact with mathematicians, Escher expanded his vocabulary of ambiguous forms. He used the Möbius strip, the Klein bottle, knots and various forms of polygons. *Circle Limit I,* a hyperbolic (non-Euclidian) construction, was developed in 1958 in an exchange of letters with Coxeter [*see illustration at top left on opposite page*]. It gave Escher a chance to represent "the limits of infinite smallness," as he termed it. *Heaven and Hell,* done in 1960, belongs to the same series [*see illustration at top right on opposite page*].

In the 1950's Escher returned to sources from the psychology of visual perception in a group of prints dealing with reversible perspectives. The 1957 lithograph *Cube with Magic Ribbons* combines the reversible Necker cube (a discovery of the 19th-century Swiss mineralogist L. A. Necker) with the crater illusion [*see bottom illustration on page 134*]. In 1938 the Finnish psychologist Kai von Fieandt published a study on apparent changes in depth perception from concave to convex depending on different directions of light. For his experiments he used small knobs shaped

"STARS," a 1948 wood engraving done in the style of the early 17th century, celebrates Escher's identification with Johannes Kepler's neo-Platonic belief in an underlying mathematical order in the universe. The print is in Roosevelt collection at the National Gallery.

"CIRCLE LIMIT I," a woodcut designed by Escher in 1958, was based on a non-Euclidean mathematical construction developed in an exchange of letters with the mathematician H. S. M. Coxeter. The reproduction is made from a print in the Gemeentemuseum.

"HEAVEN AND HELL," a 1960 Escher woodcut in which the figure-ground ambiguity mirrors an ambiguity of meaning (good and evil), belongs to the same series of mathematically derived designs. The reproduction is from a print in the Gemeentemuseum.

just like those appearing on Escher's band [see top illustration on page 134]. Escher must have known von Fieandt's experiments. The artist explains: "If we follow...the strips of buttonlike protuberances...with the eye, then these nodules surreptitiously change from convex to concave."

Concave and Convex [see top illustration on page 144] belongs to the same group of prints where reversible perspectives, or "inversions," as Escher called them, are the topic. The cluster of cubes on the flag announces the basic visual motif of the composition. In this 1955 lithograph Escher plays with the ambiguity of volumes on the flat picture plane; they switch from solid to hollow,

from inward to outward, from roof to ceiling—like the symbol on the flag.

In 1958 Escher created Belvedere, an impossible building, also based on the reversible Necker cube [see bottom illustration on page 145]. By the end of the 19th century the Necker cube had become one of the most popular and most frequently debated optical illusions

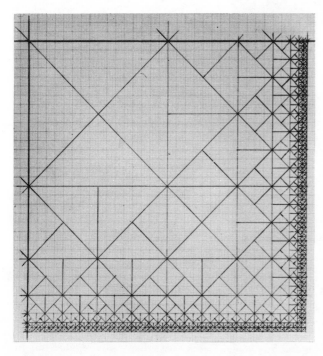

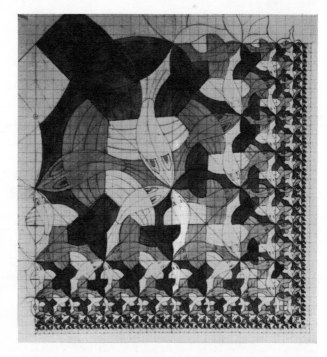

STUDIES for Escher's 1964 woodcut Square Limit reveal that this design was carried out by simply dividing surface after surface in

half, up to the limit of visibility at the outer edge. This reproduction is from the original drawing in the Gemeentemuseum.

"CONCAVE AND CONVEX," a lithograph designed by Escher in 1955, also makes use of reversible perspectives to bring out the ambiguity of volumes portrayed on the flat picture plane. The original print is in the Rosenwald collection at the National Gallery.

EIGHTEENTH-CENTURY ENGRAVING by Giovanni Battista Piranesi, one of a series titled *Carceri* (*Prisons*), is distinguished by perspective aberrations of a type similar to those in Escher's prints. Escher actually owned a set of Piranesi's *Carceri*, but he discounted their influence on his own work, pointing out that he was much more inspired by experiments on visual perception. This detail of a print catalogued Plate XI, 2nd State is reproduced here by courtesy of the Museum of Fine Arts in Boston (gift of Miss Ellen Bullard).

in the psychological literature. To emphasize the theme of the fantastic piece of architecture, the boy on the bench contemplates the reversible cube in his hands and on paper. The corners that are flipping forward and backward during reversals are connected by diagonals, just as in Necker's original 1832 drawing [*see top illustration on next page*]. In *Belvedere*, however, Escher not only uses reversible perspective but also introduces perceptual impossibility, which obstructs the two perceptual interpretations of the cube simultaneously. This technique resembles the constructions of impossible figures published in 1958 by L. S. Penrose and R. Penrose in the *British Journal of Psychology*, acknowledged by Escher as a source for his 1960 lithograph *Ascending and Descending*.

The Schröder stairs, another 19th-century reversible-perspective illusion, first published by H. Schröder in 1858 [*see top illustration on page 146*], is the theme of Escher's 1953 lithograph *Relativity* [*see middle illustration on page 146*]. The stairs show the characteristic shading that facilitates reversals, so that they look either like a staircase going up or an overhang of wall coming down. For the inhabitants of this structure the stairs lead up and down at the same time.

These compositions resemble certain 18th-century engravings, particularly Giovanni Battista Piranesi's *Carceri* (*Prisons*), with their obsessional repetitions and their shifting viewpoints that break up the unity of Renaissance perspective, thus giving a hallucinatory quality to these architectural dreams [*see bottom illustration at left*]. Note in the distance in the upper left quadrant of Piranesi's print a light-shaded underside of an arch. Or is it a walkway leading to a set of stairs? In *Concave and Convex* Escher employs the same motif in both orientations. Escher actually owned a set of Piranesi's engravings, according to his son, George A. Escher, who relates the following revealing story about his father and *Belvedere*:

"One evening, it must have been late 1958, we were looking at the *Carceri* by Piranesi, which he greatly admired and of which he owned a posthumously printed set. We had been hunting for the many perspective aberrations of the same nature as occur in *Belvedere* and I asked him whether these had inspired him to make that print. No, he said, he had been aware of these oddities since long, but had always considered them as carelessness due to the reputed furious pace at which Piranesi had produced the prints during an illness. They had never awakened the particular twist of fantasy which gave birth to *Belvedere*. That, he said, was the direct consequence of noting somewhere...a picture of the reversible...cube."

Nothing could confirm more closely the essentials of Escher's art. As I have tried to show, the artist was fascinated by certain phenomena from experimental work on vision. These were the intellectual starting points for his inventions. Once gripped by one of his "visual ideas" he would spend sleepless nights, writes his son, "trying to bring some vague concept to clarity.... For weeks he would refuse to talk about what he was doing and lock his studio, whether he was there or not." The perspective displacements in Piranesi's *Carceri* or the ambiguities in the reversible patterns of the tiles of the Alhambra were exciting to him because he felt a kinship with these works reaching back over the centuries, but they were not his primary sources.

It is quite apparent that Escher's use of principles derived from the contemporary psychology of visual perception meant much more to him than a new set of themes or artistic techniques. Escher himself described the profound change that occurred in his style between 1936 and 1938 as if it had been the result of a religious conversion: "There came a moment when it seemed as though scales fell from my eyes...I became gripped by a desire the existence of which I had never suspected. Ideas came into my head quite unrelated to graphic art, notions which so fascinated me that I longed to communicate them to other people." It is no contradiction that this sudden revelation had been foreshadowed in Escher's much earlier application of Rubin's original ideas in the beginning of the 1920's. Artistic ideas, like scientific ideas, have a way of going underground only to reemerge with full force at a later stage.

Once gained, Escher's insights stayed with him into his final years. Even 30 years after his first contact with Koffka's work, when Escher was 70 years old, he expressed himself entirely in Koffka's terms (in his 1968 essay "Approaches to Infinity"): "No one can draw a line that is not a boundary line; every line splits a singularity into a plurality. Every closed contour, no matter what its shape, whether a perfect circle or an irregular random form, evokes in addition the notions of 'inside' and 'outside' and the suggestion of 'near' and 'far away,' of 'object' and 'background.'"

Here Escher refers not only to the

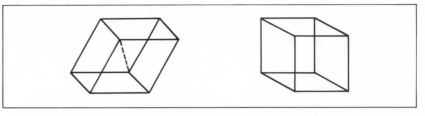

NECKER CUBE, a famous reversible-perspective illusion, was first described in 1832 by the Swiss mineralogist L. A. Necker, who noticed the reversals in his drawings of crystals.

"BELVEDERE," a 1958 lithograph by Escher, is also based on the ambiguous geometry of the Necker cube. The reversible cube, in which the corners that flip forward and backward during reversals are connected by diagonals, appears in three different forms in this print: in the impossible architecture of the building itself, in the model held by the boy sitting on the bench in front of the building and in the drawing on the piece of paper lying on the floor. The reproduction is from a print in the Roosevelt collection at the National Gallery.

SCHRÖDER STAIRS, another 19th-century reversible-perspective diagram, was first published in 1858 by H. Schröder, who pointed out that the shading facilitates the reversals.

"RELATIVITY," a 1953 Escher lithograph, shows reversals similar to those in the diagram at top. The reproduction is from a print in the Rosenwald collection at the National Gallery.

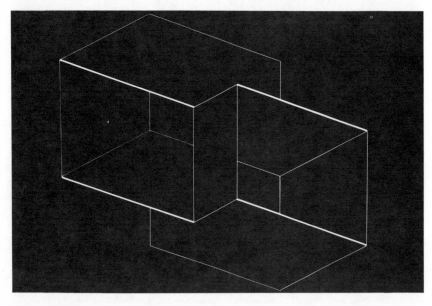

"STRUCTURAL CONSTELLATION," a laminated-plastic construction by Josef Albers, can also be traced to certain reversible-perspective diagrams in the psychological literature.

principle of protruding figure and receding ground, and the double function of contours, but also to well-known Gestalt investigations on closed-contour figures and the problem of *"unum* and *duo* organization" of surface subdivisions analyzed by Wertheimer and Koffka. Regular subdivisions, as in Escher's studies for *Square Limit* of 1964 [*see bottom illustration on page 143*], could be carried out by simply dividing surface after surface in half, up to the limit of visibility at the outer edge. Therefore Escher could say with Koffka: "Every line splits a singularity into a plurality."

The figure-ground ambiguity of Rubin, Koffka and Harrower provided the decisive impetus for Escher to give up the traditional Renaissance picture space. Although he held on to the recognizable image of beast or man for his reversible units, he arrived at a new—sometimes surreal—emphasis on the flat picture surface, a development that the great innovators of 20th-century art had reached at a much earlier date. Picasso and Braque painted their first Cubist pictures between 1907 and 1909; Kandinsky's first abstract color compositions date from 1911. The interdigitation of shapes and their symbolic interpretation in Escher's graphic work, however, can be traced to a trend antedating the modern movement, namely the flat positive and negative patterns of Art Nouveau—often equally charged with meaning and in vogue just before and after the turn of the century.

Escher's contact with the visual experiments of the Gestalt psychologists is not an isolated instance. Joseph Albers' striking constructions on laminated plastic and many of his drawings can be traced to similar prototypes from the psychological literature [*see bottom illustration at right*]. Such ambiguous forms had become a focus of renewed interest at the Bauhaus in Dessau, Germany, in 1929 and 1930, when lectures on Gestalt psychology were offered at this influential school of design. Albers, first a student and then a teacher at the Bauhaus from 1920 until its closing by the Nazis in 1933, became fascinated by reversible perspectives. Beginning in 1931, abstract reversible-line constructions have continued to fascinate him throughout his artistic career.

In the 1930's (almost contemporaneously with Escher) Albers and Vasarely, both precursors of the "Op art" movement (which Albers prefers to call "perceptual art"), created paintings and woodcuts displaying the ambiguity of figure and ground. Yet it is apparent that the intellectual stimulation provided by Gestalt theory manifests itself in very different ways, depending on the artist's choice and predisposition. Albers and Vasarely continue the abstract tradition of modern art by giving it a new direction through insights gained from investigations on vision and visual perception. Escher instead extended the decorative tradition of Art Nouveau coupled with the Symbolist movement. It is perhaps no accident that Art Nouveau patterns are similarly repetitive and crowd the flat surface, just as Escher's inventions do.

Uncovering Escher's sources does not diminish the fascination of his work. Indeed, it underscores how directly the awe we experience before his compositions derives from the perplexing ambiguity of his scientific prototypes. By employing motifs from contemporary attempts at the scientific analysis of form perception, the artist plays with stripped-down mechanisms of perception and reflects on his own visual means.

Similarly, the abstract perceptual artist of the 1960's reflects on the presumed functional property of our visual apparatus by making his patterns vibrate with repetitive line and color stimuli. It is remarkable that such art culminated at the very time when physiologists of the brain began to demonstrate mechanisms for primitive "feature detection" in the cerebral visual pathways [see "The Visual Cortex of the Brain," by D. H. Hubel; SCIENTIFIC AMERICAN Offprint 168]. As the British information theorist D. M. MacKay has pointed out, complementary mechanisms of form perception (similar to complementary color perception) play a role in these scintillating patterns [see top illustration at right]. These effects were adopted by the Op-art painters in their provocative arrays of lines. Without any other visual clues to guide us, these patterns make the feature-extracting machinery in the human visual system reverberate *in vacuo*.

Escher instead clings tenaciously to meaningful, if fantastic, patterns and invites the viewer to repeat the basic figure-ground experiments of the Gestalt school. This can best be seen in the four-color woodcut *Sun and Moon*, which combines the Symbolist yearnings of the turn of the century with demonstrations of ambiguity in the perceptual process [see bottom illustration at right]. If you focus on the light birds, the crescent of the moon appears and night prevails; if you focus on the dark birds, the sun will shine.

"RAY PATTERN," published originally in *Nature* in 1957 by the British information theorist D. M. MacKay, influenced the work of the Op artists of the 1960's. A scintillating pattern of fine lines appears to run at right angles to the rays, indicating that a line-detecting mechanism of form perception complementary to the ray pattern has been stimulated.

"SUN AND MOON," a four-color woodcut designed by Escher in 1948, epitomizes, in the author's view, "the symbolist yearnings of the turn of the century with...demonstrations of ambiguity in the visual process." Reproduction is from a print in the Gemeentemuseum.

III

MEMORY, LEARNING, AND THINKING

III   MEMORY, LEARNING, AND THINKING

INTRODUCTION

This section covers a wide range of cognitive activities—learning, memory, and the ability to use symbols in language and thought. In its broadest sense learning refers to a relatively permanent change in behavior that occurs as a result of experience—organisms "learn" when they adapt their behavior in response to changes in the environment. Learning capacity is thus an important factor in an organism's ability to survive. Learning entails memory; if nothing were retained from experience, there could be no learning. Higher organisms, with complex nervous systems, can store memories from events long past and use such memories to think about and solve present problems. Thinking requires the ability to use symbols to represent objects and events. Most often these symbols are in the form of language. Symbolization permits us to represent the past in our consciousness and, thus, to seek solutions to unsolved problems.

In the first article in this section, "The Control of Short-Term Memory," Richard Atkinson and Richard Shiffrin offer a theory of how new information is acquired by humans and how that information is retained over time. They propose two types of memory mechanisms: one for immediate information (a telephone number just looked up) and one for repeated information (your own telephone number). These two storage mechanisms are labeled "short-term" and "long-term" memory. Long-term memory stores such items as your name, the words and grammar of language, addition and multiplication tables, and important events in your life. Except for occasional mental blocking on a word or the name of an acquaintance, these memories are relatively permanent. In contrast, the telephone number you have just looked up, the definition the instructor has just given in class, or the name of a stranger to whom you have just been introduced remain with you in short-term memory only; unless you make a conscious effort to focus your attention on such information, it is quickly lost. Using this distinction between short- and long-term memory, the authors formulate a theory to account for a range of psychological data.

In "How We Remember What We See" Ralph Haber breaks down even further the memory process for visual information. He suggests that a visual display generates an iconic (visual) image in the brain that precedes its representation in short-term memory. Although the iconic image lasts for less than a second, during this time information is extracted from it and transferred to short-term memory. A brief visual presentation of a word, for example, will generate an icon that can be scanned, appropriately coded, and operated on by the subject even after the stimulus has disappeared. The coding operation might involve transforming the printed word into spoken form. The spoken form will be stored in short-term memory, whence it may be forgotten; if it receives additional attention in the form of rehearsal or further coding, it may be transferred to long-term memory for more permanent storage. Haber describes some interesting experiments indicating that pictorial and linguistic information may be coded differently.

The ability to keep track of our location in space by remembering where we have been also involves a form of short-term memory. Animals who forage for food seem able to remember places they have visited and thus avoid returning to a previously inspected spot. In "Spatial Memory" David Olton investigates the strategies that rats use in solving such spatial problems. His experiments indicate that rats learn a kind of "spatial map" that enables them to understand the relations among places in their environment (as opposed to remembering a list of places). Olton goes further to identify a structure in the center of the brain called the hippocampus (after the Greek word for *sea horse* because of its shape) as the center for this kind of memory.

If the reader has an animal at home that needs to be trained, the article by B. F. Skinner, "How to Teach Animals," will prove informative. Skinner gives a step-by-step description of a procedure for modifying behavior called *operant conditioning*. The principle is to provide immediate reinforcement, in the form of food or praise, for any act that approaches desired behavior. (The same principle, of course, is applicable to the social training of children.) By requiring progressively closer approximation to the desired behavior, it is possible to "shape" the animal's behavior in a relatively short period of time. The principles of operant conditioning have been applied extensively in a variety of learning situations, adding much to our understanding of the conditions that produce optimal learning. They have also been used to help individuals with emotional and behavioral problems. A later article in this volume ("Behavioral Psychotherapy" by Albert Bandura, Section IV) describes the use of operant conditioning techniques in treating human subjects with psychological disorders.

One of our most remarkable cognitive accomplishments is the ability to communicate through language. As verbally facile adults, we fail to appreciate the complexity of the task confronting a child learning to speak. He or she must dissect the language heard into its minimal units of sound and meaning, discover the rules for combining sounds into words, learn the meanings of individual words and the rules for combining words into meaningful sentences, and acquire the vocal intonations acceptable in his or her social group. That the average child has mastered this task quite well by the age of five is truly astonishing. In "The Acquisition of Language" Breyne Moskowitz discusses the nature of language and how children learn to use it. The orderliness and speed with which children learn their native language have convinced some experts that the human brain is innately programed for language learning. But whatever built-in propensities there may be, experience plays a major role—as Moskowitz points out.

Some experts believe that the ability to learn language is not only innate, but unique to the human species. They acknowledge that other species have communication systems but argue that these are qualitatively different from ours. This view has been challenged by a number of experimenters who have succeeded in teaching "language"—in the form of a sign language used by the deaf or the manipulation of objects representing linguistic symbols—to gorillas and chimpanzees. Such a project was undertaken by Ann and David Premack ("Teaching Language to an Ape") who taught a young chimpanzee named Sarah to communicate by means of colored plastic symbols representing words. Sarah mastered a vocabulary of some 130 "words." These included not only the names of objects, adjectives, and verbs but also concepts (such as "same" and "different") and conditionals (such as "if-then"). And she was able to combine them in sentences. Although Sarah's ability in no way matches that of a human adult, it compares quite favorably with the performance of a two-year-old child. The method used to teach Sarah to communicate has been used successfully with people who have language difficulties caused by brain damage.

In "Specialization of the Human Brain" Norman Geschwind discusses the relationship between some of our higher faculties—such as language, memory, musical ability, and the perception of visual patterns—and specific regions of the brain. He describes some intriguing research indicating that the two halves of the brain, the right and left cerebral hemispheres, are specialized for quite different functions.

15

The Control of Short-Term Memory

by Richard C. Atkinson and Richard M. Shiffrin
August 1971

*Memory has two components: short-term and
long-term. Control processes such as "rehearsal"
are essential to the transfer of information from
the short-term store to the long-term one*

The notion that the system by which information is stored in memory and retrieved from it can be divided into two components dates back to the 19th century. Theories distinguishing between two different kinds of memory were proposed by the English associationists James Mill and John Stuart Mill and by such early experimental psychologists as Wilhelm Wundt and Ernst Meumann in Germany and William James in the U.S. Reflecting on their own mental processes, they discerned a clear difference between thoughts currently in consciousness and thoughts that could be brought to consciousness only after a search of memory that was often laborious. (For example, the sentence you are reading is in your current awareness; the name of the baseball team that won the 1968

World Series may be in your memory, but to retrieve it takes some effort, and you may not be able to retrieve it at all.)

The two-component concept of memory was intuitively attractive, and yet it was largely discarded when psychology turned to behaviorism, which emphasized research on animals rather than humans. The distinction between short-term memory and long-term memory received little further consideration until the 1950's, when such psychologists as Donald E. Broadbent in England, D. O. Hebb in Canada and George A. Miller in the U.S. reintroduced it [see "Information and Memory," by George A. Miller; SCIENTIFIC AMERICAN Offprint 419]. The concurrent development of computer models of behavior and of mathematical psychology accelerated

the growth of interest in the two-process viewpoint, which is now undergoing considerable theoretical development and is the subject of a large research effort. In particular, the short-term memory system, or short-term store (STS), has been given a position of pivotal importance. That is because the processes carried out in the short-term store are under the immediate control of the subject and govern the flow of information in the memory system; they can be called into play at the subject's discretion, with enormous consequences for performance.

Some control processes are used in many situations by everyone and others are used only in special circumstances. "Rehearsal" is an overt or covert repetition of information—as in remembering a telephone number until it can be writ-

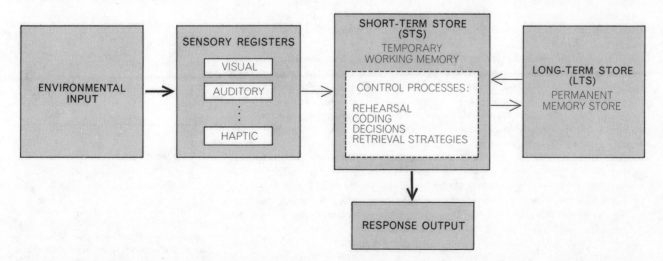

INFORMATION FLOW through the memory system is conceived of as beginning with the processing of environmental inputs in sensory registers (receptors plus internal elements) and entry into the short-term store (STS). While it remains there the information may be copied into the long-term store (LTS), and associated information that is in the long-term store may be activated and entered into the short-term store. If a triangle is seen, for example, the name "triangle" may be called up. Control processes in the short-term store affect these transfers into and out of the long-term store and govern learning, retrieval of information and forgetting.

ten down, remembering the names of a group of people to whom one has just been introduced or copying a passage from a book. "Coding" refers to a class of control processes in which the information to be remembered is put in a context of additional, easily retrievable information, such as a mnemonic phrase or sentence. "Imaging" is a control process in which verbal information is remembered through visual images; for example, Cicero suggested learning long lists (or speeches) by placing each member of the list in a visual representation of successive rooms of a well-known building. There are other control processes, including decision rules, organizational schemes, retrieval strategies and problem-solving techniques; some of them will be encountered in this article. The point to keep in mind is the optional nature of control processes. In contrast to permanent structural components of the memory system, the control processes are selected at the subject's discretion; they may vary not only with different tasks but also from one encounter with the same task to the next.

We believe that the overall memory system is best described in terms of the flow of information into and out of short-term storage and the subject's control of that flow, and this conception has been central to our experimental and theoretical investigation of memory. All phases of memory are assumed to consist of small units of information that are associatively related. A set of closely interrelated information units is termed an image or a trace. Note that "image" does not necessarily imply a visual representation; if the letter-number pair TKM–4 is presented for memory, the image that is stored might include the size of the card on which the pair is printed, the type of print, the sound of the various symbols, the semantic codes and numerous other units of information.

Information from the environment is accepted and processed by the various sensory systems and is entered into the short-term store, where it remains for a period of time that is usually under the control of the subject. By rehearsing one or more items the subject can keep them in the short-term store, but the number that can be maintained in this way is strictly limited; most people can maintain seven to nine digits, for example. Once an image is lost from the short-term store it cannot thereafter be recovered from it. While information resides in short-term storage it may be copied into

the long-term store (LTS), which is assumed to be a relatively permanent memory from which information is not lost. While an image is in short-term storage, closely related information in the long-term store is activated and entered in the short-term store too. Information entering the short-term store from the sensory systems comes from a specific modality—visual, auditory or whatever—but associations from the long-term store in all modalities are activated to join it. For instance, an item may be presented visually, but immediately after input its verbal "name" and associated meanings will be activated from the long-term store and placed in the short-term one [see illustration on opposite page].

Our account of short-term and long-term storage does not require that the two stores necessarily be in different parts of the brain or involve different physiological structures. One might consider the short-term store simply as being a temporary activation of some portion of the long-term store. In our thinking we tend to equate the short-term store with "consciousness," that is, the thoughts and information of which we are currently aware can be considered part of the contents of the short-term store. (Such a statement lies in the realm of phenomenology and cannot be verified scientifically, but thinking of the short-term store in this way may help the reader to conceptualize the system.) Because consciousness is equated with the short-term store and because control processes are centered in and act through it, the short-term store is considered a working memory: a system in which decisions are made, problems are solved and information flow is directed. Retrieval of information from short-term storage is quite fast and accurate. Experiments by Saul Sternberg of the Bell Telephone Laboratories and by others have shown that the retrieval time for information in short-term storage such as letters and numbers ranges from 10 to 30 milliseconds per character.

The retrieval of information from long-term storage is considerably more complicated. So much information is contained in the long-term store that the major problem is finding access to some small subset of the information that contains the desired image, just as one must find a particular book in a library before it can be scanned for the desired information. We propose that the subject activates a likely subset of information, places it in the short-term store and then scans that store for the desired image. The image may not be present in the

current subset, and so the retrieval process becomes a search in which various subsets are successively activated and scanned [see illustration below]. On the basis of the information presented to him the subject selects the appropriate "probe information" and places it in the short-term store. A "search set," or subset of information in the long-term store closely associated with the probe, is then activated and put in the short-term store. The subject selects from the search set some image, which is then examined. The information extracted from the selected image is utilized for a decision: has the desired information

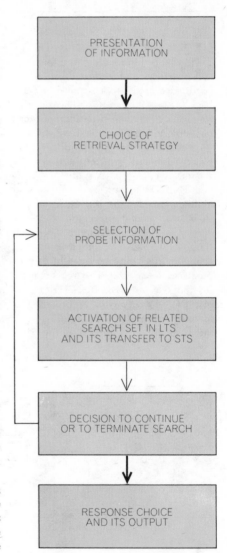

RETRIEVAL from the long-term store requires a choice of strategy and selection of certain information as a "probe" that is placed in the short-term store. The probe activates a "search set" of information in the long-term store. The search set is placed in the short-term store and is examined for the desired information. If it is not found, search is halted or recycled with new probe.

been found? If so, the search is terminated.

If the information has not been found, the subject may decide that continuation is unlikely to be productive or he may decide to continue. If he does, he begins the next cycle of the search by again selecting a probe, which may or may not be the same probe used in the preceding cycle depending on the subject's strategy. For example, a subject asked to search for states of the U.S. starting with the letter *M* may do so by generating states at random and checking their first letter (in which case the same probe information can be used in each search cycle), or he may generate successive states in a regular geographic order (in which case the probe information is systematically changed from one cycle to the next). It can be shown that strategies in which the probe information is systematically changed will result more often in successful retrieval but will take longer than alternative "random" strategies. (Note that the Freudian concept of repressed memories can be considered as being an inability of the subject to generate an appropriate probe.)

This portrayal of the memory system almost entirely in terms of the operations of the short-term store is quite intentional. In our view information storage and retrieval are best described in terms of the flow of information through the short-term store and in terms of the subject's control of the flow. One of the most important of these control processes is rehearsal. Through overt or covert repetition of information, rehearsal either increases the momentary strength of information in the short-term store or otherwise delays its loss. Rehearsal can be shown not only to maintain information in short-term storage but also to control transfer from the short-term store to the long-term one. We shall present several experiments concerned with an analysis of the rehearsal process.

The research in question involves a memory paradigm known as "free recall," which is similar to the task you face when you are asked to name the people present at the last large party you went to. In the typical experimental procedure a list of random items, usually common English words, is presented to the subject one at a time. Later the subject attempts to recall as many words as possible in any order. Many psychologists have worked on free recall, with major research efforts carried out by

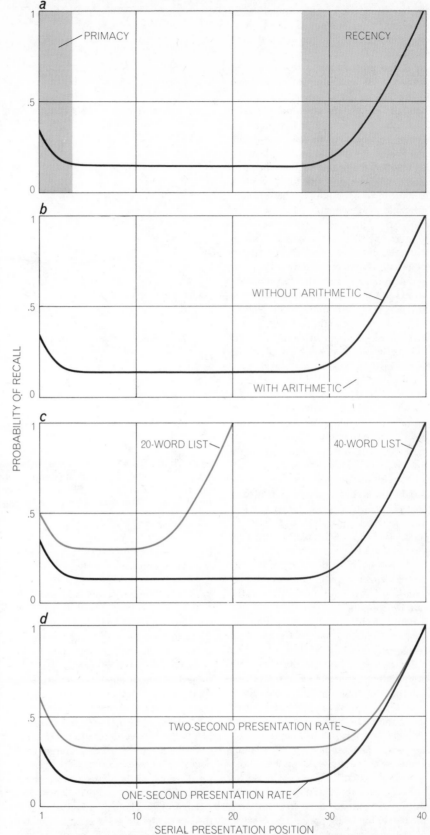

PROBABILITY OF RECALL in free-recall experiments varies in a characteristic way with an item's serial position in a list: a "primacy effect" and a "recency effect" are apparent (*a*). If an arithmetic task is interpolated between presentation and recall, the recency effect disappears (*b*). Words in long lists are recalled less well than words in short lists (*c*). Slower presentation also results in better recall (*d*). The curves are idealized ones based on experiments by James W. Deese Bennet Murdock, Leo Postman and Murray Glanzer.

Bennet Murdock of the University of Toronto, Endel Tulving of Yale University and Murray Glanzer of New York University. The result of principal interest is the probability of recalling each item in a list as a function of its place in the list, or "serial-presentation position." Plotting this function yields a U-shaped curve [see "a" in illustration on preceding page]. The increased probability of recall for the first few words in the list is called the primacy effect; the large increase for the last eight to 12 words is called the recency effect. There is considerable evidence that the recency effect is due to retrieval from short-term storage and that the earlier portions of the serial-position curve reflect retrieval from long-term storage only. In one experimental procedure the subject is required to carry out a difficult arithmetic task for 30 seconds immediately following presentation of the list and then is asked to recall. One can assume that the arithmetic task causes the loss of all the words in short-term storage, so that recall reflects retrieval from long-term storage only. The recency effect is eliminated when this experiment is performed; the earlier portions of the serial-position curve are unaffected [b]. If variables that influence the long-term store but not the short-term one are manipulated, the recency portion of the serial-position curve should be relatively unaffected, whereas the earlier portions of the curve should show changes. One such variable is the number of words in the presented list. A word in a longer list is less likely to be recalled, but the recency effect is quite unaffected by list length [c]. Similarly, increases in the rate of presentation decrease the likelihood of recalling words preceding the recency region but leave the recency effect largely unchanged [d].

In free-recall experiments many lists are usually presented in a session. If the subject is asked at the end of the session to recall all the words presented during the session, we would expect his recall to reflect retrieval from long-term storage only. The probability of recalling words as a function of their serial position within each list can be plotted for end-of-session recall and compared with the serial-position curve for recall immediately following presentation [see illustration on this page]. For the delayed-recall curve the primacy effect remains, but the recency effect is eliminated, as predicted. In summary, the recency region appears to reflect retrieval from both short-term and long-term storage whereas the serial-position curve preced-

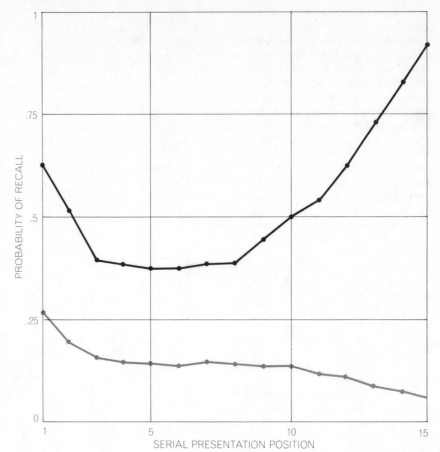

EFFECT OF DELAY is tested by asking subjects to recall at the end of a session all words from the entire session, and then plotting probability of recall against serial position within each list. An experiment by Fergus Craik compares immediate recall (*black*) with delayed recall (*color*). The delayed-recall curve emphasizes transitory nature of recency effect.

ing the recency region reflects retrieval from long-term storage only.

In 1965, at a conference sponsored by the New York Academy of Sciences, we put forward a mathematical model explaining these and other effects in terms of a rehearsal process. The model assumed that in a free-recall task the subject sets up a rehearsal buffer in the short-term store that can hold only a fixed number of items. At the start of the presentation of a list the buffer is empty; successive items are entered until the buffer is filled. Thereafter, as each new item enters the rehearsal buffer it replaces one of the items already there. (Which item is replaced depends on a number of psychological factors, but in the model the decision is approximated by a random process.) The items that are still being rehearsed in the short-term store when the last item is presented are the ones that are immediately recalled by the subject, giving rise to the recency effect. The transfer of information from the short-term to the long-term store is

postulated to be a function of the length of time an item resides in the rehearsal buffer; the longer the time period, the more rehearsal the item receives and therefore the greater the transfer of information to long-term storage. Since items presented first in a list enter an empty or partly empty rehearsal buffer, they remain longer than later items and consequently receive additional rehearsal. This extra rehearsal causes more transfer of information to long-term storage for the first items, giving rise to the primacy effect.

This rehearsal model was given a formal mathematical statement and was fitted to a wide array of experiments, and it provided an excellent quantitative account of a great many results in free recall, including those discussed in this article. A more direct confirmation of the model has recently been provided by Dewey Rundus of Stanford University. He carried out free-recall experiments in which subjects rehearsed aloud during list presentation. This overt rehearsal was tape-recorded and was compared with the recall results. The number of different words contained in the "rehearsal set" (the items overtly rehearsed between successive presentations) was one after the first word was presented and then rose until the fourth word; from the fourth word on the number of different words in the rehearsal set remained fairly constant (averaging about 3.3) until the end of the list. The subjects almost always reported the members of the most recent rehearsal set when the list ended and recall began. A close correspondence is evident between the number of rehearsals and the recall probability for words preceding the recency effect; in the recency region, however, a sharp disparity occurs [*see illustrations below*]. The hypothesis that

long-term storage is a function of the number of rehearsals can be checked in other ways. The recall probability for a word preceding the recency region was plotted as a function of the number of rehearsals received by that word; the result was an almost linear, sharply increasing function. And words presented in the middle of the list given the same number of rehearsals as the first item presented had the same recall probability as that first item.

With efficacy of rehearsal established both for storing information in the long-term store and for maintaining information in the short-term store, we did an experiment in which the subjects' rehearsal was manipulated directly. Our subjects were trained to engage in one

of two types of rehearsal. In the first (a one-item rehearsal set) the most recently presented item was rehearsed exactly three times before presentation of the next item; no other items were rehearsed. In the second (a three-item rehearsal set) the subject rehearsed the three most recently presented items once each before presentation of the next item, so that the first rehearsal set contained three rehearsals of the first word, the second rehearsal set contained two rehearsals of the second word and one rehearsal of the first word, and all subsequent sets contained one rehearsal of each of the three most recent items [*see illustration on following page*].

When only one item is rehearsed at a time, each item receives an identical number of rehearsals and the primacy effect disappears, as predicted. Note that the recency effect appears for items preceding the last item even though the last item is the only one in the last rehearsal set. This indicates that even when items are dropped from rehearsal, it takes an additional period of time for them to be completely lost from short-term storage. The curve for the three-item rehearsal condition shows the effect also. The last rehearsal set contains the last three items presented and these are recalled perfectly, but a recency effect is still seen for items preceding these three. It should also be noted that a primacy effect occurs in the three-rehearsal condition. This was predicted because the first item received a total of five rehearsals rather than three. A delayed-recall test for all words was given at the end of the experimental session. The data confirmed that long-term-store retrieval closely parallels the number of rehearsals given an item during presentation, for both rehearsal schemes.

These results strongly implicate rehearsal in the maintenance of information in the short-term store and the transfer of that information to the long-term system. The question then arises: What are the forgetting and transfer characteristics of the short-term store in the absence of rehearsal? One can control rehearsal experimentally by blocking it with a difficult verbal task such as arithmetic. For example, Lloyd R. Peterson and Margaret Peterson of Indiana University [see "Short-Term Memory," by Lloyd R. Peterson; SCIENTIFIC AMERICAN Offprint 499] presented a set of three letters (a trigram) to be remembered; the subject next engaged in a period of arithmetic and then was asked to recall as many letters of the trigram

ITEM PRESENTED	ITEMS REHEARSED (REHEARSAL SET)
1 REACTION	REACTION, REACTION, REACTION, REACTION
2 HOOF	HOOF, REACTION, HOOF, REACTION
3 BLESSING	BLESSING, HOOF, REACTION
4 RESEARCH	RESEARCH, REACTION, HOOF, RESEARCH
5 CANDY	CANDY, HOOF, RESEARCH, REACTION
6 HARDSHIP	HARDSHIP, HOOF, HARDSHIP, HOOF
7 KINDNESS	KINDNESS, CANDY, HARDSHIP, HOOF
8 NONSENSE	NONSENSE, KINDNESS, CANDY, HARDSHIP
⋮	⋮
20 CELLAR	CELLAR, ALCOHOL, MISERY, CELLAR

OVERT-REHEARSAL experiment by Dewey Rundus shows the effect of rehearsal on transfer into long-term storage. The subject rehearses aloud. A partial listing of items rehearsed in one instance shows typical result: early items receive more rehearsals than later items.

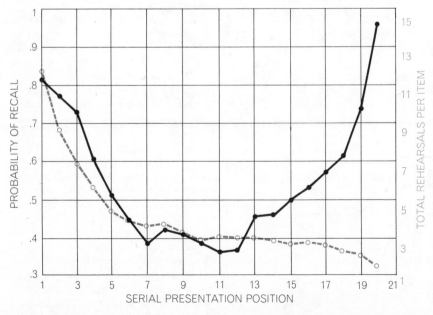

EFFECT OF REHEARSAL is demonstrated by comparison of an item's probability of recall (*black*) with the total number of rehearsals item receives (*color*). The two are related in regions reflecting retrieval from long-term storage (preceding recency region). That is, long-term storage efficacy depends on number of rehearsals and is reflected in retrieval.

ONE-ITEM REHEARSAL SCHEME

SERIAL POSITION	ITEM PRESENTED	ITEMS REHEARSED	TOTAL REHEARSALS PER ITEM
1	A	AAA	3
2	B	BBB	3
3	C	CCC	3
4	D	DDD	3
5	E	EEE	3
6	F	FFF	3
.	.	.	.
.	.	.	.
.	.	.	.
14	N	NNN	3
15	O	OOO	3
16	P	PPP	3

THREE-ITEM REHEARSAL SCHEME

SERIAL POSITION	ITEM PRESENTED	ITEMS REHEARSED	TOTAL REHEARSALS PER ITEM
1	A	AAA	5
2	B	BBA	4
3	C	CBA	3
4	D	DCB	3
5	E	EDC	3
6	F	FED	3
.	.	.	.
.	.	.	.
.	.	.	.
14	N	NML	3
15	O	ONM	2
16	P	PON	1

NUMBER OF REHEARSALS is controlled with two schemes. In one (*top*) only the current item is rehearsed and all items have three rehearsals. In the other (*bottom*) the latest three items are rehearsed; early ones have extra rehearsals. (Letters represent words.)

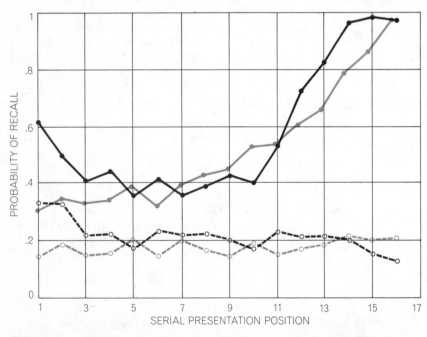

PRIMACY EFFECT disappears with one-item rehearsal (*color*), in which all items have equal rehearsal, but remains with three-item rehearsal (*black*). Recency effect is pronounced for both schemes in immediate recall (*solid lines*). Curves for delayed recall (*broken lines*), which reflect only retrieval from long-term storage, parallel the number of rehearsals.

as possible. When the probability of recall is plotted as a function of the duration of the arithmetic task, the loss observed over time is similar to that of the recency effect in free recall [*see top illustration on next page*]. Short-term-store loss caused by an arithmetic task, then, is similar to loss from short-term storage caused by a series of intervening words to be remembered. The flat portion of the curve reflects the retrieval of the trigram from long-term storage alone and the earlier portions of the curve represent retrieval from both short-term and long-term storage; the loss of the trigram from short-term storage is represented by the decreasing probability of recall prior to the asymptote.

Does the forgetting observed during arithmetic reflect an automatic decay of short-term storage that occurs inevitably in the absence of rehearsal or is the intervening activity the cause of the loss? There is evidence that the amount of new material introduced between presentation and test is a much more important determinant of loss from short-term storage than simply the elapsed time between presentation and test. This finding is subject to at least two explanations. The first holds that the activity intervening between presentation and test is the *direct* cause of an item's loss from short-term storage. The second explanation proposes that the rate of intervening activity merely affects the number of rehearsals that can be given the item to be remembered and thus *indirectly* determines the rate of loss.

It has recently become possible to choose between these two explanations of loss from the short-term store. Judith Reitman of the University of Michigan substituted a signal-detection task for the arithmetic task in the Petersons' procedure. The task consisted in responding whenever a weak tone was heard against a continuous background of "white" noise. Surprisingly, no loss from short-term storage was observed after 15 seconds of the task, even though subjects reported no rehearsal during the signal detection. This suggests that loss from the short-term store is due to the type of interference during the intervening interval: signal detection does not cause loss but verbal arithmetic does. Another important issue that could potentially be resolved with the Reitman procedure concerns the transfer of information from the short-term to the long-term store: Does transfer occur only at initial presentation and at subsequent rehearsals, or does it occur throughout the period during which the information resides in the short-term store, regardless of rehearsals?

To answer these questions, the following experiment was carried out. A consonant pentagram (a set of five consonants, such as *QJXFK*) was presented for 2.5 seconds for the subject to memorize. This was followed by a signal-detection task in which pure tones were presented at random intervals against a continuous background of white noise. The subjects pressed a key whenever they thought they detected a tone. (The task proved to be difficult; only about three-fourths of the tones presented were correctly detected.) The signal-detection period lasted for either one second, eight seconds or 40 seconds, with tones sounded on the average every 2.5 seconds. In conditions 1, 2 and 3 the subjects were tested on the consonant pentagram immediately after the signal detection; in conditions 4, 5 and 6, however, they were required to carry out 30 seconds of difficult arithmetic following the signal detection before being tested [*see middle illustration at right*]. In order to increase the likelihood that rehearsal would not occur, we paid the subjects for performing well on signal detection and for doing their arithmetic accurately but not for their success in remembering letters. In addition they were instructed not to rehearse letters during signal detection or arithmetic. They reported afterward that they were not consciously aware of rehearsing. Because the question of rehearsal is quite important, we nevertheless went on to do an additional control experiment in which all the same conditions applied but the subjects were told to rehearse the pentagram aloud following each detection of a tone.

The results indicate that arithmetic causes the pentagram information to be lost from the short-term store but that in the absence of the arithmetic the signal-detection task alone causes no loss [*see bottom illustration at right*]. What then does produce forgetting from the short-term store? It is not just the analysis of any information input, since signal detection is a difficult information-processing task but causes no forgetting. And time alone causes no noticeable forgetting. Yet verbal information (arithmetic) does cause a large loss. Mrs. Reitman's conclusion appears to be correct: forgetting is caused by the entry into the short-term store of other, similar information.

What about the effect of rehearsal? In the arithmetic situation performance improves if subjects rehearse overtly

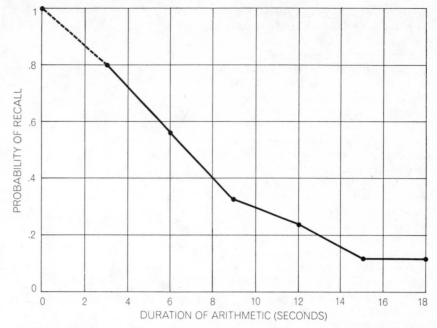

ARITHMETIC TASK before recall reduces the probability of recall. Lloyd R. Peterson and Margaret Peterson charted recall probability against duration of arithmetic. The probability falls off with duration until it levels off when recall reflects retrieval from long-term storage alone. Does curve reflect only lack of rehearsal or also nature of intervening task?

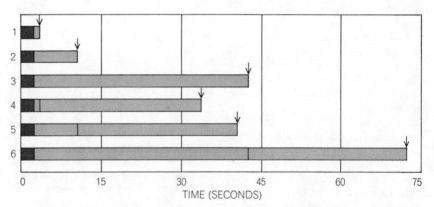

TWO TASKS were combined in an experiment with these six conditions. Five consonants were presented for 2.5 seconds (*dark gray*), followed by a signal-detection task for one second, eight seconds or 40 seconds (*color*), followed in three cases by arithmetic (*light gray*). Then came the test (*arrows*). Rehearsal during detection was included in a control version.

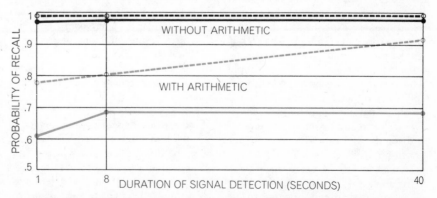

NATURE OF TASKS is seen to have an effect. In the absence of arithmetic, signal detection leaves the short-term store virtually unaffected, with rehearsal (*broken black curve*) or without (*solid black*). Arithmetic, however, causes loss from the short-term store (*color*); decreased recall shown reflects retrieval from long-term store only. Retrieval improves with duration of signal detection if there is rehearsal, which increases transfer to the long-term store (*broken colored curve*) but not in the absence of rehearsal (*solid color*).

during the signal-detection period. Presumably the rehearsal transfers information about the pentagram to the long-term store; the additional transfer during the long signal-detection period is reflected in the retrieval scores, and the rehearsal curve rises. The no-rehearsal curve is horizontal over the last 32 seconds of signal detection, however, confirming that no rehearsal was occurring during that period. The fact that the lowest curve is flat over the last 32 seconds has important implications for transfer from the short-term store to the long-term. It indicates that essentially no transfer occurred during this period even though, as the results in the absence of arithmetic show, the trace remained in the short-term store. Hence the presence of a trace in the short-term store is alone not enough to result in transfer to the long-term store. Apparently transfer to the long-term system occurs primarily during or shortly after rehearsals. (The rise in the lowest curve over the first eight seconds may indicate that the transfer effects of a presentation or rehearsal take at least a few seconds to reach completion.)

The emphasis we have given to rote rehearsal should not imply that other control processes are of lesser importance. Although much evidence indicates that transfer from short-term storage to long-term is strongly dependent on rehearsals, effective later retrieval from long-term storage can be shown to be highly dependent on the type of information rehearsed. Coding is really the choosing of particular information to be rehearsed in the short-term store. In general, coding strategies consist in adding appropriately chosen information from long-term storage to a trace to be remembered and then rehearsing the entire complex in the short-term store. Suppose you are given (as is typical in memory experiments) the stimulus-response pair HRM–4; later HRM will be presented alone and you will be expected to respond "4." If you simply rehearse HRM–4 several times, your ability to respond correctly later will probably not be high. Suppose, however, HRM reminds you of "homeroom" and you think of various aspects of your fourth-grade classroom. Your retrieval performance will be greatly enhanced. Why? First of all, the amount and range of information stored appears to be greater with coding than with rote rehearsal. Moreover, the coding operation provides a straightforward means by which you can gain access to an appropriate and small region of memory

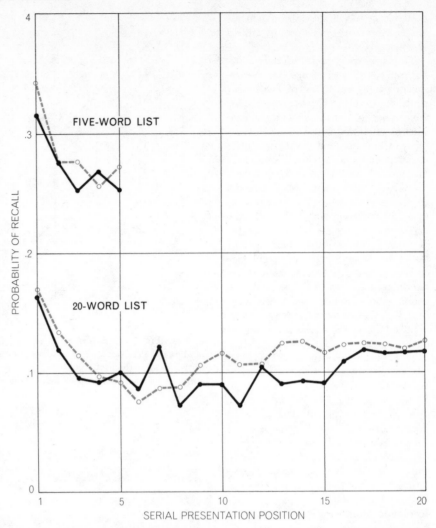

LENGTH OF LIST rather than amount of "interference" governs recall probability. Subjects were asked to recall the list before the one just studied. Five-word lists (*top*) were recalled better than 20-word lists (*bottom*) whether they were followed by intervening lists of five words (*black*) or of 20 words (*color*). The data are averages from three experiments.

during retrieval. In the above example, when HRM is presented at the moment of test, you are likely to notice, just as during the initial presentation, that HRM is similar to "homeroom." You can then use "homeroom" (and the current temporal context) as a further probe and would almost certainly access "fourth grade" and so generate the correct response.

As the discussion of coding suggests, the key to retrieval is the selection of probe information that will activate an appropriate search set from the long-term store. Since in our view the long-term store is a relatively permanent repository, forgetting is assumed to result from an inadequate selection of probe information and a consequent failure of the retrieval process. There are two basic ways in which the probe selection

may prove inadequate. First, the wrong probe may be selected. For instance, you might be asked to name the star of a particular motion picture. The name actually begins with T but you decide that it begins with A and include A in the probe information used to access the long-term store. As a result the correct name may not be included in the search set that is drawn into the short-term store and retrieval will not succeed.

Second, if the probe is such that an extremely large region of memory is accessed, then retrieval may fail even though the desired trace is included in the search set. For example, if you are asked to name a fruit that sounds like a word meaning "to look at," you might say "pear." If you are asked to name a living thing that sounds like a word meaning "to look at," the probability of your coming up with "pear" will be greatly reduced. Again, you are more likely to remember a "John Smith" if you met him at a party with five other people than if there had been 20 people at the party. This effect can be explained on grounds other than a failure of memory search, however. It could be argued that more attention was given to "John Smith" at the smaller party. Or if the permanence of long-term storage is not accepted, it could be argued that the names of the many other people met at the larger party erode or destroy the memory trace for "John Smith." Are these objections reasonable? The John Smith example is analogous to the situation in free recall where words in long lists are less well recalled from long-term storage than words in short lists.

The problem, then, is to show that the list-length effect in free recall is dependent on the choice of probe information rather than on either the number of words intervening between presentation and recall or the differential storage given words in lists of different size. The second issue is disposed of rather easily: in many free-recall experiments that vary list length, the subjects do not know at the beginning of the list what the length of the list will be. It is therefore unlikely that they store different amounts of information for the first several words in lists of differing length. Nevertheless, as we pointed out, the first several words are recalled at different levels.

To dispose of the "interference" explanation, which implicates the number of words between presentation and recall, is more difficult. Until fairly recently, as a matter of fact, interference theories of forgetting have been predominant [see "Forgetting," by Benton J. Underwood, SCIENTIFIC AMERICAN Offprint 482, and "The Interference Theory of Forgetting," by John Ceraso, Offprint 509]. In these theories forgetting has often been seen as a matter of erosion of the memory trace, usually by items presented following the item to be remembered but also by items preceding the item to be remembered. (The list-length effect might be explained in these terms, since the average item in a long list is preceded and followed by more items than the average item in a short list.) On the other hand, the retrieval model presented in this article assumes long-term storage to be permanent; it maintains that the strength of long-term traces is independent of list length and that forgetting results from the fact that the temporal-contextual probe cues used to access any given list tend to elicit a larger search set for longer lists, thereby producing less efficient retrieval.

In order to distinguish between the retrieval and the interference explanations, we presented lists of varying lengths and had the subject attempt to recall not the list just studied (as in the typical free-recall procedure) but the list before the last. This procedure makes it possible to separate the effect of the size of the list being recalled from the effect of the number of words intervening between presentation and recall. A large or a small list to be recalled can be followed by either a large or a small intervening list. The retrieval model predicts that recall probability will be dependent on the size of the list being recalled. The interference model predicts that performance will be largely determined by the number of words in the intervening list.

We used lists of five and of 20 words and presented them in four combina-tions: 5–5, 5–20, 20–5, 20–20; the first number gives the size of the list being recalled and the second number the size of the intervening list. One result is that there is no recency effect [see illustration on preceding page]. This would be expected since there is another list and another recall intervening between presentation and recall; the intervening activity causes the words in the tested list to be lost from short-term storage and so the curves represent retrieval from long-term storage only. The significant finding is that words in lists five words long are recalled much better than words in lists 20 words long, and the length of the intervening list has little, if any, effect. The retrieval model can predict these results only if a probe is available to access the requested list. It seems likely in this experiment that the subject has available at test appropriate cues (probably temporal in nature) to enable him to select probe information pertaining to the desired list. If the experimental procedure were changed so that the subject was asked to recall the 10th preceding list, then selection of an adequate probe would no longer be possible. The results demonstrate the importance of probe selection, a control process of the short-term store.

The model of memory we have described, which integrates the system around the operations of the short-term store, is not in any sense a final theory. As experimental techniques and mathematical models have become increasingly sophisticated, memory theory has undergone progressive changes, and there is no doubt that this trend will continue. We nevertheless think it is likely that the short-term store and its control processes will be found to be central.

16

How We Remember What We See

by Ralph Norman Haber
May 1970

It depends on whether what we see is pictorial (scenes, photographs and so forth) or linguistic (words, numbers and so on). Experiments indicate that the linguistic memory is different from the pictorial

Visual perception is as much concerned with remembering what we have seen as with the act of seeing itself. When I look at a picture, I am aware that I am seeing it, and I can describe the experience of seeing. I can also remember what I saw after the picture is no longer there. How does this kind of perceptual memory work? Is it perhaps a process involving several steps in sequence, or one involving only one step during which many processes occur in parallel? Are scenes, faces and pictures remembered differently from linguistic material such as words and numbers?

In seeking to answer such questions my colleagues and I at the University of Rochester and workers in other laboratories have been studying the process of visual memory in human subjects. Our tools include tachistoscopes (devices that can display a series of images in rapid succession), slide projectors and screens, instruments for following eye movements, instruments for measuring the time needed to respond to stimuli, and various kinds of pictorial and linguistic material. These experiments are beginning to reveal several important characteristics of the visual memory process. Among the most significant of these findings is the suggestion that there is one kind of memory for pictorial material and another for linguistic.

The capacity of memory for pictures may be unlimited. Common experience suggests that this is so. For example, almost everyone has had the experience of recognizing a face he saw only briefly years before. (It is significant, as we shall see, that the name is usually harder to recall.) The reality of such experiences is supported by experiment. In one such experiment subjects were able to recognize as many as 600 pictures they had seen for only a short period of time.

More recently Lionel G. Standing and I have conducted an experiment showing that at least four times this amount of material can be recognized.

In our test of visual memory capacity subjects were shown 2,560 photographic slides at the rate of one every 10 seconds during viewing sessions held on consecutive days. Suspecting that fatigue might have some effect on performance, we had some of our volunteers follow a rigorous viewing schedule that consisted in looking at 1,280 pictures a day during four-hour sessions on two consecutive days. The rest of the subjects viewed only 640 pictures a day during two-hour sessions on four consecutive days.

One hour after a subject had seen the last of the slides he was shown 280 pairs of pictures. One member of each pair was a picture from the series the subject had already seen. The other was from a similar set, but it had never been shown to the subject. When the subjects were asked to say which of the two pictures they had seen before, 85 to 95 percent of their choices were correct. Surprisingly, subjects whose endurance had been pressed did as well as subjects who had followed a more leisurely viewing schedule. In another version of the experiment the high scores were maintained even when the pictures were shown as their mirror image during the identification sessions, so that the right-hand side became the left-hand side. The scores diminished only slightly when the subjects were asked if the pictures had been reversed [*see illustration on page 164*].

Although a person may remember almost any picture he has ever seen, he frequently is unable to recall details from a specific image when asked to do so. In another experiment Matthew H. Erdelyi and I attempted to find out what happens to these omitted details. Are they never seen in the first place? Are they seen but then forgotten, or are they seen and remembered but in such a way that they are not retrievable under normal circumstances? In order to find out each subject was briefly shown a very detailed picture and then was asked to recall both in words and in a drawing all of the picture he could remember seeing. When he said he could remember no more, we asked him nondirective questions until his ability to recall all further details seemed exhausted. (For example: "You drew a man standing here; can you describe his clothing?" "You left the lower right-hand corner of the drawing blank; can you remember anything in the picture down there?")

After this initial questioning half of the subjects were individually engaged in a 30-minute game of darts, described as an unrelated experiment. Each of the remaining subjects was asked to lean back in his chair, stare at a projection screen, relax and report whatever words came to his mind. The first 10 words spoken by the subject were written down on separate cards. Each card was then handed one at a time to the subject, who was asked first to associate more words to it, and then to express any thoughts that came to his mind in relation to the word. The entire association exercise usually lasted about 30 minutes.

Following either the dart game or the word-association task, each subject was asked again to try to recall the picture by talking about it and redrawing it. The same kinds of probing questions were asked. All the subjects were given a rationale for the interpolated task. The dart-throwers were told that we expected their memory to improve because they had spent 30 minutes thinking about something unrelated, and the word-associators were told that we expected their memory to improve because they had just spent 30 minutes intensively exercising it.

We found that the dart-throwers' ability to recall more pictorial detail neither improved nor deteriorated. Each word-associator, however, recovered a number of details he had left out of his earlier recall. We also analyzed the content of the associations themselves, and we found that if a previously unrecalled detail was prominent in the associations, it was more likely to be recovered on the subsequent recall. These results, in addition to those from other parts of the experiment, indicate that some information about fine details is maintained in memory even though it may not normally be available for report. If this were not so, even the most intense memory-jogging and free association would have failed to yield more detail than was originally reported.

Another conclusion can be drawn from this experiment. It would appear that the pictures were not originally stored in the form of words. If they had been, the details would have been recalled during the first questioning. Instead a period of intense associative activity was required during which the subject was able to attach words to the pictorial images so that the individual details of the picture could be recalled.

The first of these experiments with pictorial stimuli suggests that recognition of pictures is essentially perfect. The results would probably have been the same if we had used 25,000 pictures instead of 2,500. The second experiment indicates that such recognition is based on some type of representation in memory that is maintained without labels, words, names or the need for rehearsal. If the representation were linguistic, subjects asked to recall the details of a picture in words or other symbols should remember much more than they actually do. The test results also suggest that since the pictures are not stored in words they cannot be recalled in words either, at least not in much detail, unless the memory is stirred by an activity such as the free-association exercise.

One implication of these findings is that if techniques could be found to facilitate an attaching of words to visual images, recall might dramatically improve. Some people believe they have this ability, for example politicians who seem to be able to associate a name with every face they ever saw. Freud argued

VISUAL MEMORY EXPERIMENT required a test subject to look at 280 pairs of photographic slides. Each pair consisted of one slide that had been shown to subject before in a series of 2,560 viewed at the rate of one every 10 seconds. Subject presses button that signals that he thinks slide on left was one he had seen. Subjects remembered nearly all the slides they had been shown.

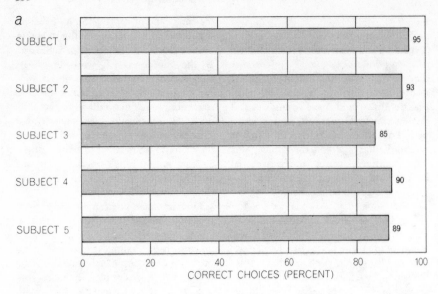

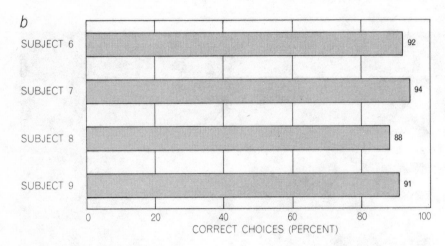

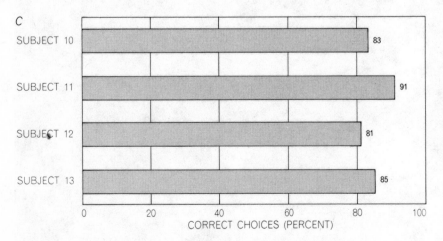

RESULTS OF VISUAL MEMORY EXPERIMENT indicate that the capacity for remembering pictures may be unlimited. Subjects in *a* recognized between 85 and 95 percent of the 2,560 slides they had previously viewed. In order to determine whether fatigue would reduce memory capacity, subjects No. 4 and No. 5 viewed 1,280 slides a day on each of two days, whereas subjects No. 1, No. 2 and No. 3 viewed only 640 slides a day on each of four days. Surprisingly, there was no significant difference between the scores of the two groups. Subjects in *b* looked at slides shown in mirror-image orientation, so that left became right, yet they were still able to identify slides as accurately as the subjects in *a* did. Subjects in *c* were also shown slides that had been reversed. When they were asked if the orientation of each photograph had been changed, the subjects responded correctly in most instances.

strongly that free association was an ideal way to recover irretrievable memories. Although Freud was concerned with repressed memories rather than with merely irretrievable ones, a more general statement is possible: The recall of previous stimulation may fail because we do not use words to remember pictures or feelings, and therefore we have difficulty using words to describe the memory later.

When the pictorial memory process is compared with the process by which words, numbers and other symbols are remembered, it becomes clear that the two systems are probably very different. Each kind of memory handles material that is perceived when light stimulates the retina, generating impulses that are then coded, organized and sent to the brain. In the case of pictures the image is received and stored permanently in pictorial form. Where words or other symbols are concerned the first step of memory is to take the stimulus out of its visual, pictorial form, code the items and extract their meaning. The collection of letters making up a printed word is not remembered as an image of distinct letters on a page; they are stored and recalled as the word itself. And words are remembered as ideas, not as a literal collection of words. A road sign is not remembered as a brightly colored panel with an arrow or a warning on it but as a message to stop, slow down or turn.

This particular memory process accounts for the ease with which a reader may overlook spelling errors in printed text. Instead of visualizing the word as it actually appears in physical reality, the reader tends almost immediately to extract the word itself from the printed characters and thus does not see the error. By the same token an unskilled proofreader may overlook the fact that a single letter in a word is printed in a typeface different from the face of the rest of the letters because he sees not the physical character but the spelling of the word.

The process of extracting linguistic material from its representational form and storing it conceptually appears to consist of several steps [*see top illustration, page 166*]. The first step is a brief moment of "iconic," or visual, storage. As we shall see, this storage lasts less than a second after perception. During this time the image may be scanned and coded. (For instance, a word may be taken out of the form of a collection of letters and translated into spoken form.) This item is then stored in the short-term memory. From the short-term memory the item is passed on to the long-term memory.

The short-term memory can probably hold from four to six unrelated items without decay, but beyond that number some kind of rehearsal is needed to prevent loss. A common example of rehearsal is our need to repeat a telephone number we have just looked up or heard as we hurry to the telephone to dial it. The seven digits cannot survive in the memory for more than a few seconds without some repetition. Another strategy for increasing the capacity of the short-term memory consists in recoding the item to be remembered. A long series of letters can be more easily held in the short-term memory, for instance, if they are made into an acronym or a word. In this case the word rather than the individual letters is remembered.

How does the material move from the short-term memory to the long-term one? Recoding from the names of the items to their meanings, a semantic coding, probably underlies this transition. No further maintenance is needed to hold

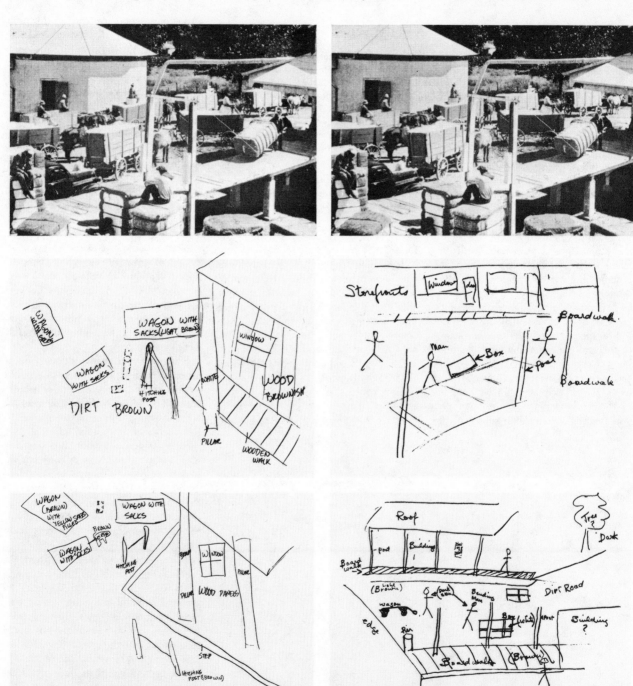

RECALL OF DETAIL indicates that pictures, faces and other pictorial material are stored in the memory as images. In this experiment two subjects were shown the same photograph of a rural scene (*pictures at top*) and each was asked to recall as much of the picture as he could by describing and drawing it (*middle picture*). At this point both subjects displayed similar levels of recall. One subject then threw darts for half an hour while the other tried to recall more details by thinking about the picture and speaking whatever words came to mind. Afterward both subjects were asked to redraw the picture. Drawing at lower left by dart-thrower indicates that his memory was relatively unchanged by his activity. Drawing at right by other subject contains much detail not present in his earlier drawing, indicating that the memory exercise helped him to attach words to the pictorial detail in his memory. If such details had been stored in the form of words rather than pictures, both subjects should have remembered all of them at first recall.

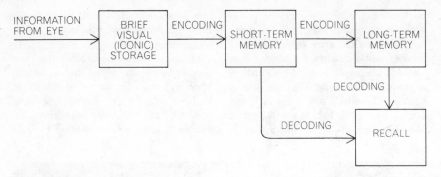

MEMORY PROCESS for words, numbers and other linguistic material has several stages. At left information such as a printed word seen by the eye is briefly stored as it actually looks. While this visual image lasts the word can be scanned, even if the original stimulus has disappeared. At center, during scanning, the word is encoded into its name (the letters *c*, *a* and *t* may become the word "cat") and is then entered in the short-term memory. At right the word enters the long-term memory, perhaps by being encoded again, this time from its name into its meaning. At lower right word is recalled by being decoded into its name.

the information in recallable form at this point, although the information may have to be coded back into names if it is to be recalled. The evidence does not yet indicate whether awareness of seeing the stimulus is synonymous with the iconic storage or short-term memory, or is something that happens with or after semantic coding.

This model of the linguistic memory process is a rather generalized one. Many specific models have been proposed, and the experimental evidence is not yet complete enough to choose between them. Nevertheless, several recent experiments have clarified what happens in the early stages. One problem that was investigated was the source of the

errors that are made when an individual is asked to recall several items in a large display. Do such omissions indicate a limited memory capacity or are they due to a failure to perceive some of the items?

It is known that only four to six items can be remembered without the aid of rehearsal or recoding. Thus it seems possible that whereas all the objects might have been perceived at first, some were simply lost because there was no room for them in the short-term memory. Items might also be lost at later stages in the memory process.

How could these hypotheses be tested? How, in other words, could failure to perceive be experimentally distinguished

from some limitation of memory capacity? One cannot solve the problem merely by asking the subject if he saw every item in the display when it was first perceived. If a subject's memory capacity is too limited to contain all the items in a display, he will not be able to recall whether or not he perceived each of them initially.

An experimental approach to this problem, developed a century ago by N. Baxt, was rediscovered by George Sperling of the Bell Telephone Laboratories. In one of Sperling's experiments based on Baxt's method the subject was presented with an array of letters in a tachistoscope. The array remained visible for about 50 milliseconds. Once the display ended, the subject was asked to remember all the letters until a marker appeared that indicated the position of from one to four of the letters that he was to report. If there was no delay, that is, if the indicator came on immediately after the termination of the display, the subject made virtually no errors. This period of error-free reporting lasted for approximately 250 milliseconds (a quarter of a second). As the delay between the end of the display and the appearance of the indicator increased, however, so did the frequency of the subject's errors.

Some important conclusions about the memory process and the source of the errors can be drawn from these results. If recall is perfect at the instant after the tachistoscopic flash of the array ends, it follows that nearly all the information in the display has probably been stored in the memory. If the storage were not virtually complete, the subject would be unable to recall some items because those indicated for report are selected randomly. There is accordingly no way for the subject to remember only those items to be selected for recall.

It can also be concluded from the highly accurate recall that the initial perception, that is, the image conveyed by the visual system to the memory system, must itself be accurate. If perception were not detailed and inclusive, the iconic image in the memory would contain errors and so would the recall. The initial perception, then, cannot be the source of the errors.

Since the subject is never asked to report more than four items, a quantity within the capacity of the short-term memory, the errors and omissions subjects make when they try to recall items from a large display must apparently originate in the later processing stages of the memory, not in the initial iconic-

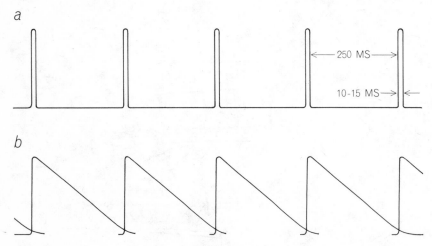

VISUAL IMAGE in an observer's memory makes a flash of light appear to persist after it has actually faded. In one experiment demonstrating such persistence a subject watched a train of flashes, each lasting between 10 and 15 milliseconds and spaced 250 milliseconds apart. In *a* flashes are represented by peaks. In *b* the images excited by the flashes are represented by curves indicating how the flashes looked to subject. The curves show that a visual image is excited by each flash (*sharply rising phase*). This image persists in the memory, fading gradually over 250 milliseconds so that it outlasts the flash itself. Because one image is still perceptible when the next image begins (*intersections of falling and rising curves*) flashes appear to subject to blend into each other, forming a flickering train.

storage stage or in a limitation on reporting by the subject.

These experiments suggested, but did not directly confirm, that the iconic image persists in the memory for about a quarter of a second. Standing and I devised two further experiments that provided this confirmation. Our results also confirm that the iconic image is visual. We argued that if a visual representation actually persisted for 250 milliseconds or so after the termination of the flash, it should be possible to have a subject estimate this persistence directly. We knew that it is not possible, however, to ask him to provide a judgment of absolute duration. With suitable adjustment in intensity, flashes lasting from one nanosecond (10^{-9} second) to 10 milliseconds (10^{-2} second) seem equal. We have tried two other procedures, both considerably more direct than Sperling's estimates.

Our first experiment tested the assumption that a brief flash of light creates an iconic image that persists in the memory for perhaps 250 milliseconds after the stimulus has ended. If this were so, it could be predicted that when the interval between flashes is equal to or slightly shorter than the duration of the iconic image, the subject should report that no flash completely faded away before the next one began. The train of flashes might appear to be flickering, but there should be no completely dark intervals between the flashes. We tested this prediction by recycling a briefly presented small black-on-white circle in one channel of a two-channel tachistoscope. The other channel was set at the same luminance as the one with the circle, in order to keep the subject's eyes adapted to light. The flash presenting the circle lasted from 10 to 15 milliseconds. A number of trains of flashes were presented, each with a different interval between flashes. After the subject had viewed a particular train of flashes he was asked to indicate if the circle completely faded away each time before it reappeared. As long as the interval between flashes did not exceed about 250 milliseconds all the subjects reported that the form never completely faded away. Intervals longer than 250 milliseconds produced reports of complete fading.

What effect, if any, did the length of the flash itself have on the duration of the iconic image? We found that for relatively short presentation times ranging between four and 200 milliseconds (well above threshold) the iconic image still persisted for about 250 milliseconds. In other words, the duration of the iconic image seemed to be independent of

TACHISTOSCOPE (*tall box at right*) is a viewing chamber in which an experimental subject watches rapidly changing stimuli such as images or light flashes. Apparatus at left controls timing and presentation of the stimuli. The subject also wears earphones through which he hears clicking sounds. He controls the tone generator that produces the clicks so that one coincides with the onset of an image and the other with the termination. Such experiments reveal how the memory processes letters, numbers and similar material.

the duration of the original stimulus, at least for very brief stimuli.

Our evidence for the existence of an iconic image seemed to be falling very neatly into place. None of the tests we had conducted so far, however, excluded the possibility that we were measuring the properties of a retinal image rather than an image formed during the first stages of the memory process. In order to eliminate this possibility—or to substantiate it—we devised another procedure. In this variation of the experiment the first flash of a train was presented to the right eye while the left eye's vision was blocked; then the right eye's vision would be blocked while the next flash was delivered to the left eye, and so forth. Under these conditions subjects

still needed about 250 milliseconds between flashes. This result clearly indicates that although there may be some persistence at the retinal level, the iconic image exists centrally, after the information from the two eyes has been combined. If this were not so, the flashes would have had to be only 125 milliseconds apart (250 milliseconds to each eye separately).

In our next experiment we attempted to refine and extend our earlier results. Following a plan suggested by Sperling, we used a three-channel tachistoscope. One channel was a blank illuminated field, the second displayed the target whose duration was to be estimated by the subject and the third presented random designs (the visual equivalent of "noise"). The subject wore earphones through which he heard a brief click at about the time the target was presented in the tachistoscope. His task was to turn a knob so that he judged the click and the beginning of the flash to come at exactly the same time. There was a click-flash presentation every few seconds. When the subject was satisfied with the match between the click and the beginning of the display, he had to repeat the procedure, but this time he had to match the click to the end of the display. The difference in the timing of the clicks thus represented the subject's estimate of the duration of the display.

As we expected, the second click followed the actual termination of the very brief display by about 200 milliseconds, indicating that the iconic image is of that duration. It will be recalled that in the preceding experiment the duration of the iconic image was independent of the duration of a flash less than 200 milliseconds long. In this experiment the persistence of the image decreased, however, as the stimulus's duration increased. When the display lasted for 500 milliseconds, the image persisted for less than 50 milliseconds. The iconic image associated with a one-second flash is less than 30 milliseconds. An iconic image lasts longer than about 250 milliseconds—for 400 milliseconds, in fact—only when the subject is dark-adapted.

Both of these studies are in close agreement with the more cumbersome estimates in the literature. They confirm the fact that the memory process seems to increase the effective length of all brief flashes to at least 200 milliseconds. If the flashes are already that long, further increases are minimized. The studies also clearly demonstrate that the brief storage Sperling postulated is in fact visual, since subjects describe the iconically stored image as if they were talking about the flash itself.

What other factors determine the length of this visual storage? Can it be lengthened or shortened under normal as well as experimental circumstances? What role does it play in the extraction of information from visual stimuli? It should be obvious that a brief period of visual storage, effectively extending a stimulus for less than a second, will be useful only when that extension provides some critical advantage. Are perceivers only asked to describe the effects of brief flashes when experimental psychologists present such flashes? Have we perhaps invented a concept of visual storage that serves no function in nature (except perhaps to read in the dark dur-

ing a lightning storm)? I believe quite the contrary. There are many rapidly presented visual stimuli encountered in the environment. For literate adults the most important and continuing visual experience is reading, and reading if nothing else is a task of viewing a rapid succession of brief visual exposures containing large amounts of information.

Evidence that the persistent iconic image aids in reading and therefore in similar visual tasks has been suggested by many workers. These investigators have found that a slow reader or someone reading slowly fixes his eyes on each word for about a quarter of a second. A faster reader also fixes his eyes for about the same amount of time. Such a fast reader attains his higher speed by reducing the number of fixations, that is, he looks at and processes several words instead of one word during each fixation. Both kinds of reader need from 30 to 50 milliseconds to shift their eyes from one fixation point to the next.

It would seem, then, that both fast and slow readers need about a quarter of a second to perceive and extract the information contained in any word. Since the length of this interval is under the reader's control, the conclusion can be drawn that the interval constitutes the adequate minimum processing time for encoding linguistic material into the memory. If this is true, it follows that a visual storage medium might serve the purpose of prolonging a stimulus that does not last long enough to be recognized otherwise. It should not be regarded as mere coincidence that the duration of iconic storage and the minimum fixation time in reading are both about a quarter of a second.

Evidence supporting this line of reasoning is beginning to accumulate, but it is still by no means adequate. Part of the evidence concerns how an iconic image is erased and what effect erasure has on information processing. If a persistent iconic image helps the viewer to process information, there should also be a way to erase the iconic image when it has served its purpose. If there were no erasing process, a reader or someone rapidly scanning the faces in a crowd might be hampered by the persistence of an iconic image from the last stimulus as he tried to assimilate a new one.

A large number of experiments show that superimposing a new visual pattern or a visual noise field over the old one will in fact wipe out the iconic image, thereby interfering with or actually stopping the processing of information contained in the pattern. This will normally

ADAPTATION CHANNEL

IMAGE CHANNEL

SOUND

DURATION OF VISUAL IMAGE is measured. In an experiment shown schematically the subject was asked to match a clicking sound (*bottom*) to the onset of a repeated stimulus consisting of a black circle on a

ADAPTATION CHANNEL

IMAGE CHANNEL

SOUND

LONG-LASTING STIMULUS in the tachistoscope produces a brief visual image in the memory. In *a* subject has already adjusted

ADAPTATION CHANNEL

VISUAL NOISE CHANNEL

IMAGE CHANNEL

SOUND

VISUAL IMAGE IS ERASED by the appearance of a new stimulus. In *a* black circle is presented for 50 milliseconds, an interval normally long enough to produce a

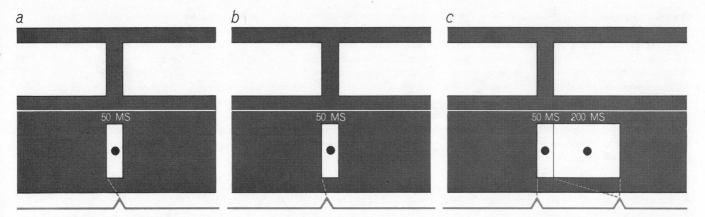

white field displayed in the tachistoscope. Adaptation field in the tachistoscope (*top*) keeps the subject's eyes adjusted to a given light level. In *a* the subject hears a click after he sees the stimulus. In *b* subject has begun to make the click coincide with the onset of the next image. In *c* adjustment has been made and subject has

also matched a second click with what he perceives as the end of the stimulus. Actually the click marks the end of the visual image in the subject's memory rather than the end of the stimulus itself, which has faded out 200 milliseconds earlier. This interval from fade-out to click therefore represents duration of the visual image.

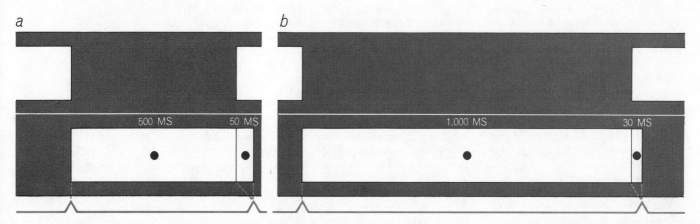

one click so that it coincides with the beginning of the stimulus and another so that it coincides with the perceived end. The stimulus actually lasts for 500 milliseconds. The interval between clicks,

however, is about 550 milliseconds, an indication that the visual image lasts 50 milliseconds. In *b*, when stimulus lasts twice as long as in *a*, visual image it excites is still shorter, about 30 milliseconds.

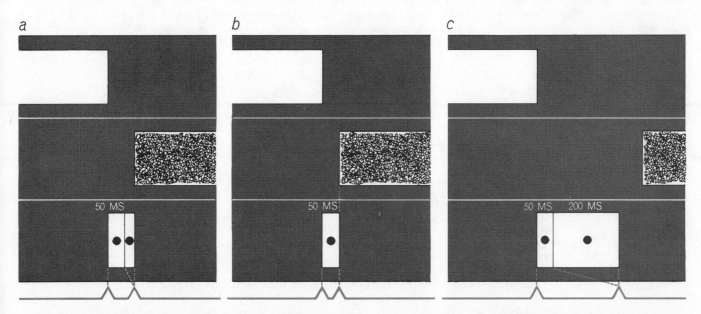

200-millisecond visual image. In this instance, however, visual noise (a random pattern of letters) appears. This new stimulus ends the visual image of the black circle after only a few milliseconds. Therefore interval between clicks is only slightly longer

than the duration of the stimulus. In *b* noise begins as circle vanishes, so that interval between clicks equals the duration of stimulus, indicating that there is no visual image at all. In *c* the noise has no effect on image because it begins after the image has faded.

happen in reading when the eyes focus on a new portion of print. The new stimulus wipes out the iconic image of the old, so that the way is cleared for the processing of new material.

The experiment of the click-flash pairings is relevant to this issue. The third channel of the tachistoscope in another condition of that study presented visual noise in the form of random patterns. At various times after the flash this visual noise channel was turned on. If the new stimulus (visual noise) erased the image of the old stimulus, as we expected, then the time interval between the two clicks should be reduced if visual noise arrives before the iconic image has had time to fade. Specifically, if the visual noise coincides with the end of the flash, the time interval between the clicks should be no longer than the flash itself. Conversely, if the visual noise were delayed beyond the normal persistence of the iconic image, the subject's performance should not be affected. This is exactly what was found.

This task did not require the subject to extract information; he was asked only to estimate how much time he would need to extract the information. The results provide fairly direct support for the erasive and therefore process-stopping effect of visual noise.

Even more convincing, however, is the fact that when one display is removed and another is presented to the subject before he has time to process the image, he reports that he was aware of seeing the first stimulus but did not have enough time to recognize it. This result can be obtained whether the display is followed by visual noise or by more information. It can be concluded that the visual noise reduces a subject's

time for extracting information, not the time available for perceiving the stimulus; the quarter-second occupied by the iconic image is not needed for seeing a display but for processing its content.

This effect was most clearly shown in a sequential word-recognition experiment. As the subject watched, each letter of a word appeared in succession on the screen of an electroluminescent panel, each in the same location so that the second letter should destroy the persistence of the first, the third letter the persistence of the second and so on. In this way the rate of presentation effectively controlled the time the subject had for processing each letter. The rate was varied from 20 milliseconds per letter to 300 milliseconds per letter. It was not surprising that the probability of recognizing each letter was higher for the slower rates of presentation. More important (and more relevant to this argument) was the finding that for each rate it did not matter whether the time from the onset of one letter to the onset of the next was used entirely for presenting the letter or whether the letter was presented for just a few milliseconds. Once a letter is seen, further viewing time is irrelevant as long as its persistence is unimpaired. The extra time is used to process the information that is already secured.

Finally, several experiments dating back to an earlier one of Sperling's have shown that when the interval between the onset of the stimulus and the arrival of visual noise is varied so that the time available for processing the content of the stimulus is also varied, a nearly linear function is revealed between processing time and the number of items the perceiver can recognize. In

an experiment conducted in my laboratory we have shown that this relationship is much more apparent in subjects without practice in this particular task; it is attenuated after they acquire more experience. In the first few days of the experiment it appears that the perceiver needs about 10 milliseconds of processing time to recognize each letter after having some time to perceive all the letters and set up the iconic storage. For the particular displays we used, this perception and setup time was about 50 milliseconds. Thus a four-letter word requires about 90 milliseconds of time before the visual noise arrives in order for each of its letters to be correctly recognized. After several days, however, four letters require little more time than one does. This suggests that perceivers are developing more efficient strategies for processing information as they become familiar with the task and the items to be recognized.

Clearly much is happening in the first few milliseconds after the onset of a visual stimulus that is to be encoded into verbal memory. It can also be seen that the memory process can be regarded as a system concerned with information processing that consists of several stages and has its own time constants for extraction, decay, mode of persistence, susceptibility to interference or erasure, and the like. Viewing the memory process in this way is likely to lead investigators to design still other experiments that will yield a basic understanding of visual perception. Such knowledge is important for its own sake, but I hope it is also clear how much our knowledge of reading and other visual skills is ultimately related to our understanding of visual perception and information processing.

Spatial Memory

by David S. Olton
June 1977

Among the many things animals are able to remember is where they have been. Experiments with rats suggest that this kind of memory is localized in the region of the brain known as the hippocampus

The ability of an animal to keep track of its location in space by remembering where it has been is a basic component of intelligent behavior. According to modern concepts of memory, this ability involves a form of short-term memory, called working memory, that stores information as it is being worked on, or processed. (A common verbal example is remembering a telephone number obtained from a directory as you dial the number.) How is spatial memory programmed? Is it localized in some specific part of the brain? Is it associated with the activity of specific nerve cells? Such questions have now been at least partly answered by psychological and physiological experiments with rodents.

The importance of spatial memory for the survival of an animal is suggested by the behavior of the Hawaiian honeycreeper, a bird that feeds on nectar from flowers. Each of the flowers in the bird's territory may provide nectar on numerous visits, but the supply of nectar on any one visit is limited and time must pass before it is replaced. If the bird returns to the flower during this time, it finds little or no nectar. The optimal strategy is therefore to visit the other flowers before returning to the first one, giving each flower the longest possible time to replace its nectar. Alan C. Kamil of the University of Massachusetts, who has studied the Hawaiian honeycreeper in its natural habitat, has found that it tends to follow such a strategy: it does significantly better than chance at remembering the locations of flowers it has recently visited, rarely returning to them until enough time has passed for the nectar to be replenished.

The importance of spatial memory has also been demonstrated by laboratory experiments. When rewards and punishments are consistently located in a particular place, experimental animals quickly learn to obtain the rewards and avoid the punishments. Even when the rewards and punishments are correlated with some stimulus other than spatial location (such as a light), the animal will still attempt to solve the task first on the basis of its spatial characteristics, for example consistently turning right or left rather than responding to the location of the light. Only after the attempt at a spatial solution has failed does the animal begin to try other strategies.

To obtain some understanding of how animals use working memory to solve spatial problems, my colleagues and I at Johns Hopkins University developed a new experimental procedure that would enable us to study working memory. We based our experimental design on the spatial maze, an apparatus that has been employed for testing animal behavior since the turn of the century. Such mazes vary considerably in complexity, from a simple *T* to a miniature replica of the famous hedge maze at Hampton Court outside London. The late Edward C. Tolman of the University of California at Berkeley was a strong advocate of using mazes to explore the cognitive abilities of animals; he believed the major component of an animal's solution of a problem is its ability to discover the experimenter's instructions. Mazes are particularly useful in this regard because the instructions are inherent in the apparatus itself.

In our experiments we wanted to give rodents instructions that were essentially the same as the spatial strategy of the honeycreeper: Remember a list of places where food can be found and then visit each place once before returning to the first one. To make these instructions clear to the animals we developed a maze with eight radiating arms elevated on stilts. At the start of a test a food pellet was placed at the end of each arm. The animal was then put in the center of the apparatus and allowed to choose the arms freely until it had obtained all eight pellets. The optimal strategy is clearly to visit each arm once and not to return to it, thus visiting all eight arms in the first eight choices. In this way the animal can get the eight food pellets with the least amount of running through the maze.

So far the animals we have tested in the radial-arm maze have been mostly laboratory rats, but we have obtained similar results with the first-generation offspring of wild rats and with gerbils. All the animals learned rapidly and performed well. After a few days of being trained to run on the elevated alleyways, they made an average of 6.8 correct responses in the first eight choices; after 20 days they had improved to an average of 7.8 correct responses. Since the animal returned to the center platform after each response and therefore had all eight arms available on every choice, the probability of its making at least seven correct responses by chance in the first eight choices was very low (.07). Yet by the end of the testing every animal performed this well for 10 consecutive days (a probability of $.07^{10}$), making it extremely unlikely that mere chance was involved in its performance.

There were two main theoretical explanations for the excellent performance of rodents in the radial maze. Either they were identifying the position of the visited arms by comparing them with landmarks in the surrounding room or they were following some simpler strategy that required them to store a smaller amount of information in their working memory. One such strategy would be to use an algorithm, or rule, such as "Choose adjacent arms in a clockwise direction." Only the general strategy would have to be kept in the working memory; the specific arms chosen could be forgotten immediately after each choice. Another strategy would be to use the rodent equivalent of a check mark, perhaps a scent label left at the entrance to a visited arm. The particular choice could then be forgotten because the label would serve as a permanent reminder.

The algorithm hypothesis was easy to dismiss because the daily sequence of choices was not consistent enough for the accurate choice behavior to depend on a particular rule. The possibility that the rats were marking visited arms with a label of some kind was harder to evaluate and required an additional experiment. For this purpose we regarded landmarks in the surrounding room and the hypothetical labels within the maze as being "relevant-redundant" cues: relevant, because either might guide choice behavior, and redundant, because in the usual testing situation both cues always occurred together. In order to evaluate the relative importance of the two types of cue we separated them and made them nonredundant. We did so by allowing the animal to make three choices and then rotating the maze (with the animal confined in the center) to a new po-

sition, thereby separating the place cues (which remained the same) and the hypothetical labels (which moved with the maze). The three arms already chosen were rebaited so that all the arms again contained food pellets, and the animal was allowed to choose freely among the arms until it had chosen five more of them (for a total of eight). We found that the animals tended to avoid the first three spatial locations, even though the maze rotation had placed arms that had not previously been visited and hence would have lacked labels in these locations. The results therefore indicated

that the animals were not following a maze-labeling strategy.

We next wondered whether the rats were learning a spatial map that enabled them to understand the relations among all the parts of the maze, or whether they were simply learning some kind of list of places that were unrelated and independent. To determine which was the case John A. Walker, a graduate student at Johns Hopkins, designed a testing procedure with a four-arm maze. The rat was first placed at the end of an arm and allowed to obtain the food pel-

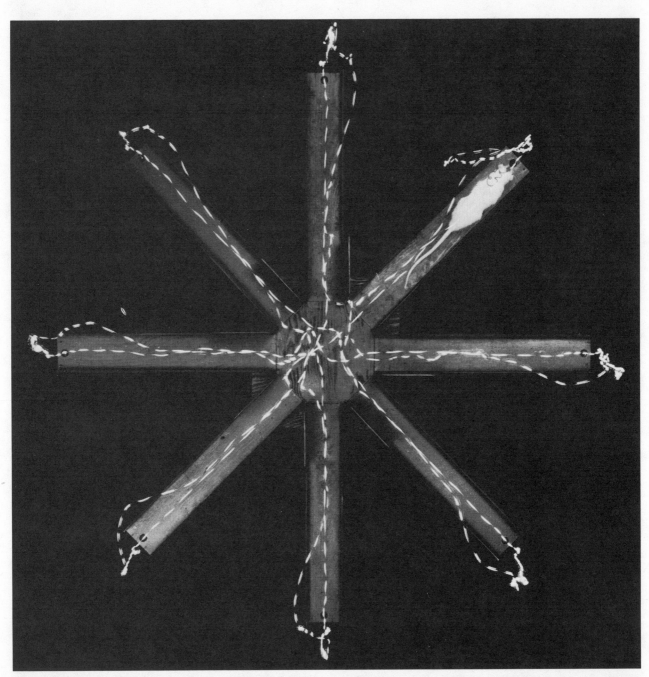

PATH OF NORMAL RAT as it travels through an eight-arm spatial maze is shown in this two-minute time exposure made in the author's laboratory by affixing a flashing light to the animal's head. Optimal strategy is to visit each arm once, picking up food pellet at the far end. This task requires the animal to keep track of the spatial locations it has visited by storing them in short-term, or "working," memory.

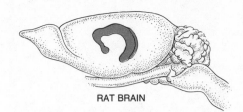

RAT BRAIN

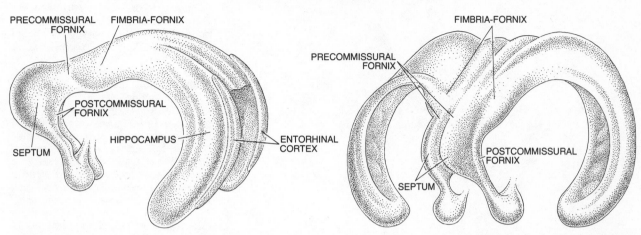

PRECOMMISSURAL FORNIX

FIMBRIA-FORNIX

POSTCOMMISSURAL FORNIX

SEPTUM

HIPPOCAMPUS

ENTORHINAL CORTEX

FIMBRIA-FORNIX

PRECOMMISSURAL FORNIX

POSTCOMMISSURAL FORNIX

SEPTUM

HIPPOCAMPUS is a structure in the center of the rat brain. It is named after the Greek word for sea horse because it is shaped some-what like one. It is connected to deep brain structures by way of the fornix and to higher brain structures by way of the entorhinal cortex.

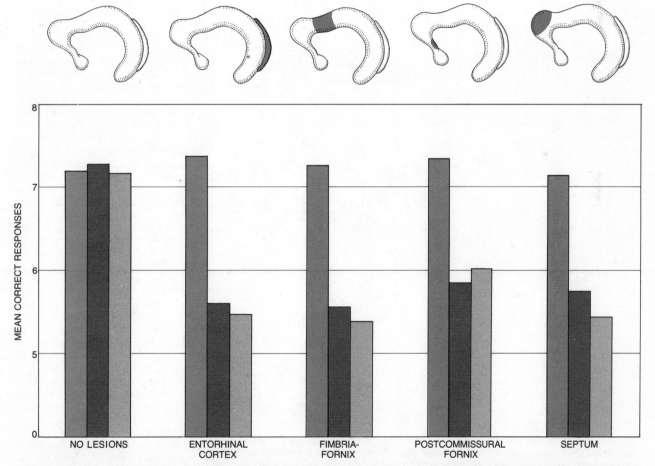

MEAN CORRECT RESPONSES

NO LESIONS   ENTORHINAL CORTEX   FIMBRIA-FORNIX   POSTCOMMISSURAL FORNIX   SEPTUM

LESIONS IN THE HIPPOCAMPUS cause rodents to perform poorly on radial-arm maze compared with normal performance (*color*), suggesting that the hippocampus is essential for spatial working memory. The disruptive effect is specific to the hippocampus (lesions in other brain regions have little or no effect) and is the same four days after surgery (*dark gray*) or 50 days after it (*light gray*). Damage to any part of the hippocampal circuit produces a similar behavioral disturbance, limiting the number of possible "circuit diagrams."

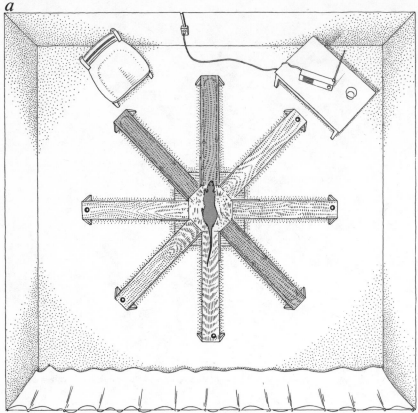

a

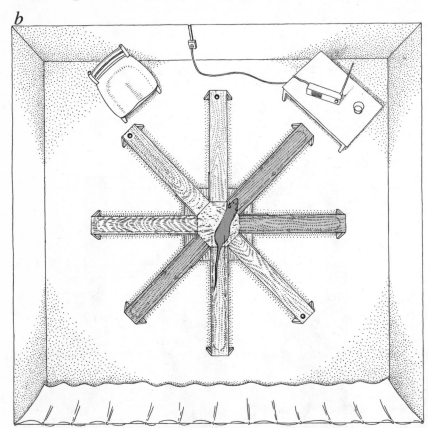

b

MAZE-ROTATION EXPERIMENT shows that rats do not identify visited arms by marking them with a pheromone, or scent. The rat was first allowed to choose three arms (*a*). The maze was then rotated until the chosen arms (*color*) were correlated with unchosen spatial locations. The arms were rebaited and the animal was allowed to make five more choices (*b*). Instead of avoiding arms previously visited (as the scent-marking theory would predict) the animal chose the five unvisited spatial locations even though that meant returning to visited arms. This suggests that the animals remember arms by correlating them with stimuli in surrounding room.

let there rather than having to run out on the arm of its own accord. After the initial placement the animal was returned to the center platform and allowed to choose among the arms freely. The animal could therefore remember where it had been only on the basis of spatial stimuli at the end of one arm and had to make the rest of the choices on the basis of stimuli at the entrance to the arms. Only by successfully making the association between the two sets of spatial stimuli could the animal correctly solve the problem.

We found that the animals had no difficulty with this procedure. After a few days of adapting to being placed at the end of the arms, they chose just as well as they did in the usual procedure and did not return to the arm on which they had been placed. These results suggested that the animals had indeed learned a map of the maze that enabled them to understand the spatial relations between the various parts of it. Moreover, since the animals were placed at the end of an arm, they never had the opportunity to leave a label identifying that arm, again demonstrating the absence of an intramaze labeling strategy.

To further explore the nature of the spatial memory we did a series of experiments to see if the animals' memory for the list of visited arms had some characteristics in common with those described for human learning of items in a list. One of these characteristics is that the capacity of working memory is limited: the more items that are stored, the worse the memory for those items is. When we tested rats on the eight-arm maze and also on a 17-arm maze, we found in both there was a significant decline in the probability of a correct response as the number of choices increased.

There were two possible theoretical explanations for the decline in accuracy of choice behavior during a test. The first was that the memory trace gradually decayed with time, rather like a fading photograph, so that the memory of the early choices diminished toward the end of the test and increased the likelihood of a return to those arms. The second was that information was not forgotten because of the passage of time per se but because the storage of the earlier choices in working memory interfered with the storage of the later choices. In order to distinguish between these two explanations we separated time and choices by varying the amount of time required for the animals to complete a test.

In some experiments we approximately doubled the duration of the test by placing guillotine doors at the entrance to each arm. The doors were lowered after each choice, confining the animal to the center of the maze for about 20 seconds. In other experiments the testing time was cut approximately in half by providing the animals with water on the central platform, facilitating the ingestion of the dry pellets. Under these conditions the memory-trace-decay hypothesis would predict that the animals would perform better than normal when the test was shorter and worse than normal when the test was longer, whereas the interference theory would predict that such manipulations would have no effect because the number of choices the animal made was not altered.

We found that the animals performed no better or worse than usual when the testing time was shortened or lengthened. Moreover, additional experiments demonstrated little or no decay of spatial working memory for periods of up to an hour. Thus it appears that short-term forgetting in this task results from interference among the items to be remembered rather than from a decay of the memory trace.

Another characteristic of working memory we have examined is the effect of the order in which items are entered in memory. As an example, consider having to learn a list composed of the following eight words: house, cat, car, love, desk, wall, card, patch. If you are like most people, you will remember the first two words on the list and the last two words better than the words in the middle. Hence the order in which items are entered into memory may affect the accuracy of their recall.

With this human psychological phenomenon in mind we looked for a serial-order effect on the spatial-memory store in rodents by examining choice performance to see whether the animals made fewer mistakes involving the first few or the last few choices in a test. Such a distinction did not seem to be present; when there was an error, it was as likely to be made by repeating the first or the last choices as by repeating choices in the middle. Thus either rodents do not store their spatial choices in a particular serial order or serial storage does not affect the accuracy of their recall as it does in man.

Finally, we investigated the ability of the animals to isolate spatial information from one test so that it did not interfere with their performance on a later test. Since the capacity of working memory is limited, it should ideally be cleared of all old and unnecessary information as rapidly as possible so that a maximum amount of new information can be stored. In experiments with human subjects this process is called resetting. To determine whether rodents could also reset working memory by eliminating old information at the end of a test we gave the animals eight tests on the eight-arm maze in immediate succession, letting the animal know a

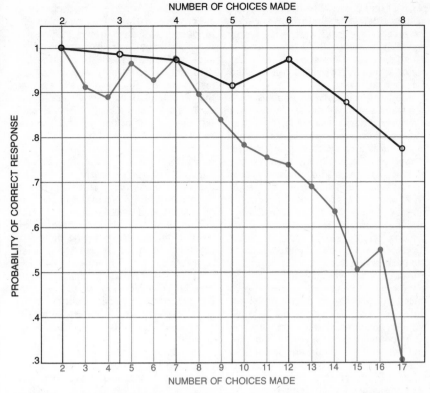

ACCURACY OF CHOICES DECLINES in a test as the number of correct choices increases, a phenomenon that can be observed both in the eight-arm maze (*black*) and the 17-arm maze (*color*). Experiments by the author suggest that this decline is due to an interference among the items stored in working memory rather than to a time-dependent decay of the memory trace.

given test was over by removing it briefly from the apparatus. We found that although accuracy of choice among the arms decreased as we expected within each test as the number of choices increased, it recovered markedly at the beginning of the next test, indicating that the animals were indeed resetting their working memory between tests.

Once we had achieved our aim of establishing an adequate test of spatial working memory in animals we turned our attention to the brain mechanisms underlying this kind of memory. We were particularly interested in the region of the brain named the hippocampus (after the Greek for sea horse, which it resembles in curving around the core of the brain). Experiments I had conducted with Robert L. Isaacson at the University of Michigan had suggested that following damage to the hippocampus rats have difficulty distinguishing between the left and the right half of a simple maze, whereas normal animals do not. Several other investigators, particularly Helen Mahut of Northeastern University, also noted the peculiar difficulty animals with damage to the hippocampus had with spatial tasks.

The first formal theoretical statement of the role of the hippocampus in spatial behavior was made by John O'Keefe and Lynn Nadel of University College London, who provided experimental evidence that the hippocampus forms the spatial map animals use to guide themselves through space. In one experiment with Abraham H. Black of McMaster University they trained rats to run from one small compartment to another to avoid shock. They found that normal animals learned to associate the shock with the spatial location of the compartment in the room but that rats with damage to the hippocampal system appeared to ignore completely the spatial characteristics of the task. Since rats in the radial-arm maze rely on spatial information to choose each arm, we thought it would be valuable to observe the effect of experimental damage to the hippocampus on the accuracy of choice.

Rats have a large and well-formed hippocampus, and its connections to other parts of the rat brain have been extensively studied by Walle J. H. Nauta of the Massachusetts Institute of Technology and Theodor W. Blackstad of the University of Aarhus. A major connection is in the entorhinal cortex, which lies in back of the hippocampus and connects it to the areas of the cerebral cortex that are involved in processing sensory information. A second connection is by way of the fornix (meaning arch) to the deep brain structures involved in motivation and emotion. The fornix is divided into two parts: an upper part that passes through the septum in the center of the brain and is called the precommissural fornix, and a lower one that bypasses the septum and is called the postcommissural fornix. The region where the two parts join is called the fimbria-fornix.

In our experiments the animals were first trained in the radial-arm maze until their performance was stable. Then they were anesthetized and lesions were made surgically by cutting one of the hippocampal connections. Control animals underwent all the surgical procedures except the production of a lesion. After several days for recovery from the surgery the animals were retested in the radial-arm maze. There were two test periods: one beginning four days after surgery to examine the acute effects of the brain lesion and the other beginning 50 days after surgery to determine whether the behavioral deficits produced by the lesion might diminish with time. In both cases we wanted to know whether an animal that had been operated on could perform as well as one that had not, and if it could not perform as well, exactly how its performance was affected by the brain damage.

In the control animals there was no significant effect of the surgery itself. Lesions in the cerebral cortex, an area not immediately related to the hippo-campus, had essentially no behavioral effect. Destruction of any part of the hippocampal system, however, caused a profound impairment in maze performance both during the testing period immediately after surgery and during the testing period 50 days later. Lesions in the caudate nucleus, another nonhippo-campal area, had a slight disruptive effect but not one of the same magnitude as lesions in the hippocampus.

The lack of major effects of damage in other brain areas indicates that impairment of spatial performance is not caused by disrupting just any system in the rodent brain; it seems to be particularly associated with damage to the hippocampal system. Another point of interest is the similarity in the degree of the deficit after the destruction of each connection to the hippocampus. One could postulate many different circuit diagrams of hippocampal function, but the fact that behavior is disrupted in the same way after any lesion in the hippocampal system limits the number of acceptable alternatives.

The changes produced by the lesions appear to be irreversible, even though the hippocampus has proved to be a very "plastic" brain area, reorganizing itself after many different types of damage. Gary S. Lynch of the University of California at Irvine and Oswald Stew-ard of the University of Virginia have demonstrated that after destruction of either the body of the fornix or the ento-rhinal area many of the fibers in the hippocampus sprout and put out new connections in a few days. Since in our experiments the animals did not perform any better 50 days after surgery than they had immediately afterward, plastic changes in the hippocampus appear to have no functional importance for the animal in this type of task.

Having shown that animals with their hippocampal function disrupted by lesions had great difficulty performing well in the radial-arm maze, we attempted to characterize the difficulty. Several possible explanations were quickly eliminated. After brain damage the animals were just as coordinated in the maze as before and showed no tendency to fall off the arms or miss them altogether. In fact, the animals ran slightly faster than usual and with no hesitation, indicating that the impaired choice behavior did not result from some primary sensory or motor deficit.

Many experiments, such as those of Isaacson (who is now at the University of Florida), have characterized animals with hippocampal damage as "persever-ating," or returning to make the same error time after time, more often than would be expected by chance. In our experiments too animals with damage to the hippocampus exhibited remarkable repetitions of choice sequences, a behavior that was almost never observed in normal animals. One rat, for example, chose arms 2, 4, 6 and 8 on the first four choices and then repeated the same sequence twice more before making the next correct response. Another animal chose opposite arms, responding first to Arm 1 and then to Arm 5, and repeated the sequence five times. These are the types of behavior one would expect if the animals were actively perseverating in their choices.

The significance of perseveration is still an open question. At present there seem to be two alternative explanations for this striking effect of lesions in the hippocampus. First, it is possible that damage to the hippocampus does not destroy spatial memory but instead disrupts other cognitive functions. In that case the animal would be able to discriminate between correct and incorrect choices but its decision-making ability would be out of phase, like that of a speculator in the stock market who consistently buys long before a stock goes down and sells short before a stock goes up. The second possibility is that the lesions in the hippocampus do destroy spatial memory and that the rats, instead of behaving on the basis of spatial stimuli, try to compensate by using a different set of stimuli to control their

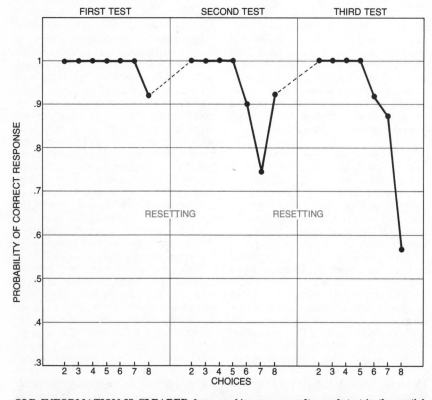

OLD INFORMATION IS CLEARED from working memory after each test in the spatial maze so that a maximum amount of new information can be stored. Called resetting, this process was demonstrated by giving a rat a series of tests in the eight-arm maze (removing the animal briefly from apparatus between tests). Choice accuracy returned to maximum level at the beginning of each test, indicating that old choices were not interfering with new ones.

behavior, such as a learned sequence of muscular movements or a place-cue strategy.

To understand this latter concept consider a person in New York City who wants to travel first to San Francisco, then to Miami and then back to New York. If he has formed a cognitive map of the U.S., he knows that San Francisco is west of New York and Miami is south. Therefore he would know that he should drive west to San Francisco and then in a southeasterly direction to Miami. The traveler could also make the trip, however, without having any idea where he is. Instead of relying on his knowledge of geography he could follow a cue strategy based on the fact that New York and San Francisco are connected by Route 80 and New York and Miami are connected by Route 95. That strategy would be successful in getting him to his destination, but once he was in San Francisco he would have no idea how to get directly to Miami, and he would have to retrace his path by way of Route 80 to New York and then take Route 95 south to Miami.

O'Keefe and Nadel have suggested that the hippocampus is responsible for creating the spatial map and that other brain structures mediate cue learning.

To support their view they conducted an experiment testing two groups of rats in a circular maze. One group was trained to use spatial stimuli, as in our usual experiments with radial-arm mazes. The other group was given an explicit cue (a stand with a light on it) to mark the location of the food. Normal animals and animals with lesions in the fornix were trained in both tasks. The fornix lesions produced the expected behavioral deficit in the group that learned with spatial stimuli but had little effect on the group that learned with the light cue. These results suggested that if we could modify the radial-arm maze to make it a cue-

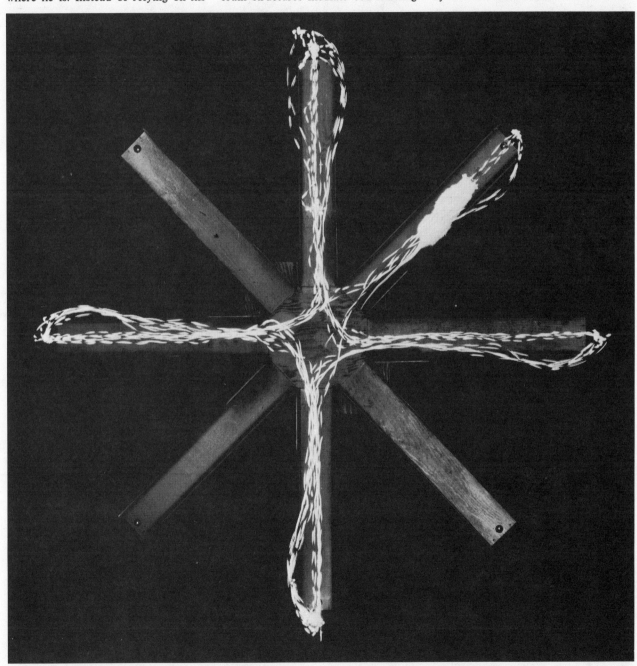

ABNORMAL MAZE BEHAVIOR of a rat with a lesion in the fornix is shown in this time exposure. The striking repetition of a sequence of choices, termed perseveration, is often seen in such animals. It may be that damage to the hippocampus destroys the animal's ability to learn a cognitive map of the maze, forcing it to rely on a simpler strategy such as repeating a sequence of muscular movements.

learning task rather than a spatial one, animals with fornix damage should perform no worse than normal animals.

To test this prediction we altered the 17-arm maze so that it could be solved by cue learning. At the outside end of each arm we put a small drawbridge that was an extension of the arm and could be raised or lowered. The food pellet was placed on a pedestal beyond the end of the arm so that the ani-

mal had to cross the bridge to get the food. At the beginning of each test the drawbridge on every arm was raised. When the animal went out on an arm to get food, it pushed the drawbridge down, ran across it to pick up the pellet and then returned to the center. The drawbridge stayed down for the remainder of the test, so that the rat did not have to remember each of the arms chosen because the position of the drawbridge could function as a cue to guide

his choices correctly. When the rat was deciding which arm to choose next, it needed only to look down each arm. If the drawbridge was up, the rat would know it should choose that arm.

So far we have only preliminary evidence from a few animals, but the results strongly support O'Keefe and Nadel's predictions. All the rats were first trained to respond correctly, one group with drawbridges and the other without. Lesions were then made in their fornix.

ADDITION OF DRAWBRIDGES enables animals to successfully solve the 17-arm maze without having to learn a cognitive map of its layout in space. At the start of a test the drawbridge at the end of each arm is up and the animal must push it down and run across it in order to obtain the food on the pedestal beyond. The lowered bridge serves from then on as a visual cue, informing the animal that it has already visited an arm. Rats with lesions in the hippocampus perform poorly in conventional mazes but perform well in modified maze. This result suggests that although the hippocampus is required for learning a cognitive map of the environment, other brain regions mediate simpler strategies (such as cue learning) that enable the animal to find its way through the spatial maze without knowing where it is.

Rats tested in the usual spatial procedure without the drawbridge cues showed a severe impairment after the lesions and performed no better than chance even on the second choice. Lesioned rats tested with drawbridge cues; on the other hand, showed at most only a transient impairment that might have been due to the effects of the operation itself. Within a few days they were performing without error, choosing only those arms with the drawbridge up and avoiding all the arms with the drawbridge down. These results demonstrate that animals with damage to the hippocampus show an impairment only in those procedures that might involve spatial memory, not in every testing procedure in the radial-arm maze. When rats with lesions in the hippocampus are given an alternative strategy based on cue learning, they have no difficulty in performing as well as normal animals.

Another way of approaching the relation between brain structures and behavioral functions is to obtain recordings of brain activity while the animals are engaged in the appropriate behavior. If the brain structure is important in the function required for the performance of the behavior, the electrical activity of the nerve cells making up the structure ought to be correlated with that behavior.

James B. Ranck, Jr., of the Downstate Medical Center of the State University of New York and O'Keefe, Nadel and their colleagues have obtained considerable information about the types of behavior that are correlated with electrical

activity in the hippocampus. Most relevant to our maze experiments are O'Keefe's findings that the activity of some cells in the hippocampus is strongly correlated with the animal's position in space. O'Keefe called these cells "place units" to emphasize the fact that their activity depended on the animal's position in the apparatus and not on the type of behavior being displayed by the animal in that position. Whether the animal was eating, drinking, grooming, running or just standing still seemed to make no difference to the cell. As long as the rat was in a particular place in the apparatus the cell was active, and whenever the rat left that place the cell was quiet.

Since rats use spatial stimuli to solve the radial-arm maze, we decided to search for place units in the hippocampus while the animals were running in the maze. To test the hypothesis that nerve cells in the hippocampus mediate spatial memory in our task I collaborated with Phillip J. Best and Michael H. Branch of the University of Virginia on a series of neurophysiological experiments. We first trained animals in the radial-arm maze with a procedure of partial reinforcement in which food was placed randomly at the ends of the arms. The optimal strategy for the animal was thus to move continually about the apparatus, checking the end of each arm to determine if food had been replaced there. The animals learned this behavior quite rapidly, and for periods of several hours they would regularly explore all the arms of the maze.

We then surgically attached a microelectrode mounting to each animal's skull. The mounting, developed by Ranck, was very light and caused no discomfort or interference. Several days after surgery we attached a tungsten wire microelectrode to the mounting and lowered it into the brain. All but three microns (three thousandths of a millimeter) at the tip of the electrode was insulated, so that we could record from single nerve cells. The insertion procedure was essentially blind: we merely lowered the electrode into the hippocampus until the activity of a single cell was detected. After the recording experiment had been completed we made a spot lesion by passing a relatively small amount of current through the tip of the electrode. Hence we were later able to identify the precise area of the hippocampus we had been recording from by slicing the brain and staining the tissue.

When we located a cell in the hippocampus with the electrode, the rat was allowed to run freely in the radial-arm maze while the cell's activity was recorded, amplified and displayed on an oscilloscope screen. We found that many cells in the hippocampus responded selectively to certain arms of the maze either by an increase in their rate of firing when the rat chose an arm or by an abrupt decrease in the rate of firing below the average level of activity. One cell, for example, was relatively inactive when the animal started on Arm 5, became very active on arms 2 and 3, quiet-

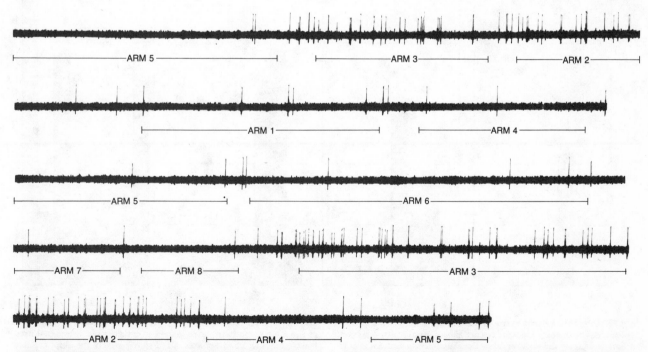

OSCILLOSCOPE TRACE shows the activity of a single cell in the hippocampus as the rat runs freely in the radial-arm maze. The cell's activity, which was recorded by means of an implanted metal electrode, is strikingly correlated with the rat's position in space. Cell's firing rate is slow when animal starts on Arm 5, speeds up on arms 2 and 3, slows down on other arms and increases again on Arm 3.

ed down on the other arms and became active again on arms 2 and 3.

Using this procedure and recording for periods of several hours with each cell, we classified arms as being either "on" or "off." This usage followed one that is generally applied to the receptive fields of nerve cells in the visual or auditory regions of the cerebral cortex to identify the types of visual or auditory stimuli that cause these cells to modify their firing rate significantly. In our experiments an "on" arm was an arm in the maze where the cell fired more rapidly; an "off" arm was one where the cell fired more slowly. For an arm to be considered either "on" or "off" it had to meet two criteria. The first was that the mean rate of activity when the animal was on the arm had to be at least three standard errors of the mean greater or less than the overall mean rate, since the likelihood of a rate change that large occurring by chance is very small (.002). The second was that the mean rate of activity on an arm had to be consistently different from the overall mean rate each time the animal entered the arm, so as to ensure that the large increased or decreased rate of firing was not a random effect but was consistent over a period of time.

For example, for one cell we recorded from, arms 2 and 3 passed both criteria for being an "on" arm, arms 1, 4, 6, 7 and 8 passed both criteria for being an "off" arm and Arm 5 did not meet at least one of the two criteria. The receptive field of this cell therefore divided the radial-arm maze into a small "on" field and a larger "off" field.

How do we know that the only behavioral correlate of a hippocampal cell's activity is the animal's position in space? The answer is that we do not. One of the difficulties with any recording experiment is that the investigators do not have the time or the opportunity to ask the cell about every possible stimulus. In short, one can never be certain whether one has found the only behavioral correlate or receptive field of a given brain cell. We did, however, carry out a number of tests to ensure that some irrelevant part of the experimental procedure was not particularly influencing the cell's activity. We distracted the animal in various ways, picking it up, clapping our hands, flashing lights and moving around in the testing chamber and the adjoining room. We altered the animal's expectations about reinforcement by attracting it to an arm with food held in front of it with tweezers, by placing food in unusual positions in the maze (such as in the middle of an arm) or by occasionally putting food at the end of the arm only after the animal had already checked the food cup and found that it was empty.

Throughout all of these modifications the activity recorded from the cell in the hippocampus was stable; the only obvious behavior that was correlated with the amount of activity in the nerve cell was the position of the animal in the maze. This was true even when the general motivation of the animal changed as the animal became satiated. Running behavior clearly waxed and waned in cycles, the animal sometimes responding slowly and pausing to groom itself or to rest, and sometimes responding rapidly and running through all eight choices in about 30 seconds. Still the activity of the cells in the hippocampus remained consistent. As a final control we also recorded from cells in other brain structures and found no correlation between spatial location and the cells' firing rate. In short, the cells we recorded from in the hippocampus looked just like those O'Keefe described as place units. The activity of the cell was correlated with the animal's position in the apparatus, regardless of the type of behavior we observed in that position.

The types of receptive fields we have measured for cells in the hippocampus range from a simple one with a single "on" arm to a complex one with alternating "on" and "off" arms. So far these receptive fields do not fall into any obvious categories as those of the visual system do. There are obvious differences among individual cells in terms of their overall rate of activity, the number and discreteness of their "on" and "off" arms and the magnitude of the change in the cell firing rate when the animal enters an

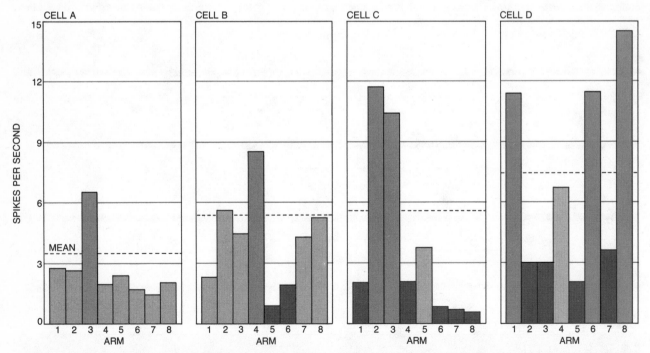

SPATIAL STIMULI that excite or inhibit the firing of four prototypical cells in the rat hippocampus are shown graphically. Each set of bars represents the eight arms of the radial-arm maze. An arm is classified as being "on" (*color*) for a given cell if, when the animal enters that arm, the cell's firing rate increases by at least three standard errors of the mean away from the overall mean rate. An "off" arm (*dark gray*) must consistently produce a decrease in firing rate of the same magnitude. Arms in neither category are considered neutral (*light gray*). The responses of individual cells in the hippocampus to spatial position vary greatly. Cell *A* has a very simple response pattern with a single "on" arm. Cell *D*, however, has a complex pattern with alternating "on" and "off" arms. *B* and *C* are in between.

arm, but grouping cells into categories based on these different response characteristics must await more extensive experimental information.

How does a place unit know where in space it should be active? O'Keefe and his colleagues have addressed this question by testing animals in a dimly lighted chamber with black walls. On each of the walls was displayed a single prominent stimulus: a light, a rotating fan, a loudspeaker emitting sound and a white card, all of which together activated the place unit. Removal of any one of the four stimuli had little effect on the cell's activity, presumably because the remaining three stimuli allowed successful orientation. When any three of the stimuli were removed, however, the cell's firing pattern became erratic and unpredictable. These findings suggest that place units receive information from a constellation of spatial stimuli in the environment rather than from just one stimulus. Thus each place unit recognizes a particular spatial location by "triangulating" among stimuli in different parts of the environment, much as a surveyor or a navigator determines his location in space by measuring the relative positions of fixed landmarks.

We have looked primarily at place units in our experiments, but other types of cells in the hippocampus have also been described. It is known from the work of Case H. Vanderwolf of the University of Western Ontario that when animals are engaged in voluntary behavior such as exploring and running, their hippocampus exhibits a rhythmically varying electric potential known as the theta rhythm. Ranck identified a group of cells in the hippocampus whose activity is strongly correlated with this rhythm. O'Keefe and Black subsequently found that when they trained rats to jump from the floor of a cage to a small ledge, and then varied the distance between the floor and the ledge, the frequency of the rhythmic firing of these cells was related to the distance the animal had to jump in order to reach the ledge. When they placed small weights on the animal's back to vary the amount of force required to make a jump, the activity of the cells did not change, indicating that the distance of the jump was the critical variable. O'Keefe accordingly named the rhythmically firing cells "displace units," since their activity depended on the distance the animal was about to move. Hence it appears that the hippocampus has at least two classes of cells: place units that reflect where the animal is at the present time and displace units that reflect the distance it is about to move in the environment.

In sum, our experiments with brain lesions and those with nerve-cell recordings suggest that the hippocampus plays an important role in spatial working memory and provide support for O'Keefe and Nadel's spatial-map hypothesis as well. Without the hippocampus the ability of rats to perform the radial-maze task correctly is severely impaired. With the hippocampus intact the rats do well, and the activity of nerve cells within the hippocampus is strongly correlated with the animals' position in space.

As with many experiments, the information we have obtained now raises an entirely new set of questions. Some of them have to do with the performance of normal animals. Why did the rats not adopt any of the strategies that might have made the task easier for them? Was it because of a limitation of rodent cognitive processes or the task's being so simple that it did not provide a sufficient challenge? Other questions have to do with the physiological bases of spatial working memory. Our results suggest an important role for the hippocampus, but the late Hans-Lukas Teuber of M.I.T. and Brenda A. Milner of the Montreal Neurological Institute have suggested that other parts of the brain, such as the parietal lobe, may be involved in spatial memory, at least in man. What are the factors responsible for this apparent discrepancy between the brain mechanisms of spatial behavior in human beings and in rodents?

Future research must also consider the way in which the cellular organization of the hippocampus enables it to store and retrieve spatial information. Per Andersen of the University of Oslo has demonstrated that the hippocampus contains many small and complex circuits, and Leonard E. Jarrard of Washington and Lee University is currently examining their function by making discrete lesions in the hippocampus that selectively disrupt particular circuits. He has found that lesions in different circuits have markedly different behavioral effects. For example, a particular lesion appears to disrupt the acquisition of spatial memory but not its retention. These results suggest that a more subtle level of anatomical and functional analysis must be pursued if we are to understand the role of the hippocampus in the programming of spatial memory.

One tantalizing piece of anatomical evidence relating to the idea of the hippocampus as a memory system is the organization of the synaptic connections linking the hippocampus to the fornix and to the entorhinal area. The connections distribute themselves in a regular manner from the front of the hippocampus to the back, and the pathways that make the connections run at right angles to other pathways within the hippocampus so as to form an extensive and highly structured network. This arrangement of nerve fibers has reminded many people of the wires running at right angles to one another in the core memory of a computer, where a "bit" of information can be stored at each intersection of the wires. Although it is unlikely that the hippocampal system stores information the same way, its structural resemblance to a computer memory raises still other questions about the memory mechanisms of the brain.

How to Teach Animals

18

December 1951

*Some simple techniques of the psychological
laboratory can also be used in the home. They
can train a dog to dance, a pigeon to play a toy
piano and will illuminate the learning process in man*

TEACHING, it is often said, is an art, but we have increasing reason to hope that it may eventually become a science. We have already discovered enough about the nature of learning to devise training techniques which are much more effective and give more reliable results than the rule-of-thumb methods of the past. Tested on animals, the new techniques have proved superior to traditional methods of professional animal trainers; they yield more remarkable results with much less effort.

It takes rather subtle laboratory conditions to test an animal's full learning capacity, but the reader will be surprised at how much he can accomplish even under informal circumstances at home. Since nearly everyone at some time or other has tried, or wished he

knew how, to train a dog, a cat or some other animal, perhaps the most useful way to explain the learning process is to describe some simple experiments which the reader can perform himself.

"Catch your rabbit" is the first item in a well-known recipe for rabbit stew. Your first move, of course, is to choose an experimental subject. Any available animal—a cat, a dog, a pigeon, a mouse, a parrot, a chicken, a pig—will do. (Children or other members of your family may also be available, but it is suggested that you save them until you have had practice with less valuable material.) Suppose you choose a dog.

The second thing you will need is something your subject wants, say food. This serves as a reward or—to use a term which is less likely to be misunder-

stood—a "reinforcement" for the desired behavior. Many things besides food are reinforcing—for example, simply letting the dog out for a run—but food is usually the easiest to administer in the kind of experiment to be described here. If you use food, you must of course perform the experiment when the dog is hungry, perhaps just before his dinnertime.

The reinforcement gives you a means of control over the behavior of the animal. It rests on the simple principle that whenever something reinforces a particular activity of an organism, it increases the chances that the organism will repeat that behavior. This makes it possible to shape an animal's behavior almost as a sculptor shapes a lump of clay. There is, of course, nothing new in this principle. What is new is a better understanding

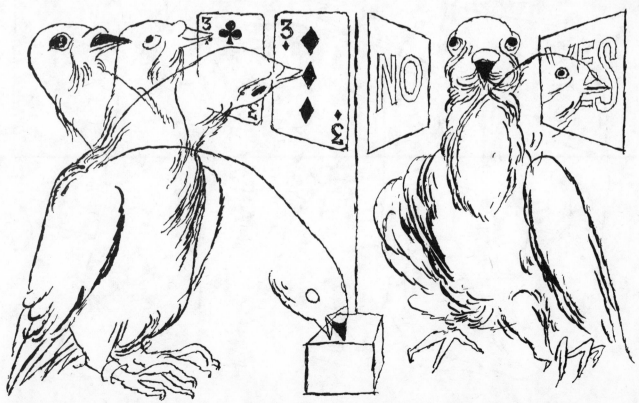

PIGEON can be taught to choose one card rather than another and even apparently to read. This is done by "reinforcing" the animal when it pecks the right card and turning out the light when it pecks the wrong one.

of the conditions under which reinforcement works best.

To be effective a reinforcement must be given almost simultaneously with the desired behavior; a delay of even one second destroys much of the effect. This means that the offer of food in the usual way is likely to be ineffective; it is not fast enough. The best way to reinforce the behavior with the necessary speed is to use a "conditioned" reinforcer. This is a signal which the animal is conditioned to associate with food. The animal is always given food immediately after the signal, and the signal itself then becomes the reinforcer. The better the association between the two events, the better the result.

For the conditioned reinforcer you need a clear signal which can be given instantly and to which the subject is sure to respond. It may be a noise or a flash of light. A whistle is not effective because of the time it takes to draw a breath before blowing it. A visual signal like a wave of the arm may not always be seen by the animal. A convenient signal is a rap on a table with a small hard object or the noise of a high-pitched device such as a "cricket."

YOU are now ready to start the experiment with your dog. Work in a convenient place as free as possible from distraction. Let us say that you have chosen a "cricket" as your conditioned reinforcer. To build up the effect of the reinforcer begin by tossing a few scraps of food, one at a time and not oftener than once or twice a minute, where the dog may eat them. Use scraps of food so small that 30 or 40 will not greatly reduce the animal's hunger. As soon as the dog eats each scrap readily and without delay, begin to pair the cricket with the food. Sound the cricket and then toss a piece of food. Wait half a minute or so and repeat. Sound the cricket suddenly, without any preparatory movements such as reaching for food.

At this stage your subject will probably show well-marked begging behavior. It may watch you intently, perhaps jump on you, and so on. You must break up this behavior, because it will interfere with other parts of the experiment. Never sound the cricket or give food when the dog is close to you or facing you. Wait until it turns away, then reinforce. Your conditioned reinforcer is working properly when your subject turns immediately and approaches the spot where it receives food. Test this several times. Wait until the dog is in a fairly unusual position, then sound the signal. Time spent in making sure the dog immediately approaches the food will later be saved manyfold.

Now, having established the noise as the reinforcer, you may begin teaching the dog. To get the feel of the technique start with some simple task, such as getting the dog to approach the handle on a low cupboard door and touch it with its nose. At first you reinforce any activity which would be part of the final completed act of approaching and touching the handle of the cupboard. The only permissible contact between you and the dog is *via* the cricket and the food. Do not touch the dog, talk to it, coax it, "draw its attention" or interfere in any other way with the experiment. If your subject just sits, you may have to begin by reinforcing any movement, however slight. As soon as the dog moves, sound the cricket and give food. Remember that your reaction time is important. Try to reinforce as nearly simultaneously with the movement as possible.

After your subject is moving freely about, reinforce any turn toward the cupboard. Almost immediately you will notice a change in its behavior. It will begin to face toward the cupboard most of the time. Then begin to reinforce only when the dog moves nearer the cupboard. (If you withhold reinforcement too long at this stage, you may lose the facing response. If so, go back and pick it up.) In a very short time—perhaps a minute or two—you should have the dog standing close to the cupboard. Now begin to pay attention to its head. Reinforce any movement that brings the nose close to the handle. You will have to make special efforts now to reduce the time between the movement and the reinforcement to the very minimum. Presently the dog will touch the handle with its nose, and after reinforcement it will repeat this behavior so long as it remains hungry.

DOG can easily be trained to touch its nose to the handle of a cupboard with the aid of a mechanical "cricket." The experimenter holds the cricket in one hand and a bit of food in the other. When the dog makes any move-

Usually it takes no more than five minutes, even for a beginner, to teach a dog this behavior. Moreover, the dog does not have to be particularly smart to learn it; contrary to the usual view, all normal dogs will learn with about equal facility by this conditioning technique.

Before going on with other experiments test the effect of your conditioned reinforcer again two or three times. If the dog responds quickly and eats without delay you may safely continue. You should "extinguish" the response the dog has already learned, however, before teaching it another. Stop reinforcing the act of touching the cupboard handle until the dog abandons this activity.

As a second test, let us say, you want to teach the dog to lift its head in the air and turn around to the right. The general procedure is the same, but you may need some help in sharpening your observation of the behavior to be reinforced. As a guide to the height to which the dog's head is to be raised, sight some horizontal line on the wall across the room. Whenever the dog, in its random movements, lifts its head above this line, reinforce immediately. You will soon see the head rising above the line more and more frequently. Now raise your sights slightly and reinforce only when the dog's head rises above the new level. By a series of gradual steps you can get the dog to hold its head much higher than usual. After this you can begin to emphasize any turning movement in a clockwise direction while the

head is high. Eventually the dog should execute a kind of dance step. If you use available food carefully, a single session should suffice for setting up this behavior.

HAVING tested your ability to produce these simple responses, you may feel confident enough to approach a more complex assignment. This time suppose you try working with a pigeon. Pigeons do not tame easily. You will probably want a cage to help control the bird, and for this you can rig up a large cardboard carton with a screen or lattice top and windows cut in the side for observing the bird. It is much less disturbing to the bird if you watch it from below its line of vision than if you peer at it from above. In general keep yourself out of the experimental situation as much as possible. You may still use a cricket as a conditioned reinforcer, and feed the bird by dropping a few grains of pigeon feed into a small dish through a hole in the wall. It may take several daily feedings to get the bird to eat readily and to respond quickly to the cricket.

Your assignment is to teach the pigeon to identify the visual patterns on playing cards. To begin with, hang a single card on a nail on the wall of the cage a few inches above the floor so that the pigeon can easily peck it. After you have trained the bird to peck the card by reinforcing the movements that lead to that end, change the card and again reinforce the

peck. If you shuffle the cards and present them at random, the pigeon will learn to peck any card offered.

Now begin to teach it to discriminate among the cards. Let us say you are using diamonds and clubs (excluding face cards and aces) and want the bird to select diamonds. Reinforce only when the card presented is a diamond, never when it is a club. Almost immediately the bird will begin to show a preference for diamonds. You can speed up its progress toward complete rejection of clubs by discontinuing the experiment for a moment (a mild form of punishment) whenever it pecks a club. A good conditioned punishment is simply to turn off the light or cover or remove the card. After half a minute replace the card or turn on the light and continue the experiment. Under these conditions the response which is positively reinforced with food remains part of the repertoire of the bird, while the response that leads to a blackout quickly disappears.

There is an amusing variation of this experiment by which you can make it appear that a pigeon can be taught to read. You simply use two printed cards bearing the words PECK and DON'T PECK, respectively. By reinforcing responses to PECK and blacking out when the bird pecks DON'T PECK, it is quite easy to train the bird to obey the commands on the cards.

The pigeon can also be taught the somewhat more "intellectual" performance of matching a sample object. Let us

ment toward the handle, the experimenter sounds the cricket and tosses the food. Babies are just as smart as dogs in learning such tricks. At right a baby is taught to lift its arm when a lamp is turned off and on.

say the sample to be matched is a certain card. Fasten three cards to a board, with one above and the two others side by side just below it. The board is placed so that the bird can reach all the cards through windows cut in the side of the cage. After training the bird to peck a card of any kind impartially in all three positions, present the three chosen cards. The sample to be matched, say the three of diamonds, is at the top, and below it put a three of diamonds and a three of clubs. If the bird pecks the sample three of diamonds at the top, do nothing. If it pecks the matching three of diamonds below, reinforce it; if it pecks the three of clubs, black out. After each correct response and reinforcement, switch the positions of the two lower cards. The pigeon should soon match the sample each time. Conversely, it can also be taught to select the card that does not match the sample. It is important to reinforce correct choices immediately. Your own behavior must be letter-perfect if you are to expect perfection from your subject. The task can be made easier if the pigeon is conditioned to peck the sample card before you begin to train it to match the sample.

IN A MORE elaborate variation of this experiment we have found it possible to make a pigeon choose among four words so that it appears to "name the suit" of the sample card. You prepare four cards about the size of small calling cards, each bearing in block letters the name of a suit: SPADES, HEARTS, DIAMONDS and CLUBS. Fasten these side by side in a row and teach the pigeon to peck them by reinforcing in the usual way. Now arrange a sample playing card just above them. Cover the name cards and reinforce the pigeon a few times for pecking the sample. Now present, say, the three of diamonds as the sample. When the pigeon pecks it, immediately uncover the name cards. If the pigeon pecks DIAMONDS, reinforce instantly. If it pecks a wrong name instead, black out for half a minute and then resume the experiment with the three of diamonds still in place and the name cards covered. After a correct choice, change the sample card to a different suit while the pigeon is eating. Always keep the names covered until the sample card has been pecked. Within a short time you should have the bird following the full sequence of pecking the sample and then the appropriate name card. As time passes the correct name will be pecked more and more frequently and, if you do not too often reinforce wrong responses or neglect to reinforce right ones, the pigeon should soon become letter-perfect.

A toy piano offers interesting possibilities for performances of a more artistic nature. Reinforce any movement of the pigeon that leads toward its pressing a key. Then, by using reinforcements and blackouts appropriately, narrow the response to a given key. Then build up a two-note sequence by reinforcing only when the sequence has been completed and by blacking out when any other combination of keys is struck. The two-note sequence will quickly emerge. Other notes may then be added. Pigeons, chickens, small dogs and cats have been taught in this way to play tunes of four or five notes. The situation soon becomes too complicated, however, for the casual experimenter. You will find it difficult to control the tempo, and the reinforcing contingencies become very complex. The limit of such an experiment is determined as much by the experimenter's skill as by that of the animal. In the laboratory we have been able to provide assistance to the experimenter by setting up complicated devices which always reinforce consistently and avoid exhaustion of the experimenter's patience.

The increased precision of the laboratory also makes it possible to guarantee performance up to the point of almost complete certainty. When relevant conditions have been controlled, the behavior of the organism is fully determined. Behavior may be sustained in full strength for many hours by utilizing different schedules of reinforcement. Some of these correspond to the contingencies established in industry in daily wages or in piece-work pay; others resemble the subtle but powerful contingencies of gambling devices, which are notorious for their ability to command sustained behavior.

THE human baby is an excellent subject in experiments of the kind described here. You will not need to interfere with feeding schedules or create any other state of deprivation, because the human infant can be reinforced by very trivial environmental events; it does not need such a reward as food. Almost any "feed-back" from the environment is reinforcing if it is not too intense. A crumpled newspaper, a pan and a spoon, or any convenient noisemaker quickly generates appropriate behavior, often amusing in its violence. The baby's rattle is based upon this principle.

One reinforcer to which babies often respond is the flashing on and off of a table lamp. Select some arbitrary response—for example, lifting the hand. Whenever the baby lifts its hand, flash the light. In a short time a well-defined response will be generated. (Human babies are just as "smart" as dogs or pigeons in this respect.) Incidentally, the baby will enjoy the experiment.

The same principle is at work in the behavior of older children and adults. Important among human reinforcements are those aspects of the behavior of others, often very subtle, that we call "attention," "approval" and "affection."

Behavior which is successful in achieving these reinforcements may come to dominate the repertoire of the individual.

All this may be easily used—and just as easily misused—in our relations with other people. To the reader who is anxious to advance to the human subject a word of caution is in order. Reinforcement is only one of the procedures through which we alter behavior. To use it, we must build up some degree of deprivation or at least permit a deprivation to prevail which it is within our power to reduce. We must embark upon a program in which we sometimes apply relevant reinforcement and sometimes withhold it. In doing this, we are quite likely to generate emotional effects. Unfortunately the science of behavior is not yet as successful in controlling emotion as it is in shaping practical behavior.

A scientific analysis can, however, bring about a better understanding of personal relations. We are almost always reinforcing the behavior of others, whether we mean to or not. A familiar problem is that of the child who seems to take an almost pathological delight in annoying its parents. In many cases this is the result of conditioning which is very similar to the animal training we have discussed. The attention, approval and affection that a mother gives a child are all extremely powerful reinforcements. Any behavior of the child that produces these consequences is likely to be strengthened. The mother may unwittingly promote the very behavior she does not want. For example, when she is busy she is likely not to respond to a call or request made in a quiet tone of voice. She may answer the child only when it raises its voice. The average intensity of the child's vocal behavior therefore moves up to another level—precisely as the head of the dog in our experiment was raised to a new height. Eventually the mother gets used to this level and again reinforces only louder instances. This vicious circle brings about louder and louder behavior. The child's voice may also vary in intonation, and any change in the direction of unpleasantness is more likely to get the attention of the mother and is therefore strengthened. One might even say that "annoying" behavior is just that behavior which is especially effective in arousing another person to action. The mother behaves, in fact, as if she had been given the assignment to teach the child to be annoying! The remedy in such a case is simply for the mother to make sure that she responds with attention and affection to most if not all the responses of the child which are of acceptable intensity and tone of voice and that she never reinforces the annoying forms of behavior.

The Acquisition of Language

19

by Breyne Arlene Moskowitz
November 1978

*How do children learn to speak? It seems they do so
in a highly methodical way: they break the language
down into its simplest parts and develop the rules they
need to put the parts together*

An adult who finds herself in a group of people speaking an unfamiliar foreign language may feel quite uncomfortable. The strange language sounds like gibberish: mysterious strings of sound, rising and falling in unpredictable patterns. Each person speaking the language knows when to speak, how to construct the strings and how to interpret other people's strings, but the individual who does not know anything about the language cannot pick out separate words or sounds, let alone discern meanings. She may feel overwhelmed, ignorant and even childlike. It is possible that she is returning to a vague memory from her very early childhood, because the experience of an adult listening to a foreign language comes close to duplicating the experience of an infant listening to the "foreign" language spoken by everyone around her. Like the adult, the child is confronted with the task of learning a language about which she knows nothing.

The task of acquiring language is one for which the adult has lost most of her aptitude but one the child will perform with remarkable skill. Within a short span of time and with almost no direct instruction the child will analyze the language completely. In fact, although many subtle refinements are added between the ages of five and 10, most children have completed the greater part of the basic language-acquisition process by the age of five. By that time a child will have dissected the language into its minimal separable units of sound and meaning; she will have discovered the rules for recombining sounds into words, the meanings of individual words and the rules for recombining words into meaningful sentences, and she will have internalized the intricate patterns of taking turns in dialogue. All in all she will have established herself linguistically as a full-fledged member of a social community, informed about the most subtle details of her native language as it is spoken in a wide variety of situations.

The speed with which children accomplish the complex process of language acquisition is particularly impressive. Ten linguists working full time for 10 years to analyze the structure of the English language could not program a computer with the ability for language acquired by an average child in the first 10 or even five years of life. In spite of the scale of the task and even in spite of adverse conditions—emotional instability, physical disability and so on—children learn to speak. How do they go about it? By what process does a child learn language?

What Is Language?

In order to understand how language is learned it is necessary to understand what language is. The issue is confused by two factors. First, language is learned in early childhood, and adults have few memories of the intense effort that went into the learning process, just as they do not remember the process of learning to walk. Second, adults do have conscious memories of being taught the few grammatical rules that are prescribed as "correct" usage, or the norms of "standard" language. It is difficult for adults to dissociate their memories of school lessons from those of true language learning, but the rules learned in school are only the conventions of an educated society. They are arbitrary finishing touches of embroidery on a thick fabric of language that each child weaves for herself before arriving in the English teacher's classroom. The fabric is grammar: the set of rules that describe how to structure language.

The grammar of language includes rules of phonology, which describe how to put sounds together to form words; rules of syntax, which describe how to put words together to form sentences; rules of semantics, which describe how to interpret the meaning of words and sentences, and rules of pragmatics, which describe how to participate in a conversation, how to sequence sentences and how to anticipate the information needed by an interlocutor. The

internal grammar each adult has constructed is identical with that of every other adult in all but a few superficial details. Therefore each adult can create or understand an infinite number of sentences she has never heard before. She knows what is acceptable as a word or a sentence and what is not acceptable, and her judgments on these issues concur with those of other adults. For example, speakers of English generally agree that the sentence "Ideas green sleep colorless furiously" is ungrammatical and that the sentence "Colorless green ideas sleep furiously" is grammatical but makes no sense semantically. There is similar agreement on the grammatical relations represented by word order. For example, it is clear that the sentences "John hit Mary" and "Mary hit John" have different meanings although they consist of the same words, and that the sentence "Flying planes can be dangerous" has two possible meanings. At the level of individual words all adult speakers can agree that "brick" is an English word, that "blick" is not an English word but could be one (that is, there is an accidental gap in the adult lexicon, or internal vocabulary) and that "bnick" is not an English word and could not be one.

How children go about learning the grammar that makes communication possible has always fascinated adults, particularly parents, psychologists and investigators of language. Until recently diary keeping was the primary method of study in this area. For example, in 1877 Charles Darwin published an account of his son's development that includes notes on language learning. Unfortunately most of the diarists used inconsistent or incomplete notations to record what they heard (or what they thought they heard), and most of the diaries were only partial listings of emerging types of sentences with inadequate information on developing word meanings. Although the very best of them, such as W. F. Leopold's classic *Speech Development of a Bilingual Child,* continue to be a rich resource for contemporary investigators, advances in audio and video recording equipment have made modern diaries generally much more valuable. In the 1960's, however, new discoveries inspired linguists and psychologists to approach the study of language acquisition in a new, systematic way, oriented less toward long-term diary keeping and more toward a search for the patterns in a child's speech at any given time.

An event that revolutionized linguistics was the publication in 1957 of Noam Chomsky's *Syntactic Structures*. Chomsky's investigation of the structure of grammars revealed that language systems were far deeper and more complex than had been suspected. And of course if linguistics was more complicated, then language learning had to be more complicated. In the 21 years since the publication of *Syntactic Structures* the disciplines of linguistics and child language have come of age. The study of the acquisition of language has benefited not only from the increasingly sophisticated understanding of linguistics but also from the improved understanding of cognitive development as it is related to language. The improvements in recording technology have made experimentation in this area more reliable and more detailed, so that investigators framing new and deeper questions are able to accurately capture both rare occurrences and developing structures.

The picture that is emerging from the more sophisticated investigations reveals the child as an active language learner, continually analyzing what she hears and proceeding in a methodical, predictable way to put together the jigsaw puzzle of language. Different children learn language in similar ways. It is not known how many processes are involved in language learning, but the few that have been observed appear repeatedly, from child to child and from language to language. All the examples I shall discuss here concern children who are learning English, but identical processes have been observed in children learning French, Russian, Finnish, Chinese, Zulu and many other languages.

Children learn the systems of grammar—phonology, syntax, semantics, lexicon and pragmatics—by breaking each system down into its smallest combinable parts and then developing rules for combining the parts. In the first two years of life a child spends much time working on one part of the task, disassembling the language to find the separate sounds that can be put together to form words and the separate words that can be put together to form sentences. After the age of two the basic process continues to be refined, and many more sounds and words are produced. The other part of language acquisition—developing rules for combining the basic elements of language—is carried out in a very methodical way: the most general rules are hypothesized first, and as time passes they are successively narrowed down by the addition of more precise rules applying to a more restricted set of sentences. The procedure is the same in any area of language learning, whether the child is acquiring syntax or phonology or semantics. For example, at the earliest stage of acquiring negatives a child does not have at her command the same range of negative structures that an adult does. She has constructed only a single very general rule: Attach "no" to the beginning of any sentence constructed by the other rules of grammar.

At this stage all negative sentences will be formed according to that rule.

Throughout the acquisition process a child continually revises and refines the rules of her internal grammar, learning increasingly detailed subrules until she achieves a set of rules that enables her to create the full array of complex, adult sentences. The process of refinement continues at least until the age of 10 and probably considerably longer for most children. By the time a child is six or seven, however, the changes in her grammar may be so subtle and sophisticated that they go unnoticed. In general children approach language learning economically, devoting their energy to broad issues before dealing with specific ones. They cope with clear-cut questions first and sort out the details later, and they may adopt any one of a variety of methods for circumventing details of a language system they have not yet dealt with.

Prerequisites for Language

Although some children verbalize much more than others and some increase the length of their utterances much faster than others, all children overgeneralize a single rule before learning to apply it more narrowly and before constructing other less widely applicable rules, and all children speak in one-word sentences before they speak in two-word sentences. The similarities in language learning for different children and different languages are so great that many linguists have believed at one time or another that the human brain is preprogrammed for language learning. Some linguists continue to believe language is innate and only the surface details of the particular language spoken in a child's environment need to be learned. The speed with which children learn language gives this view much appeal. As more parallels between language and other areas of cognition are revealed, however, there is greater reason to believe any language specialization that exists in the child is only one aspect of more general cognitive abilities of the brain.

Whatever the built-in properties the brain brings to the task of language learning may be, it is now known that a child who hears no language learns no language, and that a child learns only the language spoken in her environment. Most infants coo and babble during the first six months of life, but congenitally deaf children have been observed to cease babbling after six months, whereas normal infants continue to babble. A child does not learn language, however, simply by hearing it spoken. A boy with normal hearing but with deaf parents who communicated by the American Sign Language was exposed to television every day so that he would learn English. Because the child

(1)	BOY	CAT	MAN	HOUSE	FOOT FEET
(2)			MEN		
(3)	BOYS	CATS	MANS	HOUSE	FOOTS FEETS
(4)	BOYSəZ	CATSəZ CATəZ	MANSəZ MENəZ	HOUSəZ	FOOTSəZ FEETSəZ
(5)	BOYS	CATS	MANS	HOUSES	FEETS
(6)	BOYS	CATS	MEN	HOUSES	FEET

SORTING OUT OF COMPETING PRONUNCIATIONS that results in the correct plural forms of nouns takes place in the six stages shown in this illustration. Children usually learn the singular forms of nouns first (*1*), although in some cases an irregular plural form such as "feet" may be learned as a singular or as a free variant of a singular. Other irregular plurals may appear for a brief period (*2*), but soon they are replaced by plurals made according to the most general rule possible: To make a noun plural add the sound "s" or "z" to it (*3*). Words such as "house" or "rose," which already end in an "s"- or "z"-like sound, are usually left in their singular forms at this stage. When words of this type do not have irregular plural forms, adults make them plural by adding an "əz" sound. (The vowel "ə" is pronounced like the unstressed word "a.") Some children demonstrate their mastery of this usage by tacking "əz" endings indiscriminately onto nouns (*4*). That stage is brief and use of the ending is quickly narrowed down (*5*). At this point only irregular plurals remain to be learned, and since no new rule-making is needed, children may go on to harder problems and leave final stage (*6*) for later.

was asthmatic and was confined to his home he interacted only with people at home, where his family and all their visitors communicated in sign language. By the age of three he was fluent in sign language but neither understood nor spoke English. It appears that in order to learn a language a child must also be able to interact with real people in that language. A television set does not suffice as the sole medium for language learning because, even though it can ask questions, it cannot respond to a child's answers. A child, then, can develop language only if there is language in her environment and if she can employ that language to communicate with other people in her immediate environment.

Caretaker Speech

In constructing a grammar children have only a limited amount of information available to them, namely the language they hear spoken around them. (Until about the age of three a child models her language on that of her parents; afterward the language of her peer group tends to become more important.) There is no question, however, that the language environments children inhabit are restructured, usually unintentionally, by the adults who take care of them. Recent studies show that there are several ways caretakers systematically modify the child's environment, making the task of language acquisition simpler.

Caretaker speech is a distinct speech register that differs from others in its simplified vocabulary, the systematic phonological simplification of some words, higher pitch, exaggerated intonation, short, simple sentences and a high proportion of questions (among mothers) or imperatives (among fathers). Speech with the first two characteristics is formally designated Baby Talk. Baby Talk is a subsystem of caretaker speech that has been studied over a wide range of languages and cultures. Its characteristics appear to be universal: in languages as diverse as English, Arabic, Comanche and Gilyak (a Paleo-Siberian language) there are simplified vocabulary items for terms relating to food, toys, animals and body functions. Some words are phonologically simplified, frequently by the duplication of syllables, as in "wawa" for "water" and "choochoo" for "train," or by the reduction of consonant clusters, as in "tummy" for "stomach" and "scambled eggs" for "scrambled eggs." (Many types of phonological simplification seem to mimic the phonological structure of an infant's own early vocabulary.)

Perhaps the most pervasive characteristic of caretaker speech is its syntactic simplification. While a child is still babbling, adults may address long, complex sentences to her, but as soon as she begins to utter meaningful, identifiable

(1)	WALK	PLAY	NEED	COME	GO
(2)				CAME	WENT
(3)	WALKED	PLAYED	NEED	COMED	GOED
(4)	WALKEDəD	PLAYEDəD	NEEDəD	CAMEDəD COMEDəD	GOED WENTəD
(5)	WALKED	PLAYED	NEEDED	COMED	GOED
(6)	WALKED	PLAYED	NEEDED	CAME	WENT

DEVELOPMENT OF PAST-TENSE FORMS OF VERBS also takes place in six stages. After the present-tense forms are learned (*1*) irregular past-tense forms may appear briefly (*2*). The first and most general rule that is postulated is: To put a verb into the past tense add a "t" or "d" sound (*3*). In adult speech verbs such as "want" or "need," which already end in a "t" or "d" sound, are put into the past tense by adding "əd" sound. Many children go through brief stage in which they add "əd" endings to any existing verb forms (*4*). Once the use of "əd" ending has been narrowed down (*5*), only irregular past-tense forms remain to be learned (*6*).

words they almost invariably speak to her in very simple sentences. Over the next few years of the child's language development the speech addressed to her by her caretakers may well be describable by a grammar only six months in advance of her own.

The functions of the various language modifications in caretaker speech are not equally apparent. It is possible that higher pitch and exaggerated intonation serve to alert a child to pay attention to what she is hearing. As for Baby Talk, there is no reason to believe the use of phonologically simplified words in any way affects a child's learning of pronunciation. Baby Talk may have only a psychological function, marking speech as being affectionate. On the other hand, syntactic simplification has a clear function. Consider the speech adults address to other adults; it is full of false starts and long, rambling, highly complex sentences. It is not surprising that elaborate theories of innate language ability arose during the years when linguists examined the speech adults addressed to adults and assumed that the speech addressed to children was similar. Indeed, it is hard to imagine how a child could derive the rules of language from such input. The wide study of caretaker speech conducted over the past eight years has shown that children do not face this problem. Rather it appears they construct their initial grammars on the basis of the short, simple, grammatical sentences that are addressed to them in the first year or two they speak.

Correcting Language

Caretakers simplify children's language-analysis task in other ways. For example, adults talk with other adults about complex ideas, but they talk with children about the here and now, minimizing discussion of feelings, displaced events and so on. Adults accept children's syntactic and phonological "errors," which are a normal part of the acquisition process. It is important to understand that when children make such errors, they are not producing flawed or incomplete replicas of adult sentences; they are producing sentences that are correct and grammatical with respect to their own current internalized grammar. Indeed, children's errors are essential data for students of child language because it is the consistent departures from the adult model that indicate the nature of a child's current hypotheses about the grammar of language. There are a number of memorized, unanalyzed sentences in any child's output of language. If a child says, "Nobody likes me," there is no way of knowing whether she has memorized the sentence intact or has figured out the rules for constructing the sentence. On the other hand, a sentence such as "Nobody don't like me" is clearly not a memorized form but one that reflects an intermediate stage of a developing grammar.

Since each child's utterances at a particular stage are from her own point of view grammatically correct, it is not surprising that children are fairly impervious to the correction of their language by adults, indeed to any attempts to teach them language. Consider the boy who lamented to his mother, "Nobody don't like me." His mother seized the opportunity to correct him, replying, "Nobody likes me." The child repeated his original version and the mother her modified one a total of eight times until in desperation the mother said, "Now listen carefully! Nobody likes me." Finally her son got the idea and dutifully replied, "Oh! Nobody don't likes me." As the example demonstrates, children do not always understand exactly what it is the adult is correcting. The information the adult is trying to impart may be at odds with the information in the child's head, namely the rules the child is postulating for producing language. The surface correction of a sentence does not give the child a clue about how to revise the rule that produced the sentence.

It seems to be virtually impossible to speed up the language-learning process. Experiments conducted by Russian investigators show that it is extremely difficult to teach children a detail of language more than a few days before they would learn it themselves. Adults sometimes do, of course, attempt to teach children rules of language, expecting them to learn by imitation, but Courtney B. Cazden of Harvard University found that children benefit less from frequent adult correction of their errors than from true conversational interaction. Indeed, correcting errors can interrupt that interaction, which is, after all, the function of language. (One way children may try to secure such interaction is by asking "Why?" Children go through a stage of asking a question repeatedly. It serves to keep the conversation going, which may be the child's real aim. For example, a two-and-a-half-year-old named Stanford asked "Why?" and was given the nonsense answer: "Because the moon is made of green cheese." Although the response was not at all germane to the conversation, Stanford was happy with it and again asked "Why?" Many silly answers later the adult had tired of the conversation but Stanford had not. He was clearly not seeking information. What he needed was to practice the form of social conversation before dealing with its function. Asking "Why?" served that purpose well.)

In point of fact adults rarely correct children's ungrammatical sentences. For example, one mother, on hearing "Tommy fall my truck down," turned to Tommy with "Did you fall Stevie's truck down?" Since imitation seems to have little role in the language-acquisition process, however, it is probably just as well that most adults are either too charmed by children's errors or too busy to correct them.

Practice does appear to have an important function in the child's language-learning process. Many children have been observed purposefully practicing language when they are alone, for example in a crib or a playpen. Ruth H. Weir of Stanford University hid a tape recorder in her son's bedroom and recorded his talk after he was put to bed. She found that he played with words and phrases, stringing together sequences of similar sounds and of variations on a phrase or on the use of a word: "What color . . . what color blanket . . . what color mop . . . what color glass . . . what color TV . . . red ant . . . fire . . . like lipstick . . . blanket . . . now the blue blanket . . . what color TV . . . what color horse . . . then what color table . . . then what color fire . . . here yellow spoon." Children who do not have much opportunity to be alone may use dialogue in a similar fashion. When Weir tried to record the bedtime monologues of her second child, whose room adjoined that of the first, she obtained through-the-wall conversations instead.

The One-Word Stage

The first stage of child language is one in which the maximum sentence length is one word; it is followed by a stage in which the maximum sentence length is two words. Early in the one-word stage there are only a few words in a child's vocabulary, but as months go by her lexicon expands with increasing rapidity. The early words are primarily concrete nouns and verbs; more abstract words such as adjectives are acquired later. By the time the child is uttering two-word sentences with some regularity, her lexicon may include hundreds of words.

When a child can say only one word at a time and knows only five words in all, choosing which one to say may not be a complex task. But how does she decide which word to say when she knows 100 words or more? Patricia M. Greenfield of the University of California at Los Angeles and Joshua H. Smith of Stanford have suggested that an important criterion is informativeness, that is, the child selects a word reflecting what is new in a particular situation. Greenfield and Smith also found that a newly acquired word is first used for naming and only later for asking for something.

Superficially the one-word stage

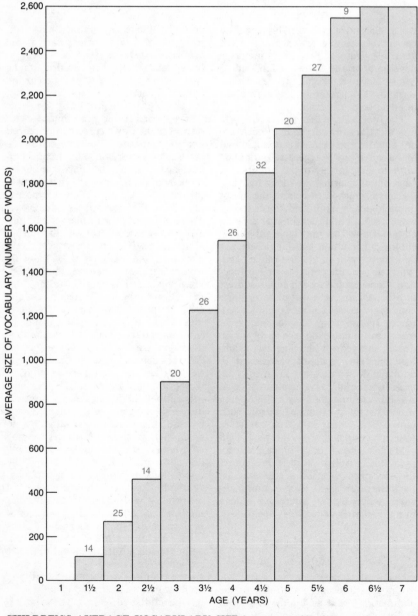

CHILDREN'S AVERAGE VOCABULARY SIZE increases rapidly between the ages of one and a half and six and a half. The number of children tested in each sample age group is shown in color. Data are based on work done by Madorah E. Smith of University of Hawaii.

seems easy to understand: a child says one word at a time, and so each word is a complete sentence with its own sentence intonation. Ten years ago a child in the one-word stage was thought to be learning word meanings but not syntax. Recently, however, students of child language have seen less of a distinction between the one-word stage as a period of word learning and the subsequent period, beginning with the two-word stage, as one of syntax acquisition. It now seems clear that the infant is engaged in an enormous amount of syntactic analysis in the one-word stage, and indeed that her syntactic abilities are reflected in her utterances and in her accurate perception of multiword sentences addressed to her.

Ronald Scollon of the University of Hawaii and Lois Bloom of Columbia University have pointed out independently that important patterns in word choice in the one-word stage can be found by examining larger segments of children's speech. Scollon observed that a 19-month-old named Brenda was able to use a vertical construction (a series of one-word sentences) to express what an adult might say with a horizontal construction (a multiword sentence). Brenda's pronunciation, which is represented phonetically below, was imperfect and Scollon did not understand her words at the time. Later, when he transcribed the tape of their conversation, he heard the sound of a passing car immediately preceding the conversation and was able to identify Brenda's words as follows:

Brenda: "Car [pronounced 'ka']. Car. Car. Car."
Scollon: "What?"
Brenda: "Go. Go."
Scollon: [Undecipherable.]
Brenda: "Bus [pronounced 'baish']. Bus. Bus. Bus. Bus. Bus. Bus. Bus."
Scollon: "What? Oh, bicycle? Is that what you said?"
Brenda: "Not ['na']."
Scollon: "No?"
Brenda: "Not."
Scollon: "No. I got it wrong."

Brenda was not yet able to combine two words syntactically to express "Hearing that car reminds me that we went on the bus yesterday. No, not on a bicycle." She could express that concept, however, by combining words sequentially. Thus the one-word stage is not just a time for learning the meaning of words. In that period a child is developing hypotheses about putting words together in sentences, and she is already putting sentences together in meaningful groups. The next step will be to put two words together to form a single sentence.

The Two-Word Stage

The two-word stage is a time for experimenting with many binary semantic-syntactic relations such as possessor-

possessed ("Mommy sock"), actor-action ("Cat sleeping") and action-object ("Drink soup"). When two-word sentences first began to appear in Brenda's speech, they were primarily of the following forms: subject noun and verb (as in "Monster go"), verb and object (as in "Read it") and verb or noun and location (as in "Bring home" and "Tree down"). She also continued to use vertical constructions in the two-word stage, providing herself with a means of expressing ideas that were still too advanced for her syntax. Therefore once again a description of Brenda's isolated sentences does not show her full abilities at this point in her linguistic development. Consider a later conversation Scollon had with Brenda:

Brenda: "Tape corder. Use it. Use it."
Scollon: "Use it for what?"
Brenda: "Talk. Corder talk. Brenda talk."

Brenda's use of vertical constructions to express concepts she is still unable to encode syntactically is just one example of a strategy employed by children in all areas of cognitive development. As Jean Piaget of the University of Geneva and Dan I. Slobin of the University of California at Berkeley put it, new forms are used for old functions and new functions are expressed by old forms. Long before Brenda acquired the complex syntactic form "Use the tape recorder to record me talking" she was able to use her old forms—two-word sentences and vertical construction—to express the new function. Later, when that function was old, she would develop new forms to express it. The controlled dovetailing of form and function can be observed in all areas of language acquisition. For example, before children acquire the past tense they may employ adverbs of time such as "yesterday" with present-tense verbs to express past time, saying "I do it yesterday" before "I dood it."

Bloom has provided a rare view of an intermediate stage between the one-word and the two-word stages in which the two-word construction—a new form—served only an old function. For several weeks Bloom's daughter Alison uttered two-word sentences all of which included the word "wida." Bloom tried hard to find the meaning of "wida" before realizing that it had no meaning. It was, she concluded, simply a placeholder. This case is the clearest ever reported of a new form preceding new functions. The two-word stage is an important time for practicing functions that will later have expanded forms and practicing forms that will later expand their functions.

Telegraphic Speech

There is no three-word stage in child language. For a few years after the end of the two-word stage children do produce rather short sentences, but the al-

STAGE 1	No . . . wipe finger.
	No a boy bed.
	No singing song.
	No the sun shining.
	No money.
	No sit there.
	No play that.
	No fall!
	Not . . . fit.
	Not a teddy bear.
	More . . . no.
	Wear mitten no.
STAGE 2	I can't catch you.
	I can't see you.
	We can't talk.
	You can't dance.
	I don't want it.
	I don't like him.
	I don't know his name.
	No pinch me.
	Book say no.
	Touch the snow no.
	This a radiator no.
	No square . . . is clown.
	Don't bite me yet.
	Don't leave me.
	Don't wake me up . . . again.
	He not little, he big.
	That no fish school.
	That no Mommy.
	There no squirrels.
	He no bite you.
	I no want envelope.
	I no taste them.
STAGE 3	We can't make another broom.
	I don't want cover on it.
	I gave him some so he won't cry.
	No, I don't have a book.
	I am not a doctor.
	It's not cold.
	Don't put the two wings on.
	I didn't did it.
	You didn't caught me.
	I not hurt him.
	Ask me if I not made mistake.
	Because I don't want somebody to wake me up.
	I didn't see something.
	I isn't . . . I not sad.
	This not ice cream.
	This no good.
	I not crying.
	That not turning.
	He not taking the walls down.

THREE STAGES in the acquisition of negative sentences were studied by Ursula Bellugi of the Salk Institute for Biological Studies and Edward S. Klima of the University of California at San Diego. They observed that in the first stage almost all negative sentences appear to be formulated according to the rule: Attach "no" or "not" to the beginning of a sentence to make it negative. In the second stage additional rules are postulated that allow the formation of sentences in which "no," "not," "can't" and "don't" appear after the subject and before the verb. In the third stage several issues remain to be worked out, in particular the agreement of pronouns in negative sentences (*dark color*), the inclusion of the forms of the verb "to be" (*gray*) and the correct use of the auxiliary "do" (*white*). In adult speech the auxiliary "do" often carries tense and other functional markings such as the negative; children in third stage may replace it by "not" or use it redundantly to mark tense that is already marked on the main verb.

most inviolable length constraints that characterized the first two stages have disappeared. The absence of a three-word stage has not been satisfactorily explained as yet; the answer may have to do with the fact that many basic semantic relations are binary and few are ternary. In any case a great deal is known about the sequential development in the language of the period following the two-word stage. Roger Brown of Harvard has named that language telegraphic speech. (It should be noted that there is no specific age at which a child enters any of these stages of language acquisition and further that there is no particular correlation between intelligence and speed of acquisition.)

Early telegraphic speech is characterized by short, simple sentences made up primarily of content words: words that are rich in semantic content, usually nouns and verbs. The speech is called telegraphic because the sentences lack function "words": tense endings on verbs and plural endings on nouns, prepositions, conjunctions, articles and so on. As the telegraphic-speech stage progresses, function words are gradually added to sentences. This process has possibly been studied more thoroughly than any other in language acquisition, and a fairly predictable order in the addition of function words has been observed. The same principles that govern the order of acquisition of function words in English have been shown to operate in many other languages, including some, such as Finnish and Russian, that express the same grammatical relations with particularly rich systems of noun and verb suffixes.

In English many grammatical relations are represented by a fixed word order. For example, in the sentence "The dog followed Jamie to school" it is clear it is the dog that did the following. Normal word order in English requires that the subject come before the verb, and so people who speak English recognize "the dog" as the subject of the sentence. In other languages a noun may be marked as a subject not by its position with respect to the other words in the sentence but by a noun suffix, so that in adult sentences word order may be quite flexible. Until children begin to acquire suffixes and other function words, however, they employ fixed word order to express grammatical relations no matter how flexible adult word order may be. In English the strong propensity to follow word order rigidly shows up in children's interpretations of passive sentences such as "Jamie was followed by the dog." At an early age children may interpret some passive sentences correctly, but by age three they begin to ignore the function words such as "was" and "by" in passive sentences and adopt the fixed word-order interpretation. In other words, since "Jamie" appears before the verb, Jamie is assumed to be the actor, or the noun doing the following.

Function Words

In spite of its grammatical dependence on word order, the English language makes use of enough function words to illustrate the basic principles that determine the order in which such words are acquired. The progressive tense ending "-ing," as in "He going," is acquired first, long before the present-tense third-person singular ending "-s," as in "He goes." The "-s" itself is acquired long before the past tense endings, as in "He goed." Once again the child proves to be a sensible linguist, learning first the tense that exhibits the least variation in form. The "-ing" ending is pronounced only one way, regard-

CHILD'S LEXICAL ITEM	FIRST REFERENTS	OTHER REFERENTS IN ORDER OF OCCURRENCE	GENERAL AREA OF SEMANTIC EXTENSION
MOOI	MOON	CAKE ROUND MARKS ON WINDOWS WRITING ON WINDOWS AND IN BOOKS ROUND SHAPES IN BOOKS TOOLING ON LEATHER BOOK COVERS ROUND POSTMARKS LETTER "O"	SHAPE
BOW-WOW	DOG	FUR PIECE WITH GLASS EYES FATHER'S CUFFLINKS PEARL BUTTONS ON DRESS BATH THERMOMETER	SHAPE
KOTIBAIZ	BARS OF COT	LARGE TOY ABACUS TOAST RACK WITH PARALLEL BARS PICTURE OF BUILDING WITH COLUMNS	SHAPE
BÉBÉ	REFLECTION OF CHILD (SELF) IN MIRROR	PHOTOGRAPH OF SELF ALL PHOTOGRAPHS ALL PICTURES ALL BOOKS WITH PICTURES ALL BOOKS	SHAPE
VOV-VOV	DOG	KITTENS HENS ALL ANIMALS AT A ZOO PICTURE OF PIGS DANCING	SHAPE
ASS	GOAT WITH ROUGH HIDE ON WHEELS	THINGS THAT MOVE: ANIMALS, SISTER, WAGON... ALL MOVING THINGS ALL THINGS WITH A ROUGH SURFACE	MOVEMENT TEXTURE
TUTU	TRAIN	ENGINE MOVING TRAIN JOURNEY	MOVEMENT
FLY	FLY	SPECKS OF DIRT DUST ALL SMALL INSECTS CHILD'S OWN TOES CRUMBS OF BREAD A TOAD	SIZE
QUACK	DUCK ON WATER	ALL BIRDS AND INSECTS ALL COINS (AFTER SEEING AN EAGLE ON THE FACE OF A COIN)	SIZE
KOKO	COCKEREL'S CROWING	TUNES PLAYED ON A VIOLIN TUNES PLAYED ON A PIANO TUNES PLAYED ON AN ACCORDION TUNES PLAYED ON A PHONOGRAPH ALL MUSIC MERRY-GO-ROUND	SOUND
DANY	SOUND OF A BELL	CLOCK TELEPHONE DOORBELLS	SOUND

CHILDREN OVERGENERALIZE WORD MEANINGS, using words they acquire early in place of words they have not yet acquired. Eve V. Clark of Stanford University has observed that when a word first appears in a child's lexicon, it refers to a specific object but the child quickly extends semantic domain of word, using it to refer to many other things. Eventually meaning of the word is narrowed down until it coincides with adult usage. Clark found that children most frequently base the semantic extension of a word on shape of its first referent.

less of the pronunciation of the verb to which it is attached. The verb endings "-s" and "-ed," however, vary in their pronunciation: compare "cuts (s)," "cuddles (z)," "crushes (əz)," "walked (t)," "played (d)" and "halted (əd)." (The vowel "ə," called "shwa," is pronounced like the unstressed word "a.") Furthermore, present progressive ("-ing") forms are used with greater frequency than any other tense in the speech children hear. Finally, no verb has an irregular "-ing" form, but some verbs do have irregular third-person present-tense singular forms and many have irregular past-tense forms. (The same pattern of learning earliest those forms that exhibit the least variation shows up much more dramatically in languages such as Finnish and Russian, where the paradigms of inflection are much richer.)

The past tense is acquired after the progressive and present tenses, because the relative time it represents is conceptually more difficult. The future tense ("will" and a verb) is formed regularly in English and is as predictable as the progressive tense, but it is a much more abstract concept than the past tense. Therefore it is acquired much later. In the same way the prepositions "in" and "on" appear earlier than any others, at about the same time as "-ing," but prepositions such as "behind" and "in front of," whose correct usage depends on the speaker's frame of reference, are acquired much later.

It is particularly interesting to note that there are three English morphemes that are pronounced identically but are acquired at different times. They are the plural "-s," the possessive "-s" and the third-person singular tense ending "-s," and they are acquired in the order of listing. Roman Jakobson of Harvard has suggested that the explanation of this phenomenon has to do with the complexity of the different relations the morphemes signal: the singular-plural distinction is at the word level, the possessive relates two nouns at the phrase level and the tense ending relates a noun and a verb at the clause level.

The forms of the verb "to be"—"is," "are" and so on—are among the last of the function words to be acquired, particularly in their present-tense forms. Past- and future-tense forms of "to be" carry tense information, of course, but present-tense forms are essentially meaningless, and omitting them is a very sensible strategy for a child who must maximize the information content of a sentence and place priorities on linguistic structures still to be tackled.

Plurals

When there are competing pronunciations available, as in the case of the plural and past tenses, the process of sorting them out also follows a predictable pattern. Consider the acquisition of the English plural, in which six distinct stages can be observed. In English, as in many other (but not all) languages, nouns have both singular and plural forms. Children usually use the singular forms first, both in situations where the singular form would be appropriate and in situations where the plural form would be appropriate. In instances where the plural form is irregular in the adult model, however, a child may not recognize it as such and may use it in place of the singular or as a free variant of the singular. Thus in the first stage of acquisition, before either the concept of a plu-ral or the linguistic devices for expressing a plural are acquired, a child may say "two cat" or point to "one feet."

When plurals begin to appear regularly, the child forms them according to the most general rule of English plural formation. At this point it is the child's overgeneralization of the rule, resulting in words such as "mans," "foots" or "feets," that shows she has hypothesized the rule: Add the sound /s/ or /z/ to the end of a word to make it plural. (The slashes indicate pronounced sounds, which are not to be confused with the letters used in spelling.)

For many children the overgeneralized forms of the irregular nouns are actually the earliest /s/ and /z/ plurals to appear, preceding "boys," "cats" and other regular forms by hours or days. The period of overgeneralization is considered to be the third stage in the acquisition of plurals because for many children there is an intermediate second stage in which irregular plurals such as "men" actually do appear. Concerned parents may regard the change from the second-stage "men" to the third-stage "mans" as a regression, but in reality it demonstrates progress from an individual memorized item to the application of a general rule.

In the third stage the small number of words that already end in a sound resembling /s/ or /z/, such as "house," "rose" and "bush," are used without any plural ending. Adults normally make such words plural by adding the suffix /əz/. Children usually relegate this detail to the remainder pile, to be dealt with at a later time. When they return to the problem, there is often a short fourth stage of perhaps a day, in which the child delightedly demonstrates her

(1) Laura (2:2): Her want some more. Her want some more candy.	(4) Andrew (2:0): Put that on. Andrew put that on.	(7) Jamie (6:0): Jamie: Why are you doing that? Mother: What? Jamie: Why are you writing what I say down? Mother: What? Jamie: Why are you writing down what I say?
(2) Laura (2:2): Where my tiger? Where my tiger book?	(5) Andrew (2:1): All wet. This shoe all wet.	(8) Jamie (6:3): Jamie: Who do you think is the importantest kid in the world except me? Mother: What did you say, Jamie? Jamie: Who do you think is the specialest kid in the world not counting me?
(3) Laura (2:2): Let's dooz this. Let's do this. Let's do this puzzle.	(6) Benjy (2:3): Broke it. Broke it. Broke it I did.	(9) Jamie (6:6): Jamie: Who are you versing? Adult: What? Jamie: I wanted to know who he was playing against. (10) Jamie (6:10): Jamie: I figured something you might like out. Mother: What did you say? Jamie: I figured out something you might like.

CHILDREN CORRECT THEIR SPEECH in ways that reflect the improvements they are currently making on their internal grammar. For example, Laura (*1–3*) is increasing the length of her sentences, encoding more information by embellishing a noun phrase. Andrew (*4, 5*) and Benjy (*6*) appear to be adding subjects to familiar verb-phrase sentences. Jamie (*7–10*) seems to be working on much more subtle refinements such as the placement of verb particles, for example the "down" of "writing down." (Each child's age at time of correction is given in years and months.) Corrections shown here were recorded by Judy S. Reilly of University of California at Los Angeles.

solution by tacking /əz/ endings indiscriminately onto nouns no matter what sound they end in and no matter how many other plural markings they may already have. A child may wake up one morning and throw herself into this stage with all the zeal of a kitten playing with its first ball of string.

Within a few days the novelty wears off and the child enters a less flamboyant fifth stage, in which only irregular plurals still deviate from the model forms. The rapid progression through the fourth stage does not mean that she suddenly focused her attention on the problem of /əz/ plurals. It is more likely that she had the problem at the back of her mind throughout the third stage. She was probably silently formulating hypotheses about the occurrence of /əz/ and testing them against the plurals she was hearing. Finding the right rule required discovering the phonological specification of the class of nouns that take /əz/ plurals.

Arriving at the sixth and final stage in the acquisition of plurals does not require the formulation of any new rules. All that is needed is the simple memorizing of irregular forms. Being rational, the child relegates such minor details to the lowest-priority remainder pile and turns her attention to more interesting linguistic questions. Hence a five-year-old may still not have entered the last stage. In fact, a child in the penultimate stage may not be at all receptive to being taught irregular plurals. For example, a child named Erica pointed to a picture of some "mouses," and her mother corrected her by saying "mice." Erica and her mother each repeated their own version two more times, and then Erica resolved the standoff by turning to a picture of "ducks." She avoided the picture of the mice for several days. Two years later, of course, Erica was perfectly able to say "mice."

Negative Sentences

One of the pioneering language-acquisition studies of the 1960's was undertaken at Harvard by a research group headed by Brown. The group studied the development in the language of three children over a period of several years. Two members of the group, Ursula Bellugi and Edward S. Klima, looked specifically at the changes in the children's negative sentences over the course of the project. They found that negative structures, like other subsystems of the syntactic component of grammar, are acquired in an orderly, rule-governed way.

When the project began, the forms of negative sentences the children employed were quite simple. It appeared that they had incorporated the following rule into their grammar: To make a sentence negative attach "no" or "not" to the beginning of it. On rare occasions,

possibly when a child had forgotten to anticipate the negative, "no" could be attached to the end of a sentence, but negative words could not appear inside a sentence.

In the next stage the children continued to follow this rule, but they had also hypothesized and incorporated into their grammars more complex rules that allowed them to generate sentences in which the negatives "no," "not," "can't" and "don't" appeared after the subject and before the verb. These rules constituted quite an advance over attaching a negative word externally to a sentence. Furthermore, some of the primitive imperative sentences constructed at this stage began with "don't" rather than "no." On the other hand, "can't" never appeared at the beginning of a sentence, and neither "can" nor "do" appeared as an auxiliary, as they do in adult speech: "I can do it." These facts suggest that at this point "can't" and "don't" were unanalyzed negative forms rather than contractions of "cannot" and "do not," but that although "can't" and "don't" each seemed to be interchangeable with "no," they were no longer interchangeable with each other.

In the third stage of acquiring negatives many more details of the negative system had appeared in the children's speech. The main feature of the system that still remained to be worked out was the use of pronouns in negative sentences. At this stage the children said "I didn't see something" and "I don't want somebody to wake me up." The pronouns "somebody" and "something" were later replaced with "nobody" and "nothing" and ultimately with the properly concorded forms "anybody" and "anything."

Many features of telegraphic speech were still evident in the third stage. The form "is" of the verb "to be" was frequently omitted, as in "This no good." In adult speech the auxiliary "do" often functions as a dummy verb to carry tense and other markings; for example, in "I didn't see it," "do" carries the tense and the negative. In the children's speech at this stage "do" appeared occasionally, but the children had not yet figured out its entire function. Therefore in some sentences the auxiliary "do" was omitted and the negative "not" appeared alone, as in "I not hurt him." In other sentences, such as "I didn't did it," the negative auxiliary form of "do" appears to be correct but is actually an unanalyzed, memorized item; at this stage the tense is regularly marked on the main verb, which in this example happens also to be "do."

Many children acquire negatives in the same way that the children in the Harvard study did, but subsequent investigations have shown that there is more than one way to learn a language. Carol B. Lord of U.C.L.A. identified a quite different strategy employed by a

two-year-old named Jennifer. From 24 to 28 months Jennifer used "no" only as a single-word utterance. In order to produce a negative sentence she simply spoke an ordinary sentence with a higher pitch. For example, "I want put it on" spoken with a high pitch meant "I don't want to put it on." Lord noticed that many of the negative sentences adults addressed to Jennifer were spoken with an elevated pitch. Children tend to pay more attention to the beginning and ending of sentences, and in adult speech negative words usually appear in the middle of sentences. With good reason, then, Jennifer seemed to have hypothesized that one makes a sentence negative by uttering it with a higher pitch. Other children have been found to follow the same strategy. There are clearly variations in the hypotheses children make in the process of constructing grammar.

Semantics

Up to this point I have mainly discussed the acquisition of syntactic rules, in part because in the years following the publication of Chomsky's *Syntactic Structures* child-language research in this area flourished. Syntactic rules, which govern the ordering of words in a sentence, are not all a child needs to know about language, however, and after the first flush of excitement over Chomsky's work investigators began to ask questions about other areas of language acquisition. Consider the development of the rules of semantics, which govern the way words are interpreted. Eve V. Clark of Stanford reexamined old diary studies and noticed that the development in the meaning of words during the first several months of the one-word stage seemed to follow a basic pattern.

The first time children in the studies used a word, Clark noted, it seemed to be as a proper noun, as the name of a specific object. Almost immediately, however, the children generalized the word based on some feature of the original object and used it to refer to many other objects. For example, a child named Hildegard first used "tick-tock" as the name for her father's watch, but she quickly broadened the meaning of the word, first to include all clocks, then all watches, then a gas meter, then a fire-hose wound on a spool and then a bathroom scale with a round dial. Her generalizations appear to be based on her observation of common features of shape: roundness, dials and so on. In general the children in the diary studies overextended meanings based on similarities of movement, texture, size and, most frequently, shape.

As the children progressed, the meanings of words were narrowed down until eventually they more or less coincided with the meanings accepted by adult speakers of the language. The narrow-

CHILDREN'S SPEECH IS STUDIED to determine what grammatical rules, which describe how language is structured, they have developed. The author, shown here recording the language output of two young children, works with children in their homes so that their speech is as unconstrained as possible. The search for the regularities in children's language has revealed that in any area of language ac-quisition they follow the same basic procedure: hypothesizing rules, trying them out and then modifying them. Children formulate the most general rules first and apply them across the board; narrower rules are added later, with exceptions and highly irregular forms. Examples discussed in article concern children learning English, but same process has been observed in children learning other languages.

ing-down process has not been studied intensively, but it seems likely that the process has no fixed end point. Rather it appears that the meanings of words continue to expand and contract through adulthood, long after other types of language acquisition have ceased.

One of the problems encountered in trying to understand the acquisition of semantics is that it is often difficult to determine the precise meaning a child has constructed for a word. Some interesting observations have been made, however, concerning the development of the meanings of the pairs of words that function as opposites in adult language. Margaret Donaldson and George Balfour of the University of Edinburgh asked children from three to five years old which one of two cardboard trees had "more" apples on it. They asked other children of the same age which tree had "less" apples. (Each child was interviewed individually.) Almost all the children in both groups responded by pointing to the tree with more apples on it. Moreover, the children who had been asked to point to the tree with "less" apples showed no hesitation in choosing the tree with more apples. They did not act as though they did not know the meaning of "less"; rather they acted as if they did know the meaning and "less" meant "more."

Subsequent studies have revealed similar systematic error making in the acquisition of other pairs of opposites such as "same" and "different," "big" and "little," "wide" and "narrow" and "tall" and "short." In every case the pattern of learning is the same: one word of the pair is learned first and its meaning is overextended to apply to the other word in the pair. The first word learned is always the unmarked word of the pair, that is, the word adults use when they do not want to indicate either one of the opposites. (For example, in the case of "wide" and "narrow," "wide" is the unmarked word: asking "How wide is the road?" does not suggest that the road is wide, but asking "How narrow is the road?" does suggest that the road is narrow.)

Clark observed a more intricate pattern of error production in the acquisition of the words "before" and "after." Consider the four different types of sentence represented by (1) "He jumped the gate before he patted the dog," (2) "Before he patted the dog he jumped the gate," (3) "He patted the dog after he jumped the gate" and (4) "After he jumped the gate he patted the dog." Clark found that the way the children she observed interpreted sentences such as these could be divided into four stages.

In the first stage the children disregarded the words "before" and "after" in all four of these sentence types and assumed that the event of the first clause took place before the event of the sec-

ond clause. With this order-of-mention strategy the first and fourth sentence types were interpreted correctly but the second and third sentence types were not. In the second stage sentences using "before" were interpreted correctly but an order-of-mention strategy was still adopted for sentences that used "after." Hence sentences of the fourth type were interpreted correctly but sentences of the third type were not. In the next stage both the third and the fourth sentence types were interpreted incorrectly, suggesting that the children had adopted the strategy that "after" actually meant "before." Finally, in the fourth stage both "before" and "after" were interpreted appropriately.

It appears, then, that in learning the meaning of a pair of words such as "more" and "less" or "before" and "after" children acquire first the part of the meaning that is common to both words and only later the part of the meaning that distinguishes the two. Linguists have not yet developed satisfactory ways of separating the components of meaning that make up a single word, but it seems clear that when such components can be identified, it will be established that, for example, "more" and "less" have a large number of components in common and differ only in a single component specifying the pole of the dimension. Beyond the studies of opposites there has been little investigation of the period of semantic acquisition that follows the early period of rampant overgeneralization. How children past the early stage learn the meanings of other kinds of words is still not well understood.

Phonology

Just as children overgeneralize word meanings and sentence structures, so do they overgeneralize sounds, using sounds they have learned in place of sounds they have not yet acquired. Just as a child may use the word "not" correctly in one sentence but instead of another negative word in a second sentence, so may she correctly contrast /p/ and /b/ at the beginnings of words but employ /p/ at the ends of words, regardless of whether the adult models end with /p/ or /b/. Children also acquire the details of the phonological system in very regular ways. The ways in which they acquire individual sounds, however, are highly idiosyncratic, and so for many years the patterns eluded diarists, who tended to look only at the order in which sounds were acquired. Jakobson made a major advance in this area by suggesting that it was not individual sounds children acquire in an orderly way but the distinctive features of sound, that is, the minimal differences, or contrasts, between sounds. In other words, when a child begins to contrast /p/ and /b/, she also begins to contrast

all the other pairs of sounds that, like /p/ and /b/, differ only in the absence or presence of vocal-cord vibration. In English these pairs include /t/ and /d/, and /k/ and the hard /g/. It is the acquisition of this contrast and not of the six individual sounds that is predictable. Jakobson's extensive examination of the diary data for a wide variety of languages supported his theory. Almost all current work in phonological theory rests on the theory of distinctive features that grew out of his work.

My own recent work suggests that phonological units even more basic than the distinctive features play an important part in the early acquisition process. At an early stage, when there are relatively few words in a child's repertory, unanalyzed syllables appear to be the basic unit of the sound system. By designating these syllables as unanalyzed I mean that the child is not able to separate them into their component consonants and vowels. Only later in the acquisition process does such division into smaller units become possible. The gradual discovery of successively smaller units that can form the basis of the phonological system is an important part of the process.

At an even earlier stage, before a child has uttered any words, she is accomplishing a great deal of linguistic learning, working with a unit of phonological organization even more primitive than the syllable. That unit can be defined in terms of pitch contours. By the late babbling period children already control the intonation, or pitch modulation, contours of the language they are learning. At that stage the child sounds as if she is uttering reasonably long sentences, and adult listeners may have the impression they are not quite catching the child's words. There are no words to catch, only random strings of babbled sounds with recognizable, correctly produced question or statement intonation contours. The sounds may accidentally be similar to some of those found in adult English. These sentence-length utterances are called sentence units, and in the phonological system of the child at this stage they are comparable to the consonant-and-vowel segments, syllables and distinctive features that appear in the phonological systems of later stages. The syllables and segments that appear when the period of word learning begins are in no way related to the vast repertory of babbling sounds. Only the intonation contours are carried over from the babbling stage into the later period.

No matter what language environment a child grows up in, the intonation contours characteristic of adult speech in that environment are the linguistic information learned earliest. Some recent studies suggest that it is possible to identify the language environment of a child from her babbling intonation during the second year of life. Other studies suggest that children can be distinguished at an even earlier age on the basis of whether or not their language environment is a tone language, that is, a language in which words spoken with different pitches are identifiable as different words, even though they may have the same sequence of consonants and vowels. To put it another way, "ma" spoken with a high pitch and "ma" spoken with a low pitch can be as different to someone speaking a tone language as "ma" and "pa" are to someone speaking English. (Many African and Asian languages are tone languages.) Tones are learned very early, and entire tone systems are mastered long before other areas of phonology. The extremely early acquisition of pitch patterns may help to explain the difficulty adults have in learning the intonation of a second language.

Phonetics

There is one significant way in which the acquisition of phonology differs from the acquisition of other language systems. As a child is acquiring the phonological system she must also learn the phonetic realization of the system: the actual details of physiological and acoustic phonetics, which call for the coordination of a complex set of muscle movements. Some children complete the process of learning how to pronounce things earlier than others, but differences of this kind are usually not related to the learning of the phonological system. Brown had what has become a classic conversation with a child who referred to a "fis." Brown repeated "fis," and the child indignantly corrected him, saying "fis." After several such exchanges Brown tried "fish," and the child, finally satisfied, replied, "Yes, fis." It is clear that although the child was still not able to pronounce the distinction between the sounds "s" and "sh," he knew such a systematic phonological distinction existed. Such phonetic muddying of the phonological waters complicates the study of this area of acquisition. Since the child's knowledge of the phonological system may not show up in her speech, it is not easy to determine what a child knows about the system without engaging in complex experimentation and creative hypothesizing.

Children whose phonological system produces only simple words such as "mama" and "papa" actually have a greater phonetic repertory than their utterances suggest. Evidence of that repertory is found in the late babbling stage, when children are working with sentence units and are making a large array of sounds. They do not lose their phonetic ability overnight, but they must constrain it systematically. Going on to the next-higher stage of language learning, the phonological system, is more important to the child than the details of facile pronunciation. Much later, after the phonological system has been acquired, the details of pronunciation receive more attention.

In the period following the babbling period the persisting phonetic facility gets less and less exercise. The vast majority of a child's utterances fail to reflect her real ability to pronounce things accurately; they do, however, reflect her growing ability to pronounce things systematically. (For a child who grows up learning only one language the movements of the muscles of the vocal tract ultimately become so overpracticed that it is difficult to learn new pronunciations during adulthood. On the other hand, people who learn at least two languages in early childhood appear to retain a greater flexibility of the vocal musculature and are more likely to learn to speak an additional language in their adult years without the "accent" of their native language.)

In learning to pronounce, then, a child must acquire a sound system that includes the divergent systems of phonology and phonetics. The acquisition of phonology differs from that of phonetics in requiring the creation of a representation of language in the mind of the child. This representation is necessary because of the abstract nature of the units of phonological structure. From only the acoustic signal of adult language the child must derive successively more abstract phonological units: first intonations, then syllables, then distinctive features and finally consonant-and-vowel segments. There are, for example, few clear segment boundaries in the acoustic signal the child receives, and so the consonant-and-vowel units could hardly be derived if the child had no internal representation of language.

At the same time that a child is building a phonological representation of language she is learning to manipulate all the phonetic variations of language, learning to produce each one precisely and automatically. The dual process of phonetics and phonology acquisition is one of the most difficult in all of language learning. Indeed, although a great deal of syntactic and semantic acquisition has yet to take place, it is usually at the completion of the process of learning to pronounce that adults consider a child to be a full-fledged language speaker and stop using any form of caretaker speech.

Abnormal Language Development

There seems to be little question that the human brain is best suited to language learning before puberty. Foreign languages are certainly learned most easily at that time. Furthermore, it has been observed that people who learn more than one language in childhood have an easier time learning additional languages in later years. It seems to be extremely important for a child to exercise the language-learning faculty. Children who are not exposed to any learnable language during the crucial years, for example children who are deaf before they can speak, generally grow up with the handicap of having little or no language. The handicap is unnecessary: deaf children of deaf parents who communicate by means of the American Sign Language do not grow up without language. They live in an environment where they can make full use of their language-learning abilities, and they are reasonably fluent in sign language by age three, right on the developmental schedule. Deaf children who grow up communicating by means of sign language have a much easier time learning English as a second language than deaf children in oral-speech programs learning English as a first language.

The study of child language acquisition has made important contributions to the study of abnormal speech development. Some investigators of child language have looked at children whose language development is abnormal in the hope of finding the conditions that are necessary and sufficient for normal development; others have looked at the development of language in normal children in the hope of helping children whose language development is abnormal. It now appears that many of the severe language abnormalities found in children can in some way be traced to interruptions of the normal acquisition process. The improved understanding of the normal process is being exploited to create treatment programs for children with such problems. In the past therapeutic methods for children with language problems have emphasized the memorizing of language routines, but methods now being developed would allow a child to work with her own language-learning abilities. For example, the American Sign Language has been taught successfully to several autistic children. Many of these nonverbal and antisocial children have learned in this way to communicate with therapists, in some cases becoming more socially responsive. (Why sign language should be so successful with some autistic children is unclear; it may have to do with the fact that a sign lasts longer than an auditory signal.)

There are still many questions to be answered in the various areas I have discussed, but in general a great deal of progress has been made in understanding child language over the past 20 years. The study of the acquisition of language has come of age. It is now a genuinely interdisciplinary field where psychologists, neurosurgeons and linguists work together to penetrate the mechanisms of perception and cognition as well as the mechanisms of language.

20 Teaching Language to an Ape

by Ann James Premack and David Premack
October 1972

Sarah, a young chimpanzee, has a reading and writing vocabulary of about 130 "words." Her understanding goes beyond the meaning of words and includes the concepts of class and sentence structure

Over the past 40 years several efforts have been made to teach a chimpanzee human language. In the early 1930's Winthrop and Luella Kellogg raised a female chimpanzee named Gua along with their infant son; at the age of 16 months Gua could understand about 100 words, but she never did try to speak them. In the 1940's Keith and Cathy Hayes raised a chimpanzee named Vicki in their home; she learned a large number of words and with some difficulty could mouth the words "mama," "papa" and "cup." More recently Allen and Beatrice Gardner have taught their chimpanzee Washoe to communicate in the American Sign Language with her fingers and hands. Since 1966 in our laboratory at the University of California at Santa Barbara we have been teaching Sarah to read and write with variously shaped and colored pieces of plastic, each representing a word; Sarah has a vocabulary of about 130 terms that she uses with a reliability of between 75 and 80 percent.

Why try to teach human language to an ape? In our own case the motive was to better define the fundamental nature of language. It is often said that language is unique to the human species. Yet it is now well known that many other animals have elaborate communication systems of their own. It seems clear that language is a general system of which human language is a particular, albeit remarkably refined, form. Indeed, it is possible that certain features of human language that are considered to be uniquely human belong to the more general system, and that these features can be distinguished from those that are unique to the human information-processing regime. If, for example, an ape can be taught the rudiments of human language, it should clarify the dividing line between the general system and the human one.

There was much evidence that the chimpanzee was a good candidate for the acquisition of language before we began our project. In their natural environment chimpanzees have an extensive vocal "call system." In captivity the chimpanzee has been taught to sort pictures into classes: animate and inanimate, old and young, male and female. Moreover, the animal can classify the same item in different ways depending

SARAH, after reading the message "Sarah insert apple pail banana dish" on the magnetic board, performed the appropriate actions. To be able to make the correct interpretation that she should put the apple in the pail and the banana in the dish (not the apple, pail and banana in the dish) the chimpanzee had to understand sentence structure rather than just word order. In actual tests most symbols were colored (*see illustration on page 201*).

on the alternatives offered. Watermelon is classified as fruit in one set of alternatives, as food in another set and as big in a third set. On the basis of these demonstrated conceptual abilities we made the assumption that the chimpanzee could be taught not only the names of specific members of a class but also the names for the classes themselves.

It is not necessary for the names to be vocal. They can just as well be based on gestures, written letters or colored stones. The important thing is to shape the language to fit the information-processing capacities of the chimpanzee. To a large extent teaching language to an animal is simply mapping out the conceptual structures the animal already possesses. By using a system of naming that suits the chimpanzee we hope to find out more about its conceptual world. Ultimately the benefit of language experiments with animals will be realized in an understanding of intelligence in terms not of scores on tests but of the underlying brain mechanisms. Only then can cognitive mechanisms for classifying stimuli, for storing and retrieving information and for problem-solving be studied in a comparative way.

The first step in teaching language is to exploit knowledge that is already present. In teaching Sarah we first mapped the simple social transaction of giving, which is something the chimpanzee does both in nature and in the laboratory. Considered in terms of cognitive and perceptual elements, the verb "give" involves a relation between two individuals and one object, that is, between the donor, the recipient and the object being transferred. In order to carry out the act of giving an animal must recognize the difference between individuals (between "Mary" and "Randy") and must perceive the difference between donors and recipients (between "Mary gives Randy" and "Randy gives Mary"). In order to be able to map out the entire transaction of giving the animal has to distinguish agents from objects, agents from one another, objects from one another and itself from others.

The trainer began the process of mapping the social transaction by placing a slice of banana between himself and Sarah. The chimpanzee, which was then about five years old, was allowed to eat the tasty morsel while the trainer looked on affectionately. After the transaction had become routine, a language element consisting of a pink plastic square was placed close to Sarah while the slice of banana was moved beyond her reach. To obtain the fruit Sarah now had to put the plastic piece on a "language board" on the side of her cage. (The board was magnetic and the plastic square was backed with a thin piece of steel so that it would stick.) After Sarah had learned this routine the fruit was changed to an apple and she had to place a blue plastic word for apple on the board. Later several other fruits, the verb "give" and the plastic words that named each of them were introduced.

To be certain that Sarah knew the meaning of "give" it was necessary to contrast "give" with other verbs, such as "wash," "cut" and "insert." When Sarah indicated "Give apple," she was given a piece of apple. When she put "Wash apple" on the board, the apple was placed in a bowl of water and washed. In that way Sarah learned what action went with what verb.

In the first stage Sarah was required to put only one word on the board; the name of the fruit was a sufficient indicator of the social transaction. When names for different actions—verbs—were introduced, Sarah had to place two words on the board in vertical sequence. In order to be given an apple she had to write "Give apple." When recipients were named, two-word sentences were not accepted by the trainer; Sarah had to use three words. There were several trainers, and Sarah had to learn the name of each one. To facilitate the teaching of personal names, both the chimpanzees and the trainers wore their plastic-word names on a string necklace. Sarah learned the names of some of the recipients the hard way. Once she wrote "Give apple Gussie," and the trainer promptly gave the apple to another chimpanzee named Gussie. Sarah never repeated the sentence. At every stage she was required to observe the proper word sequence. "Give apple" was accepted but "Apple give" was not. When donors were to be named, Sarah had to identify all the members of the social transaction: "Mary give apple Sarah."

The interrogative was introduced with the help of the concepts "same" and "different." Sarah was given a cup and a spoon. When another cup was added, she was taught to put the two cups together. Other sets of three objects were given to her, and she had to pair the two objects that were alike. Then she was taught to place the plastic word for "same" between any two similar objects and the plastic word for "different" between unlike objects. Next what amounted to a question mark was placed between pairs of objects. This plastic shape (which bore no resemblance to the usual kind of question mark) made the question explicit rather than implicit, as it had been in the simple matching tests. When the interrogative element was placed between a pair of cups, it meant: "What is the relation between cup A and cup B?" The choices provided Sarah were the plastic words "same" and "different." She learned to remove the interrogative particle and substitute the correct word [see top illustration on page 202]. Sarah was able to transfer what she had learned and apply the word "same" or "different" to numerous pairs of objects that had not been used in her training.

Any construction is potentially a question. From the viewpoint of structural linguistics any construction where one or more elements are deleted becomes a question. The constructions we used with Sarah were "A same A" and "A different B." Elements in these constructions were removed and the deletion was marked with the interrogative symbol; Sarah was then supplied with a choice of missing elements with which she could restore the construction to its familiar form. In principle interrogation can be taught either by removing an element from a familiar situation in the animal's world or by removing the element from a language that maps the animal's world. It is probable that one can induce questions by purposively removing key elements from a familiar situation. Suppose a chimpanzee received its daily ration of food at a specific time and place, and then one day the food was not there. A chimpanzee trained in the interrogative might inquire "Where is my food?" or, in Sarah's case, "My food is?" Sarah was never put in a situation that might induce such interrogation because for our purposes it was easier to teach Sarah to answer questions.

At first Sarah learned all her words in the context of social exchange. Later, when she had learned the concepts "name of" and "not name of," it was possible to introduce new words in a more direct way. To teach her that objects had names, the plastic word for "apple" and a real apple were placed on the table and Sarah was required to put the plastic word for "name of" between them. The same procedure was repeated for banana. After she had responded correctly several times, the symbol for "apple" and a real banana were placed on the table and Sarah had to put "not

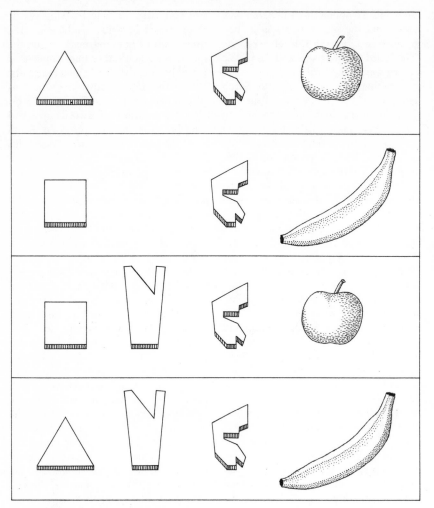

TEACHING LANGUAGE WITH LANGUAGE was the next step. Sarah was taught to put the symbol for "name of" between the word for "apple" and an apple and also between the word for "banana" and a banana. She learned the concept "not name of" in the same way. Thereafter Sarah could be taught new nouns by introducing them with "name of."

name of" between them. After she was able to perform both operations correctly new nouns could be taught quickly and explicitly. The plastic words for "raisin" and "name of" could be placed next to a real raisin and Sarah would learn the noun. Evidence of such learning came when Sarah subsequently requested "Mary give raisin Sarah" or set down "Raisin different apple."

An equally interesting linguistic leap occurred when Sarah learned the predicate adjective and could write such sentences as "Red color of apple," "Round shape of apple" and "Large size of apple." When asked for the relation between "Apple is red ? Red color of apple" and given "same" and "different" as choices, she judged the sentences to be the same. When given "Apple is red ? Apple is round," she judged the sentences to be different. The distinctions between similar and different, first learned with actual objects, was later applied by Sarah in linguistic constructions.

In English the conditional consists of the discontinuous elements "if-then," which are inconvenient and conceptually unnecessary. In symbolic logic the conditional consists of the single sign ⊃, and we taught Sarah the conditional relation with the use of a single plastic word. Before being given language training in the conditional, she was given contingency training in which she was rewarded for doing one thing but not another. For example, she was given a choice between an apple and a banana, and only when she chose the apple was she given chocolate (which she dearly loved). "If apple, then chocolate, if banana, then no chocolate" were the relations she learned; the same relations were subsequently used in sentences to teach her the name for the conditional relation.

The subject was introduced with the

written construction: "Sarah take apple ? Mary give chocolate Sarah." Sarah was provided with only one plastic word: the conditional particle. She had to remove the question mark and substitute the conditional in its place to earn the apple and the chocolate. Now she was presented with: "Sarah take banana ? Mary no give chocolate Sarah." Again only the conditional symbol was provided. When Sarah replaced the question mark with the conditional symbol, she received a banana but no chocolate. After several such tests she was given a series of trials on each of the following pairs of sentences: "Sarah take apple if-then Mary give chocolate Sarah" coupled with "Sarah take banana if-then Mary no give chocolate Sarah," or "Sarah take apple if-then Mary no give chocolate Sarah" coupled with "Sarah take banana if-then Mary give chocolate Sarah."

At first Sarah made many errors, taking the wrong fruit and failing to get her beloved chocolate. After several of her strategies had failed she paid closer attention to the sentences and began choosing the fruit that gave her the chocolate. Once the conditional relation had been learned she was able to apply it to other types of sentence, for example "Mary take red if-then Sarah take apple" and "Mary take green if-then Sarah take banana." Here Sarah had to watch Mary's choice closely in order to take the correct action. With the paired sentences "Red is on green if-then Sarah take apple" and "Green is on red if-then Sarah take banana," which involved a change in the position of two colored cards, Sarah was not confused and performed well.

As a preliminary to learning the class concepts of color, shape and size Sarah was taught to identify members of the classes red and yellow, round and square and large and small. Objects that varied in most dimensions but had a particular property in common were used. Thus for teaching the word "red" a set of dissimilar, unnamed objects (a ball, a toy car, a Life Saver and so on) that had no property in common except redness were put before the chimpanzee. The only plastic word available to her was "red." After several trials on identifying red with a set of red objects and yellow with a set of yellow objects, Sarah was shifted to trials where she had to choose between "red" and "yellow" when she was shown a colored object. Finally completely new red and yellow objects were presented to her, including small cards that were identical except for their color.

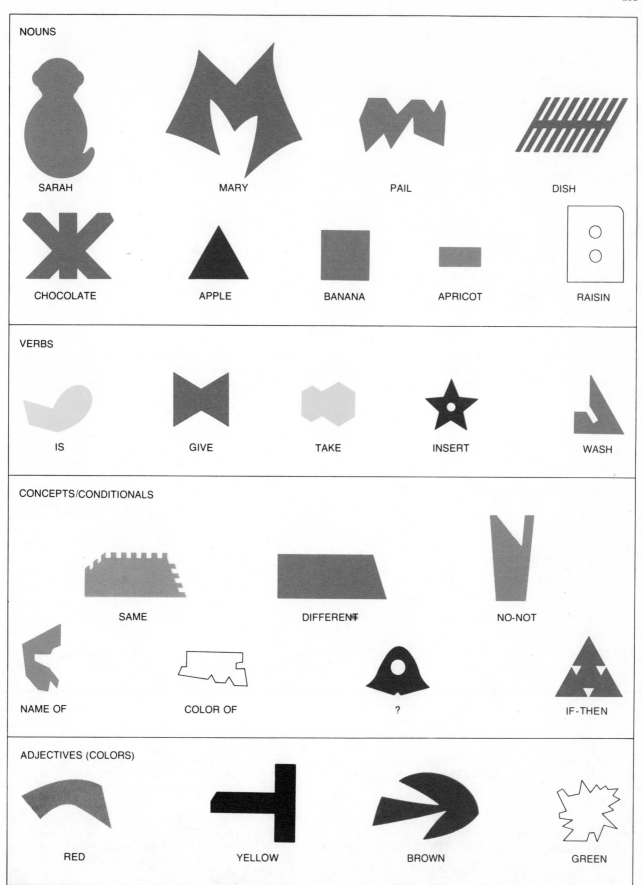

NOUNS

SARAH   MARY   PAIL   DISH

CHOCOLATE   APPLE   BANANA   APRICOT   RAISIN

VERBS

IS   GIVE   TAKE   INSERT   WASH

CONCEPTS/CONDITIONALS

SAME   DIFFERENT   NO-NOT

NAME OF   COLOR OF   ?   IF-THEN

ADJECTIVES (COLORS)

RED   YELLOW   BROWN   GREEN

PLASTIC SYMBOLS that varied in color, shape and size were chosen as the language units to be taught to Sarah. The plastic pieces were backed with metal so that they would adhere to a magnetic board. Each plastic symbol stood for a specific word or concept. A "Chinese" convention of writing sentences vertically from top to bottom was adopted because at the beginning of her training Sarah seemed to prefer it. Sarah had to put the words in proper sequence but the orientation of the word symbols was not important.

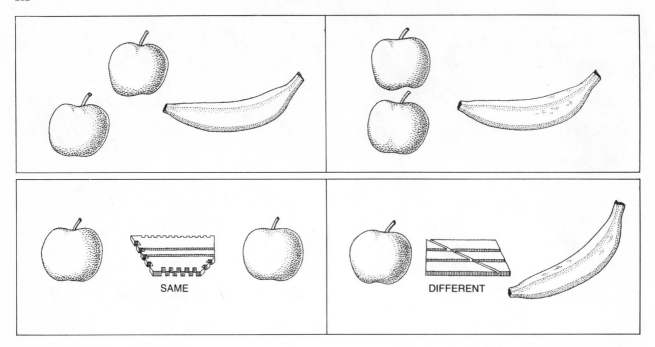

CONCEPTS "SAME" AND "DIFFERENT" were introduced into Sarah's vocabulary by teaching her to pair objects that were alike (*top illustration*). Then two identical objects, for example apples, were placed before her and she was given plastic word for "same" and induced to place word between the two objects. She was also taught to place the word for "different" between unlike objects.

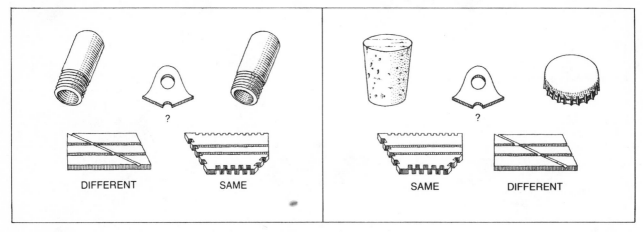

THE INTERROGATIVE was introduced with the help of the concepts "same" and "different." A plastic piece that meant "question mark" was placed between two objects and Sarah had to replace it with either the word for "same" or the word for "different."

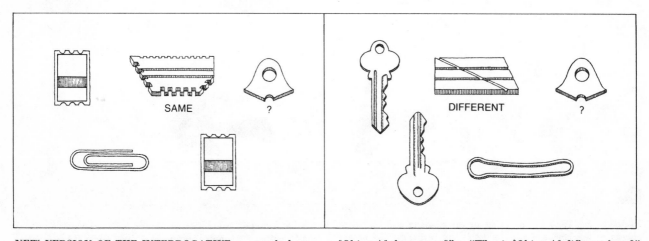

NEW VERSION OF THE INTERROGATIVE was taught by arranging an object and plastic symbols to form questions: "What is [Object A] the same as?" or "What is [Object A] different from?" Sarah had to replace question marker with the appropriate object.

Again she performed at her usual level of accuracy.

Sarah was subsequently taught the names of shapes, "round" and "square," as well as the size names "large" and "small." These words formed the basis for teaching her the names of the class concepts "color of," "shape of" and "size of." Given the interrogative "Red ? apple" or "Yellow ? banana," Sarah was required to substitute the plastic word for "color of" for the question mark. In teaching class names a good many sentences were not written on the board but were presented as hybrids. The hybrid sentences consisted of a combination of plastic words and real objects arranged in the proper sentence sequence on Sarah's worktable. Typical sentences were "Yellow ?" beside a real yellow balloon or "Red ?" beside a red wood block.

The hybrid sentences did not deter Sarah in the least. Her good performance showed that she was able to move with facility from symbols for objects to actual objects. Her behavior with hybrid constructions recalls the activity of young children, who sometimes combine spoken words with real objects they are unable to name by pointing at the objects.

Was Sarah able to think in the plastic-word language? Could she store information using the plastic words or use them to solve certain kinds of problem that she could not solve otherwise? Additional research is needed before we shall have definitive answers, but Sarah's performance suggests that the answers to both questions may be a qualified yes. To think with language requires being able to generate the meaning of words in the absence of their external representation. For Sarah to be able to match "apple" to an actual apple or "Mary" to a picture of Mary indicates that she knows the meaning of these words. It does not prove, however, that when she is given the word "apple" and no apple is present, she can think "apple," that is, mentally represent the meaning of the word to herself. The ability to achieve such mental representation is of major importance because it frees language from simple dependence on the outside world. It involves displacement: the ability to talk about things that are not actually there. That is a critical feature of language.

The hint that Sarah was able to understand words in the absence of their external referents came early in her language training. When she was given a piece of fruit and two plastic words, she was required to put the correct word for the fruit on the board before she was allowed to eat it. Surprisingly often, however, she chose the wrong word. It then dawned on us that her poor performance might be due not to errors but to her trying to express her preferences in fruit. We conducted a series of tests to determine her fruit preferences, using actual fruits in one test and only fruit names in the other. Sarah's choices between the words were much the same as her choices between the actual fruits. This result strongly suggests that she could generate the meaning of the fruit names from the plastic symbols alone.

We obtained clearer evidence at a later stage of Sarah's language training. In the same way that she could use

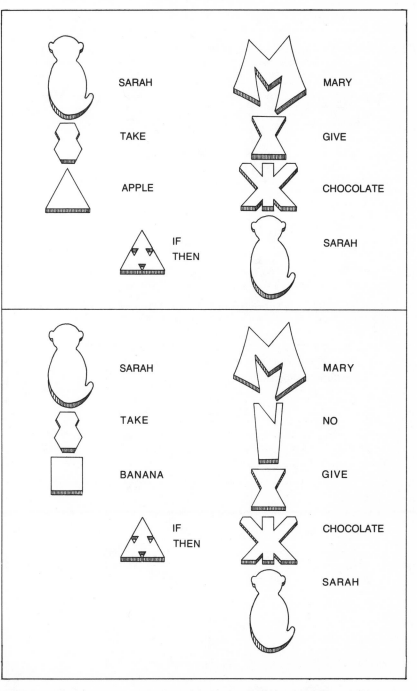

CONDITIONAL RELATION, which in English is expressed "if...then," was taught to Sarah as a single word. The plastic symbol for the conditional relation was placed between two sentences. Sarah had to pay attention to the meaning of both sentences very closely in order to make the choice that would give her a reward. Once the conditional relation was learned by means of this procedure, the chimpanzee was able to apply it to other situations.

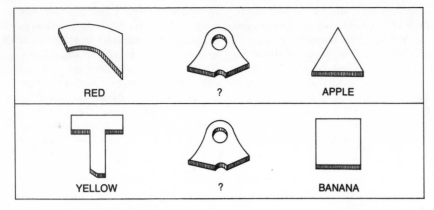

CLASS CONCEPT OF COLOR was taught with the aid of sentences such as "Red ? apple" and "Yellow ? banana." Sarah had to replace the interrogative symbol with "color of."

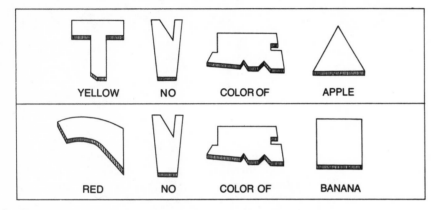

NEGATIVE CONCEPT was introduced with "no-not." When asked "Yellow ? apple" or "Red ? banana," Sarah had to replace interrogative symbol with "color of" or "not color of."

ALTERNATIVE FEATURES			
		🍎	△
RED	GREEN	RED	RED
○	□	○	○
⌑	⬜	⌑	⌑
⌑	○	○	○

FEATURE ANALYSIS of an actual apple and the plastic word for "apple" was conducted. Sarah was shown an apple or the word and made to choose from alternative features: red or green, round or square, square with stem or plain square and square with stem or round. Sarah gave plastic word for "apple" same attributes she had earlier assigned to apple.

"name of" to learn new nouns, she was able to use "color of" to learn the names of new colors. For instance, the names "brown" and "green" were introduced in the sentences "Brown color of chocolate" and "Green color of grape." The only new words at this point were "brown" and "green." Later Sarah was confronted with four disks, only one of which was brown, and when she was instructed with the plastic symbols "Take brown," she took the brown disk. Since chocolate was not present at any time during the introduction of the color name "brown," the word "chocolate" in the definition must have been sufficient to have Sarah generate or picture the property brown.

What form does Sarah's supposed internal representation take? Some indication is provided by the results of a test of ability to analyze the features of an object. First Sarah was shown an actual apple and was given a series of paired comparisons that described the features of the apple, such as red v. green, round v. square and so on. She had to pick the descriptive feature that belonged to the apple. Her feature analysis of a real apple agreed nicely with our own, which is evidence of the interesting fact that a chimpanzee is capable of decomposing a complex object into features. Next the apple was removed and the blue plastic triangle that was the word for "apple" was placed before her and again she was given a paired-comparison test. She assigned the same features to the word that she had earlier assigned to the object. Her feature analysis revealed that it was not the physical properties of the word (blue and triangle) that she was describing but rather the object that was represented by the word [see bottom illustration at left].

To test Sarah's sentence comprehension she was taught to correctly follow these written instructions: "Sarah insert apple pail," "Sarah insert banana pail," "Sarah insert apple dish" and "Sarah insert banana dish." Next instructions were combined in a one-line vertical sequence ("Sarah insert apple pail Sarah insert banana dish"). The chimpanzee responded appropriately. Then the second "Sarah" and the second verb "insert" were deleted to yield the compound sentence: "Sarah insert apple pail banana dish." Sarah followed the complicated instructions at her usual level of accuracy.

The test with the compound sentence is of considerable importance, because it provides the answer to whether or not

Sarah could understand the notion of constituent structure: the hierarchical organization of a sentence. The correct interpretation of the compound sentence was "Sarah put the apple in the pail and the banana in the dish." To take the correct actions Sarah must understand that "apple" and "pail" go together but not "pail" and "banana," even though the terms appear side by side. Moreover, she must understand that the verb "insert" is at a higher level of organization and refers to both "apple" and "banana." Finally, Sarah must understand that she, as the head noun, must carry out all the actions. If Sarah were capable only of linking words in a simple chain, she would never be able to interpret the compound sentence with its deletions. The fact is that she interprets them correctly. If a child were to carry out the instructions in the same way, we would not hesitate to say that he recognizes the various levels of sentence organization: that the subject dominates the predicate and the verb in the predicate dominates the objects.

Sarah had managed to learn a code, a simple language that nevertheless included some of the characteristic features of natural language. Each step of the training program was made as simple as possible. The objective was to reduce complex notions to a series of simple and highly learnable steps. The same program that was used to teach Sarah to communicate has been successfully applied with people who have language difficulties caused by brain damage. It may also be of benefit to the autistic child.

In assessing the results of the experiment with Sarah one must be careful not to require of Sarah what one would require of a human adult. Compared with a two-year-old child, however, Sarah holds her own in language ability. In fact, language demands were made of Sarah that would never be made of a child. Man is understandably prejudiced in favor of his own species, and members of other species must perform Herculean feats before they are recognized as having similar abilities, particularly language abilities. Linguists and others who study the development of language tend to exaggerate the child's understanding of language and to be extremely skeptical of the experimentally demonstrated language abilities of the chimpanzee. It is our hope that our findings will dispel such prejudices and lead to new attempts to teach suitable languages to animals other than man.

21

Specializations of the Human Brain

by Norman Geschwind
September 1979

Certain higher faculties, such as language, depend on specialized regions in the human brain. On a larger scale the two cerebral hemispheres are specialized for different kinds of mental activity

The nervous systems of all animals have a number of basic functions in common, most notably the control of movement and the analysis of sensation. What distinguishes the human brain is the variety of more specialized activities it is capable of learning. The preeminent example is language: no one is born knowing a language, but virtually everyone learns to speak and to understand the spoken word, and people of all cultures can be taught to write and to read. Music is also universal in man: people with no formal training are able to recognize and to reproduce dozens of melodies. Similarly, almost everyone can draw simple figures, and the ability to make accurate renderings is not rare.

At least some of these higher functions of the human brain are governed by dedicated networks of neurons. It has been known for more than 100 years, for example, that at least two delimited regions of the cerebral cortex are essential to linguistic competence; they seem to be organized explicitly for the processing of verbal information. Certain structures on the inner surface of the underside of the temporal lobe, including the hippocampus, are apparently necessary for the long-term retention of memories. In some cases the functional specialization of a neural system seems to be quite narrowly defined: hence one area on both sides of the human cerebral cortex is concerned primarily with the recognition of faces. It is likely that other mental activities are also associated with particular neural networks. Musical and artistic abilities, for example, appear to depend on specialized systems in the brain, although the circuitry has not yet been worked out.

Another distinctive characteristic of the human brain is the allocation of functions to the two cerebral hemispheres. That the human brain is not fully symmetrical in its functioning could be guessed from at least one observation of daily experience: most of the human population favors the right hand, which is controlled by the left side of the brain. Linguistic abilities also reside mainly on the left side. For these reasons the left cerebral hemisphere was once said to be the dominant one and the right side of the brain was thought to be subservient. In recent years this concept has been revised as it has become apparent that each hemisphere has its own specialized talents. Those for which the right cortex is dominant include some features of aptitudes for music and for the recognition of complex visual patterns. The right hemisphere is also the more important one for the expression and recognition of emotion. In the past few years these functional asymmetries have been matched with anatomical ones, and a start has been made on exploring their prevalence in species other than man.

In man as in other mammalian species large areas of the cerebral cortex are given over to comparatively elementary sensory and motor functions. An arch that extends roughly from ear to ear across the roof of the brain is the primary motor cortex, which exercises voluntary control over the muscles. Parallel to this arch and just behind it is the primary somatic sensory area, where signals are received from the skin, the bones, the joints and the muscles. Almost every region of the body is represented by a corresponding region in both the primary motor cortex and the somatic sensory cortex. At the back of the brain, and particularly on the inner surface of the occipital lobes, is the primary visual cortex. The primary auditory areas are in the temporal lobes; olfaction is focused in a region on the underside of the frontal lobes.

The primary motor and sensory areas are specialized in the sense that each one is dedicated to a specified function, but the functions themselves are of general utility, and the areas are called on in a great variety of activities. Moreover, homologous areas are found in all species that have a well-developed cerebral cortex. My main concern in this article is with certain regions of the cortex that govern a narrower range of behavior. Some of these highly specialized areas may be common to many species but others may be uniquely human.

A series of experiments dealing with learning in monkeys illustrates how fine the functional distinction can be between two networks of neurons. A monkey can be taught to choose consistently one object or pattern from a pair. The task is made somewhat more difficult if the objects are presented and then withdrawn and the monkey is allowed to indicate its choice only after a delay during which the objects are hidden behind a screen. It has been found that performance on this test is impaired markedly if a small region of the frontal lobes is destroyed on both sides of the brain. Difficulty can also be introduced into the experiment by making the patterns complex but allowing a choice to be made while the patterns are still in sight. Damage to a quite different area of the cortex reduces ability to carry out this task, but it has no effect on the delay test.

These experiments also illustrate one of the principal means for acquiring information about the functions of the brain. When a particular site is damaged by disease or injury, a well-defined deficiency in behavior sometimes ensues. In many cases one may conclude that some aspects of the behavior affected are normally dependent on the part of the brain that has been destroyed. In man the commonest cause of brain damage is cerebral thrombosis, or stroke: the occlusion of arteries in the brain, which results in the death of the tissues the blocked arteries supply. By 1920 the study of patients who had sustained such damage had led to the identification of several functional regions of the brain, including the language areas.

The study of the effects of damage to the brain is still an important method of investigating brain function, but other techniques have since been developed. One of the most important was brought to a high level of development by the German neurosurgeon Otfrid Foerster and by Wilder Penfield of the Montreal Neurological Institute. They studied the responses in the conscious patient un-

REPRODUCED BY LEFT HAND
(RIGHT HEMISPHERE)

MODEL PATTERN

REPRODUCED BY RIGHT HAND
(LEFT HEMISPHERE)

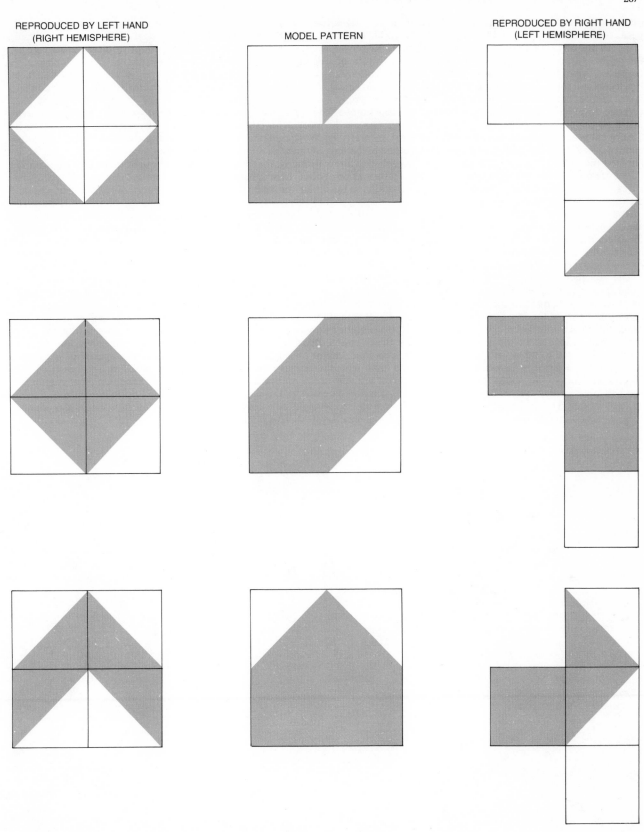

CAPABILITIES OF THE TWO HEMISPHERES of the human cerebral cortex were tested in a subject whose hemispheres had been surgically isolated from each other. The surgical procedure consisted in cutting the two main bundles of nerve fibers that connect the hemispheres: the corpus callosum and the anterior commissure. In the test each of the patterns in the middle column was presented to the subject, who was asked to reproduce it by assembling colored blocks. The assembly was carried out either with the right hand alone (which communicates mainly with the left hemisphere) or with the left hand alone (which is controlled primarily by the right hemisphere). Errors were equally frequent with either hand, but the kinds of error typical of each hand were quite different. The results suggest that each side of the brain may bring a separate set of skills to bear on such a task, a finding consistent with other evidence that the hemispheres are specialized for different functions. What is equally apparent, however, is that neither hemisphere alone is competent in the analysis of such patterns; the two hemispheres must cooperate. The test was conducted by Edith Kaplan of the Boston Veterans Administration Hospital.

dergoing brain surgery that follow electrical stimulation of various sites in the brain. In this way they were able to map the regions responsible for a number of functions. Apart from the importance of this technique for the study of the brain, it is of clinical benefit since it enables the surgeon to avoid areas where damage might be crippling.

Surgical procedures developed for the control of severe epilepsy have also contributed much information. One method of treating persistent epileptic seizures (adopted only when other therapies have failed) is to remove the region of the cortex from which the seizures arise. The functional deficits that sometimes result from this procedure have been studied in detail by Brenda Milner of the Montreal Neurological Institute.

The specializations of the hemispheres can be studied in people who have sustained damage to the commissures that connect the two sides of the brain, the most important of these being the corpus callosum. In the first such cases, studied at the end of the 19th century by Jules Déjerine in France and by Hugo Liepmann in Germany, the damage had been caused by strokes. More recently isolation of the hemispheres by surgical sectioning of the commissures

has been employed for the relief of epilepsy. Studies of such "split brain" patients by Roger W. Sperry of the California Institute of Technology and by Michael S. Gazzaniga of the Cornell University Medical College have provided increasingly detailed knowledge of the functions of the separated hemispheres. Doreen Kimura, who is now at the University of Western Ontario, pioneered in the development of a technique, called dichotic listening, that provides information about hemispheric specialization in the intact human brain.

The specialized regions of the brain that have been investigated in the greatest detail are those involved in language. In the 1860's the French investigator Paul Broca pointed out that damage to a particular region of the cortex consistently gives rise to an aphasia, or speech disorder. The region is on the side of the frontal lobes, and it is now called the anterior language area, or simply Broca's area. Broca went on to make a second major discovery. He showed that whereas damage to this area on the left side of the brain leads to aphasia, similar damage to the corresponding area on the right side leaves the faculty of speech intact. This finding

has since been amply confirmed: well over 95 percent of the aphasias caused by brain damage result from damage to the left hemisphere.

Broca's area is adjacent to the face area of the motor cortex, which controls the muscles of the face, the tongue, the jaw and the throat. When Broca's area is destroyed by a stroke, there is almost always severe damage to the face area in the left hemisphere as well, and so it might be thought that the disruption of speech is caused by partial paralysis of the muscles required for articulation. That some other explanation is required is easily demonstrated. First, damage to the corresponding area on the right side of the brain does not cause aphasia, although a similar weakness of the facial muscles results. Furthermore, in Broca's aphasia it is known that the muscles that function poorly in speech operate normally in other tasks. The evidence is quite simple: the patient with Broca's aphasia can speak only with great difficulty, but he can sing with ease and often with elegance. The speech of a patient with Broca's aphasia also has features, such as faulty grammar, that cannot be explained by a muscular failure.

Another kind of aphasia was identified in 1874 by the German investiga-

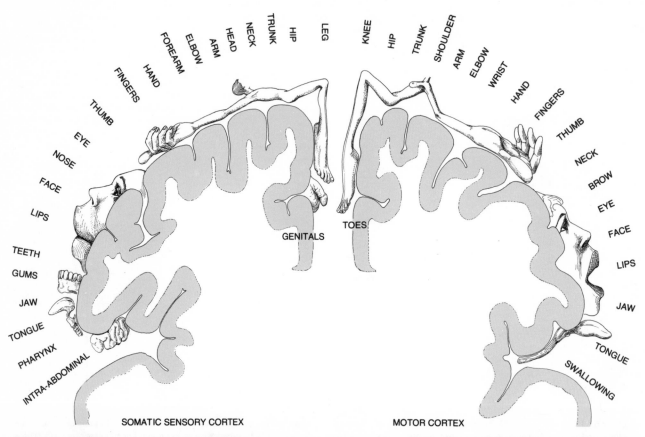

SOMATIC SENSORY AND MOTOR REGIONS of the cerebral cortex are specialized in the sense that every site in these regions can be associated with some part of the body. In other words, most of the body can be mapped onto the cortex, yielding two distorted homunculi. The distortions come about because the area of the cortex dedicated to a part of the body is proportional not to that part's actual size but to the precision with which it must be controlled. In man the motor and somatic sensory regions given over to the face and to the hands are greatly exaggerated. Only half of each cortical region is shown: the left somatic sensory area (which receives sensations primarily from the right side of the body) and the right motor cortex (which exercises control over movement in the left half of the body).

tor Carl Wernicke. It is associated with damage to another site in the cortex, also in the left hemisphere, but in the temporal lobe rather than the frontal lobe. This region, which is now called Wernicke's area, lies between the primary auditory cortex and a structure called the angular gyrus, which probably mediates between visual and auditory centers of the brain. It has since been learned that Wernicke's area and Broca's area are connected by a bundle of nerve fibers, the arcuate fasciculus.

A lesion in either Broca's area or Wernicke's area leads to a disruption of speech, but the nature of the two disorders is quite different. In Broca's aphasia speech is labored and slow and articulation is impaired. The response to a question will often make sense, but it generally cannot be expressed as a fully formed or grammatical sentence. There is particular difficulty with the inflection of verbs, with pronouns and connective words and with complex grammatical constructions. As a result the speech has a telegraphic style. For example, a patient asked about a dental appointment said, hesitantly and indistinctly: "Yes... Monday...Dad and Dick...Wednesday nine o'clock...10 o'clock...doctors...and...teeth." The same kinds of errors are made in writing.

In Wernicke's aphasia speech is phonetically and even grammatically normal, but it is semantically deviant. Words are often strung together with considerable facility and with the proper inflections, so that the utterance has the recognizable structure of a sentence. The words chosen, however, are often inappropriate, and they sometimes include nonsensical syllables or words. Even when the individual words are correct, the utterance as a whole may express its meaning in a remarkably roundabout way. A patient who was asked to describe a picture that showed two boys stealing cookies behind a woman's back reported: "Mother is away here working her work to get her better, but when she's looking the two boys looking in the other part. She's working another time."

From an analysis of these defects Wernicke formulated a model of language production in the brain. Much new information has been added in the past 100 years, but the general principles Wernicke elaborated still seem valid. In this model the underlying structure of an utterance arises in Wernicke's area. It is then transferred through the arcuate fasciculus to Broca's area, where it evokes a detailed and coordinated program for vocalization. The program is passed on to the adjacent face area of the motor cortex, which activates the appropriate muscles of the mouth, the lips, the tongue, the larynx and so on.

Wernicke's area not only has a part

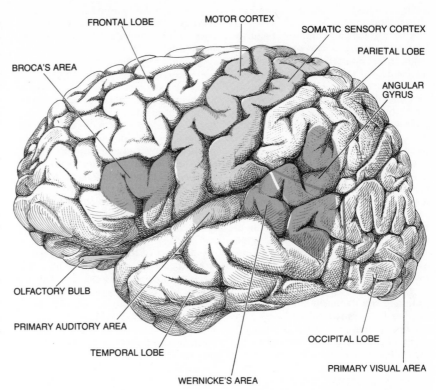

MAP OF THE HUMAN CORTEX shows regions whose functional specializations have been identified. Much of the cortex is given over to comparatively elementary functions: the generation of movement and the primary analysis of sensations. These areas, which include the motor and somatic sensory regions and the primary visual, auditory and olfactory areas, are present in all species that have a well-developed cortex and are called on in the course of many activities. Several other regions (*dark color*) are more narrowly specialized. Broca's area and Wernicke's area are involved in the production and comprehension of language. The angular gyrus is thought to mediate between visual and auditory forms of information. These functional specializations have been detected only on the left side of the brain; the corresponding areas of the right hemisphere do not have the same linguistic competence. The right hemisphere, which is not shown, has its own specialized abilities, including the analysis of some aspects of music and of complex visual patterns. The anatomical regions associated with these faculties, however, are not as well defined as the language areas. Even in the left hemisphere the assignment of functions to sites in the cortex is only approximate; some areas may have functions in addition to those indicated, and some functions may be carried out in more than one place.

in speaking but also has a major role in the comprehension of the spoken word and in reading and writing. When a word is heard, the sound is initially received in the primary auditory cortex, but the signal must pass through the adjacent Wernicke's area if it is to be understood as a verbal message. When a word is read, the visual pattern (from the primary visual cortex) is transmitted to the angular gyrus, which applies a transformation that elicits the auditory form of the word in Wernicke's area. Writing a word in response to an oral instruction requires information to be passed along the same pathways in the opposite direction: from the auditory cortex to Wernicke's area to the angular gyrus.

This model explains many of the symptoms that characterize the aphasias. A lesion in Broca's area disturbs the production of speech but has a much smaller effect on comprehension. Damage to Wernicke's area, on the other hand, disrupts all aspects of the use of language. The effects of certain rarer lesions are also in accord with the model. For example, destruction of the arcuate fasciculus, disconnecting Wernicke's area from Broca's area, leaves speech fluent and well articulated but semantically aberrant; Broca's area is operating but it is not receiving information from Wernicke's area. Because the latter center is also functional, however, comprehension of spoken and written words is almost normal. Writing is disrupted in all aphasias where speech is abnormal, but the neural circuits employed in writing are not known in detail.

Lesions in the angular gyrus have the effect of disconnecting the systems involved in auditory language and written language. Patients with injuries in certain areas of the angular gyrus may speak and understand speech normally, but they have difficulty with written language. The comprehension of a written word seems to require that the auditory form of the word be evoked in Wernicke's area. Damage to the angular gyrus seems to interrupt communication between the visual cortex and Wernicke's area, so that comprehension of written language is impaired.

Although the partitioning of linguistic functions among several sites in the cortex is now supported by much evidence, the rigidity of these assignments should not be overemphasized. The pessimistic view that damage to tissue in these areas inevitably leads to a permanent linguistic impairment is unwarranted. Actually a considerable degree of recovery is often observed. The neural tissue destroyed by an arterial thrombosis cannot be regenerated, but it seems the functions of the damaged areas can often be assumed, at least in part, by other regions. In some cases the recovery probably reflects the existence of an alternative store of learning on the opposite side of the brain, which remains dormant until the dominant side is injured. In other cases the function is taken over by neurons in areas adjacent to or surrounding the damaged site. Patrick D. Wall of University College London has shown that there is a fringe of such dormant but potentially active cells adjacent to the somatic sensory cortex, and it seems likely that similar fringe regions exist throughout the brain. Jay P. Mohr, who is now at the University of Southern Alabama, and his co-workers have shown that the prospects for recovery from Broca's aphasia are quite good provided the region destroyed is not too large. One interpretation of these findings suggests that regions bordering on Broca's area share its specialization in latent form.

Although the detailed mechanism of recovery is not known, it has been established that some groups of patients are more likely than others to regain their linguistic competence. Children, particularly children younger than eight, often make an excellent recovery. Left-handed people also make better progress than right-handers. Even among right-handers those who have left-handed parents, siblings or children are more likely to recover than those with no family history of left-handedness. The relation between handedness and recovery from damage to the language areas suggests that cerebral dominance for handedness and dominance for language are not totally independent.

A disorder of the brain that is startling because its effects are so narrowly circumscribed is prosopagnosia; it is a failure to recognize faces. In the normal individual the ability to identify people from their faces is itself quite remarkable. At a glance one can name a person from facial features alone, even though the features may change substantially over the years or may be presented in a highly distorted form, as in a caricature. In a patient with prosopagnosia this talent for association is abolished.

What is most remarkable about the disorder is its specificity. In general it is accompanied by few other neurological symptoms except for the loss of some part of the visual field, sometimes on both sides and sometimes only in the left half of space. Most mental tasks, in-

cluding those that require the processing of visual information, are done without particular difficulty; for example, the patient can usually read and correctly name seen objects. What he cannot do is look at a person or at a photograph of a face and name the person. He may even fail to recognize his wife or his children. It is not the identity of familiar people that has been lost to him, however, but only the connection between the face and the identity. When a familiar person speaks, the patient knows the voice and can say the name immediately. The perception of facial features is also unimpaired, since the patient can often describe a face in detail and can usually match a photograph made from the front with a profile of the same person. The deficiency seems to be confined to forming associations between faces and identities.

The lesions that cause prosopagnosia are as stereotyped as the disorder itself. Damage is found on the underside of both occipital lobes, extending forward to the inner surface of the temporal lobes. The implication is that some neural network within this region is specialized for the rapid and reliable recognition of human faces. It may seem that a disproportionate share of the brain's resources is being devoted to a rather limited task. It should be kept in mind, however, that the recognition of people as individuals is a valuable talent in a highly social animal, and there has probably been strong selectional pressure to improve its efficiency.

Similar capacities probably exist in other social species. Gary W. Van Hoesen, formerly in my department at the Harvard Medical School and now at the University of Iowa College of Medicine, has begun to investigate the neurological basis of face recognition in the rhesus monkey. So far he has demonstrated that the monkeys can readily discriminate between other monkeys on the basis of facial photographs. The neural structures called into play by this task have not, however, been identified.

Until recently little was known about the physiological basis of memory, one of the most important functions of the human brain. Through the study of some highly specific disorders, however, it has been possible to identify areas or structures in the brain that are involved in certain memory processes. For example, the examination of different forms of anterograde amnesia—an inability to learn new information—has revealed the role of the temporal lobes in memory. In particular, the striking disability of a patient whom Milner has studied for more than 25 years demonstrates the importance in memory of structures on the inner surface of the temporal lobes, such as the hippocampus.

In 1953 the patient had submitted to a radical surgical procedure in which

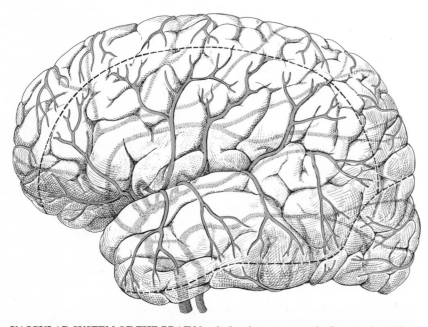

VASCULAR SYSTEM OF THE BRAIN has had an important part in the mapping of functional regions in the cerebral cortex. The normal functions of an area can often be inferred from the disturbance or impairment of behavior that results when the area is damaged. The commonest cause of such damage is the occlusion of an artery supplying the cortex, which leads to the death of the tissue nourished by that artery. Broca's area and Wernicke's area were identified in this way about 100 years ago, when patients with distinctive aphasias, or speech defects, were found by postmortem examination to have damage in those areas of the left hemisphere.

much of the hippocampus and several associated structures in both temporal lobes were destroyed. After the operation the skills and knowledge the patient had acquired up to that time remained largely intact, and he was and still is able to attend normally to ongoing events. In fact, he seems to be able to register limited amounts of new information in the usual manner. Within a short time, however, most of the newly learned information ceases to be available to him.

Milner has interviewed and tested the patient at intervals since the operation, and she has found that his severe anterograde amnesia has changed very little during that time. He has also exhibited an extensive although patchy retrograde amnesia (about the years before the operation), but that has improved appreciably. In the absence of distraction he can retain, say, a three-digit number for many minutes by means of verbal rehearsal or with the aid of an elaborate mnemonic device. Once his attention has been momentarily diverted, however, he cannot remember the number or the mnemonic device to which he devoted so much effort. He cannot even remember the task itself. Living from moment to moment, he has not been able to learn his address or to remember where the objects he uses every day are kept in his home. He fails to recognize people who have visited him regularly for many years.

The bilateral surgery that resulted in this memory impairment is, for obvious reasons, no longer done, but similar lesions on the inner surface of the temporal lobes have occasionally resulted from operations on one side of the brain in a patient with unsuspected damage to the opposite lobe. Comparable memory deficits result, and so the role of the inner surface of the temporal lobes in memory function is now widely accepted. Moreover, the fact that these patients generally retain their faculties of perception supports the distinction made by many workers between a short-term memory process and a long-term process by which more stable storage of information is achieved. It is clearly the second process that is impaired in the patients described above, but the nature of the impairment is a matter of controversy. Some think the problem is a failure of consolidation, that is, transferring information from short-term to long-term storage. Others hold that the information is transferred and stored but cannot be retrieved. The ultimate resolution of these conflicting theories will require a clearer specification of the neural circuitry of memory.

At a glance the brain appears to have perfect bilateral symmetry, like most other organs of the body. It might therefore be expected that the two halves of the brain would also be functionally equivalent, just as the two kid-

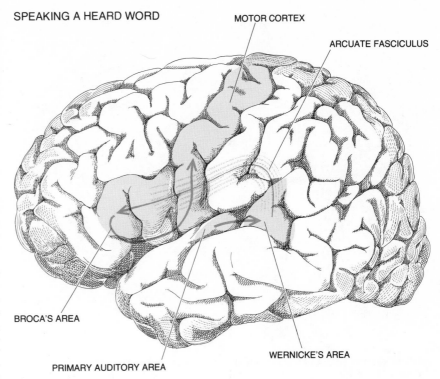

SPEAKING A HEARD WORD

MOTOR CORTEX

ARCUATE FASCICULUS

BROCA'S AREA

PRIMARY AUDITORY AREA

WERNICKE'S AREA

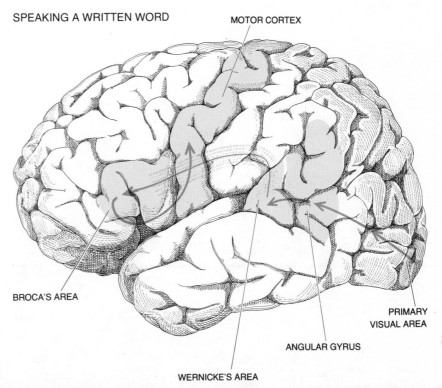

SPEAKING A WRITTEN WORD

MOTOR CORTEX

BROCA'S AREA

PRIMARY VISUAL AREA

ANGULAR GYRUS

WERNICKE'S AREA

LINGUISTIC COMPETENCE requires the cooperation of several areas of the cortex. When a word is heard (*upper diagram*), the sensation from the ears is received by the primary auditory cortex, but the word cannot be understood until the signal has been processed in Wernicke's area nearby. If the word is to be spoken, some representation of it is thought to be transmitted from Wernicke's area to Broca's area, through a bundle of nerve fibers called the arcuate fasciculus. In Broca's area the word evokes a detailed program for articulation, which is supplied to the face area of the motor cortex. The motor cortex in turn drives the muscles of the lips, the tongue, the larynx and so on. When a written word is read (*lower diagram*), the sensation is first registered by the primary visual cortex. It is then thought to be relayed to the angular gyrus, which associates the visual form of the word with the corresponding auditory pattern in Wernicke's area. Speaking the word then draws on the same systems of neurons as before.

FACIAL-RECOGNITION AREA

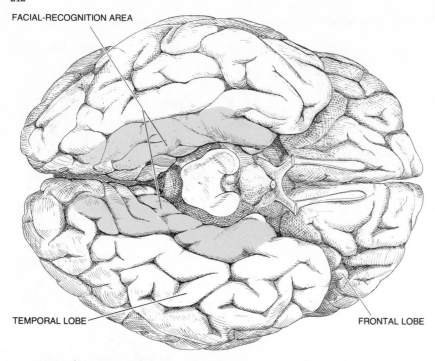

TEMPORAL LOBE

FRONTAL LOBE

RECOGNITION OF FACES is a faculty that seems to be governed by regions on the underside of the temporal and occipital lobes on both sides of the cortex, which is seen here from below. A lesion that destroys this area impairs the ability to identify a person by facial features but has almost no other effects. There is often some loss of vision, but the patient can read, can name objects on sight and can even match a full-face portrait with a profile of the same person. People can also be recognized by their voices. The only ability that is lost is the ability to recognize people by their faces, and that loss can be so severe that close relatives are not recognized.

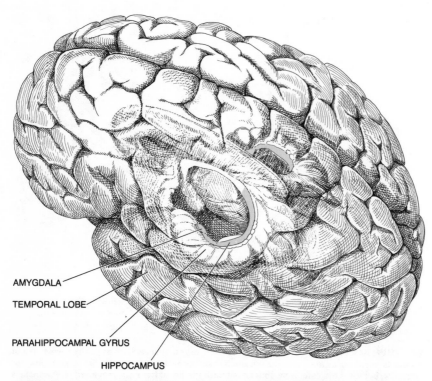

AMYGDALA

TEMPORAL LOBE

PARAHIPPOCAMPAL GYRUS

HIPPOCAMPUS

CERTAIN MEMORY PROCESSES appear to be associated with structures on the inner surface of the temporal lobes, such as the hippocampus (color). Bilateral lesions of these areas have been shown to cause a severe and lasting memory disorder characterized by the inability to learn new information. Patients with lesions of this type appear to have undiminished powers of perception, but they are largely incapable of incorporating new information into their long-term store. Acute lesions in this region of a single temporal lobe sometimes result in similar but less persistent memory disorders that reflect the contrasting specializations of the hemispheres: the type of information that cannot be learned varies according to the side the lesion is on.

neys or the two lungs are. Actually many of the more specialized functions are found in only one hemisphere or the other. Even the apparent anatomical symmetry turns out to be illusory.

In the primary motor and sensory areas of the cortex the assignment of duties to the two hemispheres follows a simple pattern: each side of the brain is concerned mainly with the opposite side of the body. Most of the nerve fibers in the pathways that radiate from the motor and somatic sensory areas cross to the opposite side of the nervous system at some point in their course. Hence the muscles of the right hand and foot are controlled primarily by the left motor cortex, and sensory impulses from the right side go mainly to the left somatic sensory cortex. Each ear has connections to the auditory cortex on both sides of the brain, but the connections to the contralateral side are stronger. The distribution of signals from the eyes is somewhat more complicated. The optic nerves are arranged so that images from the right half of space in both eyes are projected onto the left visual cortex; the left visual field from both eyes goes to the right hemisphere. As a result of this pattern of contralateral connections the sensory and motor functions of the two hemispheres are kept separate, but they are largely symmetrical. Each half of the brain is concerned with half of the body and half of the visual field.

The distribution of the more specialized functions is quite different, and it is profoundly asymmetrical. I have indicated above that linguistic ability is dependent primarily on the left hemisphere. There is reason to believe the right side of the brain is more important for the perception of melodies, one item of evidence being the ease with which aphasic patients with left-hemisphere damage can sing. The perception and analysis of nonverbal visual patterns, such as perspective drawings, is largely a function of the right hemisphere, although the left hemisphere also makes a distinctive contribution to such tasks. These asymmetries are also reflected in partial memory defects that can result from lesions in a single temporal lobe. A left temporal lobectomy can impair the ability to retain verbal material but can leave intact the ability to remember spatial locations, faces, melodies and abstract visual patterns.

In everyday life this lateralization of function can seldom be detected because information is readily passed between the hemispheres through several commissures, including the corpus callosum. Even when the interconnections are severed, the full effects of cerebral dominance can be observed only in laboratory situations, where it is possible to ensure that sensory information reaches only one hemisphere at a time and that a motor response comes from only one hemisphere. Under these conditions a

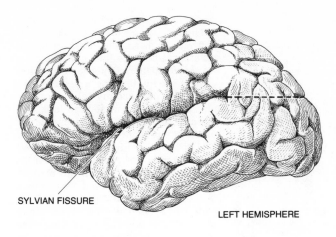

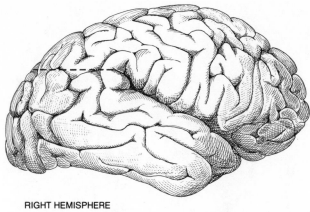

SYLVIAN FISSURE

LEFT HEMISPHERE   RIGHT HEMISPHERE

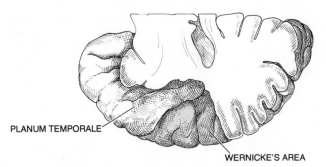

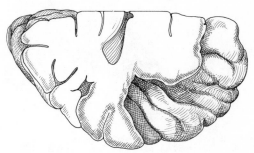

PLANUM TEMPORALE

WERNICKE'S AREA

ANATOMICAL ASYMMETRY of the cortex has been detected in the human brain and may be related to the distinctive functional specializations of the two hemispheres. One asymmetry is readily observed in the intact brain: the sylvian fissure, which defines the upper margin of the temporal lobe, rises more steeply on the right side of the brain. A more striking asymmetry is found on the planum temporale, which forms the upper surface of the temporal lobe, and which can be seen only when the sylvian fissure is opened. The posterior part of the planum temporale is usually much larger on the left side. The enlarged region is part of Wernicke's area, suggesting that the asymmetry may be related to the linguistic dominance of the left hemisphere. The distribution of the asymmetries varies with handedness.

remarkable pattern of behavior is observed. If an object is placed in a patient's left hand or if it is presented only to his left visual field, he cannot say its name. The failure is not one of recognition, since the patient is able to match related objects, but the perception received only in the right hemisphere cannot be associated with a name that is known only to the left hemisphere.

The specialization of the isolated hemispheres should not be overstated, however. The right half of the brain does have some rudimentary linguistic ability. Moreover, there are doubtless many tasks where the two hemispheres ordinarily act in concert. In one test administered after surgical isolation of the hemispheres the patient is asked to reproduce a simple pattern by assembling colored blocks. In some cases errors are frequent whether the task is completed with the left hand or the right, but they are characteristically different kinds of errors. It appears that neither hemisphere alone is competent in this task and that the two must cooperate.

One of the most surprising recent findings is that different emotional reactions follow damage to the right and left sides of the brain. Lesions in most areas on the left side are accompanied by the feelings of loss that might be expected as a result of any serious injury. The patient is disturbed by his disability and often is depressed. Damage in much of the right hemisphere sometimes leaves the patient unconcerned with his condition. Guido Gainotti of the Catholic University of Rome has made a detailed compilation of these differences in emotional response.

Emotion and "state of mind" are often associated with the structures of the limbic system, at the core of the brain, but in recent years it has been recognized that the cerebral cortex, particularly the right hemisphere of the cortex, also makes an important contribution. Lesions in the right hemisphere not only give rise to inappropriate emotional responses to the patient's own condition but also impair his recognition of emotion in others. A patient with damage on the left side may not be able to comprehend a statement, but in many cases he can still recognize the emotional tone with which it is spoken. A patient with a disorder of the right hemisphere usually understands the meaning of what is said, but he often fails to recognize that it is spoken in an angry or a humorous way.

Although cerebral dominance has been known in the human brain for more than a century, comparable asymmetries in other species have been recognized only in the past few years. A pioneer in this endeavor is Fernando Nottebohm of Rockefeller University, who has studied the neural basis of singing in songbirds. In most of the species he has studied so far, but not in all of them, the left side of the brain is more important for singing. Examples of dominance in mammals other than man have also been described, although in much less detail. Under certain conditions damage to the right side of the brain in rats alters emotional behavior, as Victor H. Denenberg of the University of Connecticut has shown. Dominance of the left cerebral cortex for some auditory tasks has been discovered in one species of monkey by James H. Dewson III, who is now at Stanford University. Michael Petersen and other investigators at the University of Michigan and at Rockefeller University have shown that the left hemisphere is dominant in the recognition of species-specific cries in Japanese macaques, which employ an unusual variety of such signals. So far, however, no definitive example of functional asymmetry has been described in the brains of the great apes, the closest relations of man.

For many years it was the prevailing view of neurologists that the func-

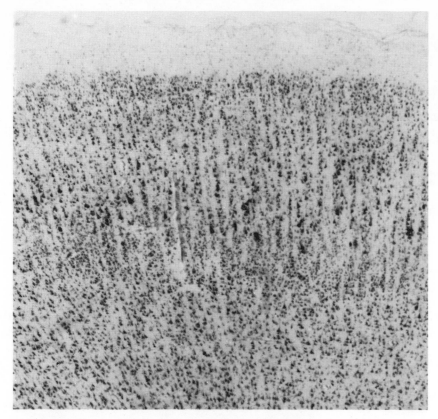

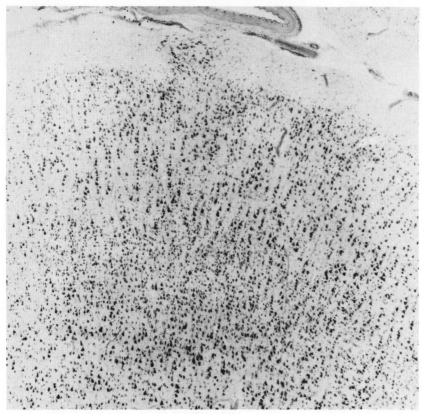

ABNORMAL CELLULAR ARCHITECTURE has been found in a language area of a patient with a developmental reading disorder. The top photomicrograph is a section of the normal cortex from the posterior portion of the planum temporale, the region that makes up part of Wernicke's area. Several layers can be perceived and the cells have a characteristic columnar organization. The bottom photograph is a section from the same region in a patient with dyslexia. One peculiarity is the presence of nerve-cell bodies in the most superficial layer (*near top of photograph*), where they are normally absent. Moreover, throughout the tissue the arrangement of cells is disrupted. The abnormality was found by Albert M. Galaburda of the Harvard Medical School and Thomas Kemper of the Boston University School of Medicine.

tional asymmetries of the brain could not be correlated with anatomical asymmetries. If there were any significant differences between the hemispheres, it was assumed, they would have been noted long ago by surgeons or pathologists. About 10 years ago my colleague Walter Levitsky and I decided to look into this matter again, following some earlier observations by the German neurologist Richard Arwed Pfeifer. We examined 100 human brains, paying particular attention to a region called the planum temporale, which lies on the upper surface of the temporal lobe and is hidden within the sylvian fissure that runs along each side of the brain. Our study was concerned only with gross anatomy, and we employed no instruments more elaborate than a camera and a ruler; nevertheless, we found unequivocal evidence of asymmetry. In general the length and orientation of the sylvian fissures is different on opposite sides of the head. What is more significant, the posterior area of the planum temporale, which forms part of Wernicke's area, is generally larger on the left side. The differences are not subtle and can easily be seen with the unaided eye.

Juhn A. Wada of the University of British Columbia subsequently showed that the asymmetry of the planum temporale can be detected in the human fetus. It therefore appears that the enlargement of the left planum cannot be a response to the development of linguistic competence in childhood. On the contrary, the superior linguistic talent of the left hemisphere may result from the anatomical bias.

More recently my colleague Albert M. Galaburda has discovered that the enlargement of the left planum can be explained in terms of the cellular organization of the tissue. On the planum is a region with a distinctive cellular architecture, designated *Tpt*. Galaburda found that the extent of the *Tpt* region is considerably greater in the left hemisphere; in the first brain he examined it was more than seven times as large on the left side as it was on the right.

Galaburda and Thomas Kemper of the Boston University School of Medicine also examined the brain of an accident victim who had suffered from persistent dyslexia. He found that the *Tpt* areas in the two hemispheres were of approximately equal size. Furthermore, the cellular structure of the *Tpt* area on the left side was abnormal. The neurons in the normal cortex are arranged in a sequence of layers, each of which has a distinctive population of cells. In the brain of the dyslexic the strata were disrupted, one conspicuous anomaly being the presence of cell bodies of neurons in the most superficial layer of the cortex, where they are normally absent. Islands of cortical tissue were also found in the white matter of the brain, where they do not belong. Although no firm conclusion can be drawn from a single case, it does seem striking that a structural abnormality would be found in the language area of a patient who was known to have a linguistic disability.

A new line of research on brain asymmetry has lately been opened by my colleague Marjorie J. LeMay. She has devised several methods for detecting anatomical asymmetry in the living person. One of these methods is cerebral arteriography, in which a substance opaque to X rays is injected into the bloodstream and the distribution of the substance is monitored as it flows through the cranial arteries. Arteriography is often employed in the diagnosis of brain tumors and other brain diseases, and the arteriograms LeMay examined had been made for diagnostic purposes. One of the cranial arteries (the middle cerebral artery) follows the groove of the sylvian fissure, and LeMay showed that the position of the artery in the arteriogram reveals the length and orientation of the fissure. She found that in most people the middle cerebral artery on the right side of the head is inclined more steeply and ultimately ascends higher than the corresponding artery on the left side.

LeMay has also detected brain asymmetries by computed axial tomography, the process whereby an image of the skull in cross section is reconstructed from a set of X-ray projections. In these images a peculiar, skewed departure from bilateral symmetry is observed. In right-handed people the right frontal lobe is usually wider than the left, but the left parietal and occipital lobes are wider than the right. The inner surface of the skull itself bulges at the right front and the left rear to accommodate the protuberances.

LeMay has even reported finding asymmetries in cranial endocasts made from the fossil skulls of Neanderthal man and other hominids. A ridge on the inner surface of the skull corresponds to the sylvian fissure; where the ridge is preserved well enough to make an impression in an endocast LeMay finds the same pattern of asymmetry that is observed in modern man, suggesting that hemispheric dominance had already emerged at least 30,000 years ago. LeMay and I have shown that asymmetries of the sylvian fissures exist in the great apes but not in monkeys. (Grace H. Yeni-Komshian and Dennis A. Benson of the Johns Hopkins University School of Medicine have reported similar findings.) If a functional correlative to this anatomical bias can be discovered, an animal model of cerebral dominance in the anthropoid apes would become available.

One of the most commonplace manifestations of cerebral dominance is also one of the most puzzling: the phenomenon of handedness. Many animals exhibit a form of handedness; for example, if a monkey is made to carry out a task with only one hand, it will consistently use the same one. In any large population of monkeys, however, left- and right-handed individuals are equally common. In the human population no more than 9 percent are left-handed. This considerable bias toward right-handedness may represent a unique specialization of the human brain.

The genetics and heritability of handedness is a controversial topic. In mice Robert V. Collins of the Jackson Laboratory in Bar Harbor, Me., has shown that continued inbreeding of right-handed animals does not increase the prevalence of right-handedness in their offspring. The pattern in man is quite different. Marian Annett of the Lanchester Polytechnic in England has proposed a theory in which one allele of a gene pair favors the development of right-handedness, but there is no complementary allele for left-handedness. In the absence of the right-favoring allele handedness is randomly determined.

Studies undertaken by LeMay and her co-workers have revealed that the distribution of brain asymmetries in left-handed people is different from that in right-handers. In right-handed individuals, and hence in most of the population, the right sylvian fissure is higher than the left in 67 percent of the brains examined. The left fissure is higher in 8 percent and the two fissures rise to approximately equal height in 25 percent. In the left-handed population a substantial majority (71 percent) have approximate symmetry of the sylvian fissures. Among the remainder the right fissure is still more likely to be the higher (21 percent v. 7 percent). The asymmetries observed by tomography also have a different distribution in right-handers and left-handers. Again in the left-handed segment of the population the asymmetries tend to be less pronounced. These findings are in qualitative agreement with the theory proposed by Annett.

If functions as narrowly defined as facial recognition are accorded specific neural networks in the brain, it seems likely that many other functions are represented in a similar way. For example, one of the major goals of child rearing is to teach a set of highly differentiated responses to emotional stimuli, such as anger and fear. The child must also be taught the appropriate responses to stimuli from its internal milieu, such as hunger or fullness of the bladder or bowel. Most children learn these patterns of behavior just as they learn a language, suggesting that here too special-purpose processors may be present. As yet little is known about such neural systems. Indeed, even as the mapping of specialized regions continues, the next major task must be confronted: that of describing their internal operation.

IV

PERSONALITY, ABNORMALITY, AND SOCIAL BEHAVIOR

IV

PERSONALITY, ABNORMALITY, AND SOCIAL BEHAVIOR

INTRODUCTION

Although the articles in this section are less closely related than those in the other sections, they are all concerned with individual differences in reacting to the environment. When we speak of personality, we usually refer to the characteristics and modes of behavior that make one individual different from others and determine his or her unique adjustment to the environment. Some of these characteristics—such as physical attributes, intelligence, and special talents—depend to a large extent on innate potentials. Others are primarily a product of the particular culture in which one is raised, as well as individual experiences with parents and peers. The potentialities present at birth are molded by life experiences to form the adult personality.

In the introduction to Section I we noted the importance of early experiences for the development of personality. Although early experiences are indeed crucial in personality formation, the role of innate attributes should not be overlooked. In "The Origin of Personality" Alexander Thomas, Stella Chess, and Herbert Birch explore the nature of inborn differences in temperament—the individual's "style" of responding to the environment. A careful study of the behavior of infants two or three months after birth found marked individual differences in style even at this early age—differences that could hardly be attributed to differences in parental treatment. For example, of two infants from the same family, one might be characteristically active, easily distracted, and willing to accept new objects and people. The other might be predominantly quiet, persistent, and unwilling to accept anything new. A follow-up study of the same children over a 14-year period indicated that, for most of the children, characteristics of temperament tended to persist. The authors propose that the important factor in shaping personality is the interaction between innate characteristics and environment. If the two influences harmonize, then healthy development will follow; if not, psychological difficulties can be expected.

Emotional stress can produce physical illness. Asthma, high blood pressure, skin eruptions, and intestinal disorders are examples of ailments that have been called psychosomatic—that is, they may stem more from emotional problems than physical ones. In "Psychological Factors in Stress and Disease" Jay Weiss investigates the conditions under which stress can lead to stomach ulcers. A series of studies that exposed rats to stress (electric shock) under different psychological conditions identified three variables that influenced ulceration: the predictability of the stress, the variety of coping responses the animal could make to avoid or escape it, and the type of feedback the coping attempts produced. Based on this and other research, the author has developed a theory that predicts when ulceration, as well as other physiological responses to stress, is most likely to occur. The theory has obvious practical implications since the principles discovered in these animal experiments may apply to humans as well.

An additional finding of Weiss's study concerns a brain chemical (norepinephrine) that serves as a neurotransmitter; animals that were able to avoid shock showed an increase in the level of brain norepinephrine, whereas helpless animals showed a decrease. The normal functioning of the brain involves numerous complex electrical and chemical processes. Recent research has enabled us to identify some of the chemicals involved in transmission of nervous impulses across the synapses that separate neurons. In "Disorders of the Human Brain" Seymour Kety discusses some of the mental disorders that appear to be related to disturbances in brain chemistry and describes how genetic and environmental factors interact to produce various pathological conditions. Of particular interest is the possibility that the major psychoses—schizophrenia and manic-depressive illness—may involve an imbalance in certain neurotransmitters.

In the article "Behavioral Psychotherapy" Albert Bandura describes a method for treating behavior disorders that departs from the more traditional approaches to psychotherapy. Whereas the latter are concerned primarily with helping the individual gain insight into the origins of his or her problems, behavioral therapy attempts to apply the principles of learning to the treatment of emotional and behavioral problems. In treating autistic children, for example, behavioral therapists reinforce desired behavior with attention or food rewards and ignore (or even punish) undesirable behavior. Such operant conditioning techniques (see the article by Skinner in Section III) have proved effective in substituting desirable for undesirable behavior. The main thesis of those who practice behavioral therapy is that behavior that departs from accepted social norms should not be viewed as a disease but as the way a person has learned to cope with environmental demands. Treatment is thus a matter of teaching new "social learning" rather than delving into the psychological traumas of childhood.

Most of our life is spent in interaction with other people. Their responses to us are a major influence on our attitudes and actions. Psychologists are interested in determining how attitudes are formed and changed, how social groups affect our attitudes and behavior, and the ways in which people interact within groups and against other groups. In "Social and Nonsocial Speech" Robert Krauss and Sam Glucksberg describe how people modify their language to take into account the characteristics of their audience. Effective social communication involves more than simply knowledge of the language itself.

In "The Role of Pupil Size in Communication" Eckhard Hess describes a unique method for measuring a person's private attitude toward some person, object, or group. Because people do not always fully or truthfully express their attitudes, an involuntary response (such as pupil dilation) can provide a clue to the individual's true feelings.

How attitudes change after a decision has been made is discussed by Leon Festinger in "Cognitive Dissonance." After we make a choice between equally attractive alternatives, we tend to change our appraisal of the alternatives in favor of our decision. For example, if you are selecting a house for purchase, you may find the two to have nearly equal advantages and disadvantages. Once you decide between the two, however, you tend to find many more advantages in favor of the house you purchased and new reasons why the other would have been a poor choice. By altering your appraisal to reduce any anxiety about having made a wrong decision, you are reducing *cognitive dissonance*. The theory of cognitive dissonance is based on the assumption that we want our behavior and attitudes to be consistent. If we find that they are inconsistent (dissonant), we try to reduce the dissonance by changing either our behavior or attitudes, or both. Festinger's theory has important implications for the way in which social pressures may produce changes in attitudes or behavior.

22

The Origin of Personality

by Alexander Thomas, Stella Chess, and Herbert G. Birch
August 1970

Children differ in temperament from birth. What is the nature of these temperamental differences, and how do they interact with environmental influences in the formation of personality?

Mothers, nurses and pediatricians are well aware that infants begin to express themselves as individuals from the time of birth. The fact that each child appears to have a characteristic temperament from his earliest days has also been suggested by Sigmund Freud and Arnold Gesell. In recent years, however, many psychiatrists and psychologists appear to have lost sight of this fact. Instead they have tended to emphasize the influence of the child's early environment when discussing the origin of the human personality.

As physicians who have had frequent occasion to examine the family background of disturbed children, we began many years ago to encounter reasons to question the prevailing one-sided emphasis on environment. We found that some children with severe psychological problems had a family upbringing that did not differ essentially from the environment of other children who developed no severe problems. On the other hand, some children were found to be free of serious personality disturbances although they had experienced severe family disorganization and poor parental care. Even in cases where parental mishandling was obviously responsible for a child's personality difficulties there was no consistent or predictable relation between the parents' treatment and the child's specific symptoms. Domineering, authoritarian handling by the parents might make one youngster anxious and submissive and another defiant and antagonistic. Such unpredictability seemed to be the direct consequence of omitting an important factor from the evaluation: the child's own temperament, that is, his own individual style of responding to the environment.

It might be inferred from these opinions that we reject the environmentalist tendency to emphasize the role of the child's surroundings and the influence of his parents (particularly the mother) as major factors in the formation of personality, and that instead we favor the constitutionalist concept of personality's being largely inborn. Actually we reject both the "nurture" and the "nature" concepts. Either by itself is too simplistic to account for the intricate play of forces that form the human character. It is our hypothesis that the personality is shaped by the constant interplay of temperament and environment.

We decided to test this concept by conducting a systematic long-term investigation of the differences in the behavioral reactions of infants. The study would be designed to determine whether or not these differences persist through childhood, and it would focus on how a child's behavioral traits interact with specific elements of his environment. Apart from satisfying scientific curiosity, answers to these questions would help parents and teachers—and psychiatrists —to promote healthy personality development.

After much preliminary exploration we developed techniques for gathering and analyzing information about individual differences in behavioral characteristics in the first few months of life, for categorizing such differences and for identifying individuality at each stage of a child's life. This technique consisted in obtaining detailed descriptions of children's behavior through structured interviews with their parents at regular intervals beginning when the child had reached an age of two to three months. Independent checks by trained observers established that the descriptions of the children's behavior supplied by the parents in these interviews could be accepted as reliable and significant.

Analyzing the data, we identified nine characteristics that could be reliably scored on a three-point scale (medium, high and low): (1) the level and extent of motor activity; (2) the rhythmicity, or degree of regularity, of functions such as eating, elimination and the cycle of sleeping and wakefulness; (3) the response to a new object or person, in terms of whether the child accepts the new experience or withdraws from it; (4) the adaptability of behavior to changes in the environment; (5) the threshold, or sensitivity, to stimuli; (6) the intensity, or energy level, of responses; (7) the child's general mood or "disposition," whether cheerful or given to crying, pleasant or cranky, friendly or unfriendly; (8) the degree of the child's distractibility from what he is doing; (9) the span of the child's attention and his persistence in an activity.

The set of ratings in these nine characteristics defines the temperament, or behavioral profile, of a child, and the profile is discernible even as early as the age of two or three months. We found that the nine qualities could be identified and rated in a wide diversity of population samples we studied: middle-class children, children of working-class Puerto Ricans, mentally retarded children, children born prematurely and children with congenital rubella ("German measles"). Other investigators in the U.S. and abroad have identified the same set of characteristics in children.

Equipped with this means of collecting and analyzing the required data on individual children through standard interviews with their parents, we proceeded to our long-term study of the development of a large group of children. We obtained the willing collaboration of 85 families, with a total of 141 children, who agreed to allow us to follow their children's development from birth over a period of years that by now extends to

HALLIE, a six-month-old experimental subject, is shown in motion picture taken during an observation session. In frames beginning at top left and running downward she pulls at rings hanging above her crib and repeatedly pushes away stuffed animal. She demonstrates a high level of concentration and persistence by rejecting animal each time it is given and continuing to play with the rings.

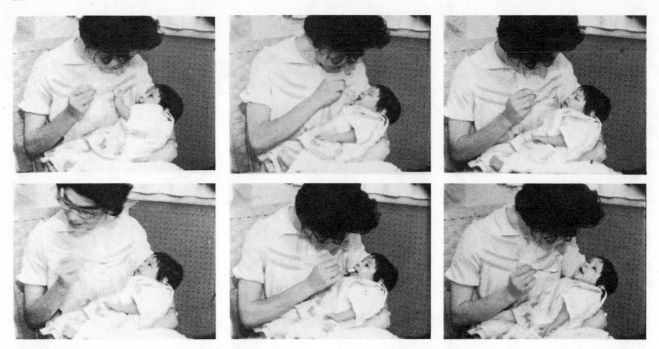

POSITIVE RESPONSE is displayed by Hallie when she was three months old as she is fed a new food, Cream of Wheat, for the first time. When her mother presents her with a spoonful of the food, she accepts it eagerly, swallows it and unhesitatingly accepts more.

more than a decade. Our parents have cooperated magnificently in all the interviews and tests, and in the 14 years since the study was started only four families (with five children) have dropped out. In order to avoid complicating the study by having to consider a diversity of socioeconomic influences we confined the study to a homogeneous group, consisting mainly of highly educated families in the professions and business occupations.

We have observed the children's development throughout their preschool period and their years in nursery and elementary school. Their parents have been interviewed at frequent intervals, so that descriptions of the children's behavior have been obtained while the parents' memory of it was still fresh. The interviews have focused on factual details of how the children behaved in specific situations, avoiding subjective interpretations as much as possible. We have supplemented the parental interviews with direct observation and with information obtained from the children's teachers. The children have also been examined with various psychological tests. Youngsters who have shown evidence of behavioral disturbances have received a complete psychiatric examination. The detailed behavioral data collected on all the children have been analyzed both in statistical and in descriptive terms.

Our preliminary exploration had already answered our first question: Chil-

dren do show distinct individuality in temperament in the first weeks of life, independently of their parents' handling or personality style. Our long-term study has now established that the original characteristics of temperament tend to persist in most children over the years. This is clearly illustrated by two striking examples. Donald exhibited an extremely high activity level almost from birth. At three months, his parents reported, he wriggled and moved about a great deal while asleep in his crib. At six months he "swam like a fish" while being bathed. At 12 months he still squirmed constantly while he was being dressed or washed. At 15 months he was "very fast and busy"; his parents found themselves "always chasing after him." At two years he was "constantly in motion, jumping and climbing." At three he would "climb like a monkey and run like an unleashed puppy." In kindergarten his teacher reported humorously that he would "hang from the walls and climb on the ceiling." By the time he was seven Donald was encountering difficulty in school because he was unable to sit still long enough to learn anything and disturbed the other children by moving rapidly about the classroom.

Clem exemplifies a child who scored high in intensity of reaction. At four and a half months he screamed every time he was bathed, according to his parents' report. His reactions were "not discriminating—all or none." At six months during feeding he screamed "at the sight of the spoon approaching his mouth." At

nine and a half months he was generally "either in a very good mood, laughing or chuckling," or else screaming. "He laughed so hard playing peekaboo he got hiccups." At two years his parents reported: "He screams bloody murder when he's being dressed." At seven they related: "When he's frustrated, as for example when he doesn't hit a ball very far, he stomps around, his voice goes up to its highest level, his eyes get red and occasionally fill with tears. Once he went up to his room when this occurred and screamed for half an hour."

Of course a child's temperament is not immutable. In the course of his development the environmental circumstances may heighten, diminish or otherwise modify his reactions and behavior. For example, behavior may become routinized in various areas so that the basic temperamental characteristics are no longer evident in these situations. Most children come to accept and even take pleasure in the bath, whatever their initial reactions may have been. The characteristics usually remain present, however, and may assert themselves in new situations even in the form of an unexpected and mystifying reaction. An illustration is the case of a 10-year-old girl who had been well adjusted to school. Entering the fifth grade, Grace was transferred from a small school to a large new one that was strongly departmentalized and much more formal. The change threw her into a state of acute fear and worry. Her parents were

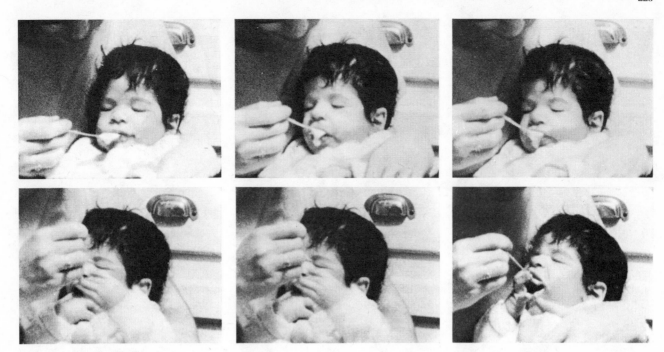

NEGATIVE RESPONSE is demonstrated by Hallie's younger brother, Russ, during his first exposure to a cereal at three months of age. He refuses to swallow the new food, spits it out, pushes the spoon away, grimaces and tilts his head away from the spoon.

puzzled, because Grace had many friends and had been doing very well in her studies. On reviewing her history, however, we found that she had shown withdrawal reactions to new situations during infancy and also on entrance into kindergarten and the first and second grades. Her parents and Grace had forgotten about these early reactions, because from the third grade on she was entirely happy in school. In the light of the early history it now became apparent that Grace's fear at the transfer to the new school, confronting her with a new scholastic setup, new fellow-students and a new level of academic demand, arose from her fundamental tendency to withdraw from new situations and to be slow to adapt to them.

Not all the children in our study have shown a basic constancy of temperament. In some there have apparently been changes in certain characteristics as time has passed. We are analyzing the data in these cases to try to determine if changes in the children's life situations or in specific stresses are responsible for the apparent fluctuations in temperament. We may find that inconsistency in temperament is itself a basic characteristic in some children.

When we analyzed the behavioral profiles of the children in an endeavor to find correlations among the nine individual attributes, we found that certain characteristics did cluster together. The clusters defined three general types of temperament (although some of the children did not fit into any of the three).

One type is characterized by positiveness in mood, regularity in bodily functions, a low or moderate intensity of reaction, adaptability and a positive approach to, rather than withdrawal from, new situations. In infancy these children quickly establish regular sleeping and feeding schedules, are generally cheerful and adapt quickly to new routines, new foods and new people. As they grow older they learn the rules of new games quickly, participate readily in new activities and adapt easily to school. We named this group the "easy children," because they present so few problems in care and training. Approximately 40 percent of the children in our total sample could be placed in this category.

In contrast, we found another constellation of characteristics that described "difficult children." These children are irregular in bodily functions, are usually intense in their reactions, tend to withdraw in the face of new stimuli, are slow to adapt to changes in the environment and are generally negative in mood. As infants they are often irregular in feeding and sleeping, are slow to accept new foods, take a long time to adjust to new routines or activities and tend to cry a great deal. Their crying and their laughter are characteristically loud. Frustration usually sends them into a violent tantrum. These children are, of course, a trial to their parents and require a high degree of consistency and tolerance in their up-

bringing. They comprised about 10 percent of the children in our sample.

The third type of temperament is displayed by those children we call "slow to warm up." They typically have a low activity level, tend to withdraw on their first exposure to new stimuli, are slow to adapt, are somewhat negative in mood and respond to situations with a low intensity of reaction. They made up 15 percent of the population sample we studied. Hence 65 percent of the children could be described as belonging to one or another of the three categories we were able to define; the rest had mixtures of traits that did not add up to a general characterization.

Among the 141 children comprising our total sample, 42 presented behavioral problems that called for psychiatric attention. Not surprisingly, the group of "difficult children" accounted for the largest proportion of these cases, the "slow to warm up children" for the next-largest proportion and the "easy children" for the smallest proportion. About 70 percent of the "difficult children" developed behavioral problems, whereas only 18 percent of the "easy children" did so.

In general easy children respond favorably to various child-rearing styles. Under certain conditions, however, their ready adaptability to parental handling may itself lead to the development of a behavioral problem. Having adapted readily to the parents' standards and expectations early in life, the child on moving into the world of his peers and

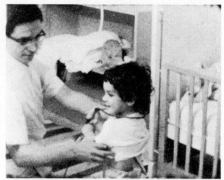

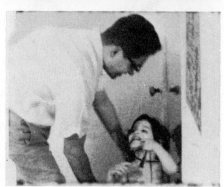

TWO YEARS OLD, Hallie plays with her father as he tries to change her clothes. He gets shirt off after struggling to lift it over her head, but she holds on with cord. She runs away, provoking chase, and tries to escape as he buttons her shirt. Hallie displays

school may find that the demands of these environments conflict sharply with the behavior patterns he has learned at home. If the conflict between the two sets of demands is severe, the child may be unable to make an adaptation that reconciles the double standard.

The possible results of such a dissonance are illustrated in the case of an "easy child" we shall call Isobel. Reared by parents who placed great value on individuality, imagination and self-expression, she developed these qualities to a high degree. When she entered school, however, her work fell far below her intellectual capabilities. She had difficulties not only in learning but also in making friends. It was found that the problems arose from her resistance to taking instruction from her teacher and to accepting her schoolmates' preferences in play. Once the nature of the conflict was recognized it was easily remedied in this case. We advised the parents to combine their encouragement of Isobel's assertions of individuality with efforts to teach her how to join constructively in activities with her teacher and schoolmates. The parents adopted this strategy, and within six months Isobel began to function well in school life.

In the case of difficult children the handling problem is present from the outset. The parents must cope with the child's irregularity and the slowness with which he adapts in order to establish conformity to the family's rules of living. If the parents are inconsistent, impatient or punitive in their handling of the child, he is much more likely to react negatively than other children are. Only by exceptionally objective, consistent treatment, taking full account of the child's temperament, can he be brought to get along easily with others and to learn appropriate behavior. This may take a long time, but with skillful handling such children do learn the rules and function well. The essential requirement is that the parents recognize the need for unusually painstaking handling; tactics that

work well with other children may fail for the difficult child.

For children in the "slow to warm up" category the key to successful development is allowing the child to adapt to the environment at his own pace. If the teacher or parents of such a child pressure him to move quickly into new situations, the insistence is likely to intensify his natural tendency to withdraw. On the other hand, he does need encouragement and opportunity to try new experiences. Bobby was a case in point. His parents never encouraged him to participate in anything new; they simply withdrew things he did not like. When, as an infant, he rejected a new food by letting it

TYPE OF CHILD	ACTIVITY LEVEL	RHYTHMICITY	DISTRACTIBILITY
	The proportion of active periods to inactive ones.	Regularity of hunger, excretion, sleep and wakefulness.	The degree to which extraneous stimuli alter behavior.
"EASY"	VARIES	VERY REGULAR	VARIES
"SLOW TO WARM UP"	LOW TO MODERATE	VARIES	VARIES
"DIFFICULT"	VARIES	IRREGULAR	VARIES

TEMPERAMENT of a child allows him to be classified as "easy," "slow to warm up" or "difficult" according to how he rates in certain key categories in the authors' nine-point

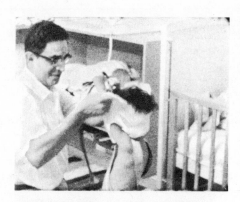

many temperamental characteristics such as intensity, positive mood and high activity.

dribble out of his mouth, they eliminated it from his diet. When he backed away from other children in the playground, they kept him at home. By the age of 10 Bobby was living on a diet consisting mainly of hamburgers, applesauce and medium-boiled eggs, and in play he was a "loner." Any activity that required exposure to new people or new demands was distasteful or even impossible for him. Yet he was adept and took pleasure in activities he could pursue by himself and at his own speed.

In general our studies indicate that a demand that conflicts excessively with any temperamental characteristics and capacities is likely to place a child under heavy and even unbearable stress. This means that parents and teachers need to recognize what a specific child can and cannot do. A child with a high activity level, for example, should not be required to sit still through an eight-hour automobile trip; frequent stops should be made to allow him to run around and give vent to his energy. A persistent child who does not like to be distracted from a project should not be expected to come running when he is called unless he has been told in advance how much time he will have before he is called.

Obviously a detailed knowledge of a child's temperamental characteristics can be of great help to parents in handling the child and avoiding the development of behavioral problems. A highly adaptable child can be expected to accept new foods without resistance and even welcome them. On the other hand, a nonadaptable, intense child may need to have the same food offered at each meal for several days until he comes to accept it; if the mother takes away a rejected food, tries it again some weeks later and again retreats in the face of protests, the child simply learns that by fussing enough he will have his way. An adaptable child who is caught sticking things into electric sockets may need only one lecture on the danger to give up this practice; an easily distractible child may merely need to have his attention diverted to some other activity; a persistent child may have to be removed bodily from the hazard.

Understanding a child's temperament is equally crucial in the school situation. His temperamental traits affect both his approach to a learning task and the way he interacts with his teacher and classmates. If the school's demands on him go against the grain of these traits, learning may be difficult indeed. Hence the teacher has a need to know not only the child's capacities for learning but also his temperamental style.

A pupil who wriggles about a great deal, plays continually with his pencils and other objects and involves himself in activities with the student next to him—in short, a child with a high activity level—obviously requires special handling. If the teacher decides the child does not want to learn and treats him accordingly, the youngster is apt to conclude that he is stupid or unlikable and react with even worse behavior. The teacher is best advised to avoid expressions of annoyance and to provide the child with constructive channels for his energy, such as running necessary errands, cleaning the blackboard and so on. Similarly, a "slow to warm up" child requires patience, encouragement and repeated exposure to a learning task until he becomes familiar with it and comfortable in attacking it. Children with the "difficult" constellation of traits of course present the most taxing problem. They respond poorly to a permissive, *laissez faire* attitude in the teacher and angrily to learning tasks they cannot master immediately. The teacher needs to be firm and patient; once the child has been tided over the period (which may be long) of learning rules or becoming familiar with a new task, he will function well and confidently. *Laissez faire* treatment is also detrimental for youngsters who are low in persistence and easily distracted from their work. Such a child will do poorly if few demands are made and little achievement is expected of him. He must be required to function up to his abilities.

The paramount conclusion from our studies is that the debate over the relative importance of nature and nurture only confuses the issue. What is important is the interaction between the two—between the child's own character-

APPROACH WITHDRAWAL	ADAPTABILITY	ATTENTION SPAN AND PERSISTENCE	INTENSITY OF REACTION	THRESHOLD OF RESPONSIVENESS	QUALITY OF MOOD
The response to a new object or person.	The ease with which a child adapts to changes in his environment.	The amount of time devoted to an activity, and the effect of distraction on the activity.	The energy of response, regardless of its quality or direction.	The intensity of stimulation required to evoke a discernible response.	The amount of friendly, pleasant, joyful behavior as contrasted with unpleasant, unfriendly behavior.
POSITIVE APPROACH	VERY ADAPTABLE	HIGH OR LOW	LOW OR MILD	HIGH OR LOW	POSITIVE
PARTIAL WITHDRAWAL	SLOWLY ADAPTABLE	HIGH OR LOW	MILD	HIGH OR LOW	SLIGHTLY NEGATIVE
WITHDRAWAL	SLOWLY ADAPTABLE	HIGH OR LOW	INTENSE	HIGH OR LOW	NEGATIVE

personality index (*color*). The categories are only a general guide to temperament. Of the 141 subjects 65 percent could be categorized, but 35 percent displayed a mixture of traits. Such a child might, for example, be rated "easy" in some ways and "difficult" in others.

TEMPERAMENTAL QUALITY	RATING	2 MONTHS	6 MONTHS
ACTIVITY LEVEL	HIGH	Moves often in sleep. Wriggles when diaper is changed.	Tries to stand in tub and splashes. Bounces in crib. Crawls after dog.
	LOW	Does not move when being dressed or during sleep.	Passive in bath. Plays quietly in crib and falls asleep.
RHYTHMICITY	REGULAR	Has been on four-hour feeding schedule since birth. Regular bowel movement.	Is asleep at 6:30 every night. Awakes at 7:00 A.M. Food intake is constant.
	IRREGULAR	Awakes at a different time each morning. Size of feedings varies.	Length of nap varies; so does food intake.
DISTRACTIBILITY	DISTRACTIBLE	Will stop crying for food if rocked. Stops fussing if given pacifier when diaper is being changed.	Stops crying when mother sings. Will remain still while clothing is changed if given a toy.
	NOT DISTRACTIBLE	Will not stop crying when diaper is changed. Fusses after eating, even if rocked.	Stops crying only after dressing is finished. Cries until given bottle.
APPROACH/WITHDRAWAL	POSITIVE	Smiles and licks washcloth. Has always liked bottle.	Likes new foods. Enjoyed first bath in a large tub. Smiles and gurgles.
	NEGATIVE	Rejected cereal the first time. Cries when strangers appear.	Smiles and babbles at strangers. Plays with new toys immediately.
ADAPTABILITY	ADAPTIVE	Was passive during first bath; now enjoys bathing. Smiles at nurse.	Used to dislike new foods; now accepts them well.
	NOT ADAPTIVE	Still startled by sudden, sharp noise. Resists diapering.	Does not cooperate with dressing. Fusses and cries when left with sitter.
ATTENTION SPAN AND PERSISTENCE	LONG	If soiled, continues to cry until changed. Repeatedly rejects water if he wants milk.	Watches toy mobile over crib intently. "Coos" frequently.
	SHORT	Cries when awakened but stops almost immediately. Objects only mildly if cereal precedes bottle.	Sucks pacifier for only a few minutes and spits it out.
INTENSITY OF REACTION	INTENSE	Cries when diapers are wet. Rejects food vigorously when satisfied.	Cries loudly at the sound of thunder. Makes sucking movements when vitamins are administered.
	MILD	Does not cry when diapers are wet. Whimpers instead of crying when hungry.	Does not kick often in tub. Does not smile. Screams and kicks when temperature is taken.
THRESHOLD OF RESPONSIVENESS	LOW	Stops sucking on bottle when approached.	Refuses fruit he likes when vitamins are added. Hides head from bright light.
	HIGH	Is not startled by loud noises. Takes bottle and breast equally well.	Eats everything. Does not object to diapers being wet or soiled.
QUALITY OF MOOD	POSITIVE	Smacks lips when first tasting new food. Smiles at parents.	Plays and splashes in bath. Smiles at everyone.
	NEGATIVE	Fusses after nursing. Cries when carriage is rocked.	Cries when taken from tub. Cries when given food she does not like.

BEHAVIOR of a child reveals that he has a distinct temperament early in life. These reports taken from interviews with the parents of the children studied by the authors show that temperamental differences are apparent when a child is only two months old. As a child grows his temperament tends to remain constant in quality: if he wriggles while his diaper is being changed at two months,

istics and his environment. If the two influences are harmonized, one can expect healthy development of the child; if they are dissonant, behavioral problems are almost sure to ensue.

It follows that the pediatrician who undertakes to supervise the care of a newborn child should familiarize himself with his young patient's temperamental as well as physical characteristics. He will then be able to provide the parents with appropriate advice on weaning, toilet training and the handling of other needs as the child develops. Similarly, if a behavioral disorder arises, the psychiatrist will need to understand both the child's temperament and the environmental demands in conflict with it in order to find a helpful course of action. His function then will often be to guide rather than "treat" the parents.

1 YEAR	2 YEARS	5 YEARS	10 YEARS
Talks rapidly. Eats eagerly. Climbs into everything.	Climbs furniture. Explores. Gets in and out of bed while being put to sleep.	Leaves table often during meals. Always runs.	Plays ball and engages in other sports. Cannot sit still long enough to do homework.
Finishes bottle slowly. Goes to sleep easily. Allows nail-cutting without fussing.	Enjoys quiet play with puzzles. Can listen to records for hours.	Takes a long time to dress. Sits quietly on long automobile rides.	Likes chess and reading. Eats very slowly.
Naps after lunch each day. Always drinks bottle before bed.	Eats a big lunch each day. Always has a snack before bedtime.	Falls asleep when put to bed. Bowel movement regular.	Eats only at mealtimes. Sleeps the same amount of time each night.
Will not fall asleep for an hour or more. Moves bowels at a different time each day.	Nap time changes from day to day. Toilet training is difficult because bowel movement is unpredictable.	Food intake varies; so does time of bowel movement.	Food intake varies. Falls asleep at a different time each night.
Cries when face is washed unless it is made into a game.	Will stop tantrum if another activity is suggested.	Can be coaxed out of forbidden activity by being led into something else.	Needs absolute silence for homework. Has a hard time choosing a shirt in a store because they all appeal to him.
Cries when toy is taken away and rejects substitute.	Screams if refused some desired object. Ignores mother's calling.	Seems not to hear if involved in favorite activity. Cries for a long time when hurt.	Can read a book while television set is at high volume. Does chores on schedule.
Approaches strangers readily. Sleeps well in new surroundings.	Slept well the first time he stayed overnight at grandparents' house.	Entered school building unhesitatingly. Tries new foods.	Went to camp happily. Loved to ski the first time.
Stiffened when placed on sled. Will not sleep in strange beds.	Avoids strange children in the playground. Whimpers first time at beach. Will not go into water.	Hid behind mother when entering school.	Severely homesick at camp during first days. Does not like new activities.
Was afraid of toy animals at first; now plays with them happily.	Obeys quickly. Stayed contentedly with grandparents for a week.	Hesitated to go to nursery school at first; now goes eagerly. Slept well on camping trip.	Likes camp, although homesick during first days. Learns enthusiastically.
Continues to reject new foods each time they are offered.	Cries and screams each time hair is cut. Disobeys persistently.	Has to be hand led into classroom each day. Bounces on bed in spite of spankings.	Does not adjust well to new school or new teacher; comes home late for dinner even when punished.
Plays by self in playpen for more than an hour. Listens to singing for long periods.	Works on a puzzle until it is completed. Watches when shown how to do something.	Practiced riding a two-wheeled bicycle for hours until he mastered it. Spent over an hour reading a book.	Reads for two hours before sleeping. Does homework carefully.
Loses interest in a toy after a few minutes. Gives up easily if she falls while attempting to walk.	Gives up easily if a toy is hard to use. Asks for help immediately if undressing becomes difficult.	Still cannot tie his shoes because he gives up when he is not successful. Fidgets when parents read to him.	Gets up frequently from homework for a snack. Never finishes a book.
Laughs hard when father plays roughly. Screamed and kicked when temperature was taken.	Yells if he feels excitement or delight. Cries loudly if a toy is taken away.	Rushes to greet father. Gets hiccups from laughing hard.	Tears up an entire page of homework if one mistake is made. Slams door of room when teased by younger brother.
Does not fuss much when clothing is pulled on over head.	When another child hit her, she looked surprised, did not hit back.	Drops eyes and remains silent when given a firm parental "No." Does not laugh much.	When a mistake is made in a model airplane, corrects it quietly. Does not comment when reprimanded.
Spits out food he does not like. Giggles when tickled.	Runs to door when father comes home. Must always be tucked tightly into bed.	Always notices when mother puts new dress on for first time. Refuses milk if it is not ice-cold.	Rejects fatty foods. Adjusts shower until water is at exactly the right temperature.
Eats food he likes even if mixed with disliked food. Can be left easily with strangers.	Can be left with anyone. Falls to sleep easily on either back or stomach.	Does not hear loud, sudden noises when reading. Does not object to injections.	Never complains when sick. Eats all foods.
Takes bottle; reaches for it and smiles. Laughs loudly when playing peekaboo.	Plays with sister; laughs and giggles. Smiles when he succeeds in putting shoes on.	Laughs loudly while watching television cartoons. Smiles at everyone.	Enjoys new accomplishments. Laughs when reading a funny passage aloud.
Cries when given injections. Cries when left alone.	Cries and squirms when given haircut. Cries when mother leaves.	Objects to putting boots on. Cries when frustrated.	Cries when he cannot solve a homework problem. Very "weepy" if he does not get enough sleep.

his high activity level is likely to be expressed at one year through eager eating and a tendency "to climb into everything." A five-year-old child who behaved quietly in infancy may dress slowly and be able to sit quietly and happily during long automobile rides. Color indicates those temperamental characteristics that are crucial to classifying a child as "easy," "slow to warm up" and "difficult."

Most parents, once they are informed of the facts, can change their handling to achieve a healthier interaction with the child.

Theory and practice in psychiatry must take into full account the individual and his uniqueness: how children differ and how these differences act to influence their psychological growth. A given environment will not have the identical functional meaning for all children. Much will depend on the temperamental makeup of the child. As we learn more about how specific parental attitudes and practices and other specific factors in the environment of the child interact with specific temperamental, mental and physical attributes of individual children, it should become considerably easier to foster the child's healthy development.

23

Psychological Factors in Stress and Disease

by Jay M. Weiss
June 1972

A new technique separates the psychological and physical factors in stressful conditions. In studies with rats the psychological factors were the main cause of stomach ulcers and other disorders

One of the most intriguing ideas in medicine is that psychological processes affect disease. This concept is not new; it dates back to antiquity, and it has always been controversial. To counter those skeptics who believed that "no state of mind ever affected the humors of the blood," Daniel Hack Tuke, a noted 19th-century London physician, compiled an exhaustive volume, *Illustrations of the Influence of the Mind on the Body*. He concluded:

"We have seen that the influence of the mind upon the body is no transient power; that *in health* it may exalt the sensory functions, or suspend them altogether; excite the nervous system so as to cause the various forms of convulsive action of the voluntary muscles, or to depress it so as to render them powerless; may stimulate or paralyze the muscles of organic life, and the processes of Nutrition and Secretion—causing even death; that *in disease* it may restore the functions which it takes away in health, reinnervating the sensory and motor nerves, exciting healthy vascularity and nervous power, and assisting the *vis medicatrix Naturae* to throw off disease action or absorb morbid deposits." Through the years many other individuals have voiced their belief in the importance of psychological factors in disease, and they have carved out the field known as psychosomatic medicine. It is a field filled with questions, and we are still seeking better evidence on the role of the psychological factors.

Our ability to determine the influence of psychological factors on disease entered a new phase recently with the application of experimental techniques. Formerly the evidence that psychological factors influence disease came from the observations of astute clinicians who noted that certain psychological conditions seemed to be associated with particular organic disorders or with the increased severity of disorders. But such evidence, no matter how compelling, is correlational in nature. Although a psychological characteristic or event may coincide with the onset or advance of a disorder, one cannot be certain that it actually has any effect on the disease process; the psychological event may simply occur together with the disease or may even be caused by the disease. In addition it is always possible that the apparent correlation between the psychological variable and the disease is spurious; that among the myriad of other factors in the physical makeup of the patient and in his life situation lies a different critical element the observer has failed to detect. Such considerations can be ruled out only by accounting for every possible element in the disease process, which obviously is impractical.

The development of experimental techniques for inducing disease states in animals has made the task of determining whether or not psychological factors affect disease much easier. When an investigator can establish conditions that will cause a pathology to develop in experimental animals in the laboratory, he does not have to wait for the disease to arise and then attempt to determine if a particular factor had been important; instead he can introduce that factor directly into his conditions and see if it does indeed affect the development of the disease. Moreover, the use of experimental procedures enables the investigator to deal with the numerous other variables that might influence the disease. Even so, the investigator certainly cannot regulate or even be aware of all the variables that affect a disease. Such variables will, however, be distributed randomly throughout the entire population of experimental subjects. When the experimenter applies some treatment to one randomly selected group of subjects and not to another, he knows that any consistent difference between the treatment group and the control group will have been caused by the experimental treatment and not by the other variables, since those variables are distributed randomly throughout both groups.

Recently I have been studying the influence of psychological factors on certain experimentally induced disorders, particularly the development of gastric lesions or stomach ulcers. As the prob-

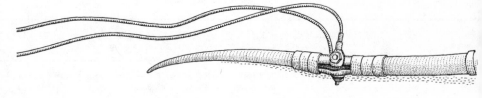

TRANSPARENT-PLASTIC CHAMBER is one type of apparatus used in stress ulcer experiments with rats. The rat is housed in the chamber for the entire 48-hour stress session.

lem of gastrointestinal ulcers has become more widespread (the disease currently causes more than 10,000 deaths each year in the U.S. and afflicts one out of every 20 persons at some point in their life) pathologists have continued to refine techniques of studying ulceration experimentally. Within the past 15 years, beginning with the pioneering work of Serge Bonfils and his associates at the Institut d'Hygiène in Paris, investigators have discovered that experimental animals can develop gastric lesions under stressful environmental conditions. The finding that lesions can be induced by manipulating an animal's external environment opened the way for experimental study of the psychological conditions that are brought about by stressful environmental events.

The experimental techniques had to be refined still further, however, for studying the influence of psychological variables. The reason is that when experimental animals are exposed to an environmental stressor (a stressor is a stress-inducing agent), the effects of psy-

chological variables may be confounded with the effects of the physical stressors. For example, suppose rats are made to swim for an hour in a tank from which they cannot escape, and these animals then develop organic pathology whereas control animals (those not exposed to the swim stressor) show no pathology at all. Although it is evident that the pathology was induced by the swim stressor, how can we assess the role of any psychological factor in producing this pathology? Certainly the pathology might have been affected by the fear the animal experienced, by its inability to escape, by the constant threat of drowning. But what about the extraordinary muscular exertion the stressful situation required, with its attendant debilitation and exhaustion of tissue resources? Clearly in such an experiment it is not possible to determine if psychological variables influenced the development of pathology, since the pathology might have been due simply to the direct impact of the swim stressor itself. Thus in order to study the role of psychological factors one must

devise a means of assessing the importance of psychological variables apart from the impact of the physical stressor on the organism.

The method I have used is to expose two or more animals simultaneously to exactly the same physical stressor, with each animal in a different psychological condition. I then look to see if a consistent difference results from these conditions; such a difference must be due to psychological variables since all the animals received the same physical stressor. To illustrate this technique, let us consider an experiment on the effects of the predictability of an electric shock on ulceration.

Two rats received electric shocks simultaneously through electrodes placed on their tail, while a third rat served as a control and received no shocks. Of the two rats receiving shocks, one heard a beeping tone that began 10 seconds before each shock. The other rat also heard the tone, but the tone sounded randomly with respect to the

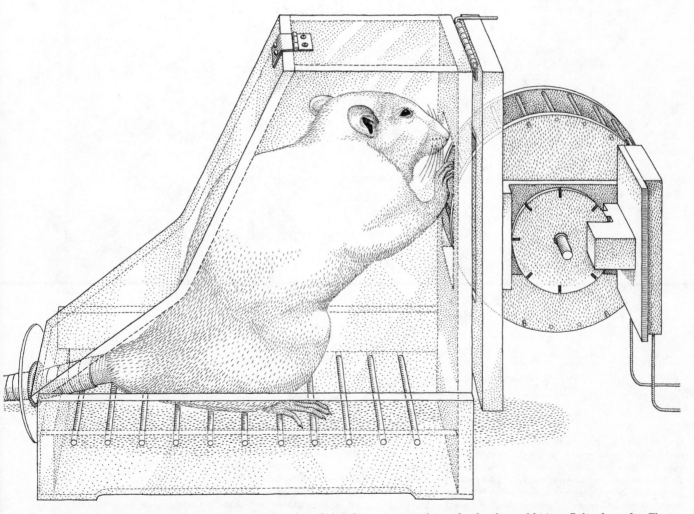

Shocks are delivered through electrodes attached to the tail. A disk secured to the tail by a piece of tubing prevents the rat from pull-ing its tail into the chamber and biting off the electrodes. The rat receives no food during the experiment, but water is available.

shock. Thus both these animals received the same shocks, but one could predict when the shocks would occur whereas the other could not. Since the physical stressor was the same for the two animals, any consistent difference between them in the amount of ulceration would be the result of the difference in the predictability of the stressor, the psychological variable being studied.

This raises a most important point: If such experiments are to be valid, one must be sure that the physical stressor, in this case the electric shock, is the same for all animals in the test. When these studies were begun, the standard way of administering electric shock to experimental rats was to place them on a grid floor whose bars were electrically charged. That method of delivering an electric shock was clearly inadequate for the present experiments, since rats can lessen the shock on a grid floor by changing their posture or can even terminate the shock completely by jumping. The experimenter is faced with a serious problem if one group of rats is able to perform such maneuvers more effectively than another group. In the predictability experiment, for example, the rats that are able to predict shock would surely have been able to prepare for such postural changes more effectively than the rats that were unable to predict shock, so that the groups would have differed with respect not only to the predictability of the stressor but also to the amount of shock received. That would essentially invalidate the experiment. The tail electrode, which is used in all the experiments discussed here, was developed specifically to avoid the possibility of unequal shock. Because the electrode is fixed to the tail, the rat cannot reduce or avoid the shock by moving about. In addition, with the fixed electrode it is possible to wire the electrodes of matched animals in series, so that both animals are part of the same circuit. Thus all the shocks received by the matched subjects are equal in duration and have an identical current intensity, which appears to be the critical element in determining the discomfort of shock.

As was to be expected, the control rats that received no shock developed very little gastric ulceration or none. A

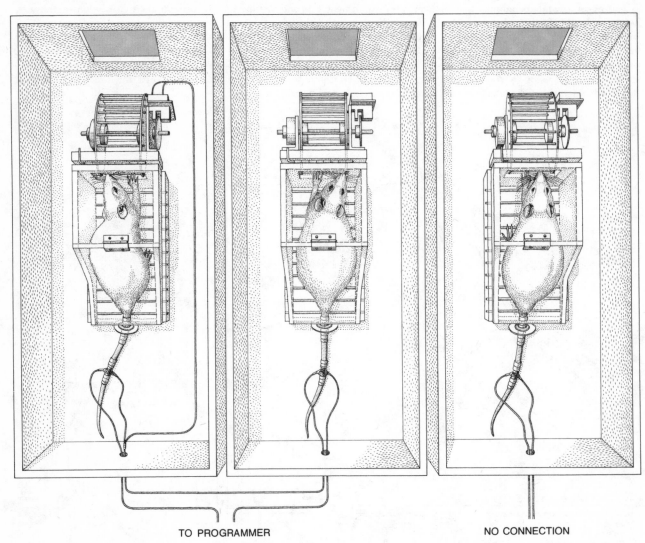

TO PROGRAMMER   NO CONNECTION

BASIC TRIPLET PARADIGM for the ulceration experiments consists in placing three rats, matched for weight and age, in individual soundproof compartments with one-way-mirror windows. Each rat is prepared in exactly the same way and then randomly assigned to one of the three experimental conditions: avoidance-escape, yoked and control. In this illustration the rat on the left is the avoidance-escape subject. It can terminate the programmed shock by turning the wheel. Moreover, turning the wheel between shocks will postpone the shock. The rat in the center is electrically wired in series to the first rat, so that when the first rat receives a shock, the yoked rat simultaneously receives a shock of the same intensity and duration. The actions of the yoked rat do not affect the shock sequence. The electrodes on the tail of the control rat on the right are not connected, and this rat does not receive shocks at any time. At the end of the experimental session the rats are sacrificed and the length of their gastric lesions is measured.

striking result of the experiment was that rats able to predict when the shocks would occur also showed relatively little ulceration, whereas those that received the same shocks unpredictably showed a considerable amount of ulceration [*see top illustration at right*]. In short, the results demonstrated clearly that the psychological variable of predictability, rather than the shock itself, was the main determinant of ulcer severity.

Even though some rats in the foregoing experiment could predict the shock, they were helpless in that they could not avoid the shock. How will stress reactions, such as gastric ulcers, be altered if an animal has control over a stressor instead of being helpless? A recent series of experiments conducted in our laboratory at Rockefeller University has yielded a considerable amount of new information on effects of coping behavior, and also has given us some insight into why these effects arise.

To study the effects of coping behavior, three rats underwent experimental treatment simultaneously, just as in the predictability experiment. Two of the rats again received exactly the same shocks through fixed tail electrodes wired in series, while the third rat served as a nonshock control. In the coping experiments, however, the difference between the two rats receiving shock was not based on predictability (all matched shocked rats in these experiments received the same signals) but rather was based on the fact that one rat could avoid or escape the shock whereas the other could not do anything to escape it.

Since albino rats tend to lose weight when stressed, at first I simply measured the effects of avoidance-escape versus helplessness in terms of changes in the rate of weight gain. In this experimental arrangement one rat of each shocked pair could avoid the shock by jumping onto a platform at the rear of its enclosure during a warning signal, thereby preventing the shock from being given to itself or its partner. If the avoidance-escape rat failed to jump in time, so that shock occurred, it could still jump onto the platform to terminate the shock for itself and its partner. Thus the avoidance-escape rat could affect the occurrence and duration of shock by its responses, whereas its partner, called the yoked subject, received exactly the same shocks but was helpless: its responses had no effect at all on shock. The control rat, which received no shock, was simply allowed to explore its apparatus during the experiment. It is important to note that in all these experiments the three rats were assigned to their respec-

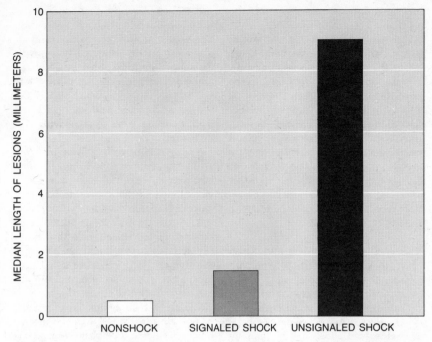

PREDICTABILITY EXPERIMENT showed that if a rat could predict when shocks would occur, it developed less gastric ulceration than a rat that received the same shocks unpredictably. One rat heard a "beep" before each shock, whereas for the other rat the "beep" occurred randomly with respect to the shock. A third rat, a control subject, heard the sound but received no shocks. Thus the only difference between the rats receiving shocks was psychological, and this psychological variable strongly affected the degree of ulceration.

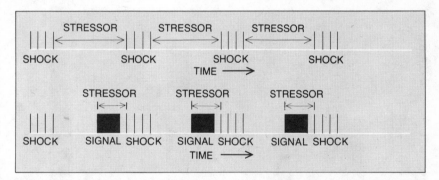

STRESSFUL SITUATION (called "stressor") is created by the electric shock and the stimuli associated with the shock. When there is no warning-signal stimulus, the stressor condition extends through the entire time between shocks. When a warning of the shock is given, however, the stressor condition tends to be restricted to the warning signal.

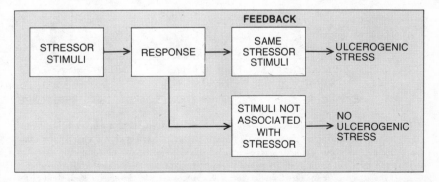

COPING ATTEMPTS OR RESPONSES made by the rat in trying to escape from the stressor are related to ulcerogenic stress only if the responses fail to produce stimuli that are not associated with the stressor. If coping responses produce stimuli not associated with the stressor, the rat receives relevant feedback and ulcerogenic stress does not occur.

tive condition randomly just before the first trial.

The results showed that the yoked, helpless rats lost considerably more weight than the avoidance-escape rats. Over the several days of test sessions the yoked, helpless rats suffered an 80 percent reduction from "normal" weight gain (as measured in the control rats), whereas the reduction of weight gain in the avoidance-escape rats was only 30 percent. Again a psychological factor, in this case a difference in coping behavior, exerted a more powerful influence on stress responses than the occurrence of the physical stressor did.

A second experiment was immediately undertaken to test the generality of these findings, employing a different apparatus and measuring a different pathological response: gastric ulceration. In this case the avoidance-escape rat could avoid shock not by jumping onto a platform but by reaching through a hole in a small restraint cage to touch a panel mounted just outside. The avoidance-escape animal again had a yoked

partner, which received the same shocks but was helpless, and a nonshock control. The rats were subjected to one continuous stress session lasting 21 hours, with the shocks—each preceded by a signal—scheduled to occur at the rate of one per minute. After the conclusion of the session all animals were sacrificed and their stomachs were examined for gastric lesions.

The effects of coping behavior were again found to be beneficial. The rats that were able to avoid and escape shock were found to show considerably less gastric ulceration than their yoked, helpless partners. And again the results pointed up how remarkable the effects of coping behavior could be. Whereas the stomach of the average avoidance-escape rat was found to have 1.6 millimeters of lesioned tissue, the average yoked rat had 4.5 millimeters of lesions, or roughly three times as much ulceration as the average avoidance-escape rat.

In both avoidance-escape experiments the shock was always preceded by a warning, so that the rats could predict when a shock was going to occur. Hence

the avoidance-escape rat always had a signal to inform it when to respond. What would happen if there was no signal before the shock? Would the avoidance-escape rat again show less ulceration than a yoked subject?

To find out a large experiment was conducted in which three different warning-signal conditions were set up: no warning signal, a single uniform signal preceding the shock as in the earlier experiments, and a series of different signals that acted like a clock and therefore gave more information about when a shock would occur than the single uniform signal did. For these studies each rat was placed in a chamber with a large wheel [see illustration on pages 228 and 229]. If the avoidance-escape rat turned the wheel at the front of the apparatus, the shock was postponed for 200 seconds, or if shock had begun, it was immediately terminated and the next shock did not occur for 200 seconds. Thus the avoidance-escape conditions were exactly the same except for the difference in the warning signals. Each avoidance-escape rat had a yoked, helpless partner and both received exactly the same signals and shocks. A rat that never received a shock also was included in every case as a control subject.

The results showed that regardless of the warning-signal condition avoidance-escape rats developed less gastric ulceration than yoked, helpless rats [see illustration at left]. Although the presence of a warning signal did reduce ulceration in both avoidance-escape and yoked groups, the avoidance-escape rats always developed less ulceration.

All the experimental findings on coping behavior that I have described up to this point have been opposite to the result found by Joseph V. Brady, Robert Porter and their colleagues in an experiment with monkeys [see "Ulcers in 'Executive' Monkeys," by Joseph V. Brady; SCIENTIFIC AMERICAN Offprint 425]. They reported that in four pairs of monkeys the animals that could avoid shock by pressing a lever developed severe gastrointestinal ulcers and died, whereas yoked animals that received the same shocks but could not perform the avoidance response survived with no apparent ill effects. Why were these results so markedly different?

With careful study of the data from the 180 rats that were used in the coping-behavior and warning-signal experiment, it was possible to develop a theory that may explain how coping behavior affects gastric ulceration. This theory can account for the results I have

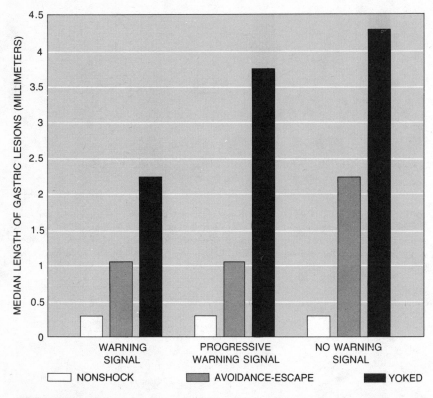

"HELPLESS" RATS develop more ulcers than their counterparts that can avoid or escape shock by performing a simple task, even though both rats have received exactly the same shocks. In all situations the avoidance-escape rat could terminate or postpone the shock by turning the wheel in front of it; its yoked partner received the same shocks but was unable to affect the shock sequence by its behavior. The control rat was never shocked. Regardless of the warning-signal conditions, rats that could do something to stop the shock developed less ulceration than their yoked, helpless mates. Ulceration was more extensive in both groups when there was no warning signal. The yoked, helpless rats unexpectedly developed almost as much ulceration with the progressive warning signal as with no warning signal.

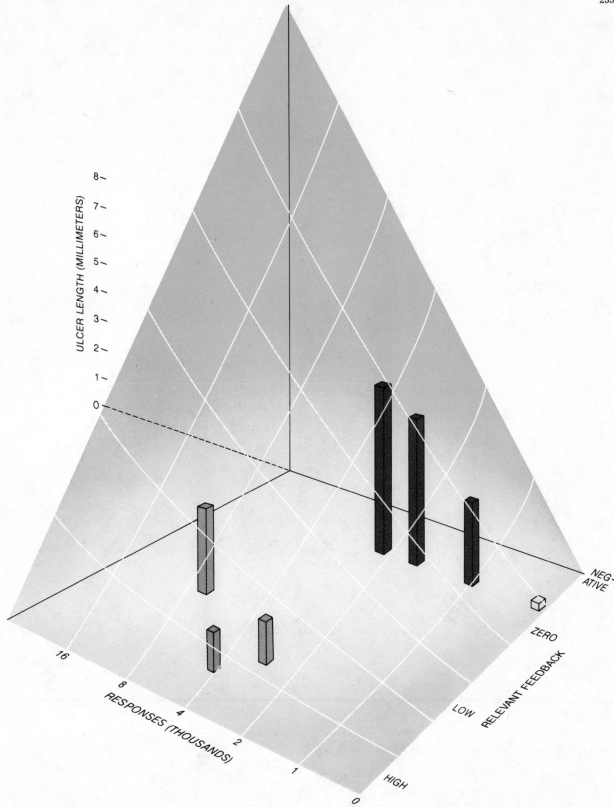

RESPONSE RATE was found to be related to the amount of ulceration: the greater the number of responses, the more the ulceration. Moreover, increasing the amount of relevant feedback decreases ulceration. Combining these variables produces this three-dimensional graph. Here data from the illustration on the opposite page are replotted. The yoked, helpless rats given the progressive warning signal (*middle black bar*) made more responses than helpless rats given only a brief warning signal (*lowest black bar*). Helpless rats shocked without a warning signal made more responses than the other helpless rats and had the highest ulceration (*tallest black bar*). The single white bar represents the control rats that received no shocks in all three conditions, since their response rate and ulceration was nearly the same in all cases. (They developed some ulceration because they too were in a mildly stressful condition.) The avoidance-escape rats that received no warning signal made the greatest number of coping responses and had a high amount of ulceration (*tallest gray bar*). The avoidance-escape rats given the progressive warning signal (high feedback) made more responses (*middle gray bar*) than avoidance-escape rats that heard the brief warning signal before the shock (*right gray bar*).

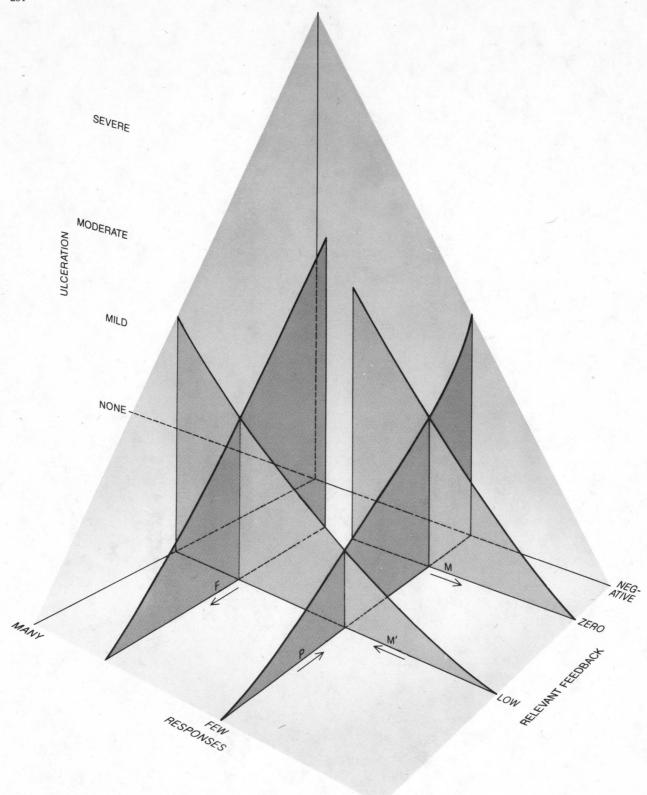

SEVERE

MODERATE

ULCERATION

MILD

NONE

MANY

FEW
RESPONSES

F

P

M'

M

NEG-
ATIVE

ZERO

LOW

RELEVANT FEEDBACK

PREDICTIVE MODEL of the relation between responses, feedback and ulceration is shown here. It predicts that the highest rate of ulceration will occur when the number of coping responses is very high and the feedback is very low or negative. The model can explain why the "executive" monkeys developed more ulcers than their "helpless" counterparts. The executive monkeys could postpone a shock by pressing a lever. Their response rate was quite high, but the amount of relevant feedback they received was low. Thus increased response rate along the low-feedback plane (*M' in illustration*) led to increased ulceration in the executive monkeys. For the "helpless" monkeys, even though they received zero feedback (*Plane M*), their low response rate put them in the low-ulceration area. Similarly, if a high-relevant-feedback situation is changed into a negative-relevant-feedback situation (for example, a previously correct response suddenly begins to produce punishment), the model predicts a rapid increase in ulceration (*Plane P*) even at low levels of response. Finally, increasing feedback to a very high level should reduce ulceration to a very low amount (*Plane F*) even if the response rate is high. Results of experiments conducted to test these predictions are shown on page 236.

obtained and also can reconcile the seemingly contradictory results of the "executive monkey" experiment.

The theory states that stress ulceration is a function of two variables: the number of coping attempts or responses an animal makes, and the amount of appropriate, or "relevant," feedback these coping attempts produce. When an animal is presented with a stressor stimulus, the animal will make coping attempts or responses. The first proposition is simply that the more responses one observes, the greater is the ulcerogenic (ulcer-producing) stress. (Note that this does not say that the behavioral responses themselves cause ulceration, only that the amount of coping behavior and the amount of ulcerogenic stress tend to rise together.) If the responses, however, immediately produce appropriate feedback —that is, if the responses bring about stimuli that have no connection with the stressor—ulcerogenic stress will not occur. On the other hand, if the responses fail to produce such stimuli, then ulcerogenic stress will occur [see bottom illustration on page 231].

Perhaps the most important concept in this theory is that of feedback. The appropriate feedback is called relevant feedback. It consists of stimuli that are not associated with the stressful situation. Relevant feedback occurs when a response produces stimuli that differ from the stressor. The amount of relevant feedback produced depends on how different the stimulus situation becomes and how far removed these new stimuli are from any association with the stressor.

We can now specify how the two variables, responding and relevant feedback, are related to ulceration. Ulceration increases as the number of responses increases, and ulceration decreases as the amount of relevant feedback increases. Combining these two produces a function that forms a three-dimensional plane [see illustration on page 233]. From this model one can predict the amount of ulceration that is expected to occur in any stressful situation by specifying the number of coping attempts or responses the animal makes and the amount of relevant feedback these responses produce.

The model explains why animals able to perform effective coping responses usually develop fewer ulcers than helpless animals. Whenever a helpless animal makes a coping attempt, the response necessarily produces no relevant feedback because it has no effect on the stimuli of the animal's environment. Thus if helpless animals make an appreciable number of coping attempts, which many of them do, they will develop ulcers because of the lack of relevant feedback. Animals that have control in a stressful situation, however, do receive relevant feedback when they respond. In my experiments, for example, the avoidance-escape rats could terminate warning signals and shocks (thereby producing silence and the absence of shocks), so that their responses produced stimuli that were dissociated from the stressor. Hence animals in control of a stressor can usually make many responses and not develop ulcers because they normally receive a substantial amount of relevant feedback for responding.

It is evident that, according to the theory, the effectiveness of coping behavior in preventing ulceration depends on the relevant feedback that coping responses produce; simply to have control over the stressor is in and of itself not beneficial. This means that conditions certainly can exist wherein an animal that has control will ulcerate severely. Specifically, in cases of low relevant feedback ulceration will be severe if the number of responses made is high [see illustration on opposite page].

I believe the foregoing statement tells us precisely why the executive monkeys died of severe gastrointestinal ulceration while performing an avoidance response. First of all, the responding of the monkeys was maintained at a very high rate in that experiment because they had to respond once every 20 seconds to avoid shock. In addition, the executives were actually selected for their high rate of responding. On the basis of a test before the experiment began, the monkey in each pair that responded at the higher rate was made the avoidance animal while its slower partner was assigned to the yoked position. Thus on the basis of their response rate the executive monkeys were more ulcer-prone from the beginning than their yoked partners. With regard to the relevant feedback for responding, the feedback for avoidance responding was quite low. There were no warning signals, and so the executives' rapid-fire responses could not turn off any external signals and therefore did not change the external-stimulus environment at all. As a result the relevant feedback came entirely from internal cues. Evidently this feedback was not sufficient to counteract the extremely high response condition, so that the executive animals developed ulcers and died. At the same time the yoked animals probably made very few responses or coping attempts because the shocks were few and far between, thanks to the high responding of the executives. It is no wonder, then, that the yoked animals in this case survived with no apparent ill effects.

Further evidence in support of this model has emerged, both in an analysis of earlier experiments and in new direct tests with rats. Reviewing those experiments in which hyperactive avoidance-escape rats happened to be paired with low-responding yoked rats under conditions similar to those of the executive-monkey experiment, I found that high-responding avoidance-escape animals developed more ulceration than their helpless partners, which replicated the results of the monkey pairs [see top illustration on next page]. I then went on to test the model directly by examining the effects of very poor relevant feedback and excellent relevant feedback.

The first experiment examined the effects of very poor relevant feedback, which should, of course, produce severe ulceration. In this case avoidance-escape rats, having spent 24 hours in a normal avoidance situation with a warning signal, were given a brief pulse of shock every time they performed the correct response. Although the avoidance-escape rats had control over the stressor, their responses now produced the wrong kind of feedback: the stressor stimulus itself. The feedback in this condition is even worse than it is in the zero-relevant-feedback, or helplessness, condition. The results showed that even though these rats had control over the stressor, they developed severe gastric ulceration, in fact more ulceration than helpless animals receiving the same shocks [see middle illustration on next page].

Having found that very poor feedback would cause severe ulceration, I conducted an experiment to determine if excellent feedback could reduce and possibly eliminate ulceration in a stressful situation. Initially the shock was administered without a warning signal, and under this condition the avoidance-escape rats will normally develop a considerable amount of gastric ulceration. Presumably ulceration occurs because the relevant feedback for responding is low, as in the case of the executive monkeys. Then a brief tone was added to the experiment. When the rat now performed its coping response, it not only postponed shock but also sounded the tone. Because the tone immediately followed the response, and the response postponed the shock, the tone was not associated with the shock. Thus the tone produced a change in the stimulus situa-

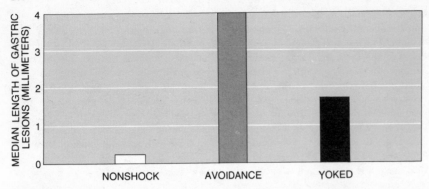

REPLICATION of the executive-monkey situation with data from experiments in which rats received unsignaled shocks offers support for the theoretical model of ulcerogenic stress. Matched pairs of high-responding avoidance rats and low-responding yoked rats were statistically selected and their ulcers measured. As the model predicts, the avoidance rats showed higher ulceration and the low-responding yoked rats had less ulceration.

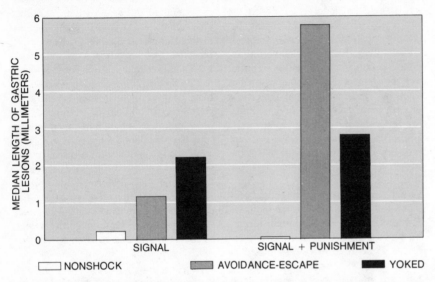

☐ NONSHOCK ▨ AVOIDANCE-ESCAPE ■ YOKED

NEGATIVE RELEVANT FEEDBACK produces severe ulceration even when the animal has control over the shock. In the warning-signal condition avoidance-escape rats learned to perform a response to avoid a shock whenever a tone sounded. In the punishment situation during the last half of the experiment the rats received a shock every time they performed the previously learned correct response. With this negative relevant feedback the avoidance-escape rats developed more ulcers than their yoked, helpless mates did.

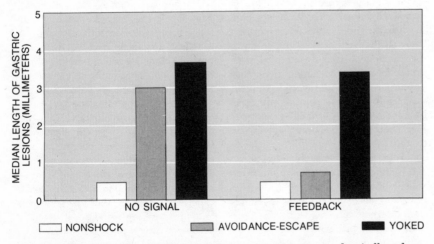

☐ NONSHOCK ▨ AVOIDANCE-ESCAPE ■ YOKED

EXCELLENT RELEVANT FEEDBACK following a correct response drastically reduces the amount of ulceration in rats. In the no-signal condition the avoidance-escape rat could postpone the shock by turning a wheel but there was no feedback other than the absence of shock. In the feedback condition a signal followed immediately after every correct response. The number of responses by avoidance-escape rats in both conditions was the same.

tion that constituted excellent relevant feedback. The result was striking. Although the rats in this situation received about as many shocks as the counterparts that were not given the tone feedback, they developed a small amount of ulceration; in fact, they developed only slightly more ulceration than controls receiving no shocks at all did [*see bottom illustration at left*].

Hence by manipulating the feedback consequences of responding, rats could be made to develop extensive gastric ulceration in an otherwise nonulcerogenic condition or could be protected almost completely from developing ulcers in a condition that was normally quite ulcerogenic. The fact that these results are consistent with the proposed model means that we are beginning to develop some idea of why the remarkable effects of psychological variables in stress situations occur.

It appears that the principles discovered in these animal experiments may operate in human situations as well. For example, Ronald Champion of the University of Sydney and James Geer and his associates at the State University of New York at Stony Brook have shown that if people are given inescapable shocks, the individuals who think they can terminate these shocks by clenching a fist or pressing a button show less emotional arousal as measured by electrical skin resistance than individuals who receive the same shocks and are also asked to clench a fist or press the button but are told that the shocks are inescapable. These findings can be explained using the model derived from the animal experiments, again emphasizing the role of relevant feedback. The people who thought they had control over the shock perceived their responses as producing the shock-free condition, that is, they saw their responses as producing relevant feedback. In contrast, the people who thought they were helpless necessarily perceived their responses as producing no relevant feedback. Thus for humans, as for rats, the same variables seem important in describing the effects of behavior in stress situations. On the other hand, the experiments with humans alert us to how important higher cognitive processes are in people, showing that verbal instructions and self-evaluation can determine feedback from behavior, which will subsequently affect bodily stress reactions.

Other stress responses have been measured in addition to gastric ulceration, for example the level of plasma corticosterone in the blood and the amount of body weight the animals lost during the stress session. In many instances the results reflect those found with gastric ulcers, showing that ulceration may be only one manifestation of a more general systemic stress response. The correlation between measures is by no means perfect, so that it is evident that all physiological systems participating in stress reactions are not affected in the same way by a given stress condition. Certain systems in the body may be severely taxed by one set of conditions whereas other systems may be hardly affected at all, or actually may be benefited. For example, I have observed that heart weight tends to decrease in certain conditions, and this effect is seen more often in animals that are able to avoid and escape shock. We do not yet even know what this change indicates, but it suggests that certain conditions protecting one organ system, such as the gastrointestinal tract, might adversely affect another, such as the cardiovascular system.

Perhaps the most exciting biochemical system we have begun to study involves the catecholamines of the central nervous system. Eric A. Stone, Nell Harrell and I have studied changes in the level of norepinephrine in the brain. This substance is a suspected neurotransmitter that is thought to play a major role in mediating active, assertive responses, and several investigators have suggested that depletion of norepinephrine is instrumental in bringing about depression in humans. We found that animals able to avoid and escape shock showed an increase in the level of brain norepinephrine, whereas helpless animals, which received the same shocks, showed a decrease in norepinephrine. At the same time Martin Seligman, Steven Maier and Richard L. Solomon of the University of Pennsylvania have found that dogs given inescapable shocks will subsequently show signs of behavioral depression, but that dogs that are able to avoid and escape shocks do not show such depression. It may well be that the causal sequence leading from "helplessness" to behavioral depression depends on biochemical changes in the central nervous system, such as changes in brain norepinephrine. This would indicate that depressed behavior often can be perpetuated in a vicious circle: the inability to cope alters neural biochemistry, which further accentuates depression, increasing the inability to cope, which further alters neural biochemistry, and so on. We need to know more about this cycle and how to break it.

24 Disorders of the Human Brain

by Seymour S. Kety
September 1979

They can result from inherited metabolic defect, vascular disease, infection, tumor and trauma. The frontier in the study of mental illness is the relation between genetic and environmental factors

In a structure as complex as the human brain a multitude of things can go wrong. The wonder is that for most people the brain functions effectively and unceasingly for more than 60 years. It speaks for the resiliency, redundancy and self-restorative nature of the brain's mechanisms. The fact remains that disorders of the brain do sometimes arise in its structural architecture or in its electrical and chemical processes. More than a century ago pathologists were able to recognize disorders that involve damage to the gross anatomical structure of the brain, damage resulting from hemorrhage, pressure, displacement, inflammation, degeneration and atrophy. The microscope and selective chemical stains made it possible to see how morphological damage contributes to the starvation, degeneration and death of neurons and to the interruption of the pathways connecting them.

Investigations of brain disorders were hampered for many years by the absence of techniques for studying the living brain. What little was known about such disorders came from studies at autopsy. The discovery of X rays at the end of the 19th century enabled investigators to look inside the living brain. Gross structural defects in the ventricles, or cavities, of the brain can now be detected by pneumoencephalography: the X-ray technique in which the fluid that normally surrounds the brain and fills the ventricles is replaced with air to reveal their shape. In another approach, cerebral angiography, an X-ray-opaque dye is injected into the bloodstream so that pathological displacement of the blood vessels in the brain can be observed with X rays. Conventional radiography, invaluable as it is, suffers from a major drawback: on the developed film the X-ray projections of abnormalities can overlap those of the normal structures, making it difficult or even impossible to distinguish them from one another. This is particularly true when the X-ray densities of neighboring structures are similar, as is often the case with a tumor and the surrounding healthy tissue.

The development of the CAT scan (computed axial tomography) has surmounted that shortcoming. The CAT scan is a synthetic technique that combines X-ray readings taken from many different angles to yield a faithful representation of the internal structure of the living brain in cross section. The scan reveals enlarged and atrophied normal structures and any abnormal masses such as tumors and hemorrhages.

By the middle of this century electrical techniques had emerged as important tools for prospecting the brain. The messages the brain receives from the sense organs, the directives it sends to them and the messages between the billions of neurons within the brain are all carried by electrical signals. The electric fields near the surface of the brain can be picked up and amplified by the electroencephalograph. In this way disturbances in the electrical activity of the brain can be traced to specific locations.

Over the past two decades investigations of brain function have been extended to chemical processes. The utilization of energy by the brain can be studied by measurements of blood flow and of oxygen and glucose consumption. The recent work of Niels A. Lassen of the Bispebjerg Hospital in Copenhagen and David H. Ingvar of the University of Copenhagen makes it possible to see in cathode-ray-tube images how the circulation of blood in different regions of the brain changes rapidly in response to specific mental activities, such as reading aloud or reading silently. Louis Sokoloff and his co-workers at the National Institute of Mental Health have developed techniques for measuring the metabolism of glucose at any point in the brain. Because functional activity is closely related to blood flow and is intimately related to glucose utilization, such techniques provide a means for mapping the living brain in terms of the functional activity of its components.

At the level of the neuron, brain disorders can arise from anomalous chemical processes operating at the synapses between neurons. Disturbances in the synthesis, release or inactivation of a particular chemical transmitter or disturbances in the sensitivity of a transmitter's postsynaptic receptors can result in synaptic dysfunction. Such dysfunction need not be accompanied by morphological changes on either the gross or the microscopic level. The recent development of histofluorescent and immunofluorescent techniques, which in effect stain for specific transmitters or their enzymes, has made it possible to demonstrate and measure the effect of a transmitter on individual neurons. New chemical techniques employing radioactive isotopes can assay the number and the sensitivity of postsynaptic receptors, and powerful analytical instruments can examine brain fluid, cerebrospinal fluid, blood and urine for almost infinitesimal traces of transmitters and their metabolites.

Perfectly tuned and smoothly functioning synapses are essential to the successful operation of such complex mental processes as perception, cognition, affect and judgment. Since such processes are often disturbed in mental illness increased knowledge of them should help to unravel the mysteries of mental disorders. Only recently have these new techniques for studying the chemistry of the synapse been applied to mental disorders such as schizophrenia and manic-depressive psychosis. I think it is quite possible that these investigative tools may do for psychiatry what the older techniques have done for neurology.

Pathological processes in the brain can be brought about by a wide variety of proximate and remote causative factors that are often classified as being either genetic or environmental. Since every characteristic of a living organism ultimately depends on a complex interaction of genetic and environmental influences, it may seem futile to try to disentangle them. It is nonetheless possible to differentiate them by seeing how much each influence contributes to the variance in a particular characteristic. For example, language ability requires a highly developed mechanism in the brain, a mechanism that clearly depends

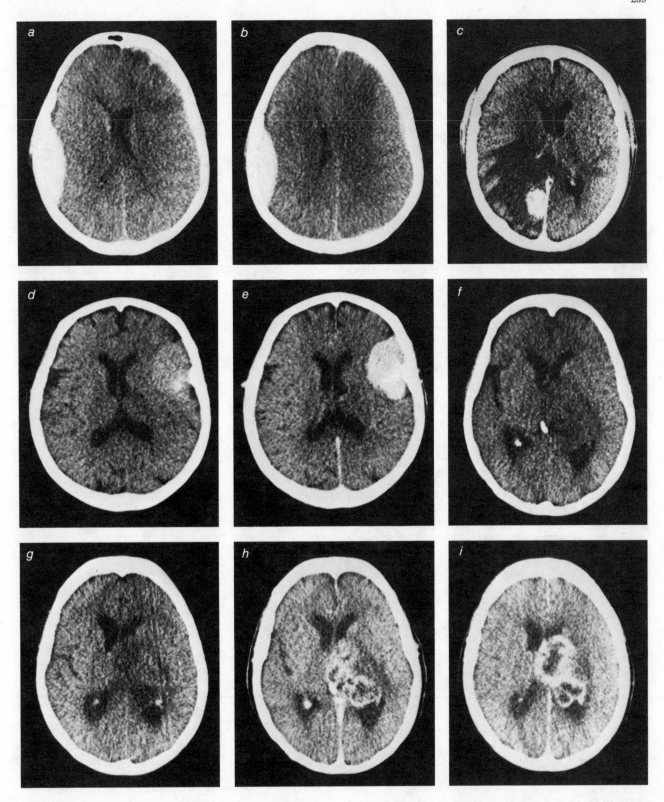

CAT SCAN (computed axial tomography) combines X-ray readings taken from many different angles to yield a representation of the living brain in cross section. The injection of an iodine solution into the venous system improves the contrast between different structures appearing in the scan. In scans *a* and *b* iodine was not needed to bring out a dense fresh blood clot between the brain and the skull. The hemorrhage was caused by a blow to that part of the skull. Diagonally opposite the clot is a shallow pool of blood on the surface of the brain or just inside it. The pool resulted from "contra coup" injury to the brain on the side opposite the blow. The ventricles (*center*) were compressed by the swelling of both halves of the brain. In scan *c* iodine brought out a tumor (*lower center*) of a patient suffering from cancer metastases. To the right of the tumor nodule is a normal vein, which stands out because it contains iodine-enriched blood. The ventricles have been displaced by the swelling of the tissues surrounding the tumor. In scan *d* a meningioma (a benign tumor) is fairly faint without iodine. Inside the tumor is a small island of calcium. Hyperostosis, an accumulation of bone close to the tumor, is characteristic of a meningioma. In scan *e* iodine greatly enhanced the same tumor. The thin white line running through the tumor was generated by the scanning apparatus for measurement purposes. In scans *f* and *g* a malignant tumor (*center*) can scarcely be seen without the aid of iodine, but in scans *h* and *i*, made with iodine, it shows up clearly as a patchy area. The ventricles have been displaced and indented. In scan *f* a calcified pineal gland (*center*) has also been slightly displaced. The white ring-like zones of iodine enhancement are characteristic of a malignant tumor. The nine CAT scans were provided through the courtesy of Fred J. Hodges III of the Johns Hopkins University School of Medicine.

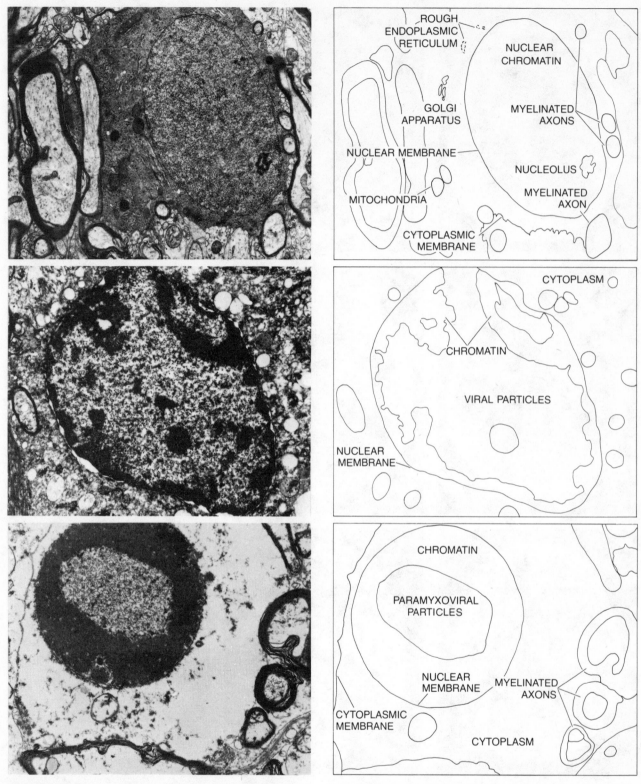

GLIAL CELL, which manufactures and maintains the fatty layer of myelin that sheathes the axons of the central nervous system, can be implicated in brain disorders. At the top left is an electron micrograph of a normal glial cell; it is a relatively dark cell with densely packed intracellular organelles, including mitochondria, "rough" endoplasmic reticulum and a well-defined Golgi apparatus. At the top right is a map of the organelles. In this normal cell chromatin, which incorporates the genetic material, is evenly dispersed throughout the nucleus. At the periphery of the cell are parts of several myelinated axons; the myelin is a direct extension of the glial cell's specialized cytoplasmic membrane. At the middle left is a glial cell from a person suffering from chronic lymphocytic leukemia. The organelles of the cell are much disrupted. The cell, which is in tissue removed at autopsy, has an enlarged and displaced nucleus, condensed chromatin and numerous viral particles that were destroying the cell. As a result the myelin of the axons was no longer being maintained. The progressive demyelination of major neural pathways gives rise to disease symptoms. About four months before the patient died he complained of decreased vision (which progressed to blindness in his left visual field), of inability to recognize faces and of inability to read. He suffered ultimately from complete blindness, mild confusion and bilateral motor dysfunction. At the bottom left is a glial cell, which is in tissue removed at autopsy, from a person suffering from subacute sclerosing panencephalitis. Here the individual organelles in the glial cell can no longer be distinguished, although the adjacent myelinated axons are still distinct. The chromatin is clumped and is displaced by particles characteristic of a paramyxovirus. The electron micrographs were made by Jerry S. Wolinsky of the Johns Hopkins School of Medicine.

on genetic processes. Yet the particular language a person speaks is not genetically determined but is accounted for almost entirely by the environmental factor of acculturation. On the other hand, there are genetic defects affecting the brain that require specific dietary conditions to bring them on. If these conditions are ubiquitous, the variance between the normal individual and the abnormal one will be entirely accounted for by the genetic factor; hence the disorder is classified as a genetic disease. Of course, most human characteristics cannot be categorized so easily. They seem to fall somewhere between the two extremes.

Genes determine the amino acid sequences that form proteins. It is these protein molecules, synthesized at specific sites and times, that serve as the structural materials and the enzyme catalysts responsible for the development and operation of the brain. Many disorders of the central nervous system, particularly those resulting in mental retardation, are known to be genetic in origin. For example, phenylketonuria and galactosemia are both caused by genetically determined enzyme deficiencies. In both diseases an enzyme deficiency makes toxic a component of the diet that is ordinarily beneficial. An infant born with phenylketonuria lacks the enzyme phenylalanine hydroxylase, which is responsible for the further metabolism of phenylalanine in the body. As a result excessive quantities of this essential amino acid accumulate in the blood and tissues, interfering with the development and operation of the brain.

In galactosemia the infant appears normal at birth, but within a few days or weeks of milk feeding it develops anorexia, vomiting and growth failure that may lead to death from wasting and inanition. Untreated survivors are often stunted and mentally retarded. Galactosemia is caused by the absence of an enzyme essential to the further metabolism of the sugar galactose, which therefore accumulates in abnormal amounts. The deleterious effects of these diseases can be eliminated by altering the environment, namely by removing the offending substance (phenylalanine or galactose) from the diet for at least the period of infancy when the brain grows and develops the most.

Some genetic disorders are sex-linked. Lesch-Nyhan syndrome, characterized by purposeless and uncontrollable movements, mental retardation and self-destructive psychotic behavior, is the result of an enzyme deficiency. An absent or defective gene on the X chromosome is responsible. The disorder affects only males because they have only one X chromosome. (In females, who have two X chromosomes, the absent or defective gene, if it is present on one X chromosome, has no effect because

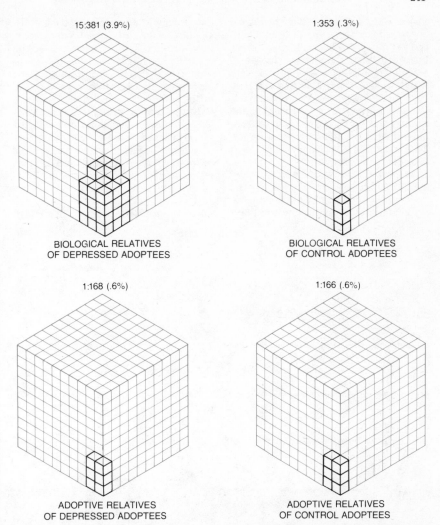

15:381 (3.9%)

BIOLOGICAL RELATIVES
OF DEPRESSED ADOPTEES

1:353 (.3%)

BIOLOGICAL RELATIVES
OF CONTROL ADOPTEES

1:168 (.6%)

ADOPTIVE RELATIVES
OF DEPRESSED ADOPTEES

1:166 (.6%)

ADOPTIVE RELATIVES
OF CONTROL ADOPTEES

HIGHER INCIDENCE OF SUICIDE in biological relatives of adoptees who suffered from depression compared with the incidence in their adoptive relatives and in the relatives of control adoptees who had no mental illness suggests a genetic factor in suicide. Each ratio shows the number of relatives who committed suicide with respect to the total number of relatives. Data come from a study by the author, David Rosenthal of National Institute of Mental Health, Fini Schulsinger of University of Copenhagen and Paul H. Wender of University of Utah.

there is a normal gene on the other X chromosome.)

Brain disorders can result not only from a deficiency of genetic material but also from an excess. Extra X or Y chromosomes are associated with syndromes involving mild intellectual and personality disorders. In Down's syndrome, which afflicts about one out of every 700 newborn infants, there is an extra chromosome No. 21. Such children suffer from retarded physical and mental development.

Genetic disorders do not necessarily reveal themselves at birth. For example, the symptoms of Huntington's chorea, namely uncontrolled movements and mental deterioration, appear for the first time between the ages of 30 and 50. The disease, which depends almost entirely on a dominant genetic trait, leads to gross atrophy of the corpus striatum in the brain and to neuron degeneration in the caudate and the other deep neural nuclei and in the frontal cerebral cortex.

In 1968 Linus Pauling proposed that

there are genetically determined differences in the amount of vitamins people need. He suggested that the differences might result in disorders of the central nervous system, including the brain. This hypothesis is exemplified by several rare childhood neurological syndromes in which a genetically determined failure to absorb or process a particular vitamin creates a severe vitamin deficiency that adversely affects the central nervous system. These syndromes can be treated successfully by administering large doses of the particular vitamin involved. Pauling suggested that such a mechanism might be the cause of schizophrenia, but there is little evidence that an increased requirement of any vitamin is characteristic of the disorder.

The major psychoses, including schizophrenia and the affective disorders, are considerably commoner than the disorders mentioned above. In these psychoses genetic factors seem to play a major role, although their biological consequences have not yet been identified, as they have been for many other brain disorders. Ever since schizophrenia and manic-depressive illness were first described nearly a century ago, they have been known to run in families. Roughly 10 percent of the parents, the siblings and the offspring of an afflicted individual also suffer from the disorder. That was often taken to mean that such disorders are hereditary.

A family, however, shares environmental influences as well as genetic ones, and so the mere fact that a disease runs in families says little about its etiol-

ogy. Pellagra, a vitamin-deficiency disease that in the early decades of this century accounted for 10 percent of the mentally ill in the U.S., also afflicts families, so that it was once thought to be hereditary. In 1915 Joseph Goldberger of the U.S. Public Health Service demonstrated that the principal cause of pellagra is a severe deficiency in the diet of the B vitamin niacin. Since members of a family usually eat the same kinds of food, the disease ran in families. Pellagra has been almost entirely eradicated by dietary intervention.

Evidence of a genetic etiology for schizophrenia and for manic-depressive

disease comes from studies of the incidence of these disorders in identical twins (who share all their genes) and in fraternal twins (who share about half of the same genes). In identical twins both disorders show a high concordance rate (almost 50 percent), but in fraternal twins the rate (about 10 percent) is no different from that in all siblings. Recent studies have concentrated on adopted individuals whose genetic endowment can be investigated through their biological relatives and whose environmental influences can be examined through their adoptive relatives.

Such studies indicate that both schizo-

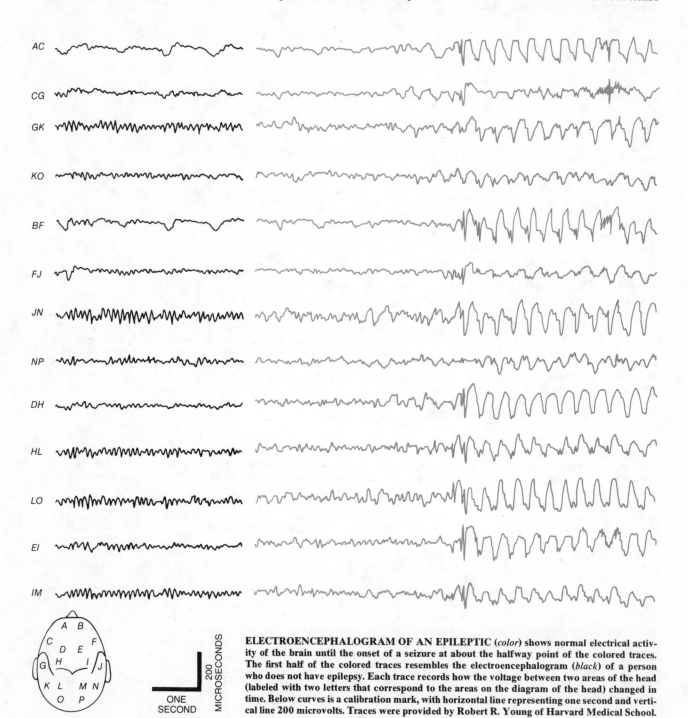

ELECTROENCEPHALOGRAM OF AN EPILEPTIC (*color*) shows normal electrical activity of the brain until the onset of a seizure at about the halfway point of the colored traces. The first half of the colored traces resembles the electroencephalogram (*black*) of a person who does not have epilepsy. Each trace records how the voltage between two areas of the head (labeled with two letters that correspond to the areas on the diagram of the head) changed in time. Below curves is a calibration mark, with horizontal line representing one second and vertical line 200 microvolts. Traces were provided by Robert R. Young of Harvard Medical School.

phrenia and manic-depressive disorder run in the biological families and not in the adoptive ones. The rate of mental illness in the adoptive relatives who lived with the affected adoptee is the same as the rate of mental illness in the general population. This finding in conjunction with the higher concordance rate in identical twins indicates the importance of genetic factors in schizophrenia and manic-depressive disorder, although it does not rule out the possibility of various environmental factors also playing a major etiological role. Since genes can express themselves only through biochemical mechanisms, the importance of genetic factors in mental disorders constitutes compelling evidence for biochemical substrates in these disorders, although such substrates have not yet been specifically identified.

Studies of biological and adoptive families suggest the presence of a significant genetic factor in chronic alcoholism, in which an environmental agent, namely alcohol, has an obvious role, and in suicide, in which many kinds of environmental influences are undoubtedly involved. The genetic factors in such disorders might explain why not everyone exposed to alcohol becomes addicted and why only a fraction of the people who find themselves in apparently hopeless situations choose to commit suicide.

Since all etiological factors that are not genetic must be environmental, the latter category spans a broad range of influences that differ in quality, intensity and the times in the life of an individual during which they exert their effects. Such factors first come into play in the uterine environment. In the complex metamorphosis from the fertilized ovum to the newborn infant, chemical and physical processes operate at every stage to allow the expression of the genetic program. All kinds of environmental deficiencies and disturbances can interfere with this expression and thwart the normal development of the central nervous system.

Many forms of cerebral palsy and mental retardation owe their origin to abnormalities in the fetal environment or in the process of birth. If rubella, or "German measles," is transmitted from the mother to the fetus in the first trimester of pregnancy, the disease can cause mental retardation and possibly infantile autism. If cytomegalovirus, which in adults is fairly common and usually innocuous, infects the brain of the fetus, it may lead to deafness and subnormal intelligence. Kernicterus, a fetal jaundice resulting from Rh incompatibility between the mother and the fetus, can cause hearing loss, cerebral palsy and mental retardation, although the incidence of such complications has been greatly reduced by diagnostic and prophylactic intervention. Hormonal disorders in the mother and her exposure to certain drugs and other foreign substances have been shown to give rise to abnormalities in the fetus. It is also likely that severe malnutrition or maternal exposure to alcohol and other toxins could disturb the normal development of the fetal brain.

Bacterial infections are a chief cause of cerebral disorders at all stages of life, although the control of infection by antibiotics has almost entirely eradicated many severe disorders, such as the general paresis, or extreme insanity, that resulted from syphilis and the often fatal meningitis, or inflammation of the membranes enclosing the brain, that resulted from tuberculosis and other bacterial infections.

Viral diseases cannot be treated as effectively as bacterial infections can, so that acute and often fatal encephalitis is occasionally associated with such viral diseases as measles, mumps, influenza and herpes. Poliomyelitis, an infection of the motor neurons, is a viral disorder of the central nervous system that has been almost completely eradicated by the development of effective vaccines. The influenza epidemic that swept the world in 1918 left in its wake countless people who gradually developed a form of Parkinson's disease, characterized by a severe dysfunction of motor control. The strain of influenza virus had a special predilection for invading the extrapyramidal system of the brain and seems to be the first recorded example of a viral infection of the nervous system that lay dormant for several years before giving rise to deleterious effects.

Recently the cause of several other disorders has been traced to latent or slow viral infections of the nervous system. For example, kuru is a slowly progressive neurological disorder that is limited to a small tribe in New Guinea. Kuru runs in families, and so it was thought to be genetic until D. Carleton Gajdusek of the National Institutes of Health established its viral etiology by showing that chimpanzees inoculated with brain tissue from infected individuals also developed the disease.

Creutzfeldt-Jakob disease, a rare dementia of middle age, is another slowly progressive disorder that is viral in origin. Alzheimer's disease, a much commoner type of senile dementia, resembles Creutzfeldt-Jakob disease in many of its clinical and neuropathological features. Several laboratories are investigating the possibility that a viral agent is responsible for Alzheimer's disease. Herpes and cytomegalovirus are examples of other viruses that can remain dormant in the nervous system for years before producing neurological or mental symptoms. There is also evidence that some forms of schizophrenia may be viral in origin.

The history of psychiatry and neurology provides numerous cases of cerebral disorders caused by toxic chemicals. The Mad Hatter was not a creature of Lewis Carroll's remarkable imagination but a fictional victim of an occupational disease of the 18th and 19th centuries. Hatmakers who were exposed daily to mercury used in the preparation of felt suffered a toxic psychosis. Other heavy metals are also known to disturb the nervous system. Manganese causes a form of Parkinson's disease and lead causes disturbances of the peripheral nerves and the brain. Lead poisoning in children (chiefly from the ingestion of lead-based paint) can give rise to behavioral abnormalities and learning disabilities.

In the Middle Ages bread made of rye infested with ergot, a parasitic fungus, was responsible for epidemics of madness. This plant parasite is now known to contain several alkaloids that have a potent effect on the nervous system. The powerful hallucinogen LSD is a synthetic derivative of one of them.

In addition to exogenous poisons and drugs, endogenous substances that are made in the body as the result of some disease can be toxic to the brain. Untreated diabetes and severe or terminal kidney or liver failure can result in the production of toxic substances that cause confusion, delirium and ultimately coma. Porphyria is a rare metabolic disorder of genetic origin in which the buildup of porphyrins interferes with mental processes. The madness of King George III has been attributed to porphyria.

Although the processes of immunity defend the body against infection, the immune response occasionally goes awry, resulting in a variety of disorders, some of which involve the brain. Allergic disorders such as asthma and hay fever are the commonest immune diseases. The root of disorders such as rheumatoid arthritis, lupus erythematosus and other collagen diseases is a faulty immune response directed against normal tissue. Such an autoimmune process has been definitively implicated in one neuropsychiatric illness: myasthenia gravis, a severe neuromuscular disorder characterized by sporadic muscular fatigability and weakness. The disease invades the neuromuscular junction, where the transmitter acetylcholine is released and acts on receptors in muscle-cell membranes in order to trigger muscular contraction. Recent work indicates that in this disorder an autoimmune process impairs receptor function and reduces the efficiency of the neuromuscular junction. It is also possible that an autoimmune process is responsible for multiple sclerosis. The evidence comes from a laboratory-animal model of an autoimmune disease, called experimental allergic encephalomyelitis, that resembles multiple sclerosis in its behavioral symptoms and neuropathology.

The most prevalent brain disorders are due to deficiencies in the supply of blood. The energy requirements of the brain are among the highest in the body. The brain needs a fifth of the heart's output of blood and a fifth of the oxygen consumed by the entire body at rest. Although rare congenital defects can disturb the vascular system of the brain, the commonest disturbance is atherosclerosis, the poorly understood disorder of the blood vessels that can affect the heart, the kidneys and the limbs as well as the brain. Atherosclerosis can lead to a narrowing of the bore and an eventual thrombosis of a blood vessel, which results in a gradual or a sudden diminution in the blood supply of an area of the brain and hence in abnormal functioning of that area. The wall of an atherosclerotic vessel can also rupture, causing a cerebral hemorrhage. The symptoms of thrombosis or cerebral hemorrhage vary greatly, depending on what areas and processes of the brain are affected. Some of the effects of a hemorrhage are the result of pressure, which acts to oppose the blood flow and to displace and distort the complex architecture of the brain. Tumors and head injuries can operate the same way.

Epilepsy, characterized by the simultaneous and rhythmic firing of large numbers of neurons, is a neuropsychiatric disorder for which the primary and proximate causes are still largely unknown. The origin of one kind of epilepsy has been traced to a scar, usually on the surface of the brain, that is the result of injury or infection. The scar tissue serves as the focus of abnormal electrical activity, which spreads over a large field of adjacent normal neurons. In most kinds of epilepsy, however, scars or other lesions have not been found. Here there is accumulating evidence that the defect is a chemical one involving one or more transmitters, particularly GABA (gamma-aminobutyric acid), the major inhibitory transmitter in the central nervous system.

As for the major psychoses (schizophrenia and manic-depressive illness), their etiology is still not known. In their severe and classical form they can resemble disorders of the brain. The individual symptoms or the entire syndrome of a psychiatric disorder can sometimes be seen in the early stages of a recognized neurological disorder such as Huntington's chorea.

A chemical dimension of mental illness is most clearly suggested by the studies I have mentioned that revealed the importance of genetic factors in the etiology of the major psychoses. The biochemical processes through which these genetic factors express themselves have not been established, although there are promising indications that they operate at certain synapses in the brain. Drugs that act on the brain can alleviate the symptoms of depression, mania and schizophrenia as well as create them. Such drugs act specifically on synaptic processes. The drugs that remove certain transmitters (dopamine, norepinephrine and serotonin) from their synapses cause depression, whereas the drugs used to treat clinical depression all tend to elevate the levels of these transmitters or to enhance their function. The hypothesis that some forms of depression are the result of a deficiency of these transmitters or of other transmitters that interact with them is a plausible one, and studies of metabolites in urine and cerebrospinal fluid tend to support it.

By the same token the drugs that are effective in relieving the psychotic symptoms of schizophrenia all damp the activity of dopamine synapses,

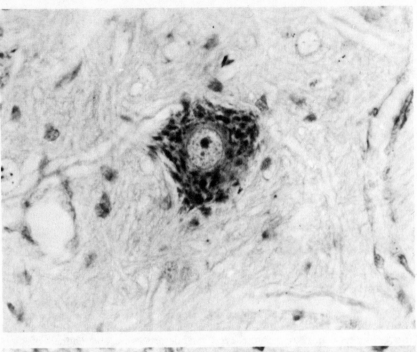

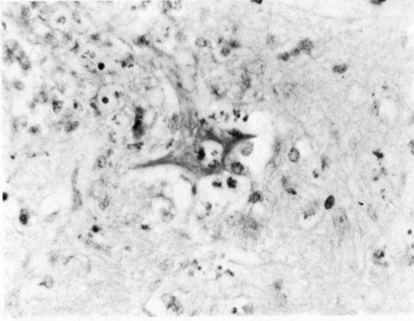

POLIOMYELITIS, a viral infection of the motor neurons, has been almost eradicated by the development of vaccines. In the electron micrograph at the top is a normal anterior-horn cell in the spinal cord of a rhesus monkey; it is characterized by massive Nissl bodies in the cytoplasm, a centrally located nucleus and dispersed chromatin. In the micrograph at the bottom is an anterior-horn cell from a monkey in a late stage of poliomyelitis. The cell is irreversibly injured. The micrographs were provided by David Bodian of Johns Hopkins School of Medicine.

whereas amphetamine, which gives rise to a toxic psychosis that closely resembles schizophrenia, increases the level of dopamine at these synapses. Although clear evidence of an excess of dopamine in the brain of schizophrenics is lacking, it is possible that other conditions might exist in the brain of schizophrenics that would have an effect similar to the one produced by an excess of dopamine, conditions such as an oversensitivity of dopamine receptors or a deficiency in the activity of another transmitter that normally opposes dopamine. All these possibilities call for much further investigation.

Psychological and social factors undoubtedly play an important role in these psychiatric disorders. There can be no doubt that such influences alter the manifestations, severity, duration and course of such disorders, and that in many instances they can precipitate them. Several plausible hypotheses have been put forward on a possible interaction between environmental factors and a biological predisposition for mental illness. The environmental influences that have been suggested or implicated as playing some etiological role in mental illness include, in addition to psychological factors, physiological difficulties during the prenatal period, birth injuries, infectious disease and certain toxins. Such influences have a differential social distribution. Most are commoner among the lower socioeconomic groups because of crowding, poor hygiene and inadequate medical care. Schizophrenia in particular is known to be twice as prevalent among the poor who live in large cities than it is in the rest of the population.

The successful treatment or prevention of a brain disorder depends largely on how much is known about it. The effects of a tumor or of a sclerotic blood vessel can sometimes be alleviated by corrective measures, but more specific treatment or prevention of a disorder calls for an understanding of the fundamental mechanisms involved. Parkinson's disease, whose symptoms cripple about 50,000 people in the U.S. per year, is a good example of how knowledge of the underlying neurobiological processes at fault in a particular disorder can give rise to a successful method of treatment. Parkinson's disease is a progressive chronic condition that once meant death or severe disability for its victims. The disease begins with an involuntary shaking of the arms. The jerky tremor spreads to the other extremities and to the neck and the jaw. The back stiffens and the muscles become so rigid that the sufferer walks with a strange shuffle. In the final stages of the disease the sufferer is bedridden, unable to walk or feed himself and unable to talk because of facial paralysis.

The work of Arvid Carlsson of the University of Göteborg and Oleh Hornykiewicz of the University of Vienna revealed that the cause of the disease is the progressive destruction of the neuron pathways that are characterized by the transmitter dopamine. As a result a deficiency of dopamine was found at the pathway synapses in the corpus striatum, a structure near the center of the brain that modulates movement.

This information enabled investigators to develop an effective treatment. It was known that although dopamine itself would not pass through the membrane that separates brain tissue from the blood, its chemical precursor, L-DOPA, would. When L-DOPA is administered orally, it enters the bloodstream from the intestine and travels to the brain, where it is taken up and converted into dopamine. In clinical trials with large doses of L-DOPA George C. Cotzias of the Brookhaven National Laboratory found that the symptoms of the disorder were dramatically relieved. The therapeutic doses of L-DOPA are quite large (as much as 8,000 milligrams a day), so that many adverse side effects result from the action of dopamine on other parts of the body. Modified forms of the treatment have been developed recently that introduce fewer adverse complications.

The treatment of Parkinson's disease constitutes one of the major medical triumphs that resulted from fundamental research in biochemistry and neuroscience. Yet even before the underlying mechanism of a brain disorder is understood an effective treatment will sometimes be discovered fortuitously. That was the case with the antidepressant and antipsychotic drugs that sparked the development of psychopharmacology, revolutionizing the treatment of mental illness. Knowledge of the actions of these drugs on chemical synapses facilitates the development of more effective drugs with fewer side effects. Epilepsy, whose underlying causes and mechanisms are still not understood, is successfully treated with Dilantin, a drug that was discovered in a systematic search with electrophysiological techniques.

As understanding of a particular disorder increases with deliberate investigation and the steady accumulation of basic knowledge, new treatments and ultimately methods of prevention are developed. That has been the case with infectious diseases of the brain, such as general paresis, poliomyelitis, meningitis and certain kinds of encephalitis, where identification of the etiological agent made possible vaccine prophylaxis and antibiotic therapy. It was the case even earlier with pellagra. One may reasonably expect it will also happen for those brain disorders that are still shrouded in mystery.

Behavioral Psychotherapy

by Albert Bandura
March 1967

Abnormal behavior can be thought of not as a symptom of a hidden illness but as a problem of "social learning," and can be treated directly by methods that are derived from principles of learning

In recent years there has been a fundamental departure from conventional views regarding the nature, causes and treatment of psychological disorders. Most theories of maladaptive behavior are based on the disease concept, according to which abnormalities in behavior are considered to be symptoms of an underlying neurosis or psychic illness. Today many psychotherapists are advancing the view that behavior that is harmful to the individual or departs widely from accepted social and ethical norms should be viewed not as some kind of disease but as a way—which the person has learned—of coping with environmental demands. Treatment then becomes a problem in "social learning." The abnormal behavior can be dealt with directly, and in seeking to modify it the therapist can call on principles of learning that are based on experimentation and are subject to testing and verification.

The concepts of symptom and disease are quite appropriate in physical disorders. Changes in tissues or in their functioning do in fact occur, and they can be verified whether or not there are external manifestations. Where psychological problems are concerned, however, analogy with physical disease can be misleading. The psychic conditions that are assumed to underlie behavioral malfunctioning are merely abstractions from the behavior that are given substance and often endowed with powerful motivating properties. Each of the many conventional theories of psychopathology has its own favored set of hypothetical internal agents. Psychotherapists of differing theoretical background and affiliation tend to find evidence for their own preferred psychodynamic agents but not for those cited by other schools. Freudians unearth Oedipus complexes Ad-

lerians discover inferiority feelings with compensatory power-strivings, Rogerians find inappropriate self-concepts and existentialists are likely to diagnose existential crises and anxieties.

A correlate of the disease approach is the assumption that in order to gain lasting benefits from psychotherapy the client must achieve awareness of the concealed forces causing his actions, and the development of this insight is usually one of the primary goals of conventional therapy. A study of the results of psychotherapy made by Ralph W. Heine at the University of Chicago School of Medicine suggested, however, that a client's insights and emergent "unconscious" could be predicted more accurately from knowledge of his therapist's theoretical system than from the client's actual developmental history. It would seem from this finding and others that insight may primarily represent a conversion to the therapist's point of view rather than a process of self-discovery. It is therefore not surprising that insight can be achieved without any real effect on the difficulties for which the patient originally sought help. A chronic stutterer converted to Freudianism or Jungianism—or to any other theoretical system—will not necessarily begin to speak fluently. His stuttering behavior is more likely to be eliminated by the necessary relearning experiences than by the gradual discovery of predetermined insights.

Stuttering is a well-defined motor behavior, but I should make it clear that what are called behavioral therapies apply to the full range of psychological events: attitudinal and emotional as well as motor. Some forms of behavioral therapy bring about major changes in people's actions by modifying their emotional responses; on the other hand,

enduring changes in attitude can be most successfully effected through modifications in overt behavior. In the final analysis all modes of psychotherapy are behavioral, since the client's behavior—broadly defined to include conceptual, emotional and motor expression—is the only reality the psychotherapist can deal with and modify. Indeed, while conventional therapists are promoting insights, they may simultaneously (if inadvertently) reward desirable patterns of behavior and show disapproval of abnormal behavior; they may reduce anxieties through their supportive reactions to a client's statements; they exhibit attitudes, values and patterns of behavior that a client is inclined to emulate. Many of the therapeutic changes that occur in conventional psychotherapy may therefore arise primarily from the unwitting application of social-learning principles. The point is that these beneficial results can be obtained more readily when the principles are applied in a more considered and systematic way. I shall describe a number of different approaches to treatment based on learning principles and review some studies, many of them controlled investigations, in which such procedures have been tested.

In our research at Stanford University we have found that almost any learning outcome that results from direct experience can also come about on a vicarious basis through observation of other people's behavior and its consequences for them. Indeed, providing an appropriate "model" may accelerate the learning process, and one method of social-learning therapy is therefore based on modeling the desired behavior. This is particularly suitable in the treatment of gross deficits in behavior, as in the case of a child (usually diagnosed as

PRINCIPLES OF LEARNING are utilized in the simple course of therapy suggested by these drawings. An extremely withdrawn pre-kindergarten boy whose solitary play is usually "reinforced" by the teacher's solicitude (*a*) is instead rewarded for joining a group by the teacher's devoting her full attention to him and the group (*b*). When the original reinforcement is resumed as a check on the treatment, he reverts to his former behavior (*c*). Then the therapeutic reinforcement is reinstituted and the desired behavior is well established (*d*). In time the child's enjoyment of his new behavior maintains his sociable interaction without special attention (*e*).

schizophrenic or autistic) who does not speak, interact with other people or even respond to their presence.

O. Ivar Lovaas of the University of California at Los Angeles has recently devised modeling procedures that hold promise of developing the intellectual and interpersonal capabilities of schizophrenic children. In teaching a mute child to talk, for example, the therapist first rewards any visual attentiveness and even random sounds made by the child. When vocalization has been increased, the rewards are limited to occasions on which sounds are made in response to a sound uttered by the therapist, and then to precise verbal reproduction of specific sounds, words and phrases modeled by the therapist. When the child has acquired a vocabulary and can imitate new words easily, the therapist goes on to teach the meaning of words, grammatical structure and even abstract verbal concepts by the modeling procedures. Lovaas has also taught schizophrenic children a variety of skills and social patterns of behavior by modeling the desired behavior and rewarding the child when he emulates it. The most impressive thing about this form of treatment is that it can be conducted under the supervision of nurses, students and parents, to whom the methods are easily taught.

In a very different application of modeling principles, George A. Kelly of Brandeis University conceived a role-enactment form of therapy for adults who want to develop new personality characteristics. The client is provided with a personality sketch and given demonstrations of the desired behavior; he then has opportunities to practice the new patterns in a protected therapeutic situation before being encouraged to apply them as he goes about his everyday life.

Often therapists, instead of having to fill a behavioral vacuum, have the problem of eliminating strongly established abnormal behavior. In an early study at the University of Iowa, Gertrude E. Chittenden tested the efficacy of a symbolic modeling procedure for dealing with children's hyperaggressive reactions to frustration. It has been widely assumed that either witnessing or participating in aggressive behavior serves to reduce, at least temporarily, the incidence of such behavior. The overall evidence from studies conducted in our laboratory and elsewhere strongly indicates that psychotherapies employing these conventional "cathartic" procedures may actually be increasing aggres-

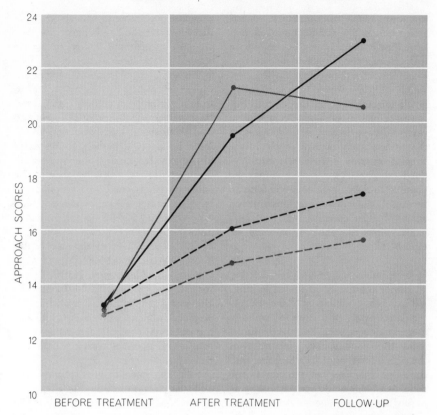

FEAR OF DOGS, as measured by an "approach score," abated most for children who watched displays in which "models" played with dogs in a party atmosphere (*solid black curve*) or in a neutral context (*solid gray*). The change was less for children who were merely in the party atmosphere (*broken black*) or who saw no child models (*broken gray*).

sive tendencies rather than reducing them. In contrast, therapy based on social-learning principles concentrates at the outset on developing constructive alternative modes of behavior. Chittenden had domineering and hyperaggressive children watch a series of scenes in which dolls representing preschool children exhibited first aggressive reactions to common frustrating situations and then cooperative reactions; the consequences of the aggressive reactions were shown as being unpleasant and those of the cooperative ones as being rewarding. Children for whom the different reactions and consequences were modeled showed a lasting decrease in aggressive, domineering behavior compared with a group of similarly hyperaggressive children who received no treatment.

We have found that phobias and inhibitions can be eliminated by having the fearful person observe a graduated sequence of modeled activities beginning with presentations that are easily tolerated. In a controlled test of this therapy, nursery school children who were afraid of dogs (according to their parents' statements and tests of "dog avoidance" behavior) were assigned to one of four groups. Children in the first group par-

ticipated in eight brief sessions in which they watched a child without fear interact more and more closely with a dog—approaching it, playing with it, petting it and so on—with the entire procedure taking place in a "positive" party setting designed to counteract anxiety reactions. The second group saw the same sequence but in a neutral context. In order for us to assess the effects of exposure to the dog alone the third group saw the dog in a party setting but without the child model; the fourth joined the party activities but was not exposed to either the model or the dog.

The tests for avoidance behavior were readministered after the completion of treatment and again a month later. The tests were quite severe, requiring the child not only to touch, pet and walk a dog but also to remain alone in a room with it, to hand-feed it and finally to climb into a playpen with the animal. The test scores showed that most of the children who had received the modeling treatment had essentially lost their fear of dogs [*see illustration on this page*]. The favorable results were largely confirmed by a second experiment in which the same modeled behavior was presented to some children in filmed performances while children in a control group watched a different motion picture. Finally the control children, whose fear of dogs had remained unchanged, were shown the therapeutic movies, after which their fear was in turn substantially diminished. One of the obvious advantages of the modeling technique in psychotherapy is that it lends itself to the treatment of groups of people. Moreover, the success of the filmed version of the modeling suggests that it may be possible to develop therapeutic films to be used in preventive programs directed against certain common fears and anxieties before they became strongly established.

There is increasing evidence that behavior commonly attributed to internal psychic conditions is in fact largely regulated by its own external, environmental consequences. Positive reinforcement—the modification of behavior through alteration of its rewarding outcomes—is therefore an important procedure in behavioral therapy. The techniques are those of operant conditioning, which was developed largely by B. F. Skinner and his colleagues at Harvard University.

Three elements are necessary to the proper implementation of operant conditioning in psychotherapy. The first is that the reinforcement, or incentive, system must be capable of maintaining the client's motivation and responsiveness; the system can involve tangible rewards, opportunities to engage in enjoyable activities, praise and attention or the satisfaction of a job well done. The second is that the reinforcement must be made conditional on the occurrence of the desired behavior, correctly timed and applied on a regular basis. The third is that there must be a dependable way to elicit the desired behavior either by demonstrating it or by rewarding small improvements in the direction of more complex forms of behavior.

The application of these elements is illustrated by a case reported by Arthur W. Staats, then at Arizona State University, and William H. Butterfield. They treated a 14-year-old delinquent boy who, in addition to having a long history of aggressive, destructive behavior, had never received a passing grade in eight and a half years of school and who read at the second-grade level. He was considered to be uneducable, incorrigible and mentally retarded.

The therapists undertook to teach him to read—first single words, then sentences and finally brief stories. For each

word the boy learned he received points that he saved and "exchanged" for phonograph records and other things he wanted or for sums of money. In four and a half months he made notable advances in reading-test scores [see illustration below]. Moreover, the brief treatment program produced generalized educational and psychological effects: he received passing grades in all his subjects for the first time and his aggressively defiant behavior ceased. The entire program, which was administered by a probation officer, involved a total expenditure of $20.31 for the exchange items!

The effectiveness of operant conditioning was demonstrated most convincingly by Florence R. Harris, Montrose M. Wolf and Donald M. Baer at the University of Washington. In their method grossly abnormal behavior in children is successively eliminated, reinstated and eliminated again by varying its social consequences.

First the psychologists observe the child in question to note the frequency of the behavior disorder, the context in which it occurs and the reaction of the teacher. In one case an extremely withdrawn little boy in nursery school spent about 80 percent of the time in solitary activities. Observation revealed that the teacher unwittingly "reinforced" his solitary behavior by paying a great deal of attention to him, consoling him and encouraging him to play with the other children. When he did happen to join the others, the teacher took no particular notice.

In the second phase of the program a new set of reinforcement practices is substituted. In the case of the solitary little boy, for example, the teacher stopped rewarding solitary play with attention and support. Instead, whenever the child sought out other children, the teacher immediately joined the group and gave it her full attention. Soon the boy was spending about 60 percent of his time playing with the other children.

After the desired change in behavior has been produced, the original reinforcement practices are reinstated to determine if the original behavior was in fact maintained by its social consequences. In this third stage, for example, the teacher again paid no attention to the child's sociability but instead responded with comforting ministrations and concern whenever he was alone. The effect of this traditional "mental hygiene" treatment was to increase the child's withdrawal to the original high level.

Finally the therapeutic activity is reintroduced, the abnormal behavior is eliminated and the desired behavior pattern is generously reinforced until it is well enough established to be maintained by its own implicit satisfactions. Once the little boy was again playing with other children the teacher was able to reduce her direct involvement with the group; the child derived increasing enjoyment from his new behavior pattern and eventually maintained it without any special attention.

Children with a wide variety of be-

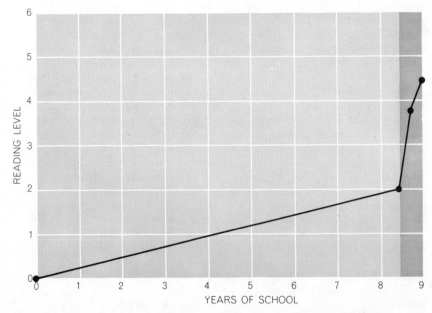

DELINQUENT ADOLESCENT BOY was reading at the second-grade level after more than eight years in school. In half a year of therapy his reading level had more than doubled.

havior disorders have participated in this form of treatment, and in each case their maladaptive behavior was eliminated, reinstated and removed a second time by alterations in the teacher's "social responsiveness." Clearly child-rearing and therapeutic practices should be evaluated carefully in terms of the effects they have on their recipients rather than in terms of the humanitarian intent of teachers or psychotherapists.

Certain widespread psychological problems must be treated primarily at the social rather than the individual level. By altering the reinforcement contingencies of a social group it may be possible to affect the behavior of each member in beneficial ways, whereas working with individuals would yield trifling results. Recently incentive programs have been applied on a group basis in psychiatric hospitals and in institutions for retarded children and for delinquent adolescents. Operant conditioning therapies have, for example, restored some social competence and self-reliance in severely impaired psychiatric patients. The traditional hospital routine tends to reinforce docile behavior and

dependence; the therapy rewards self-sufficiency, social relations and progress in vocational training. At the Anna State Hospital in Illinois, Teodoro Ayllon and Nathan H. Azrin found that psychotic patients would work productively in the rehabilitation program if activities and material comforts they wanted were made dependent on the completion of their assignments; the patients quickly lapsed into their customary lethargy when the incentives were discontinued and the privileges were made available routinely as before [see illustration on page 252].

There is an obverse side to the positive-reinforcement method. Abnormal behavior that persists because it leads to rewarding outcomes can often be eliminated simply by withholding the usual positive reinforcement. Tantrums, hyperaggressive behavior, chronic eating problems, psychosomatic and hypochondriacal complaints, psychotic talk and even the bizarre behavior of autistic children have been found to abate gradually when the solicitous concern they usually evoke is not forthcoming. This process is greatly facilitated if alterna-

tive behavior patterns are rewarded at the same time.

A third major category of therapeutic methods derived from learning theory is based on the principle of "counterconditioning." These methods are appropriate for treating the conditions most frequently seen in a conventional interview-therapy practice: anxiety reactions, chronic tensions, inhibitions, phobias and psychosomatic reactions. The objective in counterconditioning is to induce strong positive responses in the presence of stimuli that ordinarily arouse fear or other unfavorable reactions in the client. As positive responses are repeatedly associated with the threatening events, the anxiety is gradually eliminated. Although psychotherapeutic applications of this principle were reported by Mary Cover Jones as long ago as 1924, the approach received little attention until some 30 years later, when Joseph Wolpe, now at the Temple University School of Medicine, worked out procedures that increased the range of disorders subject to treatment by counterconditioning.

In Wolpe's "desensitization" method

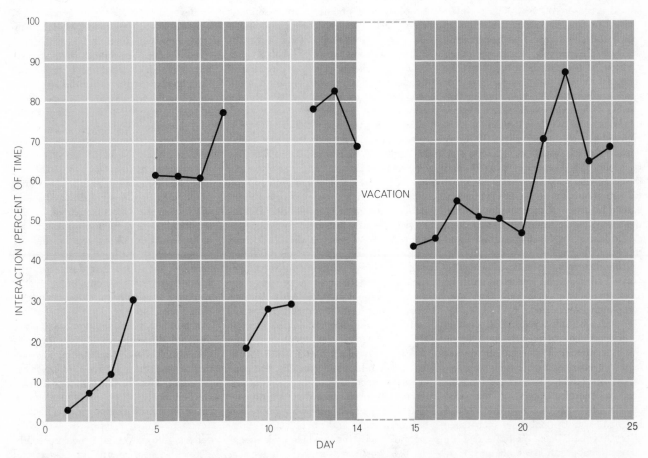

IMPROVEMENT in the behavior of the withdrawn child (*see illustration on page 248*) is indicated by the increasing time spent in social interaction. Before treatment began and during the time when his solitary play was rewarded with attention he was usually alone (*light colored areas*), but he played with others when such behavior was reinforced by the teacher's responses (*dark areas*).

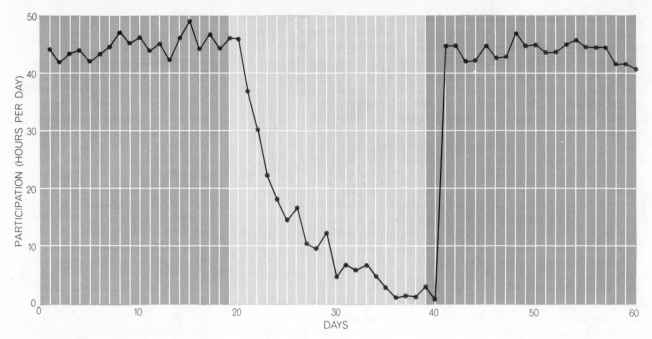

PARTICIPATION in rehabilitation activities increased for a group of 44 schizophrenic patients when privileges were made conditional on their successful completion of assignments (*dark colored areas*), and decreased when the same rewards were provided whether or not they took part in the activities (*light area*). The colored spots indicate the total number of hours of participation each day.

the therapist—working with information obtained from interviews and psychological tests—first constructs a "hierarchy," or ranked list, of situations to which the client reacts with increasing degrees of anxiety (or avoidance or inhibition, as the case may be). Then the therapist induces in the client a state of deep muscular relaxation—a state incompatible with anxiety—and asks the client to visualize the weakest item in the hierarchy of anxiety-arousing stimuli. If any tension results, the client is told to stop imagining the threatening situation and the relaxation process is resumed; if the relaxation remains unimpaired in the imagined presence of the stimulus, the patient is presented with the next item in the hierarchy. So it goes throughout the graduated series, with the intensity of the disturbing situations being increased from session to session until the most threatening situations have been completely neutralized.

Favorable clinical reports on counterconditioning have recently been borne out by a number of experimental studies in which changes in behavior were assessed objectively. Arnold A. Lazarus, now at Temple University, evaluated clients afflicted with acrophobia (fear of heights), claustrophobia or impotence after they had been treated either by conventional group psychotherapy or by group desensitization. Of the 18 clients treated by desensitization, 13 completely recovered from their phobias. The con-

ventional treatment was successful in only two out of 17 cases, and of the 15 people whose phobias were essentially unmodified 10 were thereupon treated successfully by group desensitization. A follow-up study indicated that 80 percent of the clients for whom desensitization had been successful maintained their recovery as measured by a stringent criterion: the recurrence of even weak phobic responses was rated as a failure.

At the University of Illinois, Gordon L. Paul studied the relative efficacy of counterconditioning and conventional methods in treating college students who suffered from extreme anxiety about public speaking. One group received interview therapy intended to produce insight. A second group underwent desensitization treatments in which relaxation was associated with imagined public-speaking situations of a progressively more threatening nature. A third group was given a form of placebo treatment, and a control group had no treatment at all.

After six weeks the students' response to a stressful public-speaking test was evaluated according to three sets of criteria: their own reports as to just how disturbed they felt, physiological indicators of anxiety and an objective judgment of the extent to which their speaking behavior was disrupted. Students in all three of the treatment conditions showed less behavior indicative of anxiety, and reported less distress, than the

untreated control group. Only the students in the counterconditioned group achieved a significant reduction in physiological arousal compared with the controls, however. In each case the counterconditioned group showed greater improvement than the insight group and the placebo group, which did not differ significantly from each other [*see illustration on page 253*]. In a follow-up period the counterconditioned students reported experiencing less anxiety about speaking than the other three groups. An interesting aspect of this study was that the therapists, who in their regular practice favored insight-directed methods, rated the students treated by desensitization as most improved and also indicated a better prognosis for them. A subsequent study by Paul and Donald Shannon indicated that desensitization administered on a group basis can be similarly effective in eliminating disabling anxieties.

A number of current investigations are directed at identifying the specific components of counterconditioning therapy that account for its success. In these experiments Gerald C. Davison and Earl D. Schubot of Stanford and Peter J. Lang of the University of Wisconsin devise treatment procedures with well-defined differences and then make objective measurements of behavioral changes. The preliminary results of their studies suggest that the critical factor is the close association of relaxation with the stimuli that arouse anxiety, particularly in the treatment of severe anxiety disorders.

I have been discussing specific kinds of procedures for rather specific psychological problems. Many people seeking psychotherapy present multiple problems, and these call for combinations of procedures. (The developments in behavioral therapy in some respects parallel those in medicine, where all-purpose therapies of limited efficacy were eventually replaced by powerful specific procedures designed to treat particular physical disorders.) The treatment process is not piecemeal, since favorable changes in one area of behavior tend to produce beneficial modifications in other areas. In many instances a circumscribed problem has wide social consequences, and a change in such an area can have pervasive psychological effects.

Psychotherapists who think in terms of diseases often assume that the direct modification of abnormal behavior may result in what they call "symptom substitution." The available evidence reveals, however, that induced behavioral changes at least persist in themselves and often have favorable effects on other areas of psychological functioning. To be sure, a poorly designed course of therapy aimed only at eliminating maladaptive behavior patterns does not in itself guarantee that desired modes of response will take their place. The client may revert to alternative and equally unsatisfactory courses of action, and the therapist may be faced with the task of eliminating a succession of ineffective patterns of behavior. This problem can be forestalled by including procedures

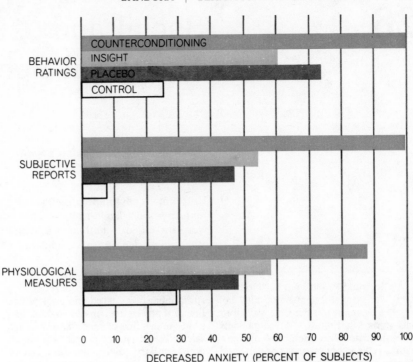

PUBLIC-SPEAKING phobia was treated by counterconditioning, by an "insight" method and by a placebo treatment. There was also an untreated control group. The chart gives the percent of subjects who showed decreased anxiety (according to three different criteria).

in the original treatment that are designed to foster desirable alternative modes of behavior.

Preliminary applications of social-learning approaches to psychotherapy indicate that these methods hold considerable promise; they need to be developed further, extended to the treatment of multiple problems and evaluated after a sufficient period has elapsed. Many new methods of psychotherapy have been introduced enthusiastically and then have been retired by controlled studies. The fact that social-learning

therapies are based on established principles of behavior and are subjected to experimental study at each stage of development gives us reason to expect them to weather the test of time. The day may not be far off when psychological disorders will be treated not in hospitals or mental hygiene clinics but in comprehensive "learning centers," when clients will be considered not patients suffering from hidden psychic pathologies but responsible people who participate actively in developing their own potentialities.

26 Social and Nonsocial Speech

by Robert M. Krauss and Sam Glucksberg
February 1977

*In order to communicate effectively with others
children must learn not only the language itself but
also the use of social speech, which takes into account
the knowledge and perspective of another person*

As Bertrand Russell put it, "No matter how eloquent a dog may be, he cannot tell me that his father was poor but honest." All organisms communicate with members of their own species in one way or another, and some of the nonhuman signaling systems can be impressively complex and efficient, but they are limited in a fundamental sense: each species has a repertory that is pretty much restricted to a fixed set of messages with a fixed set of meanings. It cannot construct novel messages in order to communicate new concepts—or even clichés about honest poverty.

Unlike other species, human beings seem to be capable of communicating about virtually anything, whether or not they have the precise words available for doing so. If our vocabulary happens not to contain the standard term for denoting a particular concept, we are usually able to invent some way of expressing our meaning, perhaps by the use of metaphor or circumlocution. Scholars, pedants and bureaucrats, among others, devise terms for new inventions, discoveries or concepts, assigning meanings in a deliberate and explicit fashion. Young children also frequently find themselves forced to invent ways to talk about things whose names are not yet part of their repertory. Although the terms children invent lack the explicit definitions that characterize technical terminology, they are often perversely accurate and considerably more entertaining—as when the daughter of one of us communicated her discovery of her father's bald spot by proclaiming: "Daddy has a hole in his hair."

All of us are under continuous pressure to invent new ways of communicating with others. The necessity comes in part from the nature of language itself. Although it is not obvious until one thinks about it, the nature of language is not such that for each word there is one and only one thing (or class of things) to which it can be applied. It is also not such that each thing can be referred to by one and only one word. For example, the word "line" can be used, given the appropriate context, to refer to a straight line or a curved line, a telephone line or a power line, an ideological line, a salesman's line of merchandise or his sales talk, a queue of people or a line of type. Similarly, any given thing can be referred to by any number of different words or phrases. Even a 10-cent piece can be called just that or "dime," "money," "change," "that coin" and so on.

The point is that the relation between the reference, or verbal expression, and the referent, or the thing referred to, is not in the nature of an unequivocal code. In the Morse code, for example, three dots followed by a momentary pause and then by three dashes invariably denotes the letter sequence *SO*. No word, let alone a phrase or sentence, in any natural language bears any such invariant relation to a thing or concept it may denote.

We learn at least two rather different kinds of things when we learn our language. We learn the language itself, which means learning its sound system, its syntax and its vocabulary. We must also learn how to manipulate the language for communicating concepts effectively and efficiently, and that is not quite the same thing as having learned the language. One way to appreciate this distinction is to contrast social messages with nonsocial ones. Nonsocial messages are messages that are not intended to communicate information to another person; they can be expressed in the abbreviated, idiosyncratic, private language one uses in writing a reminder to oneself. Since nonsocial speech is not directed to another person, the knowledge and perspective of a particular recipient need not be considered in its formulation. People who speak nonsocial speech would be likely to address young children in precisely the same way they speak to adults, or to address laymen in the same way they speak to colleagues in their profession. An ornithologist speaking social speech directs a child's attention to a nearby "robin redbreast"; he does not ask, "Do you see that *Turdus migratorius?*" Social messages are

characterized by variability because they take into account both the nature of the audience and the context of the conversation.

That people do take the characteristics of their audience into account is not difficult to demonstrate. Douglas Kingsbury, who was then an undergraduate at Harvard University, casually approached randomly selected passersby on the streets of Cambridge and asked them the way to Central Square. To some he addressed the question, "Can you tell me how to get to Central Square?" in a nondescript local accent. The typical response was brief and direct, containing neither more nor less information than the situation seemed to require. Does this reflect the brusqueness and impersonality of modern urban

GIVING DIRECTIONS on a busy city street, passersby communicate socially. Asked for

life? Not at all. When Kingsbury prefaced his question with the statement "I'm from out of town," the same busy Cantabrigians gave him involved and explicit instructions, describing landmarks he would encounter en route and telling him how he could be sure he was in Central Square when he reached it. Interestingly, Kingsbury found he could achieve the same effect if he signaled his ignorance of local geography implicitly by adopting a rural Missouri accent, which is exotic enough in Cambridge to indicate quite clearly: "I'm from out of town."

What those Cambridge pedestrians were demonstrating was their implicit knowledge of how to use language communicatively. They did not say the same thing even when they were talking about the same thing—how to get from point x to point y. They tailored what they said and how they said it to suit what they understood to be the knowledge and perspective of their listener. In the same way adults tailor what they say in accordance with whether they are talking to children or to other adults. Noam Chomsky of the Massachusetts Institute of Technology and others have held that language skills must be acquired by means of some "innate language-acquisition device," because, among other reasons, children surely could not learn a language by exposure to the kind of speech adults typically inflict on one another, which is syntactically complex, fragmented and virtually incomprehensible out of context. Catherine E. Snow

of McGill University, pondering the Chomsky view, decided to compare the ways adult women talk to older children and to younger ones. When they were talking to younger children, the women she studied, whether or not they were experienced mothers, spoke in short and syntactically simple sentences. As a result a two-year-old was likely to hear—and understand, and learn language skills from—this kind of talk: "That's a lion. And the lion's name is Leo. Leo lives in a big house. Leo goes for a walk every morning. And he always takes his cane along." The women knew quite well that it would be pointless to express the same ideas to a two-year-old in the form: "That's a lion named Leo, who lives in a spacious house and makes it a practice to take a constitutional every morning, invariably accompanied by his cane."

How and when do children learn to employ language so as to suit the demands of a particular listener and the particular circumstances of a conversation? We decided to investigate the question by means of a communication task one of us (Krauss) had designed some years before. The object of the original research had been to assess the efficiency of communication between adults over a noisy or otherwise degraded communication channel. Along with the findings on that question the research revealed certain patterns to which adult communications tend to conform, and those patterns became our

prototypical model for assessing children's communication skills.

The communication task involved a speaker and a listener separated by an opaque barrier. In the adult version the speaker had in front of him a page showing a set of designs numbered in order from one through six. The listener had in front of him the same designs, arranged differently on the page and not numbered. The task called for the speaker to describe each design and give its number so that the listener could identify his copies and number them correspondingly. The measure of the accuracy of communication was the extent to which the listener's set was correctly numbered; one measure of the efficiency of the communication was the number of words required by the speaker and listener to accomplish the task.

What made the task more than trivial was that the designs were deliberately constructed so as not to have either short or familiar "names." The six forms are easy to distinguish from one another, but they do not evoke simple and unequivocal descriptions. Adults nonetheless found the task trivially easy, whether they were college sophomores practiced in the ways of psychological experiments or raw Army recruits. Even with no feedback, or knowledge of the results, provided by the experimenter, pairs of adults made virtually no errors on their very first try.

In addition to accuracy the adult performance was characterized by the development of an efficient social (in con-

directions in an offhand manner by a person who appears to be a native, people answer briefly and directly (a). When the questioner announces himself as being—or when he appears to be—from out of town, however, people answer at length and give explicit detail (b).

It's like a spaceman's helmet; its got two things....

ADULT COMMUNICATION TASK required a speaker (*left*) to describe six odd designs on a sheet of paper in front of him and give the number associated with each; a listener (*right*) on the other side of an opaque barrier had to assign the correct number to copies of same designs.

FORM	INITIAL DESCRIPTION	SHORTER VERSION	SHORTEST VERSION
1	Looks like a motor from a motorboat. It has a thing hanging down with two teeth.	Motorboat with teeth.	Motorboat.
2	It looks like two worms or snakes looking at each other. The bottom part looks like the rocker from a rocking chair.	Two worms looking at each other.	Two worms.
3	It's a zigzag with lines going in all different directions.	The zigzag with lines.	Zigzag.
4	It's like a spaceman's helmet; it's got two things going up the sides.	The spaceman's helmet.	Helmet.
5	This one looks something like a horse's head.	The horse's head.	The horse.
6	It's an upside-down cup. It's got two triangles, one on top of the other.	An upside-down cup.	The cup.

ADULT SPEAKERS communicated successfully by giving detailed descriptions the first time a design was encountered, taking into consideration the listener's difficulty in identifying the unfamiliar forms. When the same form appeared in successive trials, speakers shortened their descriptions, as shown by these examples, and continued to be well understood by listeners.

trast to a linguistic) code, much as rock musicians or molecular biologists develop their own specialized jargon. At the beginning of the communicative interaction the speaker's language was detailed, redundant, even prolix. For example, the first time one adult speaker talked about a certain form he described it in nine words; he required fewer words when the same pattern showed up in a subsequent trial, and by the fourth trial he had settled on one word to get his message across. The original descriptive phrase was always an effective reference: on hearing it other people could accurately select the intended referent. The short final message, on the other hand, was adequate only for those listeners who had earlier heard the redundant original message; it did not usually communicate much to someone who had not participated in the social interaction from the beginning.

With these two characteristics—the accuracy and the social-language development—of adult pair communication in mind we set out to see what young children would do in a comparable task in the form of a stack-the-blocks game. The speaker has before him a peg and a dispenser, with a transparent front, holding six blocks; each block has a hole through it and is labeled with an identifying design. The listener has another peg and has duplicates of the six blocks placed randomly on his table. The speaker must take one block at a time from the base of his dispenser, put it on the peg and tell his partner which block to stack on his own peg. This continues until all six blocks have been stacked on both the speaker's and the listener's pegs.

We began with nursery-school children. First we made sure that they could play the game when each block depicted a familiar animal or household object instead of the strange, hard-to-describe designs that had been presented to the adults. Then we substituted blocks with the strange designs on them. An experimenter acted as the speaker and described the designs as they had been described by an adult in the original experiment. When one typical set of initial descriptions [*see bottom illustration at left*] was read off to children from 52 to 63 months old, none of the children made any errors. They continued to perform accurately even when, in subsequent trials, the messages were shortened systematically as they had been in the adult interactions from which they were taken.

When young children played the game with each other, however, not one of the six pairs of children we tested could complete a single errorless trial, even when we pointed out the errors they had made after each trial. Unlike adults, these young speakers used short and idiosyncratic messages at the outset; rarely if ever did they begin with an elaborate and redundant message. There was a notable lack of communality of description among the various speakers as well as a lack of obvious relation between reference and referent. Given such meager and idiosyncratic descriptions it is not surprising that the young listeners could not select the right blocks. Indeed, we wondered whether or not the speakers themselves knew what they were talking about. Did they assign those names blindly and randomly or did they do so in ways that were somehow meaningful, if only to themselves?

One indication that the messages were not random was the very consistency of the naming. Once a child had assigned a name to a referent, he virtually never changed it during the course of the game. Would a young speaker understand his own names, however, if he were put in the role of a listener? We looked into that by reversing roles, putting the erstwhile speaker in the role of the listener, with an experimenter in the role of the speaker. The experimenter-speaker instructed the child, identifying each form with the same name the child had previously provided. To our surprise none of the five children we tested made any errors, either during the first session in which they had generated the name or after a three-week period during which there was no intervening practice or study. Clearly a speaker's own descriptions were meaningful to him—but not to anyone else, because these young children had not yet learned how to use their language to develop a socially shared and mutually comprehensible code.

How long does it take before children reach adult levels of competence in this task? In our first attempt to trace development toward adult competence Hugh O'Brien, who was then an undergraduate at Princeton University, tested matched-age pairs of children from kindergarten through fifth grade on the same problem we had given the nursery-school children. Each pair of children played the game for eight successive blocks of two trials each.

The results were somewhat surprising. Kindergartners performed no better than nursery-school children and displayed the same lack of improvement with practice. Considering that adults make virtually no errors on the very first trial, the performance of children in the first, third and fifth grades is even more surprising: they were no better than kindergartners on the first trial. The older children did show marked improvement with practice, but it seemed clear that even the fifth-graders (who were about 10 years old) did not approach the adult level. This finding is all the more striking because the children were given full information about their performance after each trial, whereas the adults had

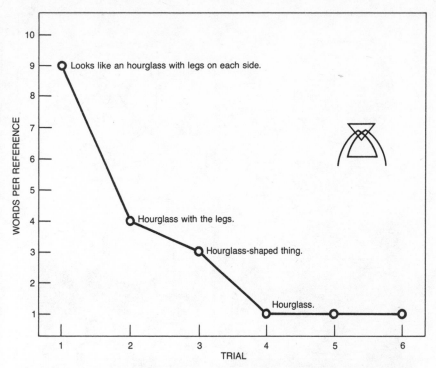

PROCESS OF SHORTENING referred to in the preceding illustration, in effect the tacit development of a two-person social code, is illustrated for one speaker's description of one form.

been given none at all. How well would older children do under the no-feedback conditions?

We proceeded to test children from grades three through nine in the Princeton school system on the block-stacking version of the task, but without giving them any information about how they were doing. We were again surprised at the generally low level of performance. Ten pairs of children in each of the four grades were tested. The proportion of pairs performing perfectly on the first three trials ranged from about 25 to 42 percent [see bottom illustration on page 259]. The third-graders did not improve at all over the course of 15 trials, and the fifth- and seventh-graders improved very little. Ninth-graders, although they showed dramatic improvement in successive trials, still did not attain the virtually perfect accuracy that adults display from the very first trial.

What factors might account for the remarkably inept performance of our youngest subjects and for the older children's surprisingly slow attainment of adult competence? When we first began working with very young children, we concluded somewhat naïvely that the primary factor accounting for communicative failures in our experimental situation was "childhood egocentrism," a term coined by the Swiss developmental psychologist Jean Piaget to describe the thought and speech typical of an early stage of cognitive development. In its simplest terms egocentric behavior is characterized by the inability to detach oneself from one's own point of view

and take into account the perspective of someone else. It is as though the egocentric child thought that others know precisely what he himself knows and believe what he himself believes—in short, that others are just like himself. Clearly egocentrism must be a matter of degree; by the age of two most children are aware that adults are more knowledgeable, more skillful and unquestionably more powerful. We thought, however, that young children may fail to appreciate that someone else may not be more knowledgeable, may indeed not know something they themselves know, and that what is apparent and perceptible to themselves may not be so obvious to someone else.

In this sense the messages generated by our youngest subjects could aptly be described as egocentric. They are meaningful to the speaker who generated them but cannot be understood by anyone who does not share the particular perspective of the speaker. We observed a particularly striking example of this kind of interaction in a session with a pair of four-year-olds:

Speaker (referring to one of the geometric figures): "It's a bird."

Listener: "Is this it?"

Speaker: "No."

Neither child could actually see the other child or the other child's stimulus materials, but their interaction gives no evidence of that fact.

Tempting as such an explanation for the poor performance of young children may be, it is unsatisfactory for a number of reasons. First, numerous attempts to find correlations between standard mea-

Daddy's shirt....

CHILDREN'S VERSION required the speaker to describe the design on blocks appearing at the base of a dispenser and then to stack the blocks on a peg. The listener's task was to select the correct blocks from a randomly ordered collection and stack them in the same order. The youngest speakers gave noncommunicative descriptions that were usually misunderstood.

FORM	CHILD				
	1	2	3	4	5
1	Man's legs	Airplane	Drapeholder	Zebra	Flying saucer
2	Mother's hat	Ring	Keyhold	Lion	Snake
3	Somebody running	Eagle	Throwing sticks	Strip-stripe	Wire
4	Daddy's shirt	Milk jug	Shoe hold	Coffeepot	Dog
5	Another Daddy's shirt	Bird	Dress hold	Dress	Knife
6	Mother's dress	Ideal	Digger hold	Caterpillar	Ghost

TYPICAL INITIAL DESCRIPTIONS offered by five nursery-school speakers for each of the forms are shown here. Unlike adult descriptions, they were brief and highly idiosyncratic.

sures of egocentrism and performance in communication tasks have failed to produce convincing results. Second, by the age of eight most children should be beyond the point where egocentrism is an important factor in their behavior, and yet 13- and 14-year-olds did not perform with adult competence in our task. Although egocentrism may contribute to the poor performance of younger children, it cannot account for the overall pattern of performance we have observed. And in any case egocentrism is essentially a descriptive notion: it characterizes certain kinds of behavior but does not tell why they are displayed.

How, then, is one to explain the differences in communication performance that we find among children of different ages and between children and adults? Do children truly lack the capacity to role-play (to temporarily assume another person's perspective), which seems to be required for effective performance in any but the most routine and stereotyped communication situations? Or is it rather that children—even four-year-olds—have the ability to role-play but for one reason or another do not deploy the ability in certain experimental contexts? Perhaps these children have yet to learn under what circumstances role-playing is particularly important for effective communication. Or perhaps they fail to do so when the task is overly demanding cognitively, that is, when it overloads their information-processing capacity.

Recent work in our own laboratories and in those of other investigators seems to strongly implicate the latter possibility. As we simplify the communication task, and thereby reduce the sheer cognitive load the child must deal with, the performance of even very young children begins to approach the adult level of competence. This suggests that the poor performance of children in particular communication situations may stem from something other than a generalized inability to take into account the perspective of another person. When the demands of the task are relatively light, children do engage in social, nonegocentric speech, and they communicate rather successfully. As the demands become heavier children may still attempt to employ social-communication strategies, but they do so less effectively than adults. Finally, when the demands of the task become heavy enough, children may not have the opportunity to bring into play the social-communication skills they possess.

If this seems strange, it is well to keep in mind that even mature and articulate adults can find themselves in situations where they fail to take another person's knowledge and perspective into account. Consider the American tourist in a foreign country who asks, "Where is

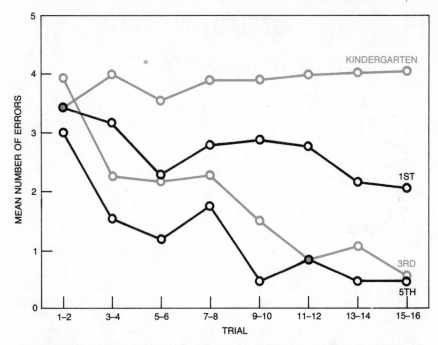

ELEMENTARY-SCHOOL CHILDREN performed badly on their initial trials. Kindergartners did not improve with practice. Children in the first, third and fifth grades did improve, with the help of comments from the experimenter pointing out the mistakes they had been making.

the men's room?" and, on receiving no answer because his informant speaks no English, proceeds to shout, "Men's room, toilet, where?" Such an adult is not very different from the child who tries to communicate an unfamiliar geometric form by calling it "Daddy's shirt." Both the tourist and the child are ordinarily able to distinguish social from nonsocial speech and to communicate socially, and yet both may find themselves so overwhelmed by the demands of the particular situation that they do not bring that ability into play.

What we see developing so slowly in our studies of children's communication is a constellation of knowledge and skills that reflects the child's interaction with the world and with other people and cultures. The social use of language depends as much on that knowledge as it does on knowledge of language itself.

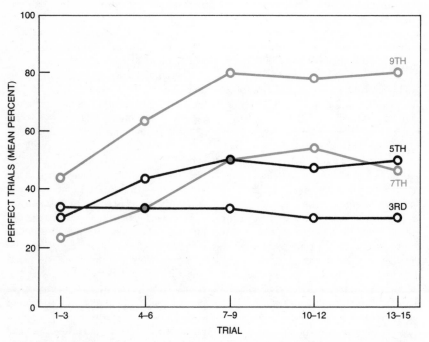

OLDER CHILDREN, tested on the block version but without feedback from experimenters, did not match adult performance. Only the ninth-graders showed significant improvement.

27

The Role of Pupil Size in Communication ·

by Eckhard H. Hess
November 1975

Changes in attitude can be detected by measuring changes in pupil size. It now appears that enlarged or constricted pupils can also affect the attitude and responses of the person who observes them

When we say that someone's eyes are soft, hard, beady, cold or warm, we are in most instances referring only to a certain aspect of that person's eyes: the size of the pupils. The commonplace idea that the eyes can express emotion has been confirmed by experiment. Ten years ago I described in these pages how the viewing of a pleasing image is accompanied by a measurable dilation of the viewer's pupils, and how in general changes in pupil size are objectively correlated with emotions and mental activity [see "Attitude and Pupil Size," by Eckhard H. Hess; Scientific American; Offprint 493]. More recently I have been interested in another aspect of changes in pupil size: the role of such changes in nonverbal communication. I have found that pupil size serves as a signal between individuals, usually at an unconscious level. It is obvious that the eyes play many roles in nonverbal communication, as when someone averts his eyes in talking with someone else. Here, however, I am referring only to the role of the pupil.

The changes in emotions and mental activity revealed by changes in pupil size are clearly associated with changes in attitude. Accordingly the measurement of changes in pupil size, which I have named pupillometrics, has become a useful tool in the study of attitudinal change. In my laboratory at the University of Chicago changes in pupil size are measured while the subject views slides projected on a screen. In order to adapt the subject's eyes to the brightness of the stimulus slide, he is first shown a control slide that has the same average brightness as the stimulus slide that is to follow. The subject views the control slide for 10 seconds and then the stimulus slide for 10 seconds. The difference between the average size of the pupil when

the subject is viewing the control slide and its average size when he is viewing the stimulus slide is recorded as the pupil response. One of our methods for measuring pupil size is to photograph the subject's eye during the experiment with a motion-picture camera. Later the film is projected on a screen and the pupil size is measured with a millimeter scale. We have also been using an electronic pupillometer that scans the eye and automatically measures the diameter of the pupil while the experiment is in progress.

The usefulness of pupillometrics in the study of attitudinal change has recently been further validated by the results of a study in my laboratory by Paul W. Beaver. He presented color slides of several kinds of food to 20 people who had missed their previous lunch or dinner and who had not eaten at all for the past five to eight hours. Another group of 20 subjects who had eaten lunch or dinner two hours before were also shown the slides. When the pupil responses of the viewers were measured, it was found that the increase in pupil diameter among the hungry subjects was greater than that among the sated subjects. In fact, in some instances the sated subjects showed a constriction of the pupil. The results demonstrate that even a temporary change in attitude can be detected by measuring pupil response.

Our studies of the pupil as an indicator of attitude led us to consider the possibility that one person uses another person's pupil size as a source of information about that person's feelings or attitudes. In one experiment I showed two photographs of an attractive young woman to a group of men. The photographs were identical except that in one the woman's pupils had been retouched

to make them larger and in the other they had been retouched to make them smaller. None of the men reported noticing the difference in pupil size, but when they were asked to describe the woman, they said that the woman in the picture with the large pupils was "soft," "more feminine" or "pretty." The same woman in the picture with the small pupils was described as being "hard," "selfish" or "cold." There could be little doubt that the large pupils made the woman more attractive to the men.

Women used to put the drug belladonna, meaning "beautiful lady," into their eyes because they thought it made them more beautiful. The active principle of belladonna is atropine, which causes the pupils to dilate. Indeed, an eyewash preparation containing atropine was popular among women not many years ago, until the U.S. Food and Drug Administration put a stop to its sale.

Where did the notion that larger pupils make a woman look more attractive come from? It would be easy to dismiss it as mere folklore, but it clearly has a basis in reality. For one thing, younger people have larger pupils than older people, so that large pupils are associated with an obvious constituent of physical attractiveness. What is really appealing about large pupils in a woman, however, is that they are an indicator of interest, which can be interpreted as sexual interest. Moreover, when men view a picture of a woman with large pupils, their own pupils dilate. In other words, seeing large pupils gives rise to larger pupils.

The pupil responses of men and women, all stably married and presumably heterosexual, were investigated by Thomas M. Simms, who was then working at the University of Toronto. The subjects were shown two pictures of a man, one with large pupils and the other

PHOTOGRAPHS OF TWO WOMEN were retouched so that each woman had large pupils in one photograph and small pupils in the other. Male subjects were shown eight different pairs of the photographs: all the possible combinations of the two women. As subjects viewed each pair they were asked in which of the two pictures did the woman appear to be more sympathetic, more selfish, happier, angrier, warmer, sadder, more attractive, more unfriendly and so on. When the question concerned a positive attribute, male subjects tended to choose the photograph of the woman with the large pupils. When the question concerned a negative attribute, they tended to choose the photograph of the woman with the small pupils. Neither woman, however, was consistently chosen as being the more attractive or the more unfriendly. The selection in most instances appeared to be made unconsciously on basis of pupil size.

with small pupils. They were also shown two pictures of a woman, one with large pupils and the other with small pupils. The pupils of the male subjects dilated the most when they viewed the picture of the woman with the large pupils. Similarly, the pupils of the women dilated the most when they viewed the picture of the man with large pupils. With both men and women the dilation in response to the picture of a person of the opposite sex with small pupils was much less.

Even more interesting were the pupil responses of the men and women to the pictures of the person of their own sex. The men showed almost no increase in pupil size as they viewed either picture of the man. The women, on the other hand, showed a smaller pupil response to the picture of the woman with the large pupils than they did to the picture of the woman with the small pupils. This finding is supported by the results of another study carried out by Robert A. Hicks, Tom Reaney and Lynn Hill of California State University at San Jose. In interviews with a group of women they found that the women preferred a picture of a woman who had small pupils to a picture of the same woman with large pupils. These findings suggest that women's magazines will not increase their newsstand sales by printing pictures of women with large pupils on the cover.

Additional evidence comes from a study conducted by John W. Stass and Frank N. Willis, Jr., of the University of Missouri at Kansas City. They introduced a subject to two individuals of the opposite sex and asked the subject to select one of them as a partner for an ex-periment. One of the proposed partners had been given eye drops to dilate his pupils; the other had not. Both men and women tended to choose the person with the large pupils. Stass and Willis also observed that eye contact—a direct exchange of gazes—during the introduction was a factor that increased the likelihood that the individual with the large pupils would be chosen. Most of the subjects were not able, however, to say whether they had used the large pupils or the eye contact as the basis for choosing their partner.

A study of men who identified themselves as homosexuals, conducted by Simms at the University of Toronto, further confirms the effect of pupil size in sexual communication. Simms found that male homosexuals distinctly prefer a picture of a woman with constricted pupils to a picture of the same woman with dilated pupils. Apparently the signal of sexual interest that is transmitted by the dilated pupils of a woman does not appeal to male homosexuals.

Another interesting finding by Simms is that heterosexual "Don Juans," men who identified themselves as being more interested in having sexual relations with many women than in forming a lasting relationship with one woman, have the same pupil response to pictures of women with large and small pupils that male homosexuals do. This finding suggests that such men also have an aversion to women whose pupils indicate sexual interest.

In the experiments I have been describing the test pictures were retouched photographs of a complete face. I set out to examine whether or not similar responses might be elicited by a purely schematic pair of eyes. Because of my interest in ethology, the study of the biological basis of behavior, I wondered if large pupils might not act as a "releaser." Ethologists have shown that a small portion of an animal may in itself be sufficient to release a specific pattern of behavior in another animal. For example, a robin will usually attack another robin that intrudes on its territory. David Lack of the University of Oxford found that a robin will also attack a single red feather that is put in an upright position in some strategic place such as a tree limb. The feather, which apparently symbolizes the red breast of a robin, releases the attack behavior of another robin. Could the size of the pupils release a pattern of behavior that is innate or perhaps learned very early in life?

I drew three kinds of schematic eyes that consisted simply of a circle with a

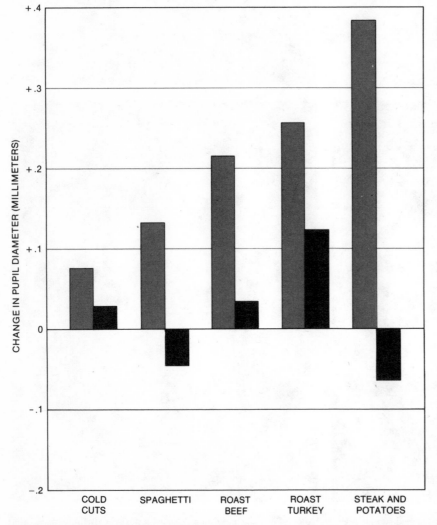

DIFFERENCES IN PUPIL RESPONSE of hungry subjects (*gray bars*) and of sated subjects (*black bars*) to color slides of various foods are shown. The subjects first viewed a control slide, then a slide of a food, and the change in pupil size was measured. The hungry subjects had not eaten at all for from five to eight hours. The sated subjects had eaten a meal two hours before. All the food slides produced dilation of the pupils in hungry subjects, whereas in two instances the slides produced a constriction of the pupils in the sated subjects. The results indicate the pupil response can be a valid measure of attitude change.

round black area in its center. One set of schematic eyes had small pupils, a second set had medium-sized pupils and the third set had large pupils. I prepared slides that displayed each size of pupil first as a single eye, then as a pair of eyes and finally as three eyes. In the slide showing a pair of eyes the two circles were slightly separated so that they would resemble a pair of eyes in a face. In the slide showing three eyes the spacing of the circles was the same as that of the two eyes of the pair.

I showed the schematic eyes to a group of subjects and observed how they responded in terms of their own pupil size. The responses to the single eye and the triple eye did not vary systematically in relation to the size of the schematic pupils. When I displayed the paired eyes, however, there was a significant

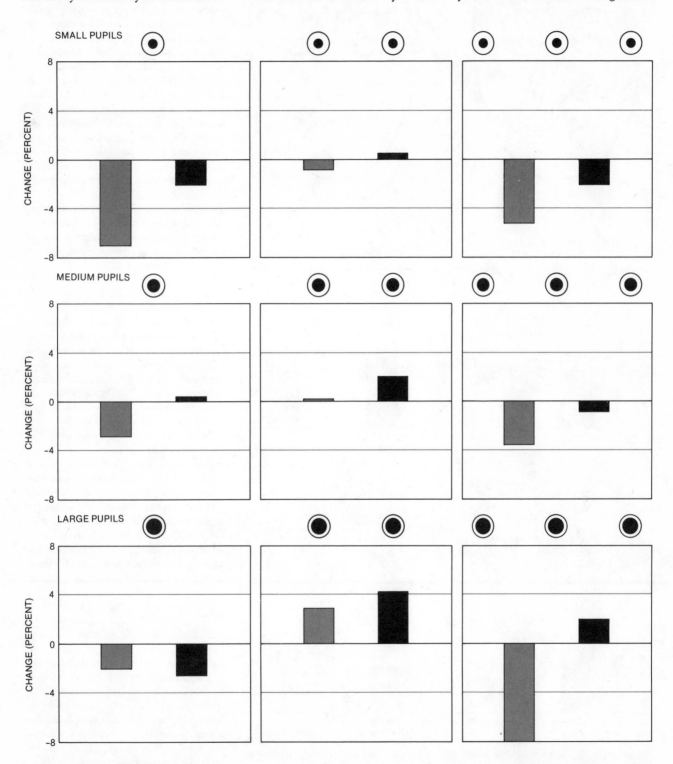

SCHEMATIC EYES with small, medium and large pupils were tested to determine their effect on the pupil size of subjects who viewed them. The pupil responses of men (*gray bars*) and women (*black bars*) to the single eye and the triple eyes did not vary systematically in relation to the size of the pupil in the schematic eyes. The paired schematic eyes, however, produced a significant change in the size of the subjects' pupils. The paired eyes with the largest pupils caused the largest dilation. The finding that schematic eyes with large pupils will cause dilation suggests that observing large pupils releases a pattern of behavior that may be innate.

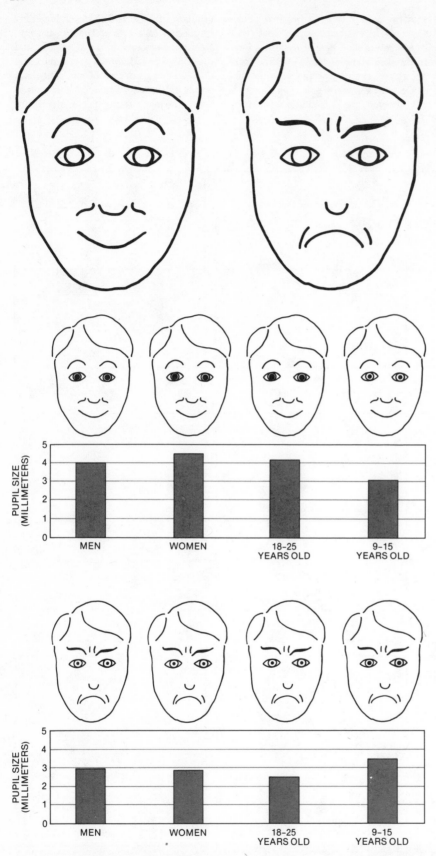

DRAWINGS OF TWO FACES WITHOUT PUPILS were given to subjects who were asked to draw in the size of pupil that best fits the face. One face was smiling and the other was scowling. Men and women drew larger pupils on the happy face than on the scowling face, and so did a group of college students ranging in age from 18 to 25 years. Younger people between the ages of nine and 15 tended to draw pupils of about the same size on both faces, which indicates that they do not attribute different meanings to pupils of different sizes.

change in the dilation of the subjects' pupils. The paired schematic eyes that had the largest pupils caused the viewers' pupils to dilate much more than paired schematic eyes with smaller pupils did. In female subjects the dilation of the pupils was greater than that in male subjects. The fact that even a pair of schematic eyes will give rise to a dilation of the pupils strongly suggests that the dilation response is innate and not learned.

Similar results were obtained in an experiment with schematic eyes by Richard G. Coss of the University of California at Los Angeles. He, however, got a smaller pupil-dilation response to the paired schematic eyes than I did, possibly because he had placed the schematic eyes so close together that they did not resemble a pair of eyes in a face.

In children the absolute—not relative— size of the pupils is larger than it is in adults. Whatever other reasons there are for this difference, having large pupils is probably advantageous to a child in that it makes him more appealing to the adults who take care of him. Very young children have other features that may release the caring response in adults. An infant's head is large in proportion to his body. His eyes are large and are located below the middle of his face. His limbs are short and fat. The "lovable" cartoon characters created by Walt Disney and other artists tend strongly to have these babyish features and large pupils.

While studying the behavior of infants Janet Bare Ashear of the University of Chicago noticed that she seemed to elicit more smiles from infants than some of her fellow workers did. It turned out that in average room lighting her pupils were larger than those of most other people. To find out if large pupils in an adult do affect the smiling behavior of infants, she arranged to visit 16 infants in their homes. The infants were between three months and three and a half months old, an age when they smile at adults and have not yet developed a fear of strangers. Ashear made two visits to each home, and on each visit she interacted with the infant, talking and smiling, and recorded the number of times the infant smiled. On one of her visits she had her pupils artificially dilated with the drug phenylephrine hydrochloride. On the other visit her pupils had been artificially constricted with another drug, pilocarpine hydrochloride.

The infants smiled more often when Ashear's pupils were dilated than they did when her pupils were constricted. Although the experiment was only a pilot study and was obviously open to experimenter bias, the results nonetheless suggest that in infants the positive response to large pupils may not be learned but is part of the infants' perceptual development. Perhaps large pupils act as a releaser in infants as well as in adults.

An unexpected result of Ashear's pilot study was the reactions of the mothers. When the experimenter's pupils were constricted, the mothers said that she appeared to be "harsh," "hard," "brassy," "cold," "evasive" and "sneaky." One of the mothers said that Ashear appeared to be trying to hide something from her. When Ashear came with dilated pupils, she was described as being "naïve," "young," "open," "soft" and "gentle."

Children's books sometimes have illustrations that make use of different pupil sizes to depict good and bad characters. One finds that the "wicked witch" has tiny pupils and the "beautiful princess" very large pupils. There is an interesting difference between older books for children and more recent ones. Many of the older books have illustrations in which the pupils of the characters are rendered in various sizes; many of the newer books have illustrations in which the pupils of the characters are the same size.

I have conducted an experiment with drawings of faces that have no pupils. The faces were drawn about three-fourths the size of an average adult face. One face was smiling and the other was scowling. When I gave these faces to 10 men and 10 women and asked them to "draw in the size of pupils that you think best fits the face," I found that 15 of 20 subjects drew larger pupils on the happy face than on the scowling face [see illustration on preceding page].

I also had students in several of my classes draw pupils on the same two faces. The results were unequivocal: 47 of 50 students drew larger pupils on the happy face than they did on the scowling one. When I tested a group of younger people, between the ages of nine and 15, I found that they tended to draw the pupils on both faces the same size; in fact, the pupils on the scowling face were on the average slightly larger.

One of my students, James Dickson McLean, investigated the response of individuals ranging in age from six to 22 to drawings of faces that had pupils of different sizes. In one experiment the subjects were asked to choose the "happier" of two female faces. One face had large pupils and the other had small ones. McLean found that up to the age of 14 a person does not necessarily perceive larger pupils as being happier than smaller pupils. His finding agrees with the results I obtained in my study of youngsters between the ages of nine and 15. McLean concluded that the turning point for attributing different meanings to pupils of different sizes comes at about the age of 14. It may be, however, that the answers given by children reflect not their actual perception but their understanding of the question (or lack of understanding). By testing the pupil responses of children to pictures of faces with large pupils and small pupils, we

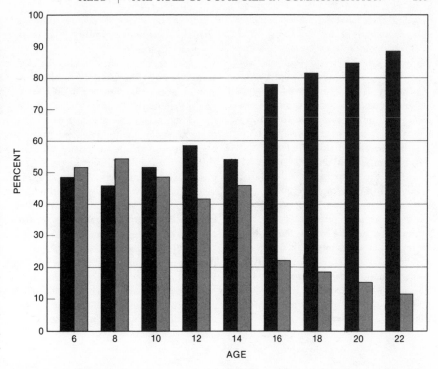

AGE DIFFERENCES in perceiving a face with large pupils as being happier than a face with small pupils were found in study of individuals ranging in age from six to 22. The subjects were shown drawings of two faces and were asked to choose the happier one. Subjects up to the age of 14 were just as likely to choose the face with the small pupils (*gray bars*) as the one with the large pupils (*black bars*). Subjects who were 16 years of age or older, however, strongly tended to choose the face with the larger pupils as being the happier one.

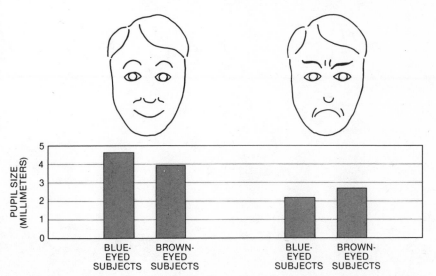

BLUE-EYED SUBJECTS drew larger pupils on a sketch of a happy face and smaller pupils on a scowling face than brown-eyed subjects. In addition, when viewing a picture that normally causes dilation or constriction, blue-eyed people show a greater change in pupil size.

may find they have the same dilation responses that adults do.

Of particular interest was another finding by McLean: blue-eyed subjects were more likely to judge large pupils as being happy than brown-eyed subjects. When we asked another group of subjects to fill in the pupils on drawings of happy faces and angry ones, we found that the blue-eyed subjects drew larger "happy" pupils and smaller "angry" pupils than the brown-eyed subjects [see bottom illustration on page 265].
We also found that blue-eyed people have a stronger pupil response than brown-eyed people when they view a picture that causes pupil dilation or constriction. To be more precise, with respect to the total range of response from the smallest pupil size to the largest the range is greater for blue-eyed people than it is for brown-eyed people. (This

statement applies, of course, only to changes in pupil size resulting from emotions or attitudes.)

I shall conclude with the results of a study we have just completed. We took two identical photographs of a woman and in one made the pupils large and in the other made the pupils small. The same was done with a second pair of photographs of another woman. We showed these photographs in pairs to a group of male subjects. As the subjects viewed each pair they were asked which of the two women was more attractive, more selfish, happier, more unfriendly and so on. The subjects were shown eight different pairs of photographs, that is, all the possible combinations of the two women.

Neither woman was consistently chosen as being the more attractive or the more selfish or whatever. The subjects,

however, strongly tended to choose the photograph with the large pupils when the question concerned a positive attribute. When the question concerned a negative attribute, the subjects tended to choose the photograph with the small pupils. The tendency to associate positive attributes with large pupils and negative attributes with small pupils was stronger in blue-eyed subjects than in brown-eyed subjects.

Why do blue-eyed people respond more to large and small pupils than brown-eyed people? It is of course easier to see a pupil surrounded by a blue iris than it is to see one surrounded by a brown iris. Perhaps it is not unwarranted to assume that the response has been favored by evolutionary selection more in blue-eyed people than in brown-eyed people.

Cognitive Dissonance

by Leon Festinger
October 1962

*It is the subject of a new theory based on experiments
showing that the grass is usually not greener on the
other side of the fence and that grapes are sourest
when they are in easy reach*

There is an experiment in psychology that you can perform easily in your own home if you have a child three or four years old. Buy two toys that you are fairly sure will be equally attractive to the child. Show them both to him and say: "Here are two nice toys. This one is for you to keep. The other I must give back to the store." You then hand the child the toy that is his to keep and ask: "Which of the two toys do you like better?" Studies have shown that in such a situation most children will tell you they prefer the toy they are to keep.

This response of children seems to conflict with the old saying that the grass is always greener on the other side of the fence. Do adults respond in the same way under similar circumstances or does the adage indeed become true as we grow older? The question is of considerable interest because the adult world is filled with choices and alternative courses of action that are often about equally attractive. When they make a choice of a college or a car or a spouse or a home or a political candidate, do most people remain satisfied with their choice or do they tend to wish they had made a different one? Naturally any choice may turn out to be a bad one on the basis of some objective measurement, but the question is: Does some psychological process come into play immediately after the making of a choice that colors one's attitude, either favorably or unfavorably, toward the decision?

To illuminate this question there is another experiment one can do at home, this time using an adult as a subject rather than a child. Buy two presents for your wife, again choosing things you are reasonably sure she will find about equally attractive. Find some plausible excuse for having both of them in your possession, show them to your wife and ask her to tell you how attractive each one is to her. After you have obtained a good measurement of attractiveness, tell her that she can have one of them, whichever she chooses. The other you will return to the store. After she has made her choice, ask her once more to evaluate the attractiveness of each of them. If you compare the evaluations of attractiveness before and after the choice, you will probably find that the chosen present has increased in attractiveness and the rejected one decreased.

Such behavior can be explained by a new theory concerning "cognitive dissonance." This theory centers around the idea that if a person knows various things that are not psychologically consistent with one another, he will, in a variety of ways, try to make them more consistent. Two items of information that psychologically do not fit together are said to be in a dissonant relation to each other. The items of information may be about behavior, feelings, opinions, things in the environment and so on. The word "cognitive" simply emphasizes that the theory deals with relations among items of information.

Such items can of course be changed. A person can change his opinion; he can change his behavior, thereby changing the information he has about it; he can even distort his perception and his information about the world around him. Changes in items of information that produce or restore consistency are referred to as dissonance-reducing changes.

Cognitive dissonance is a motivating state of affairs. Just as hunger impels a person to eat, so does dissonance impel a person to change his opinions or his behavior. The world, however, is much

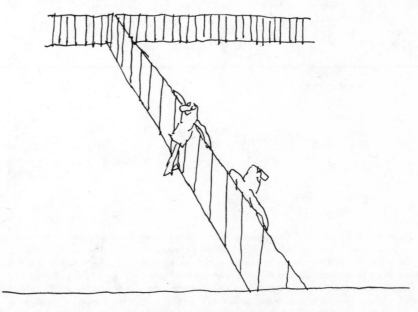

The grass is not always greener on the other side of the fence

Consequences of making a decision between two reasonably attractive alternatives

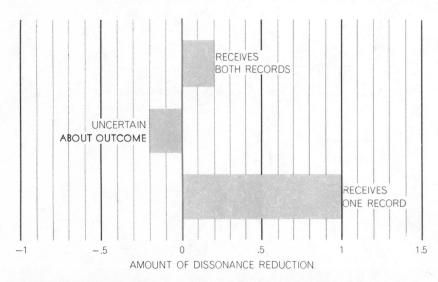

AMOUNT OF DISSONANCE REDUCTION

DISSONANCE REDUCTION is a psychological phenomenon found to occur after a person has made a choice between two approximately equal alternatives. The effect of the phenomenon is to enhance the attractiveness of the chosen object or chosen course of action. The chart summarizes the results of an experiment in which high school girls rated the attractiveness of 12 "hit" records before and after choosing one of them as a gift. Substantial dissonance reduction occurred under only one of three experimental conditions described in the text. Under two other conditions no systematic reduction was observed.

more effectively arranged for hunger reduction than it is for dissonance reduction. It is almost always possible to find something to eat. It is not always easy to reduce dissonance. Sometimes it may be very difficult or even impossible to change behavior or opinions that are involved in dissonant relations. Consequently there are circumstances in which appreciable dissonance may persist for long periods.

To understand cognitive dissonance as a motivating state, it is necessary to have a clearer conception of the conditions that produce it. The simplest definition of dissonance can, perhaps, be given in terms of a person's expectations. In the course of our lives we have all accumulated a large number of expectations about what things go together and what things do not. When such an expectation is not fulfilled, dissonance occurs.

For example, a person standing unprotected in the rain would expect to get wet. If he found himself in the rain and he was not getting wet, there would exist dissonance between these two pieces of information. This unlikely example is one where the expectations of different people would all be uniform. There are obviously many instances where different people would not share the same expectations. Someone who is very self-confident might expect to succeed at whatever he tried, whereas someone who had a low opinion of himself might normally expect to fail. Under these circumstances what would produce dissonance for one person might produce consonance for another. In experimental investigations, of course, an effort is made to provide situations in which expectations are rather uniform.

Perhaps the best way to explain the theory of cognitive dissonance is to show its application to specific situations. The rest of this article, therefore, will be devoted to a discussion of three examples of cognitive dissonance. I shall discuss the effects of making a decision, of lying and of temptation. These three examples by no means cover all the situations in which dissonance can be created. Indeed, it seldom happens that everything a person knows about an action he has taken is perfectly consistent with his having taken it. The three examples, however, may serve to illustrate the range of situations in which dissonance can be expected to occur. They will also serve to show the kinds of dissonance-reduction effects that are obtained under a special circumstance: when dissonance involves the person's behavior and the action in question is difficult to change.

Let us consider first the consequences of making a decision. Imagine the situation of a person who has carefully weighed two reasonably attractive alternatives and then chosen one of them— a decision that, for our purposes, can be regarded as irrevocable. All the information this person has concerning the attractive features of the rejected alternative (and the possible unattractive features of the chosen alternative) are now inconsistent, or dissonant, with the knowledge that he has made the given choice. It is true that the person also knows many things that are consistent or consonant with the choice he has made, which is to say all the attractive features of the chosen alternative and unattractive features of the rejected one. Nevertheless, some dissonance exists and after the decision the individual will try to reduce the dissonance.

There are two major ways in which the individual can reduce dissonance in this situation. He can persuade himself that the attractive features of the rejected alternative are not really so attractive as he had originally thought, and that the unattractive features of the chosen alternative are not really unattractive. He can also provide additional justification for his choice by exaggerating the attractive features of the chosen alternative and the unattractive features of the rejected alternative. In other words, according to the theory the process of dissonance reduction should lead, after the decision, to an increase in the desirability of the chosen alternative and a decrease in the desirability of the rejected alternative.

This phenomenon has been demonstrated in a variety of experiments. A brief description of one of these will suffice to illustrate the precise nature of the effect. In an experiment performed by Jon Jecker of Stanford University, high school girls were asked to rate the attractiveness of each of 12 "hit" records. For each girl two records that she had rated as being only moderately attractive were selected and she was asked which of the two she would like as a gift. After having made her choice, the girl again rated the attractiveness of all the records. The dissonance created by the decision could be reduced by increasing the attractiveness of the chosen record and decreasing the attractiveness of the rejected record. Consequently a measurement of dissonance reduction could be obtained by summing both of these kinds of changes in ratings made before and after the decision.

Different experimental variations were employed in this experiment in order to examine the dynamics of the process of dissonance reduction. Let us look at three of these experimental variations. In all three conditions the girls, when they were making their choice, were given to understand there was a slight possibility that they might actually be given both records. In one condition they were asked to rerate the

records after they had made their choice but before they knew definitely whether they would receive both records or only the one they chose. The results for this condition should indicate whether dissonance reduction begins with having made the choice or whether it is suspended until the uncertainty is resolved. In a second condition the girls were actually given both records after their choice and were then asked to rerate

Further consequences of making a difficult decision

all the records. Since they had received both records and therefore no dissonance existed following the decision, there should be no evidence of dissonance reduction in this condition. In a third condition the girls were given only the record they chose and were then asked to do the rerating. This, of course, resembles the normal outcome of a decision and the usual dissonance reduction should occur.

The chart on page 268 shows the results for these three conditions. When the girls are uncertain as to the outcome, or when they receive both records, there is no dissonance reduction—that is, no systematic change in attractiveness of the chosen and rejected records. The results in both conditions are very close to zero—one slightly positive, the other slightly negative. When they receive only the record they chose, however, there is a large systematic change in rating to reduce dissonance Since dissonance reduction is only observed in this last experimental condition, it is evident that dissonance reduction does not occur during the process of making

a decision but only after the decision is made and the outcome is clear.

Let us turn now to the consequences of lying. There are many circumstances in which, for one reason or another, an individual publicly states something that is at variance with his private belief. Here again one can expect dissonance to arise. There is an inconsistency between knowing that one really believes one thing and knowing that one has publicly stated something quite different. Again, to be sure, the individual knows things that are consonant with his overt, public behavior. All the reasons that induced him to make the public statement are consonant with his having made it and provide him with some justification for his behavior. Nevertheless, some dissonance exists and, according to the theory, there will be attempts to reduce it. The degree to which the dissonance is bothersome for the individual will depend on two things. The more deviant his public statement is from his private belief, the greater will be the dissonance. The greater the amount of justification the person has for having made the public statement, the less bothersome the dissonance will be.

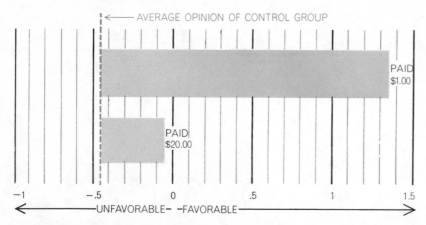

CONSEQUENCES OF LYING are found to vary, depending on whether the justification for the lie is large or small. In this experiment students were persuaded to tell others that a boring experience was really fun. Those in one group were paid only $1 for their cooperation; in a second group, $20. The low-paid students, having least justification for lying, experienced most dissonance and reduced it by coming to regard the experience favorably.

How can the dissonance be reduced? One method is obvious. The individual can remove the dissonance by retracting his public statement. But let us consider only those instances in which the public statement, once made, cannot be changed or withdrawn; in other words, in which the behavior is irrevocable. Under such circumstances the major avenue for reduction of the dissonance is change of private opinion. That is, if the private opinion were changed so that it agreed with what was publicly stated, obviously the dissonance would be gone. The theory thus leads us to expect that after having made an irrevocable public statement at variance with his private belief, a person will tend to change his private belief to bring it into line with his public statement. Furthermore, the degree to which he changes his private belief will depend on the amount of justification or the amount of pressure for making the public statement initially. The less the original justification or pressure, the greater the dissonance and the more the person's private belief can be expected to change.

An experiment recently conducted at Stanford University by James M. Carlsmith and me illustrates the nature of this effect. In the experiment, college students were induced to make a statement at variance with their own belief. It was done by using students who had

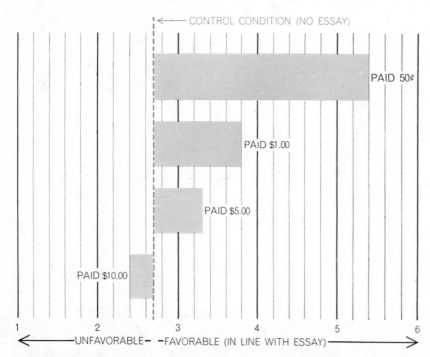

GRADED CHANGE OF OPINION was produced by paying subjects various sums for writing essays advocating opinions contrary to their beliefs. When examined later, students paid the least had changed their opinion the most to agree with what they had written. Only the highest paid group held to their original opinion more strongly than did a control group.

volunteered to participate in an experiment to measure "motor performance." The purported experiment lasted an hour and was a boring and fatiguing session. At the end of the hour the experimenter thanked the subject for his participation, indicating that the experiment was over. The real purpose of the hour-long session, however, was to provide each subject with an identical experience about which he would have an unfavorable opinion.

At the end of the fatiguing hour the experimenter enlisted the subject's aid in preparing the next person for the experiment. The subject was led to believe that, for experimental purposes, the next person was supposed to be given the impression that the hour's session was going to be very interesting and lots of fun. The subject was persuaded to help in this deception by telling the next subject, who was waiting in an adjoining room, that he himself had just finished the hour and that it had indeed been very interesting and lots of fun. The first subject was then interviewed by someone else to determine his actual private opinion of the experiment.

Two experimental conditions were run that differed only in the amount of pressure, or justification given the subject for stating a public opinion at variance with his private belief. All subjects, of course, had the justification of helping to conduct a scientific experiment. In addition to this, half of the subjects were paid $1 for their help—a relatively small amount of money; the other subjects were paid $20—a rather large sum for the work involved. From the theory we would expect that the subjects who were paid only $1, having less justification for their action, would have more dissonance and would change their private beliefs more in order to reduce the dissonance. In other words, we would expect the greatest change in private opinion among the subjects given the least tangible incentive for changing.

The upper illustration on the opposite page shows the results of the experiment. The broken line in the chart shows the results for a control group of subjects. These subjects participated in the hour-long session and then were asked to give their private opinion of it. Their generally unfavorable views are to be expected when no dissonance is induced between private belief and public statement. It is clear from the chart that introducing such dissonance produced a change of opinion so that the subjects who were asked to take part in a deception finally came to think better of the session than did the control subjects. It

The effect of rewards on lying

is also clear that only in the condition where they were paid a dollar is this opinion change appreciable. When they were paid a lot of money, the justification for misrepresenting private belief is high and there is correspondingly less change of opinion to reduce dissonance.

Another way to summarize the result is to say that those who are highly rewarded for doing something that involves dissonance change their opinion less in the direction of agreeing with what they did than those who are given very little reward. This result may seem surprising, since we are used to thinking that reward is effective in creating change. It must be remembered, however, that the critical factor here is that the reward is being used to induce a behavior that is dissonant with private opinion.

To show that this result is valid and not just a function of the particular situation or the particular sums of money used for reward, Arthur R. Cohen of New York University conducted a similar experiment in a different context. Cohen paid subjects to write essays advocating an opinion contrary to what

they really believed. Subjects were paid either $10, $5, $1 or 50 cents to do this. To measure the extent to which dissonance was reduced by their changing their opinion, each subject was then given a questionnaire, which he left unsigned, to determine his private opinion on the issue. The extent to which the subjects reduced dissonance by changing their opinion to agree with what they wrote in the essay is shown in the lower illustration on the opposite page. Once again it is clear that the smaller the original justification for engaging in the dissonance-producing action, the greater the subsequent change in private opinion to bring it into line with the action.

The final set of experiments I shall discuss deals with the consequences of resisting temptation. What happens when a person wants something and discovers that he cannot have it? Does he now want it even more or does he persuade himself that it is really not worth having? Sometimes our common general understanding of human behavior can provide at least crude answers to such questions. In this case, however, our common understanding is ambiguous, because it supplies two contradictory answers. Everyone knows the meaning of the term "sour grapes"; it is the attitude taken by a person who persuades himself that he really does not want what he cannot have. But we are also familiar with the opposite reaction. The child who is not allowed to eat candy and hence loves candy passionately; the woman who adores expensive clothes even though she cannot afford to own them; the man who has a hopeless obsession for a woman who spurns his attentions. Everyone "understands" the behavior of the person who longs for what he cannot have.

Obviously one cannot say one of these reactions is wrong and the other is right; they both occur. One might at least, however, try to answer the question: Under what circumstances does one reaction take place and not the other? If we examine the question from the point of view of the theory of dissonance, a partial answer begins to emerge.

Imagine the psychological situation that exists for an individual who is tempted to engage in a certain action but for one reason or another refrains. An analysis of the situation here reveals its similarity to the other dissonance-producing situations. An individual's knowledge concerning the attractive aspects of the activity toward which he was tempted is dissonant with the knowledge that he has refrained from engaging in the activity. Once more, of course, the individual has some knowledge that is consonant with his behavior in the situation. All the pressures, reasons and justifications for refraining are consonant with his actual behavior. Nevertheless, the dissonance does exist, and there will be psychological activity oriented toward reducing this dissonance.

As we have already seen in connection with other illustrations, one major way to reduce dissonance is to change one's opinions and evaluations in order to bring them closer in line with one's actual behavior. Therefore when there is

dissonance produced by resisting temptation, it can be reduced by derogating or devaluing the activity toward which one was tempted. This derivation from the theory clearly implies the sour-grapes attitude, but both theory and experiment tell us that such dissonance-reducing effects will occur only when there was insufficient original justification for the behavior. Where the original justification for refraining from the action was great, little dissonance would have occurred and there would have been correspondingly little change of opinion in order to reduce dissonance. Therefore one might expect that if a person had resisted temptation in a situation of strong prohibition or strong threatened punishment, little dissonance would have been created and one would not observe the sour-grapes effect. One would expect this effect only if the person resisted temptation under conditions of weak deterrent.

This line of reasoning leaves open the question of when the reverse effect occurs—that is, the situation in which desire for the "unattainable" object is increased. Experimentally it is possible to look at both effects. This was done by Elliot Aronson and Carlsmith, at Stanford University, in an experiment that sheds considerable light on the problem. The experiment was performed with children who were about four years old. Each child was individually brought into a large playroom in which there were five toys on a table. After the child had had an opportunity to play briefly with each toy, he was asked to rank the five in order of attractiveness. The toy that the child liked second best was then left on the table and the other four toys were spread around on the floor. The experimenter told the child that he had to leave for a few minutes to do an errand but would be back soon. The experimenter then left the room for 10 minutes. Various techniques were employed to "prohibit" the child from playing with the particular toy that he liked second best while the experimenter was out of the room.

For different children this prohibition was instituted in three different ways. In one condition there was no temptation at all; the experimenter told the child he could play with any of the toys in the room and then took the second-best toy with him when he left. In the other two conditions temptation was present: the second-best toy was left on the table in the experimenter's absence. The children were told they could play with any of the toys in the room except

Temptation accompanied by a severe threat

Temptation accompanied by a mild threat

the one on the table. The children in one group were threatened with mild punishment if they violated the prohibition, whereas those in the other group were threatened with more severe punishment. (The actual nature of the punishment was left unspecified.)

During his absence from the room the experimenter observed each child through a one-way mirror. None of the children in the temptation conditions played with the prohibited toy. After 10 minutes were up the experimenter returned to the playroom and each child was again allowed to play briefly with each of the five toys. The attractiveness of each toy for the child was again measured. By comparing the before and after measurements of the attractiveness of the toy the child originally liked second best, one can assess the effects of the prohibition. The results are shown in the chart on this page.

When there was no temptation—that is, when the prohibited toy was not physically present—there was of course no dissonance, and the preponderant result is an increase in the attractiveness of the prohibited toy. When the temptation is present but the prohibition is enforced by means of a severe threat of punishment, there is likewise little dissonance created by refraining, and again the preponderant result is an increase in the attractiveness of the prohibited toy. In other words, it seems clear that a prohibition that is enforced in such a way as not to introduce dissonance results in a greater desire for the prohibited activity.

The results are quite different, however, when the prohibition is enforced by only a mild threat of punishment. Here we see the result to be expected from the theory of dissonance. Because the justification for refraining from playing with the toy is relatively weak, there is appreciable dissonance between the child's knowledge that the toy is attractive and his actual behavior. The tendency to reduce this dissonance is strong enough to more than overcome the effect apparent in the other two conditions. Here, as a result of dissonance reduction, we see an appreciable sour-grapes phenomenon.

The theory of cognitive dissonance obviously has many implications for everyday life. In addition to throwing light on one's own behavior, it would seem to carry useful lessons for everyone concerned with understanding human behavior in a world where everything is not black and white.

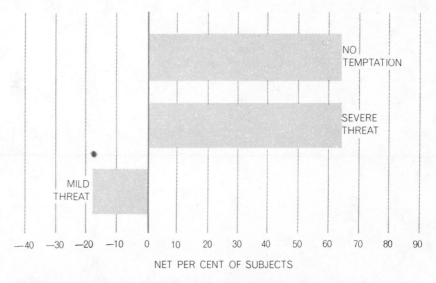

Consequences of resisting temptation when deterrence varies

CONSEQUENCES OF TEMPTATION were explored by prohibiting children from playing with a desirable toy. Later the children were asked to re-evaluate the attractiveness of the forbidden toy. In one case the prohibition was enforced by removing the toy from the child's presence. In the second case the prohibition took the form of a threat of severe punishment; in the third case, a threat of mild punishment. The chart shows the net per cent of children who thought the forbidden toy more attractive after the experiment than before. ("Net per cent" means the per cent who found the toy more attractive minus the per cent who found it less so.) Evidently only those threatened mildly experienced much dissonance, and they reduced it by downgrading toy's desirability. Others thought the toy more desirable.

BIBLIOGRAPHIES

I BIOLOGICAL AND DEVELOPMENTAL DETERMINERS OF BEHAVIOR

1. Small Systems of Neurons

GENETIC DISSECTION OF BEHAVIOR. Seymour Benzer in *Scientific American*, Vol. 229, No. 6, pages 24–37; December, 1978.

THE NERVOUS SYSTEM OF THE LEECH. John G. Nicholls and David Van Essen in *Scientific American*, Vol. 230, No. 1, pages 38–48; January, 1974.

THE NEUROBIOLOGY OF CRICKET SONG. David Bentley and Ronald R. Hoy in *Scientific American*, Vol. 231, No. 2, pages 34–44; August, 1974.

CELLULAR BASIS OF BEHAVIOR: AN INTRODUCTION TO BEHAVIORAL NEUROBIOLOGY. Eric R. Kandel. W. H. Freeman and Company, 1976.

CELLULAR INSIGHTS INTO BEHAVIOR AND LEARNING. Eric R. Kandel in *The Harvey Lectures*, Series 73, pages 29–92; 1979.

2. Brain Changes in Response to Experience

CHEMICAL AND ANATOMICAL PLASTICITY OF BRAIN. Edward L. Bennett, Marian C. Diamond, David Krech and Mark R. Rosenzweig in *Science*, Vol. 146, No. 3644, pages 610–619; October 30, 1964.

EFFECTS OF ENVIRONMENT ON DEVELOPMENT OF BRAIN AND BEHAVIOR. Mark R. Rosenzweig in *Biopsychology of Development*, edited by Ethel Tobach. Academic Press, 1971.

ENVIRONMENTAL INFLUENCES ON BRAIN AND BEHAVIOR OF YEAR-OLD RATS. Walter H. Riege in *Developmental Psychobiology*, Vol. 4, No. 2, pages 157–167; 1971.

QUANTITATIVE SYNAPTIC CHANGES WITH DIFFERENTIAL EXPERIENCE IN RAT BRAIN. Kjeld Møllgaard, Marian C. Diamond, Edward L. Bennett, Mark R. Rosenzweig and Bernice Lindner in *International Journal of Neuroscience*, Vol. 2, No. 2, pages 113–128; August, 1971.

3. The Reward System of the Brain

THE ORGANIZATION OF THE ASCENDING CATECHOLAMINE NEURON SYSTEMS IN THE RAT BRAIN AS REVEALED BY THE GLYOXYLIC ACID FLUORESCENCE METHOD. Olle Lindvall and Anders Björklund in *Acta Physiologica Scandinavica Supplementum 412*, pages 1–48; 1974.

BRAIN STIMULATION REWARD. Albert Wauquier and Edmund T. Rolls. North-Holland Publishing Company, 1976.

DRIVES AND REINFORCEMENTS: BEHAVIORAL STUDIES OF HYPOTHALAMIC FUNCTIONS. James Olds. Raven Press, 1977.

THE ROLE OF PREFRONTAL CORTEX IN INTRACRANIAL SELF-STIMULATION. Aryeh Routtenberg and Rebecca Santos-Anderson in *Handbook of Psychopharmacology: Vol. 8*, edited by Leslie L. Iversen, Susan D. Iversen and Solomon H. Snyder. Plenum Press, 1977.

4. Brain Mechanisms of Vision

MODALITY AND TOPOGRAPHIC PROPERTIES OF SINGLE NEURONS OF CAT'S SOMATIC SENSORY CORTEX. V. B. Mountcastle in *The Journal of Neurophysiology*, Vol. 20, No. 4, pages 408–434; July, 1957.

RECEPTIVE FIELDS AND FUNCTIONAL ARCHITECTURE OF MONKEY STRIATE CORTEX. D. H. Hubel and T. N. Wiesel in *The Journal of Physiology*, Vol. 195, No. 2, pages 215–244; November, 1968.

FERRIER LECTURE: FUNCTIONAL ARCHITECTURE OF MACAQUE MONKEY VISUAL CORTEX. D. H. Hubel and T. N. Wiesel in *Proceedings of the Royal Society of London, Series B*, Vol. 198, pages 1–59; 1977.

ANATOMICAL DEMONSTRATION OF ORIENTATION COLUMNS IN MACAQUE MONKEY. David H. Hubel, Torsten N. Wiesel and Michael P. Stryker in *The Journal of Comparative Neurology*, Vol. 177, No. 3, pages 361–379; February 1, 1978.

5. "Imprinting" in a Natural Laboratory

"Imprinting" in Animals. Eckhard H. Hess in *Scientific American*, Vol. 198, No. 3, pages 81–90; March, 1958.

Imprinting in Birds. Eckhard H. Hess in *Science*, Vol. 146, No. 3648, pages 1128–1139; November 27, 1964.

Innate Factors in Imprinting. Eckhard H. Hess and Dorle B. Hess in *Psychonomic Science*, Vol. 14, No. 3, pages 129–130; February 10, 1969.

Development of Species Identification in Birds: An Inquiry into the Prenatal Determinants of Perception. Gilbert Gottlieb. University of Chicago Press, 1971.

Natural History of Imprinting. Eckhard H. Hess in *Integrative Events in Life Processes: Annals of the New York Academy of Sciences*, Vol. 193, in press.

6. The Object in the World of the Infant

The Construction of Reality in the Child. Jean Piaget. Basic Books, Inc., 1954.

The Child and Modern Physics. Jean Piaget in *Scientific American*, Vol. 196, No. 3, pages 46–51; March, 1957.

Causalité, Permanence et Réalité Phénoménales: Etudes de Psychologie Expérimentale. A. Michotte. Louvain, Belgium: Publications Universitaires, 1962.

The Nature of Perceptual Adaptation. Irvin Rock. Basic Books, Inc., 1966.

The Visual World of Infants. T. G. R. Bower in *Scientific American*, Vol. 215, No. 6, pages 80–92; December, 1966.

Space Perception in Early Infancy: Perception within a Common Auditory-Visual Space. Eric Aronson and Shelley Rosenbloom in *Science*, Vol. 172, No. 3988, pages 1161–1163; June 11, 1971.

7. Repetitive Processes in Child Development

The Child and Modern Physics. Jean Piaget in *Scientific American*, Vol. 196, No. 3, pages 46–51; March, 1957.

Plasticity in Sensory-Motor Systems. Richard Held in *Scientific American*, Vol. 213, No. 5, pages 84–94; November, 1965.

Conservation of Weight in Infants. Pierre Mounoud and T. G. R. Bower in *Cognition*, Vol. 3, No. 1, pages 29–40; 1974–1975.

A Primer of Infant Development. T. G. R. Bower. W. H. Freeman and Company, 1977.

II PERCEPTION AND AWARENESS

8. The Processes of Vision

The Kinetic Depth Effect. H. Wallach and D. N. O'Connell in *Journal of Experimental Psychology*, Vol. 45, No. 4, pages 205–218; April 1953.

The Relation of Eye Movements, Body Motility and External Stimuli to Dream Content. William Dement and Edward A. Wolpert in *Journal of Experimental Psychology*, Vol. 55, No. 6, pages 543–553; June, 1958.

The Senses Considered as Perceptual Systems. James J. Gibson. Houghton Mifflin, 1966.

Cognitive Psychology. Ulric Neisser. Appleton-Century-Crofts, 1967.

9. Negative Aftereffects in Visual Perception

Comparison of Normalization Theory and Neural Enhancement Explanation of Negative Aftereffects. Ray Over in *Psychological Bulletin*, Vol. 75, No. 4, pages 225–243; April, 1971.

Handbook of Perception, Vol. I: Historical and Philosophical Roots of Perception. Edited by Edward C. Carterette and Morton P. Friedman. Academic Press, 1973.

Sight and Mind: An Introduction to Visual Perception. Lloyd Kaufman. Oxford University Press, 1974.

What Does Visual Perception Tell Us about Visual Coding? Stuart M. Anstis in *Handbook of Psychobiology*, edited by Michael S. Gazzaniga and Colin Blakemore. Academic Press, 1975.

McCollough Effects: Experimental Findings and Theoretical Accounts. D. Skowko, B. N. Timney, T. A. Gentry and R. B. Morant in *Psychological Bulletin*, Vol. 82, No. 4, pages 497–510; July, 1975.

10. Visual Illusions

Sensation and Perception in the History of Experimental Psychology. Edwin Garrigues Boring. Appleton-Century, 1942.

Optical Illusions. S. Tolansky. Pergamon, 1964.

Eye and Brain. R. L. Gregory. McGraw-Hill, 1966.

Will Seeing Machines Have Illusions? R. L. Gregory in *Machine Intelligence I*, edited by N. L. Collins and Donald Michie. American Elsevier, 1967.

11. Multistability in Perception

THE ANALYSIS OF SENSATIONS AND THE RELATION OF THE PHYSICAL TO THE PSYCHICAL. Ernst Mach. Dover Publications, Inc., 1959.

AMBIGUITY OF FORM: OLD AND NEW. Gerald H. Fisher in *Perception and Psychophysics*, Vol. 4, No. 3, pages 189–192; September, 1968.

TRIANGLES AS AMBIGUOUS FIGURES. Fred Attneave in *The American Journal of Psychology*, Vol. 81, No. 3, pages 447–453; September, 1968.

12. The Perception of Disoriented Figures

RECOGNITION UNDER OBJECTIVE REVERSAL. George V. N. Dearborn in *The Psychological Review*, Vol. 6, No. 4, pages 395–406; July, 1899.

THE ANALYSIS OF SENSATIONS AND THE RELATION OF THE PHYSICAL TO THE PSYCHICAL. Ernst Mach, translated from the German by C. M. Williams. Dover Publications, Inc., 1959.

ORIENTATION AND SHAPE I AND II in *Human Spatial Orientation*. I. P. Howard and W. B. Templeton. John Wiley & Sons, Inc., 1966.

SIMILARITY IN VISUALLY PERCEIVED FORMS. Erich Goldmeier in *Psychological Issues*, Vol. 8, No. 1, Monograph 29; 1972.

ORIENTATION AND FORM. Irvin Rock. Academic Press, 1974.

13. Hallucinations

MESCAL AND MECHANISMS OF HALLUCINATIONS. Heinrich Klüver. The University of Chicago Press, 1966.

HASHISH AND MENTAL ILLNESS. J. J. Moreau. Raven Press, 1973.

HALLUCINATIONS: BEHAVIOR, EXPERIENCE AND THEORY. Edited by Ronald K. Siegel and Louis Jolyon West. John Wiley & Sons, Inc., 1975.

14. Sources of Ambiguity in the Prints of Maurits C. Escher

SOME FACTORS DETERMINING FIGURE-GROUND ARTICULATION. M. R. Harrower in *British Journal of Psychology*, Vol. 26, No. 4, pages 407–424; 1936.

PERCEPTION. Hans-Lukas Teuber in *Handbook of Physiology: Section 1—Neurophysiology, Vol. 3*. Edited by H. W. Magoun. Williams & Wilkins, 1961.

THE GRAPHIC WORK OF M. C. ESCHER. M. C. Escher. Ballantine Books, Inc., 1971.

THE WORLD OF M. C. ESCHER, edited by J. L. Locher. Harry N. Abrams, Inc., 1971.

NEW ASPECTS OF PAUL KLEE'S BAUHAUS STYLE. M. L. Teuber in *Paul Klee, Paintings and Watercolors from the Bauhaus Years, 1921–1931*. Des Moines Art Center, 1973.

III MEMORY, LEARNING, AND THINKING

15. The Control of Short-term Memory

HUMAN MEMORY: A PROPOSED SYSTEM AND ITS CONTROL PROCESSES. R. C. Atkinson and R. M. Shiffrin in *Advances in the Psychology of Learning and Motivation Research and Theory: Vol. II*, edited by K. W. Spence and J. T. Spence. Academic Press, 1968.

MEMORY SEARCH. Richard M. Shiffrin in *Models of Human Memory*, edited by Donald A. Norman. Academic Press, 1970.

FORGETTING: TRACE EROSION OR RETRIEVAL FAILURE. Richard M. Shiffrin in *Science*, Vol. 168, No. 3939, pages 1601–1603; June 26, 1970.

HUMAN MEMORY AND THE CONCEPT OF REINFORCEMENT. R. C. Atkinson and T. D. Wickens in *The Nature of Reinforcement*, edited by R. Glaser. Academic Press, 1971.

AN ANALYSIS OF REHEARSAL PROCESSES IN FREE RECALL. D. Rundus in *Journal of Experimental Psychology*, Vol. 89, pages 63–77; July, 1971.

16. How We Remember What We See

EMERGENCE AND RECOVERY OF INITIALLY UNAVAILABLE PERCEPTUAL MATERIAL. Ralph Norman Haber and Mathew Hugh Erdelyi in *Journal of Verbal Learning and Verbal Behavior*, Vol. 6, No. 4, pages 618–628; August, 1967.

DIRECT MEASURES OF SHORT-TERM VISUAL STORAGE. Ralph Norman Haber and L. G. Standing in *The Quarterly Journal of Experimental Psychology*, Vol. 21, Part 1, pages 43–54; February, 1969.

PROCESSING OF SEQUENTIALLY PRESENTED LETTERS. Ralph Norman Haber and Linda Sue Nathanson in *Perception and Psychophysics*, Vol. 5, No. 6, pages 359–361; June, 1969.

17. Spatial Memory

MAPS IN THE BRAIN. John O'Keefe and Lynn Nadel in *New Scientist*, Vol. 62, No. 903, pages 749–751; June 27, 1974.

BEHAVIORAL CORRELATES AND FIRING REPERTOIRE OF NEURONS IN THE DORSAL HIPPOCAMPAL FORMATION AND SEPTUM OF UNRESTRAINED RATS. James B. Ranck, Jr., in *The Hippocampus*, edited by Robert L. Isaacson and Karl H. Pribram. Plenum Press, 1975.

HIPPOCAMPAL ELECTRICAL ACTIVITY AND BEHAVIOR. A. H. Black in *The Hippocampus: Vol. II*, edited by Robert L. Isaacson and Karl H. Pribram. Plenum Press, 1975.

REMEMBRANCE OF PLACES PASSED: SPATIAL MEMORY IN RATS. David S. Olton and Robert J. Samuelson in *Journal of Experimental Psychology: Animal Behavior Processes*, Vol. 2, No. 2, pages 97–116; April, 1976.

18. How to Teach Animals

THE BEHAVIOR OF ORGANISMS. B. F. Skinner. Appleton-Century-Crofts, 1938.

19. The Acquisition of Language

THE ACQUISITION OF LANGUAGE: THE STUDY OF DEVELOPMENTAL PSYCHOLINGUISTICS. David McNeill. Harper & Row, Publishers, 1970.

LANGUAGE, STRUCTURE AND LANGUAGE USE: ESSAYS BY CHARLES A. FERGUSON. Selected and introduced by Anwar S. Dil. Stanford University Press, 1971.

A FIRST LANGUAGE: THE EARLY STAGES. Roger Brown. Harvard University Press, 1973.

ONE WORD AT A TIME. Lois Bloom. Mouton, 1975.

20. Teaching Language to an Ape

SYNTACTIC STRUCTURES. Noam Chomsky. Mouton & Co., 1957.

THE GENESIS OF LANGUAGE. Edited by F. Smith and G. A. Miller. The M.I.T. Press, 1966.

BEHAVIOR OF NONHUMAN PRIMATES: VOLS. III–IV. Edited by Fred Stollnitz and Allan M. Schrier. Academic Press, 1971.

LANGUAGE IN CHIMPANZEE? David Premack in *Science*, Vol. 172, No. 3985, pages 808–822; May 21, 1971.

A FIRST LANGUAGE: THE EARLY STAGES. Roger Brown. Harvard University Press, 1973.

21. Specializations of the Human Brain

EMOTIONAL BEHAVIOR AND HEMISPHERIC SIDE OF THE LESION. G. Gainotti in *Cortex*, Vol. 8, No. 1, pages 41–55; March, 1972.

SELECTED PAPERS ON LANGUAGE AND THE BRAIN. Norman Geschwind. D. Reidel Publishing Co., 1974.

THE INTEGRATED MIND. Michael S. Gazzaniga and Joseph E. Ledoux. Plenum Press, 1978.

RIGHT-LEFT ASYMMETRIES IN THE BRAIN. Albert M. Galaburda, Marjorie LeMay, Thomas L. Kemper and Norman Geschwind in *Science*, Vol. 199, No. 4311, pages 852–856; February 24, 1978.

IV PERSONALITY, ABNORMALITY, AND SOCIAL BEHAVIOR

22. The Origin of Personality

BIRTH TO MATURITY: A STUDY IN PSYCHOLOGICAL DEVELOPMENT. Jerome Kagan and H. A. Moss. Wiley, 1962.

THE WIDENING WORLD OF CHILDHOOD: PATHS TOWARD MASTERY. Lois Barclay Murphy. Basic Books, 1962.

YOUR CHILD IS A PERSON: A PSYCHOLOGICAL APPROACH TO PARENTHOOD WITHOUT GUILT. Stella Chess, Alexander Thomas and Herbert G. Birch. Viking Press, 1965.

TEMPERAMENT AND BEHAVIOR DISORDERS IN CHILDREN. Alexander Thomas, Stella Chess and Herbert G. Birch. New York University Press, 1968.

TEMPERAMENT AND DEVELOPMENT. Alexander Thomas and Stella Chess. Brunner/Mazel, 1977.

23. Psychological Factors in Stress and Disease

SOMATIC EFFECTS OF PREDICTABLE AND UNPREDICTABLE SHOCK. Jay M. Weiss in *Psychosomatic Medicine*, Vol. 32, pages 397–408; 1970.

EXPERIMENTALLY INDUCED GASTRIC LESIONS: RESULTS AND IMPLICATIONS OF STUDIES IN ANIMALS. Robert Ader in *Advances in Psychosomatic Medicine*, Vol. 6, pages 1–39; 1971.

EFFECTS OF COPING BEHAVIOR IN DIFFERENT WARNING SIGNAL CONDITIONS ON STRESS PATHOLOGY IN RATS. Jay M. Weiss in *Journal of Comparative and Physiological Psychology*, Vol. 77, No. 1, pages 1–30; October, 1971.

24. Disorders of the Human Brain

THE BIOLOGY OF MENTAL DEFECT. L. S. Penrose, with a preface by J. B. S. Haldane. Grune & Stratton, 1962.

MADNESS AND THE BRAIN. Solomon H. Snyder. McGraw-Hill Book Company, 1974.

BRAIN WORK: THE COUPLING OF FUNCTION, METABOLISM AND BLOOD FLOW IN THE BRAIN. Edited by David H. Ingvar and Niels A. Lassen. Munksgaard, 1975.

THE BIOLOGICAL ROOTS OF MENTAL ILLNESS: THEIR RAMIFICATIONS THROUGH CEREBRAL METABOLISM, SYNAPTIC ACTIVITY, GENETICS, AND THE ENVIRONMENT. Seymour S. Kety in *The Harvey Lectures*, Series 71, pages 1–22; 1978.

GENETIC TRANSMISSION OF SCHIZOPHRENIA. Dennis K. Kinney and Steven Matthysse in *Annual Review of Medicine*, Vol. 29, pages 459–473; 1978.

25. Behavioral Psychotherapy

BEHAVIORAL MODIFICATIONS THROUGH MODELING PROCEDURES. Albert Bandura in *Research in Behavior Modification*, edited by Leonard Krasner and Leonard P. Ullmann. Holt, Rinehart & Winston, 1965.

EXPERIEMNTS IN BEHAVIOR THERAPY. H. J. Eysenck. Pergamon Press, 1964.

PRINCIPLES OF BEHAVIOR MODIFICATION. Albert Bandura. Holt, Rinehart & Winston, 1969.

PSYCHOTHERAPY BY RECIPROCAL INHIBITION. Joseph Wolpe. Stanford University Press, 1958.

SOCIAL LEARNING AND PERSONALITY DEVELOPMENT. Albert Bandura and Richard H. Walters. Holt, Rinehart & Winston, 1963.

SOCIAL LEARNING THEORY. Albert Bandura. Prentice-Hall, 1977.

26. Social and Nonsocial Speech

SPEECH ACTS: AN ESSAY IN THE PHILOSOPHY OF LANGUAGE. John Searle. Cambridge University Press, 1969.

COGNITIVE BASIS OF LANGUAGE LEARNING IN INFANTS. John Macnamara in *Psychological Review*, Vol. 79, No. 1, pages 1–13; January, 1972.

MOTHERS' SPEECH TO CHILDREN LEARNING LANGUAGE. Catherine E. Snow in *Child Development*, Vol. 43, No. 2, pages 549–565; June, 1972.

THE DEVELOPMENT OF COMMUNICATION SKILLS: MODIFICATIONS IN THE SPEECH OF YOUNG CHILDREN AS A FUNCTION OF LISTENER. Marilyn Shatz and Rochel Gelman in *Monographs of the Society for Research in Child Development*, Vol. 38, No. 5; 1973.

THE DEVELOPMENT OF ROLE-TAKING AND COMMUNICATION SKILLS IN CHILDREN. John H. Flavell in collaboration with Patricia T. Botkin, Charles L. Fry, Jr., John W. Wright and Paul E. Jarvis. Robert E. Krieger Publishing Company, 1975.

27. The Role of Pupil Size in Communication

ATTITUDE AND PUPIL SIZE. Eckhard H. Hess in *Scientific American*, Vol. 212, No. 4, pages 46–54; April, 1965.

PSYCHOLOGICAL SIGNIFICANCE OF PUPILLARY MOVEMENTS. Bram C. Goldwater in *Psychological Bulletin*, Vol. 77, No. 5, pages 340–355; May, 1972.

PUPILLOMETRICS: A METHOD OF STUDYING MENTAL, EMOTIONAL AND SENSORY PROCESSES. Eckhard H. Hess in *Handbook of Psychophysiology*, edited by N. S. Greenfield and R. A. Sternbach. Holt, Rinehart and Winston, 1973.

28. Cognitive Dissonance

COGNITIVE CONSEQUENCES OF FORCED COMPLIANCE. Leon Festinger and James M. Carlsmith in *The Journal of Abnormal and Social Psychology*, Vol. 58, No. 2, pages 203–210; March, 1959.

PREPARATORY ACTION AND BELIEF IN THE PROBABLE OCCURRENCE OF FUTURE EVENTS. Ruby B. Yaryan and Leon Festinger in *The Journal of Abnormal and Social Psychology*, Vol. 63, No. 3, pages 603–606; November, 1961.

A THEORY OF COGNITIVE DISSONANCE. Leon Festinger. Row, Peterson, 1957.

WHEN PROPHECY FAILS. Leon Festinger, Henry W. Riecken and Stanley Schachter. University of Minnesota Press, 1956.

INDEX